SIXTH EDITION

Psychology for Living

Adjustment, Growth, and Behavior Today

◆ ◆ ◆

Eastwood Atwater
Karen Grover Duffy

Prentice Hall, Upper Saddle River, New Jersey 07458

Library of Congress Cataloging-in-Publication Data

Atwater, Eastwood, (date)
   Psychology for living : adjustment, growth, and behavior today /
Eastwood Atwater, Karen Grover Duffy.—6th ed.
    p. cm.
   ISBN 0-13-958778-0
   1. Adjustment (Psychology)   2. Adulthood—Psychological aspects.
3. Interpersonal relations.   4. Self-actualization (Psychology)
I. Duffy, Karen Grover. II. Title.
BF335.A88 1999
158—dc21
                                   98-15321
                                   CIP

Editor in Chief: Nancy Roberts
Executive Editor: Bill Webber
Assistant Editor: Jennifer Cohen
Vice President and Director of Production
  and Manufacturing: Barbara Kittle
Senior Managing Editor: Bonnie Biller
Production Liaison: Fran Russello
Project Manager: Linda B. Pawelchak
Manufacturing Manager: Nick Sklitsis
Prepress and Manufacturing Buyer: Lynn Pearlman
Cover Director: Jayne Conte
Cover Design: Anthony Gemmellaro
Cover Art: Diana Ong.-Chinese/USA (B. 1940).
  "Parts Equal the Whole I"/SuperStock
Director, Image Resource Center: Lori Morris-Nantz
Photo Research Supervisor: Melinda Lee Reo
Image Permission Supervisor: Kay Dellosa
Photo Researcher: Diana Gongora
Electronic Art Creation: Burmar Technological Corp.
Senior Marketing Manager: Michael Alread
Copy Editing: Susan Korb/Proofreading: Nancy Menges

Acknowledgments may be found on page 493, which constitutes an
extension of this copyright page.

This book was set in 10.5/12 Bembo by Carlisle Communications, LTD
and was printed and bound by Courier Companies, Inc.
The cover was printed by Phoenix Color Corp.

Printed in the United States of America
10 9 8 7 6 5 4 3

ISBN 0-13-958778-0

Prentice-Hall International (UK) Limited, *London*
Prentice-Hall of Australia Pty. Limited, *Sydney*
Prentice-Hall Canada Inc., *Toronto*
Prentice-Hall Hispanoamericana, S.A., *Mexico*
Prentice-Hall of India Private Limited, *New Delhi*
Prentice-hall of Japan, Inc., *Tokyo*
Simon & Schuster Asia Pte. Ltd., *Singapore*
Editora Prentice-Hall do Brasil, Ltda., *Rio de Janeiro*

To
Eastwood Atwater,
for the humanity and wisdom
he so generously and kindly
shared with us

Brief Contents

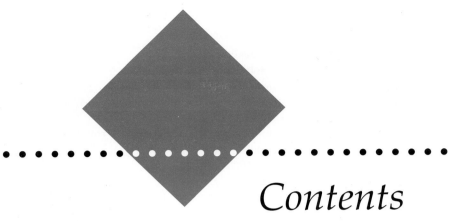

Contents

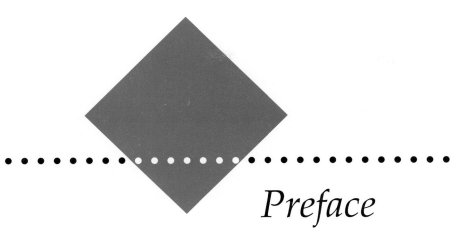

Preface

This book is intended for those who are interested in applying psychological insights and principles to their own lives as a way of achieving a better understanding of themselves and living more effectively. To this end, we've included material from the major perspectives of psychology, including the psychodynamic, cognitive-behavioral, and humanistic viewpoints. Since a well-rounded text cuts across several branches of psychology, we've included contributions from clinical, personality, social, and developmental psychology, as well as from the important fields of cognitive, biological, and health psychology.

Throughout the book, we've often presented differing views on the same issue, along with questions, that are designed to stimulate the reader's critical thought. Our aim is to increase readers' understanding as well as their knowledge, in order that they may continue learning on their own.

Major features of this sixth edition are as follows.

 ## New Content

We have made three significant changes in the book with regard to content and chapter ordering. First, the chapters on motivation and emotion have been combined. So as not to make this chapter too lengthy, some material from the last edition was moved to other chapters. For example, the material on sleeping and dreaming from the former chapter on motivation has been moved to the chapter on health. Second, we have removed the chapter on cultural diversity. Instead, information on cultural diversity, gender similarities and differences, and minorities is integrated throughout all other chapters. The third change is that a new chapter on groups is included in this edition. This chapter pertains to group dynamics, including group processes such as communication and social influence, leadership, and problems in groups such as conflict and groupthink.

Another new feature of this edition is increased use of cases to reify the material. Each chapter begins with a vignette about an individual. Whereas the vignettes are fictional, the individual described is based on a composite of several real persons. The case is fully worked into the text to better illustrate many of the main points. Where appropriate, other cases are also detailed. The cases, then, both make real and exemplify the material being discussed. We have also made a concerted effort to create diverse cases representing our diverse audience of readers.

◆ Learning Aids

Several features have been introduced to assist the student in making the best use of this book:

- A *How to Study* section at the beginning of the book provides suggestions for studying and taking tests.
- *Chapter outlines* at the beginning of each chapter give students an overview of what will be covered.
- *Learning objectives* identify what students are expected to attain in regard to knowledge, understanding, and application.
- A *glossary* at the end of the book defines key terms in the text.
- *End-of-the-chapter summaries,* arranged by major headings, help the reader to grasp the main points of the chapter.
- *Self-tests,* consisting of 10 multiple-choice questions, help students to assess their understanding of the material covered.

APPLICATIONS

- *One or two self-scoring inventories* in each chapter enable students to apply the concepts and principles covered in the text to themselves.
- *End-of-the-chapter exercises* heighten the student's involvement in the material.
- *Questions for self-reflection* encourage students to relate the material in the text to themselves.

FOR FURTHER INFORMATION

A new feature at the end of each chapter is a list of ways to explore topics electronically. One of the points the text establishes is that we have moved into a technological information age. World Wide Web sites as well as usenet information are available.

Also included are a half-dozen recommended readings, together with a brief description of their contents, intended for those who wish to pursue a given topic in greater depth.

INSTRUCTOR'S MANUAL

A separately bound Instructor's Manual is also available. Each chapter in the learning aids section includes a chapter overview, class activities, discussion questions, lecture suggestions, and audiovisual resources. For each chapter in the test item section, there are representative multiple-choice questions, essay questions, short-answer questions, and true-false items.

The following reviewers are acknowledged for their helpful comments: Susan O. Bolman, Norwalk Community Technical College; Emory Holland, Montgomery County Community College; Diane Kawagoe, California State University-Fresno; Cheryl S. McFadden, York Technical College; Robert J. Mitchell, Waukesha County Technical College; Douglas J. Narby, Louisiana State University-Eunice; Cary Schawel, Oakton Community College; and David Wright, Brigham Young University.

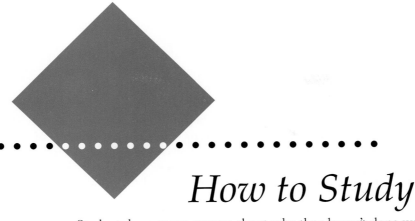

How to Study

Students have many excuses about why they haven't done well on a test. Occasionally, they will admit outright, "I just didn't study." But more often, they will say, "I really *studied* for that test. I can't understand why I did so poorly." A common problem is waiting until the last minute to study. But in many instances, students just don't know *how to study*. Whether or not you fall into this category, chances are you could improve your studying habits by applying one of the following time-honored methods of studying.

 ## The PQ4R Method

The PQ4R method gets its name from the six overlapping stages for studying material such as textbook chapters—**p**review, **q**uestion, **r**ead, **r**eflect, **r**ecite, and **r**eview.[1] Extensive experience has shown that this method can improve your understanding and memory, and thus your test performance.

PREVIEW

It's a good idea to look over the chapter as a whole before you begin it. When you read a novel, you usually start at the beginning and read straight through so as not to spoil the surprise ending. But with concepts and factual material, it's just the opposite. Here, it's important to get an idea of the material as a whole so you can put the details in context as you read.

- First, look over the table of contents.
- Next, skim through the chapter, looking at the headings and subheadings.
- Then, read the chapter summary.
- Finally, decide how much you want to read at a sitting.

QUESTION

Once you've looked over the chapter, you may be curious about the material. A helpful technique is to ask yourself questions about the material. Then read the chapter with the aim of finding the answers to your questions. One way to do this is to turn each boldfaced heading and subheading into a question. For example, the first major heading and subheadings in Chapter 4 are

[1] E. L. Thomas and H. A. Robinson, *Improving Memory in Every Class; A Sourcebook for Teachers* (Boston: Allyn & Bacon, 1972).

Understanding Stress
  Meaning of Stress
  Measuring Stress
  Personal, Situational Factors

Now use these headings and subheadings to think up some questions. Here are some examples: What does the term *stress* mean? Does stress refer to external forces or to something within? What are the most stressful events in our lives? Why do some individuals find the same event more stressful than others? Your use of such questions may prove even more effective if you jot them down, and then, as you read, write down your answers.

READ

Make it a point to understand what you're reading, digesting the material in one section before proceeding to the next. Skimming through material without comprehending it leads to superficial understanding at best, but more often, to downright confusion. In contrast, when you take the time to understand what you read, you'll also retain it better. If you're not clear about the meaning of a word, check the glossary of terms at the end of the book. If you can't find the word in the glossary, look it up in one of the better dictionaries such as *Webster's New World Dictionary*. Also, feel free to make explanatory notes to yourself in the margins of the pages of your textbook.

REFLECT

A good way to improve your understanding of something is to pause periodically and reflect on it. Ask yourself: Do I really understand this material? Could I explain it to someone else? If the answer is no, reread the material.

It's also helpful to mark or underline key passages in the chapter. This makes you an active participant in reading and provides you with key passages to review for tests. Some students prefer to mark or underline as they read. Others prefer to read through the material, and then to go back and highlight the most important points. We prefer the latter approach, because we usually have a better idea of the key passages after we've read through the material. Here are some suggestions for marking or underlining:

- Read through each section before marking or underlining.
- Mark only key passages or ideas.
- Use a marker or pen. Pencil often smears.

RECITE

Perhaps you've had this experience: You look up someone's telephone number, but no sooner have you closed the phone book than you've forgotten the number. You reopen the book and find the number again. But this time as you close the book, you repeat the number to yourself, either silently or audibly. You're improving your memory through *recitation*—the act of repeating or speaking aloud.

Recitation improves your memory in several ways. First, by focusing your attention on the page a bit longer, you can encode the material better, thereby ensuring accurate storage of the material. Repeated practice may also help you to retrieve the material when you need it.

There are several ways to use recitation. First, the act of reflection, or asking questions about the material, mentioned earlier, is itself a form of recitation. Second, you may also recite by closing the book and mentally recalling what you've just read. A third way is to recite aloud, either by discussing the material with a classmate, or by sharing your reactions or asking questions about it in class. A fourth way is to make a written outline of what you've read. We highly recommend this method because it forces you to select the main ideas in the material. Occasionally, students attempt to escape the thinking process by simply copying down the headings and subheadings, including little else. Others include too much detail, which becomes distracting. Instead, be selective. You should be able to outline an entire chapter of this book in just several written pages, depending, of course, on how large you write. The entire process of selecting the major ideas and writing them down is an excellent form of recitation. It also provides you with a handy guide to review for the test.

The amount of time spent on recitation depends on the material covered. When you're trying to remember isolated bits of information, like names or numbers, up to 80 percent of your time should be spent in recitation. But when you're learning ideas or concepts that are highly meaningful and well-organized, perhaps you would spend only 20 percent of your time in recitation. Personal experience will help you to determine which method of recitation works best for you.

REVIEW

When you're ready to review, reread the summary at the end of the chapter to give yourself a sense of the material as a whole. Then look back over the material in the chapter, paying special attention to the key ideas you've marked or underlined under each heading and subheading. If you've made a written outline of the chapter, review this, too. Ideally, you should review the material periodically, to offset the rapid decline in retention once you've learned something. It's recommended that you review the material within 24 hours of the initial reading, and then again 72 hours later. After this, it's a good idea to review the material about once a week until you're tested on it.

When you're ready, do the self-test at the end of each chapter. Then check your responses against the list of correct answers provided in the back of this book. When you miss a question, it's important to go back and look up the correct answer. Otherwise, you may make the same mistake again. You may observe that the order of test items parallels the sequence of material in the chapter, thus facilitating your use of the self-test for study purposes.

 ## Where and When to Study

Once the semester is under way, you're ready to plan your study schedule. Consider your class schedule, the workload in each course, and other commitments, such as a part-time job or family responsibilities. Be realistic. Don't try to study too much material at one time.

First, it's important to find a place to study that is free from distractions. Then use this place only for studying. In this way, you'll develop a set of associations that will strengthen your study habits. One of the worst places to study is on your bed. The bed is associated with fatigue; thus, you may find yourself falling asleep rather than studying. When you find yourself daydreaming or worrying about something else, take a short break, and return when you're ready to study. When you finish studying, leave this place. By consistently doing this, you'll associate this place with studying and feel more like studying there.

It's also important to set aside particular times for study. You may wish to study for a given block of time and quit at the end of this period regardless of how much you've read. Or, you may want to study until you've covered a certain amount of material. Either way, it's best to study in reasonable blocks of time, about 1 to 3 hours. After a long stretch you may have difficulty concentrating on the material at hand. That's why it's a good idea to take a short break at least once an hour, or even on the half-hour when you're covering very difficult material. Also, you might select other things you enjoy doing, and make them contingent on completing your study goal for a given time slot. For instance, if you'd like to call a friend or watch television, do your studying first. Then make your call or watch TV as a reward to yourself.

Above all, don't procrastinate. Distribute your study times realistically so you don't try to absorb too much material at a time. For instance, if you must cover four chapters in this book for a test, plan to read no more than one chapter in a given time slot. Spacing out your study time cuts down on boredom and fatigue and also allows your memory time to consolidate the material. Your mind may continue absorbing the material in the intervals between study periods. This is especially important to keep in mind when you're learning complex or difficult material.

 ## Taking Tests

When taking a test, stay calm and reasonably relaxed. By keeping your anxiety at a mild to moderate level, you minimize its interference with your thinking process. If you encounter a question that makes you especially anxious, note this on the question sheet. Then proceed to do the remaining questions before returning to tackle the difficult question(s). Realizing that you've completed most of the test helps you to concentrate on the more difficult items.

Regardless of the type of test, take time to read the questions carefully. Make certain you understand what the instructor is asking. Don't read things into a question, making it more complicated than it is. If the item looks particularly confusing, raise your hand and ask the instructor to rephrase the item. Be sure also to read every single choice for multiple-choice questions before selecting the correct one.

Before answering an essay question, take a few moments to jot down a brief outline on the back of a page. This helps to keep your thoughts on the subject while you write. If your test includes both multiple-choice and essay questions, first outline the essay question. Then complete the multiple-choice questions before writing out the essay answer.

After you've read a multiple-choice question and selected an answer, it's best to reread the question making certain your answer matches the question. This helps to avoid simple "forgetting" mistakes, because material stays in our short-term memory for only about 30 seconds. By the time you've decided on the correct answer, chances are you've forgotten the exact wording of the question. Consequently, it's helpful to reread the question before marking your answer. This time, read the answer choices in reverse order, too.

Learn to eliminate incorrect answers before settling on the correct one. For instance, if there are four possible answers, eliminate the two that are the least plausible. With only two remaining answers to choose from, you have a 50-50 chance of selecting the correct one. Answers containing words like *always, never, only, must,* and *totally* often imply sweeping assertions and can usually be eliminated early on.

Should you ever change your answer? It all depends. If you have studied reasonably well and feel good about your answer, stick with it. However, if you have strong doubts about an answer, especially if you're not well informed on the subject, it might pay to reconsider. At the same time, a lot depends on the individual. In going over tests with students, we've found that anxious, impulsive students may initially choose an incorrect answer and would benefit from taking another look at their answer. On the other hand, students who lack self-confidence will often change a correct answer to an incorrect one because they distrust their own abilities. As a result, we suggest keeping track of the answers you change. Then go over each test, recording the number of answers you changed from wrong to right, and vice versa. Then take this information into consideration throughout future test taking.

Finally, there are other ways you can learn from your test results. If your instructor goes over the test in class, make it a point to attend that day. Find out what you missed, and, equally important, why. Were the questions different from what you expected, requiring, say, the understanding of concepts rather than factual information? If you didn't do well on an essay test, ask your instructor how you can do better next time. Try not to waste time making excuses or blaming your instructor or yourself. Find out what you need to *do* in order to improve your test performance next time. Then modify your study habits and test taking accordingly. Good luck!

About the Authors

Eastwood Atwater was a professor of psychology at Montgomery County Community College and lectured at Gwynedd-Mercy College. He also conducted a private practice in psychology. His Ph.D. was from the University of Chicago, where he studied with Carl Rogers. Dr. Atwater belonged to several professional associations. He was also the author of several books, including two other textbooks: *Adolescence,* 4th edition, and *Human Relations.* Dr. Atwater died in 1996.

Karen Duffy is a Distinguished Service Professor at the State University of New York, College at Geneseo. She received her Ph.D. in social and personality psychology from Michigan State University. Dr. Duffy is a family mediator for the New York Unified Court System. She has also served on the executive committee for the New York State Employees Assistance Program, as well as on a board of directors for a shelter for domestic violence and an educational committee for a family planning agency, and she has consulted to a variety of work settings on stress management, EAPs, and other work issues. She is a member of the American Psychological Society and the Eastern Psychological Association. Dr. Duffy has authored several other books, including *Community Mediation: A Handbook for Practitioners and Researchers* and *Community Psychology.* She also edits the annual editions for *Psychology* and *Personal Growth and Behavior.*

CHAPTER 1

Self-Direction in a Changing World

◆ **Social Change**
   A postindustrial society
   An uncertain but optimistic
      future
   Other social changes

◆ **Challenge of Self-Direction**
   The ambiguity of personal
      freedom
   Taking charge of our lives
   The new rules

◆ **Orientation of This Book**
   Continuity and change
   How we experience personal
      growth
   Beyond individualism

●●●●●●●●●●●●

After completing this chapter, you should be able to

1. Describe several characteristics of the postindustrial society.
2. Explain Fromm's twofold meaning of human freedom.
3. Discuss what it means to take charge of your life.
4. Describe some of the changing values associated with the "new rules."
5. List several personal traits, each of which are most and least likely to change throughout adulthood.
6. Describe the three-phase cycle by which we experience personal growth.
7. Discuss what is meant by the reassessment of the search for self-fulfillment.

Change has always been an important part of our American way of life. To understand the impact of change, let's look at two college students, Zachary and Karen, related by blood but separated by 130 years.

Zachary is a freshman in college in 1880. He is among the privileged few to attend college, mostly because his family is sufficiently well off to send him to school. Zachary travels to college by train, passing through miles of farmland and forests along the way. He keeps in touch with his family by letters. At school he reads by gaslight and handwrites all his term papers. There are only a few women on campus because higher education is considered inappropriate for them. Zachary hopes to be a physician, an occupation pretty much closed to women in the 1800s. Some women do attend Zachary's college but major in home economics, teacher education, and more traditional female majors. Zachary lives at a boardinghouse for college students. He takes his meals there but studies at the library. There are no computers or other technology such as photocopiers in the library. Zachary goes to the card catalogs to find what he needs. He copies everything as well as writes his papers by hand.

Karen, a fourth-generation descendant of Zachary, is a first-year college student in 1998. Since her parents' divorce, she has lived with her mother and sister. She is able to attend college mostly because of financial aid. Karen travels back and forth to college by plane several times a year, passing over a megalopolis spread out over several hundred miles. To keep in touch with her family, she has only to pick up the telephone and push buttons or send an electronic message via computer. Electricity lights up the room in which Karen reads and powers the computer she uses for term papers and correspondence. She lives in a coed dorm. Also, she is accustomed to mingling with students from different ethnic and racial groups on campus, about half of them being women. Karen uses the library as Zachary did, but she is fortunate to have an electronic card catalog, photocopiers, electronic abstract searches, and access to the information highway known as the World Wide Web. Karen also hopes to be a physician as did Zachary. She hopes, however, to specialize in gynecology, something Zachary would never dream of.

Social Change

Both Zachary and Karen have lived in periods of rapid **social change.** In Zachary's era, America shifted from an agrarian society to an urban one, and numerous inventions made transportation and communication more rapid and available. During his lifetime America became transformed from a frontier society to an industrial giant. Karen, in turn, takes technological change for granted. She believes that medical advances will soon have a cure for many life-threatening illnesses, including AIDS. She is also aware that the shortages of fossil fuels and pollution may eventually change the world she knows. Meanwhile, she has learned that rapid social change is normal and inevitable, though she occasionally wonders what lies ahead.

All of us now realize that the galloping rate of technological and social change is worldwide and has far-reaching effects. Social change seems to be a pervasive condition of our time (Christensen & Robinson, 1989). Most of the Third World nations want to develop economically as fast as possible. Meanwhile, people in every country are growing up in a world of greater interdependence. The revolution in communication, in particular, is recreating the world in the image of a "global village," in which every aspect of life—every thought, act, and institution—is being reconsidered in light of what is happening to people in other parts of the world.

A POSTINDUSTRIAL SOCIETY

The more economically developed nations such as the United States as Karen knows it are experiencing massive social changes of their own. Although people recognize the fact of change, they often disagree on the direction in which we're headed (Reich, 1995). Some assume that the world as we know it will last indefinitely and that all the changes around us will not shake the familiar social, economic, and political structures that hold our society together. A larger proportion of people, however, fed by a steady diet of bad news about crime, economic problems, world crises, and the threat of nuclear destruction, have adopted a bleaker view (Couch, 1996). Some of them feel that no one is really in control and that society is falling apart. Some also fear that today's solutions might become tomorrow's problems (Keys & Frank, 1987).

In the first of his three books, *Future Shock,* Alvin Toffler (1971) wrote about the disorientation and stress brought on by trying to cope with too many changes in too short a time. In his next book, *The Third Wave,* Alvin Toffler (1980) presented another, more optimistic view of where society is headed. He held that many of the technological and social changes we experienced in the 1980s and 1990s were neither isolated nor random. Instead, they are part of a larger pattern of an emerging civilization. Viewing history as a succession of rolling waves of change, Toffler now sees a major new wave

TABLE 1–1
CHANGES IN TYPES OF EMPLOYMENT OPPORTUNITIES
ACROSS THREE DECADES (IN THOUSANDS)

Type of Employment	1970	1980	1994
Manufacturing	20,746	21,942	20,157
Retail	15,008	20,191	25,699
Finance	3,945	5,993	8,141
Services	20,385	28,752	42,986

SOURCE: Adapted from U.S. Bureau of the Census (1995). *Statistical Abstract of the United States, 1995* (115th ed.). Washington, DC: U.S. Government Printing Office, p. 416.

sweeping over economically advanced nations. Today, Toffler believes we are in the midst of a third wave of major social change that is radically altering the way we live. We are moving into a **postindustrial** and **technological society,** with new ground rules for almost everything. Although the pattern of social change is complex and continues to evolve, the postindustrial period differs from the industrial primarily in the dominance of the **service industries** in contrast to the dominance of manufacturing and agriculture. (See Table 1–1.) All forms of labor will be affected by automation and computerized systems. The increasing need for technical solutions places a premium on intellectual and technical knowledge. In turn, educated, middle-class workers will make up a larger proportion of the work force. And finally, government and centralized political direction will dominate the postindustrial era as business dominated the industrial era. In his most recent book in this trilogy, *Power Shift,* Toffler (1990) suggests that there exists a crucial relationship between knowledge and power. He says that "knowledge is the source of the highest-quality power [and it] is gaining importance with every fleeting nanosecond" (p. 470). Those who have knowledge do and will have a valuable kind of power, a power quite different from that afforded by wealth or violence. Learning, then, must become a "way of being," especially if the future might be full of "white water" or unpredictability (Vaill, 1996). American schools are beginning to address this shift in power and the need for technology by increasing the number of computers available to children. Table 1–2 shows this rapid increase.

One problem related to increasing people's knowledge and use of technology is that some people fear technology. Such fear is called **technophobia.** For example, some people are apprehensive about using computers because they fear they will break the computers, make costly errors, look stupid, or lose control (Bloom, 1985). Pilisuk and Acredolo (1988) found that those who exhibit the highest levels of technophobia are women, minority group members, and individuals with the lowest levels of education. In other words, those individuals who are already the most powerless and who have the least experience with technology fear it most; they are perhaps also the very individuals who could benefit most from knowledge about technology in terms of their own individual career advancement.

Do you recognize any of these signs of the postindustrial society? Which are the most evident to you? As Popenoe (1989) points out, the notion of the postindustrial society is not without its critics. For instance, because of the recent political climate in the United States, some individuals are opposed to the idea of increased centralization and government control (Reich, 1995). Also, critics note that many features of the postindustrial society are not so different from those of the industrialized societies. Such problems as worker alienation, social and economic inequality, racism, and poverty in the

TABLE 1–2
INSTRUCTIONAL USE OF COMPUTERS IN ELEMENTARY AND SECONDARY SCHOOLS

Item	Unit	1985	1992
Computers used for instruction	per 1,000	1,034	3,536
Schools using computers	Percent	86	100
Schools with 15 or more computers	Percent	24	80

SOURCE: Adapted from U.S. Bureau of the Census (1995). *Statistical Abstract of the United States, 1995* (115th ed.). Washington, DC: U.S. Government Printing Office, p. 169.

big cities are still with us. Then, too, some feel that projections of postindustrial trends assume an overly optimistic view of the future. High government deficits, inflation, unemployment, and energy shortages suggest that we do not have unlimited horizons, any more than do Third World countries. As a result, a more pessimistic view of the future for advanced societies has emerged in recent decades, which strongly encourages us to reevaluate our growth-oriented priorities, to conserve, and to alter our lifestyles. Otherwise, the world in the twenty-first century will be more crowded, more polluted, less stable ecologically, and more vulnerable to disruptions.

AN UNCERTAIN BUT OPTIMISTIC FUTURE

Actually, how each of us understands the characteristic changes and trends in today's world is somewhat like the proverbial problem of whether we perceive a partly filled glass as half empty or half full. Pessimists tend to see the glass as half empty; optimists see

Our decisions are only as good as the information they are based on.

TABLE 1–3
WORLD AND U.S. POPULATION (IN THOUSANDS)

Geographic Location	1980	2000 (Projected)
World	4,457,463	6,169,794
United States	227,726	276,621

SOURCE: Adapted from U.S. Bureau of the Census (1995). *Statistical Abstract of the United States, 1995* (115th ed.). Washington, DC: U.S. Government Printing Office, pp. 845, 847.

it as half full. Similarly, social forecasters, who speculate on the long-term future, admit that we live in uncertain times, but they still project an optimistic view nevertheless. Although they do not necessarily agree on what the future holds for us, they typically see it as promising.

Social forecasters such as Alvin Toffler view many of the problems of our time as the growing pains of success rather than the harbingers of doom. Thus, the problems of overcrowding, economic inequality, environmental pollution, scarcity of resources, and poverty cannot be dismissed. But they should be seen as temporary or regional phenomena with which society must deal rather than the inevitable foreboding fate of civilization.

For instance, in the eighteenth and nineteenth centuries, Thomas Malthus first predicted the dire consequences of overpopulation. He theorized that whereas human population grew at a geometric rate (2, 4, 8, 16, etc.), food supplies increased only at an arithmetic rate (2, 3, 4, 5, etc.). Consequently, when population growth exceeded the food supply, Malthus predicted disasters such as famine, plague, and war would increase the death rate, thereby reducing the population to a level that is commensurate with the food supply. Malthus proposed that such disasters might be avoided by more moral means, such as marriage later in life and abstinence from sex. But Malthus did not foresee the invention of effective birth-control methods or the revolutionary changes in agriculture that have increased food production (Popenoe, 1989). Although world population growth continues to be a problem, it has somewhat stabilized in recent years, in part because of the success of birth-control programs in the developing nations. (See Table 1–3.)

OTHER SOCIAL CHANGES

Although both Karen and Zachary were affected by new technologies in their lifetimes, the technological changes Karen experienced were quite different. The changes in Zachary's lifetime pertained mostly to manufacturing and agriculture, whereas those in Karen's lifetime are related primarily to communication. Thus, despite surges in the world population the world seems smaller to Karen than it did to Zachary.

What other changes can we expect in the global village we know as the world? One change related to continued population expansion is pollution and other worries about the health of our environment. According to Donella Meadows (1991), author of *The Global Citizen,* 60 percent of the world's peoples do not have access to fresh drinking water. Each day there are 80 square miles less of tropical rain forest. Each minute 60 million barrels of nonrenewable oil are burned. Each day between 10 and 100 species of life become extinct because their habitats have been destroyed by humans. For more of

Pollution is an ongoing threat to the world in which we live.

what Meadows has to say, see Box 1–1. Only strict conservation measures can save our planet. The problem of pollution and exhaustion of natural resources in one country is also a problem for all other countries.

Another dramatic change is the increase in the heterogeneity of the population in the United States. An increasing number of immigrants from various regions of the world are entering this country. With them they bring a wealth of cultural ideas, languages, and customs. Accommodating these individuals will not be easy, in particular because some Americans are closed minded and rather ignorant of or insensitive to other cultures. Table 1–4 demonstrates the changes across decades in the composition of the American populace. Because of the swell in **cultural diversity** in this country, in this book we will offer information about various racial and ethnic groups in America and how they cope with problems of adjustment.

TABLE 1–4
POPULATION CHARACTERISTICS OF THE UNITED STATES (IN PERCENTS)

Date	White	Black	Hispanic	Other
1980	85.9	11.8	6.4	2.3
2000 (projected)	81.9	12.8	11.3	5.3

SOURCE: Adapted from U.S. Bureau of the Census (1995). *Statistical Abstract of the United States, 1995* (115th ed.). Washington, DC: U.S. Government Printing Office, p. 14.

BOX 1–1

THE WORLD IN TWO PAGES

Each *day* on this planet 35,000 people die of starvation, 26,000 of them children. This human toll is equivalent to 100 fully loaded 747-jets crashing every day. It is the same number of deaths every three days as were caused by the Hiroshima atomic bomb explosion. And each day, because of population growth, there are 220,000 more mouths to feed.

Yet enough food is *already* raised each year to feed not only the current human population of 5.2 billion, but also the population of 6.1 billion expected by the year 2000.

Each *day* 57 million tons of topsoil are lost to erosion, enough to cover more than my entire town of Plainfield, New Hampshire, to a depth of 8 inches. Each *day* there are 70 square miles more of desert, each four years an area greater than West Germany.

Yet the amount of food produced on the planet has doubled in the past thirty-five years. Hundreds of thousands of farmers know and practice agricultural technologies that preserve the soil, minimize the use of harmful chemicals, and still produce high yields. If their techniques could be widely adopted, world food production could be doubled again.

In the Third World 60 percent of the people do not have access to clean drinking water, which causes billions of preventable illnesses, infections, and deaths each year. One-fourth of the world's freshwater runoff is now made unusable by pollution.

Yet the amount of money that could provide clean water to everyone is only one-third the amount the world spends on cigarettes. The annual stable freshwater runoff of the planet is sufficient to supply double the present rate of human use—more if water is conserved or if unnecessary pollution is stopped.

Each *day* there are 80 square miles less of tropical forest. The annual loss of forest is equal to an area larger than Maine or Indiana. This forest loss results in soil erosion, flooding and drought, siltation of water reservoirs, extinction of species, and enhancement of the greenhouse effect.

Yet much of that deforestation is economically unviable, sustained only by the subsidies of governments that do not understand the direct economic value of a living forest. Saving the forest would actually make money for some of the poorest nations of the world.

Each *minute* 60 million barrels of oil—which is nonrenewable—are burned. We pay for it in spills, toxic wastes, foreign debt, urban air pollution, acid rain, and the release of carbon dioxide into the atmosphere at such rates as to threaten a global climate change.

Yet the world could produce all its current goods and services with at most one-fourth of the energy it now uses just by using it more efficiently. Two thousand times our total global energy consumption arrives free from the sun each day; it is infinitely renewable and nonpolluting.

Each *day* on this planet $2 billion is spent on armaments.

Each *day* between ten and one hundred species of life become extinct because their habitats have been destroyed by human activity.

SOURCE: Meadows, D. H. (1991). *The Global Citizen*. Washington, DC: Island Press. Reprinted with permission.

Because of its diversity, the United States possesses a wealth of cultures, languages, and customs. Sensitivity to and understanding of others' cultures are important for successful living today.

 ## Challenge of Self-Direction

These rapid social changes and the growing importance of information and access to technology heighten the challenge of **self-direction,** that is, the need to learn more about ourselves and our world as a means of directing our lives more effectively. For example, like Karen, the young woman you met in the opening vignette, some individuals find using computers to be an exciting challenge and actively seek out their use and actively try to learn more about computers. Others view computers as a threat and complain about having to use them or react passively to them (Staufer, 1992). We can respond to many life events in the same way: threat or challenge.

This is especially true for people in democratic and **individualistic societies.** Individualistic societies, a term utilized throughout this text, are societies in which individual gain is appreciated more than general societal gain. Individualistic societies can be contrasted to **collectivist societies,** where collective or societal gain is cherished over individual advancement. Many Eastern and Asian cultures are collective societies. In mainstream American culture, we enjoy greater personal freedom and challenge and take greater pride in personal achievements than do people in Eastern societies who better know what is expected of them and their position in society. By the same token we as Americans may be more vulnerable to insecurity, confusion, and loneliness.

THE AMBIGUITY OF PERSONAL FREEDOM

Nobody has written more eloquently about the ambiguity of human freedom than Erich Fromm (1963), the distinguished psychoanalyst. His experience of growing up in Germany during the Nazi regime and his subsequent move to the United States gave him tremendous insight into the problems of totalitarianism and human freedom. One of Fromm's basic ideas is that human freedom has a twofold meaning for people in the modern world: (1) the freedom "from" traditional authorities such as the state, and (2) the freedom "for" actualizing one's individual destiny. Fromm holds that although people in advanced societies have been freed from the bonds of preindividualistic society, which gave them both security and limitations, they have not gained freedom in the positive sense of realizing their individual selves, that is, the optimal expression of their intellectual, emotional, and social potential. If anything, the trend toward more human rights and personal freedom has accelerated, whereas the traditional sources of security, such as the closely knit family and the authoritative church and school, are themselves changing. As a result, we have more freedom to direct our lives—from the details of daily life to the more crucial choices such as our careers. But at times, the challenge of self-direction makes us feel more anxious, insecure, and isolated. Fromm contends that such isolation is so unbearable that many people are inclined to escape from the burden of freedom into new dependencies, such as looking to experts and the government for assistance or to conformity with the crowd.

The ambiguity of human freedom is especially evident when making important life choices, for example, who we want to be and how we want to live our lives. We may find ourselves becoming anxious and "freezing up" in the face of important decisions. We can use the term **decidophobia,** a term coined by Walter Kaufmann (1973), for the fear of making important life choices. Kaufmann suggested that most of us, at one time or another, have used the following strategies to avoid making serious, fateful decisions in our lives, that is, actualizing our positive freedom. A common strategy is drifting. Instead of choosing how to live, people simply drift along, either by living according to the status quo or by dropping out, as do those whose lives are guided by no ties, code, tradition, or major purpose. Another strategy is based on shared decision making, as in committees, marriage and family life, and assumed agreement among friends. Instead of really making a decision, people just talk until something happens. They presume a consensus, often never questioning it. But if things turn out badly, no one feels responsible: Each merely went along. Another frequently used strategy is based on an appeal to some type of authority—an expert, a movement, a religion, or some institution. Although individuals may experience a tension between their loyalty and their personal conscience, they find innumerable ways to justify either alternative.

Truly autonomous people rely on none of these strategies. Some psychologists call these truly autonomous, optimal beings **self-actualized** individuals. (We describe self-actualization in more detail in the next chapter.) Autonomous or actualized individuals accept responsibility for their lives and carefully scrutinize the alternatives available to them. But they also keep their eyes open and have the courage to admit when they are wrong and need to change. Many Russian writers working in Soviet times, such as Alexander Solzhenitsyn, are examples of truly autonomous persons who made one fateful decision after another in order to maintain personal integrity, often against overwhelming odds in the oppressive Soviet society of their day. Box 1–2 contains a story about another Soviet writer named Joseph Brodsky, an eventual Nobel Prize winner in literature who faced terrible repercussions because of his strong desire to be an author. For most of today's Russians who live in a more democratic society, self-actualization is

BOX 1–2

JOSEPH BRODSKY

On February 18, 1964, in Leningrad, in the Dzerzhinsky district court—a grubby room with a spit-covered floor—there began the hearing of Joseph Brodsky, who was already well-known in the city. The twenty-three-year-old Brodsky was charged with "malicious parasitism"—that is, being out of a job—which was a violation of Soviet law. Tall and thin, with red hair and bright cheeks, Brodsky (with a guard next to him) spoke calmly, trying to explain to an ignorant and hostile judge that his work was writing poetry. She and Brodsky had the following exchange, which was written down clandestinely by the sympathetic journalist Frida Vigdorova.

JUDGE: And who recognized that you are a poet? Who listed you among poets?
BRODSKY: No one. (*Dispassionately.*) Who listed me a member of the human race?
JUDGE: Did you study this?
BRODSKY: What?
JUDGE: To be a poet? Did you try to graduate from a school where they prepare . . . where they teach . . .
BRODSKY: I don't think that it comes from education.
JUDGE: What then?
BRODSKY: I think that it's . . . (*bewildered*) . . . from God.

This was like something out of Kafka or an absurdist play. The judge sent Brodsky under police escort to a psychiatric hospital to determine his sanity. Things were very tough there: he was forcibly given sulfur injections, which caused the slightest movement to be unbearably painful.

A favorite amusement of the male nurses was to wrap Brodsky in a sheet, dip him in an icy bath, and then toss him, still wrapped in the sheet, alongside a radiator. They called this the "cold-damp envelope." As it dried, the sheet tore off Brodsky's skin. His roommate committed suicide by slitting his veins with a razor at night, and Brodsky was afraid that he would never leave the hospital alive. His sufferings during that terrible period are reflected in the long philosophical poem "Gorbunov and Gorchakov."

Forensic psychiatrists found Brodsky sane, and he went back to court. The same judge who committed him asked him, "What good have you done for your homeland?"

Brodsky replied with quiet persistence, "I wrote poetry. That is my work. I am convinced . . . I believe that what I write will be of service to people, and not only now but for future generations."

All Brodsky's attempts to explain fell on deaf ears. The predetermined sentence read, in part, "Brodsky systematically does not fulfill the duties of a Soviet man in the production of material goods. . . . He wrote and recited his decadent poems. From the report of the Commission on Work with Young Writers, it is clear that Brodsky is not a poet. . . . Brodsky is to be sent to remote areas for a term of five years at forced labor."

SOURCE: Reprinted with the permission of The Free Press, a Division of Simon & Schuster, from *St. Petersburg: A Cultural History* by Solomon Volkov. Copyright © 1995 by Solomon Volkov.

also a possibility. However, whether the Russian people respond in a timely and active fashion to the challenge of democracy and defend their new way of life depends on whether they understand that they, not the government, hold fate in their hands (Balakrishnan, 1993).

TAKING CHARGE OF OUR LIVES

Today, people all over the world are pursuing a similar odyssey of freedom. A dramatic example is the bold leadership of Gorbachev and Yeltsin in introducing capitalism and democracy into the newly formed Commonwealth of Independent States. Much of the dissatisfaction that occurs in other countries reflects people's desire for the greater freedom and economic opportunity they see in the more economically advanced societies. Similarly, many of the people who immigrate to the United States seek the very freedoms we take for granted.

Surveys indicate that the majority of Americans feel they have more freedom and control over their lives than their parents did. As for the two individuals in our opening vignette, Karen probably experiences more freedom as well as more control than did Zachary. Most people today feel their parents' lives were hemmed in by all kinds of social, educational, and economic constraints that they themselves have escaped. For instance, Thomas (1986) found that three-fourths of all respondents, and 81 percent of the 18- to 29-year-olds, definitely say they have more control over their lives than their parents did. People, however, do not necessarily feel they are better off financially than their parents. But they do believe they have more options in the important areas of education, work, sex, marriage, family, friends, travel, possessions, where to live, and how to live. Would you agree?

Exercising our positive freedom means facing up to the necessity of decision making in our lives, especially the life choices that shape our destinies. At the same time, the fear of making the wrong decision in front of others is so great that many youths speak of "keeping my options open," living in an "extended holding pattern," and being "leery of commitment." Much of this reaction is understandable in light of the uncertainties of our age; however, research has indeed demonstrated that individuals extrinsically motivated by financial success, an appealing appearance, or social recognition have lower vitality, lower self-actualizing potential, and report more physical (health) symptoms than individuals who are more intrinsically or internally inspired. Intrinsically motivated, autonomous individuals appear to be more healthy, self-accepting, and community minded (Kasser & Ryan, 1996).

Taking charge of our lives means that we can and must choose for ourselves. No decision, by default, becomes a decision in fact. Also, we must make choices within a time-bound existence, so that some of our choices might fall short of the ideal. Thankfully, not all decisions are written in stone. We can and often do change many decisions as we grow and mature. Meanwhile, the realization that our decisions are only as good as the information they are based on reminds us again of the value of education and critical thinking skills.

Acting on our positive freedom also means assuming responsibility for our choices, without blaming others or fate for what happens to us. In fact, those who are self-actualized or internally motivated experience less interpersonal distress and more interpersonal closeness (Sheffield, Carey, Patenaude, & Lambert, 1995), perhaps because they are less likely to blame others. Interestingly, self-actualization correlates with **altruism** or the desire to help others at cost to the helper (Sharma & Rosha, 1992). Admittedly, we had no choice about being thrust into the world, but we have a great deal of choice in the manner in which we live. Yet, we often hear people say such things as "I can't help it because that's the way I am" or "Naturally I'm this way because of the way I grew up." These people fail to realize that free choice and responsibility go hand in hand. As a constant reminder of this fact, Viktor Frankl (1978) suggests that the Statue of Liberty on the East Coast be supplemented by the Statue of Responsibility on the West Coast.

Self-realization also involves taking calculated risks and making commitments in spite of uncertainty. Growth involves stepping into unfamiliar and potentially dangerous situations, thereby leaving us more vulnerable to hurt and disappointment. Individuals who are perfectionists are especially prone not to take risks and to low levels of actualization. Self-actualizers are more tolerant of failure (Flett, Hewitt, Blankstein, & Mosher, 1991). How perfectionistic are you? Figure 1–1 presents the "Almost Perfect Scale" so that you can learn about yourself and your perfectionism.

The decision to grow or actualize our potential often has to be made in spite of these dangers and therefore requires courage. Theologian Paul Tillich calls this the "courage to be," that is, the courage to affirm ourselves and our possibilities in spite of the risks involved—a theme also found in the writings of psychologists like Carl Rogers and Rollo May.

In less obvious ways, of course, we run a risk whenever we avoid growing. Each time we pass up an opportunity to develop a new skill or value security over challenge, we run the risk of becoming stagnant or succumbing to boredom, the breeding ground of so many of today's scourges of drugs, violence, and irresponsible sex. When we habitually suppress or deny the inherent growth tendency of the human organism itself, we risk becoming maladaptive, sometimes in obvious ways, sometimes in subtle ways, sometimes immediately, or sometimes later in life. Much research supports these notions. Fortunately, higher education, one mechanism for growth that you as well as Zachary and Karen are taking advantage of, helps individuals self-actualize (Barnes & Srinivas, 1993; MacKay & Kuh, 1994). Maslow (1968) once observed that many of the characteristic disorders of our time such as the "stunted person," the "amoral person," or the "apathetic person" result from the fundamental failure to grow.

THE NEW RULES

Fortunately, the times in which we live afford a more supportive, if hazardous, environment for actualizing our positive freedom. This, in turn, heightens the challenge of self-direction. The cumulative impact of social changes has given rise to new social values and **new rules** by which people live. Generally, this change means a reduced concern with adapting to things as they are and a greater interest in shaping the environment to meet one's own needs and goals. This shift in values should not be seen as merely an increase in self-centeredness and self-indulgence—the excesses of the "me generation"—as its critics claim. It is true that many people are preoccupied with themselves today. But the increase in self-centeredness may prove to be an incidental feature of the transition phase from the old rules to a synthesis of the old and new.

A more central feature is the modification of the basic **giving/getting pact** (Yankelovich, 1981) or the agreement between individuals and their environment. This pact consists of the unwritten rules governing what we give in our personal relationships, work, and community and what we expect in return. It is rarely made explicit. Rather, we take it so much for granted that we hardly realize how extensive and powerful it is, until it begins to change.

FIGURE 1–1

THE ALMOST PERFECT SCALE

INSTRUCTIONS: If you strongly disagree with the following statements, circle 1; if you strongly agree with the following statements, circle 7. For variation in degree of disagreement or agreement, circle the appropriate numbers between 2 and 6.

Standards and Order

1. I am an orderly person.

   1   2   3   4   5   6   7
   strongly disagree   strongly agree

2. I have high standards for my performance at work or at school.

   1   2   3   4   5   6   7
   strongly disagree   strongly agree

3. I have to admit that basically I'm a perfectionist.

   1   2   3   4   5   6   7
   strongly disagree   strongly agree

4. It bothers me to be distracted when I have work to do.

   1   2   3   4   5   6   7
   strongly disagree   strongly agree

5. I think things should be put away in their place.

   1   2   3   4   5   6   7
   strongly disagree   strongly agree

6. I have trouble leaving things incomplete.

   1   2   3   4   5   6   7
   strongly disagree   strongly agree

7. I like to always be organized and disciplined.

   1   2   3   4   5   6   7
   strongly disagree   strongly agree

8. I often think it is easier to do something myself than it is to get someone else to do it.

   1   2   3   4   5   6   7
   strongly disagree   strongly agree

9. I like to be very careful and precise when I measure things.

   1   2   3   4   5   6   7
   strongly disagree   strongly agree

10. I try to do my best at everything I do.

       1   2   3   4   5   6   7

    strongly disagree   strongly agree

11. Neatness is important to me.

       1   2   3   4   5   6   7

    strongly disagree   strongly agree

12. I like to make lists of tasks I have to do and then check them off as I do them.

       1   2   3   4   5   6   7

    strongly disagree   strongly agree

Relationships

13. I wish I had closer relationships with my friends.

       1   2   3   4   5   6   7

    strongly disagree   strongly agree

14. I hate to cry.

       1   2   3   4   5   6   7

    strongly disagree   strongly agree

15. When I have a problem, I should be able to solve it by myself.

       1   2   3   4   5   6   7

    strongly disagree   strongly agree

16. Seeking the help of a counselor would be hard.

       1   2   3   4   5   6   7

    strongly disagree   strongly agree

17. Relationships seem easier for other people.

       1   2   3   4   5   6   7

    strongly disagree   strongly agree

18. When it comes to emotions, I want to understand them so I can get rid of them.

       1   2   3   4   5   6   7

    strongly disagree   strongly agree

19. Sometimes I feel like I could cry but I don't want to.

       1   2   3   4   5   6   7

    strongly disagree   strongly agree

20. It is no good to let strong feelings show.

       1   2   3   4   5   6   7

    strongly disagree   strongly agree

21. I find it hard to talk about my feelings.

 1 2 3 4 5 6 7
 strongly disagree   strongly agree

22. I feel uncomfortable in intimate relationships.

 1 2 3 4 5 6 7
 strongly disagree   strongly agree

23. Some people have told me I seem cold and distant.

 1 2 3 4 5 6 7
 strongly disagree   strongly agree

24. There are very few people in the world to whom I closely relate.

 1 2 3 4 5 6 7
 strongly disagree   strongly agree

Anxiety

25. I have trouble relaxing.

 1 2 3 4 5 6 7
 strongly disagree   strongly agree

26. I am fearful of making mistakes.

 1 2 3 4 5 6 7
 strongly disagree   strongly agree

27. When I think of things I have to do, I feel anxious.

 1 2 3 4 5 6 7
 strongly disagree   strongly agree

28. I often feel anxious when I strive to complete a task.

 1 2 3 4 5 6 7
 strongly disagree   strongly agree

Procrastination

29. I tend to procrastinate so long that I never have enough time to do things right.

 1 2 3 4 5 6 7
 strongly disagree   strongly agree

30. Other people seem to be more efficient than I am.

 1 2 3 4 5 6 7
 strongly disagree   strongly agree

31. I tend to put things off for as long as I can.

    1   2   3   4   5   6   7

  strongly disagree   strongly agree

32. My standards are so high that often I procrastinate.

    1   2   3   4   5   6   7

  strongly disagree   strongly agree

SCORING: Add your total points for each question. The higher your score, the more your tendency toward perfectionism. To understand where you are most perfectionistic, examine your scores for each area (Standards and Order; Relationships; Anxiety; Procrastination). Extreme perfectionists score high in all four areas.

SOURCE: Johnson, D. P., & Slaney, R. B. (1996). Perfectionism: Scale development and a study of perfectionistic clients in counseling. *Journal of College Student Development, 37* (1), 29-41. Reproduced with permission. Direct correspondence to Robert B. Slaney, Department of Counselor Education, Counseling Psychology and Rehabilitation Services, 314 Cedar Building, The Pennsylvania State University, University Park, PA 16802.

The old giving/getting pact, which was in effect throughout much of this century, was based on self-denial and loyalty to society much as in today's collective societies. It might be paraphrased this way: "I'll work hard and honor my commitments. I'll stifle my frustrations and suppress my own desires. Instead, I'll do what is expected of me. I'll put the needs of society and others before my own. I realize I give a lot, but what I get in return is well worth it—an ever-rising standard of living, a loyal spouse and kids, a good job, and a nice home. And last but not least, I'm proud to be an American, a citizen of the greatest country on earth." Much of this ethic was at the heart of the American dream—the opportunity to get ahead through hard work and loyalty, or to have your children do so; the belief in working for delayed rewards; and conformity to existing social norms.

But now millions of Americans have grown wary of the demands for further sacrifices, which they believe may no longer be warranted. Americans seem to be becoming more individualistic and egocentric. They feel the old rules needlessly restrict the individual at the expense of large institutions, especially big business and government, which use their power to advance their own interests. Consequently, more Americans are engaged in correcting the imbalance. They are modifying the basic giving/getting pact in order to get more in return for their efforts. Although these changes may be seen more clearly among members of the younger generation, who have grown up taking the newer values for granted, such changes have also filtered into the population at large and affect people of every age and social class.

The new giving/getting pact is based on the pursuit of personal fulfillment and individual rights. The majority of Americans are now engaged in the pursuit of **self-fulfillment** or self-direction in some way. In fact, there is emerging evidence that self-direction is one of several universal human values found across many cultures (S. Schwartz, 1994). Figure 1–2 names and depicts the relationship of many of the universal human values. Pay close attention to self-direction and its relationship to openness to change and stimulation.

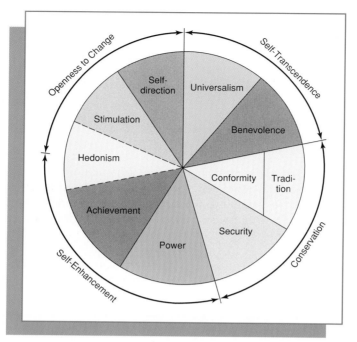

FIGURE 1–2

Universal human values. Theoretical model of relations among motivational types of values, higher order value types, and bipolar value dimensions.
SOURCE: Schwartz, S. H. (1992). Universals in the content and structure of values: Theoretical advances and empirical tests in 20 countries. In M. Zanna (Ed.), *Advances in Experimental Social Psychology, 25*, 1–65. Orlando, FL: Academic. Reprinted with permission.

There is also greater impatience to satisfy one's goals. Individuals scoff when told of the need to "pay your dues" through hard work to achieve success in a career or happiness in a marriage. They want success and happiness now. Or to paraphrase the more self-centered seekers, "I want it *all* now." The "future" orientation of earlier generations—with the assumption that things are getting better and better—has been superseded by a "now" orientation, by living fully in the present, haunted by the world's uncertain future.

Still another change is the greater assertiveness of individuals, who are more concerned with their personal rights than with social responsibilities. As a result, more individuals are now relentlessly pursuing their own interests and goals, hopefully without violating the rights of others. However, when conflicts of interest arise, participants are less willing to deny themselves anything to accommodate others, as if adhering to a new moral principle—"I have a duty to myself."

 Orientation of This Book

Each of us faces the challenge of reconciling the old and new rules. We must honor the old values of hard work, frugality, and moderation to get an education and secure our jobs and, thus, the means to enjoy the new values associated with self-fulfillment, that is personal pleasure and expressiveness. In many ways these two sets of values contradict each other, making it difficult to reconcile them. This task is hard enough for reasonably well-educated and well-informed individuals. It is even more confusing and upsetting to the less educated, who anticipate more dramatic and negative social changes than do college-educated people (DeStefano, 1990).

People who seek guidance from popular self-help books, television shows that entertain more than they educate, and movements that blend pop psychology with quasi-religious thought do not always fare well. Many of these sources oversimplify the process of personal and social change, generating grossly unrealistic expectations and, ultimately, disappointment.

In contrast, a textbook on psychology can provide sound principles of development and behavior. Throughout this book we shall attempt to show how the principles and findings of contemporary psychology can help us to better understand ourselves and others, and thus to cope more effectively with our environment and fulfill more of our human potential.

This statement does not mean that personal growth can be achieved by simply reading a book on the subject. Nor does mere exposure to scientific knowledge guarantee that you will use it. For instance, despite evidence that cigarette smoking is hazardous to one's health and the fact that most individuals who smoke can state that they know smoking is harmful, cigarettes are widely used in our society. Modern psychology can provide dependable information about ourselves and our world, but the mastery and effective use of this knowledge is up to the reader. Let us next look at some issues related to seeking self-direction.

CONTINUITY AND CHANGE

A key issue for psychologists and the public alike is the extent to which people change while growing up. Can our personalities really change? Or do they simply mellow? A generation ago psychologists and the public alike assumed that genes and early experiences are the decisive influences on development, so that once we reach adulthood we tend to remain that way. Then, during the 1960s and 1970s, new findings as well as social trends suggested that people tend to continue growing throughout their adult lives. Today, authorities acknowledge that there is both continuity and change in development, but they differ on which is predominant.

Robert McCrae and Paul Costa (1994) have found some evidence for the stability of personality throughout the life span. The highest degree of stability was found in the domain of introversion-extroversion, which reflects gregariousness, warmth, and assertiveness. There is almost as much stability in the area of "neuroticism," which includes such traits as anxiety, depression, and hostility. Thus, individuals who are expressive and outgoing in their teens are apt to remain that way as adults, as are those who are inhibited and shy in their teens. **Longitudinal studies** indicate slight drops over the course of adulthood in anxiety, hostility, and impulsiveness. That is, individuals change somewhat because of their personal maturity and life experiences, but the differences between themselves and others remain much the same. For instance, an impulsive 20-year-old like Karen, the medical student from the chapter opening, may be a bit less impulsive by the time she is 55, but she is still likely to be more impulsive than her agemates. As people grow older, their stability becomes more evident. Thus, there is more stability from 30 to 40 than there is from 20 to 30 years of age. Part of the reason is that we select environments and marry people who help sustain our traits (Caspi & Herbener, 1990).

Other researchers, such as Kagan (1989), acknowledge the importance of stability but emphasize the variability or change that occurs in development. They question the extent to which the persistence of traits reflects inherited predispositions and childhood influences or, instead, patterns of social roles and expectations that people get locked into. They point out that only certain traits have been shown to be relatively stable, most notably, aspects of social and emotional style, such as introversion-extroversion, anxiety, and depression. At the same time, Kagan (1989) has found that people are much more likely to change in other aspects, especially their self-esteem, sense of personal mastery or control over their environment, and their values. The emphasis on the potential for change has been seized on by those who want to foster change, from weight watchers to social watchers, all of whom stress openness to change throughout the course of adulthood.

In the final analysis, the tension between continuity and change is found not only in academic debates but also in each of us. How much we change depends greatly on the different priorities we assign to stability or change, that is, our ideas about who we want to be and how we want to live our lives. Thus, people with traditional values tend to exhibit a high degree of stability in their lives *unless* something happens to make them change. The events most likely to change deeply ingrained patterns are usually quite dramatic, such as an unwanted divorce, the death of a child, failure in one's career, or being taken hostage in a crisis. In these cases, individuals may become motivated to make marked changes in their outlook and personality. In contrast, those who put more value on personal growth may continue changing to a greater extent throughout their lives *unless* they become stuck somewhere. For instance, a coal miner who spends 10 hours a day for 30 years under the earth may have little opportunity for personal growth. However, we are now in the midst of a revolution in human development away from the traditional pattern of continuity toward greater change throughout our life span. Medical advances, such as plastic surgery and organ transplants, as well as the techniques of behavior change and the encouragement of change provided by thousands of support groups are part of this trend.

HOW WE EXPERIENCE PERSONAL GROWTH

To believe we can change is one thing. Actively to pursue and achieve personal change is something else, because the experience of change can be confusing and unsettling. To understand and facilitate **personal growth,** Sidney Jourard (1975) has given us a **phenomenology** of growth, or an account of how we subjectively experience it. Like all patterns of development, our inner experience of growth tends to be uneven, with spurts and plateaus. We may be willing to try out something new one minute and feel a need for consolidating our gains the next. Because we experience our inner world more as a continuous flow of ideas, feelings, and meanings, we are more apt to realize that we've grown in retrospect than while we're in the midst of a particular growth cycle.

The experience of growth tends to follow a three-phase cycle. Typically, it begins with (1) acknowledging some change within ourselves or our surroundings, which evokes (2) a sense of dissonance or dissatisfaction within, which in turn leads us to (3) reorganize our experience in some way, such as adopting a new attitude toward ourselves or others.

1. Acknowledging change.   Growth usually begins with the acknowledgment of change. Actually, changes occur all the time, but we're not always aware of them. A constant awareness of change would be too disturbing. Instead, we strive to construct an image of ourselves and our world that pictures reality as more stable and under our control than it really is. As a result, we become more acutely aware of changes at some moments than at others. Sometimes we become aware of change rather suddenly, for example, by receiving an unexpected compliment or criticism. Times of uncertainty and decision making also remind us that more changes will be forthcoming, for example, when we are wrestling with the choice of a college major or a career. Taking on new responsibilities like marriage, parenthood, or a promotion at work is a major source of growth. Disappointment and failure, such as being fired from a job without warning, force us to acknowledge change. The common denominator in all these experiences is the realization that things are different from what they were—or what we believed or expected they would be.

2. A sense of dissonance or dissatisfaction.   Whether or not the awareness of change leads to growth depends on how we react. Sometimes we may respond to change defensively, with little awareness of our real feelings, such as the man who dismisses his failure to get a promotion at work by saying, "I really didn't want it anyway." Because this man is denying his feelings about the change, he minimizes the possibility for growth. In contrast, when we feel disappointment from such experiences, we may be aroused or motivated to further change. Thus, the growth cycle is often triggered by disappointment and failure. For example, the agony of failing a test or course and seeking remedial help may drive a student to learn more effective reading and study habits. Of course, we may also grow under happier conditions, when our feelings of discomfort come from unmet growth needs rather than from dissatisfaction. Consider a woman like Karen, the young college student at the beginning of the chapter, who wants to go to medical school because she feels more women doctors are needed, rather than because she feels that she won't be quite as successful as a lawyer.

This phase of growth is inevitably accompanied by a certain degree of anxiety and discomfort. When our motive for growth proceeds out of a sense of challenge or mastery, such as when we take up a new sport, we may simply be stimulated and mildly apprehensive about the outcome. But when our motive springs from profound dissatisfaction with ourselves, our feelings tend to be more agonizing. Either way, the old saying "How can something that feels so bad be so good?" reminds us that these unsettling feelings are more often than not a necessary part of achieving some desired goal.

3. Reorganizing our experience.   In conventional terms this phase is often expressed as acquiring new ideas and then altering our attitudes, behaviors, and values. In some instances, such as the discovery that most people feel anxious about tests, additional knowledge or insight may alter our understanding of ourselves or others. Or we may become aware of our own largely unconscious processes, such as the realization that our chronic sense of anxiety during tests masks an undue fear of criticism and failure. Or we may adopt a new attitude toward another person, becoming more willing to listen to someone's criticism because we know that the person wants to help rather than hurt us. Growth may also take the form of new self-perceptions, such as the increased self-acceptance and confidence that comes with an achievement like getting a degree. The main point is that each inner adjustment or change we make affects the whole of our experience, so that growth consists in the continuous reorganization of that experience.

We're more apt to have positive, gratifying feelings at this point than in the earlier stages. We're also more likely to understand how we've grown. As Kierkegaard, an existentialist philosopher, once said, "Life is necessarily understood in a backward direction, but it must be lived in a forward direction." Perhaps you have looked back at a very trying time in your life that eventually led to growth and said to yourself, "Now I realize what was happening in my life."

BEYOND INDIVIDUALISM

Growth is supposed to enlarge our self-understanding and enhance our relationships with others. But there's always the risk of becoming overly absorbed with ourselves in the process. It's not surprising, then, that the notion of self-fulfillment, especially the popularized versions, has attracted its share of criticism. Even our definitions of success are changing—from self-improvement through hard work and delayed pleasures to egocentrism, with its desire for immediate rewards. Admittedly, there's some truth to this criticism.

However, in their book *Habits of the Heart,* Bellah, Madsen, Sullivan, Swidler, and Tipton (1985) point to a still more basic issue, namely, the mistaken notion of rugged and radical **individualism** associated with self-fulfillment. Throughout extensive interviews with Americans, they found very few selfish, narcissistic "me generation" people. What they did find was that the language of individualism, the primary American language of self-understanding, limits the way people think. Although individualism has long been a central value in American life, the notion of self-fulfillment is too often understood as an exaggerated extension of individualism. As a result, more than ever before, we insist on "finding our true selves independent of any culture or social influence, being responsible to that self alone, and making its fulfillment the very meaning of our lives" (p. 150).

At the same time we are becoming less committed to the common purposes of society, as is true for collectivist societies or earlier periods of American life where self-orientation is and was held in check by strong ties to the family, church, and local community. But now that these ties are weakening, people are putting aside the public concerns that are necessary for the survival of a free, democratic society.

The contradiction between the lone individual and the necessary social context of life is repeatedly expressed in surveys of Americans' attitudes. For instance, when George Gallup (1991) and his pollsters asked Americans, "Are you generally satisfied/dissatisfied with the way things are going in your personal life?" more than three-fourths said they were satisfied with their personal lives. But when asked about the way things were going in the United States, barely half responded in this way. Similarly, in another Gallup survey, Americans were asked how optimistic or pessimistic they felt about their own futures and that of the world. Again, 44 percent felt very optimistic about their own futures. Only half as many, however, felt very optimistic about the future of the world (DeStefano, 1990). Apparently, people fail to realize the contradictions in their views. How can you personally expect a bright financial future despite a mounting national deficit, unemployment, and poverty? Also, how realistic is it to expect a happy family life while being surrounded by a rising divorce rate and harder times for working parents?

Meanwhile, a major reassessment of the search for self-fulfillment may be giving rise to a more realistic view of life and personal fulfillment. Millions of Americans are discovering, often by painful experience, that preoccupation with their personal needs is not a direct path to fulfillment. But their life experiments are not leading them back toward a stifling of the self, as in the past; nor are they retreating to the cultivation of their own gardens without regard for the rest of the world. Instead, we may be in the midst

Life's deepest satisfactions come through our relationships with others.

of developing new rules of living, which involve a realignment of the claims of self and society. The heart of this new outlook is the realization that personal fulfillment can be achieved only in relation to others—through a web of shared meanings that transcend the isolated individual. Personal fulfillment in the deeper sense of the term requires commitments that endure over long periods of time. These may be commitments to loved ones, family, friends, career, ideas, beliefs, social causes, nature, places, or adventures—depending on the individual and his or her values. The term *commitment* shifts the focus away from unduly individualistic notions of the self, either self-denial or self-fulfillment, toward the more inclusive self-in-relationships or connectedness with others.

Similarly, as Bellah et al. (1985) point out, we need to look beyond the language of radical individualism to the deeper truth that we do not find ourselves independently of other people and institutions but through them: "We discover who we are face to face and side by side with others" (p. 84) at home, at work, and in the larger community. Almost all of our activity occurs in relationships, groups, and community, structured by institutions and interpreted by cultural meaning. The isolated, unencumbered self is an empty abstraction. Even the positive aspects of our individualism are dependent in countless ways on a social context that sustains us even when we are not fully aware of it. Although most of the people interviewed in Bellah's study extolled autonomy and self-fulfillment, they did not imagine that the good life could be achieved alone. Instead, "Those we interviewed would almost all agree that connectedness to others in work, love, and community is essential to happiness, self-esteem, and moral worth" (p. 84).

In retrospect, it appears that the traditional rules of living put an undue burden on the individual, suppressing personal desires for the sake of social adjustment. As a corrective, the self-fulfillment movement has given greater importance to the individual and the satisfaction of personal needs, though too often fostering a radical individualism as well. However, as we've seen, human fulfillment is more complex than popularly portrayed and requires a better balance between the claims of self and society. Hans Selye (1980), the noted authority on stress, once observed that people suffering from a stress-linked illness also have a warped view of life—one that emphasizes either too much sacrifice or too much selfishness. A one-sided approach to life won't do. Throughout this book we'll explore the major areas of personality, growth, and behavior. But every realm of life requires a constant striving to achieve that level of give and take between ourselves and others that ensures a truly satisfying life.

SUMMARY

SOCIAL CHANGE

We began the chapter by describing how rapid technological and social changes are having far-reaching effects throughout the world. The revolution in communication, in particular, is giving rise to a global outlook in which people in Third World countries are influenced by what they see in the more economically developed countries, and we, in turn, are affected by what happens to them.

Economically developed nations, such as the United States, are moving into a postindustrial era, with the service industries becoming dominant and a premium put on intellectual and technical knowledge. Similarly, the **information age** drives us to create, process, or distribute information. Social forecasters admit we live in uncertain times, but they tend to have an optimistic view of the future. The biggest challenge is how to prepare people to live and work in the new service-oriented information society that demands high-tech skills and more education. Women, minorities, and less-educated individuals may actually fear technology or have technophobia.

CHALLENGE OF SELF-DIRECTION

Living in a rapidly changing society poses an even greater challenge to self-direction of individuals than was the case in the past. Yet, as Fromm reminds us, we have been more successful in achieving freedom "from" traditional authorities than in using this freedom "for" actualizing our individual destinies. The challenge of self-direction is so demanding that we tend to escape from making important choices by looking to the experts or conforming to the crowd. In contrast, taking charge of our lives means facing up to the importance of decision making, taking calculated risks for the sake of growth, and assuming full responsibility for our lives.

The "new rules" in today's individualistic societies accentuate the challenge of self-direction. As a result, people are increasingly questioning the old rules that emphasize social conformity and self-denial. Instead, they are busily pursuing their individual rights and, in varying degrees, self-fulfillment. A major change is that people want and expect more out of life in return for their efforts.

ORIENTATION OF THIS BOOK

The search for self-fulfillment creates a predicament for the individual as well as the nation, challenging us to reconcile the old and new values. People looking to self-help books tend to find an oversimplified idea of self-fulfillment, leading to unrealistic expectations that end in disappointment. In contrast, the field of psychology offers sound principles and tested knowledge that may help in realistic self-direction and growth.

According to psychology, the tendencies toward both continuity and change are present in each of us. How much you and I change depends greatly on the different priorities we assign to stability or change. At the same time, we live in an era in which personal growth occurs more widely than previously recognized.

The subjective experience of growth involves a three-phase cycle: (1) the acknowledgment of change within ourselves or our environment, (2) a sense of dissonance or dissatisfaction within, which in turn leads to (3) reorganizing our experience in some way, such as adopting a new attitude toward ourselves or others.

Critics claim that the self-fulfillment movement encourages people to become unduly self-centered and individualistic and, thus, to withdraw from the social involvement necessary for a democratic society. Today, however, a major reassessment of the self-fulfillment movement is under way, giving rise to a more realistic view of life and personal fulfillment. The heart of the new outlook calls for a realignment of the claims of self and society so that personal fulfillment can be realized only in relation to others—through a web of shared meanings that transcend the isolated individual.

SELF-TEST

1. The postindustrial society is characterized by the dominance of
   a. machines
   b. unemployment
   c. service and information industries
   d. blue-collar workers

2. In the United States there is a trend toward
   a. fewer human rights
   b. ethnic diversity
   c. conformity to authority
   d. greater materialism

3. Most service workers are dealing primarily with
   a. information
   b. health care
   c. machines
   d. finances

4. Who suffers most from technophobia?
   a. mid-level managers
   b. white-collar workers
   c. children
   d. minorities and women

5. An individualistic society
   a. is exemplified by American culture
   b. regards social gain as important
   c. is exemplified by China
   d. is the same as a collectivist society

6. The "old rules" governing Americans were based on self-denial and
   a. loyalty to society   c. personal fulfillment
   b. a "now" orientation   d. individual rights

7. Which of the following characteristics is the most likely to change throughout adulthood?
   a. gregariousness   c. self-esteem
   b. anxiety   d. neuroticism

8. According to Sidney Jourard, the subjective experience of growth begins with
   a. a sense of dissonance   c. a commitment to change
   b. acknowledging change   d. reorganizing experience

9. Surveys show that the majority of Americans are pleased with the direction of
   a. their personal lives   c. their country
   b. national politics   d. world progress

10. The reassessment of the self-fulfillment movement implies that personal fulfillment can be realized only in
    a. educated people   c. relation to others
    b. middle or late adulthood   d. perfectionistic people

EXERCISES

1. *Social change.* Select two or three societal changes that are having the greatest impact on your life, and write a page or so about how your life is affected by these changes. For example, think about how a computer has altered your academic, business, and personal life.

2. *Change as a challenge or threat.* Select some change that has occurred in your environment recently, such as a new professor or layoffs at work. Then write a page or so describing how you feel about this change, especially whether you see it as a challenge or a threat. (People who are psychologically hardy tend to perceive change mostly as a challenge, feel personally involved in whatever they are doing, and have a sense of personal control over their lives.)

3. *Identify your giving/getting pact.* Select some aspect of your life, whether job, a friendship, or marriage. Then describe in a few paragraphs how much you're prepared to give to this relationship and how much you expect in return. To what extent is your giving/getting pact based on the old rules or the new rules of self-fulfillment?

4. *How important is self-fulfillment to you?* Think about what you do that is fulfilling. What are your life goals? Are they other-centered or self-centered? What do you do to actively meet these goals?

5. *An experience of personal growth.* In a page or so describe some experience of personal growth in relation to Jourard's three phases of the growth cycle: (a) awareness of change, (b) a sense of inner dissatisfaction, and (c) the resulting reorganization of your experience.

6. *Self-fulfillment and personal and social involvement.* Select some area of your life that has been very gratifying to you (an accomplishment, relationship, etc.) and describe the extent to which your sense of fulfillment depended on involvement with others.

QUESTIONS FOR SELF-REFLECTION

1. Are you more optimistic about your own personal future than that of our society or the world?
2. Are you so concerned to keep your options open that you may suffer from the inability to make decisions? Are you too perfectionistic?
3. How much control do you feel you have over your life?
4. Would you agree that many of the ground rules in our society are changing?
5. Have you met people who act as if there are *no* rules, that anything goes?
6. How important are self-fulfillment values to you?
7. Do you expect more out of life than your parents did?
8. To what extent are you reconciling the old and new values described in this book?
9. Can you remember a difficult time in your life and, in retrospect, realize it was a time of growth?
10. Would you agree that personal fulfillment is achieved mostly in and through our relationships with others?

FOR FURTHER INFORMATION

RECOMMENDED READINGS

BELLAH, R. N., MADSEN, R., SULLIVAN, W. M., SWIDLER, A., & TIPTON, S. M. (1985). *Habits of the heart*. Berkeley: University of California Press. An intellectually stimulating account of individualism and commitment in American life.

FREY, S. (1994). *Psychotrends: What kind of people are we becoming?* New York: Simon & Schuster. One man's view of how Americans are changing.

LAUER, R. H., & LAUER, J. C. (1988). *Watersheds*. Boston: Little, Brown. Considers a variety of life crises as potential opportunities for personal growth.

STOCK, G. (1985). *The book of questions*. New York: Workman Publishing. Challenging questions that may stimulate self-discovery and growth.

ZEY, M. (1994). *Seizing the future: How the coming revolution in science, technology, and industry will expand the frontiers of human potential and reshape the planet*. New York: Simon & Schuster. A look at the future of the world if the technology and information revolution continues.

WEBSITES AND THE INTERNET

http://www.launchsite.come/freedom.htm: A launch pad for other sites related to freedom of speech, civil rights, social activism, and so forth.

http://www.mcs.net/~zupko/popculture.htm: A location where popular American culture in its ever-changing forms is tracked.

http://www.cpsr.org/dox/: A site supported by computer professionals concerned about the responsible use of technology in society.

http://futurec.xtc.net/: Interested in the future or the concept of global community? This is the site for you.

http://www.safari.net/~pam/netanon/: Although some fear technology, others become addicted to it, especially to surfing the Web. If you are an addict, this is the spot for you.

CHAPTER 2

Personality and Social Development

After completing this chapter, you should be able to

1. Discuss the relative importance of genetic influences on personality.
2. Explain what is meant by the ego, superego, and id.
3. List the developmental tasks of Erikson's eight stages of psychosocial development.
4. Explain Bandura's concept of modeling and social learning.
5. Identify five types of cognitive variables that influence behavior.
6. Explain Maslow's concept of self-actualization.
7. Discuss some of the reasons people aren't more fully actualized.

Ken was on the fast track. He graduated from a prestigious private college in the Northeast. After college, Ken continued to law school and finished second in his class. From law school, Ken joined a large law firm. Although he knew he was at the bottom of the hierarchy, Ken had designs on eventually becoming a partner in one of the old, respected firms and ultimately to found his own respected firm. This meant that he had to make several moves in terms of jobs and geography, but Ken remained undaunted in his quest for prestige. Despite the fact that Ken was enthusiastically moving ahead with his career plans, he felt a sense of loneliness that led him to his first girlfriend, Audra, a young woman who was a lawyer in one of the firms for which Ken worked. Audra knew about Ken's drive, and she admired that in him. She, too, was determined that she would be successful. They both dreamed of founding their own law firm. Because of their career plans, neither of them wanted children.

When Ken was 49 years old, he came home one day and announced to Audra that he was thoroughly disenchanted with his career and his life. As he unfolded his angst to the astonished Audra, he made clear that the stress, the unpredictability of the practice of law, and the geographic relocations were killing him. He longed for a quieter, less frenetic life or, as he expressed it, a "saner" life. He begged Audra to move to Oregon with him. He said that he had been reading a magazine for wine enthusiasts and had seen a winery for sale. He wanted the two of them to buy the winery and live right on site.

 A Perspectival Approach

"Why do you think people do this—make seemingly dramatic and sudden changes in their lives?" "Do most people make these changes or at least fantasize about them?" When we ask students these questions, their answers vary tremendously. One person says, "Maybe they're trying to prove something." "Frankly, I think they're crazy," adds another student. "If I had a lot of money, the last thing I'd do is to risk my life savings on a business like a vineyard." Still another person says, "Like the man said, perhaps they're distressed and need a change." Actually, how each of us would interpret this incident depends a great deal on our own views of personality.

In a similar way, psychologists approach personality from different viewpoints or **perspectives**—angles of vision. Although there are dozens of different theories of personality, most of them can be grouped into four basic types: the biological, psychodynamic, social-cognitive (including behavioral), and humanistic perspectives. Each perspective emphasizes certain aspects of **personality,** but no one perspective provides the complete truth. Attempting to prove which view is more correct, especially on issues that admit to no simple test of truth, is a waste of energy. Instead, it's more helpful to learn the best that each perspective has to offer. For what each view offers us is an *optimal range* of explanations about personality. That is, each perspective explains some aspects especially well, while minimizing, if not neglecting, others. For instance, the biological perspective reminds us of the obvious but often overlooked genetic influence on personality. The psychodynamic perspective calls attention to our unconscious needs and conflicts as well as the influence of earlier stages of development on our lives. In contrast, the social-cognitive perspective highlights the importance of learning and the environment, as well as the practical strategies for modifying our behavior. The humanistic perspective emphasizes the enormous potential for freedom and growth in each of us, thereby encouraging us to engage in the lifelong process of self-actualization. Thus, by examining the distinctive viewpoints of all four perspectives, we may arrive at a more inclusive, well-balanced understanding of personality.

 ## The Biological Perspective

One of the earliest ways to understand personality, the **biological perspective,** has been the study of **temperament**—the inherited disposition to behave in a particular way. Hippocrates, the Greek physician who is considered to be the pioneer of modern medicine, classified people according to four body types, depending on which body fluids were believed to predominate: melancholic (depressed), sanguine (cheerful), phlegmatic (unemotional), or choleric (irritable). Later, William Sheldon (1954) used extensive **correlational studies** to classify people by body types that were thought to be closely linked to temperament types. The plump "endomorphs" tend to be relaxed and easygoing. The muscular "mesomorphs" are more energetic and aggressive, and the thin "ectomorphs" are high-strung and solitary. In actuality, each person has a different combination of the various temperaments, which is further modified by his or her lifestyle and environment. Although Sheldon's studies yielded strong positive associations between body and temperament types, others have found merely positive but weak associations, suggesting that such temperament types tend to be stereotypes that exaggerate a kernel of truth (L. A. Tucker, 1983).

Today, the rapid increase in knowledge about brain functioning and **genes** provides more substantial scientific evidence for the biological basis of personality. Extensive comparisons of twins, whether reared together or apart, have shown clear evidence of genetic influences on personality. For instance, Ken had a twin brother, Paul. Both had similar hairstyles, mustaches, and aviator glasses. Each made his living as a white-collar professional. And, interestingly, they both liked the same wine, chardonnay.

Overall genetic influences account, on average, for between 25 to 50 percent of the differences in personal characteristics among the general population (Bouchard, Lykken, McGue, Segal, & Tellegen, 1990; Plomin & Rende, 1991; Scarr, 1987). (See Figure 2–1.) The rest is determined by interaction with the environment. In actuality, the specific percentage attributed to **heredity** varies greatly among different traits and different individuals. For example, although Ken and his twin Paul were similar in some respects, they differed in others. Paul wanted children; he considered them a wonderful addition to his life. Ken, on the other hand, decided that children would interfere with his climb up the law career ladder. Although genetic factors have been cited for a wide range of characteristics including alcoholism, depression, and phobias, the evidence is especially strong for such characteristics as intelligence, sociability, emotionality, and activity level (Bouchard et al., 1990; Plomin & Rende, 1991). In Darwinian theory, if a characteristic is inherited it should be adaptive, that is, help us cope with our physical and social world and thus aid our survival. Perhaps this theory helps to explain why characteristics such as intelligence, sociability, and activity level are partly inherited, in that they enhance our adaptability or adjustment.

Lest you jump to the conclusion, as some lay people do, that heredity is more important than **environment,** consider this: Studies of twins and others in adoptive families have shown that people who grow up together do *not* strongly resemble one another in personality, whether they are biologically related or not (Rowe, 1990). Each person tends to be unique. Such findings raise puzzling questions. Why do the shared pool of genes together with a common environment have so little effect on siblings' personalities? Is it because each individual receives a different combination of genes? Or perhaps individuals seek out environments that are most suitable for their inherited personality dispositions. Then, too, could it be that each child experiences the same home environment somewhat differently? Apparently, this is the case, with each person's unique experiences being a substantial influence on his or her personality. What affects a child is not so much his or her parents as how each child perceives and reacts to them, in addition to their siblings and peers, as well as to other social and cultural influences.

As a result, it makes more sense to speak of the **nature–nurture issue** as nature via (through) nurture rather than nature versus nurture. That is, personality is a product of both inherited temperament and environment. How much or how little of our response potential we develop depends greatly on our interaction with the environment, especially our selection and reaction to particular environments. However, there are limits to how much temperament can be modified by environment. In the long run, even intense environmental pressure cannot radically alter a pronounced temperamental disposition.

APPLYING IT TO YOURSELF

According to the biological perspective, up to half of our personal traits may be attributable to genetic influences. But since most of us spend our formative years in a family with a common pool of genes, it is difficult to tell how much a given characteristic reflects our heredity and how much it reflects our environment or early training. Much depends on the specific characteristic. As we've seen, characteristics like intelligence and sociability have a marked genetic influence. But even these characteristics are determined not so much by a single gene as by a complex combination of genes that gives rise to a range of response potential. How much or how little of our response potential we develop depends largely on our interaction with the environment. For instance, a first-born female might earn high grades and go on to become a physician. Her sister, however, who is equally smart but impatient with long years of schooling, may

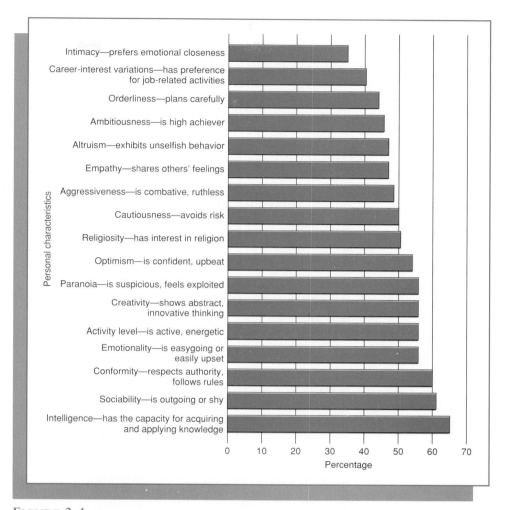

FIGURE 2–1

Extent to which genetic influences account for personality differences in the general population. SOURCE: Adapted from data in Bouchard, T. J., Lykken, D. T., McGue, M., Segal, N. L., & Tellegen, A. (1990). Sources of human psychological differences: The Minnesota study of twins reared apart. *Science, 250,* 223–228; Plomin, R., & Rende, R. (1991). Human behavioral genetics. *Annual Review of Psychology, 42,* 161–190; Rowe, D. C. (1990). As the twig is bent? The myth of child-rearing influences on personality development. *Journal of Counseling and Development, 68,* 606–611.

choose a paramedical career as an emergency medical technician. Both sisters may continue to get similar scores on the same intelligence test, but their achievements may be regarded differently because of the status and money associated with their respective careers.

Have you ever considered the dominant traits in your family tree? At the next family gathering, you might observe that someone, perhaps a favorite uncle or aunt, exhibits the same warmth and sociability that you do. You might wonder why you are more similar to a more distant relative in this trait than to your parents or siblings. The answer may be heredity. Realizing the importance of heredity, some prospective marital partners make sure to meet their fiancé's extended family as well as parents, to get a better idea of the pool of shared genes their children will inherit. Suppose something like depression runs in your family. Do you wonder how much at risk you would be? Even though genetic factors are likely to account for a predisposition to this disorder, they do not, in themselves, determine its appearance. Other influences, such as increased levels of stress, are usually involved in triggering the disorder. We will discuss this disorder and others in Chapter 13.

 ## The Psychodynamic Perspective

Psychodynamic theory consists of a group of related theories that view personality and behavior in terms of the dynamics, or interaction, of the driving forces of personality—such as desires, anxieties, conflicts, and defenses. According to this viewpoint, individuals are inevitably caught in the clash between the conflicting forces of life, such as between impulses and inhibitions or between individuals and society. Although different psychodynamic theories emphasize different aspects of personality, most agree that the basic dynamics of personality include conflict between two opposing forces: **anxiety** (which results from the clash of desire and inhibitions) and **defenses** against the desires that arouse anxiety. Since Freud's ideas provide the core concepts for this perspective, we'll devote much of our discussion to his ideas. But we'll also indicate

Sigmund Freud—founder of psychoanalysis.

some of the ways in which later psychodynamic theories have modified and expanded Freud's views.

Freud (1933) compared personality to an iceberg in which only the surface tip shows: Most of the psychic activity remains unconscious. Since behavior originates in unconscious impulses, psychology in its search for the causes of behavior cannot simply rely on observations of the individual, much less the person's self-reports. Instead, the psychologist must interpret the individual's behavior, revealing its intrapsychic motives. Thus, every aspect of behavior, whether humor, dreams, or works of art, can be interpreted in terms of its surface meaning or of its true, unconscious meaning. Throughout his writings, Freud characteristically interpreted various human behaviors in terms of their deeper, unconscious meanings. The existence of the unconscious, after remaining a controversial concept for decades, is finally commonly accepted in psychology (Allen, 1997).

The goal of psychoanalytic or Freudian therapy was to help patients, through the same approach, to gain insight and mastery of their unconscious motives. To understand the psychodynamic point of view, we'll describe several aspects of Freud's thought, including the structure of the mind or personality, the dynamics of personality, and the development of personality. We will discuss psychoanalysis and the other therapies mentioned later in more detail in Chapter 14.

STRUCTURE OF PERSONALITY

Freud held that the **structure of personality** consists of three interacting processes: the id, the ego, and the superego. (See Figure 2–2.) Because each has different goals, their interaction often takes the form of conflict. The **id** is the unconscious reservoir of psychic energy for the overall personality and the source of its later development—the ego and superego. All the drives that make up the id are derived from the two primal instincts: the "life," or sex, instinct and the "death," or aggressive, instinct. Freud regarded the sex drive as the major source of psychic energy, affecting the entire personality, including the need for affection, love of family and friends, and the urge toward creativity, as well as erotic behavior. The id operates entirely on the **pleasure principle,** taking no account of reason, reality, or morality.

The **ego** is a direct outgrowth of the id and functions as a manager of personality, enabling the individual to cope with the conflicting demands of the id, the superego, and society. Accordingly, the ego operates on the basis of the **reality principle**, with the primary concern for the individual's well-being. When a desire from the id bids for expression, the ego looks for a potential means of gratifying the desire in a socially satisfying way. The ego anticipates the consequences of such action and then either acts accordingly or delays gratification, as the case may be. Ken always wanted to be wealthy (a very id-like desire), but he knew that only a socially acceptable means for obtaining wealth would assure his future. This was one of the driving forces behind his desire to go to law school.

The **superego** is that part of the personality that has been shaped by the moral standards of society as transmitted by the parents. It is roughly equivalent to "conscience," though much of it remains unconscious. As such, the superego takes no more account of reality than does the id and, instead, operates in accordance with the principle of *perfection*. Thus, the effects of the superego on personality tend to be harsh and punitive, or hypermoral. Much of the repression of unacceptable impulses is carried out by the superego directly or by the ego at the urging of the superego. Ken, for example, often

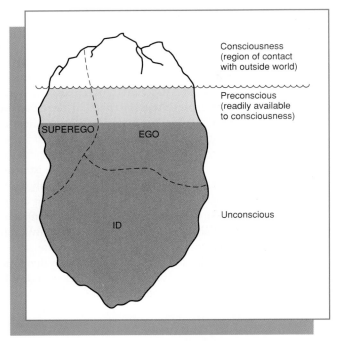

Consciousness
(region of contact
with outside world)

Preconscious
(readily available
to consciousness)

SUPEREGO

EGO

Unconscious

ID

FIGURE 2–2
Freud's view of the psyche.

thought about cheating on his college exams and law school cases, but his superego was sufficiently strong so that he knew not to cheat.

The id, ego, and superego are not entities or even parts of the mind. They are best seen as metaphors or names that Freud gave to highly complex psychological processes that make up our mental life.

PERSONALITY DYNAMICS

According to Freud's view of **personality dynamics,** the ego, id, and superego are often in *conflict* with one another, so that individuals commonly experience *ambivalence*—being pulled in opposing directions simultaneously. Ordinarily, the ego keeps the conflict at a manageable level, giving the id and superego their due consideration. But at times, the urges of the id or the judgments of the superego threaten to usurp the ego's control, resulting in unacceptable feelings or behavior. When this happens, the ego experiences anxiety.

Anxiety is an alarm signal, analogous to the sense of pain in the body, that warns the ego of danger. Freud distinguished three types of anxiety according to the source of danger. In **reality anxiety** the individual (1) is threatened by something that occurs in the external world, (2) experiences the appropriate anxiety, and (3) acts accordingly. In **neurotic anxiety** the ego senses that some impulses of the id are threatening to get out of control, tempting the individual to do something he or she will be punished for. In **moral anxiety** the person feels guilty about something he or she has done—either real or imagined. Sometimes the ego handles anxiety in a direct, realistic way, such as studying to reduce one's anxiety about an important exam. However, the most common response to anxiety is avoidance, covering it up through reliance on the ego defenses.

Defense mechanisms are unconscious reactions that automatically reduce the level of anxiety, thereby helping the individual to cope with the situation at hand. **Repression,** or the blocking of unacceptable desires or memories from awareness, is the fundamental defense underlying all others. We'll identify some of the other ego defense mechanisms in Chapter 4. But here, it is important to point out that the defense mechanisms in themselves are neither good nor bad. Up to a point, they are adaptive mechanisms, helping us to cope with psychological threat. Beyond that, defenses become self-defeating, as in the case of people who habitually make excuses or blame others for their own failures rather than correcting their own inadequacies. Ken at least did not seem defensive about his desire to move to Oregon; for example, he did not blame Audra nor anyone at his law firm. He merely realized that the stress of achieving high grades and then of practicing law was wearing on him.

Slips of the tongue are another way that the unconscious expresses itself. In fact, such slips today are often called Freudian slips. Box 2–1 presents more information about these interesting bungles that are so common in our daily lives.

A major characteristic of personality dynamics is the constant shift or displacement of psychic energy from one aspect of the personality to another. Freud thought that only a certain amount of energy is available to the organism, but it may be focused or displaced onto different objects. For example, if Ken had been angry at his boss but fearful of saying so, he may have displaced his anger onto a safer object by banging his fist on the desk or arguing with Audra when he arrived home. Thus, much of the adaptability of personality consists in the transformation of motives through the redistribution of psychic energy.

BOX 2–1

SLIPS OF THE TONGUE

Most of us are familiar with those embarrassing slips of the tongue—called Freudian slips—in which we say (or write) something we didn't intend. Are these slips simply accidental mistakes? Or do they reveal something of our "real" or unconscious motives, as Sigmund Freud contended? Consider the following examples. When one heavily sedated male patient bumped into an attractive female nurse, he exclaimed, "Pardon me, madam. I've been heavily seduced." Or consider the line in a newspaper announcement about a forthcoming wedding—"The wrestling will take place at 8 o'clock at the First Baptist Church" (Feist, 1985, p. 51).

Although many psychologists would disagree with Freud's interpretations of such slips of the tongue, there is considerable evidence that emotional factors may contribute to such verbal mistakes. For instance, in one experiment male subjects completed sentences such as "Tension mounted at the end, when the symphony reached its _____." When the test was administered by a man, most subjects completed the sentence with a word like *finale* or *conclusion*. But when the test was given by an attractive female, subjects were more likely to use the word *climax* (Morris, 1988).

Can you recall some of your own slips of the tongue? Do you think your mistake was partly due to emotional factors?

DEVELOPMENT OF PERSONALITY

Since Freud regarded the **libido,** the psychic energy of the sex drive, as fundamental to the entire personality, he interpreted the **development of personality** on the basis of the sequential process of **psychosexual stages.** In each stage, the child seeks to gratify the drive for pleasure in the various body zones: the mouth, the anus, and the genitals. The manner in which children handle the conflict between their impulses and environmental restrictions is decisive for adult personality. Too little or too much gratification may result in **fixation,** by which the personality becomes emotionally fixed at a particular anxiety-ridden stage and continues to act out symbolically the wishes that were overly inhibited or indulged.

The **oral stage** occurs during the first year of life, during which the mouth becomes the primary means of gratifying the desires of the id. Although infants must suck milk from the breast (or bottle) to survive, their mouths soon become a means to satisfying sucking pleasure and, to some extent, aggressive impulses. Thus, the various ways infants achieve gratification through sucking or holding on lay the foundations for later adult personality traits such as acquisitiveness and tenacity. Fixation at this stage may result in the passive personality associated with addictive eating, smoking, or drinking or in the sarcastic person who is always criticizing everyone else's ideas without offering any of his or her own.

The **anal stage** occurs during the second year of life, when the child's major source of physical pleasure becomes the releasing or retaining of feces. Caught between the pleasurable urges of the id and parental demands, the child may experience considerable anxiety and conflict. Fixation in the early phase of this stage may result in adult tendencies toward disorderly, messy behavior. By contrast, fixation in the later phase of this stage would give rise to the stubborn, compulsively orderly personality.

The **phallic stage,** which extends from the third to the fifth or sixth year, is the period in which the child experiences sensual pleasure through handling of his or her genitals. Again, too little or too much gratification sets the stage for later difficulties, such as the individual who feels guilty about his or her sexuality or engages in sex to reduce anxiety. The phallic stage is especially important because of the occurrence of the Oedipus complex for boys and the Electra complex for girls during this period. In the Greek legend, King Oedipus unwittingly kills a man who turns out to be his father and marries a woman he later discovers is his mother. And Electra, the legendary daughter of King Agamemnon, longs for him after his death and plots the revenge of his killers—her mother and her mother's lover. Interestingly, Audra was a bit like Ken's mother in that she was tall, had dark hair, possessed a warm personality, was very intelligent, but not particularly affectionate.

Similarly, children during the phallic stage are sexually attracted to the opposite-sex parent and envy the same-sex parent. The unconscious conflict arouses considerable anxiety in children of both sexes, though in due time in most cases, it is resolved as spontaneously as it emerged. Instead of trying to possess the opposite-sex parent and risk losing the love of the same-sex parent, the child settles for identification with the same-sex parent. In so doing, children incorporate that parent's sexual orientation, mannerisms, and values. Furthermore, the resolution of the Oedipus conflict results in the formation of the superego. Examples of people who suffer from unresolved Oedipal conflicts are the male Don Juan, who "loves 'em and leaves 'em" without ever getting close to his partners, and the actively seductive female who continues to feel guilty about sex.

The **latency period** takes place between about 5 years and 12 years of age. During this time the child's interests turn away from erogenous satisfactions, with early sexual feelings being forgotten and sexual urges lying relatively dormant. Paul and Ken as boys were typical examples of this stage. They had absolutely no interest in the opposite sex; in fact, they thought that girls were absolutely silly and that contact with them should be avoided at all costs.

The **genital stage** begins with the onset of puberty and sexual maturation, from about 12 years of age on. In this period the individual's sexual interests are reawakened and focus on gratification through genital or sexual activity. In the well-adjusted adult the experiences of the oral, anal, and phallic stages have become incorporated into genital strivings so that he or she is capable of genuine love and adult sexual satisfaction. Ken, for example, outgrew his resistance to girls and as a young man was very happy to have found Audra. However, most adult problems with sex derive from fixations at the earlier oral, anal, or phallic stage. Some examples of such fixations are people who are cynical about sex and enter into lustful relationships as ends in themselves or those who withdraw from all sexual relationships.

MODIFICATIONS

Many of Freud's followers were original thinkers in their own right who revised and expanded his views. Although post-Freudian thought developed in many different directions, two trends are especially significant. First, there has been a greater emphasis on the ego. Many of the later psychodynamic thinkers deemphasized sex, the unconscious, and the deterministic aspects of Freud's views. Instead, they stressed the goals and self-directed aspects of development. Carl Jung held that the purpose of insight is not simply to gain rational control over the id and the source of psychic energy. It is also to help the individual discover and develop his or her wholeness and individuation. Heinz Hartman stressed that the ego develops independently of the id and has its own autonomous functions. He held that many of the cognitive functions, such as memory, perception, and learning, are "conflict-free." Accordingly, the psychodynamic approach to behavior should focus on the ego and the relationship between the conflict-free functions as well as the conflict-resolving functions, such as the defenses.

A second trend in the revision of Freud has been a more positive emphasis on the individual's social interactions. Freud had interpreted the child's social interactions in relation to the forces of the id. Later thinkers, especially Harry Stack Sullivan and Karen Horney, emphasized the importance of social relationships in their own right. Eric Erikson, a psychologist showcased in Box 2–2, altered Freud's theory to contain more developmental stages as well as to emphasize social rather than intrapsychic conflicts.

More recently, St. Clair (1986) and others have emphasized object-relations theory, which shows how early self/other patterns decisively influence later interpersonal relationships. These revisions of Freud's thought have enriched the psychodynamic perspective and brought it closer to the other branches of psychology, with their current emphasis on cognitive functions and social influences.

EVALUATION

Many of Freud's ideas remained controversial during his lifetime. Later, during the heyday of Freud's popularity, his views were often reified and accepted without question.

BOX 2–2

ERIKSON'S EIGHT STAGES OF PSYCHOSEXUAL DEVELOPMENT

Erik Erikson has widened the potential application of psychodynamic theory by transforming Freud's psychosexual theory of development into a more inclusive view of personality development. Whereas Freud focused on the child's psychosexual development with the family, Erikson takes into account the individual's psychosocial relationships within the larger society. And whereas Freud's stages covered only the years between birth and puberty, Erikson's stages extend throughout adulthood into old age. Each of the eight psychosocial stages is presented as a polarity, with a positive ability to be achieved along with a related threat or vulnerability. Personality development is sequential, with one's overall personality composed of the strengths and weaknesses acquired during each of the following stages.

1. *Trust versus mistrust.* If children's physical and emotional needs are met in the first year of life, they learn to trust people around them. If not, they become anxious and mistrustful of their environment.

2. *Autonomy versus doubt and shame.* As parents encourage children to walk, talk, and do things for themselves through the second and third years of life, the children will develop age-appropriate autonomy. But if the parents are coercive or over-protective, children will experience self-doubt and feel ashamed of themselves.

3. *Initiative versus guilt.* During the fourth and fifth years of development, children readily roam about and make new friends. If such efforts are supported by the parents, children will enjoy exploring their environment. However, if such actions are unduly restricted or punished, children may become passive and guilt-ridden about taking the initiative.

4. *Industry versus inferiority.* From about 6 to 11 years of age, children enjoy developing various abilities at home, school, and play. The more competent they become in dealing with their environment, the better they feel about themselves as persons. Undue frustration and failure evoke the sense of inferiority or worthlessness.

5. *Identity versus role confusion.* Throughout adolescence, roughly 12 to 18 years of age, individuals are busily redefining their identities in ways that incorporate the various changes occurring in their bodies, minds, and sexual development. The more successful they are in this task, the stronger their sense of personal identity. The more difficulty experienced, the more confusion adolescents feel about who they are and what they may become.

6. *Intimacy versus isolation.* As family ties are loosened during early adulthood, individuals need to form satisfying, close relationships with peers of both sexes. The inability to establish satisfying relationships with friends, including a lover or spouse, results in a painful sense of isolation or loneliness.

7. *Generativity versus stagnation.* By middle age, individuals are especially ready to develop generativity—the ability to look beyond one's self, family, and job and to contribute to the welfare of others. The person who succeeds in doing so may continue being productive and happy. The person who doesn't tends to become self-absorbed.

8. *Integrity versus despair.* In late adulthood, individuals tend to look back upon their lives as a whole. To the extent they have achieved a satisfying life, they will feel happy with themselves in old age. But if they feel that their life has been disappointing and a failure, despair will be the result.

SOURCE: Erikson, E. H. (1963). *Childhood and Society* (2nd ed.). New York: W. W. Norton.

With the critical assessment of Freud's views in recent years, people have sometimes gone to the opposite extreme, dismissing Freud prematurely without ever understanding him. Freud's thought is not something, however, that must be accepted or rejected as a whole. Instead, it is a complex structure with many parts, some of which deserve to be accepted, some deserve to be rejected, and still others are in need of revision (Cramer, 1991).

A major criticism of Freud is that many of his ideas are vague and speculative, and thus hard to test. How do you prove or disprove the notion that sex is instinctive or that an abstract concept such as the unconscious exists—especially when people are not aware of its existence? Most theorists have abandoned the idea of instincts and tend to regard the sex drive as a complex blend of biological, psychological, and social components that function in relation to many other motives. A related criticism is that Freud's views were derived from clinical experience, lacked experimental support, and were based on inferences and interpretations of selected cases that involved disturbed people. In contrast, the field of psychology today includes both experimental and clinical approaches, with a concern for representative sampling and empirical methods of verification. For example, contemporary research has shown that dreams serve a variety of functions other than wish fulfillment, as Freud suggested, such as serving memory, problem solving, and neurological discharge (Hobson, 1988). Still another criticism of Freud's approach is that it amounts to a reductionistic interpretation of human behavior. Every aspect of behavior is interpreted on the basis of animal instincts, childhood experience, and deterministic forces. As we've seen, many of these latter criticisms have been taken to heart and corrected by Freud's followers.

It should also be pointed out that Freud's ideas and those of the psychodynamic perspective in general have made substantial contributions to our understanding of behavior. First, such an approach has directed our attention to the inner life, to our memories, dreams, fantasies, and self-deceptions. It has helped to bring about the "psychological age," in which we take for granted the adaptive value of insight and self-knowledge. Second, Freud helped to remove the mystique of abnormal behavior by showing that disturbed behaviors stem from the same impulses and developmental processes as normal behavior. The big difference is the lopsided distribution of psychic energy, with the ego being overwhelmed by the id or superego in abnormal behavior. Third, Freud's use of insight in the helping process has spawned, in addition to orthodox psychoanalysis, a vast array of insight therapies that now include group therapy, marital therapy, and family therapy. Finally, the impact of Freud's thought has been felt far beyond professional psychology, so that terms like *repression, unconscious, ego,* and *rationalization* have become everyday usage.

APPLYING IT TO YOURSELF

According to the psychodynamic perspective, each of us is driven by motives, needs, and conflicts we're not fully aware of. Accordingly, at times we're beset by ambivalence and indecision, such as whether we really want to remain in a given relationship or job or not. One of the most commonly asked questions of psychologists is "Can you love and hate the same person?" Most psychodynamic therapists would say yes because of the unconscious and often conflicting urges inherent in human nature.

However, much of the way we cope with life and relate to others depends on how we've grown up. That is, each of us tends to act out of our psychic character or adult personality. This aspect, in turn, has evolved through a developmental process in which early experiences have had a significant bearing on our present functioning, especially if our childhood experiences were marked by trauma or maladaptive relationships.

At the same time, it's normal to have "problems." Even Freud had them, being afflicted by migraine headaches, nicotine addiction, and a variety of other symptoms he himself labeled "neurotic" (E. Jones, 1953). But the various symptoms of maladjustment, whether Freud's or ours, share a common feature: The individual's ego and coping defenses are weakened, making that person vulnerable to further maladjustment. In extreme cases, the individual's defenses break down, overwhelming the ego with archaic impulses and with anxiety, leading to one of the severe psychological disorders.

Optimal **adjustment** comes from strengthening the ego and the attendant reality orientation, that is, learning to live in the world as it is rather than fantasizing about life. Essentially, this consists of increasing our self-understanding and self-mastery, so that we can make meaningful accommodations between our deepest needs and desires and the social demands made of us. Our goal should be to maximize the satisfaction of our needs while minimizing guilt and self-defeating tendencies. But at best, this involves a series of practical concessions through the successful management of the inherently conflicting forces of life—rather than the achievement of some idealized self-actualization. As a result, Freud observed that if we are able "to love and to work"—to establish satisfying relationships and find meaningful work—we are indeed fortunate.

 ## The Social-Cognitive Perspective

The **social-cognitive perspective** is a broad term that includes behavioral and social learning theory as well as cognitive psychology. The early behavioral psychologists relied on scientific laboratory methods to observe behavior. As such, they focused on how behavior is learned; hence, the terms **learning theory** and **behaviorism** are often associated with their approach. Some, like Dollard and Miller (1950), sought to integrate Freud's basic ideas with their laboratory approach and retained an emphasis on human behavior. But most learning theorists, following the pioneering efforts by John Watson and B. F. Skinner, focused on the mechanics of behavior, especially the importance of reinforcement, in a way that excluded human consciousness. Thus, many of their findings were based on animal studies and dealt with the more elementary types of learning.

However, in recent years behavioral research has shifted to complex human behavior and real-life problems. In the process, learning concepts are being expanded and integrated with ideas and findings in other areas of psychology—especially cognitive psychology. As a result, there is more of an emphasis on the interaction between individuals and their environment, as well as on how their elaborate cognitive abilities affect learning and behavior.

SOCIAL LEARNING THEORIES

Albert Bandura (1986) and others have demonstrated that much of what we know and do is acquired through a process of **observational learning.** This is a process in which we learn by observing other people, or "models," and events without any direct reward or reinforcement. Such learning depends on four components: attention, retention, reproduction, and motivation. Obviously, it is essential that we attend or pay attention to the distinctive features of the behavior modeled. Yet such behavior would have little impact if we did not also remember or retain it after watching it. Then, too, when the behavior involves complex motor activities (as in driving a car or playing tennis), the observer also must put together physically the components of the action, a process re-

Albert Bandura—leading social learning theorist.

quiring accurate self-observation and feedback during rehearsal. Finally, to transfer the knowledge to performance, we must have the motivation to enact the behaviors that we have learned. Although observational learning may occur because of an intrinsic desire to acquire the observed behaviors, such learning is often combined with direct reinforcement to enhance learning. As a concrete example of this, let us again examine Ken's decision to leave the practice of law. What is interesting from the social learning perspective is that another lawyer in Ken's firm had left the firm the year before due to a stress-related illness. When Ken inquired about this man, he discovered that the man did not return to the practice of law even after he recovered. Instead the man moved to Vermont where he opened an ice cream parlor. Perhaps this individual provided a model for Ken.

Bandura (1973) has paid special attention to how aggressive behavior may be acquired through observational learning. In one study, he compared overly aggressive boys who were in trouble with the law with better-adjusted boys. He found that much of the former's behavior could be explained by their home atmosphere. More specifically, he found that the fathers of overly aggressive boys were more rejecting of their sons, so that their sons became less dependent on them and spent less time with them. Parents of overly aggressive boys were also more likely to use harsh, physical punishment so that their sons were more apt to imitate their parents' aggressive behavior than their verbal warnings to the contrary. These parents also tended to encourage their sons in aggressive behavior, such as standing up for their rights or leading with their fists. In contrast, parents of the better-adjusted boys showed more accepting attitudes toward their sons, explained their discipline and demands, and were less likely to use physical punishment. As a result, these boys tended to develop more inner controls of their aggression, that is, an adequate conscience and a sense of guilt, so that they kept their aggressive behavior well within the bounds of the law.

However, once a given trait or behavior has been learned, as Bandura observed, it is not necessarily expressed uniformly in all situations. A lot depends on the extent to

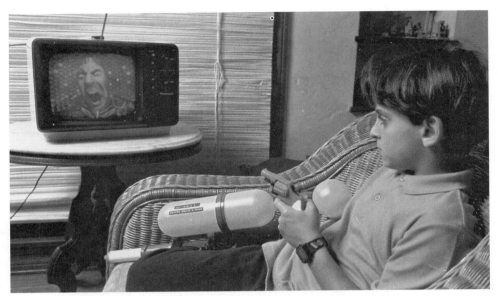

Social learning theory suggests that children learn violence from television. Children can also learn positive behaviors from television.

which the behavior is valued or rewarded in various situations. For instance, whereas physical aggressiveness may be encouraged among boys sparring in the gym, it will not be tolerated in response to one's parents or younger siblings. Consequently, current behavior is best understood in terms of the interaction between one's acquired traits (or past learning) and the present situation. In fact, our behavior is often shaped more by the requirements of the particular situation we happen to be in at the moment than by some inner trait. Thus, the same individual may act aggressively in sports, compliantly in the classroom, and democratically when socializing with his or her friends.

COGNITION AND BEHAVIOR

In recent years, psychologists have begun exploring the impact of cognition on behavior. Essentially, **cognition** has to do with the processing of information, and it includes a variety of processes such as selective attention, information gathering, memory, and motivation. Psychologists are studying cognition as a means of understanding those processes that mediate between the environmental stimulus and the individual's response. They believe that the impact of a stimulus depends on more than its objective physical characteristics. It also depends on contextual clues such as how it is presented and the meaning it has for the individual. In other words, many learning theorists recognize that behavior is influenced by the total stimulus complex, not just some single stimulus acting in isolation.

Walter Mischel (1986) suggests that there are five basic categories of cognitive variables that influence our response to a given stimulus:

1. *Competencies.* Each of us has a different combination of abilities and skills that shapes our responses to events. When a car battery doesn't work, one person takes the bus to work; another person, with a different set of skills, borrows battery-jumper cables to get the car started.

2. *Encoding strategies.* We also have different ways of perceiving and categorizing experiences that shape our responses. For example, when looking at a teenager's messy room, one mother fusses and fumes with no results. But another calmly takes it in stride with the realization that people at this age are preoccupied with other matters.

3. *Expectancies.* Learning experiences lead each of us to form different expectations that help to determine our reactions to events. One person buys state lottery tickets, hoping to win a million dollars; another person, realizing the overwhelming odds against winning such a fortune, is content to buy tickets occasionally for "fun"—or doesn't buy them at all.

4. *Personal values.* Our sense of priorities and values also shapes our decisions and actions. Thus, when office politics become intolerable, one worker quits but another worker takes it in stride.

5. *Self-regulatory systems.* We also formulate plans, goals, and strategies that influence our actions. For instance, whereas some people regard foreign languages as a waste of time, others may find such knowledge useful for foreign travel or business transactions.

The recognition that cognitive variables intervene between our behavior and the environment means that we are active, complex organisms and that our behavior is affected by a host of complicating factors. Bandura (1986) refers to the mutual interaction between the various components of learning as "reciprocal determinism." That is, the internal personal-cognitive variables, environmental influences, and behaviors all operate as interlocking determinants of one another. For example, our eating habits (or behaviors) are influenced by the family in which we grew up (environmental factors), which are also influenced by our past personal eating habits and preferences (a personal-cognitive factor). All these influences are mutual. Consequently, if we should learn more about nutrition (a personal-cognitive factor), this would affect which types of restaurants we would seek (an environmental factor), which in turn would shape our present eating patterns (or behavior). Such a view gives us a richer, more realistic understanding of human existence than the earlier learning theories.

More recently, Bandura (1997) has added another important concept to his theoretical notions, self-efficacy. **Self-efficacy** is the belief in one's capacity to organize and execute the courses of action required to produce given attainments. Ken, the lawyer in the opening sketch, can once again be used as an example. When Ken first sprang his idea of moving to Oregon on Audra, Ken argued persuasively and confidently that both of them could easily make this career change. Ken was sure that they both had the intelligence to make this other business succeed even though neither of them had any experience as wine makers. We would assume, then, that Ken was high in self-efficacy.

Our overall functioning is enhanced by high self-efficacy (Wiedenfeld et al., 1990). Self-efficacy as a cognitive process affects our achievement, our physical and mental health, our career development, and even our voting behavior. Self-efficacy is discussed further in Chapter 3, "Motivation and Emotion."

EVALUATION

A primary objection to learning theorists, especially those who adhere strictly to the principles of classical and operant conditioning, is that they oversimplify human life. By reducing human experience to bits of measurable behavior, they portray us as mechanistic and passive, thereby excluding much of what makes people human. However, much of the criticism of learning theory has been blunted by the development of the social learning approach, especially with its emphasis on cognitive variables. In fact, cognitive psychologists have been criticized by strict behaviorists for compromising the empirical method. In response, cognitive psychologists contend that a distinction should be made between methodological behaviorism (which may investigate any type of behavior that is measurable) and the commitment to a philosophical behaviorism that automatically rules out the study of inner experience. Furthermore, by recognizing the complexity of our cognitive life and the importance of interpersonal, real-life settings, social learning psychologists have expanded the behavioral approach to include more of the richness of human life, including the possibilities of human freedom.

One of the major contributions of learning theory has been to advance psychology as a science. By insisting on a method of investigation that focuses on actual, measurable behavior that is subject to being retested, learning theorists have given new credibility to the scientific study of human behavior. Learning therapists have also produced many effective treatment strategies that are less time-consuming and expensive than traditional methods, such as systematic desensitization. Finally, the social learning view reminds us of the importance of situational factors and of the fact that behavior usually results from an interaction of inner dispositions and environmental influences.

APPLYING IT TO YOURSELF

According to the social-cognitive perspective, much of our personality and behavior patterns have been acquired through interaction with our environment, especially the significant people in our lives. Although past experience may affect our present functioning, it need not determine our lives. That is, through the learning process many of the same mechanisms that are involved in childhood or maladaptive behavior can be used to improve our present adjustment. For instance, someone who acquired the smoking habit by imitating his or her parents or peers in the adolescent years may, by the same token, give up this habit as an adult when sufficiently motivated and encouraged by positive models in the present.

Unlike the psychodynamic view, which holds that we always act out of "character," social-cognitive learning theorists emphasize the importance of the environment and the present situation. Thus, we often act the way we do because of specific influences in our immediate situation, whether at work or at home. As such, maladaptive behavior is often more attributable to inadequate circumstances and faulty learning than the deficiencies in one's deeper psychological makeup. And conversely, the possibility of change involves seeking out a more positive or promising environment, such as a new job or career, as well as learning new skills. Also, when judging ourselves or others, it's important to take into consideration one's circumstances at the time rather than blaming one's motives.

Optimal adjustment consists of maximizing our competencies and coping skills, along with improving interactions with our environment. Problems and conflict, whether intrapsychic or interpersonal, need not be considered inevitable. Instead, they may be dealt with through the lifelong learning process. Thus, changes in our personality and behavior are not only possible but also actually occur fairly continuously, especially in an environment conducive to growth. Accordingly, it's best to see ourselves as active creatures with a tremendous capacity to learn, especially when we make the full use of our minds (or "cognitive variables") and continue to increase our repertoire of problem-solving and relationship-enhancing skills.

The Humanistic Perspective

Although the psychodynamic and social-cognitive perspectives differ in many respects, they agree on one point, namely, that human behavior can be broken down into separate components. More specifically, both approaches seek to identify the causal relationships in human behavior in a manner similar to the natural sciences. For instance, if Ken or Audra were having difficulty getting along with their bosses at work, both psychodynamic and behavioral theorists would reduce the problem to special causal factors, such as sexual conflicts at home or to learning experiences. In contrast, psychologists in the **humanistic perspective** claim that these other approaches leave out much of what makes human existence distinctive, such as the meaning and richness of subjective experience, the holistic characteristics of experience, and the capacity to choose and determine ourselves.

During the 1950s and 1960s, when many thinkers became concerned about modern technology's threat to human values, humanistic psychology achieved national prominence as the **third force in psychology,** an alternative to the deterministic outlook of psychodynamic and behavioral psychology. Humanistic psychology consists of a group of related theories and therapies that emphasize the values of human freedom and the individual. We'll describe three main ideas in the humanistic perspective: the phenomenal self, human freedom, and self-actualization.

THE PHENOMENAL SELF

The term *phenomenon* refers to that which is apparent to or perceived by the senses—in short, reality as experienced by the individual. Carl Rogers (1980), a leading humanistic psychologist, emphasizes that it is this "perceived reality," rather than absolute reality, that is the basis of behavior. Essentially, human behavior is the goal-directed attempt by the organism to satisfy its needs as it experiences or perceives them. In other words, how we see and interpret events in our environment determines how we react to them.

Two key concepts in Rogers's phenomenological theory of personality are the **organismic actualizing tendency** and the **phenomenal self,** or the self-concept. Rogers assumes the existence of an actualizing tendency at the biological level—the human organism's tendency to develop and fulfill itself. In the course of actualizing itself, the organism engages in a valuing process. Experiences that are perceived as enhancing are valued positively and sought after; those that are perceived as blocking fulfillment are valued negatively and avoided. The degree to which individuals trust this valuing process depends in a large measure on their self-concept, especially the self-image derived from one's experience with significant others during the formative years of childhood. As children become aware of themselves, they automatically develop a need for positive regard or acceptance. However, parental acceptance tends to come with strings attached, and the child incorporates these "conditions of worth" into his or her self-concept. From now on, this extraneous valuing process competes with the organismic valuing process. If the conditions of worth are few and reasonable, the self engages in a variety of experiences and, in cooperation with the organismic valuing process, can judge independently which are enhancing and which are not. However, if the conditions of self-worth are many and severely limiting, they serve to screen out much of the organism's experience, whereby the self distorts and denies much of its overall experience.

Carl Rogers—founder of
person-centered psychology.

The resulting tension between the self-concept and the organismic valuing tendency is the major source of maladjustment. The basic problem is the discrepancy between the organism's tendency to value experiences on the basis of what is good or desirable to fulfill its basic needs and the self's tendency to value experiences selectively, screening out experiences that don't conform to these conditions of worth. In fact, research has shown that when there exists a major discrepancy between what we would like to be and who we really are, depression results (Higgins, Bond, Klein, & Strauman, 1986).

Ken, for example, grew up feeling he had to be successful to be accepted by his parents. As a result, he spent many years denying his anger toward his parents as well as the need to relax and be himself. When Ken first told Audra about his desire to leave the practice of law and to move to Oregon, she asked him first to consider counseling. He agreed. After he had discovered his buried anger in therapy, he said, *"So much hurt and anger came out of me that I never really knew existed.* I continued to feel this way until one night I was sitting and thinking and I realized that I had been trying to find the real me for a long time." Here, Ken's denial of his own thoughts and feelings had become so strong that the self-alienation was thwarting his own growth. Interestingly, even after Ken finished his counseling, he still wanted to move to Oregon and give up the practice of law.

Rogers (1951) developed person-centered therapy as a way of bringing about a more harmonious interaction between the self and the inherent actualizing tendency of the organism. In this approach, the therapist adopts the attitude of **unconditional positive regard** or unconditional positive acceptance toward clients and, through empathetic listening, helps them get in touch with their own thoughts, feelings, and needs. In the climate of acceptance, clients can relax the defenses of the self and explore their thoughts and feelings more freely, thereby bringing their self-perceptions more in line with the basic actualizing tendency of the organism. In the process, clients become more trusting of their own experiences, more self-directed, and more fully functioning personalities. In the context of child development, Harrington, Block, and Block (1987) have found that children reared in more supportive environments are more creative, perhaps because they can be more fully functioning in these environments. These ideas about supportive environments and psychological growth will be explained in greater detail in the chapters on self-concept and therapy.

HUMAN FREEDOM

Another major characteristic of the humanistic perspective is the insistence on **human freedom** as opposed to the deterministic viewpoint prevalent in much of psychology. From an existentialist stance, Rollo May (1977) explains that self-consciousness itself makes possible freedom of choice. That is, given our high level of self-awareness and capability for symbolic thinking—the use of ideas, images, and words—we already have at our disposal the capacity to transcend blind obedience to impulses or environmental demands. More specifically, human freedom consists in "the capacity to pause in the face of various stimuli, and then to throw one's weight toward this response rather than that one" (p. 7). The failure to accept this human freedom, on the one hand, results in the denial of our true selves. We experience a kind of spiritual death in which life becomes meaningless, and we surrender our lives to the claims of institutions, materialistic comforts, and technological control. On the other hand, when we affirm our human freedom we begin to live authentically, that is, living in the here and now, making basic choices in a less than perfect world, accepting ourselves as a process of becoming, and being responsible for our lives. We cannot blame our problems on our childhood, past misfortune, or restrictive circumstances.

Rogers (1980) adds that the freedom that we prize so much includes an inner quality, something that exists within us, aside from the degree of outward choices we often think of as freedom. It is an inner, subjective freedom through which each of us realizes, "I can live my own life, here and now, by my own choices." Rogers says, "My experience in therapy and in groups makes it impossible for me to deny the reality and significance of human choice. To me it is not an illusion that man is to some degree the architect of himself" (p. 57).

SELF-ACTUALIZATION

Still another idea in the humanistic perspective is the concept of **self-actualization**—the process of fulfilling our inborn potential. Before reading further, you might find it interesting to assess your own level of personal growth by completing the Self-Actualization Survey in Figure 2–3. This instrument measures such characteristics as autonomy and self-acceptance, which are closely associated with the concept of self-actualization.

The term *self-actualization* is usually associated with Abraham Maslow, who gave it its fullest explanation. Maslow, like Rogers, assumes the existence of an actualizing tendency in the organism at the biological level. Accordingly, each person has an inherent need to actualize his or her potentialities. However, for Maslow, the core of such growth needs functions in relation to a hierarchy of needs. Only as the individual's most basic needs are met do the higher growth needs become a potent force in motivation. As long as the individual's needs of hunger, safety, and human companionship remain unsatisfied, the person's existence is governed mostly by deficiency motivation. But once these needs are relatively satisfied, the individual becomes more aware of his or her growth motivation and of the need to fulfill needs such as autonomy and creativity. Ken, for ex-

FIGURE 2–3

SELF-ACTUALIZATION SURVEY

INSTRUCTIONS: Indicate your agreement or disagreement with each of the following statements by placing the appropriate number in the blanks before each item. Then consult the scoring key at the end of the chapter to get your score and what it means.

1 = disagree

2 = somewhat disagree

3 = somewhat agree

4 = agree

_____ 1. I do not feel ashamed of any of my emotions.

_____ 2. I feel I must do what others expect me to do.

_____ 3. I believe that people are essentially good and can be trusted.

_____ 4. I feel free to be angry at those I love.

_____ 5. It is always necessary that others approve of what I do.

_____ 6. I don't accept my own weaknesses.

_____ 7. I can like people without having to approve of them.

_____ 8. I fear failure.

_____ 9. I avoid attempts to analyze and simplify complex domains.

_____ 10. It is better to be yourself than to be popular.

_____ 11. I have no mission in life to which I feel especially dedicated.

_____ 12. I can express my feelings even when they may result in undesirable consequences.

_____ 13. I do not feel responsible to help anybody.

_____ 14. I am bothered by fears of being inadequate.

_____ 15. I am loved because I give love.

SOURCE: A. Jones & R. Crandall. "Validation of a Short Index of Self-Actualization," *Personality and Social Psychology Bulletin, 12* (1986), 63–73. Copyright © 1986 Sage Publications. Reprinted by Permission of Sage Publications, Inc.

ample, had little to worry about in terms of his physical and safety needs. He also felt that he belonged in society and that he and Audra belonged together. However, as he became aware that these needs had been satisfied, he felt a strong need to find himself, to know himself better. It was through self-realization that he understood the high level of distress and unhappiness he was experiencing in the law profession. Ken was fortunate in this respect; it can otherwise take an entire lifetime for growth needs to unfold, so that self-actualization is more of a lifelong process than a readily attainable goal.

Maslow (1971) held that some people have reached a healthier, more optimal level of functioning than the average person. He called them self-actualizing people and held that their study may teach us much about our potential for growth. Such people are relatively free from major psychological problems and have made the best possible use of their talents and strengths. Compared to the average person, self-actualizing people have certain characteristics in common, such as a continued freshness of appreciation of everyday realities; greater acceptance of themselves and others; high creativity, though not necessarily in the arts; and high resistance to conformity. If self-actualization is in-

Abraham Maslow—the most ardent spokesperson for self-actualization.

deed such a positive process, we should seek out means by which to become more actualized. Box 2–3 suggests strategies you can use to enhance your optimal being.

People with an incomplete understanding of Maslow often have misconceptions of self-actualization. For instance, in one survey students were asked, "Would you like to be self-actualizing? Why or why not?" Three-fourths of the students said yes. But the answers of both groups reflected mistaken but widely held notions about self-actualization. Some of the affirmative respondents explained that being actualized would bring them peace of mind, give them control over their own minds, and make them powerful people. Some of those who responded no felt that self-actualizing people, having met all their goals, would have nothing to live for. As one person said, "No, not anytime soon, but yes before I die. I have so much to live for and I want to have a good time before I reach self-actualization" (Feist, 1985). However, Maslow made it clear that self-actualizing people are not perfect. They remain vulnerable to the existential concerns and problems that plague everyone. At times they can be boring, irritating, or depressed. Essentially, self-actualizing people are like the rest of us but without the inhibited capabilities so characteristic of the average person.

A major criticism of Maslow's views is often voiced this way: "If each of us has an inborn actualizing tendency, why aren't people more self-actualized?" Maslow (1971) himself pondered this question and offered several possible explanations. First, one factor

---

BOX 2–3

SUGGESTIONS FOR BECOMING MORE SELF-ACTUALIZING

1. Experience life fully in the present moment rather than dwelling on the past or worrying about the future.

2. Make choices that will enhance growth by taking reasonable risks that will develop your potential rather than by sticking with the safe and secure.

3. Listen to your needs and reactions, and trust your own experience.

4. Be honest with yourself and with other people.

5. Strive to do your best in accomplishing the tangible goals in everyday life.

6. Be assertive in expressing your needs, ideas, and values.

7. Recognize and live by the inspiration of special moments or peak experiences in which you feel especially close to fulfilling your potential.

8. Be open to new experiences. Identify your defenses and be willing to put them aside in order to revise your expectations, ideas, and values.

9. Commit yourself to concerns and causes outside yourself inasmuch as self-actualization comes more as a byproduct of developing your full capacities than from the egocentric pursuit of growth itself.

10. Remember that self-actualization is a lifelong process; it is never fully achieved.

SOURCE: Based on Maslow, A. H. (1971). *The Farther Reaches of Human Nature.* New York: Viking.

---

that blocks growth is the Jonah complex, or the fear of becoming one's best self. Just as the biblical Jonah tried to escape his destiny, so each of us tends to fear success, partly because such experiences can be overwhelming and because of the demands that come with them. Ken, for example, was just about to reach the pinnacle of his career, yet he was afraid that he might not quite achieve this so he wanted to give up and move to Oregon.

Second, our inner core of growth needs is relatively weak and undeveloped, making it hard to discover and easily stifled by discouraging circumstances. Many people fail to actualize themselves because of the lack of supportive circumstances. However, countless people have been significantly creative despite deprived circumstances, and Maslow acknowledged that it is something of a mystery why affluence releases some people for growth while stunting others. As a result, Maslow suggested that a favorable environment is not enough to ensure growth. Individuals must also have an intense desire to grow, to offset the apathy and resistance to growth.

All things considered, Maslow envisioned personal development as a struggle between growth-fostering forces and growth-discouraging forces, such as fear of the unfamiliar. He felt that our society discourages growth by overvaluing safety. Instead, he suggested that we should minimize the attractions of security and maximize its dangers, such as boredom and stagnation. At the same time he felt we should emphasize the attractiveness of growth while minimizing its dangers. Maslow (1968) repeatedly emphasized that "growth is, *in itself,* a rewarding and exciting process, thereby overcoming much of our resistance to self-actualization" (p. 30).

EVALUATION

The primary criticism of the humanistic perspective is that it is unscientific. Critics contend that much of the information is gained from humanistic therapy and from studies based on self-reports, resulting in formulations that are incomplete, lacking scientific precision and a comprehensive analysis of the causes of behavior. A related criticism is that the phenomenological position, with its emphasis on the individual's freedom, removes the perceiver from the causal chain and therefore from scientific scrutiny.

To such charges, humanistic psychologists would reply that as long as the scientific method is restricted to methods borrowed from the natural sciences, the fault lies more in the use of the wrong tools than in the subjects investigated. Leading psychologists, such as Maslow and Rogers, have long argued that the study of the individual and of personal relationships calls for a more comprehensive and flexible view of the scientific method. Speaking on this topic, Rogers (1985) described some of the recent developments in many fields of science that are bringing about a broader view of science, a view that recognizes that there is no *one* scientific method that is always best. The linear, cause-effect, behavioristic model is not being thrown out. But it is being viewed as a method that although adequate for investigating some questions, is clearly inappropriate for others. Similarly, the phenomenological approach is increasingly recognized as an excellent way of investigating issues that have to do with the living, acting, whole human being.

Humanistic psychologists have made a tremendous contribution to the larger field of psychology and society by tackling issues of urgent concern to all human beings, such as individual freedom, autonomy, love, and personal growth and values. They have also called our attention to the constructive side of psychology. Individuals are now being viewed in the light of their potential for health and fulfillment as well as in terms of their vulnerabilities and maladjustments.

APPLYING IT TO YOURSELF

Humanistic psychologists encourage us to see ourselves in terms of our positive potential, or what we can become. As such, they are more concerned with our personal growth than with sheer survival. Problems and conflicts are neither necessary nor inevitable. When these occur, it's apt to be because of our restrictive self-images, faulty choices, or an unsupportive environment. Consequently, we may improve ourselves by changing the way we see ourselves and achieving more of the potential control we have over our lives. Furthermore, such changes occur more readily in an environment conducive to growth, whether a challenging job or a happy marriage, not simply in psychotherapy.

Adjustment is rarely interpreted in terms of conventional conformity to society because of the high value placed on the individual. In fact, much of the maladjustment in life occurs because we live as if there were no inherent potential for something better. In terms of Rogers's phenomenal self, we risk becoming maladjusted when we accept our limited, defensive self as the inevitable state of existence rather than achieving greater self-acceptance and self-direction. In terms of May's human freedom, much of our difficulties comes from the refusal to face up to the important choices in our lives, if only by default. And in terms of Maslow's concept of self-actualization, a good part of our maladjustment comes from settling for the conventional life based on security and boredom rather than on the more challenging choices that foster growth.

Optimal adjustment is achieved by making choices that will enhance growth and by taking reasonable risks that will develop our potential. However, we must remember that self-actualization is a lifelong process that is only imperfectly realized in anyone's experience. Yet most people find the growth experience inherently gratifying, despite their imperfections. For instance, Maslow himself had an unhappy childhood; felt his ideas of self-actualizing people were not fully appreciated; and suffered from chronic fatigue, which only later in life was diagnosed as a form of hypoglycemia. At 56, Maslow said, "If anyone were to ask me, 'Are you a happy man?' I'd say 'yes, yes!' Am I lucky? . . . The darling of fortune? Sitting as high up as a human being ever has? Yes!" (G. Leonard, 1991, p. 21). And Ken and Audra? They moved to Oregon and were very happy they made the change.

SUMMARY

A PERSPECTIVAL APPROACH

Psychologists approach personality, adjustment, and growth from differing perspectives, each of which offers an optimal range of explanations rather than the complete truth. Thus, by examining the distinctive contributions of all four major perspectives, we may attain a more inclusive, balanced understanding of personality and behavior.

THE BIOLOGICAL PERSPECTIVE

Extensive studies of twins and others have shown that genetic influences account for between 25 percent and 50 percent of the differences in personal characteristics among the general population. At the same time, how much or how little of our response potential we develop depends greatly on the interaction with our environment. As a result, we should speak of nature via or through nurture rather than nature versus nurture.

THE PSYCHODYNAMIC PERSPECTIVE

According to the psychodynamic view, individuals are inevitably caught up in the interplay between conflicting forces of life, such as our unconscious drives and the ego's defenses, as well as the tension between the individual and society. The ego is the managerial part of the psyche that enables the individual to cope with the conflicting demands of the id, the superego, and society. Since the ego, the id, and the superego are often in conflict, individuals commonly experience anxiety as well as the various ego-defense mechanisms that reduce it. Personality develops through a sequential process, and the manner in which the child handles the characteristic developmental conflicts has a decisive influence on his or her adult personality. Many of Freud's followers have deemphasized sex and the unconscious and given greater emphasis to the managerial functions of the ego as well as to interpersonal relationships. In the psychodynamic view, optimal adjustment consists of increasing the individual's self-mastery and the attendant reality orientation.

THE SOCIAL-COGNITIVE PERSPECTIVE

Learning theorists deemphasize the biological basis of behavior and instead focus on how behavior is learned through interaction with the environment. They contend that most of our personality and behavior is acquired through such processes as observational learning, with or without direct reinforcement. Furthermore, the recognition of cognitive variables that intervene between the environment and our behavior suggests that learning is affected by more complex factors than an isolated stimulus, as was the belief in early behavioral theory. Bandura has characterized the mutual interaction among the various components of learning—personal-cognitive variables, environment, and behavior—as reciprocal determinism. In this view, humans have a tremendous capacity to learn and change, especially when they make full use of their minds and maximize their competencies in dealing with the environment. Self-efficacy is one means for accomplishing growth and change.

THE HUMANISTIC PERSPECTIVE

Humanistic psychologists emphasize the wholistic characteristics of human experiences, such as human freedom and self-actualization. Rogers's theory of the phenomenal self stresses the importance of perceived reality, especially the way individuals perceive and experience themselves in relation to their environment. In May's view, we begin to live authentically only as we affirm our inherent human freedom and take responsibility for our lives. Both Maslow and Rogers hold that each person has an inherent need to actualize his or her potentialities but that self-actualization is more of a lifelong process that enhances the meaning of life rather than a readily attainable goal.

SCORING KEY FOR THE SELF-ACTUALIZATION SURVEY

The Self-Actualization Survey measures four aspects of self-actualization: autonomy, self-acceptance, acceptance of your emotions, and trust and responsibility in interpersonal relations.

To get your score, responses placed before items 2, 5, 6, 8, 9, 11, 13, and 14 should be reversed (4 = 1, 3 = 2, 2 = 3, 1 = 4). Then add the resulting numbers to the responses before the rest of the items. Total scores can range from 15 to 60. College students had an average score of 45.60.

Females tend to score slightly higher than males. Also, scores on this survey are positively related with other scales. Thus, high scorers on this index tend to live in the present rather than in the past, with guilt and regret, or in the future, with overidealized goals and fears. High scorers also tend to be inner-directed, extraverted, and rational in their thoughts and behaviors.

SELF-TEST

1. Which one of the following traits is most strongly affected by genetic influences?
   - a. intelligence
   - b. frugality
   - c. impulsiveness
   - d. shrewdness

2. The part of the Freudian psyche that operates entirely on the pleasure principle is the
   - a. ego
   - b. id
   - c. superego
   - d. ego ideal

3. According to Freud, the emotional alarm signal that warns the ego of danger is
   - a. anxiety
   - b. the superego
   - c. the id
   - d. repression

4. In contrast to Freud's approach, Erikson focuses on the individual's
   - a. childhood experiences
   - b. psychosexual development
   - c. psychopathology
   - d. psychosocial development

5. The process by which people may acquire new behaviors without any direct reinforcement is called
   - a. self-actualization
   - b. observational learning
   - c. the conditioned response
   - d. operant learning

6. Which one of the following categories is included in Mischel's list of cognitive variables?
   - a. self-concept
   - b. human freedom
   - c. fantasy
   - d. encodings

7. From the social-cognitive perspective, optimal adjustment is achieved through maximizing the individual's
   - a. management of inner conflicts
   - b. self-actualizing drive
   - c. competencies and coping skills
   - d. self-esteem

8. Carl Rogers holds that human behavior is determined primarily by
   - a. perceived reality
   - b. social reinforcers
   - c. ego defenses
   - d. biological drives

9. According to Maslow, self-actualization
   - a. is rarely experienced before middle age
   - b. occurs among half of the population
   - c. is a lifelong process
   - d. is an easily achievable goal

10. Humanistic psychologists view the person's optimal adjustment in regard to the process of
    - a. social learning
    - b. self-actualization
    - c. impulse control
    - d. overcoming inner conflicts

EXERCISES

1. *Which of Erikson's stages are you in?* Write approximately a page explaining how well you're mastering the appropriate developmental task for your stage, according to Erikson's theory. How important do you regard this task for someone at your stage of life? If possible, comment on how your past development affects your experience in the present stage of development.

2. *The important people in your life.* Describe several of the important people, including your parents, who have most influenced your past development. What are these people like? What effect did they have on your development? To what extent has your personality been learned? To what extent do you think it is determined by inheritance?

3. *Self-actualization.* Reread Maslow's 10 suggestions for actualizing yourself more fully. Then apply them to your present personality and behavior. Make an honest assessment of yourself in each of these 10 areas. In which area are you the most fully actualized? In which area is further growth most needed?

4. *Barriers to personal growth.* Each of the four major perspectives covered in this chapter offers a different view of the barriers to personal growth. The biological view reminds us of the importance of heredity, for example, our temperament; the psychodynamic view stresses unconscious conflicts and fixations; the social learning view emphasizes faulty models, environments, and maladaptive behavior; and the humanistic view highlights the importance of restricted self-concepts and self-actualization. Write a paragraph or so explaining how each of these views may help to account for the barriers to your personal growth.

5. *Human freedom.* Select a specific situation in which you exercised your human freedom in the face of restricted circumstances. Then write a page or so about your experience. How much do you agree or disagree with the view expressed by May and Rogers, that is, that we possess an inner freedom of choice over and above the available options in our environment?

6. *Which major perspective most reflects your views?* Select one of the four major perspectives that is the most compatible with your own thoughts on adjustment and growth. Then write a page or so explaining why you prefer this viewpoint. To what extent are you receptive to viewpoints different from your own? Would you agree that no one perspective possesses the whole truth?

QUESTIONS FOR SELF-REFLECTION

1. Are there personal characteristics that seem to run in your family tree?

2. Do you agree with Freud that personality is like a submerged iceberg—with only the tip surfacing in awareness?

3. Do you sometimes experience ambivalence—being pulled in opposite ways simultaneously?

4. Do you believe that much of the inconsistency in people's behavior can be explained by situational factors?

5. When psychologists label their perspective "cognitive," what does this term mean to you?

6. How would you explain the difference between Bandura's social learning view and Rogers's humanistic view?

7. Are you as convinced as Rogers that we have within ourselves vast resources for self-understanding and growth?

8. Would you agree that self-actualization is always "in process" rather than complete?

9. Why do you think people aren't more fully self-actualized?

10. Would you agree that no single psychological perspective has a monopoly on truth?

FOR FURTHER INFORMATION

RECOMMENDED READINGS

BANDURA, A. (1997). *Self-efficacy: The exercise of control.* New York: W. H. Freeman. Major ideas and applications of self-efficacy by the leading authority in the field.

FREUD, S. (1965). *New introductory lectures on psychoanalysis* (J. Strachey, Trans. & Ed.). New York: W. W. Norton. A lucid overview of Freud's major ideas about personality and therapy.

HARARY, K., & DONAHUE, E. (1994). *Who do you think you are?* San Francisco: Harper. A book about understanding your personality and processes that affect it.

HETHERINGTON, T. F., & WEINBERGER, J. L. (1994). *Can personality change?* Washington, DC: American Psychological Association. Discusses from a scientific perspective whether personality remains stable across the lifespan or changes as a matter of life experience.

ROGERS, C. (1980). *A way of being.* Boston: Houghton Mifflin. Rogers describes his personal development and major ideas associated with his person-centered approach to therapy and life.

WEBSITES AND THE INTERNET

http:www.hgmp.mrc.ac.uk/: The website for the human genome project, which is trying to document all of the genes on human chromosomes.

http://parenttime.com: A fairly new on-line parenting site that can be customized for the child's age. Tips on child rearing from experts such as Dr. Benjamin Spock.

http://www.cs.washington.edu/homes/raj/dream.html: If you've had a dream you'd like to know more about or want to read about others' dreams, this is the web location for you.

http://plaza.interport.net/nypsan/freudarc.html: Want to know more about Freud? This site has the answers.

http://www.2h.com/Tests/personality.phtml: From here you can take a variety of personality tests on-line to do some self-discovering.

Motivation and Emotion

After completing this chapter, you should be able to

1. Describe Maslow's hierarchy of needs.
2. Describe several different ways in which sensation-seeking behavior is manifested.
3. List factors that affect our achievement motivation.
4. Discuss the importance of goals in personal motivation.
5. Identify the four components of emotions.
6. Explain the basic cognitive appraisal theory of emotions.
7. List the four components of an "I" message.
8. Describe methods for managing unproductive emotions.
9. Discuss several factors that are related and unrelated to happiness.

Vasu is one of those students never to be forgotten. A pleasant and rather slender young man, he sat in the rear of the classroom next to the door. He was friendly, articulate, and eager to learn. He spoke up in class whenever he was there, but his attendance record was very spotty. On the day of the first test in the fall, Vasu called Professor Gold's office and said that he was too sick to take the test. Professor Gold agreed to give Vasu a makeup test. The same thing happened on the day of the second test and the day of the paper. Before the third test, Professor Gold inquired whether Vasu would be able to take the examination at the scheduled time. Vasu said he thought so, but on the appointed day, he again did not show. Vasu's professor finally called him into her office; she wanted to know why Vasu was missing classes and assignments.

Understanding Motivation
•••••••••••

Most of us can sympathize with Vasu. Sometimes we do the task at hand, especially when it will bring us closer to some desired goal, such as graduating from school. Yet at other times, we may feel little or no motivation for what we're supposed to do. We procrastinate, we make excuses, and we waste precious time. Not surprisingly, parents, teachers, and managers in the workplace are interested in learning how to motivate people.

Essentially, **motivation** ("to move") has to do with *energizing* and *directing* our efforts toward a meaningful goal. Our motivation is affected by many influences, some of them rather obvious but others less so. We'll begin by discussing a popular theory of motivation, Abraham Maslow's theory. Then we'll briefly explore some of our basic **needs,** like hunger. In a later section, we'll consider several basic **motives** that are shaped mostly by learning and the environment, like achievement motivation. Later we'll look at the issue of personal motivation.

Most psychologists consider that emotions and motivation are closely linked. When we feel happy, we are eager to continue to feel happy. When we are sad, we are motivated to end the sadness as quickly as possible. In the last few parts of the chapter, we will turn our attention to emotions—what they are and how they are expressed verbally and nonverbally. We will next attend to specific emotions that are problematic to adjustment such as anxiety, anger, and jealousy. To end the chapter on an upbeat note, we will finish with information on happiness.

A HIERARCHY OF NEEDS

Our understanding of motivation may be enhanced by a look at Maslow's growth model of motivation, the **hierarchy of needs.** Maslow (1970) suggests that our needs and motives function in a hierarchical manner from the bottom up according to how crucial the need is for survival. The higher needs are experienced only to the degree that the more basic ones have been relatively satisfied. He describes five levels of needs as follows: (1) *Physiological needs* include the need for food, sleep, and sex; (2) *safety needs* include the need for protection from bodily harm and security from threat, as well as the need for order and stability; (3) *love and belongingness needs* include the need for acceptance, affection, and approval; (4) *esteem needs* refer to the need for self-respect and the sense of achievement; and (5) *self-actualization needs* include a variety of needs such as the need for autonomy, uniqueness, aliveness, beauty, and justice in our lives. Figure 3–1 depicts Maslow's need hierarchy. Notice that the top is narrower than the bottom, indicating that fewer individuals have the top needs satisfied.

Maslow holds that the lowest level of unmet needs remains the most urgent, commanding our attention and efforts. Once a given level of need is satisfied, we become motivated more by the unmet needs at the next-higher level. Thus, as we satisfy our

Eating is a primary need, but when food is abundant, eating often becomes a social activity.

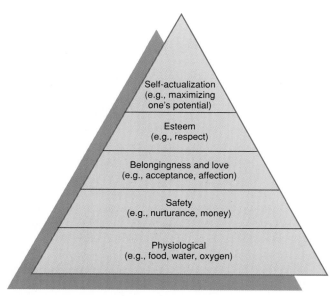

FIGURE 3–1

Maslow's hierarchy of needs. The needs are arranged
hierarchically from the bottom up according to how crucial the
need is for survival. The higher needs are experienced only to the
degree that the more basic ones have been relatively satisfied.
SOURCE: Diagram "Hierarchy of Needs" from *Motivation and Personality,* 3rd
ed. by Abraham H. Maslow. Copyright 1954, 1987 by Harper & Row,
Publishers, Inc. Copyright © 1970 by Abraham H. Maslow. Reprinted by
permission of Addison Wesley Educational Publishers Inc.

needs for food and shelter we become more concerned about things like job security.
At the same time Maslow points out that our needs are only relatively satisfied. He once
estimated that the average person is only 85 percent satisfied in terms of physiological
needs, 70 percent in safety needs, 50 percent in love needs, 40 percent in esteem needs,
and only 10 percent in self-growth needs.

An important implication of Maslow's growth model of motivation is that we aren't
content to achieve a stable, harmonious state. Instead once we've reached a relative level
of satisfaction, biologically and psychologically, we're increasingly motivated by growth
needs. This theory helps to explain why successful people are rarely satisfied to rest on
their previous accomplishments. They're constantly striving to attain something better.
Likewise, people who are happily retired seldom sit around doing nothing; they're forever developing new interests and deepening their relationships with others. It seems
we're happiest when we're growing and actualizing ourselves.

INDIVIDUAL DIFFERENCES

Although each of us desires the creature comforts of food and sleep, as well as higher
goals such as success in our jobs, the relative strengths of such motives differ from one
person to another. Accordingly, we need to think in terms of the individual's personal
hierarchy of motives as well as Maslow's generalized pattern. Which motives have top
priority in a given person will depend on factors such as inborn disposition, culture,

personal values, gender roles, and past experiences. For example, firstborn individuals tend to have a more intensive achievement motivation than their brothers and sisters, mostly because of the greater attention they received from their parents while growing up. In contrast, individuals who have been deprived of love and affection as children may be more motivated by the desire for approval than achievement.

Our motives also change over time depending on the **motive targets** around us—people toward whom our motives are directed. For example, at work you may have a strong motive to compete with your associates. In your leisure hours you may be more concerned about being accepted by your friends. Then again, at home you may feel inclined toward intimacy and sexual involvement with your lover or spouse. As a result, our motives are constantly changing throughout the day, as we move from one situation to another. Furthermore, an individual's motives tend to vary across the entire lifespan, mostly because of one's experience and personal growth. As a result, we often invest more or less of ourselves in the same career or a relationship like marriage as we grow older.

BASIC NEEDS

Like all other organisms, you and Vasu must eat, drink, and avoid extreme pain and injury if you are to survive. Although sex is not essential to our personal survival, it is necessary for the survival of the species. Such needs, though shaped by learning in varying degrees, have a clear physiological basis. As a result, they are variously labeled **basic needs, primary drives,** or **survival motives.**

For the sake of example, we will discuss here only two basic needs, hunger and thirst. When you go without food or water for half a day, you feel hungry and thirsty—right? If you were deprived of food even longer, the effect would be more marked. People who are deprived of food for a long period of time become less efficient in their thinking and behavior. They become apathetic, irritable, and depressed. The desire for food dominates their daytime activities as well as their daydreams. Fortunately, most of us never experience this extreme state, although we realize how important food is. Water is even more crucial to our survival. Although we can survive for weeks on minimal food, we can live only a few days without water.

Our eating and drinking behaviors are affected by a part of the brain known as the **hypothalamus.** Eating is also affected by a variety of learned influences. In fact, some individuals learn to like food all too well and cannot control their eating or find dieting difficult. Try the self-test in Figure 3–2 to determine how much you know about weight control. Some of the more common cues about which we learn are the smell, sight, and taste of food; emotional stress; and self-control (over our eating habits). Culture also plays a large role in learning various eating habits. Most Americans, for example, prefer white eggs to brown ones; the brown ones appear dirty. On the other hand, Russians do not mind eating brown eggs; in fact, most of the eggs they eat have brown shells.

There are other basic needs, such as the need for sleep, for clean air to breathe, and some would say for sex. Some of these other motives will be addressed in other chapters. Let us move on to other types of motives closer to the top of Maslow's hierarchy.

PSYCHOSOCIAL MOTIVES

The psychosocial motives have less to do with physical survival and more to do with our sense of well-being and psychological competence in dealing with our environment. Some—such as the motives for stimulation, curiosity, and exploration—seem to be

FIGURE 3–2

How Much Do You Know About Weight Control?

Answer true or false to each of the following statements. Then check your responses with the correct answers and explanations at the end of the chapter.

true	**false**	
———	———	1. Taking a brisk 10-minute walk not only burns up calories but also increases our energy.
———	———	2. Most obese people who lose weight regain it within 3 years.
———	———	3. People with pear-shaped bodies (ample hips and thighs) are less at risk for heart disease, diabetes, and gallstones than those with apple-shaped bodies (pot bellies).
———	———	4. Once we become fat, we need less food to maintain our weight than we did to attain it.
———	———	5. Fasting all day and eating just one big meal is an excellent way to lose weight.
———	———	6. The body burns calories most rapidly when exercise takes place within 3 hours after a meal.
———	———	7. Hunger pangs in the stomach become more intense the first 3 to 4 days after the last meal and gradually weaken thereafter.
———	———	8. Regular exercise momentarily burns up calories but does not affect our resting metabolism.
———	———	9. Most obese people lack willpower or turn to food as a substitution for other satisfactions.
———	———	10. The basic strategy for losing weight is to burn up more calories than you consume.

largely inborn and are sometimes labeled **stimulus needs.** Others, like the achievement motive, are shaped more extensively by psychological, cultural, and social influences. Because of the complexity of human behavior, there is no one authoritative list of our psychological and social motives. Some of these motives will be covered in other chapters, such as our sexual motives, affiliative motives, and the need for personal freedom and control. Here, we'll focus on two of the psychosocial motives not covered elsewhere, namely, the need for stimulation and for achievement.

Stimulation.   We need both sensory and social stimulation. People deprived of both—for instance, prisoners in solitary confinement and subjects in sensory deprivation experiments—display symptoms of stress, including distorted perceptions. They see and hear strange things; they hallucinate, have delusions, and fear losing their sanity. Military personnel in lonely outposts have shown similar reactions, though to a lesser degree. Most of us are rarely placed in a situation in which we suffer from extreme sensory or social isolation. But even after several hours of studying alone, you may feel a need to listen to the radio, call someone on the phone, or talk to your roommate, mostly for the stimulation involved.

Perhaps you've noticed how some people have a greater need for trying novel experiences and meeting new people. Others prefer more peaceful activities, such as reading or stamp collecting. Marvin Zuckerman (1990a) attributes such differences in human behavior to the relative strength of the **sensation–seeking motive.** Zuckerman believes our sensation-seeking motive may be partly dependent on biological factors, like brain stimulation and hormone secretions, so that each of us has an optimal arousal level. Whenever we find ourselves in situations that arouse us to a significantly lesser or greater extent than our optimal arousal, we become uncomfortable. If not sufficiently aroused, we seek greater stimulation; if we're overly aroused, we try to reduce the stimulation. Partly because of the biological basis, sensation seeking is at a peak during the college years and tends to diminish with age. Zuckerman's Sensation-Seeking Scale is presented in Figure 3–3, if you would like to test your desire for high levels of stimulation.

Sensation-seeking behavior may be manifested in several different ways:

1. *Thrill and adventure seeking.* Risky sports, speeding, and physical violence
2. *Experience seeking.* Drug use, novel experiences, and nonconformity

Some individuals purposely seek thrilling activities.

FIGURE 3–3

THE SENSATION-SEEKING SCALE

For each of the items below, circle the choice, A or B, that best describes your likes or dislikes, or the way you feel.

1. A. I would like a job that requires a lot of traveling.
   B. I would prefer a job in one location.

2. A. I am invigorated by a brisk, cold day.
   B. I can't wait to get indoors on a cold day.

3. A. I get bored seeing the same old faces.
   B. I like the comfortable familiarity of everyday friends.

4. A. I would prefer living in an ideal society in which everyone is safe, secure, and happy.
   B. I would have preferred living in the unsettled days of our history.

5. A. I sometimes like to do things that are a little frightening.
   B. A sensible person avoids activities that are dangerous.

6. A. I would not like to be hypnotized.
   B. I would like to have the experience of being hypnotized.

7. A. The most important goal of life is to live it to the fullest and experience as much as possible.
   B. The most important goal of life is to find peace and happiness.

8. A. I would like to try parachute jumping.
   B. I would never want to try jumping out of a plane, with or without a parachute.

9. A. I enter cold water gradually, giving myself time to get used to it.
   B. I like to dive or jump right into the ocean or a cold pool.

10. A. When I go on vacation, I prefer the comfort of a good room and bed.
    B. When I go on vacation, I prefer the change of camping out.

11. A. I prefer people who are emotionally expressive even if they are a bit unstable.
    B. I prefer people who are calm and even-tempered.

12. A. A good painting should shock or jolt the senses.
    B. A good painting should give one a feeling of peace and security.

13. A. People who ride motorcycles must have some kind of unconscious need to hurt themselves.
    B. I would like to drive or ride a motorcycle.

After you have completed the scale, consult the directions at the end of this chapter to figure your score and to determine its meaning.

SOURCE: M. Zuckerman, "The Search for High Sensation," *Psychology Today* (February 1978). Reprinted with permission from *PSYCHOLOGY TODAY MAGAZINE*. Copyright © 1978 (Sussex Publishers, Inc.). Reprinted with permission.

3. *Disinhibition.* Extraverted sensation seeking

4. *Boredom susceptibility.* Low tolerance for experiences that are constant or repetitive

In mainstream American culture, risk taking, bravado, and sensation seeking predominate. There are, however, individual differences in sensation-seeking and risk-taking behavior. Although both men and women can be sensation seekers, studies have demonstrated that men often score higher than women on Zuckerman's scale (Wills, Vacaro, & McNamara, 1994) and that men are more prone to boredom (a part of sensation seeking) than women (Vodanovich & Kass, 1990). The latter study also showed a decrease in tendency to feel bored as individuals aged.

Differences in sensation seeking may also influence the way we relate to one another. Low-sensation seekers may feel that high-sensation seekers are foolhardy and hungry for attention. In contrast, high-sensation seekers may feel that low-sensation seekers are timid and boring. Such differences also influence the choice of friends and marital partners, each type tending to marry its own kind. In fact, compatibility on this trait appears to be an important predictor of marital adjustment. Couples in which one partner has a very high SS score and the other a very low score have a high potential for marital disharmony (Farley, 1986).

Achievement. Perhaps you've noticed how your friends differ in achievement motivation. Some relish taking on a challenge. No matter what the task, they strive to do their best. Others seem to be happy just getting the job over and done with. In our opening case, Vasu had a strong motive to succeed, but something interfered with fulfilling this desire.

Achievement motivation is the desire to accomplish or master something difficult or challenging as independently and successfully as possible. Actually, achievement motivation is a complex combination of factors. Two elements are the **desire for success** or the urge to succeed and the counteracting **fear of failure,** fear that we will be humiliated by shortcoming. Each of us has a different mixture of these two tendencies, mostly because of our personal makeup and past experiences. As a result, people differ in the difficulties of the tasks they choose. For example, someone who has a strong desire for success and a low fear of failure is more apt to choose moderately difficult but realistic tasks, thus maximizing the chances of success. But another person with an intense desire for success coupled with a high fear of failure will set a much lower goal and perhaps be more anxious about achieving these goals.

Although our achievement motivation remains fairly stable over time, it may vary according to several factors, an important one of which is self-efficacy. In his book on the subject, Albert Bandura (1997) defines *self-efficacy* as beliefs in one's capabilities to organize and execute the courses of action required to produce given attainments. Self-efficacy affects our cognitive health, athletic, and career functioning. For example, athletes must learn the required skills, survive a highly competitive selection process, and then execute their skills perfectly in each game. Any and all of these processes can be affected by a sense of self-agency or self-efficacy.

"I can do it" is what the efficacious person says. But where does this come from? Bandura says families can provide experiences that build self-agency. First, young children try to get adults to produce desired outcomes that the children themselves cannot produce. Second, parents need to be responsive to their children's behavior and create opportunities for efficacious actions by providing an enriched physical environment, freedom for exploration, and varied mastery experiences. In this manner, children learn healthy self-appraisal skills. When they then move out into the school environment, self-efficacy continues to unfold if the same type of environment is created. We will return to the concept of self-efficacy in several other places in this book. Figure 3–4 presents a test of your self-efficacy.

The information on self-efficacy probably holds true for most White Americans. In other cultures, self-promotion, achieving one's own goals, and competition with others is not viewed positively. Indeed, another factor that affects achievement is the prevailing environment and the social values revered in that environment. For example, Steele (1992) claims that over half of the African American college students fail to obtain their diplomas due to racial stigmatism on campuses. Very few fail to obtain degrees

---

FIGURE 3–4

THE SELF-EFFICACY SCALE

1.	When I make plans, I am certain I can make them work.	T	F
2.	One of my problems is that I cannot get down to work when I should.	T	F
3.	If I can't do a job the first time, I keep trying until I can.	T	F
4.	When I set important goals for myself, I rarely achieve them.	T	F
5.	I give up on things before completing them.	T	F
6.	I avoid facing difficulties.	T	F
7.	If something looks too complicated, I will not even bother to try it.	T	F
8.	When I have something unpleasant to do, I stick to it until I finish it.	T	F
9.	When I decide to do something, I go right to work on it.	T	F
10.	When trying to learn something new, I soon give up if I am not initially successful.	T	F
11.	When unexpected problems occur, I don't handle them too well.	T	F
12.	I avoid trying to learn new things when they look too difficult for me.	T	F
13.	Failure just makes me try harder.	T	F
14.	I feel insecure about my ability to do things.	T	F
15.	I am a self-reliant person.	T	F
16.	I give up easily.	T	F
17.	I do not seem capable of dealing with most problems that come up in life.	T	F
18.	It is difficult for me to make new friends.	T	F
19.	If I see someone I would like to meet, I go to that person instead of waiting for him or her to come to me.	T	F
20.	If I meet someone interesting who is hard to make friends with, I'll soon stop trying to make friends with that person.	T	F
21.	When I'm trying to become friends with someone who seems uninterested at first, I don't give up easily.	T	F
22.	I do not handle myself well in social gatherings.	T	F
23.	I have acquired my friends through my personal abilities at making friends.	T	F

Reproduced with permission of authors and publisher from Sherer, M., Maddux, J. E., Mercandanter, B., Prentice-Dunn, S., Jacobs, B., & Rogers, R. W. The Self-Efficacy Scale: Construction and validation. *Psychological Reports,* 1982, 51, 663–671. © Psychological Reports 1982.

because of lack of ability. Blacks and their achievements are devalued in schools and American society. As if stigmatization is not bad enough, Steele continues with the point that African American children disidentify with school; that is, to salvage their self-esteem because their achievements have been ignored, the children decide they do not like school.

In collective (as compared to individualistic) societies where individual gain is shunned in favor of the collective good, achievement motivation occurs in a different form. Achievement motivation and satisfaction are not derived from personal accomplishment. Instead, positive feelings about the self come from fulfilling tasks associated with being interdependent with relevant others (Markus & Kitayama, 1991). For example, a study with Japanese youngsters demonstrated that self-promotion in the collective society of Japan is viewed quite negatively even by young children. One peer was presented as modest whereas another was presented as a self-promoter. The more modest peer was actually perceived as more athletically competent than the self-promoter.

PERSONAL MOTIVATION

A secret of being an active, motivated person is setting personal goals and then striving hard to reach them. In one sense, goal setting comes naturally in that we are all future-oriented. We are more concerned about today and tomorrow than yesterday. Yet it takes some thought and soul searching to set personal goals or objectives, which is why a lot of people don't bother to do it. But the risk of not doing so can be costly in terms of wasted time and energy.

There are several types of personal goals:

- *Long-range goals* are concerned with the kind of life you want to live in regard to your career, marriage, and lifestyle. It's wise to keep these goals broad and flexible, especially during your college years.
- *Medium-range goals* cover the next five years or so and include the type of education you're seeking or the next step in your career or family life. You have more control over these goals, so you can tell how well you're progressing toward them and modify them accordingly.
- *Short-range goals* apply from the next month or so up to one year from now. You can set these goals quite realistically and should try hard to achieve them.
- *Mini-goals* cover anything from one day to a month. You have a lot of control over these goals and should make them specific.
- *Micro-goals* cover the next 15 minutes to a few hours. Realistically, these are the only goals over which you have direct control.

As you can see, the shorter the time span covered, the more control you have over your goals. Yet it is only through achieving the modest, short-range goals that you'll ever attain your medium- and long-range goals. Too often, people make the mistake of setting grandiose goals and then quickly become disillusioned because they're making so little progress toward achieving them. It's far better to set realistic but desirable goals; then concentrate on achieving your day-to-day goals, which will make it more possible to reach your "dream" goals. Remember also that once you've achieved a goal, it's important to set new ones.

Some individuals set large goals when they would experience less distress day by day if they set smaller goals. The informative Box 3–1 about "Daily Pleasures" discusses how we can better increase our satisfaction with life simply by indulging in small pleasures throughout the day.

BOX 3–1

DAILY PLEASURES

Pleasure seeking is a basic motive. It is no accident that animals and humans alike have several "pleasure centers" in the brain. In animals, these are associated with the pleasures of eating, drinking, and sex—activities essential for survival. Human evolution links these centers with pleasurable activities that promote our health and well-being, such as sleep, exercise, meaningful work, play, and sharing with others. So enjoying the pleasures of food, sex, and sleep rewards us twice, in immediate enjoyment and in improved health.

Awakening after a refreshing sleep is itself a pleasurable sensation. A bracing shower and warm cup of coffee help us to begin the day. For some, aerobic or warm-up exercises afford a welcome stimulus. The pleasure of eating a good meal without hurry is enhanced by the company with whom we share it.

Potential daily pleasures are numerous and vary among individuals. Obviously, some pleasures are more healthful than others.

The sensual pleasures of a bath, sauna, or swimming on a hot day are well known. One woman recalls the sensual pleasure of a warm shower on her skin after the several-day wait following surgery.

The cliché "No pain, no gain" is only partly true. Actually, the exercise necessary to keep fit is much less than people think. Walking, biking, dancing, and even gardening can boost heart rates and enhance our physical vitality.

There are also visual feasts, such as looking at a field of trees and flowers, viewing artworks, or appreciating the sometimes dazzling array of colors worn by people today.

Music has a sensual pleasure of its own. Be it rock, jazz, pop, or country, music may soothe frazzled nerves and lift us up when we're down.

In one study, people carried beepers that recorded how they felt at any moment and rated their happiness over a 6-week period. Happiness, they discovered, consists in how much time a person feels good rather than in momentary peaks of ecstasy. Thus, simple pleasures—such as feeling the sand between your toes while walking at the shore, being with a friend, or listening to your favorite music—are more closely linked with happiness than strong feelings. So, don't bet on winning the lottery or becoming the head of your company. Instead, make sure you attend to the daily healthy pleasures of taste, sound, touch, and rewarding relationships. The good feelings help to make each day more rewarding.

SOURCE: Adapted from *Healthy Pleasures,* © 1989 by Robert Ornstein, Ph.D. and David Sobel, MD. Reprinted with permission of Addison Wesley Longman.

 Emotions

We can only imagine the anxiety Vasu felt when he could not take his exams or turn his paper in on time. This anxiety probably only compounded his anguish and depression regarding the mysterious illness he developed but did not want to tell his professor about until it was diagnosed. We turn next to the study of emotions, which as mentioned earlier are motivating in and of themselves.

WHAT ARE EMOTIONS?

Authorities differ concerning how much our emotions are inborn or learned. In fact, understanding emotions continues to be a challenge, for both researchers and the average person. Today, we still lack a single, unifying theory of emotions. Nevertheless, most psychologists would agree that an **emotion** is a complex pattern of changes that includes physiological arousal, subjective feelings, cognitive processes, and behavioral reactions—all in response to a situation we perceive to be personally significant. Accordingly, an emotion has four components:

1. *Physiological arousal.* Emotions involve the brain, nervous system, and hormones, so that when you're emotionally aroused your body is aroused. Intense or constant emotional arousal uses up valuable energy and lowers our resistance to illness.
2. *Subjective feelings.* Emotions also include subjective awareness, or "feeling," that involves elements of pleasure or displeasure, liking or disliking. Thus, in studying emotions or knowing another person's feelings, we must rely heavily on that person's own self-reports.
3. *Cognitive processes.* Emotions also involve cognitive processes such as memories, perceptions, expectations, and interpretations. Our appraisal of an event plays an especially significant role in the meaning it has for us.
4. *Behavioral reactions.* Emotions also involve behavioral reactions, both expressive and instrumental. Facial expressions, as well as gestures and tones of voice, serve to communicate our feelings to others. Cries of distress and running for our lives are also adaptive responses that may enhance our chances for survival.

Most psychologists would agree that emotions underpin psychological adjustment (Keltner, Moffitt, & Stouthamer, 1995). For example, Katz and Campbell (1994) asked college students to keep diaries for two weeks about their ambivalence over expressing emotions.

Ambivalence can be of two types. Some individuals would like to express their emotions but cannot; others do express their emotions but would prefer to hold them inside. Besides tracking ambivalence, students also answered questionnaires about their adjustment and physical well-being. Katz and Campbell found that the greater the ambivalence individuals experienced over appropriateness of emotional expression, the more likely they were to experience negative life outcomes such as illnesses.

Many contemporary theories of emotion emphasize the role of cognitive factors. Thus, an experience arouses our emotions mostly when the stimuli are appraised by the individual as having personal significance. In this view, an emotional experience cannot be understood as something that happens solely in the person or in the brain but is more in our relationship to the environment. The particular emotion that is felt depends largely on how we label a given situation, that is, on how we interpret the personal meaning it has for us.

A major implication of the cognitive view of emotions is that each of us has more potential control over our feelings than popularly believed. Whenever we feel angry, jealous, or depressed, we are not simply at the mercy of our momentary feelings. Nor should we take our "gut" reactions as infallible, as important as these may be. Instead, it's better to realize that our momentary feelings are partly the result of the way we perceive and respond to an event.

EXPERIENCING EMOTIONS

Emotions are a kind of barometer of our inner world, giving us an intuitive knowledge about ourselves and our involvement with others at the moment. On the one hand, intense emotions tell us our lives are strongly affected by some person or event and prompt us to act accordingly. On the other hand, when we feel little or no emotion in a given situation, chances are our needs, goals, or values are not affected; that is, we're not "emotionally involved." Perhaps that's why we're constantly asking each other, "How do you feel about this?" or "What's your reaction to that?" Unfortunately, it's not always easy to say, is it? A major reason is that we often have trouble identifying our feelings at the moment, much less finding the right words to express them. Then, too, our emotions are in a state of constant flux, or change, so that we may feel pleased one moment and annoyed the next. Also, our feelings are often a mixture of various **primary emotions** and so defy easy labels.

On the other hand, when people in different countries, such as Greece, Poland, China, and Canada, are asked to report their experience of different emotions, all seem to place emotions along two dimensions—pleasant versus unpleasant and intensely aroused versus weakly aroused (J. A. Russell, Lewicka, & Niit, 1989). Thus, the emotions of contentment, joy, and love fall into the category of positive emotions, whereas anger, disgust, and sadness fall into the category of unpleasant emotions. On the intensity scale, rage is more intense than anger, which in turn is more intense than annoyance. It is not surprising, then, that the facial expressions accompanying several emotions are interpreted the same way across cultures. In fact, six different primary emotions are expressed universally on the human face from a very early age: anger, fear, happiness, sadness, surprise, and disgust (Ekman, 1993). Based on his cross-cultural research, Matsumoto (1992) claims that there exists a seventh universal emotion—contempt.

EXPRESSING EMOTIONS

Emotions not only move us to do things or to avoid situations but also are a primary way of communicating with others. However, it's not always safe to share our intimate feelings, much less while casually greeting a friend in the hall or on the street. Sharing our feelings is risky and makes us vulnerable to the judgment of others. Some people are so afraid of their inner feelings, they're unable to experience, much less express, their deeper emotions in times of joy or sorrow. Others, who are more in touch with their emotions, share their feelings more readily, whether in anger or in love. Whichever way we're inclined, the most important thing is to find that balance of expression and control of feelings with which we feel most comfortable.

What underlies differences in emotional expressiveness as well as ability to interpret others' expressions? Researchers have consistently found that women are better decoders than are men of others' emotions, especially of body postures (L. R. Brody & Hall, 1993). In terms of understanding our own emotional states, researchers have found that

The six basic emotions.

Anxiety   *Anger*   *Jealousy*

Happiness   *Fear*   *Disgust*

men ruminate more about upsetting events and report more inhibition of hostile feelings than women (McConatha, Lightner, & Deaner, 1994); these same researchers also found that older persons rehearse more about upsetting events and express emotions less frequently than younger individuals. As you might guess, culture also plays a role in our expressiveness. Matsumoto (1993) found that there are differences in how Black, Asian, Caucasian, and Hispanic Americans display emotions. For example, Japanese Americans report the lowest intensity of positive emotions as well as the lowest expressiveness in romantic relationships (Aune & Aune, 1996).

Another factor that makes emotions slippery is that some individuals try to deceive us. For example, a woman might try to make her friend who has just won a major award think that she is pleased when instead she is jealous. A man might express contempt for a prospective romantic partner when actually he finds her attractive but has been recently jilted by her. How can you tell if you are being deceived? One helpful cue is what psychologists call **microexpressions,** or fleeting facial expressions that last only a fraction of a second (Ekman, 1985b). One expression followed quickly by another is one key to lying. People also try hard to control their facial expressions because they know that most of us think the face is the key to the soul. Such individuals may blink more or smile more broadly in an effort to deceive (Baron & Byrne, 1997). Watching for **body leakage** where body postures rather than the face leak the truth can be revealing.

MANAGING EMOTIONS

Because emotions are related to psychological adjustment, it is desirable to manage our feelings well. Learning to express our feelings effectively involves a suitable balance between spontaneous expression and deliberate, rational control. The areas needing improvement vary somewhat from one person to another. On the one hand, people who are overly emotional and impulsive may blurt out their feelings without much thought; they need to develop better control. On the other hand, those who keep their emotions under tight control may need to loosen up, become more aware of their feelings and more comfortable expressing them. Most of us fall into this category.

We can become more adept in expressing our emotions by sharing our everyday feelings more readily. Many times we may feel pleased about something a person has done for us. Why not share this feeling? As you become accustomed to sharing your safe emotions, you'll get in better touch with your feeling life. Then when you experience an intense emotion, like anger or disgust, you may find it easier to recognize your feelings and be more willing to express them. More often than not, it's a risk worth taking. When you express your feelings openly and in a constructive manner, it helps to clear the air and facilitate communication. Sharing your feelings with an attentive person may also help to clarify them. All too often, we're not certain what we're feeling until we've expressed it and hear how others respond to what we have said.

A technique that is particularly useful for expressing intense negative emotions is the use of an **"I" message,** as explained by Tom Gordon (Gordon & Sands, 1978). Essentially, this message is saying what you honestly feel in a way that encourages others to listen and cooperate. "I" messages are especially helpful in expressing your feelings about someone whose behavior has become a problem for you. An "I" message consists of four components.

Let's break down the "I" message point by point, in more detail. First, describe the other person's objectionable behavior in specific but nonjudgmental terms. For instance, you might use the phrase "when you fail to return my book on time" instead of "you're

Family conflicts evoke intense emotions.

irresponsible." Avoid using fuzzy and accusatory responses or guessing the person's motives. Such communication only intensifies the person's resistance to changing his or her behavior.

Second, point out the specific ways in which that person's behavior affects us. In most instances, people are not deliberately trying to make life miserable for us; they simply aren't aware of the consequences of their actions. Once they become more aware of how their behavior has become a problem for us, they're usually willing to modify it.

Third, tell the person how you feel about his or her behavior in a way that "owns" your emotions. Say "I feel hurt" instead of "you hurt me." Avoid projecting your emotions onto the other person.

Finally, tell the person what you want him or her to do. For example, if you object to the casual way telephone messages are left for you, you might say something like this: "When you don't write down my telephone messages, I don't have the information I need and I feel frustrated. I'd appreciate your writing down my telephone messages." Initially, "I" messages may seem a bit contrived or stiff. But as you become more experienced in using them you'll feel more comfortable expressing your feelings in this way. Table 3.1 provides more tips on "I" messages.

Let's next look at some troubling emotions in more detail.

SPECIFIC EMOTIONS

Anxiety.   Vasu probably felt much anxiety about his examinations. Perhaps he wondered if the exams themselves made him feel sick. He perhaps was afraid to talk to Professor Gold about missing so many of her assignment deadlines.

Although **anxiety** is an unpleasant emotion, it serves as an emotional alarm signal, warning us of threat or danger. When the threat is real and can be pinpointed, such as the risk of missing an examination, anxiety may motivate us to take the necessary steps to avoid such a misfortune. Unfortunately, we often feel anxious when there is little real

TABLE 3–1
EXAMPLES OF "I" MESSAGES

Nonjudgmental description of person's behavior	Concrete effects on me	My feelings about it	What I'd prefer the person to do
1. If you don't complete what you promised to do	then I have to do it in addition to my other tasks	and I feel annoyed.	I wish you would do what you've promised.
2. Each time you criticize my work without telling me what I'm doing wrong	I don't know how to improve it	and I feel frustrated and resentful.	Tell me what I'm doing wrong so I can correct it.
3. When you change your mind at the last minute	it's too late to make other plans	and I feel angry and disappointed.	Give me more advance notice when you think things may not work out.

danger, for example, when making a speech or going to the dentist. People who are prone to chronic, or "free-floating," anxiety tend to overreact to stressful situations, thereby making them worse. Furthermore, high levels of anxiety distort our perception and thinking so that our performance is impaired. Anxiety also siphons off energy by keeping us mobilized for action when none is needed. It makes us tense and tired, thereby robbing us of much of the enjoyment of life.

Test anxiety is a familiar problem for most college students like you and Vasu. Does test anxiety help you to learn better or does it interfere with performance? A lot depends on the person and the situation. Generally, the relationship between anxiety and test performance takes the form of an inverted-U curve as depicted in Figure 3–5. That is, at low levels of anxiety, we remain unmotivated and perform well only on easy tasks. More moderate levels tend to enhance performance, at least up to a point. But at high levels of anxiety many people become distracted and overwhelmed, thereby performing more poorly on tests. At the same time, people differ widely on their optimal level of anxiety—the degree of anxiety at which they do their best. People with relatively low levels of anxiety often do their best only when challenged, as in a highly competitive situation. But those with characteristically high levels of anxiety tend to do better, at least on difficult tasks, under conditions of less pressure. Which of these two patterns

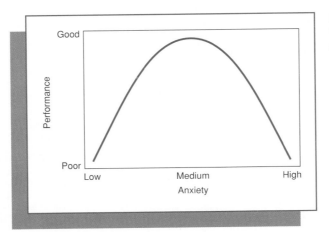

FIGURE 3–5

The relationship between anxiety and performance.

do you most resemble? Do you find it depends somewhat on the situation as well as on your own mastery of appropriate skills and motivation?

In a recent review, Zeidner (1995) found at least two important generalizations about text anxiety. First, adaptive coping in exam situations involves a flexible repertoire and combined use of several coping strategies. When one strategy does not work, the individual needs to be able to turn to another. Second, effective coping strategies should match both the context and the individual. This means that the individual needs to be comfortable with the strategy and also that the strategy should be appropriate to the level of challenge of the examination. Happily, Zeidner also reports that most students cope effectively because they utilize active coping, in which they plan study time and techniques, suppress competing activities (such as socializing with friends), and reframe the stressful event positively.

If your academic performance is hindered by test anxiety, you may benefit from a number of anxiety-reducing strategies. For instance, when you find yourself getting anxious during the test, you can employ anxiety-reducing statements such as "I know I can do it" and "I'll just take one question at a time." Another effective method for coping with test anxiety is to study and learn well. Good study techniques were reviewed in the "How to Study" section (PQ4R) at the beginning of this book.

Anger.   A basketball coach yells profanities at the referee after a controversial call. A teenage girl screams "No, no, no" at her mother. A red-faced worker slams his fist on the table to make his point during labor-management negotiations. All these people are venting **anger**—feelings of displeasure or resentment over mistreatment. Most of us have grown up with the idea that when you're angry it's healthy to "get it off your chest" or "let it all hang out." Holding anger in, goes the popular notion, leads to all kinds of problems—high blood pressure, increased risk of heart attacks, depression, and suicide.

There is *some* truth to this notion, in that people who unduly suppress their anger are more prone to high blood pressure and heart attacks. Psychologists have discovered a hostile syndrome known as the Type A personality. **Type A individuals** tend to be competitive, argumentative, and impatient as well as hostile. Type As are twice as likely as others to suffer from coronary heart disease (Booth-Kewley & Friedman, 1987). For years, psychologists believed that this whole Type A syndrome made these individuals more prone to heart attacks than their opposites, **Type Bs** or relaxed individuals. More recent research, however, has found that hostility is the primary dimension responsible for the coronary trouble (Contrada, Leventhal, & O'Leary, 1990). Type A behavior can also be manifested in children, especially boys in the United States (Compas, 1987) and is often manifested as anger, anxiety, and depression (Heft et al., 1988). Table 3–2 summarizes some of the differences between Type As and Type Bs. In fact, mainstream American culture and the prevailing theme of individualism can encourage immigrants to be more prone to Type A behavior than they ordinarily would be (Thoreson & Powell, 1992).

There is lots of evidence that we can learn to manage our anger. First, certain child-rearing practices can go a long way toward preventing inappropriate forms of anger management. Developmentally appropriate strategies for encouraging children to responsibly manage anger include modeling by parents of appropriate anger management, avoiding shaming a child's anger, and increasing the child's understanding of anger as well as the sense of control over reactions to anger-arousing events (Marion, 1994). Eliminating exposure to aggressive models also helps. For example, parents might want to monitor their child's television watching. There is much evidence that watching televised violence desensitizes us to its effects (Hearold, 1986). Individuals who are isolated

TABLE 3–2
TYPE A/TYPE B: WHICH TYPE ARE YOU?

Type A

    1. competitive

    2. always in a hurry

    3. hard-driving

    4. demands perfection of self and others

    5. ambitious, wants quick promotions

    6. is a "workaholic"—even at play

    7. hostile to others

Type B

    1. noncompetitive

    2. relaxed, in control

    3. easygoing

    4. understanding, forgiving

    5. confident and happy on the job

    6. enjoys leisure and weekends

SOURCE: From *Type A Behavior and Your Heart* by Meyer Friedman, M.D., and Ray N. Rosenman, M.D. Copyright © 1974 by Meyer Friedman. Reprinted by permission of Alfred A. Knopf, Inc.

also have difficulty managing anger. Perhaps it is the individual's failure to properly manage anger that has turned friends away. Increasing the number of social contacts and social supports so that the angry person can discuss anger with others improves anger management (Spicer & Hong, 1991; Spicer, Jackson, & Scragg, 1993).

The training of social skills where we learn to get along with others is another option. If we don't know how to respond appropriately to others, we sometimes lose our tempers. Social skills training helps individuals find alternative solutions to provocations. Such training is effective, often after only a few hours (Bienert & Schneider, 1993). For other individuals, especially physically abused individuals, therapy might be the only answer. Therapy should convey the sense that anger is destructive and that better communication and problem-solving skills and increased empathy for the target help reduce anger. Such therapy has been shown to be effective for adolescents and adults who show strong levels of anger and little control (Acton & During, 1992; Wilcox & Dowrick, 1992).

Jealousy.   Essentially, **jealousy** is a complex emotion that occurs when we fear losing a close relationship with another person or have lost it already. Jealousy is characterized by fear of loss, distrust, anxiety, and anger (Parrott & Smith, 1993). Jealousy is especially apt to occur in love and sexual relationships, so that it is popularly known as romantic jealousy. Jealousy can be contrasted with envy (Parrott & Smith), which is distinguished by feelings of inferiority, longing, resentment, and disapproval.

It is commonly thought that jealousy is a measure of devotion, and the lack of jealousy means the absence of love. Admittedly, jealousy may contribute positively, however indirectly, to close relationships like marriage. High jealousy is linked to "strong love," "establishing ground rules," and an "increased commitment" in the marriage.

However, most Americans regard jealousy as an unnecessary and destructive emotion in close relationships (Bringle, 1991).

The occurrence of jealousy depends largely on the interaction between jealousy-evoking situations and the personalities of the people involved as well as their relationship. According to Salovey and Rodin (1986), some situations are especially apt to trigger jealousy, such as the following:

- The person you like goes out with someone else.
- Someone gets closer to a person to whom you are attracted.
- Your lover or spouse tells you how sexy a former boyfriend/girlfriend was.
- Your lover or spouse visits a person he or she used to go out with.
- You find that your partner is having an affair.

How would you respond if you found yourself in these situations? How do you think your partner would respond? Apparently, a lot depends on each individual's personality, with some people being especially prone to jealousy. Individuals who readily experience jealousy are characterized by low self-esteem, high levels of anxiety, a negative view toward the world, low levels of life satisfaction, little control over their lives, low threshold of emotional arousal, and a greater sensitivity to threatening stimuli in social environments (Bringle, 1991). Also, jealousy is more common among traditionally masculine men and traditionally feminine women (Hansen, 1985), and women's but not men's jealousy is reduced when they find a romantic substitute after a terminated relationship (Mathes, 1991).

Although the potential for jealousy is inherent in our biological makeup, cultural influences carry much more weight in determining which situations provoke jealousy and how it is manifested. For instance, when jealous, the French get mad, whereas the Dutch become sad. The Germans prefer not to fight about it, and the Italians don't even want to talk about it. It appears that Americans are mostly concerned about what their friends will think (Bryson, 1991; Zummuner & Fischer, 1995).

How people appraise and cope with jealousy-evoking situations is especially important. Rusbult (1987) studied coping responses in two dimensions: whether people's responses were active or passive in regard to preserving their self-esteem, and constructive or destructive in regard to maintaining the relationship. The results showed that people who employ active, constructive responses tend to express their dissatisfaction with the relationship, with the intention of improving both the relationship as well as their own esteem—for example, "I would sit down and talk things out with my girlfriend." In contrast, a destructive response would be threatening to end the relationship, which is often a way of preserving one's self-esteem, possibly at the expense of maintaining the relationship—for example, "I would tell my boyfriend that I've had enough of his selfishness and I am leaving."

Happiness.   Imagine Vasu's happiness when his mysterious illness was finally diagnosed and successfully treated. Vasu had worked on a farm in the summer and had contracted Lyme Disease. Lyme causes unexplained joint pains, headaches, and fatigue months after the bite by the deer tick. Would Vasu remain happy? What else would contribute to his happiness? To your happiness? What in the world is happiness?

In 1995 David Myers and Ed Diener reviewed all of the available literature on happiness. The good news is that many studies reveal that happiness is more abundant than believed. **Happiness,** or what Myers and Diener called Subjective Well-Being (SWB), includes a preponderance of positive thoughts and feelings about one's life. People high in SWB have a global sense that work, marriage, and other life domains are satisfactory. They primarily experience and report pleasant rather than anxious, angry, or depressive emotions. Happy people are less self-focused, less hostile, and less vulnerable to disease. They are more loving, forgiving, trusting, energetic, decisive, creative, helpful, and sociable than unhappy people (Myers, 1993). Study after study shows that happy people have high self-esteem, a sense of personal control, optimism, and extroversion; happy people often lose a sense of time and self because they find a task challenging and absorbing (Myers & Diener, 1995). Figure 3–6 provides a self-test of happiness.

FIGURE 3–6

HAPPINESS SCALE

Part I. In general, how happy or unhappy do you usually feel? Check the one statement below that best describes your average happiness. Check just one item.

_____ 10. Extremely happy (feeling ecstatic, joyous, fantastic!)
_____ 9. Very happy (feeling really good, elated!)
_____ 8. Pretty happy (spirits high, feeling good)
_____ 7. Mildly happy (feeling fairly good, somewhat cheerful)
_____ 6. Slightly happy (just a bit above neutral)
_____ 5. Neutral (not particularly happy or unhappy)
_____ 4. Slightly unhappy (just a bit below neutral)
_____ 3. Mildly unhappy (just a little low)
_____ 2. Pretty unhappy (somewhat "blue," spirits down)
_____ 1. Very unhappy (depressed, spirits very low)
_____ 0. Extremely unhappy (utterly depressed, completely down)

Part II. On the average, what percent of the time do you feel happy? unhappy? neutral (neither happy nor unhappy)? Write down your best estimates in the spaces below. Make sure the three figures add up to 100 percent.

The percent of time I feel happy   _____%
The percent of time I feel unhappy   _____%
The percent of time I feel neutral   _____%
Total 100 %

After you have completed Parts I and II, consult the scoring directions at the end of this chapter for determining the meaning of your score.

SOURCE: M. W. Fordyce, "A Review of Research on the Happiness Measures: A Sixty Second Index of Happiness and Mental Health," *Social Indicators Research,* 1988, 20, 355–381. Reprinted by permission of Kluwer Academic Publishers.

Myers and Diener dismiss many myths about happiness. For example, research has shown that there is no one time of life that is happier or unhappier than another (Latten, 1989). Happiness does not gender discriminate either; in cross-cultural research both men and women have equal opportunities to find happiness (Michalos, 1991). There is also only a modest correlation between wealth and happiness (Diener, Sandvik, Seidlitz, & Diener, 1993). As Myers and Diener (1995) persuasively state, "[wealth's] absence can breed misery, yet its presence is no guarantee of happiness" (p. 13). Race and ethnicity are also not predictors of happiness. Crocker and Major (1989) found that despite discrimination, disadvantaged groups maintain self-esteem by valuing things that they are good at and by attributing their problems to external causes such as prejudice. Everyone, then, has the possibility for happiness. Perhaps you have wondered just how happy you are?

SUMMARY

UNDERSTANDING MOTIVATION

Maslow's hierarchy of needs is a popular theory of motivation. At the bottom are basic needs such as the need for food and the need for safety or security. The middle but narrower level involves the need for belonging or the need to fit in or to be accepted. At the top levels are self-esteem needs and self-actualizing tendencies respectively. Self-esteem needs involve the need to feel a sense of self-worth and achievement, whereas self-actualization includes a sense that we are autonomous and unique from others. These higher level needs cannot be met if the lower level needs are unfulfilled.

Hunger is an example of a basic need. Most basic needs are biological but can be shaped by learning. Psychosocial needs include the need for stimulation of which one form is sensation-seeking and achievement or the need for success. Such motives vary by the individual. Culture, gender, and other factors that influence learning shape our individual methods for responding to these needs.

EMOTIONS

Emotions are complex changes that include physical arousal and cognitive interpretations of a situation. Emotions are very important to psychological adjustment. The cognitive view of emotions is that our interpretation of them is actually more important in influencing our reaction than the actual arousal or the provoking stimulus. There are several universally expressed and recognized emotions: anger, fear, happiness, sadness, surprise, and disgust. Culture can greatly influence the intensity of the emotional expression, though. Another tricky part of emotions is that people can try to deceive us about their emotions by altering their nonverbal communications (the face and the body). We can all learn healthy methods for managing our emotions so that we express them at socially appropriate times and intensities and in appropriate ways.

Anxiety is a common unpleasant emotion, but it can serve as a useful alarm that warns us of threat. Test anxiety is especially detrimental for unprepared students, as it can diminish their performance. Being well prepared for an examination helps us overcome test anxiety.

Anger is yet another problematic emotion. Research with perpetually hostile individuals, Type As, has shown that hostility can lead to coronary disease. Learning to respond in nonhostile ways is therefore important to mental and physical health. One good method for avoiding all of this is to raise children to recognize their anger and to manage it when they are young. Parents can act as role models for their children.

Jealousy is a third negative emotion with which individuals have to cope. Jealousy often occurs in a romantic context. Jealousy is more common among traditionally sex-typed individuals. Such individuals need to learn to cope with jealousy in active and constructive ways where they express their dissatisfaction and their intention of improving the relationships.

Happiness is a positive emotion associated with subjective well-being. According to research, happiness is available to everyone regardless of sex, race, or income level. Happy people are less hostile, less vulnerable to disease, more forgiving, trusting, and energetic than unhappy people.

ANSWERS AND EXPLANATIONS TO THE QUIZ ON WEIGHT CONTROL

1. True. A daily 10-minute walk raises energy levels and reduces tension for 2 hours.
2. False. Only about half of the obese people who lose weight regain it within 3 years, though almost all of them do so by 10 years.
3. True. Excess weight in the stomach area poses a greater risk of heart disease, diabetes, and gallstones than excess weight in the hips and thighs.
4. True. Compared to other body tissues, fat tissue can be maintained with fewer calories.
5. False. This eating pattern, which is common among obese people, actually slows down metabolism.
6. True. One reason is that the calories from a recent meal are consumed before the food has an opportunity to leave the stomach and become absorbed into the body tissues.
7. True. A major finding from research on starvation.
8. False. Regular exercise not only burns up calories but increases your resting metabolism as well.
9. False. Most authorities now discount willpower as an explanation for obesity, giving greater weight to individual differences in body chemistry and genetics.
10. True. This remains the basic strategy for losing weight.

DIRECTIONS FOR SCORING THE SENSATION-SEEKING SCALE

Score 1 point for each of the following responses: 1A, 2A, 3A, 4B, 5A, 6B, 7A, 8A, 9B, 10B, 11A, 12A, 13B.

Zuckerman suggests the following interpretation:

1–3 very low SS scores
4–5 low SS scores
6–9 average SS scores
10–11 high SS scores
12–13 very high SS scores

DIRECTIONS FOR SCORING THE SELF-EFFICACY SCALE

1. T	7. F	13. T	19. T
2. F	8. T	14. F	20. F
3. T	9. T	15. T	21. T
4. F	10. F	16. F	22. F
5. F	11. F	17. F	23. T
6. F	12. F	18. F	

For each match with this key, give yourself one point. The higher your score out of 23, the higher your efficacy.

DIRECTIONS FOR SCORING THE HAPPINESS SCALE

This instrument provides a measure of the frequency and intensity of affect. The scale score in Part I and the percentages of happiness estimates in Part II are used as raw scales. The combination score that is used in happiness research requires only minimal calculation as follows:

$$\text{Combination score} = \frac{(\text{scale score} \times 10 + \text{happy percentage})}{2}$$

Mean or average scores for more than 3,000 community college students were as follows: Combination score = 61.66%; scale scores = 6.92; happy % estimate = 54.13; unhappy % estimate = 20.44; neutral % estimate = 25.43.

SELF-TEST

1. In Maslow's concept of the hierarchy of needs, the most urgent need commanding our attention is
   a. self-actualization
   b. security
   c. belongingness
   d. the lowest unmet need

2. The part of the brain that is especially responsive to the changes in blood chemistry associated with hunger is the
   - a. hypothalamus
   - b. medulla
   - c. cerebellum
   - d. frontal lobe

3. Differences in our sensation-seeking motives are thought to be partly dependent on
   - a. biological factors
   - b. educational levels
   - c. intelligence
   - d. social class

4. Individuals with a strong need for achievement tend to choose tasks with
   - a. low risks
   - b. high risks
   - c. maximum rewards
   - d. medium risks

5. Self-efficacy would be expressed by which of the following statements?
   - a. "I can do it."
   - b. "Maybe tomorrow."
   - c. "Some things are better left unsaid."
   - d. "Love is a many splendored thing."

6. The cognitive appraisal view of emotions holds that our emotions depend primarily on
   - a. how people treat us
   - b. hormonal arousal
   - c. how we interpret situations
   - d. the left side of the brain

7. The conscious, intentional control of emotions is called
   - a. denial
   - b. suppression
   - c. displacement
   - d. repression

8. Responding to someone's objectionable behavior with an "I" message normally includes our
   - a. perception of the other person's feelings
   - b. positive rather than negative emotions
   - c. judgment of the person's behavior
   - d. nonjudgmental description of his or her behavior

9. People who are the most successful in interpreting nonverbal messages are
   - a. female
   - b. masculine
   - c. high in expressiveness themselves
   - d. high in imagination

10. Jealousy is a blend of emotions, including
    - a. anticipation
    - b. disgust
    - c. love
    - d. fear of loss

EXERCISES

1. *Examine your eating habits.* Describe your eating habits in a page or so, including your responses to the following questions: How healthy are your eating habits? Do you know how many calories a day you consume? How does this figure compare with

others of your age and lifestyle? Good nutrition requires eating food from the basic food groups—bread and cereal, fruits and vegetables, dairy products, and meat. Are your meals well balanced? Do you have any bad eating habits, such as overeating at mealtimes, snacking between meals, or frequently dining in fast-food restaurants?

2. *Seek out new experiences.* Sometimes the stimulation from new experiences helps to revitalize your motivation and zest for life. You might try several of the following suggestions: Taste a food you've never tried. Take up a new sport or hobby. Invite someone out socially you would like to know better. Attend a workshop or a special course you're interested in. Perhaps you can add other ideas. Try several of these suggestions, and write about your reactions in a page or so. Would you agree that variety is the spice of life?

3. *Assess your achievement motivation.* Look at your achievement motivation in a specific area of your life—a course you're taking, your motivation in school as a whole, your job, or progress toward your career goals. Then answer the following questions:

   ◆ How strongly do you want to succeed?

   ◆ Do you believe your ability is crucial, or is success mostly a matter of luck?

   ◆ How much do you enjoy what you're doing?

   ◆ Do you have the needed skills to succeed?

   ◆ If not, what are you doing about this problem?

   Honest responses to such questions may help you to understand the strength of your achievement motivation and what's needed to increase it.

4. *Personal goals.* Do you set goals for yourself? If so, describe in a page or so some of your long-range, medium-range, and short-range goals. Even if you don't usually formulate personal goals, try writing out some of your important goals as explained in this chapter. You might find goal setting especially helpful in the areas of career, marriage, and family life.

5. *Share your everyday feelings.* Do you share your feelings as readily as you'd like? If not, you might try this exercise. A good way to begin sharing your feelings is to share some of the safe, everyday feelings. For example, whenever you're especially pleased by something another person has done for you, tell this person how you feel about it. The practice of sharing these safe feelings may help you to become more aware of and comfortable in sharing your deeper feelings.

6. *Practice sending "I" messages.* Think of several situations in which someone else's behavior has become a problem for you. Then write out the appropriate "I" messages under the respective four headings, as explained and illustrated in this chapter. If you feel comfortable doing so, you might try expressing some of these "I" messages in person.

7. *Explore the effects of anxiety in your life.* As you may recall, anxiety can have positive and negative effects in our lives. Think of at least two situations in your life, one in which anxiety stimulated you to do your best and one in which anxiety interfered with your performance. How do you account for the difference?

8. *Anger.* Recall a situation in which you became very angry. Did you tend to lose control, saying and doing things you later regretted? Or did you respond to the situation in a way that made known your grievance and helped to restore your sense of control? Looking back, what would you have done differently?

QUESTIONS FOR SELF-REFLECTION

1. What are some of the dominant motives in your life?
2. How important are incentives like money and success?
3. Has overeating or snacking between meals become a problem for you?
4. How strong is your sensation-seeking motive?
5. How strong is your achievement motive in school?
6. Are you a self-starter? Or do you work better "under pressure"?
7. What are your personal goals for the next year? What about the next five years?
8. When asked, can you readily say "how you feel"?
9. Would you characterize yourself as an emotional person?
10. Did you grow up in a home in which people expressed their feelings freely?
11. Which emotions are the hardest for you to express?
12. How do you usually cope with anxiety?
13. When it comes to anger, do you think before you speak?
14. When you feel jealous, what do you say and do?
15. What makes you happy?

FOR FURTHER INFORMATION

RECOMMENDED READINGS

BIRCH, C. (1995). *Feelings.* Sydney, Australia: University of New South Wales Press. An overview of emotions and feelings; where they originate; how we experience them; how we differentiate emotions.

FOXMAN, P. (1996). *Dancing with fear: Overcoming anxiety in a world of stress and uncertainty.* Northvale, NJ: J. Aronson. A general synopsis of information on fear and anxiety with tips on how to better cope with both.

KINDER, M. (1994). *Mastering your moods: Recognizing your emotional style and making it work for you.* New York: Simon & Schuster. Provides the reader with advice about how to identify various mood states and how to master each state and emotional style so as to benefit from them.

MYERS, D. G. (1992). *Searching for joy: Who is happy—and why.* New York: William Morrow. By a respected psychologist who furnishes the reader with advice about joy and happiness. He pays particular attention to why some people are happy and others aren't.

PINES, A. (1992). *Romantic jealousy: Understanding and conquering the shadow of love.* New York: St. Martin's Press. Ever been jealous? Most Americans have. The author explores romantic jealousy and whether such jealousy is normal and can be overcome.

WEBSITES AND THE INTERNET

http://www.proaxis.com/~katemac/faq.html: A site about polylove and polyfidelity that, of course, includes discussions about jealousy.

http://www.emc.maricopa.edu/emc_html/academics/success_guide/testanxiety.html: A site from a college that suggests tips for its students saddled with test anxiety.

Usenet: alt.angst: A site for those who want a safe place to vent negative emotions and see others' reactions or to see others emote.

http://www.algy.com/anxiety/anxiety.html: Offers support for those with intense anxiety or panic disorder.

Usenet: alt.lies: A place where you can tell the tallest tales you want as well as read others' tall tales and fibs. Perhaps with practice you'll get better at recognizing lies when they are told to you!

CHAPTER

4

Stress

After completing this chapter, you should be able to

1. Define the concept of stress.
2. Identify Selye's four variations of stress.
3. Describe the life-events method of measuring stress.
4. Understand how daily problems contribute to stress.
5. Explain Selye's concept of the general adaptation syndrome.
6. Discuss the three strategies for reducing stress through modifying your environment.
7. Describe five different ways to reduce stress through altering your lifestyle.

Steve arrives at the office late, after a harrowing 30-minute delay on the expressway. He is told the boss wants to see him right away. "I wonder what that's about?" Steve muses to himself, as he takes off his coat and heads upstairs. He's ushered inside the boss's office, only to find him pacing back and forth. The boss is furious. The big deal they were counting on with a major corporation has just fallen through. The boss makes it clear that if Steve values his job he'd better have a good explanation. Steve gropes for words. "Frankly, I'm stunned. I can't imagine what happened," he says. "Let me call and talk to the people over there and find out the story." Steve's boss continues making accusations about his incompetence and his uncertain future with the company. Steve feels enraged at being treated this way. He is tempted to punch his boss in the face but knows this is not a mature response. Instead, he returns to his office to cool off. He sits down at his desk, his stomach churning, his neck muscles tense, and his blood pressure rising. He reaches for a Maalox and an aspirin.

Understanding Stress

Steve is discovering that the modern world is no less perilous than the jungle. He feels that extra burst of adrenaline that primes his muscles and steadies his nerves for a fight. Yet the primitive "fight or flight" response used by his Stone Age ancestors is no longer appropriate. It's also dangerous. When people like Steve lash out aggressively with their fists or weapons, they jeopardize the welfare of society itself. Should they try to escape through alcohol or drugs, they only succeed in making their problems worse. Instead, they must learn how to manage stress, including the intense emotions aroused, in a more appropriate manner for our times.

Being late is stressful.

Meanwhile, stress is taking a heavy toll on the nation's well-being. Leaders of industry are alarmed about the huge costs of absenteeism, lost productivity, and increasing medical expenses, all of which are estimated to cost businesses over $75 billion a year. Stress has also become a major contributor, either directly or indirectly, to coronary heart disease, cancer, lung ailments, accidental injuries, cirrhosis of the liver, and suicide—six of the leading causes of death in the United States. In short, it seems as if our modern way of life has become a major source of stress.

Just like Steve, a majority of adult Americans experience "high stress" at one time or another. Many report that they feel "great stress" at least once or twice a week or live with high stress every day. Stress has become the price paid for being affluent and successful. Twice as many high-income as low-income people suffer from the tension of stress. Also, the more educated people are, the more likely they are to suffer great stress. Executives, managers, and professionals suffer more heavily from stress than those in most other professions.

MEANING OF STRESS

Stress is difficult to define partly because it means different things to different people. Some see stress as any external stimulus that causes wear and tear, such as the pressure to perform at work. Competitive pressures, the uncertainties of modern life, job insecurity, the threat of nuclear war—all these factors have made life increasingly stressful. At the same time, people respond to the same stressful event differently. Individuals who constantly complain or panic in the face of job pressures will experience considerably more stress than those who calmly take such things in stride. In this view, stress consists largely of *how* we respond to events, not the events themselves, so that we bring a lot of our stress on ourselves.

Although the overall experience of stress includes both stimulus and response variables, most definitions tend to emphasize one aspect of stress more than the other. Those who emphasize the stimulus factors describe stress in terms of **stressors**—the variety of external and internal stimuli that evoke stress, such as a highly competitive work environment. Other authorities emphasize the importance of our perception of and response to such events. Accordingly, **stress** can be defined as the pattern of responses an individual makes to stimulus events that disturb his or her equilibrium or exceed coping abilities. Note that it is when events disrupt our usual level of functioning and require us to make an extra effort to reestablish our equilibrium that we experience stress. Not surprisingly, it is often the combination of events, such as not being able to start our car on the morning we have an important test, that generates stress. In this case stress includes the specific efforts needed to start the car (or get a ride) and to take the test. But stress also involves the nonspecific physiological reactions that occur in response to stressful events such as the increased flow of adrenaline that mobilizes us for an extra effort. We'll discuss this factor shortly in regard to the general adaptation syndrome.

We should be careful not to equate stress with distress. Instead, stress is a many-sided phenomenon that may also have a beneficial effect. Hans Selye (1991), the noted stress researcher, has described four basic variations of stress, each with its own label. When events have a harmful effect, stress is correctly labeled **distress**. Unfortunately, much of the stress in modern society is distressful. Yet stress may also have a beneficial effect. Beginning a new job, getting married, or taking up an exciting sport like sky diving may have a stimulating effect that results in personal growth. Selye suggests we might call this **eustress**, or good stress. He has also described two more variations of stress: **Hyperstress**, or excessive stress, usually occurs when events, including positive ones, pile up and stretch the limits of our adaptability. **Hypostress**, or insufficient stress, is apt to occur when we're lacking stimulation. As a result, bored people may resort to the sensation-seeking behaviors mentioned in Chapter 3, such as experimentation with drugs. (See Figure 4–1.)

MEASURING STRESS

Because the experience of stress is so complex and varies from one situation to another, Steve's stress on the day his boss confronted him would be difficult to measure. Researchers have devised a number of ways to measure stress objectively to study its effects on our health, performance, and mortality. Generally, the various scales reflect different concepts of stress, especially in regard to which aspect should be emphasized.

Since major life events readily come to mind as obvious stressors, they were the first studied. One of the earlier instruments designed to measure stress in terms of life events was the Social Readjustment Rating Scale developed by Holmes and Rahe (1967). They realized that negative events, such as the loss of a job or the death of a loved one, are usually quite stressful. At the same time, they acknowledged that positive events such as beginning college or getting married can be stressful too. Consequently, the most important factor in this approach is the total impact of various life changes, both positive and negative, and the amount of readjustment these events require. Many studies have found that the change in life intensity, as measured by this scale, is closely linked with

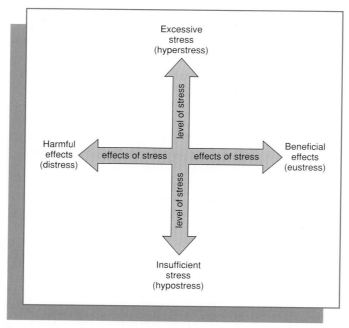

FIGURE 4–1

Selye's four basic variations of stress. SOURCE: Excerpts from *Stress Without Distress* by Hans Selye. Copyright © 1974 by Hans Selye. Reprinted by permission of HarperCollins Publishers.

the onset of various illnesses. Accordingly, the combined stress of life events has been related to sudden cardiac death, diabetes, complications of pregnancy and birth, chronic illnesses, multiple sclerosis, and many minor physical problems.

The Student Stress Scale, adapted from the Holmes and Rahe Social Readjustment Rating Scale, is shown in Table 4–1. As in the Holmes and Rahe scale, each event is given a score that represents the amount of readjustment a person has to make in his or her life as a result of the change. People with life change unit (LCU) scores of 300 and above have the highest health risk. Those scoring between 150 and 300 have a 50–50 chance of experiencing a serious health change within two years. People scoring below 150 have about a one in three chance of a serious health change (Insel & Roth, 1985). To determine your own stress score, add up the number of points corresponding to the events you have experienced in the past six months or are likely to experience in the next six months.

Despite its usefulness, the life-events approach to stress has several limitations. Steve, for example, was having a wonderful life until his supervisor challenged him. First, the particular events selected in any scale may not be equally relevant for different groups of people, such as blue-collar workers and the elderly. Second, it does not take into account how individuals *perceive* a given change, much less how well they *adapt* to it. Third, because the life-events approach is built around change, it fails to include a great deal of stress that comes with chronic or repeated conditions, such as a boring job or an unsatisfying marriage. Finally, it leaves out the "little things" in everyday life that often get to us, such as losing our car keys or snapping a shoelace while someone is waiting for us.

TABLE 4–1
STUDENT STRESS SCALE

	Past		Future
1. Death of a close family member	☐	100	☐
2. Death of a close friend	☐	73	☐
3. Divorce between parents	☐	65	☐
4. Jail term	☐	63	☐
5. Major personal injury or illness	☐	63	☐
6. Marriage	☐	58	☐
7. Fired from job	☐	50	☐
8. Failed important course	☐	47	☐
9. Change in health of a family member	☐	45	☐
10. Pregnancy	☐	45	☐
11. Sex problems	☐	44	☐
12. Serious argument with close friend	☐	40	☐
13. Change in financial status	☐	39	☐
14. Change of major	☐	39	☐
15. Trouble with parents	☐	39	☐
16. New girl- or boyfriend	☐	38	☐
17. Increased workload at school	☐	37	☐
18. Outstanding personal achievement	☐	36	☐
19. First quarter/semester in college	☐	35	☐
20. Change in living conditions	☐	31	☐
21. Serious argument with instructor	☐	30	☐
22. Lower grades than expected	☐	29	☐
23. Change in sleeping habits	☐	29	☐
24. Change in social activities	☐	29	☐
25. Change in eating habits	☐	28	☐
26. Chronic car trouble	☐	26	☐
27. Change in number of family get-togethers	☐	26	☐
28. Too many missed classes	☐	25	☐
29. Change of college	☐	24	☐
30. Dropped more than one class	☐	23	☐
31. Minor traffic violations	☐	20	☐
Total _____			

SOURCE: Adapted from Insel, P. M., & Roth, W. T. (1985). *Core Concepts in Health* (4th ed.). Palo Alto, CA: Mayfield, p. 29.

More recently, attention has turned to the measurement of stress associated with everyday difficulties, such as concerns about owing money, and daily uplifts, such as keeping in good physical shape. Steve, the individual in our opening case, was facing several hassles the day his boss confronted him. He was not only dismayed that his boss was angry, but also confused about why the big deal did not go through. Lazarus (1993) has found that daily hassles may sometimes have a greater effect on our moods and health than do the major misfortunes of life. However, people vary widely in terms of what bothers them. Among college students, the most commonly reported hassles are anxiety over tests, grades and the competition they engender, professors, studying, and finances (Murphy & Archer, 1996).

Middle-aged people are bothered more by worries over health and money. Professional people feel they have too much to do and not enough time to do it, as well as difficulty in relaxing. Daily hassles common to all groups are misplacing or losing things, worries over physical appearance, and too many things to do. Lazarus also found a strong link between daily hassles and psychological and physical health, with people who suffer frequent, intense hassles having the poorest health. Shawn (1995) had college students complete a psychological symptom checklist as well as rate their perceived control over and their ability to cope with various daily hassles. Shawn found that the frequency of daily hassles was positively associated with psychological symptomatology. That is, the more the hassles, the more psychological disturbance. Most participants tended to match the method of coping (for example, direct confrontation with the stressful stimulus) with their perceived level of control over the hassles.

A third approach to assessing life stress measures the self-perception of "global," or generalized and pervasive, stress in our lives. For example, Steve found the dispute with his boss to be very distressing; another individual might not have reacted so extremely. An example of this approach is the Perceived Stress Scale (PSS), as shown in Figure 4–2. It differs from the previous two scales in that respondents are not asked to rate the stressfulness of specific events. Instead, they are asked to rate the extent to which the demands of their present life situation are exceeding their ability to cope. Research has indicated that this scale is a better predictor of physical and psychological illnesses than life-event scales. It is an especially good predictor of incipient health problems (Cohen & Williamson, 1991).

PERSONAL, SITUATIONAL FACTORS

Our overall experience of stress is affected by a variety of personal and situational factors. Some of the more common ones are described in this chapter.

How we *perceive* a given stress may make it more or less stressful. Some people may take criticism of their work as a personal attack, become upset as Steve did, and waste a lot of energy defending themselves. Yet other people may take similar criticism as a challenge to improve their work, thereby experiencing less stress. A lot depends on our personal makeup. People plagued by inner doubt, low self-esteem, and suspiciousness may misconstrue even the routine demands of everyday life as stressful. Others, such as the Type A personality described in more detail in Chapter 3, are more likely to develop **stress–related illnesses** because of their personal traits. You will recall that Type As tend to be highly competitive, judging themselves and others by rigorous standards. They're also impatient. As a result, they keep themselves under constant stress and are more likely to develop heart disease than other people.

Another factor that can add to distress is prejudice against us because of the groups to which we belong. Saenz (1994) performed an interesting experiment that demonstrated just this. Saenz researched **tokens** or individuals who are distinctive in a group because they are not readily identified as members of the group. Examples include a male nurse working among all female nurses or an African American student in an all-white class. Saenz made participants believe they were working with students from the same school or from a rival school. Participants in the rival school group were therefore made to feel as if they were tokens. Saenz used a scrambled words or anagrams task to measure cognitive performance. She found that participants who were tokens performed worse than nontokens. She argued that the attention and time that should go into solv-

FIGURE 4–2

THE PERCEIVED-STRESS SCALE

How much stress do you feel in your life? To find out, you might compare your own self-perceived stress with that of others in a national study. Researchers Sheldon Cohen and Gail Williamson (1988), with the help of pollster Louis Harris, asked the following questions of a cross section of adult Americans.

In the last month, how often have you felt

A—unable to control the important things in your life?

0. Never
1. Almost never
2. Sometimes
3. Fairly often
4. Very often

B—confident about your ability to handle your personal problems?

0. Very often
1. Fairly often
2. Sometimes
3. Almost never
4. Never

C—that things were going your way?

0. Not very often
1. Fairly often
2. Sometimes
3. Fairly often
4. Very often

D—that difficulties were piling up so high that you could not overcome them?

0. Never
1. Almost never
2. Sometimes
3. Fairly often
4. Very often

To get your score, simply add the points indicated in questions A through D. Your score provides a crude but quick index to your experienced stress level. In Cohen and Williamson's national study, the average score for women was 4.7 points, and 4.2 for men. People with low-stress scores were slightly more likely to report themselves in good health and to be practicing good health habits, such as exercising and not smoking.

SOURCE: S. Cohen & G. M. Williamson, "Perceived Stress in a Probability Sample of the United States." In S. Spacapan & S. Oskamp (Eds.), *The Social Psychology of Health* (Newbury Park, CA: Sage, 1988). Copyright © 1988 Sage Publications. Reprinted by permission of Sage Publications.

Prejudice can lead to distress, particularly when an individual feels he or she is a token minority.

ing the task were channeled into managing how the token behaved in the group. In other words, distress from tokenism diminished performance.

Many other situational factors contribute to our experience of stress. Probably the most important is the combined effect of various life changes, as explained earlier. Car troubles, a sick child at home, and a crisis at work all at once generate more stress than any of these events alone. Unpredictable events such as an automobile accident are highly stressful. The threat of bodily harm greatly increases stress, as people taken hostage or military personnel in combat would testify. The constant alertness required of certain workers—such as air-traffic controllers, astronauts, and those working with nuclear reactors—is becoming a more common source of stress. Lack of control and a feeling of futility in a stressful situation are key factors in stress. For instance, studies of male workers whose jobs involve high psychological demands but little decision making or control over their work, such as waiters and assembly-line personnel, are five times more likely to develop coronary heart disease than workers who have greater control. (See Figure 4–3.) In contrast, managing stress successfully involves learning what you *can* do in the face of the most difficult situation, as we'll explain in the last part of this chapter.

Reactions to Stress

Stress manifests itself through a variety of symptoms. The most common sign of stress, reported by about one in four Americans (26 percent), is increased nervousness, anxiety, and tension. Almost as many people (24 percent) experience tension headaches be-

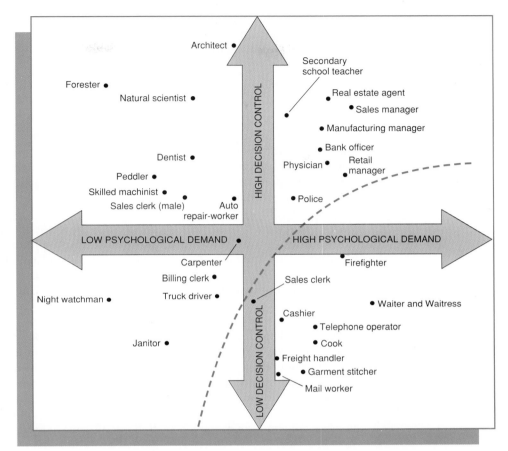

FIGURE 4–3

Some jobs are more stressful than others.   Studies of male workers suggest that those whose jobs involve high psychological demands but little decision making or control over their work, such as cooks, waiters, and assembly-line personnel, are five times more likely to develop coronary heart disease than workers who exercise greater control over their work. SOURCE: Columbia University Department of Industrial Engineering of Operations Research.

cause of stress. Another one in five (19 percent) say their stress shows up in anger and irritability with others. About 12 percent report that stress also takes its toll in fatigue. Finally, one in nine Americans (11 percent) say their stress leads to a sense of depression. Other symptoms of stress include muscle aches, stomach aches, an overall feeling of being upset, insomnia and loss of sleep, an increased heartbeat, a rise in blood pressure, compulsive eating or loss of appetite, a feeling of frustration, crying, yelling, and screaming (Harris, 1987).

Many of these symptoms are part of the body's physiological stress response, that is, the automatic, built-in reactions over which we have little control. But in some instances, the familiar symptoms of stress result from our psychological reactions to events that are more dependent on the way we perceive the world and our capacity for dealing with it. In this section, we'll examine both types of reactions, which are generally mixed in our overall experience of stress. We'll also look at how individuals differ in their characteristic responses to stress.

PHYSIOLOGICAL STRESS REACTIONS

Hans Selye (1991), a pioneer in the study of how stress affects the body, holds that in addition to the body's responses that are specific to a particular stressor (such as sweating in response to heat), there is a characteristic pattern of *nonspecific* physiological mechanisms that are activated in response to almost any stressor. Selye called this pattern the **general adaptation syndrome**. It consists of three progressive stages: the alarm reaction, the stage of resistance, and the stage of exhaustion. (See Figure 4–4.)

Alarm reaction.   In the initial emergency response to stress-provoking agents, the body attempts to restore its normal functioning. The alarm reaction consists of complicated body and biochemical changes that produce similar symptoms regardless of the type of stressor. For this reason people in the beginning stages of different illnesses often complain of common symptoms such as fever, headache, aching muscles and joints, loss of appetite, and generally tired feeling.

Stage of resistance.   If our exposure to stressful situations continues, the alarm reaction is followed by the stage in which the human organism develops an increased resistance to the stressor. The symptoms of the alarm stage disappear, and body resistance rises above its normal level to cope with the continued stress. But the price of this resistance includes increased secretions from various glands, lowered resistance to infections, and the "diseases of adaptation." Stress-induced peptic ulcers and high blood pressure are common examples, though not all cases of these disorders are induced by stress.

In an important literature review, Herbert and Cohen (1993) examined the relationship of stress to immunity. They found that stress does impair immune system functioning. The mechanisms that underlie this are not clear. Perhaps stress leads to a lack of

FIGURE 4–4
Selye's general adaptation syndrome. SOURCE: Excerpts from *Stress Without Distress* by Hans Selye. Copyright © 1974 by Hans Selye. Reprinted by permission of HarperCollins.

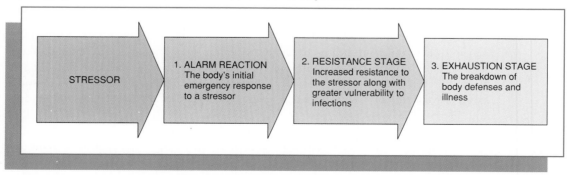

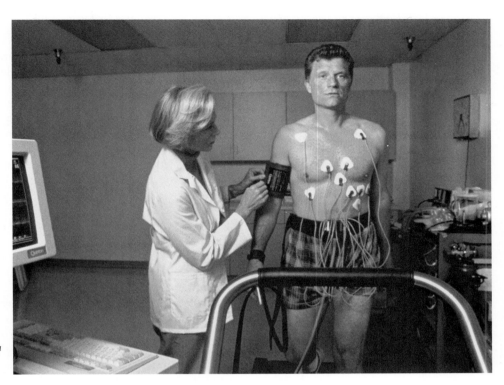

Stress affects us physiologically. A man takes a stress test to assess the effects of stress on his heart.

sleep, less interest in consuming nutritious foods, or behaviors that increase risk of infection.

Stage of exhaustion.   If chronic stress continues too long, the stage of exhaustion is reached. The body is unable to continue secreting its hormones at the increased rate, so that the organism can no longer adapt to chronic stress. Body defenses break down, adaptation energy runs out, and the physical symptoms of the alarm reaction reappear. The symptoms of this stage are similar to aging in many respects, except that the symptoms of exhaustion, depending on the severity of one's condition, are more or less reversible.

Selye (1980) originally held that the stress response occurs in reaction to various stressors, including illness. However, his theory also shows how a chronic stress reaction can *itself* lead to illness and accentuate aging. Continued arousal of the stress response uses up the body's store of adaptation energy. Although the person who is successfully coping with specific stressors may lead an active, healthy life, each experience of stress uses up some adaptation energy. Thus, it might be better to use our energy more wisely rather than wasting it on so many false alarms, which are better ignored. Also, continual stress eventually damages the various organs of the body. But different parts of our bodies do not suffer stress or age at an even rate. Instead, illness or death usually occurs when the weakest parts of our bodies give out. Each person's "weakest link" is determined partly by genetic vulnerability and partly by the type and severity of the stress experienced. In any event, reducing our level of stress may help us to lead longer and healthier lives.

PSYCHOLOGICAL REACTIONS

Unlike the body's stress reactions, our psychological reactions are shaped by learning and are heavily dependent on the way we perceive our world. Included here are a wide variety of cognitive, emotional, and behavioral responses to stress.

Because most stressors evoke anxiety—the vague, unpleasant feeling that something bad is about to happen—the most familiar psychological reactions to stress are defense mechanisms. They are called defense mechanisms, or sometimes "ego defense" mechanisms, because they are used to protect oneself from perceived threat. Although defense mechanisms are influenced by learning to some extent, they are largely automatic and unconscious reactions to keep ourselves from being overwhelmed by intense doses of psychological stress. (See Table 4–2.)

Each of us relies on such mechanisms at one time or another, especially when we feel threatened, whether the objective situation warrants it or not. As emergency reactions, they diminish our awareness of anxiety and help to maintain our sense of adequacy and self-worth in the face of threat. Yet because they also involve self-deception and a distortion of social reality, habitual reliance on defense mechanisms is maladaptive and prevents personal growth.

Once a stressor has been interpreted as threatening, a variety of cognitive functions may be adversely affected. We may become so preoccupied with the stressor that our attention and perceptions are greatly restricted. Memory is also affected because of the reduced attention given to the overall situation. Stress also interferes with our judgment, problem solving, and decision making. Whenever we're under intense stress, we tend to revert to rigid and stereotyped thinking rather than engaging in creative problem solving.

Stress also evokes a wide range of emotions, ranging from a sense of exhilaration, in the face of minor, challenging stressors, to the more familiar negative emotions of anger, fear, jealousy, and discouragement. Stressful life experiences involving separation or loss of friends and loved ones are frequently associated with depression, which will be discussed in Chapter 13. Survivors of traumatic events, such as rape victims, terror-

TABLE 4–2
DEFENSE MECHANISMS

Defense Mechanism	Definition
Repression	Excluding unacceptable ideas or feelings from consciousness
Denial	Misperceiving threatening objects or events as harmless
Fixation	Continuing a kind of gratification after one has passed through the stage at which it was appropriate
Regression	Reverting to a form of behavior that was more appropriate at an earlier stage of development
Rationalization	Justifying our unacceptable behavior with "good" reasons
Intellectualization	Reducing anxiety by analyzing threatening issues in an emotionally detached way
Projection	Attributing our unacceptable ideas or feelings to others
Displacement	Redirecting threatening ideas or impulses onto less threatening objects
Sublimation	Channeling socially unacceptable urges into acceptable behaviors
Acting out	Relieving anxiety or unpleasant tensions by expressing them in overt behavior
Reaction-formation	Developing conscious feelings and behaviors opposite to the unconscious, anxiety-arousing ones

ists' hostages, and veterans of combat, may cope well at the time but months later experience a delayed emotional reaction known as **posttraumatic stress disorder.**

How people behave under stress depends partly on the level of stress experienced. *Mild stress* energizes us to become more alert, active, and resourceful. However, *moderate stress* tends to have a disruptive effect on our lives, especially on complex behaviors such as writing a term paper. Under moderate stress, people become less sensitive to their surroundings, easily irritated, and more apt to rely on certain coping devices. (See Figure 4–5.) *Severe stress* tends to inhibit behavior and may lead to apathy and immobility, as in the severely depressed, who feel helpless in the face of overwhelming frustration or deprivation. Such immobility may be a defensive reaction that serves to reduce the harmful effects of stress. (See Figure 4–6.)

HOW DO YOU REACT TO STRESS?

Each of us reacts to stress, even the same stressor, somewhat differently. When some individuals are anxious, they are more apt to react with body symptoms. They may feel jittery, have stomach tension, a splitting headache, or diarrhea. Others react to stress more mentally. They find themselves unable to concentrate, are preoccupied by worries, and feel they are losing out on things. In many instances, people experience a mixture of physical and mental symptoms, depending on the particular stress.

FIGURE 4–5

COMMON COPING DEVICES FOR MODERATE STRESS

There are a number of ways we may attempt to alleviate stress spontaneously. Although these responses tend to occur automatically, they probably operate at a higher level of awareness than the defense mechanisms.

1. Eating, drinking, and smoking
   Examples: People who overeat, abuse alcohol or drugs, or smoke more under stress

2. Crying, laughing, or cursing
   Examples: People who find temporary relief in crying, joking before an exam, or cursing after making a mistake

3. Touching or sexual activity
   Examples: People who engage in a great deal of touching and hugging during times of grief or depressed people who seek solace in increased sexual activity

4. Dissipating tension in work or play
   Examples: People who find relief from stress through vigorous exercise, sports, or leisure activities

5. Talking it out and thinking it through
   Examples: People who reduce their tension by talking about their problems with a sympathetic listener or those who prefer to sort out things in solitude

Each of us resorts to some of these coping devices at one time or another, depending on our habits and the situation at hand. The danger is in habitually relying on one of these strategies whether it is appropriate for the circumstances or not. For instance, people who use alcoholic drinks to alleviate stress may eventually discover that their drinking has become a greater problem than the stress from which they sought relief.

FIGURE 4–6

POSTTRAUMATIC STRESS DISORDER

The types of events that trigger posttraumatic stress disorder usually lie outside the realm of ordinary human loss and grief. Examples include plane crashes, earthquakes, floods, assaults, rapes, hostage taking, torture, murders, and military combat.

Victims involuntarily reexperience the past traumatic event in dreams, which include "flashbacks" of the event accompanied by the original emotions of fear, shock, and horror. They also experience an emotional numbness to their everyday world. Frequently, they have trouble concentrating at work during the day and difficulty sleeping at night. They may also lose interest in people, feeling alienated from others.

The symptoms of this disorder may begin immediately after the traumatic event or within 6 months, as in the case of the acute form of the disorder. However, it is not unusual for the symptoms to emerge only after a much longer period, which is characteristic of the chronic or delayed forms of the disorder.

As many as one-third of the Vietnam veterans who took part in heavy combat showed signs of serious posttraumatic stress disorder—sometimes known as the Vietnam syndrome. The severity of their symptoms is partly due to two factors not present in previous wars. For one thing, civilian casualties were higher in Vietnam than in most earlier wars, leading to feelings of guilt. Then, too, the controversial nature of the Vietnam War left many returning veterans feeling unwelcome, giving rise to resentment and rage against society. As a result, Vietnam veterans have experienced above-average rates of divorce, suicide, and hospitalization for alcohol and drug abuse. Many veterans continue to have difficulties readjusting to civilian life.

There are recognized individual differences in the experience of stress and in coping. **Gender,** for example, may serve as a valuable "window" that influences not only how individuals appraise stress but also how they cope with stress (Greenglass, 1995). Greenglass suggests that there exist occupational gender segregation and unequal power and control issues that may affect how men and women perceive and cope with stress. Spurlock (1995) adds that women experience multiple and overlapping roles that can create more conflict and stress than men experience. Research has also shown that women are more likely to cope with stress through social support (sharing emotions and stress experiences with their friends) than are men (T. Butler, Giordano, & Neren, 1985). Similarly, Olah (1995) administered a situation reaction inventory that describes threats and negative life events to adolescents in India, Italy, Sweden, Hungary, and Yemen. Across cultures, girls reported more emotion-focused coping whereas boys reported more problem-focused coping. In emotion-focused coping the individual tries to alter the emotional reaction to stress, for example by expressing rather than suppressing feelings; in problem-focused coping the individual tries to change the environment or find a solution, for example by applying lessons learned from earlier experiences. Olah also found that culture plays a role in what is perceived as stressful and in adjustment to stress. European participants preferred problem-focused coping, and Asian participants reported more emotion-focused solutions.

Taking the Stress Style Test may make you more aware of your characteristic way of reacting to stress. (See Figure 4–7.) Once you get a personal grip on stress, you can deal with it more effectively. For instance, if you are the physical type, you might choose one of the following relaxers: aerobics, biking, swimming, walking, progressive relaxation, or soaking in a hot bath or sauna. However, if you're more of a cerebral type, you might try one of these relaxers: meditation, reading, crossword puzzles, television, chess or card games, or any absorbing hobby. In most cases, you may choose a combination of ways to unwind. The important thing is to find what works best for you.

Another individual difference is that some individuals seem better able to take stress in stride largely because of a different *attitude*. Studies of top executives in the Fortune 500 companies have shown that those who cope with stress most successfully have what the researchers call **psychological hardiness**—the attitude that allows them to make the most of the situation. The three trademarks of survivors are challenge, commitment, and control. The executives who did well with stress felt stimulated by change and stress (challenge). They were also intensely involved in what they were doing (commitment). And they were not usually overcome by feelings of powerlessness even in very difficult

---

FIGURE 4–7

STRESS STYLE TEST: BODY, MIND, MIXED?

Imagine yourself in a stressful situation. When you're feeling anxious, what do you typically experience? Check all that apply.

1. My heart beats faster.
2. I find it difficult to concentrate because of distracting thoughts.
3. I worry too much about things that don't really matter.
4. I feel jittery.
5. I get diarrhea.
6. I imagine terrifying scenes.
7. I can't keep anxiety-provoking pictures and images out of my mind.
8. My stomach gets tense.
9. I pace up and down nervously.
10. I'm bothered by unimportant thoughts running through my mind.
11. I become immobilized.
12. I feel I'm losing out on things because I can't make decisions fast enough.
13. I perspire.
14. I can't stop thinking worrisome thoughts.

To score:

Give yourself a Mind point if you answered yes to each of the following questions: 2, 3, 6, 7, 10, 12, 14. Give yourself a Body point for each of these: 1, 4, 5, 8, 9, 11, 13. If you have more Mind than Body points, you're a mental stress type. If you have more Body than Mind points, you're a physical stress type. Same number of each? You're a mixed reactor.

SOURCE: *The Relaxed Body Book* by Daniel Goleman (Garden City, NY: Doubleday, 1986). Copyright © 1988 by Daniel Goleman. Used with the permission of the author.

situations (control). The last is especially noteworthy. In probing the relationship among stress, physical illness, and psychological disorders, the importance of personal control recurs again and again. Being able to acknowledge heightened stress, as well as its effects on you, while maintaining reasonable control of yourself and, if possible, the situation at hand, is vital to managing stress successfully (Locke & Colligan, 1986). Note, however, that newer research on hardiness suggests that this concept may be more useful for explaining stress–coping behaviors and attitudes of men than women (Wiebe, 1991).

 ## Managing Stress

Managing stress successfully involves more than relying on the automatic, symptom-reducing reactions to stress, as helpful as these may be. Managing stress means taking charge, directing and controlling our responses to stressors, thereby modifying the overall stress. Steve, for example, realized that punching his boss was not a productive response to the distress. Instead he returned to his office to process what had happened and took an aspirin and indigestion aid. There are many other ways to cope with stress; most of them fall under two major headings: modifying our environment and altering ourselves in some way. (See Figure 4–8.)

MODIFYING YOUR ENVIRONMENT

A camera you've had on special order finally arrives. But you discover it's not exactly the model you wanted. What should you do? You could tell the clerk a mistake has been made and then proceed to order the correct model of camera. Or you could simply accept the camera on hand and leave, making sure never to buy anything in that store again. And there's still another option: You could refuse to accept the order and, instead, choose another camera more to your liking from among those already in stock.

These responses illustrate three of the basic ways to modify your environment: assertiveness, withdrawal, or compromise. Let's look at each of these strategies.

1. **Assertiveness** is the preferred way to manage stress whenever there is a reasonable possibility of success. Such an approach consists of direct attempts at modifying the stressful situation itself. Common examples are returning a defective product to a store or manufacturer or speaking up in response to an unreasonable request. (See Figure 4–9.)

   For example, if Steve were an unassertive person, he could have let his boss take advantage of him on various occasions, building up a lot of resentment in the process. Then in the moment of anger when his boss confronted him about the deal falling through, he might have lashed out aggressively, making the situation even more stressful. In contrast, assertiveness has to do with expressing rights and desires without infringing on those of others. Assertiveness is a rational and constructive way of handling stress, which in turn tends to alleviate the stress involved. Steve could have told his boss how frustrated he became when he gave conflicting orders, such as wanting to close two different deals at the same time. As might often happen, his boss might be unaware of the inconsistencies in his requests and change his ways, thereby alleviating much of Steve's stress.

FIGURE 4–8

PROBLEM-SOLVING APPROACH TO STRESS MANAGEMENT

A. Modifying Your Environment

1. Be assertive.
2. Withdraw if necessary.
3. Compromise when appropriate.
   Conformity
   Negotiation
   Substitution

B. Altering Your Lifestyle

1. Build greater stress tolerance.
2. Change your pace of life.
3. Control distressful thoughts.
4. Acquire problem-solving skills.
5. Seek social support.

FIGURE 4–9

HOW ASSERTIVE ARE YOU?

Assertiveness has to do with expressing your rights, thoughts, and feelings in a direct way without violating the rights of others. Imagine yourself in each of the following situations. What would you say?

When your parents are giving unwanted advice

When a friend asks you for a loan

When you're being pressured to buy something

When refusing an unreasonable request

When interrupted while you're speaking

In the last situation, simply to keep quiet would be nonassertive. But to blurt out "Shut up!" would be aggressive or hurtful. Instead, an assertive response might be, "Excuse me, I'd like to finish what I was saying."

Ironically, the lack of assertiveness in everyday relationships produces more resentment and alienation in the long run than assertiveness. In contrast, assertive responses not only preserve your self-respect but also facilitate good communication, which is essential for mutually satisfying relationships.

2. **Withdrawal** may be an appropriate response to stress, especially when a stressful situation cannot be successfully modified through assertiveness or compromise. By returning to his office the day his boss yelled at him, Steve practiced withdrawal. Another example of withdrawal would be the worker who actively looks for another job after getting no satisfaction from his or her supervisor. Withdrawal is neither good nor bad in itself. Much depends on how it is used. On the one hand, if someone habitually withdraws from stressful situations, that person may drift into a constricted lifestyle that prevents adequate adjustment or personal growth. On the other hand, the use of withdrawal as a *temporary* strategy may be a valuable means of coping with stress that has become overwhelming or detrimental to one's health. Some examples of temporary withdrawal are students dropping out of school until they can earn more money or marital partners agreeing to a separation while they seek counseling. When no suitable solution is forthcoming, despite the best efforts of the people involved, a permanent withdrawal may be more appropriate.

3. **Compromise** is still another adaptive response to stress. In contrast to withdrawal, compromise allows us to remain in the stressful situation but in a less active way than with an assertive approach. Compromise is most likely to be used when someone holds a higher rank or authority than another or when both participants are at a standstill. The three most common types of compromise are conformity, negotiation, and substitution.

   Conformity is one response to stressful situations. Let's say you work as a buyer for a large corporation that has just ordered a more elaborate procedure for purchasing, including much more paperwork and more signatures for approval. At the outset you detest the change. You may comply outwardly by adopting the new procedure even though you dislike it. Or you may conform to the new demands because you like your superiors and coworkers enough to accommodate to the added stress. Inasmuch as jobs are not easy to get or hold, you may take the new procedures in stride and decide that changing your attitude is the most realistic approach because endless strife and resentment may be more stressful than accommodation or outright assertion. The key question in any type of conformity response, however, is whether the price of the compromise is worth it.

   Negotiation is a more active and promising way to achieve compromise in many situations of stress. Long used in the public area of labor management and political disputes, negotiation has now become more widely used at the interpersonal level among coworkers, marriage partners, and friends. Negotiation is preferable to conformity wherever possible because it involves mutual accommodation among the participants.

   Substitution is another way to achieve compromise when negotiation or conformity is not appropriate. If a woman desires to resume her college education but has small children and cannot enroll full time, she may decide that the best alternative is to attend part time at a nearby community college. In this case, a substitute means was found to achieve the same goal. At other times, it may become necessary to choose a substitute goal. For example, the man who after several attempts is not admitted to medical school may choose some related vocational field in which there are more openings, such as pharmacy, physiotherapy, or paramedical training.

Compromise itself is neither good nor bad. Much depends on the relation between the satisfaction achieved and the price paid in the reduction of stress. Habitual compromise may bring more frustration and conflict than a more assertive approach. Too many people suffer in stale jobs or conflict-ridden marriages longer than necessary because compromise has become the easy way out. We need to take into account the long-range effects of compromise as well. A life of passive accommodation to undue stress may be more stressful than an assertive or avoidance approach.

ALTERING YOUR LIFESTYLE

Ultimately, of course, we have more control over ourselves than over our environment. As a result, we may choose to modify something about ourselves or our behavior as a way of better managing stress. There are many possibilities, including developing greater tolerance for stress, altering our everyday habits, learning to control distressful thoughts, acquiring problem-solving skills, and seeking social support.

First, build up a greater tolerance for stress. **Stress tolerance** may be defined as the degree of stress you can handle or how long you can put up with a demanding task without acting in an irrational or disorganized way. Many of the competent, successful people we admire are probably under a great deal more stress than we realize; they've simply acquired a high tolerance for it. Greater tolerance for pressure—deadlines, competition, criticism from others—usually comes with greater experience and skill at a given task. People in high-pressure jobs such as police, surgeons, and firefighters have learned how to stay calm in the face of stress through months and years of experience on the job. Our tolerance for frustration may be improved through such means as selecting reasonable goals to accomplish and adjusting our expectations to match the realities of the immediate situation. Expecting too much of ourselves is a frequent source of frustration. Each of us is disappointed with ourselves from time to time. Rather than wallow in self-pity, it's more helpful to ask what we can remedy and resolve to learn from our experience.

Another important aspect of stress tolerance is the ability to function well despite anxiety. There are many instances when it is normal to feel anxious in the face of uncertainty, such as preparing for an important exam or going for a job interview. Competence in these situations means carrying out our responsibilities despite feelings of anxiety. Evidence also strongly suggests that we can resist stress if we are more physically fit, so exercising regularly is important (Crews & Landers, 1987). Remember, mild to moderate doses of anxiety may stimulate us to do our best, though too much anxiety may interfere with our performance. In this case, you may need to control your distressful, anxiety-arousing thoughts, as explained later in this section.

Second, change your pace of life. Steve had probably experienced traffic delays before; had he only left earlier on that fateful morning, he would have experienced less stress when his boss was furious over the deal that fell through. You may bring a lot of stress on yourself by rushing around and trying to accomplish too much in too little time. A fast pace of life makes you walk, talk, conduct business, and do almost everything faster. Research by Levine (1990) has shown that pace of life in the United States is already much faster than in other countries. Only Japan seems to have a faster pace. Life on the East Coast of the United States is much faster than on the West Coast, too. Levine found that the death rate from heart disease was higher in faster-paced U.S. cities than in slower-paced cities. Slowing down serves us well then.

Frequently, we could lighten the stress by better time management. In other cases, we need to pace ourselves better. The particular adjustments needed vary with each of us. But consider the following suggestions:

+ Get up early enough to avoid rushing.
+ Set a radio-alarm clock to your favorite station.
+ Take time for breakfast.
+ Make a list of things to do; put the most important things first.
+ Allow enough time to drive to school or work without rushing.
+ Avoid scheduling all your classes back to back.
+ Walk at an unhurried pace. You'll get there just as soon.
+ Share at least one meal each day with other people.
+ Avoid the excessive use of caffeine, alcohol, or drugs.
+ Take some time to relax each day. Go for a walk, ride your bike, or take a hot bath. (See Figure 4–10.)
+ Avoid procrastination; the sooner you begin a task, the less you'll worry about it.
+ Concentrate on the task at hand.
+ Take time to talk with your friends.
+ Set aside regular times for study.
+ Schedule some relaxation for the weekends to break the cycle of stress.
+ Jot down things you don't get done that you'd like to do the next day.
+ Unwind before going to bed. Read or listen to music.

Perhaps there are other changes especially needed in your lifestyle. What are they? Add them to your list of suggestions for managing stress.

Third, learn to control distressful thoughts. Perhaps you've had the experience of glancing at the first question on a test and muttering to yourself, "I know I'm going to flunk this test." Ironically, such negative self-monitoring interferes with your performance, making you do worse on the test.

You can control distressful thoughts by using the following strategy. First, become aware of your negative, catastrophic thinking. You'll probably notice how such thoughts usually assume the worst, such as "I'll never make it," "How did I get into this mess?" or "What can I do?" Second, formulate positive thoughts that are incompatible with your distressful thoughts. Some examples are "I can do it, just take it one step at a time, and I'll keep doing my best and see how things turn out." It also helps to relax and practice deep breathing—breathing with your diaphragm. Finally, give yourself a mental pat on the back when you've successfully managed distressful thoughts. Take a few minutes to acknowledge to yourself, "I did it; it worked. I'm pleased with the progress I'm making."

Another way to manage distressing thoughts is to replace them with humorous thoughts. We do not mean that you should minimize your stress by making fun of distressing events. Rather, take some time to enjoy humor. Read some cartoons, go to lunch with a friend and tell jokes, recall funny events from your life. Humor is a valuable form of coping and can have physiological as well as psychological benefits for distressed individuals. When people laugh, there is a reduction in at least three chemicals associated with stress, and the activity of the immune system is enhanced (Morreal,

FIGURE 4–10

COUNTERACTING STRESS

There are a variety of methods for lowering the body arousal associated with stress: biofeedback, meditation, muscle relaxation, and diaphragmatic breathing.

One of the simplest techniques is diaphragmatic breathing. Essentially it consists of breathing more deeply through the diaphragm, the dome-shaped muscular sheet attached to the lower ribs, dividing the chest from the stomach. You may choose to sit in a comfortable chair or lie down. Either way, put one hand on your stomach to see that it rises and falls as you breathe through your diaphragm. Breathe in deeply, through your nose, filling your lungs as full as you can. Hold your breath for a moment. Then exhale slowly, keeping as relaxed as you can. Breathe this way for half a dozen times or so. Then breathe in the usual way for a few seconds while you think about being relaxed. Now repeat the sequence of diaphragmatic breathing and normal breathing, concentrating on the pleasant feelings of relaxation.

The next time you find yourself getting tense, practice diaphragmatic breathing for a few minutes. See how it helps you to relax.

1991). Humor can also help defuse conflict, increase morale, decrease hostility (Morreal), and reduce anxiety (Yovetich, Dale, & Hudak, 1990).

Fourth, if needed, seek help with problem-solving skills. Most colleges and communities offer a variety of workshops on topics such as assertiveness training, job-hunting skills, and stress management. Some people are wise enough to gain such training as a way of bolstering their repertoire of social skills. Others seek it only after encountering problems. Or another means for finding help is simply to turn to friends. Numerous studies have shown that we manage stress more successfully and enjoy better physical and emotional health when we have the support of a spouse, close friend, or support group (e.g., Cummins, 1988; Richey, Lovell, & Reid, 1991).

Having access to friends and support groups may help to alleviate stress in several ways. Perhaps if Steve had a trusted office mate with whom he could have shared his stressful ordeal with the boss, Steve could have coped better. Why? First, close relationships provide the opportunity to share painful feelings, which if kept to ourselves become more burdensome. Second, friends provide emotional support through their expressions of concern and affection. Third, the understanding and reassurance of our friends may bolster our self-esteem throughout the low periods of our lives. Fourth, concerned friends and support groups may provide information and advice that may help us to reach more effective solutions to our problems, especially support groups that are oriented to a particular problem such as the death of a spouse. Fifth, friends can enhance positive experiences in our lives (Duffy & Wong, 1996). We don't have to turn to friends only in times of trouble.

Of course, at times the people in our lives may cause more distress than support. Here, one thinks of the judgmental spouse or the boss, like Steve's, who puts us under even greater pressure during times of stress. Yet, on balance, people under stress who have access to close relationships enjoy greater emotional support and better health than those without close social ties.

Social support, either informal support from friends or formal support from a self-help group, can alleviate stress.

USING STRESS FOR PERSONAL GROWTH

How we choose to alter our lifestyle or modify our environment is up to us. Stress management, like stress itself, is a personal matter. Each of us faces a different combination of stressful events at work and at home. Also, each of us has our own characteristic stress tolerance, so that we experience stress differently. The important thing to remember is that we *can* do something to manage stress more effectively. We don't have to be passive victims to whom things happen. Instead, we look at ourselves as active agents who can take charge of our lives. No matter how stressful the situation, there's always something we can do to reduce the stress.

Keep in mind that stress can be a valuable means of self-understanding. We don't fully know what we can do until we have to do it. Each time we successfully get through a stressful situation, like a difficult course at school or a trying problem in our love life, we gain in self-confidence. Even experiences of disappointment and failure are sometimes blessings in disguise. Perhaps we weren't ready for the task at hand, or we were pursuing the wrong goals. Sometimes a minor failure now may save us from a bigger letdown later on.

Finally, we can make stress work for us. Remember that stress is not synonymous with distress. Too little stress and we become bored and lazy. Too much and we become tense, make mistakes, and get sick more easily. To get the most out of life, each of us needs to find our optimal level of stress and the types of stress we handle best. Properly managed, stress gives zest to life. A stressful situation may challenge us to try harder, evoking our best and bringing personal growth. Managing stress well is a lot like making music with a stringed instrument. Too little pressure and the strings moan and groan. Too much and they snap. But apply just the right pressure and we get beautiful music.

SUMMARY

UNDERSTANDING STRESS

The great majority of adult Americans experience a high level of stress at one time or another. One in four lives with high stress daily.

We've defined stress as the pattern of specific and nonspecific responses an organism makes to stimulus events that disturb its equilibrium and tax its ability to cope. However, stress may have beneficial as well as harmful effects, depending on the person and the situation.

A major source of stress is the combination of various life changes, both positive and negative, including major life events as well as daily hassles. At the same time, our overall experience of stress is affected by a variety of personal and situational factors, such as how we perceive events and the degree of control we believe we have over them.

REACTIONS TO STRESS

Some reactions to stress occur more or less spontaneously, including physiological reactions as well as certain emotional, behavioral reactions. Many of our body reactions to stress can be understood in relation to Selye's general adaptation syndrome, either in the initial alarm reaction or the successive stages of resistance or exhaustion. Psychological reactions to stress include the familiar defense mechanisms, or emergency responses, such as rationalization as well as other emotional reactions that vary somewhat with the level of stress. At the same time, each of us experiences the same stressful situations somewhat differently, depending on our particular personality and coping strategies.

MANAGING STRESS

Managing stress successfully involves more than the automatic, symptom-reducing reactions to stress, as helpful as these are. Stress management means taking charge, directing and controlling our responses to stress so that we modify the overall stress. The two major ways of doing so are modifying our environment and altering our lifestyle.

The three main ways of modifying the situational sources of stress are assertiveness, the preferred response; withdrawal, when appropriate; and compromise, especially negotiation because it involves mutual accommodation among participants.

Alleviating stress by altering our lifestyle includes building greater stress tolerance, changing our pace of life, controlling distressful thoughts, and acquiring problem-solving skills.

Finally, remember that stress is not synonymous with distress. Instead, to get the most out of life, each of us needs to find our optimal level of stress and use it as a method of growth.

SELF-TEST

1. Stress that has a beneficial effect on us is called
   a. eustress
   b. hypostress
   c. distress
   d. hyperstress

2. The single most stressful event in the Student Stress Scale is
   a. failure in an important course
   b. death of a close family member
   c. trouble with parents
   d. dropping out of college

3. The most common everyday hassle for all age groups is
   a. meeting high standards
   b. wasting time
   c. being lonely
   d. misplacing or losing things

4. Jobs like cook and telephone operator are very stressful because they combine high psychological demand with
   a. high decision control
   b. high risk taking
   c. low decision control
   d. low rewards

5. Symptoms of stress-related illnesses such as a peptic ulcer are most likely to develop in which stage of the general adaptation syndrome?
   a. exhaustion
   b. resistance
   c. alarm reaction
   d. hypostress

6. The unconscious blocking of unacceptable ideas or feelings from consciousness is called
   a. suppression
   b. rationalization
   c. repression
   d. denial

7. The single most important ability or trait in managing stress successfully is
   a. high personal control
   b. moderate anxiety tolerance
   c. low frustration tolerance
   d. low personal control

8. You're returning a defective coat recently purchased. An assertive response would be to
   a. apologize, then ask to have the coat repaired
   b. threaten to sue the store
   c. complain of the cheap merchandise
   d. ask for another coat without the defect

9. A desirable way of handling stress that involves mutual accommodation among all the participants is
   a. denial
   b. conformity
   c. negotiation
   d. withdrawal

10. The pace of life is fastest where?
    a. Boston
    b. Minneapolis
    c. Tokyo
    d. Los Angeles

EXERCISES

1. *Take an inventory of your stress.* Use the Student Stress Scale (Table 4–1) to assess the significant changes in your life. Include all the significant events that have occurred in your life during the past six months or are likely to occur in the next six months. If you've experienced stressful events not listed in the rating scale, try to assign a numerical value by comparing them to a similar event in the rating scale. Then add up your points to arrive at a total LCU score as explained in the text. When you think back over the past six months, does your level of physical health and personal functioning reflect the levels of stress indicated by your score?

2. *Daily hassles.* Jot down some of the little things in everyday life that annoy you. How does your list compare with the survey of daily hassles described in the text? Which hassles bother you the most? Select two or three of them and suggest specific ways you could make them less bothersome.

3. *Defense mechanisms.* Think of a particular situation in which you reacted defensively. Which defense mechanisms did you rely on? How well did you cope with this situation? If you face a similar situation in the future, how would you like to handle it differently?

4. *Describe your most stressful experience.* In a page or so, tell what made the incident or experience so stressful. How well did you cope with this situation?

5. *Managing stress assertively.* Recall a stressful situation that you handled in an assertive manner. Describe the situation, how you handled it, and how it turned out. An alternate exercise is to relate a similar situation that you wished you had handled in a more assertive manner. How did you react in this situation? What happened as a result? If you're faced with a similar situation in the future, how could you handle it more assertively?

6. *Altering your lifestyle.* Review the suggestions for reducing stress by changing your pace of life. If there are other changes especially needed in your daily habits, what are they? Select two or three of your suggested changes and apply them to your daily life for a week. If you find this change helpful, why not continue altering your lifestyle to reduce the stress in your everyday life?

QUESTIONS FOR SELF-REFLECTION

1. Can you recall several instances when stress had a beneficial effect?
2. Which situations do you find most distressful?
3. What are some of the "little things" that get you down?
4. Would you agree that having some control over your work activities makes them less stressful?
5. How can you tell when you're under a lot of stress?

6. When you become defensive, how do you behave?
7. Are you inclined to abuse alcohol or drugs when under stress?
8. What are some ways you've modified your environment to decrease stress?
9. Have you tried altering your lifestyle as a way of alleviating stress?
10. All things considered, how well do you manage stress?

FOR FURTHER INFORMATION

RECOMMENDED READINGS

Conduit, E. (1995). *The body under stress: Developing skills for keeping healthy.* Hillsdale, NJ: Erlbaum. A book of tips on how to cope with stress.

Davis, M. (1995). *The relaxation and stress reduction workbook.* Oakland, CA: New Harbinger Publications. A personalized guide to stress reduction.

Ellis, A. (1994). *How to keep people from pushing your buttons.* Secaucus, NJ: Carol Publishing. Noted psychologist Albert Ellis describes how to assert yourself and cope with guilt when dealing with others.

Sapolsky, R. (1994). *Why zebras don't get ulcers: A guide to stress, stress-related diseases, and coping.* New York: W. H. Freeman. Another book of tips on the physiology and psychology of stress.

Smith, J. (1993). *Understanding stress and coping.* New York: Macmillan. A scholarly approach to the study of stress.

WEBSITES AND THE INTERNET

http://www.foobar.co.uk/users/umba/stress/: Contains lots of information on stress such as the reasons for it, biological basis for stress, and tips on stress management.

http://www.callamer.com//itc/aath: A site from the American Association for Therapeutic Humor. Contains information about the benefits of humor to mental health. Also connects you to other related sites.

http://mars.superlink.net/~zorro/humor.htm: An archive of jokes and funny stories to make you laugh when under stress and to share with friends under stress.

http://www.ari.net/jec/gtower/gtower.html#mm1: One of many sites available to instruct you on relaxation.

http://www.shsu.edu/~counsel/shortr.html: Another site designed to teach you about relaxation and other therapies.

CHAPTER

5

The Body and Health

Learning Objectives

After completing this chapter, you should be able to

1. Discuss the relationship between body image and psychological well-being.
2. Discuss the major health hazards: obesity, smoking, and alcohol and drug abuse.
3. Describe the three stages of decision making in seeking medical care.
4. List at least five factors involved in taking charge of your health.
5. Describe the food pyramid.
6. Describe what makes a personal fitness program effective.
7. Discuss the role of social support in wellness.

Amanda, in her mid-30s, works at a large department store as an artist and designer. She designs some of the art for the store's newspaper and catalog advertising. She also decorates the windows and develops some of the in-store displays. When she is at her desk at work, she drinks coffee all day long. It seems she is always behind deadline so she grabs a snack on the run—often junk food from the vending machines. When she finally goes home, she is too tired to fix herself a decent meal. Instead, she sits with a glass of wine, a bag of taco chips, and some nacho dip. When the wine glass empties, she has another one or two glasses of wine. As a result, Amanda is slightly overweight though she is not obese. Complaining she doesn't have time to do so, she rarely exercises. Amanda also smokes about a pack of cigarettes a day, a habit she developed in college while sitting in the art student lounge. She thought the other students looked so sophisticated when they smoked, so she began.

Amanda is not now sick and, in fact, feels healthy enough so that she rarely complains of her health to others. But how healthy is she? Chances are she could be in much better shape. Part of the problem lies in Amanda's poor body image from being slightly overweight as well as her faulty eating and exercise habits. Also, she lacks awareness of what her sedentary and stressful lifestyle is doing to her. Then there's the mistaken notion, more subconscious than conscious, that "not being sick" means she is "well."

Body Image

Not unlike Amanda, many people lack a clear image of their bodies and do not take very good care of themselves. You'd think people would have a fairly accurate picture of their own bodies. After all, who is more familiar with our bodies than ourselves? Each day, we spend an unaccountable amount of time receiving messages from our bodies, bathing, touching, and grooming ourselves. Naturally, we acquire a great deal of information about our bodies. But we have blind spots as well, so that our body image only approximates rather than coincides with reality. A major reason is that our bodies are constantly changing, and there is a time lag in bringing our body images up to date—which is perhaps why we are fascinated by seeing ourselves in the mirror, although we are often dismayed when we look too closely. Each of us tends to hold on to more or less outdated body images, such as the aging man who has difficulty recognizing the wrinkles in his face, his thinning hair, or his sagging waistline. Our awareness of the insides of our bodies is even less well formed. Most of us have only the vaguest notions of the spatial relations between the various internal organs, much less how to interpret the significance of various aches and pains.

A major barrier is **depersonalization** or **unembodiment**—the sense of not being intimately attached to one's body. Extreme examples have been reported by people using hallucinogenic drugs. Such individuals may feel that parts of their bodies, usually their hands, do not belong to them. In less extreme ways, each of us tends to depersonalize our bodies, perhaps in part as a legacy of growing up in Western society, which emphasizes intellectual and technological achievements. A conscientious student, for example, may spend hours sitting at a desk absorbing information from a book while barely moving his or her body, sometimes warding off signs of fatigue with stimulants such as coffee. Similarly, workers like Amanda come home so tired that they will spend hours passively watching television, rarely moving their bodies except to feed themselves out of boredom or shake their foot to keep it from going to sleep. Because of our urban, technological way of life, by the time we've reached college age, about three-fourths of us have some type of physical defect that has resulted from unembodiment and disuse or misuse of our bodies. Conversely, when elderly people are taught how to breathe, sit, stand, and walk properly, many of the "symptoms of aging" disappear.

HOW WE FEEL ABOUT OUR BODIES

Traditionally, **body image** refers to the mental image we form of our own bodies. Recently, however, the term *body image* has been expanded to include how we *feel* about our bodies as well as how satisfied or dissatisfied we are with our bodies, as the case may be. Because our society puts so much emphasis on physical appearance, we might expect that many people would be dissatisfied with their bodies. Apparently, this is the case, as seen in the *Psychology Today* survey on the subject. From the nearly 4,500 people who responded to the body image survey, David Garner and his coresearchers ("A Very Revealing Picture," 1997) conducted a detailed analysis of a 3,452 person sample. All states and a few European and other countries were represented. The sample was better educated than the population at large, with over half of the respondents having attended college or having obtained an undergraduate or graduate degree. Also, because most of the respondents were Caucasian, minorities were underrepresented. Women (86 percent) were also more likely to respond than men (14 percent). The sample then is not representative of the U.S. population, so please read the following results with this knowledge in mind.

As in an earlier survey, women are still less satisfied than men with their appearance, but overall more people are dissatisfied with their bodies than ever before. In fact, the rate at which we are dissatisfied with our bodies is rapidly accelerating across time. Table 5–1 reveals some of the historic changes related to dissatisfaction with our body image.

TABLE 5–1

DISSATISFACTION WITH OUR BODIES ACROSS THREE DECADES

The dissatisfaction we feel toward our bodies has not only risen since 1972, the rate at which it's rising is accelerating.

	1972 Survey		1985 Survey		1997 Survey	
	Men	*Women*	*Men*	*Women*	*Men*	*Women*
Overall appearance	15%	25%	34%	38%	43%	56%
Height	13	13	20	17	16	16
Weight	35	48	41	55	52	66
Muscle tone	25	30	32	45	45	57
Breast/chest	18	26	28	32	38	34
Abdomen	36	50	50	57	63	71
Hips and upper thighs	12	49	21	50	29	61

SOURCE: Garner, D. M. (1997, February). The 1997 body image survey results. *Psychology Today*, p. 42. Reprinted with permission from Psychology Today Magazine, copyright © 1997 (Sussex Publishers, Inc.).

Most individuals cited their weight and dissatisfaction with their abdominal area in particular as the reason for their dissatisfaction. Interestingly, weight has different meanings for women than for men. Whereas many women reported wanting to lose weight, some men (22 percent) reported wanting to gain weight.

This relationship between dissatisfaction with body image and body weight is disturbing, especially given some of the other findings of the survey. The researchers asked a rather stark question, "How many years of your life would you trade to achieve your weight goals?" Twenty-four percent of the women and 17 percent of the men said they would sacrifice three years. Fifteen percent of the women and 11 percent of the men said they would sacrifice five years. In other words, these respondents believe that life is worth living only if you are thin.

Another question asked on the survey was whether the respondents smoke to control weight. Again, 50 percent of the women and 30 percent of the men said they smoke to lose or maintain their weight. As you will see later in the chapter, because it causes circulatory and respiratory problems as well as cancer, smoking is deadly. These smokers may indeed be giving up some life expectancy to stay thin.

Notice that in the results just described, women are more concerned about body image and weight control than men. Why? The most likely reason for such a difference is the greater emphasis in America on physical appearance for women than for men. Take Amanda's store, for example; there are three floors of clothing, makeup, perfume, and shoes for women and only a half floor for men. The *Psychology Today* survey identified the media as being a strong source for promoting thinness as an ideal way of life. Movie and TV celebrities as well as fashion models and well-known athletes were identified by many men and women as influencing their body image. Teasing by others and parental attitudes were also powerful influences on body image.

Some survey respondents were underweight. One hundred fifty-nine women in the survey were extremely thin. Forty percent of them still wanted to lose weight! Such findings suggest that women have internalized a stringent standard of slimness in regard to attractiveness, thereby making themselves more susceptible to dissatisfaction with their looks. This dissatisfaction with one's weight is only one reason among a multitude for some of the eating disorders plaguing American society (Akan & Grilo, 1995). We will look at these disorders in detail later in this chapter.

OUR IDEAL BODY

The satisfaction with our bodies is greatly influenced by our image of the ideal body, an integral part of our overall body image. Our **body ideal,** in turn, is greatly influenced by the particular body ideals prevalent in our culture. For example, in Jamaican society, plumpness is desirable, so although foreign media are present, the desire for plumpness is strong enough to counteract foreign preoccupation with thinness (D. E. Smith & Cogswell, 1994).

Every society throughout history has had somewhat different standards of beauty, but at no time in the past has there been such an intense barrage of media attention telling Americans how we should look. Magazine covers, TV ads, and films bombard us with images that reflect the standard of beauty for each sex. The ideal man is tall, large, muscular, and energetic. The ideal woman is slim, shapely, smooth-skinned, young, glamorous, and often blonde. The media define beauty so narrowly that few of us ever feel complacent or satisfied. This is especially true for Whites compared to Asians and African Americans (Akan & Grilo, 1995). The closer to the ideal body we are, the less pressure we feel to change. But those who are obviously different—the overweight, the elderly, and the physically disabled—may feel more pressure to change or hide the disliked parts of their bodies. Individuals who don't fit the images tend to have negative feelings about themselves, making it difficult for them to accept themselves as they are.

How much have you been influenced by the current emphasis on appearance and slimness? To check on your perception, you might complete the Social Attitudes Scale in Figure 5–1. Then consult the scoring key at the end of the chapter to determine the meaning of your score.

Each of us needs to construct a personal body ideal that is not too different from those in our culture but is revised to accommodate our own particular shape and features. This need becomes especially important with increasing age, so that our body ideal will allow us to see ourselves as reasonably attractive persons at each stage of life.

Unfortunately, gender differences make this task more difficult for women than men in our culture. For instance, individuals of both sexes hold body ideals that are somewhat different from their actual bodies. The average man wants to be an inch or so taller than he is and have broader shoulders and a more muscular build. The average woman wants to be an inch or so taller and somewhat thinner than she is. At the same time, there is a significant difference in the way men and women perceive the ideal body that they think is desired by members of the opposite sex compared to their self-chosen body ideals. For instance, college-aged women think men want a woman who is even thinner with larger breasts than women themselves want. Yet the type of woman men actually want is quite similar to the body ideal held by women themselves, that is, a woman who is somewhat slimmer than she actually is but with only medium-sized breasts. However, there is less discrepancy between men's perception of the ideal male body they think women want and the male figure women actually prefer. As a result, men are more apt to judge their current weight, their ideal weight, and the shape they think women prefer as quite similar (Fallon & Rozen, 1985). Furthermore, in other countries such as India, women students rate their ideal body closer to their current shapes (Fallon, 1990). Such studies suggest that when compared to men, the higher proportion of women

FIGURE 5–1

SOCIAL ATTITUDES SCALE

INSTRUCTIONS: Indicate how strongly you agree or disagree with each of the following statements. Then consult the scoring key at the end of the chapter to determine your score and what it means.

1. A man would always prefer to go out with a thin woman than one who is heavy.

Strongly agree	Agree somewhat	Agree	Neither agree nor disagree	Disagree	Disagree somewhat	Strongly disagree
___	___	___	___	___	___	___

2. Clothes are made today so that only thin people can look good.

Strongly agree	Agree somewhat	Agree	Neither agree nor disagree	Disagree	Disagree somewhat	Strongly disagree
___	___	___	___	___	___	___

3. Fat people are often unhappy.

Strongly agree	Agree somewhat	Agree	Neither agree nor disagree	Disagree	Disagree somewhat	Strongly disagree
___	___	___	___	___	___	___

4. It is not true that attractive people are more interesting, poised, and socially outgoing than unattractive people.

Strongly agree	Agree somewhat	Agree	Neither agree nor disagree	Disagree	Disagree somewhat	Strongly disagree
___	___	___	___	___	___	___

5. A pretty face will not get you very far without a slim body.

Strongly agree	Agree somewhat	Agree	Neither agree nor disagree	Disagree	Disagree somewhat	Strongly disagree
___	___	___	___	___	___	___

6. It is more important that a woman be attractive than a man.

Strongly agree	Agree somewhat	Agree	Neither agree nor disagree	Disagree	Disagree somewhat	Strongly disagree
___	___	___	___	___	___	___

7. Attractive people lead more fulfilling lives than unattractive people.

Strongly agree	Agree somewhat	Agree	Neither agree nor disagree	Disagree	Disagree somewhat	Strongly disagree
___	___	___	___	___	___	___

8. The thinner a woman is, the more attractive she is.

Strongly agree	Agree somewhat	Agree	Neither agree nor disagree	Disagree	Disagree somewhat	Strongly disagree
___	___	___	___	___	___	___

9. Attractiveness decreases the likelihood of professional success.

Strongly agree	Agree somewhat	Agree	Neither agree nor disagree	Disagree	Disagree somewhat	Strongly disagree
___	___	___	___	___	___	___

SOURCE: Judith Rodin, *Body Traps: How to Unlock the Cage of Body Obsessions.* Copyright © 1992 Judith Rodin. By permission of William Morrow & Company, Inc.

dissatisfied with their bodies may be partly attributable to our society. A major factor is our weight-obsessed culture, which bombards us with countless messages that fat is bad, which in turn encourages women to hold themselves to a stricter standard of thinness than men. All of this leads to constant dieting and an increasing incidence of serious eating disorders among women.

BODY IMAGE, AGE, AND PSYCHOLOGICAL WELL-BEING

Fortunately, the concern with appearance lessens with age. In the *Psychology Today* survey cited earlier, individuals of both sexes in their teens and 20s were the most concerned about their appearance. After this age, there was a steady decline of interest in appearance. This is good because people tend to gain weight as they age. We might expect the converse, then, that as they age, people dislike their bodies more and more. Although people become less concerned with their looks with age, they do not report a poorer body image. In fact, in the survey there was some evidence that as people age they gain insight and appreciation of their bodies' abilities. Either way, a diminished concern with looks helps us to adjust to the aging process.

 ## Psychological Factors and Physical Illness

The mutual link between how we feel about ourselves and how we feel about our bodies touches on an even larger issue, namely, the interaction between the mind and the body. Fortunately, most of us have grown up in an era in which the mind and the body are increasingly viewed as one or, at the most, two closely related aspects of the same system. Nor is this a new idea. As long ago as the fifth century B.C., Greek physicians held that whatever happened in the mind influenced the body, and vice versa. For many centuries, however, this idea was overshadowed by a dualistic notion of body and mind. The body alone was the basis of medical diagnosis and treatment; the mind was relegated to the realm of philosophers, priests, and, more recently, psychologists.

Today, however, physicians and mental health professionals alike pay greater attention to the mutual interactions of the mind-body unity. There's compelling evidence that organic factors—genes, the brain, and **neurotransmitters**—contribute to the major psychological disorders such as schizophrenia, major depression, and manic-depression (bipolar disorder). And conversely, there is substantial research indicating that psychological factors influence our susceptibility and resistance to physical illnesses. Furthermore, it is now held that psychological factors can affect *any* physical condition, not just the so-called psychosomatic illnesses. Although traditional efforts attempt to link specific diseases to single causes, such as genes, germs, and emotions, much of contemporary research assumes a systems theory perspective. In this view, human existence is made up of various subsystems and is itself an integral part of larger systems. Thus, to understand health and illness we must consider how these biological, psychological, and social systems interact, for example, as in the study of stress-related illnesses.

In this section we'll examine stress-related illnesses to see how psychological factors such as emotions and stress make us susceptible to physical illnesses. We'll also describe how stress affects the immune system and, in turn, how we may strengthen our resistance to stress. We'll also describe three of the most common health hazards associated with stress and illness: obesity, cigarette smoking, and substance abuse such as alcohol and drug abuse.

In Chapter 4 on stress, you may recall Hans Selye's concept of the *general adaptation syndrome,* the characteristic pattern of arousal by the autonomic nervous system in response to any stressful event. It is not always clear why or how individuals react as they do. What makes one person develop coronary heart disease whereas another does not? The answer is that a combination of factors including individual differences in immune systems, personalities, lifestyle preferences, and environments to which people are exposed produces illness in one person and not the other.

THE IMMUNE SYSTEM

Amanda had had a serious case of mononucleosis in college so her **immune system** had been damaged. The immune system is a complex surveillance system that defends our bodies by identifying and destroying various foreign invaders. Amanda likened herself to the proverbial canary in the coal mine. If there was a stomach flu or a cold going around, she was always first to catch it. Whereas her immune system was perhaps impaired, other individuals possess more robust immune systems.

In emphasizing the link between psychological factors such as stress and physical illnesses, it is important that we do not exceed the boundary between science and wishful thinking. Thus, stress does not *cause* illness directly. Rather, stress tends to weaken the immune system, thereby making us more vulnerable to illness. How does this happen?

First, in times of distress, psychological processes such as depression can prevent us from taking positive health-related measures such as eating well (Whisman & Kwon, 1993). Second, research has demonstrated that in stressful situations, the body's immune system functions less well. For instance, stress lowers the body's resistance to a variety of physical ailments, ranging from herpes to upper respiratory infections (Cohen & Williamson, 1991). In a typical study, Jemmett and Magloire (1988) obtained samples of the primary defensive substance against infections during and after final exams. They found that this substance (secretory immunoglobulin A) decreased during the examination period and returned to normal after the examinations. Even more provocative but controversial findings from other studies link stress and other negative emotions to serious illnesses such as cancer and death.

PERSONALITY

There is increasing evidence suggesting that we may bolster our resistance to stress and illness by harnessing the powers of the mind—our thoughts, attitudes, and emotions. Psychologists suggest that individuals who deal effectively with stress and therefore resist illness are self-healing or have **self-healing personalities.** Such individuals are happy, curious, secure, and enthusiastic about life. Other individuals as characterized by psychologists have **disease-prone personalities.** These individuals seem neurotic, insecure, and negative (Friedman, Hawley, & Tucker, 1994). For instance, four out of five cancer specialists agree that a strong will to live—a fighting spirit and a sense of hope— are important factors in longevity. Supportive evidence can be seen in a study in which patients with malignant melanoma, an insidious form of skin cancer, were divided into two groups—one serving as a control group and the other experimental. Both groups received the necessary medical and surgical attention. The main difference was that patients in the experimental group received a variety of psychological and educational instruction. By the end of six months, there was a substantial decrease in depression among patients in the experimental group compared to an increase in depression among those in the control group. Furthermore, the mood changes were accompanied by an increase in certain immune cells among those in the instructional group (Cousins, 1989).

Another personality factor that pertains to our ability to resist illness is self-efficacy, described more fully elsewhere in this book. *Self-efficacy* is the belief in one's capabilities to organize and execute the courses of action required to produce given attainments (Bandura, 1997). With regard to health behaviors, self-efficacy is that trait that enables us to adopt healthy and therefore preventive behaviors such as physical exercise or to adhere to programs designed to eliminate unhealthy habits such as smoking. Individuals high in self-efficacy are more likely to adopt healthy lifestyles and to be able to stick to their regimens when attempting to eliminate unhealthy behaviors. Just exactly how does self-efficacy function in relationship to health?

- First, a sense of efficacy can activate a wide range of biological processes that mediate human health and disease processes. For example, exposure to stressors along with the ability to control them often results in no adverse physical effects. In fact, there seem to be biochemical differences between individuals with high perceived efficacy and low perceived efficacy (Wiedenfeld et al., 1990).

- Second, people's beliefs that they can motivate themselves and regulate their own behavior play a crucial role in whether they even consider changing detrimental health habits or pursuing rehabilitative activities (Bandura, 1997). In other words, people see little point in trying to change if they do not believe they can succeed. Smokers, for example, will not even attempt to quit smoking if they believe that they don't have the personal resources to do so. Carey and Carey (1993) found that successful quitters had a stronger sense of efficacy at the outset than relapsers.

- Third, the onus for healthy lifestyles does not reside solely with individuals. With regard to self-efficacy, people are exposed to a variety of health-related messages from the media. From the media, people need knowledge about how to regulate their behavior and to develop a firm belief in their personal efficacy to engage in preventive behaviors. Compared to threatening messages, public health messages that elicit positive emotions make people feel more efficacious and optimistic about the benefits of healthy practices.

- Finally, adherence to healthy lifestyles or to rehabilitation programs once they are commenced can also be problematic. People with low self-efficacy tend to drop out more quickly and to be sporadic attendees and irregular practitioners of healthy habits (McAuley, 1991).

How can individuals develop or promote high self-efficacy? According to Albert Bandura (1997), the leading theorist on such matters, individuals must learn to monitor their own behaviors, especially the ones they wish to change. They must set short-range, attainable goals to motivate and direct their own efforts, and to enlist positive social support from others to help them sustain the efforts needed to succeed. Modeling from successful others also benefits those embarking on healthier lifestyles. Interestingly, the emotional and situational underminers of beliefs about personal efficacy seem to be very similar across cultures (Sandahl, Lindberg, & Röttenberg, 1990).

We must guard against emphasizing personality as responsible for our health to such an extent that people are made to feel guilty when they become sick or fail to get well.

As mentioned earlier, there are a multitude of other factors that contribute to our physical and mental well-being. Another such factor is lifestyle, which we will discuss next.

LIFESTYLE

In addition to stress-related illnesses such as hypertension, there are many health hazards that make us more susceptible to illness, ranging from harmful additives in the food to environmental pollutants in the air and water. Workers in certain fields are at increased risk of respiratory diseases, including miners, asbestos handlers, and metal smelters. Excessive exposure to X-rays during routine medical and dental checkups can be dangerous. And in an age of nuclear energy, there's the risk of radiation from nuclear accidents, not to mention the horrors of nuclear war. Some of these hazards, such as cigarette smoking, are more under our control than others. In fact, lifestyle kills more Americans than any other single factor; this cannot be said for other countries where environmental hazards, disease, and starvation account for more deaths. Three major health hazards that are directly associated with lifestyle and that can be controlled (though many people have difficulty doing so) are obesity, smoking, and alcohol and drug abuse.

Obesity, or an excessive amount of body fat, presents something of a paradox in our society. Nowhere is thinness more desirable than in mainstream American society, yet nowhere is obesity more prevalent probably because food is so available here compared to other countries. Amanda, the young adult from the opening story, was overweight but not obese. Her doctor knew this because he measured her with skinfold calipers. Americans are usually considered obese if they exceed the desirable weight for their height, build, and age by more than 20 percent as measured by skinfold calipers. In the United States, with about 35 percent of women being categorized as overweight, more women than men tend to be obese ("Coming to Terms," 1994). Box 5–1 discusses who is at risk for being obese.

Obesity is associated with an increased risk of illness and death from diabetes, high blood pressure, stroke, coronary heart disease, and kidney and gallbladder disorders. The

Overweight people are at greater risk for a variety of illnesses.

Box 5–1

Waistline Woes

When each person in a cross section of American adults is asked questions about his or her weight, height, and body build, the responses are hardly encouraging to a nation supposedly on a health kick.

Only 1 in 4 (23 percent) adults are within the weight range considered acceptable by health authorities. Fewer than 1 in 5 (18 percent) are underweight. But almost 6 out of 10 (59 percent) of American adults are overweight (according to the Metropolitan Life Insurance Company tables), and, as such, their health is presumably at considerable risk.

Most of the overweight people are residents of the Midwest (61 percent), those who live in small towns and the country (67 percent), those with incomes of $15,000 or below, members of racial minorities (64 percent), people 50 years of age and over (70 percent), men (66 percent), blue-collar types (62 percent), those who make little effort to maintain good nutrition (64 percent), and those who get little or no exercise (65 percent).

SOURCE: *Inside America,* Lou Harris (New York:Vintage Books, 1987), p. 11. Copyright © 1987, 1988 by Louis Harris. Reprinted by permission of Vintage Books, a division of Random House, Inc.

more overweight people are, the greater their risk. For instance, if Amanda were 40 percent overweight, she would be twice as likely to die from coronary heart disease. Also, diabetes sometimes develops as a consequence of obesity and may disappear when excess weight is lost. Very obese people suffer more surgical and anesthetic complications than leaner people. Finally, childbirth among obese women may be more risky for both mother and child.

Obesity probably results from an interaction of physiological and psychological factors. We all know overweight people who eat moderately but remain fat and thin people who eat heartily but remain slender. Although apparently some people are born to carry more fat, a lot of obesity results from overeating and insufficient exercise. There is also a variety of psychological and social factors associated with obesity. For instance, obese people tend to be more responsive to external cues, such as the visibility, availability, and smell of food, rather than the internal cues of hunger. Some individuals also eat more food when with others, especially others who are fast eaters.

People who want to lose weight must somehow help their bodies to use up more calories than they consume. The two basic ways to do so are to (1) change your diet so that you eat less, especially foods high in fat, and (2) exercise more. The benefits of crash diets are generally short-lived. To make matters worse, strict dieting tends to lower the rate of metabolism so that you can count calories carefully and still not lose weight. Instead, it's better to modify both your hunger and your metabolic rate by changing the foods you eat. For instance, carbohydrates increase metabolism and are less readily converted to body fat than the same calories eaten as fats. Furthermore, it's preferable to follow a reasonable diet aimed at a more modest weight loss—say, 1 pound a week—over a longer period of time, combined with regular exercise.

Perhaps you've heard that exercise may be self-defeating because you eat more. Actually, exercise not only burns up calories but also increases the metabolic rate, so that even when active people are not exercising, their bodies are burning up calories faster. Exercise during and after dieting is one of the few predictors of successful long-term weight loss (Brownell, 1989). In addition, many people find it easier to lose weight by joining a weight-loss club or exercising with friends, which provides guidance and support for their efforts. Finally, self-mastery plays an important role, so that individuals who acquire a greater sense of self-control over their eating and exercise habits can successfully manage their weight long after the completion of dieting and treatment programs.

Tobacco abuse continues to be a major health hazard. There is compelling evidence that cigarette smoking is a major factor in heart disease, lung cancer, emphysema, and other fatal illnesses. In addition, smoking contributes to many forms of cancer, including cancers of the mouth, larynx, bladder, and pancreas. Smokers who also drink alcohol magnify their risks of cancer even more because it enhances the carcinogenic effect of tobacco at certain sites of the body, such as the esophagus, mouth, and larynx.

Greater awareness of the health hazards of smoking and other uses of tobacco such as chewing has prompted many people to give up the habit. Only about 25 percent of the population now smokes, down from the rate of over 40 percent from 45 years ago. At the same time, these gains should not blind us to the fact that more than 3,000 teenagers begin smoking each day (Gleick, 1995). Not surprisingly, tobacco companies are under fire from the public and health officials for this increase. On a second front, many authorities are disturbed that smoking rates are even higher in other countries,

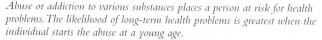

Abuse or addiction to various substances places a person at risk for health problems. The likelihood of long-term health problems is greatest when the individual starts the abuse at a young age.

many of which have citizens who cannot afford to smoke and who have inadequate health care as is.

Smoking is a difficult habit to break. Even conservative estimates imply that half or more of those who quit smoking eventually resume the habit. In addition to the psychological dependence on the smoking habit, nicotine is considered to be physically addictive. Consequently, smokers build a tolerance to nicotine and need to smoke a larger number of cigarettes or ones with a higher nicotine content to get the same effect. The average smoker smokes 20 to 30 cigarettes a day—one about every 30 to 40 minutes. And because the biological half-life of nicotine in humans is about 20 to 30 minutes, habitual smokers keep their systems primed with nicotine during most of their waking hours. Not surprisingly, withdrawal from habitual smoking, and therefore nicotine, produces a variety of symptoms, including nervousness, headaches, dizziness, fatigue, insomnia, sweating, cramps, tremors, and heart palpitations. Many famous and interesting people have been addicted to tobacco. They, too, have found the habit terribly difficult to stop. Box 5–2 is about just such a famous person.

There are many approaches to reducing **nicotine addiction.** In recent years many people have begun using the "patch," which when attached to one's arm releases nicotine into the body, thereby reducing the physical craving for a smoke. In addition, a variety of psychological and behavioral methods is available. One approach is stimulus control, in which smokers become aware of the stimuli and the situations that trigger their smoking. Then they develop alternative behaviors. For instance, Amanda usually lit a cigarette whenever she talked on the telephone. A friend suggested that she begin holding a glass of water in her right hand, thereby breaking the association between the telephone and smoking. Generally, it's better to emphasize the positive aspects of not smoking than the fear of illness, such as the desire to take charge of one's life and to maintain physical fitness. Although most smokers who give up smoking resume the habit within 6 months to a year, former smokers may increase their chance of success through the support of friends, spouses, or support groups. Then too, with sufficient motivation, many smokers may give up the habit without any formal program.

Alcohol and drug abuse continue to be major health hazards for many people. Three-fourths of American men and almost two-thirds of women drink alcoholic beverages. Approximately one-third of both sexes are light drinkers, but at least 1 out of 10

BOX 5–2

Nicotine Addiction

After a prominent physician was told that his heart arrhythmia was aggravated by his heavy smoking, up to 20 cigars a day, he decided to stop smoking. Later, describing the agony of not being able to smoke as "beyond human power to bear," he resumed smoking, though on a somewhat more moderate basis (E. Jones, 1953). Eventually, he developed cancer of the jaw and mouth, which was also associated with his smoking. However, despite 33 operations for cancer and the construction of an artificial jaw, this physician continued to smoke until his death at the age of 83. His efforts to stop smoking and the suffering he endured make him a tragic example of nicotine addiction. His name is Sigmund Freud (Altrocchi, 1980).

adults is a heavy drinker; the proportion is higher among men, especially those in the 18- to 25-year-old group. Figure 5–2 will help you assess whether you are a heavy drinker.

Alcohol use constitutes a major health hazard in many ways. Nearly two-thirds of the drivers in fatal traffic accidents have been drinking. Automobile accidents involving alcohol are a leading cause of death among youths. Furthermore, half of all the occupied beds in American hospitals are filled by people with alcohol-related ailments. In addition, chronic heavy drinking is often accompanied by poor nutrition and results in serious damage to many parts of the body such as the liver, with at least one of every five chronic heavy drinkers developing cirrhosis.

Although alcohol remains the drug of choice for a large segment of the population, we should not overlook the abuse of prescription or over-the-counter drugs. Overdose from barbiturates has become a common means of committing suicide. And people who attempt to stop taking barbiturates, or sleeping pills, often experience a rebound effect that disturbs their sleep. This rebound effect is common with many drugs, including al-

---

FIGURE 5–2

ARE YOU DRINKING TOO MUCH ALCOHOL?

Yes	No	
____	____	1. Do you often drink alone, either at home or in a bar?
____	____	2. When holding an empty glass at a party, do you always actively look for a refill instead of waiting to be offered one?
____	____	3. Do you feel you must have a drink at a particular time every day such as after work?
____	____	4. Is your drinking ever the direct result of a quarrel, or do quarrels seem to occur when you've had a drink or two?
____	____	5. Do you ever miss work or scheduled meetings because of your drinking?
____	____	6. When questioned, do you ever lie about how much you drink?
____	____	7. Do you feel physically deprived if you cannot have at least one drink every day?
____	____	8. When you're under a lot of stress, do you almost automatically take a drink to "settle your nerves"?
____	____	9. Do you sometimes crave a drink in the morning?
____	____	10. Do you sometimes have "mornings after" when you can't remember what happened the night before?

Every YES answer to the above questions should be taken as a warning sign. Two or more YES answers suggest you're on the way to becoming dependent on alcohol. Three or more YES answers indicate you may have a serious drinking problem that requires professional help.

SOURCE: Jeffrey R. M. Kunz & Asher J. Finkel (Eds.), *The American Medical Association Family Medical Guide* by the American Medical Association. (New York: Random House, 1987), p. 33. Copyright © 1982 by the American Medical Association. Reprinted by permission of Random House, Inc.

cohol. Amanda found herself awakening several hours into a deep sleep on each night that she consumed three or more glasses of wine. As many as half of all insomniacs have drug-induced insomnia as part of their problem. An excessive or prolonged use of tranquilizers, especially among the elderly, may damage the respiratory system, kidneys, and liver. Furthermore, combining alcohol with drugs tends to multiply the effect of the drug, sometimes with fatal results.

The use of illegal or street drugs poses special problems. There is no control over the strength or purity of the drug, who takes them, or the dosage. Thus, individuals may damage their bodies or take a fatal overdose by mistake. Furthermore, the tendency to use greater amounts of the mood-altering drugs over time, to offset tolerance to the drug, increases the health hazard. For instance, inasmuch as marijuana smoke contains even more carcinogenic hydrocarbons than tobacco smoke does, health authorities are concerned that heavy, prolonged use of marijuana may damage the lungs and perhaps lead to lung cancer.

People who develop problems with drugs exhibit a familiar sequential pattern. Initially, they begin using a drug with little or no awareness of what it does to their bodies. In time, they experience a loss of desired effect with an increasing frequency of usage, gradually leading to drug dependence. Those who continue using the drug suffer an eventual impairment of their health and social functioning. The pattern of progression from initial use of a drug to dependence on it may vary considerably among individuals, depending on such factors as personality, the particular drug, frequency and intensity of use, and the extent to which physical or psychological dependence occurs.

Individuals who become dependent on a drug like alcohol or marijuana exhibit characteristic symptoms of the psychoactive substance dependence disorder. Figure 5–3 lists some of the symptoms of substance dependence. Such individuals display an impaired control of and continued use of a substance despite adverse consequences. The symptoms of the dependence syndrome include, but are not limited to, the physiological symptoms of tolerance and withdrawal. In addition, some symptoms must have persisted for at least 1 month or have occurred repeatedly over a longer period of time, as in binge drinking. Furthermore, individuals may display different degrees of drug dependence—mild, moderate, or severe.

Although a wide variety of programs is available for treating drug abuse, some have a relatively high failure rate. Individuals may not be ready for the complete change in lifestyle demanded by the program, often because of denial on their part, or they may become bored and frustrated with the program or the lifestyle changes demanded of it. Most dropouts leave the residential programs in the first several weeks. A large proportion of people who enter drug treatment drop out and reenter the program at a later date, though relapse remains the rule rather than the exception. **Relapse** means a return to a previous behavior or state, in this case, a return to drinking alcohol or using drugs. The prevalence of relapse has led some cognitive-behavioral therapists to develop relapse-prevention training, which generally is incorporated into the treatment program. Substance abusers are taught how to cope with high-risk situations and to prevent small lapses from becoming full-blown relapses. Individuals are encouraged to view lapses as temporary setbacks that they can learn from and avoid in the future. For instance, Amanda went to a smoking cessation program and learned that she should avoid going to dinner with her friends who smoked. She was also taught to think, "Okay, I had a slip. But that doesn't mean I'm all through. I can get back on track." Despite the promise of this approach, more research is needed to fully evaluate the benefits of such training (Taylor & Aspinwall, 1990).

FIGURE 5–3

SYMPTOMS OF SUBSTANCE DEPENDENCE

According to the American Psychiatric Association's authoritative guide, *DSM-IV*, at least three of the following nine characteristic symptoms are necessary to make the diagnosis of a psychoactive substance dependence disorder.

1. Substance taken in larger amounts or over a longer period than the person intended.
2. Persistent desire or one or more unsuccessful efforts to cut down or control substance use.
3. A great deal of time spent obtaining the substance, taking the substance, or recovering from its effects.
4. Frequent intoxication or withdrawal symptoms when there are major role obligations at work, school, or home, or when substance use is physically hazardous.
5. Important social, occupational, or recreational activities reduced or given up because of substance use.
6. Continued use despite persistent or recurrent social, psychological, or physical problems caused or exacerbated by use of the substance.
7. Marked tolerance, that is, need for significantly increased amounts of the substance (at least a 50 percent increase) in order to achieve intoxication or desired effect, or markedly diminished effect with continued use of the same amount.

Note: The following items may not apply to cannabis, hallucinogens, or phencyclidine (PCP):

8. Characteristic withdrawal symptoms (vary with specific substances).
9. Substance often taken to relieve or avoid withdrawal symptoms.

SOURCE: Reprinted with permission from the *Diagnostic and Statistical Manual of Mental Disorders,* Fourth Edition. Copyright 1994 American Psychiatric Association.

ENVIRONMENTAL ISSUES

Various environments in which we find ourselves are more or less stressful and therefore more or less conducive to health problems. Amanda noticed, for example, that she was very distressed when her boss bellowed at her one day that she could not do anything right. The very next day, though, her employer acted as if nothing had been wrong the previous day. "What does this mean?" asked Amanda. "What could I have done differently?" Before Amanda could answer these questions, though, she was sick with a cold.

Let's analyze this situation. One reason the event was stressful to Amanda is that she felt she did nothing to promote her supervisor's ire. In other words, the situation was out of Amanda's control or was *uncontrollable.* Amanda hoped that maybe her boss had just had an upsetting morning at home and that the anger had nothing to do with her job performance. Amanda had seen her supervisor have these little tantrums before but could not predict when they would occur. *Unpredictability* is another aspect of environments that is distressing to us. If we can predict when a negative or otherwise stressful event will occur, we can brace for it, prepare for it. Not knowing when the tantrums were coming was distressing for Amanda.

Another feature of environments that is not conducive to wellness is when the factors in the environment are *ambiguous.* Recall that Amanda's boss acted angry one minute and as if nothing had happened the next. This situation is very ambiguous, again leaving Amanda wondering if she really was the cause of the outburst or if it was caused by a problem at her boss's home. Ambiguity, then, also creates distress. A final problem of stress that originates in the environment is that often the distress is *unresolvable,* that is, there is little the distressed individual can do to settle the issue or reduce the distress. Hopefully, this was not the case for Amanda; perhaps she can speak to her supervisor and come to some understanding about how to avoid instigating her supervisor's wrath in the future. In order to cope better, it is best if we avoid situations that are uncontrollable, unpredictable, ambiguous, or unresolvable. If such situations are unavoidable, as often is the case, the next best thing we can do is cope effectively with them. Coping is discussed in the next section and elsewhere in this book.

Coping With Illness

Every so often each of us has a minor health problem, which we usually treat with a variety of over-the-counter remedies like aspirin, antihistamines, and stomach medicine. However, if the problem persists, especially when it interferes with our everyday lives, we begin to consider seeing a doctor. Whether we are aware of it or not, such experiences set in motion a decision-making process that includes three stages: (1) noticing and interpreting the seriousness of our symptoms, (2) seeking professional help when needed, and (3) adhering to the prescribed treatment. In this section, we'll look at how people react to symptoms and illnesses at each of these three stages.

NOTICING AND INTERPRETING SYMPTOMS

Even healthy young adults like Amanda may experience a variety of symptoms, including nasal congestion, sore muscles, stiff joints, headaches, racing heart, dizziness, and constipation or diarrhea. Chances are that each of us has experienced one or more of these symptoms, at least to a slight degree, recently. But what do they mean? Are they simply reactions to stress? Or do such symptoms mean we're coming down with a cold or flu? When the aches and pains are more serious, the questions become more important. Is that discomfort in the chest an early warning of a heart attack or simply a bad case of indigestion? Cancer, for example, is a feared but common disease, more common than we like to think. Fortunately, cancer often gives us warning signals that can assist in early diagnosis and treatment. Learning the warning signs of cancer can save your life. Box 5–3 shares the warning signs of cancer as designated by the American Cancer Society.

Each of us differs somewhat in the tendency to label our body aches and pains as symptoms of an illness. People who habitually complain of unfounded ailments or exhibit an undue fear of illness are often called **hypochondriacs.** On the other hand, some people tend to *under*report their physical symptoms. These people are **extroverts.** People who are extroverts tend to be warm and outgoing and are sufficiently involved in life so that they don't have time to complain of their ailments. Each person's sense of well-being is a function of both clusters of traits, the relative strength of each tendency determining how we perceive and interpret our inner state. Individuals high in hypochondriasis report two or three times as many symptoms as the better-adjusted

BOX 5–3

WARNING SIGNALS OF CANCER

1. Change in bowel or bladder habits.
2. A sore that does not heal.
3. Unusual bleeding or discharge.
4. Thickening or lump in breast or elsewhere.
5. Indigestion or difficulty in swallowing.
6. Obvious change in wart or mole.
7. Nagging cough or hoarseness.

SOURCE: American Cancer Society. (1985). *Cancer Facts and Figures.* New York: Author.

people. Conversely, those high in extroversion generally report fewer ailments. We discuss the need for socializing or seeking social support in more detail later.

Psychologists have also identified other coping strategies related to health concerns. One strategy is **avoidance.** In this pattern the individual minimizes or denies that there are any symptoms to notice. Such individuals are believed to cope well with short-term stressors. On the other hand, some individuals actively confront stressors. These individuals use **confrontation** to deal with stress directly. Such individuals are believed to better cope with long-term stressors (Taylor & Clark, 1986).

One other means for coping with bad health news is through **downward comparison.** Individuals who choose to do this compare their own situation to others who are worse off. For example, Amanda smoked about a pack of cigarettes a day but found herself comparing this habit to Virginia's, a coworker who smoked almost two packs a day. You might ask yourself, "Which of these patterns does my behavior most resemble?"

There are other personal characteristics that determine typical coping styles and health-related behaviors. One is the culture in which we were reared; the other is gender. With regard to culture, for example, pain signifies different things in different cultures. In the United States many visits to doctors are prompted by the experience of pain (Turk, 1994). In some cultures, individuals attend to the intensity of pain whereas in other cultures individuals respond to what they think the pain signifies. Thus, in the latter cultures, for example, minor pain could still signal something serious.

With regard to gender, differences exist in death and illness rates between men and women, some of which are attributable to lifestyle, others attributable to what is deemed socially appropriate for men and women. In North America women live longer than men (Strickland, 1988), perhaps because men are more likely to die in car accidents and in homicides. Men are also exposed to more dangerous work environments and perhaps more stress than women (Matlin, 1996). On the other hand, women experience more symptoms and have more physical ailments than men (R. M. Kaplan, Anderson, & Wingard, 1991). Women, for example, are much more likely to experience osteoporosis (a disorder of the bones which become porous and brittle) simply because they live longer and also experience menopause (Leventhal, 1994). Why women have longer lives but higher illness rates remains a mystery. One answer lies in the fact that women are simply more likely to report symptoms to a health care provider than are men (Levanthal).

SEEKING HELP

About the only time it's easy to decide whether or not to see a doctor is when our symptoms become extreme. This tendency was brought out in a study of students' use of a college health clinic. When students felt their symptoms were minor, their willingness to go to the clinic depended mostly on their level of anxiety about school performance as well as their family and cultural background. However, when they experienced severely disabling symptoms, they almost always promptly reported to the clinic (Insel & Roth, 1985).

At the same time, the decision to seek professional help also depends on many other factors. For instance, if people believe their symptoms have a psychological rather than a physical cause, they are more reluctant to go for help. Also, if their complaints are embarrassing to talk about, like hemorrhoids, they may resist treatment. Individuals are also less likely to visit a physician if the ailment seems viral related or involves the upper half of the body. If people believe the benefits of going to the doctor are not worth the time and trouble of a visit, especially if the visit is not covered by medical insurance, they may hold back. Furthermore, the dread of a devastating or fateful diagnosis may also delay seeking help, as in the case of the football player who senses that further surgery for his recurring knee trouble may signal the end of his sports career.

Men and women also differ in their readiness to see a doctor. Women generally are more sensitive to changes in their bodies, use more prescription and nonprescription drugs, and visit physicians more often than men. Yet men have higher rates of hypertension, ulcers, heart attacks, and cancer, and as mentioned earlier significantly shorter life expectancies. One possible explanation is that men are more preoccupied with the external world and are less attentive to their bodies. Or perhaps men are more reluctant to seek professional help because it implies a "weakness" on their part (Bishop, 1984).

In deciding whether to go to a doctor, we risk making two kinds of basic mistakes: (1) We may go too quickly or too often because we overinterpret the seriousness of our physical ailments, or (2) we may ignore the symptoms of diseases that should be treated at once. Examples include a fever that is not obviously associated with a cold or stuffy nose; signs of internal bleeding such as blood in the sputum, vomit, or bowel movement; a persistent abdominal pain, especially when it is in one spot and associated with nausea; and a stiff neck that is not associated with any physical strain or injury. At the same time, many diseases are without symptoms at certain points in the course of the illness. Hypertension, diabetes, tuberculosis, heart disease, and anemia, among others, may present few or no symptoms initially. Cancer is a serious disease that presents only minor symptoms in the beginning, which is why even healthy people need periodic checkups. Box 5–4 discusses these checkups in more detail.

ADHERING TO TREATMENT

Surprisingly, as many as one-half of all adult patients do not follow or complete the doctor's prescribed treatment. For example, Amanda had a sore throat and before she had finished her medication, the soreness was gone. Thus, Amanda discontinued her med-

Box 5–4

GETTING PERIODIC CHECKUPS

Does everyone need an annual physical exam? Not necessarily. Recently, this practice has come under greater scrutiny (Insel & Roth, 1985). One reason may be the new emphasis on personal responsibility for one's health care. Probably a more obvious reason is the cost, as well as the risk, of many traditional procedures, which often outweigh the potential benefits when done routinely on a healthy person.

A favored alternative is the selective health examination (Bennett, Goldfinger, & Johnson, 1987). Which tests are done, how often, and on which individuals are often matters of judgment made in the absence of definitive research in many areas. Such exams should be conducted according to each person's special needs and health risks. For instance, a patient with a strong pattern of alcohol consumption requires more careful scrutiny for liver diseases than someone who does not drink. By the same token, a woman with a family history of breast cancer should undergo mammography examinations on a more frequent basis than other women.

Screening tests commonly done on healthy people include blood pressure measurement, cholesterol measurement, mammography (breast cancer), pap smear, stool checks for hidden blood, tonometry (glaucoma), multiple blood-screening tests, skin tests for tuberculosis, tests for sexually transmitted diseases, sigmoidoscopy (colon), electrocardiogram, and chest X-ray.

A periodic checkup by a physician every 2 to 3 years throughout mid-adult life is reasonable. Such checkups not only maintain a valuable doctor-patient relationship but also provide for a review of personal habits and health practices, a physical examination, and the teaching of self-examination (e.g., of breasts and testicles). Such visits may make us better informed and willing to take greater personal responsibility for our own health care.

ication and to her dismay, the soreness and hoarseness returned again. People may fail to follow the instructions given with the medicine, discontinue the medication too soon, as did Amanda, or ignore suggestions for a healthier lifestyle. Interestingly, neither the patient's personality nor socioeconomic class predict well who will and will not adhere to treatment plans (R. Kaplan, Sallis, & Patterson, 1993).

People may fail to adhere to the prescribed treatment for many reasons. A common reason is diminished confidence in physicians, along with other authorities such as teachers, bankers, and politicians. However, patients who have a warm relationship with their doctor and are involved in planning the treatment are more apt to comply with the doctor's orders (Goleman, 1991; Rall, Peskoff, & Byrne, 1994). Another reason patients do not follow the treatment plan is that many of them do not sufficiently understand the nature of their illness or the doctor's instructions. By contrast, when the desired treatment is explained in everyday language with easy-to-follow written instructions, patients are much more likely to cooperate. And the way the information is presented is important, too. Information can be presented or framed in negative or positive ways. A negatively framed message would be something like this: "If you don't stop smoking,

Amanda, you are likely to die at a young age." A positively framed message is "Amanda, if you stop smoking, aerobic exercise will be easier." Scientists have discovered that positively framed messages from medical practitioners are best for promoting preventive behaviors such as sticking to a health diet, whereas negatively framed messages are best for facilitating detection behaviors such as noticing pain (Rothman, Salovey, Antone, Keough, & Martin, 1993).

 ## Promoting Wellness

Until recently, people in the health-care field made little distinction between people who were "not sick" and those who were "healthy." For all practical purposes, **wellness** was the absence of sickness. However, in recent years there has been a growing realization that health is considerably more than the absence of a minor or major illness. According to the World Health Organization, **health** is ideally "a state of complete physical, mental, and social well-being and not merely the absence of disease or infirmity" (Insel & Roth, 1985, p. xvii). To be healthy is to have the full use of one's body and mind and, despite an occasional bout of illness, to be alert, energetic, and happy to be alive even in old age. As a result, health practitioners and the public alike are beginning to think more in terms of optimum health and wellness.

Optimum health is not something you can get from your doctor, guru, lover, health food, or even a wonder drug. Positive health is something that comes mostly through your own efforts, aided by good genes and regular medical care. To be well in this sense means good eating and exercise habits as well as avoiding health hazards such as smoking and the abuse of alcohol. At this point you might be interested in rating your own health habits by taking the inventory in Figure 5–4. Even the elderly and the handicapped can be considered well in the sense of practicing good health habits and making the best of their present capabilities. Realistically, wellness remains more of an ideal than something to be fully achieved. By viewing our everyday well-being in terms of the positive ideal of health, instead of merely the absence of illness, we may function better and live more zestfully than we would have otherwise.

TAKING CHARGE OF YOUR OWN HEALTH

As Americans become better educated and enjoy greater freedom of choice, generally they want to exercise greater personal control over their own health and health care. When seeing the doctor, they don't want to be told to do this or that. Instead, they want to know the evidence and reasoning involved so they can make an informed choice. They also want solid information, without getting bogged down in a lot of technical details. As would you and Amanda, most Americans would like to live a longer life, but they want to enjoy it along the way. Taking the best possible care of themselves shouldn't have to mean putting everything they enjoy on the "forbidden list." And when people are ill, they want to be able to ask the right questions and evaluate the answers themselves. When a medical decision needs to be made, they want to be a partner in making it.

A key factor is assuming greater personal responsibility for your own health, which among other things includes the following:

FIGURE 5–4

HOW DO YOUR HEALTH HABITS RATE?

Circle the appropriate number after each of the following statements, and add up the numbers to get a total score for each section. Then check the norms at the end to determine what your score means.

Eating habits	*Almost always*	*Sometimes*	*Almost never*

1. I eat a variety of foods each day, such as fruits and vegetables, whole-grain breads and cereals, lean meats, dairy products, dry peas and beans, and nuts and seeds.

	4	1	0

2. I limit the amount of fat, saturated fat, and cholesterol I eat (including fat on meats, eggs, butter, cream, shortenings, and organ meats such as liver).

	2	1	0

3. I limit the amount of salt I eat by cooking with only small amounts, not adding salt at the table, and avoiding salty snacks.

	2	1	0

4. I avoid eating too much sugar (especially frequent snacks of sticky candy or soft drinks).

	2	1	0

Eating habits score: _____

Exercise/fitness	*Almost always*	*Sometimes*	*Almost never*

1. I maintain a desired weight, avoiding overweight and underweight.

	3	1	0

2. I do vigorous exercises for 15 to 30 minutes at least three times a week (examples include running, swimming, and brisk walking).

	3	1	0

3. I do exercises that enhance my muscle tone for 15 to 30 minutes at least three times a week (examples include yoga and calisthenics).

	2	1	0

4. I use part of my leisure time participating in individual, family, or team activities that increase my level of fitness (such as gardening, bowling, golf, and baseball).

	2	1	0

Exercise/fitness score: _____

Alcohol and drugs	*Almost always*	*Sometimes*	*Almost never*

1. I avoid drinking alcoholic beverages or I drink no more than one or two drinks a day.

	4	1	0

2. I avoid using alcohol or other drugs (especially illegal drugs) as a way of handling stressful situations or the problems in my life.

	2	1	0

3. I am careful not to drink alcohol when taking certain medicines (for example, medicine for sleeping, pain, colds, and allergies).

	2	1	0

4. I read and follow the label directions when using prescribed and over-the-counter drugs.

	2	1	0

Alcohol and drugs score: _____

What your scores mean:

9–10 Excellent   6–8 Good   3–5 Mediocre   0–2 Poor

SOURCE: Adapted from U.S. Department of Health and Human Services, Public Health Service. (1981). *Health Style: A Self-Test* (PHS 81–50155). Washington, DC: Author.

* Understanding how your body works
* Knowing how the body and mind interact
* Managing stress effectively
* Developing healthy eating and exercise habits
* Monitoring your health
* Getting periodic medical checkups
* Keeping your own medical records
* Knowing the health risks related to your family history
* Being aware of health hazards in your lifestyle, workplace, and environment
* Being an active participant in your own health care

Each individual or family should have one or more appropriate resources to be used as a guide to self-care and medical matters. (See the recommended readings at the end of this chapter.) Such books contain a great deal of valuable information about the body's functioning, desirable eating and exercise habits for staying well, home health care for minor problems, and when medical help may be needed. The use of the self-diagnosis symptom charts in the *AMA Family Medical Guide* is especially helpful in determining when to seek medical assistance.

Taking charge of your own health generally involves basic changes in how you relate to the medical establishment. In traditional practice, individuals are expected to assume the "good" patient role—being cooperative, undemanding, and unquestioning. Yet such docile behavior often has a detrimental side effect. Patients are anxious and depressed when they have little control over their treatment. Furthermore, because most patients are so cooperative, doctors underestimate patients' desire for information (Krupat, 1986). People who go to the opposite extreme and adopt a "bad" patient role—complaining and demanding a lot from their doctors—may not fare much better because their aggressive behavior usually alienates medical personnel.

Instead, individuals should become active participants in their health care in a collaborative way, that is, cooperating with doctors without surrendering their own rights. The aim is to establish a working alliance between doctor and patient, with both working together for the good of the patient. Patients need to know that most doctors are willing to inform them of their medical condition and their options for treatment but that they are expected to take the initiative in asking questions. And doctors need to realize that patients who are informed of their medical problems and given an active role in deciding their course of treatment are more likely to monitor their progress and adhere to the prescribed treatment (Pomerleau & Rodin, 1986).

EATING SENSIBLY

An integral part of a health-producing personality is practicing good health habits such as sensible patterns of eating and drinking, keeping physically fit, getting adequate rest, and visiting a physician regularly. Because more people "kill themselves" with a knife and fork than by any other means, one of the best ways to promote good health is to eat sensibly. Unfortunately, Amanda is not a very good role model.

Eating sensibly involves both the amount and the kind of food we eat. The amount of food is often measured in calories—a measurement of energy produced by food when oxidized, or "burned," in the body. The number of calories needed each day depends on such factors as age, sex, size, and rate of metabolism. A woman in her early 20s with a desk job needs about 2,000 calories a day; a woman with a more active life needs about 2,300 calories. A man with a desk job uses about 2,500 calories; one with a fairly active job, such as a carpenter, needs about 2,800 calories. Men and women who are in strenuous jobs or in athletic training may need anywhere from 3,000 to 4,000 calories a day (Kunz & Finkel, 1987). Although there are as yet no definitive studies on aging and calorie consumption in humans, animal studies demonstrate that restriction of calories is beneficial in that calorie restriction postpones age-related declines, such as reduction in learning ability and protein synthesis, and also delays the onset of late-life diseases such as cancer and hypertension (Weindruch, 1996).

A well-balanced diet includes adequate amounts of six groups of substances: proteins, carbohydrates, fats—which contain calories and produce energy—and vitamins, minerals, and fibers—which are also essential to the body but do not provide energy. Although individuals vary in their nutritional needs because of factors such as their size, age, sex, and level of physical activity, a balanced diet generally includes about 55 to 60 percent carbohydrates, 30 percent fat, and 10 to 15 percent protein. However, because Americans on the average get about 35 to 40 percent of their calories as fat, most people would benefit by cutting their fat intake by about one-quarter (Bennett, Goldfinger, & Johnson, 1987).

A handy guide to eating a balanced diet is the new food guide pyramid issued by the United States Department of Agriculture in 1992. The pyramid, which replaces the familiar pie chart used since the 1940s, puts a greater emphasis on grains, vegetables, and fruits and less emphasis on foods containing fats and sugar. (See Figure 5–5.)

Breads, cereals, and pasta provide complex carbohydrates, a good source of **nutrition** and energy. Most overweight people consume too many carbohydrates in the form of high-sugar foods. A more desirable diet includes generous amounts of vegetables and fruits, which provide nutrition and energy as well as fiber.

FIGURE 5–5
The food pyramid, with servings per day. SOURCE: U.S. Department of Agriculture.

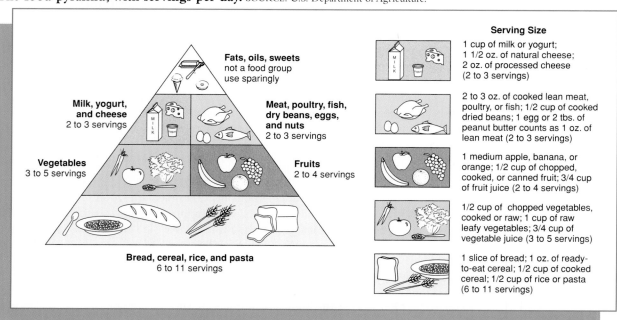

Dairy products and meat, along with other protein-laden foods, are needed in less but equal proportions for energy and the growth and repair of body tissue. However, many of these foods are relatively high in fat. Animal fats, such as those found in red meat, milk, butter, and cheese, are most highly saturated and are thought to increase the amount of cholesterol in the blood. In contrast, the fat in chicken, fish, and turkey is largely unsaturated, and most of it is in the skin, which you don't have to eat. From a healthy standpoint these polyunsaturated fats are preferable. In addition, a wide variety of vegetable protein is found in dry beans, peas, and nuts.

Fats, such as those contained in salad dressings, and sweets, consumed in candies and soft drinks, provide calories but little else nutritionally and should be used sparingly.

Our bodies also require certain amounts of vitamins and minerals. Many people take daily vitamin supplements along with their meals. Yet anyone who eats a reasonably balanced diet will get the required vitamins and minerals. In the case of salt, too much is harmful, especially if you have high blood pressure. Fortunately, there is an increasing number of low-sodium products on the market. You may also be surprised how easily you can become accustomed to food that has not been salted, either during cooking or at the table.

Since the human digestive tract is unable to digest fiber, the presence of fiber in the diet provides bulk to help the large intestine carry away body wastes. In turn, this function helps to prevent the difficulties of diverticular disease and may help prevent cancer of the large intestine. Actually, there are two kinds of fiber, each from different food sources, with varying modes of actions. On the one hand, foods rich in *bran* (whole-grain breads and cereals) contain cellulose, which usually benefits the lower bowel. On the other hand, many *fruits* (apples, oranges, and bananas) and *vegetables* (peas, carrots, and potatoes) contain pectin and gum, which tend to lower blood sugar and cholesterol (Rosenfeld, 1986).

We also need water. Perhaps you're already aware that our bodies are approximately half water. But did you know that we lose up to 4 pints of water each day? We lose water through the moisture in our breath and through sweat, urine, and bowel movements. Naturally, this liquid must be replaced; but we do not need to drink 4 pints of fluids because about 70 percent of our food is water. There is a greater risk of dehydration when we exercise, however, especially if the weather is hot.

GETTING ENOUGH SLEEP

When Amanda was in college, she sometimes stayed up all night to study for a major exam. Have you ever stayed up all night? Perhaps as Amanda once did, you've missed several consecutive nights of sleep. Although the effects of sleep deprivation vary from one person to another, they are not as drastic as we once thought. Deprived of sleep, most people make greater errors on routine tasks and experience increased drowsiness, a strong desire to sleep, and a tendency to fall asleep easily. When they finally fall asleep, chances are they'll sleep a few hours longer than usual. But extra hours of sleep won't make up the total sleep time lost. Our sleep/wake cycles follow a biochemical clock in our makeup designed to help us conserve energy. Reestablishing our natural sleep cycle is more important than trying to make up all the hours of lost sleep. We can accommodate ourselves to a variety of changes such as shift work, jet lag, and all night study sessions. These adjustments take a toll on our bodies as well as our sense of well-being. How much sleep do you need? Does it vary from other individuals' needs such as Amanda's? Although the average person sleeps about seven hours each night, the need for sleep varies from one person to another. You're probably getting enough sleep if you

BOX 5–5

CAN'T GET TO SLEEP?

Most of us have trouble falling asleep occasionally. For some, especially older adults, it's a recurring problem. Although there is no magical solution to this age-old complaint, here are some suggestions.

- Go to bed and get up at about the same time each day. Make sure you're allowing enough time for sleep.
- Relax before bedtime. Listen to music or practice yoga. But avoid strenuous exercise.
- Keep your bedroom conducive to sleep. Make sure it's quiet and dark and at a suitable temperature.
- Avoid alcohol and sleeping pills. Although these may put you to sleep sooner, they interfere with your normal sleep cycle.
- Take a lukewarm bath before bed. Hot or cold showers tend to be too stimulating. Sleep is induced when the body's core temperature falls, so you can artificially induce this by taking a warm bath.
- When you're having trouble falling asleep, count sheep or think of something pleasant that will distract you from worrying.
- Take some honey, which releases serotonin, the biochemical that induces sleep and relaxation.
- Don't stay awake fretting that sleeplessness will harm your health.
- If your home remedies don't work, seek professional help at a sleep center.

(1) wake up spontaneously, (2) feel well rested, and (3) don't have to struggle through periods of sleepiness during the day. Perhaps you have difficulty sleeping. Box 5–5 provides tips for falling asleep faster and better.

We also need to dream, though the amount of dream time diminishes as we get older. Young adults such as Amanda spend about one-fourth of their total sleep time in dreams. Each person's sleeping pattern alternates between various stages of sleep, with the deepest, most restful sleep (stage 4) occurring within the first hour or so after falling asleep. During the night, sleep alternates between **REM** (rapid eye movement) **sleep,** in which our muscles twitch and our hearts beat faster, and various stages of non-REM sleep. (See Figure 5–6.) Dreams occur more frequently and in greater vividness and detail (including color) in REM sleep. Because the stages of REM sleep and dreaming grow progressively longer toward the end of our sleep, we often awake in the morning toward the end of a dream. We may remember that last dream, but we will probably have forgotten the others unless we've learned how to recall our dreams. Amanda kept a dream diary and found that her memory for her dreams improved with time.

Do all dreams have meaning? The experts disagree. Most of us are familiar with Freud's wish-fulfillment theory, in which dreams are regarded as expressions of our repressed impulses or conflicts. Interestingly, our dreams are more likely to reflect themes of aggression, failure, and misfortune than friendliness, success, and luck. More recent and controversial neurological theories hold that dreams are mostly the result of spon-

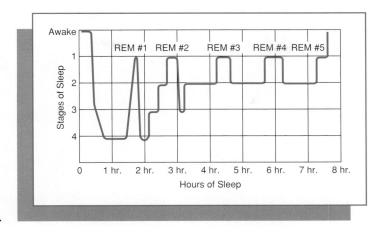

FIGURE 5–6
Stages of sleep.

taneous activity of neurons in the pons area of the brain such that dreams have little or no psychological meaning. Another theory, cognitive theory, holds that dreams are related to the processes of thinking, learning, and memory. According to this theory, the more we learn during the day, the more we need to dream at night, which may help to explain the student's familiar complaint of never having enough sleep.

KEEPING PHYSICALLY FIT

What comes to mind when you think of **physical fitness?** Do you imagine some muscular person lifting weights? Or do you think of people jogging or running along the road? Whatever you imagine, chances are that it represents only part of overall physical fitness. Actually, physical fitness is the entire human organism's ability to function efficiently and effectively, and it includes at least 11 different components (Corbin & Lindsey, 1985). There are 5 *health-related* fitness components (body composition or the ratio of muscle to fat, cardiovascular fitness, flexibility, muscular endurance, and strength) and 6 *skill-related* fitness components (agility, balance, coordination, power, reaction time, and speed). Each of these components contributes to our overall physical fitness, helping us to work more effectively, enjoy leisure activities, and stay healthy (J. D. Brown, 1991). Physical fitness also provides us with a sense of mastery and helps us overcome sad moods. In fact, fitness often inspires positive thoughts (Erber & Therriault, 1993).

Although there is some relationship among these components, people may excel in one aspect of fitness without necessarily having the others. For example, John, Amanda's brother who lifts weights, has exceptional muscular strength and power, but he does not have above-average cardiovascular fitness. In contrast, Linda, a friend of Amanda and a dance teacher, has good flexibility and coordination but lacks muscular strength in the upper part of her body.

Few of us are likely to achieve the ideal of total physical fitness. Given the limitations of time and our varied responsibilities, most of us must settle for an optimal level of fitness that will promote good health and a sense of well-being. Whatever goal we choose, we must remember that optimal physical fitness is not possible without regular exercise. Even then there is no single exercise program that is best suited for everyone. Each of us has different needs, priorities, and work schedules. In selecting your personal exercise program, you may find it helpful to observe the following points:

*It's important to keep
physically fit.*

1. *Identify your personal physical fitness needs.* A good way to do so is to consult someone in the physical education department of your college or a specialist in one of the physical fitness centers in your community. There are also books with exercises that help you to assess your fitness (see Corbin & Lindsey, 1985).

2. *Select personalized physical exercises to make exercise more enjoyable.* Choose physical activities that are related to your interests, needs, and personality. If you are a sociable person, consider a group activity such as volleyball. If you're not inclined toward competitive sports, select an activity that does not require a great deal of physical skill, such as walking, jogging, running, cycling, swimming, or home calisthenics. Finally, choose an activity that feels good to *you,* regardless of what others do.

3. *Vary your activities.* By varying your activities you can include ones that will develop different aspects of physical fitness. This variation also helps to keep exercise interesting and enjoyable. Usually, changes in the weather and the seasons along with availability of facilities suggest some variation in your exercise program.

4. *Exercise regularly.* It's best to set aside a time and place for your exercise activities, making it part of your daily routine. It's also important to perform your exercises to a level that will promote optimal fitness, usually a minimum of 20 to 30 minutes three times a week at the heart-training pulse rate. For healthy people in youth to middle age, the rule of thumb is that your *maximum* possible heart rate is 220 beats a minute *minus* your age. At least 60 percent of that heart rate is regarded as the *minimum* level to get some benefit from aerobic exercise; about 75 percent of that rate is the prudent upper level for the heart-training rate (Bennett et al., 1987). Remember to allow sufficient time to warm up to this level and wind down gradually.

5. *Periodically evaluate and modify your exercise program.* As time passes your needs and interests change. Shifts in your work schedule and family responsibilities may also dictate a change in your exercise program. Then, too, your age and overall level of stress should be kept in mind. Listen to your body. Assess how you feel.

Physical fitness is a vital part of the sense of wholeness mentioned earlier. But from all that we've said, it should also be clear that our overall well-being includes other considerations, such as our eating habits, work schedules, lifestyles, awareness of health hazards and stress, personal attitudes, and morale. We've also stressed the importance of each person taking responsibility for his or her own health, as well as recognizing the limits of our control over illness. Most important of all is the realization that the pursuit of wellness, though this is never fully achieved, may enable each of us to function better than we would have otherwise.

FINDING SOCIAL SUPPORT

One other means by which we can usually remain healthy is to affiliate with others. Individuals who are sociable such as Amanda are generally healthier than those who are not. For example, married people and those who live with others are healthier than individuals who live alone (Bishop, 1994). On the other hand, House, Lander, and Umberson (1988) studied 37,000 people in three different countries. Those individuals who were socially isolated were at greater risk for health problems than those who were socially engaged. Social support is also related to fewer sports injuries (R. E. Smith, Smoll, & Ptacek, 1990), decreased risk of heart disease in the elderly (Uchino, Kiecolt-Glaser, & Cacioppo, 1992), and better immune system functioning (Kiecolt-Glaser & Glaser, 1995). Some caution is needed here, though, because socializing and seeking

Individuals who socialize with others often report feeling healthier than those who do not affiliate with others.

social support is not for everyone. Other research demonstrates that individuals who were securely attached as children cope effectively with social support but those who were ambivalently or avoidantly attached may be uncomfortable seeking social support as adults (Mikulincer & Florian, 1995).

SUMMARY

BODY IMAGE

Although Americans may be healthier and feel fitter than ever, they are not necessarily satisfied with their looks. Weight is a major factor, with about one-half of men and women being dissatisfied with their weight. Many Americans are dissatisfied with their bodies because their weight is at odds with the prevailing ideal of slimness in our society. A somewhat higher proportion of women than men are dissatisfied with their looks, largely because our society encourages women to hold themselves to a stricter standard of thinness than men. At the same time, surveys show that men's and women's psychological well-being or self-esteem is more closely tied to their emphasis on fitness and health than to their appearance.

PSYCHOLOGICAL FACTORS AND PHYSICAL ILLNESS

The growing acceptance of the mind-body unity suggests that psychological factors may play a significant role in almost any physical ailment, not just in the traditional psychosomatic illnesses. The detrimental effects of stress tend to weaken our immune system, thereby making us more susceptible to illness. At the same time, there is increasing evidence that we may bolster our resistance to stress and illness by harnessing the powers of the mind—our thoughts, attitudes, and emotions.

Other major health hazards are obesity, cigarette smoking, and alcohol and drug abuse. Obesity, which affects about one-fourth of Americans, is associated with an increased risk of illness and death from a variety of illnesses, including diabetes, high blood pressure, and coronary heart disease. Only about one-third of all adult men and one-fourth of all adult women now smoke, a rate down from earlier years. Teenage smoking, however, is on the rise. Cigarette smoking is a major factor in heart disease, lung cancer, emphysema, and other fatal illnesses. In contrast, three-fourths of American men and almost two-thirds of women drink alcoholic beverages. Automobile accidents involving alcohol are still a leading cause of death among youths, and half of the occupied beds in American hospitals are filled by people with alcohol-related ailments.

COPING WITH ILLNESS

In evaluating the seriousness of our body complaints, we tend to rely on a decision-making process with three stages: (1) noticing and interpreting symptoms, (2) seeking professional help when needed, and (3) adhering to the prescribed treatment. Individuals differ in their tendency to label body aches and pains as symptoms, with introverted, anxious, and overly self-conscious people reporting more symptoms than better-adjusted people. People are more likely to see a doctor when they have severe, disabling symptoms rather than minor ones, especially in the lower half of the body, though men are generally more reluctant than women to do so. As many as half of those who get professional help do not complete the prescribed treatment for a variety of reasons.

PROMOTING WELLNESS

There is an increased emphasis on optimal health and wellness rather than simply the absence of illness. To be healthy is to have the full use of one's body and mind, despite an occasional bout of illness—to be alert, energetic, and happy to be alive even in old age. An important factor in the pursuit of positive health is the willingness to take charge of our own health, including greater personal responsibility in all matters pertaining to health.

An integral part of a health-producing personality is practicing good health habits. Eating sensibly involves both the amount and the kind of food we eat, including a balanced diet that provides the necessary nutrition and calories for someone of our age, size, and lifestyle. Keeping physically fit usually involves following a personalized exercise program especially suited to our interests and needs. Social contact and support is also very healthy for most people. The pursuit of wellness, though it is rarely fully achieved, may enable each of us to function better than we would have otherwise.

SCORING KEY FOR THE SOCIAL ATTITUDES SCALE

These items test how much you believe that appearance matters. Score your responses as follows:

For items 1, 2, 3, 5, 7, and 8, give yourself a zero if you said "strongly disagree"; a 1 for "disagree somewhat" and so forth; up to a 6 for "strongly agree."

For items 4, 6, and 9, reverse the scoring. In other words, give yourself a zero for "strongly agree"; a 1 for "agree somewhat" and so forth; up to a 6 for "strongly disagree."

Add together your points for all nine questions. A score of 46 or higher means that you are susceptible to being influenced by the great importance today's society places on appearance.

SELF-TEST

1. The greatest proportion of men and women feel the most dissatisfied with their
   a. face
   b. upper torso
   c. mid-torso
   d. height

2. A positive body image is strongly associated with
   a. self-esteem
   b. height
   c. intelligence
   d. sex

3. The prevalence of obesity among American adults tends to rise with higher
   a. education
   b. age
   c. socioeconomic status
   d. income

4. At least one of every five chronic heavy drinkers of alcohol develops
   a. diabetes
   b. heart attack
   c. throat cancer
   d. cirrhosis of the liver

5. People most likely to label their physical symptoms as an illness are high in
   a. neuroticism
   b. self-esteem
   c. extroversion
   d. sensation seeking

6. About half of the people who discover they have dangerously high blood pressure
   a. die within three months
   b. seek professional help for it
   c. become depressed over their condition
   d. complete the prescribed treatment

7. Assuming greater responsibility for your health involves
   a. getting periodic checkups
   b. not using doctors
   c. not asking doctors questions
   d. using only generic drugs

8. People with high blood cholesterol tend to eat a lot of food with
   a. carbohydrates
   b. proteins
   c. animal fats
   d. minerals

9. To achieve any benefit in cardiovascular fitness, you need to exercise your heart at a minimum rate of
   a. 60 percent of your maximum rate
   b. 220 minus your age
   c. 75 percent of your maximum rate
   d. 120 plus your age

10. Finding social support
    a. has no effect on health
    b. has little effect on health
    c. has negative effects on health
    d. usually has positive effects on health

EXERCISES

1. *Examine yourself in a mirror.* Undress and look at yourself in a full-length mirror. First, move up to the mirror and examine your face closely. What do you most notice about your face? Then step back and examine your entire body. Turn around slowly, looking at yourself from each side and then at your rear. Which aspects of your body do you like the most? Are there parts of your body you have difficulty accepting? All things considered, how satisfied are you with your body?

2. *Do you practice good eating habits?* Describe your eating habits in terms of the calories consumed each day and a balanced diet. If you're not sure how many calories you consume, keep a daily count for at least 3 days and take an average. How does your calorie count compare to the average for someone like yourself as indicated in the text? Do you also choose foods from each of the major food areas as described in the chapter?

3. *Describe your personal exercise habits.* How much exercise do you get in the course of your daily activities? Would you agree that everyone needs to be physically active on a regular basis? If you have a personalized exercise program, describe it in a paragraph or two. Indicate whether or not you exercise your heart to the optimal training rate for at least 20 minutes three times a week.

4. *Identify your biggest health hazard.* Are you guilty of one of the common health hazards, such as overeating, eating unbalanced meals, smoking, drinking, or drug abuse? If so, what are you doing about it? Try eliminating this hazard for 5 consecutive days and see if you feel better about yourself and your health.

5. *Do you suffer from a chronic ailment?* Do you have to cope with some type of chronic or recurring condition, such as an allergy, asthma, arthritis, hypertension, diabetes, migraine headaches, or ulcers? How well are you managing such ailments? Are you aware of the psychosocial factors that may influence your ailments, such as environmental stress and your emotions? What are you doing to improve your condition?

6. *How much control do you exercise over your health?* Do you believe you can minimize your chances of getting sick by practicing good nutrition, regular exercise, positive attitudes, and stress management? Or do you feel that coming down with a cold or the flu is mostly a matter of luck?

QUESTIONS FOR SELF-REFLECTION

1. Which part of your body or face has been the most difficult for you to accept?
2. Do you take care of your body?
3. What aspect of your eating habits would you most like to change?
4. Do you enjoy regular, vigorous physical exercise?
5. What is your worst health hazard?
6. If you're a smoker, how many times have you tried to quit? What is it that keeps you from quitting permanently?
7. Are you aware that the use of alcohol easily becomes a health hazard? Be honest; do you have a drug or alcohol problem?
8. Do you often find that a cold or flu was preceded by a period of intense emotional stress?
9. Would you agree that a healthy body and a sound mind go together?
10. Were you securely attached as a child? Do you find that you prefer social support or would you rather cope with your problems alone?

FOR FURTHER INFORMATION

RECOMMENDED READINGS

BOSTON WOMEN'S HEALTH BOOK COLLECTION. (1992). *The new our bodies, ourselves.* New York: Simon & Schuster. A comprehensive, down-to-earth book for women of all ages.

DAVIS, R. G. (1995). *The psychology of illness: In sickness and in health.* Washington, DC: American Psychological Association. An introduction to health psychology written by an expert in the field.

FRIEDMAN, H. S. (1991). *The self-healing personality: Why some people achieve health and others succumb to illness.* New York: Holt. A health psychologist's lucid account of how our genes, habits, and emotions make us prone to health or disease.

PELLETIER, K. R. (1994). *Sound mind, sound body: A new model for lifelong health.* New York: Simon & Schuster. A book that takes a long-term and psychological approach to healthier living.

WALZ, J. A. (1995). *Quick fixes to change your life: Making healthy choices.* Midland, GA: Creative Health Services. A book to guide you through your decision making for a healthy life.

WEBSITES AND THE INTERNET

http://www.health.org/index.htm: A website for links to health-related information including information on alcohol and drug abuse.

http://www.dietitian.com/ibw/ibw.html: A doctor's website where you can find personalized information about what you need to do to reach your diet goals.

http://www.healthfinder.gov: A site provided by the government that you can utilize to find information prepared by health agencies under various health topics.

http://www.cdcgov/nchswww/nchshome.htm: Another government site but this one provides health data from the National Center for Health Statistics.

http://www.amhrt.org/index.html: The link to the American Heart Association where you can find quizzes about heart disease, information about diets, and so forth.

CHAPTER

6

Self-Concept

After completing this chapter, you should be able to

1. Distinguish between self-image and ideal self.
2. Describe the core tendency toward self-consistency.
3. Identify several personal characteristics associated with high and low self-esteem.
4. Explain the self-enhancement and self-verification theories regarding feedback solicited from others.
5. Discuss how our self-concepts are affected by social and cultural influences.
6. List three ways we may use criticism for personal growth.
7. Discuss the importance of greater self-direction and self-acceptance in personal growth.

Shandra was shopping with a friend. She stopped to admire the clothes in a shop window. "Let's go in," suggested her friend. They entered the store and browsed around for a few minutes. Then Shandra tried on a pair of jeans. Looking at herself in the mirror, she noticed her hair was in disarray. She instinctively straightened it so that it appeared more the way she wanted it to look. She then noticed that she must have gained 10 or 15 pounds and that her usual size was too tight. She knew she couldn't lose that much weight in a few minutes, so she tried various ways of reconciling her appearance in the mirror with her self-image. She first asked her friend how she looked in the jeans, and her friend replied, "Not bad, but they may be a little tight around your rear end." She then tried on a larger size. But the very idea bothered her. She then decided to put off buying new clothes to avoid looking at herself in the mirror. She was also inspired to resume her weight-loss program. One thing is clear from Shandra's shopping spree—the discrepancy between self-concept and the image in the mirror has a powerful influence on behavior.

What Is the Self-Concept?

Essentially, the **self-concept** is the overall image or awareness we have of ourselves. It includes all those perceptions of "I" and "me," together with the feelings, beliefs, and values associated with them. As such, the self-concept is actually a cluster of selves, even though we habitually refer to it in the singular. Ordinarily we take our self-concept for granted, as when we are engaged in an activity at work or play. At other times we are very much aware of ourselves, as when we're making an important decision or taking on a heavy responsibility. We may become acutely self-conscious whenever we experience a discrepancy between our self-image and the way we appear to others. In

Self-image is the way we see ourselves, which may or may not be consistent with our ideal self or the way we aspire to be.

all of these instances, the self-concept exerts a powerful influence, affecting the way we perceive, judge, and behave.

The self-concept provides us with our personal identity or sense of who we are. Even though situations and people around us change, our self-concept reassures us that we are basically the same person we were yesterday. Our self-image is more real to us than our bodies, and it governs the way we experience our bodies. Our sense of identity is so important to us that we resist anyone or anything that threatens it. Even the fear of death itself may not be a fear of suffering or of the unknown so much as it is the deep fear that our personal identity will be dissolved—which is inconceivable to us.

Research on how we incorporate information about ourselves into our self-concept suggests just this, that we actively manage our self-concept such that we try to maintain a positive view of ourselves. We typically seek positive information about ourselves. Shandra was pleased, for example, that her friend said that the jeans almost fit. When confronted with ambiguous information, we generally choose to interpret it in the most positive way (Sedikides, 1993). In other words, psychologists would contend that most people adopt a self-serving attributional bias. *Attribution* is the process of attributing or ascribing the cause of some event. We can make internal attributions to the self or external attributions to the environment. With regard to ourselves, we commonly choose

self-serving attributions. Self-serving attributions are those that glorify the self or conceive of the self as causing the good outcomes that come our way. For example, we often take personal credit for our successes but blame external causes for our failures.

How many selves we choose to distinguish within our overall self-concept varies by the individual. At a general level, however, it is common to identify *body image,* the awareness of my body; the **self-image,** the self I see myself to be; the **ideal self,** the self I'd like to be; and my **social selves,** the way I feel others see me. Because body image was discussed in the last chapter, let's begin here by looking at the self-image and the ideal self. We'll examine the importance of our social selves in a later section of this chapter.

SELF-IMAGE

Self-image is the way I see myself. It is the self I think I am. It is made up of highly personal self-images. Because it is so private, each of us is an expert on our self-image—however realistic or unrealistic our perception may be.

Our self-image is made up of the many self-perceptions we have acquired growing up, especially in our formative years. It is mostly influenced by the way we are seen and treated by significant others, especially by our parents. When we were young and impressionable, we tended to internalize what they thought of us, their judgments and expectations, and regard ourselves accordingly. Ohannessian, McCauley, Lerner, Lerner, and von Eye (1994) found that young adolescents who had high levels of self-worth also had good coping techniques, peer support, and came from families with which they were satisfied. On the other hand, adolescents who had poor family adjustment were more likely to report higher levels of depression and anxiety. For example, imagine a mother who resented having to take care of her children and constantly yelled, "Don't do that, stupid!" "What's wrong with you?" "You're going to be the death of me yet." Can you imagine how her children felt about themselves after years of repeated exposure to such remarks? Would you be surprised to learn that they were troublemakers at home and at school? On the other hand, although Shandra was a young Black woman, she grew up in a supportive family who instilled in her a sense of pride about her African American heritage. They also taught Shandra that the way to a better life was through education and good grades.

We tend to revise our self-images through later experience with others, especially with our friends, teachers, and spouses. One of Shandra's friends suffered from a low opinion of herself, partly because of overly critical parents. With time, though, she began seeing herself in a new way. Through doing more things on her own and sharing with her friends, she began appreciating her good points and acquired a more positive view of herself. She even got to the point of being able to shrug off her parents' sarcastic remarks, much to her parents' amazement.

IDEAL SELF

The ideal self is the self I'd like to be, including my aspirations, moral ideals, and values. According to the psychoanalytic view, we are not fully aware of our ideal self because we have acquired much of it by identifying with parental demands and prohibitions during the formative years of childhood. Accordingly, many of the "shoulds" and "should nots" of our conscience represent unconscious and unrealistic demands that may keep us from growing up. An example is a college classmate of Shandra's, a perfectionist who felt he must make all As to please his parents.

Ordinarily, as we grow up, it's best to reexamine the shoulds and oughts we've assimilated from our parents and others during the formative years. Why? Because if our ideal self is quite different from how others see us, the result is social anxiety, an unpleasant emotion (Sanchez-Bernardos & Sanz, 1992). With experience and maturity, our aspirations should increasingly represent self-chosen goals and values that express in a healthy, adult way what we've come to expect of ourselves. Accordingly, our ideal self may serve as an incentive for us to do our best, as with Shandra's other classmate who puts forth her best effort in the hope of entering medical school rather than pleasing her parents. But if we fail to live up to our ideal self, as is often the case, it is healthy to feel we have a choice either to redouble our efforts to achieve our aspirations or to modify them in the direction of more fruitful incentives. Ordinarily, we think of having to change our self-image and behavior better to match our ideals. Indeed, our ideal self remains more consistent across time than our self-image. But in those instances when our aspirations prove to be excessive or unrealistic, it may be more appropriate for us to modify our ideal self as a way of furthering our growth and self-esteem.

How would you characterize your own ideal self? Do you tend to be idealistic and rather hard on yourself when you fall short of your aims? Or are you more down-to-earth and practically minded, shrugging off disappointments with yourself and giving it another try? To check on your perceptions, you might do the exercise on self-image and ideal self in Figure 6–1.

MULTIPLE SELVES

Actually, the overall self-concept, as indicated earlier, is an organized cluster of selves, so it would be more accurate to speak of our multiple selves. As such, the self-concept includes hundreds, perhaps thousands, of self-perceptions in varying degrees of clarity and intensity that we have acquired in growing up. Psychologists know that some individuals have more complex and differentiated selves than others (Linville, 1985). For example, Shandra's self-concept included her gender role, her racial identity, her concept of herself as a student, her attitudes and values and whether they were respected by society, and many other components. Much of the diversity of the self reflects our social roles, so that even the normal happy person wears "many masks," as we'll discuss later in this chapter. At the same time there are many other self-perceptions that are less clearly associated with social roles. Some self-images arise from the experience of our own bodies, as explained in the previous chapter. Others reflect needs, interests, traits, and habit patterns acquired through experience; and these self-images may be integrated within our overall self-concept in varying degrees. For instance, Shandra was ordinarily an easygoing person. Then one day she discovered a friend had misinterpreted her intentions. She became angry and told her friend how she felt. A couple of hours later, after an apology from her friend, she appeared calm again. Her friend thought, "She certainly has changed!" But when you stop and think, it's not that Shandra had changed so much as that she had simply expressed different *aspects* of herself at different times.

We seldom like to think of ourselves as made up of different parts or selves. Even if we acknowledge this fact in theory, we tend to forget it in practice. Making due allowance for the diversity of selves, both in ourselves and others, may help to account for some of the inconsistency in human behavior. It may also help to avoid the endless circle of blame and guilt that undermines good relationships.

Because our various selves exhibit a certain consistency or organizing pattern as a whole, we refer to them collectively as a self-concept. But it should be clear that the

FIGURE 6–1

SELF-IMAGE AND IDEAL SELF

This is an exercise to measure the correspondence between your self-image and ideal self.

Reproduce the page containing items A through P. Then cut out the 16 cards or rectangles as indicated by the lines, and put them on a table or desk in random order.

First, you're to get a profile of your self-image, or the self you see yourself to be. To do so, arrange the cards in a line, either from top to bottom or left to right. At one end, place the statement that you think describes you best. Then arrange the remaining cards in order, ranging from the next most true and so forth to the least true at the end. Then record the rank number of each item in the column labeled "self." For instance, if you placed card A in the eighth position, write "8" next to card A.

Next, repeat this procedure in regard to your ideal self. That is, arrange the cards in the order that describes the self you'd like to be, ranging from the card you wish were most true of you at one end to that which is least true of your ideal self at the other end. When you've completed your rankings, record the order of the items or cards in the column labeled "ideal."

When you finish ranking the cards and recording the numbers, consult the scoring key at the end of the chapter.

I'm a likable person A	I have sex appeal I
I'm rather self-centered at times B	I'm an anxious person J
I'm physically attractive C	I have above-average intelligence K
I have a strong need for approval D	I'm shy in groups L
I'm usually a hard worker E	I have a good sense of humor M
I daydream too much F	I'm sometimes dishonest N
I can be assertive when necessary G	I have a good disposition O
I often feel discouraged H	I gossip a lot P

Item	Self	Ideal	Differences
A			
B			
C			
D			
E			
F			
G			
H			
I			
J			
K			
L			
M			
N			
O			
P			
		Sum of differences	

self-concept is more of a hypothesis or theory we use to explain how these selves function in our experience. People with a fragmented, incoherent view of themselves—such as the severely emotionally disturbed—are often unsure of who they are and may behave in a highly inconsistent manner. In extreme cases, as with multiple personality disorders, individuals alternate between two or more distinct personalities, each with its own name, habits, memories, and behaviors. In contrast, those of us who have achieved a more desirable integration of our various selves may feel a clearer sense of personal identity and behave in a somewhat more consistent manner—"somewhat" because, as we've just described, even the healthiest person's psychic makeup includes a considerable degree of inconsistency.

 ## Core Characteristics of the Self-Concept

Critics of the notion of self-concept complain that traditional psychology regards the self-concept as a straightjacket, which once acquired during our formative years resists further efforts at change. A more appropriate approach, they contend, would be to view the self-concept as a loosely fitting garment that is continually being altered with experience. Actually, there is some truth to both views. In this section, we'll focus on the core tendency of the self-concept to maintain and perpetuate itself. In the next section, we'll look at some of the major ways our self-concepts can and do change.

Once established, the core of the self-concept exhibits a high degree of stability, as seen in the consistent ways we perceive ourselves over time (B. W. Roberts & Donahue, 1994). Peripheral aspects of the self can, and often do, change rather quickly. For example, Shandra never thought of herself as graceful. In college, she took a ballet class and found herself the best in the class and actually enjoying ballet. She came to think of herself as more graceful. The core of the self, which comprises those aspects of ourselves we regard as very important to us, tends to perpetuate itself. Shandra was very proud of her African American heritage and little could shake her pride in her racial identity. Essentially, the self-concept functions as a filter through which everything we see or hear passes. It thereby exerts a selective, circular influence on our experience, so that we tend to perceive, judge, and act in ways that are consistent with our self-concept.

SELF-CONSISTENCY

This characteristic tendency toward **self-consistency** is best understood in relation to Carl Rogers's (1980) view of the phenomenal self, as visualized in Figure 6–2. The circle on the right represents the total experience of the organism, including sensory and body experience. The circle on the left represents the self-concept, which has been acquired through interaction with significant others, mainly parents, throughout the formative years of development. It is fully available to awareness. These two circles, representing the typical or "normal" person, do not fully coincide because the self-concept develops in response to what Rogers calls "conditions of worth." That is, instead of growing up in an atmosphere of unconditional acceptance, most of us feel we are loved and accepted only if we meet certain expectations and approvals. Whatever is acceptable to our parents and other significant persons in our lives becomes incorporated into our self-concept. In turn, our self-concept functions as a filter through which everything we see or hear passes.

Experiences that are consistent with both our sensory reactions (circle B) and our self-concept (circle A) tend to be labeled or "symbolized" accurately and admitted fully

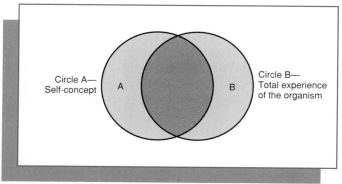

FIGURE 6–2
The interaction of the self-concept and the environment. SOURCE: From Carl R. Rogers, *Client-Centered Therapy* (Boston: Houghton Mifflin, 1951), p. 526. Copyright © 1951 by Houghton Mifflin Company. Reprinted with permission.

into our conscious awareness. These self-perceptions make up the core of our self-concept and are visualized by the shaded area, where the two circles overlap in Figure 6–2. Experiences that are not consistent with both our sensory experience and our self-concept are perceived more selectively. Such experiences are either distorted or kept from awareness.

When we experience something that is consistent with our self-concept but is not confirmed by our own sensory reactions, we perceive and label such experiences in a distorted fashion, as if they were part of us. Such experiences are visualized by the area in circle A outside the shaded area. They are part of our learned self-concept. For example, Shandra was influenced by the stereotyped gender roles in our society and believed herself to be inept at math. Each time she worked with numbers, she thought she did poorly. She readily assimilated such experiences of failure because they were consistent with her existing self-concept. Here the self-concept distorted her actual experience, so that she actually believed she was no good at math even though that distorted perception of herself was not valid.

Experiences that are not consistent with our learned self-concept are perceived as too threatening and are not even recognized as self-experiences. Consequently, they are not accurately perceived or labeled but are kept from awareness, either in part or in whole. Here, denial is roughly comparable to the concept of repression in Freudian terms and refers to an unconscious exclusion of experience because of the threat associated with it. Such experiences are visualized in the diagram by the area in circle B outside the shaded area.

Suppose Shandra, who believed she was no good at math, were required to take two semesters of math as part of her major studies. She began the course with a determination to do well, accompanied by a vague fear that she wouldn't. At first, she worked hard and even discovered to her surprise that she enjoyed the precision of mathematical thinking. Then she received her grade on her first test. A 96! "Me doing well in math?" she wondered. "How can this be? Maybe the instructor made a mistake in grading the papers. Maybe he likes me or feels sorry for me. It's probably dumb luck. It won't happen again." Like the rest of us, she would probably rely on a variety of such self-justifying mechanisms to make this experience acceptable to her existing self-concept.

In doing so she would also deny her actual experience of success, and thereby fail to discover her personal potential for math. However, suppose she completed both semesters of math with As and got a job working with computers. Chances are she would gradually revise her self-concept in a way that reflected her real ability in math, thereby incorporating aspects of herself previously denied.

SELF-ESTEEM

One of the most important aspects of the self-concept is our **self-esteem**—the personal evaluation of ourselves and the resulting feelings of worth associated with our self-concept. Self-esteem is affected by a variety of influences, ranging from formative childhood experiences in relation to our parents to our own standards or ideal self. For instance, individuals such as Shandra with high self-esteem generally were brought up by parents who were very accepting of them, expressed a lot of affection, and established firm but reasonable rules—all of which foster a positive self-image. Individuals with low self-esteem usually were brought up by parents who relied on parenting styles that were either overly strict, overly permissive, or inconsistent.

Our self-esteem is also influenced by success and failure, and perceptions of success and failure are significantly influenced by our self-esteem (J. D. Brown & Gallagher, 1992). A backlog of stored success enhances self-esteem, and repeated failure undermines it. At the same time, the impact of a particular achievement often depends on the process of social comparison with a reference group. For example, Shandra may have felt good about her ballet performance after earning the highest grade in her class. In contrast, her friend, Josie, who got an equally high grade in the same class, may feel less favorable about her performance because she compared her grade with a group of students in the advanced section of the same course. Thus, individuals with similar talents and success may vary in their self-esteem, depending on with whom they compare themselves. Table 6–1 will help you identify some of the signs of high and low self-esteem.

Although people customarily speak of self-esteem as a single entity—global esteem—our self-esteem also includes many compartmentalized or situation-specific

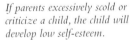

If parents excessively scold or criticize a child, the child will develop low self-esteem.

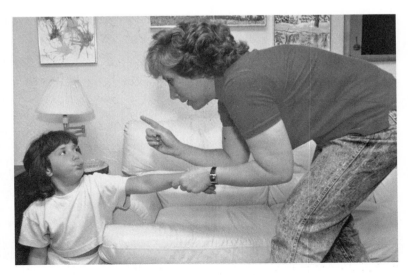

TABLE 6–1
HIGH AND LOW SELF-ESTEEM

Signs of high self-esteem	Signs of low self-esteem
Do you . . .	*Or, do you . . .*
like your appearance when you see yourself in the mirror?	avoid viewing yourself in the mirror?
feel comfortable with yourself most of the time?	feel discontented with yourself most of the time?
savor your accomplishments?	brag excessively or apologize about your achievements?
regard your failures as opportunities to learn?	make excuses for your failures?
express your opinions readily?	withhold your views, especially if asked?
listen to what others say, even if you disagree?	try to convince others of your views?
accept compliments graciously?	reject compliments or qualify them?
give credit to others when it's due?	envy others and put them down by sarcasm or gossip?
make realistic demands on yourself?	expect too much or too little of yourself?
give and receive affection generously?	withhold your affection out of fear of being hurt?

aspects, which vary according to circumstances. For instance, another of Shandra's friends, Mark, may enjoy self-confidence in playing tennis but lack confidence in regard to his writing skills in English composition. Yet another acquaintance of Shandra's, Cheryl, may feel confident in regard to her schoolwork, though this confidence also varies somewhat from one subject to another. At the same time, Cheryl may suffer from low self-esteem in regard to her weight. Thus, our overall self-esteem is more complex than ordinarily portrayed and fluctuates somewhat depending on the experiences of the moment.

Apparently, most people enjoy moderately high global self-esteem. They are generally pleased with themselves and make inferences about themselves that are slightly more positive than might be expected (Baumeister, Tice, & Hutton, 1989). Nevertheless, all of us some of the time, and a sizable minority most of the time, suffer from low self-esteem. In these instances people can be haunted by anxiety and self-doubt and report lower levels of happiness.

Self-esteem exerts a powerful influence on people's expectations, their judgments about themselves and others, and their behavior. People with high self-esteem are willing to test the validity of their inferences about themselves. Having a high level of **self-acceptance,** they tend to be accepting of others, including those with different opinions than themselves, and enjoy satisfying relationships with other people. They also expect to do well in their accomplishments, try hard, and tend to be successful in their careers. They are inclined to attribute their success to their abilities and to make due allowance for circumstances in interpreting their failures. As a result, people with high self-esteem generally enjoy a great deal of self-confidence and have a realistic assessment of their strengths and weaknesses. In contrast, people with low self-esteem are generally less willing to put their ideas about themselves to the test and are never really convinced of their own self-assessment. Furthermore, they tend to expect the worst, exert less effort on tasks—especially challenging, demanding ones—and achieve less success in their careers. Having low self-esteem, they are inclined to be overly sensitive about social rejection, often cutting others down to size by constant criticism and thereby alienating them. In turn, the preoccupation with rejection, imagined or real, further lowers their self-esteem, setting the stage for a vicious cycle of negative relationships.

Fortunately, self-esteem is not something you're born with or without. Rather, it is largely an acquired trait that you can improve, no matter how little you have to start with. Because self-esteem resides largely within yourself, ultimately you have the power to change it. However, one of the paradoxes of personal change is that only as you come to see and accept yourself as you are, warts and all, can you genuinely begin to grow. Then, too, be certain that your standards and expectations—your ideal self—against which you measure yourself are reasonable. Perfectionistic individuals who judge themselves by unrealistic standards constantly undermine their own self-esteem. Finally, although other people's reactions may influence your self-esteem through feedback and social comparison, you are the final authority on your own self-worth. As Seneca, the ancient philosopher, said, "What you think of yourself is much more important than what others think of you." To determine whether you are self-accepting, you may want to complete the scale in Figure 6–3.

FIGURE 6–3

THE SELF-ACCEPTANCE SCALE

According to proponents of self-theory, such as Carl Rogers and others, a high degree of self-acceptance and self-esteem is important to our well-being and social relationships. A high level of self-acceptance helps us to live spontaneously and to be more accepting of others. Low self-acceptance makes us more guarded and more critical of others.

Each of the following statements is suggestive of self-acceptance. After you read each statement, indicate how true or false it is for you by using the following code. Then to determine the meaning of your score, consult the scoring key at the end of the chapter.

1—completely true

2—mostly true

3—partly true, partly false

4—mostly false

5—completely false

_____ 1. I'd like it if I could find someone who would tell me how to solve my personal problems.

_____ 2. I don't question my worth as a person, even if I think others do.

_____ 3. When people say nice things about me, I find it difficult to believe they really mean it. I think maybe they aren't being sincere.

_____ 4. If there is any criticism or anyone says anything about me, I just can't take it.

_____ 5. I don't say much at social affairs because I'm afraid that people will criticize me or laugh if I say the wrong thing.

_____ 6. I realize that I'm not living very effectively, but I just don't believe I've got it in me to use my energies in better ways.

_____ 7. I look on most of the feelings and impulses I have toward people as being quite natural and acceptable.

_____ 8. Something inside me just won't let me be satisfied with any job I've done. If it turns out well, I get a smug feeling this is beneath me, I shouldn't be satisfied with it.

_____ 9. I feel different from other people. I'd like to have the feeling of security that comes from knowing I'm not too different from others.

_____ 10. I'm afraid that people I like will find out what I'm really like and be disappointed with me.

_____ 11. I am frequently bothered by feelings of inferiority.

_____ 12. Because of other people, I haven't been able to achieve as much as I should have.

_____ 13. I am quite shy and self-conscious in social situations.

_____ 14. In order to get along and be liked, I tend to be what people expect me to be rather than anything else.

_____ 15. I seem to have a real inner strength in handling things. I'm on a pretty solid foundation and it makes me pretty sure of myself.

_____ 16. I feel self-conscious when I'm with people who have a superior position to mine at work or school.

_____ 17. I think I'm neurotic or something.

_____ 18. Very often, I don't try to be friendly with people because I think they won't like me.

_____ 19. I feel that I'm a worthwhile person, on an equal level with others.

_____ 20. I can't avoid feeling guilty about the way I feel toward certain people in my life.

_____ 21. I'm not afraid of meeting new people. I feel that I'm a worthwhile person and there's no reason why they should dislike me.

_____ 22. I sort of only half believe in myself.

_____ 23. I'm very sensitive. When people say things I have a tendency to think they're criticizing me in some way, though later, when I think of it, they may not have meant anything like that.

_____ 24. I think I have certain abilities and other people say so too. But I wonder if I'm not giving them greater importance than they deserve.

_____ 25. I feel confident that I can do something about the problems that may arise in the future.

_____ 26. I tend to put on a show to impress people. I know I'm not the person I pretend to be.

_____ 27. I do not worry or condemn myself if other people pass judgment against me.

_____ 28. I don't feel very normal, but I want to feel normal.

_____ 29. When I'm in a group, I usually don't say much for fear of saying the wrong thing.

_____ 30. I have a tendency to sidestep my problems.

_____ 31. Even when people think well of me, I feel guilty because I know I must be fooling them—that if I were really myself, they wouldn't think well of me.

_____ 32. I feel that I'm on the same level as other people and that helps to establish good relations with them.

_____ 33. I feel that people are apt to react differently to me than they would normally react to other people.

_____ 34. I live too much by other people's standards.

_____ 35. When I have to speak to a group, I become self-conscious and have difficulty saying things well.

_____ 36. If I didn't always have such hard luck, I'd accomplish much more than I have.

SELF-ENHANCEMENT AND SELF-VERIFICATION

We receive a great deal of information about how people see us through our interactions with them. As a matter of fact, we often make deliberate attempts to elicit such information, whether through our actions or direct questioning. However, authorities have proposed different theories concerning the kind of reaction or feedback we solicit from others. According to **self-enhancement** theory, people will try to get positive feedback that affirms their own ideas about their positive qualities. In contrast, in accordance with **self-verification** theory, people want to preserve their own images (both positive and negative) of themselves and therefore elicit feedback that verifies or confirms their own self-perceptions. Thus, self-verification is important to us, in that it gives us a sense of stability in an unpredictable world. Also, such confirmation is vital to social interaction because if others see us as we see ourselves, they will have a better idea of how to treat us, what to expect of us, and so forth (Sileo & Baum, 1989).

To clarify the circumstances under which people engage in either of these behaviors (self-enhancement or self-verification), Swann, Pelham, and Krull (1989) conducted a series of studies to test the idea that people, regardless of their level of self-esteem, will seek favorable feedback about their positive self-views and negative feedback about their negative self-views. In one of these studies, each participant met in a group with three other people. Later, they were given a questionnaire to assess their reaction to each person, as well as feedback about the participant supposedly written by each of the three persons he or she had met. They were given three types of feedback from these partners: (1) favorable feedback on their best attribute (enhancing and verifying), (2) unfavorable feedback on their worst attribute (nonenhancing and verifying), and (3) favorable feedback on their worst attribute (enhancing but nonverifying). Afterward, each participant was asked to choose with which of the three persons he or she wanted to have more interaction.

People who like themselves are more accepting of and cooperative with others.

The researchers found that the participants preferred the enhancing and verifying partners most, followed by the nonenhancing and verifying partner, and the enhancing but nonverifying partner the least. Thus, it appears that most people prefer to hear information about themselves that is both positive and in line with their own views of themselves. That is, most people prefer and seek out positive feedback about themselves, but mostly for those attributes that they themselves view as positive because positive self-views are generally adaptive (Taylor & Brown, 1994). People will also accept negative evaluations if these confirm their own negative self-views (Sileo & Baum, 1989). In sum, people generally prefer to hear opinions that are positive but also supportive of their own views of themselves.

Is this true for women and minorities, two stigmatized groups in our society? In other words, is Shandra, a young African American woman, typical because she has high esteem or atypical? Let's look at **gender roles** and self-esteem first. Masculine traits initially appear more valued by American society, for example the traits of independence, decisiveness, and emotional stability. However, research on gender and esteem has not born out that men necessarily have higher esteem than women. In a large study of esteem and gender, Marsh and Byrne (1991) concluded that both masculine and feminine qualities contribute positively to self-concept but to different degrees depending on whether the particular aspect of self-concept is highly associated with the male sex role or the female sex role. Women's self-esteem, for example, is more affected by social relationships and men's self-esteem is more influenced by task success (Overholser, 1993). Men's and women's self-esteem levels are not necessarily different then.

Can the same be said for minorities? Is their esteem as high as that of White Americans? Based on their research, Crocker and Major (1989) say yes; self-esteem of minorities is just as high as that of Whites. The reason is that just as other individuals do, minorities also use some self-protective mechanisms for maintaining self-esteem. For example, members of **minority groups** often compare themselves to each other rather than to the White majority. Or many minority group members attribute negative feedback and failure to prejudice against their group rather than to personal failure.

 ## The Self-Concept and Personal Growth

In explaining the core characteristics of the self, we've emphasized the themes of continuity and self-consistency, which are highly valued attributes of personality, at least up to a point. As we've mentioned earlier, our self-concepts continue to change. Indeed, there is growing recognition that the cluster of selves comprised by the self-concept can and does change to a greater extent than previously realized.

Much of the change in our self-concept occurs with maturity, or the mellowing that comes with age and experience. But a great deal of change in our self-image comes from adapting to different people and situations. Different jobs, new friends, and a change in responsibilities, like marriage and parenting, all affect the way we see ourselves. Although we retain a stable core of self, the many self-perceptions that make up our overall self-concept are in a state of flux or change and are more readily influenced by current experience than previously thought. In this section, we'll explore how our self-concepts continue to change as a result of our personal aspirations, changing roles and behaviors, criticism from others, and greater self-direction.

THE SELF YOU'D LIKE TO BE

Americans spend millions of dollars every year in the hope of improving themselves, buying and trying self-help manuals and cassettes and attending workshops, not to mention academic courses in psychology. Often the changes promised in these self-help endeavors outstrip the actual help received. A comparative study of self-improvement techniques found that even though some unconventional methods such as sleep learning produce demonstrable change, others such as psychokinesis (mind over matter) exist only in the minds of the believers (M. Roberts, 1988). Shandra recognized this and decided that instead of buying books or joining Weight Watchers, she would lose weight in a way that would make her happy. She continued her ballet classes and in a year, without dieting, lost 10 pounds.

One of the more promising approaches to self-improvement consists of *visualizing* the person you'd like to become—the thin self, the confident self, or the rich self. Hazel Markus and her colleagues (Adelmann, 1988) have discovered that visualizing our "possible selves," including the desired as well as the feared selves, helps us not only to attain our goals but also to cope more effectively with the present. For instance, in one study, students were asked to imagine themselves in the future as either highly successful or a failure. They were asked to make their images as vivid as possible. One person thought of becoming a successful lawyer with her own swimming pool; another imagined working in a dead-end job in a rat-infested building. Then the students worked on difficult tasks, such as a challenging math problem or writing with their nondominant hand. The results showed that students who had imagined themselves as successful, presumably activating their positive possible selves, performed better than those who envisioned themselves as failures.

Visualizing our possible selves may also help us to cope with present life difficulties. In the same series of studies mentioned above, people who had experienced a recent life crisis, such as the breakup of a love relationship or the death of a loved one, were asked to choose between descriptions of themselves in both the present and the future. Then the participants were asked to rate how well they were recovering from their recent crises. As you might suspect, the crisis victims described their present selves mostly in negative terms. Those who were coping poorly also envisioned their future selves

Many advertisements are designed to make us unhappy with ourselves unless we use the advertised product.

even more negatively, for example, being weak and unattractive. However, those who were managing their crisis well imagined extremely positive future selves, such as being successful and attractive. A major implication is that we can create new images of ourselves, and this ability, in turn, may help us to handle our present lives more effectively.

Each of us varies in how we think of our possible selves. Some have clear-cut images of what they might be; others have ideas and feelings that are only dimly envisioned. To help realize your aim of self-improvement, you might elaborate the self or selves you'd like to be. Imagine, as vividly as possible, how you'll look, how you'll feel, and how you will act. It also helps to create an image of any feared self; that is, what would happen if you don't succeed. Think of the failed attempts to lose weight, the mediocre performances in school and at work, and the disappointments in love. In each instance, vivid mental images of our possible selves may help us to become the person we'd like to be, especially when accompanied by the appropriate efforts. Box 6–1 will help you think more about the person you would like to be.

OUR SOCIAL SELVES

One of the most common, though often underrated, ways our self-concept changes is through our interactions with people, including their perceptions and responses toward us. The term *social selves* refers to the impressions we think others have of us. It is the way we think they view us, which may or may not be an accurate representation of their views. Nevertheless, our perception of how others view us, in turn, greatly influences the way we see ourselves.

We have as many different social selves as there are distinct groups of persons about whose opinion we care, observed William James (1890/1950). As a result, we see ourselves somewhat differently with each person we meet. With a stranger, we may be guarded and unsure of ourselves, at least until we get to know what kind of person we're dealing with. A bossy, critical employer may make us feel anxious and inferior, but a close friend who admires and compliments us makes us feel confident and affectionate. It's not that we're being two-faced or untrue to ourselves. Rather, each of these people

---

BOX 6–1

VISUALIZE THE PERSON YOU'D LIKE TO BE

Select a quiet place where you can relax and have a few minutes to yourself. Then close your eyes and imagine, as vividly as possible, the kind of person you'd like to become.

How would you look?

What would you be wearing?

How would you feel?

Would you be happy, serious, or relaxed?

What would you be doing?

Where would you be?

You might repeat this exercise every night before you go to sleep—say, for a week. Do you notice any difference in yourself?

> Whenever two people meet there are really six people present. There is each person as he sees himself, each person as the other person sees him, and each person as he really is.
>
> William James

brings out a different aspect of ourselves. Realizing this fact, we might make a greater effort to seek out people who bring out the best in us and make us feel good about ourselves. For example, of all her professors, Shandra knew and liked best her ballet instructor who was very encouraging of her budding dance talent.

The way we see ourselves is also vitally affected by the way we behave in different roles and situations. Often, the way we see ourselves leads us to act in a given manner. But equally often, as Carol Tavris (1987) reminds us, we act in a certain way, and that action, in turn, changes the way we perceive ourselves and perhaps the way others see us. As a result, countless qualities—obedience, assertiveness, competitiveness, compassion, ambition, self-worth, and happiness—change remarkably with a change in our circumstances. For instance, interviews and statistics have shown that our jobs affect us more than we affect our jobs. Many aspects of work, such as routinization, the complexity of tasks, advancement, fringe benefits, and peers, significantly change our self-image, self-worth, job commitment, and moral standards. Thus, many qualities attributed to the self-concept are keyed to what we do rather than to our inner notions of what we are.

The realization that our sense of self is affected by social and cultural influences heightens the importance of our social roles and social relationships. Once we have chosen to associate with certain friends, select a lover or marriage partner, or attend a given school or job, the people involved help to shape the way we see ourselves. Are there overly critical people who devalue us? We should avoid them. Are there others who see the best in us? Perhaps we should seek them out more often. In both instances, we can change the way we see ourselves by modifying the social influences on our lives. It would be foolish to think we can change everything about ourselves in this way. But the notion of fluid, changing social selves reminds us that we have more possibilities for change and personal growth than we may be using.

LEARNING FROM CRITICISM

How do you feel when you are criticized? Do you feel angry and rejected? Do you feel resentful, even when you're in the wrong? For most people, the answer to these questions is yes. When people have been asked to finish the statement "When I am criticized . . ." typical responses include "I get upset," "I resent it," "I feel she doesn't love me anymore," and "I wonder when the ax will fall." Sound familiar? All too often, as these comments suggest, people feel that criticism is a personal attack that they must defend themselves against at all costs. As a result, they waste a lot of energy worrying about criticism, justifying themselves, and going to great lengths to avoid it.

Accepting criticism can become a valuable means of personal growth. For example, when asked to complete the statement cited earlier, some people make more positive responses. One woman said, "Criticism tells me where the other person is coming from, how he sees me, what he expects of me." An experienced executive said, "Your critics can tell you where you're going wrong before your friends can." A woman said, "When

I'm criticized, I try to figure out what the other person is trying to tell me, especially how I can improve my performance." At first, Shandra and some of her close friends thought that she had gained too much weight for ballet; however, once she realized how good she was at it, she viewed losing weight as a challenge rather than as something that prohibited her from doing well in the class. All these people have learned the valuable art of taking criticism constructively.

In the bestseller *Nobody's Perfect,* Hendrie Weisinger and Norman Lobsenz (1981) suggest many ways in which we can use criticism for personal growth. Each major strategy centers on familiar aspects of personality—our thoughts, feelings, and behavior.

- *View criticism as a valuable source of new information to be evaluated objectively.* Each time you're criticized, you don't necessarily have to rush out and change something about yourself. Instead, criticism should be taken as a cue that *may* require action. Even then, you must look beyond the surface of the criticism and ask yourself, "What is this person trying to tell me?" Ask yourself too, "How important is this criticism?" The more important the information is to you, the more likely you'll need to do something about it.

- *Consider also how many times a specific criticism is offered.* If you're frequently criticized for the same behavior by different people, there's a good chance that the criticism is valid and should be acted on.

- *Then, too, you must assess the source of criticism.* People often feel they're being criticized unfairly, especially if the other person is under a lot of stress. The more qualified the person is to judge your work, the more you should take criticism to heart. Yet even criticism spoken in frustration or anger may need to be heeded, but take into account the exaggerated emotion because of stress.

- *Weigh the pros and cons of acting on a criticism.* You should decide whether the benefits that come from acting on the criticism balance or outweigh the effort involved. For example, students who do poorly on tests may wonder whether it's worthwhile to follow the teacher's suggestion to get help in comprehension and note-taking skills. Yet if they continue to get low grades, their career goals may be in jeopardy.

- *Put the emotional energy aroused by criticism to work for you, not against you.* As mentioned earlier, emotional arousal tends to interfere with your ability to perform well, lowering your self-confidence as well. Instead, when criticized try to stay calm. Relax physically. Remind yourself that nobody is trying to hurt you. What this person is saying probably will be helpful. Then use your emotions as a source of energy to make the necessary changes. For example, whenever Shandra did something her boyfriend, Brad, disliked, he would yell, "That's stupid. How dumb can you be?" Shandra became upset and ignored his accusations as a way of justifying her actions. Gradually, Shandra learned to remain calm in the face of Brad's emotional outbursts. She would ask, "What is it you're objecting to?" or "How would you suggest handling this?" Responding in kind, Brad learned to give more specific criticisms, which Shandra found more helpful.

- *Finally, take positive steps to put the needed changes into action.* Don't waste energy defending yourself. Instead, listen carefully to what is being said. Ask for more information. Ask the person for suggested solutions to the criticism. You might ask for this information indirectly, such as, "If you were in my place, what would you do?" Or you might ask, more directly, "What would you like me to do?" People usually criticize something we're doing. But it often comes across as a personal attack because many people do not know how to give criticism constructively. So if someone says, "You're rude and inconsiderate," ask, "In what ways have I been inconsiderate?" In this way, you'll focus on something tangible that you can do, which in due time may lead to the desired changes in your self-image and reputation.

GREATER SELF-DIRECTION

Learning how to listen to others so that we'll grow and benefit from their criticism is difficult enough. Learning to listen to ourselves and be true to our own deepest desires and goals can be even more challenging, especially in a world full of people—parents, peers, politicians, and advertisers, among countless others—intent on making us into somebody else. Box 6–2 will help you learn to forgive yourself even when others won't. Carl Rogers (1961) once observed that beneath the bewildering complexity of problems

---

BOX 6–2

FORGIVING YOURSELF

Is it possible to forgive ourselves for the wrongs we've inflicted on others or the damage we've caused?

Lewis Smedes (1984), in his book *Forgive and Forget,* says it is not only possible but necessary that we forgive ourselves for past wrongs if we're to live fully in the present. Trying to evade past wrongs, repress our memories, or make excuses—not one of these has the staying power of forgiveness. Yet self-forgiveness is a difficult experience that does not usually occur overnight.

In the first place, the world works against those who would forgive themselves, because there are always people who want to see you live forever with whatever it is you've done. A lot of people want Nixon to suffer eternal punishment for what they see as his unforgivable sin.

It also takes tremendous courage to forgive ourselves. After all, who has the right to free us from the undeniable wrongs of our past? The answer is that we get the right to forgive ourselves only from the entitlements of love—the healthy acceptance of ourselves, the love and forgiveness of others, and God's healing love within us.

The process of self-forgiveness involves looking at yourself in the mirror and being specific about what you have done wrong. It's not enough to forgive yourself for being a "bad" person. Precisely what is it that you need forgiveness for?

People who can't forgive themselves or don't want to may engage in silly games. They may try to prove they're the good guys who can do no wrong. Or they try to exonerate themselves by giving lavish presents. But none of these methods works because on some level people remain stuck in their guilt.

Forgiving yourself depends on being able to say and to believe, "The past is past. I know I did wrong. I'm sorry about it," and get on with your life.

SOURCE: Lewis B. Smedes, *Forgive and Forget* (New York: Harper & Row, 1984). Copyright © 1984 by Lewis B. Smedes. Reprinted by permission of HarperCollins Publishers, Inc.

presented by his clients in therapy—the trouble with grades or an employer or indecision about an unsatisfying marriage—lies one central search. At bottom, each person, knowingly or unknowingly, is asking, "Who am I, *really?* How can I get in touch with this real self, underlying all my surface behavior? How can I become myself?" (p. 108).

Rogers (1980) has found that in the process of becoming a person, especially in psychotherapy, the individual's experience of growth follows a general pattern. The early stages of self-revision are usually characterized by a movement away from the "other-directedness" and distorted self-perceptions acquired while growing up. Individuals are busily sorting out aspects of themselves acquired under social pressure or the desire to be accepted. Some self-perceptions are affirmed and strengthened; others are modified or rejected. This process may explain the typical negativism of adolescents as well as youths in the stage of leaving home. It also accounts for the prevalence of complaints and self-disparagement so often seen in the early phases of psychotherapy.

For example, Pam, a woman in her early 30s, told her therapist how she had tried to be a good wife by giving in to her husband and how discouraging it had been. Although she had tried to meet his demands, each time he would make another, until it became an endless series of demands. In the process Pam had become overly submissive and resentful toward her husband. She had also built up a great deal of self-hatred. "I don't like myself this way," Pam said. "How can you have any self-respect when you're always giving in to someone? Yet I've always felt this is the way you have to be if you want to be loved. But I just can't live this way any longer." The disdain in her voice made it clear that Pam had already begun moving away from a self-image designed to please other people.

The later stages of self-actualization are characterized by greater self-direction and self-acceptance. Individuals become more open to and trusting of their own experience. For example, Shandra soon decided to sign up for jazz dancing and then modern dancing, both of which led her to declare a dance minor at college. As people come to accept themselves more fully, they are more accepting of others. Shandra, for example, found with time that her criticism of others' dancing gave way to generosity as she remembered her first clumsy steps in her ballet class. And most important, as individuals strive to discover themselves, they become more willing to accept themselves as a process of becoming.

First, individuals become more open to their own experiences. They become more aware of and comfortable with the complexity of their feelings. They may feel love and hatred toward the same person. Or they may feel excited and fearful about their new job. In both instances, they become more trusting of their own experience and find it a suitable source for discovering the most satisfying behavior in each immediate situation. For example, a young woman like Shandra considering marriage may ask herself about her boyfriend, "Is this the man I want as my partner in love?" As long as she feels she must justify the decision of marriage, she may see only the good qualities in her prospective mate. Greater openness to her experience would indicate that he has faults as well. The more open the young woman is to the full range of her feelings, the more she can weigh all the pros and cons of such a choice. A mistaken choice might be made. But because there is greater openness to her experience, a quicker correction can also be made. The important point is that she is choosing out of the richness of her own experience rather than out of a sense of obligation or from seeking the approval of others.

Second, as individuals accept themselves more fully, they become more accepting of others. This is a reversal of self-alienation. That is, when we fail to acknowledge or accept certain aspects of ourselves, we feel these qualities are foreign to us and we project them onto others, whom we then dislike. Thus, the man who appears to be strong and self-sufficient, while denying his own dependency needs, will feel contempt for men who allow themselves to be taken care of when weak. In contrast, a man who through therapy or a loving relationship recognizes within himself the existence of dependency needs, alongside those of adequacy and self-confidence, may be more accepting of men who exhibit their need for others. Affirming the complexity of feelings and needs within himself, he can appreciate a wider variety of people as well as the inconsistency they display in different situations.

Finally, there is a greater willingness to affirm oneself as being in a process of becoming. People enter therapy hoping to achieve some fixed state in which their problems will be resolved such that they will be more successful in their careers or their marriages will be more satisfying. It is usually a sign of progress when clients drop such fixed goals and accept a more satisfying realization that they are not a fixed entity but a process of becoming. They come to appreciate that change is the one true constant in life. People who are actualizing themselves to a high degree learn to live more in the present moment. They enjoy the richness and complexity, even the inconsistency, of life as it is, using their aspirations more as guideposts than as fixed points.

As you can see, personal growth may be unsettling at times. It involves moving away from some of the familiar self-images acquired during your formative years. And it involves seeing yourself in new ways, especially as a more self-directed person. Because each of us has different values and goals, there is no detailed guide to assure us that we are doing the right thing. Understanding the general pattern of growth, as suggested in the preceding pages, may be helpful. Feedback from others may serve as a useful mirror. Increased self-awareness also may be helpful up to a point. But it is optimal rather than constant or excessive awareness that is desirable. Most important of all, learn to *trust yourself*. Be open to your own experience. And remember, "The good life is a *process,* not a state of being. It is a direction, not a destination" (Rogers, 1961, p. 186).

SUMMARY

WHAT IS THE SELF-CONCEPT?

Essentially, the self-concept is the overall image or awareness we have of ourselves. It includes all those perceptions of "I" and "me," together with the feelings, beliefs, and values associated with them. Although the self-concept itself does not *do* anything, it exerts a tremendous influence on the way we think and act as a whole. Actually, the overall self-concept is an organized cluster of many selves, helping to explain why we do not always act consistently. It is common practice to identify the *body image* (how we perceive and feel about our body), the *self-image* (the self we see ourselves to be), the *ideal self* (the self we'd like to be), and our *social selves* (the way we feel others see us).

CORE CHARACTERISTICS OF THE SELF-CONCEPT

One of the core characteristics of the self-concept is its stability over time. That is, once formed, the self-concept tends to maintain and perpetuate itself as it is. It serves as a filter through which we view our experiences, so that experiences that are not consistent with the self-concept tend to be distorted or kept out of awareness. The tendency to think and act in a self-consistent manner is also strengthened by our self-esteem—the personal evaluation of ourselves and the resulting feelings of worth associated with the self-concept. Largely because of the self's influence, people generally prefer to hear opinions that support their own views of themselves.

THE SELF-CONCEPT AND PERSONAL GROWTH

Although we retain a stable core of self, the many selves that make up our overall self-concept are in a state of flux and are more readily influenced by current experience than previously thought; that is, our self-concept tends to change with personal growth.

We described how visualizing our future possible selves not only helps us to attain them but also aids in our present life adjustment. Also, our social selves—the impressions we think others have of us—may be improved by changing our social roles, circumstances, and the people with whom we associate. Furthermore, we may use personal criticism for growth by putting the energy it arouses to work for us rather than against us, thus using it as an opportunity to learn about ourselves and put the needed changes into action. Ultimately, personal growth involves moving away from the unwanted "other-directedness" or distorted self-perceptions acquired while growing up and moving toward greater self-acceptance and self-direction. Then we become more open to our own experiences and willing to affirm ourselves in a process of becoming. In the process, the more we accept ourselves, the more accepting we become of others.

SCORING KEY FOR THE SELF-IMAGE AND IDEAL SELF EXERCISE

To find the correspondence between your self-image and your ideal self, note the difference in the rank for each card. For example, if on card A you ranked 8 on your self-image and 2 on your ideal self, the difference would be 6. For each card, record the absolute difference between numbers without regard to pluses or minuses. Then total the numbers in the column of differences. A score in the range of 50 would be about average. A difference lower than 30 indicates a high correspondence between your self-image and your ideal self. A score of more than 80 indicates a rather low correspondence between your self-image and ideal self. However, a high score doesn't necessarily mean that you have problems. Remember, this is an exercise, not a test.

SCORING KEY FOR THE SELF-ACCEPTANCE SCALE

To score this scale, first reverse the numbers you wrote in for the following items: 2, 7, 15, 19, 21, 25, 27, and 32. For each of these items

Change a 1 to a 5.
Change a 2 to a 4.
Do not change a 3.
Change a 4 to a 2.
Change a 5 to a 1.

Then add the numbers assigned to each item to get your total score.

Interpretation of Your Score: Your score may vary from 36 to 180.

Low scores (36–110): People who score in this range express little self-acceptance and self-confidence. They may be shy and might benefit from social skills and counseling.

Average scores (111–150): Most people score in this range, though they may be more accepting in some areas than in others and more comfortable with some people than with others. They could improve their self-acceptance by challenging unrealistic expectations or improving their personal and interpersonal skills.

High scores (151–180): People who score in this range tend to be highly self-confident. Their sense of self-worth helps them meet new people and confront new challenges.

SELF-TEST

1. Which of the following includes all those perceptions of "I" and "me," together with the feelings, beliefs, and values associated with them?
   a. superego
   b. self-concept
   c. ideal self
   d. body image

2. The self-image refers to the
   a. self I'd like to be
   b. self as I think others see me
   c. self I see myself to be
   d. image I have of my body

3. Our ideal self should be
   a. modified when unduly high
   b. unattainable in principle
   c. the same as our self-image
   d. never compromised

4. Experiences that are consistent with our self-concept but are not confirmed by our "gut" reactions are
   a. admitted fully into our awareness
   b. accurately perceived and labeled
   c. kept out of awareness
   d. perceived in a distorted manner

5. Compared to people with high self-esteem, those with low self-esteem
   a. are more accepting of others
   b. report higher levels of happiness
   c. exert less effort on hard tasks
   d. report lower levels of anxiety

6. According to self-enhancement theory, we welcome positive feedback about
   a. all our qualities
   b. our positive qualities
   c. our negative qualities
   d. anything

7. Who typically has low esteem?
   a. women compared to men
   b. minorities compared to the White majority
   c. children with parents who consistently criticize
   d. all of the above

8. Our social selves refer to
   a. how we perceive other people
   b. the way we think others see us
   c. how well we get along with others
   d. the way others see us

9. The most helpful way of handling personal criticism is to regard it as something that
   a. needs immediate action
   b. reflects others' faults
   c. signals self-defense
   d. may require action

10. During the later stages of personal growth and therapy, people have a heightened sense of
    a. self-direction
    b. fixed personal goals
    c. self-criticalness
    d. future orientation

EXERCISES

1. *Self-image.* This is the self you perceive yourself to be. Using a full 8 1/2- × 11-inch page, draw two concentric circles (a circle within a circle)—the inner circle representing the core of your self-concept and the outer circle the more flexible, changeable selves. Within the inner circle list half a dozen of your most enduring aspects (traits). In the outer circle list a similar number of aspects of yourself that are more dependent on changing roles and circumstances. How would you describe your overall self-image?

2. *The self you'd like to be.* Among the various possible selves you'd like to be, including any feared self, select one specific image. Visualize it in specific terms as vividly as possible. Write down how you'd look, how you'd feel, and how you'd act. If possible, you might spend several minutes a day for a week daydreaming about your possible self. How did this affect your present self-image and adjustment?

3. *Self-esteem.* Our sense of personal worth fluctuates somewhat from one situation to another. Think of several situations or occasions in which you usually feel good about yourself and exhibit a lot of self-confidence. Then think of several situations in which you feel unsure of yourself and inferior. Can you identify the people or demands that make you feel good or bad about yourself? What are some practical steps you can take to improve your self-esteem?

4. *Identifying your social selves.* We have as many social selves, as William James observed, as there are people whose opinion we care about. Select five or six people you associate with regularly. Then identify which aspects of yourself are most readily expressed when you're with these people. Jot down some of the shared interests, typical activities, and your feelings and attitudes toward each person. Would you agree that you feel and behave somewhat differently with different people?

5. *How well do you take criticism?* Select an instance when someone criticized you and describe your experience in a page or so. Did you interpret the person's remarks as a personal attack? Or did you try to look beyond the surface of the criticism to what the person was trying to tell you? Looking back, to what extent was this a positive learning experience for you? Jot down some suggestions that will help you to benefit from personal criticism in the future.

6. *Self and ideal.* If you did the self-image and ideal self exercise in Figure 6–1, write a page or two commenting on the specific items on which you scored the highest discrepancies between your self-image and ideal self. How would you account for this score? Are you doing anything about lessening the gap?

QUESTIONS FOR SELF-REFLECTION

1. How would you describe your self-image?
2. Which aspects of your self-concept would you like to change?
3. Do you basically like yourself?
4. Are you more self-confident in some situations than in others?
5. Are you aware of how others see you?
6. When you've accepted something within yourself, are you more accepting of it in others?
7. How well do you take personal criticism?
8. What do you say when complimented by others?
9. Are you aware that self-actualization is a direction rather than a destination?
10. Do you tend to trust your own experiences?

FOR FURTHER INFORMATION

RECOMMENDED READINGS

BRANDEN, N. (1994). *The six pillars of self-esteem.* New York: Bantam. A book about establishing high esteem.

BROTHERS, J. (1994). *Positive plus: The practical plan for liking yourself better.* New York: Putnam. A book about raising self-esteem by the ever-popular author.

HAMACHEK, D. (1991). *Encounters with the self* (4th ed.). Fort Worth, TX: Harcourt Brace Jovanovich. A thorough exploration of the self-concept and its growth through the life cycle.

O'GORMAN, P. A. (1994). *Dancing backwards in high heels: How women master the art of resilience.* Center City, MN: Hazelden. Offers testimony about how contemporary women are under stress from competing roles and how those who are most resilient cope best.

RUTTER, M. (1993). *Developing minds: Challenge and continuity across the life span.* New York: Basic Books. A volume about change across the life span.

WEBSITES AND THE INTERNET

http://www.altsex.org/: A site designed to discover information about androgyny, which means being both masculine and feminine at the same time.

http://english-www.hss.cmu.edu/gender/: If you are interested in accessing lots of information about gender, here it is.

http://www.selfgrowth.com/topics.html: Interested in higher self-esteem, in fact, higher everything? This site provides much information about self-improvement and personal growth.

http://fly.hiwaay.net/~garson/selfest.htm: A website for those interested in boosting their own or their child's self-esteem. Lots of good information and essays can be found here.

http://GoZips.uakron.edu/~dje/race.htm: A site for individuals of all races to learn more about racial identity, racial harmony, and race relations.

CHAPTER

7

Meeting People
and Making Friends

After completing this chapter, you should be able to

1. Describe several factors affecting our impressions of others, including mistaken impressions.
2. Know how shyness shapes relationships.
3. Discuss the importance of physical attractiveness for interpersonal attraction.
4. Discuss the importance of mutual self-disclosure for friendship.
5. Know about the differences between same-sex and opposite-sex friendships.
6. List several major reasons friendships break up.
7. Give an example of someone who has successfully overcome his or her loneliness.

Anita and Gale were best friends. They probably would never have met were it not for their positions at Ramona Community College. Both had obtained their master's degrees in psychology, Anita in California and Gale in Minnesota. Gale's husband's job created a career move for him so she and her husband moved away from the Midwest as soon as she finished her degree. Gale grew up in a middle-class family in Minnesota where her father was a journalist and her mother an engineer. Anita grew up in Texas. Her life trajectory was not as easy as Gale's. Anita's father left her mother when Anita was very young. Anita's mother worked at various low-paying jobs. Her mother always said that she wanted her daughter to have a better life. Her daughter did. Anita's mother made sure that Anita had the opportunity to attend first a community college and then a good four-year college. Anita was encouraged by her good grades and her professors to continue her education. She pursued a master's degree and soon found herself in the position of new professor at Ramona. When Anita arrived, Gale was already a professor there. Gale was in her 40s, Anita in her late 20s. Gale was White and middle class; Anita was Hispanic American and, before acquiring her education, decidedly lower class. The two women seemingly had nothing in common, but Gale was immediately taken by this intelligent and personable young woman. Gale decided to informally mentor Anita through her early years as a fledgling professor because they were the only two women in the department. That is how their friendship began. Both women soon learned that they really did have common interests. Each enjoyed rhythm and blues, foreign films, and Tex-Mex cuisine. Their attitudes about politics and religion were very different, though. Gale was strongly Republican, rather conservative, and hardly religious. Anita was devoutly religious and a solid Democrat. Is the story of their friendship typical? How do people form friendships? Why do friendships dissolve? These and other issues are the focus of this chapter.

In our fast-paced, mobile society most people come in contact with more people than did our parents and grandparents. But we have fewer close relationships. There's a tendency to form many short-term acquaintances on the basis of shared interests and satisfactions. This is especially true for well-educated individuals who are some of the most mobile individuals in our society. Perhaps Anita and Gale never would have met had they not been so well educated; after all, each had a very different background. For instance, if you were to keep track of all the different people you come into contact with, say, during a 3-month period, you might be surprised to learn that you have met as many as several hundred people. Yet most of these contacts are fleeting and superficial.

Meeting a great variety of people enables us to develop a wide range of interests and relationships. But there is also a greater risk of loneliness. As a result, more people are now engaged in the search for closer, more satisfying social ties, that is, lasting friendships and romantic relationships. The portrayal of close relationships on television—in which people move from shouting matches to lovemaking in a matter of minutes—tends to oversimplify the realities involved. Consequently, people's expectations of intimacy, indeed their entitlement to it, often exceed their understanding of what is involved, much less their ability to attain it.

 ## Meeting People

Each of us needs both intimate as well as more superficial social relationships. On the one hand, we need a network of people to fulfill a variety of needs, such as the exchange of services and the alleviation of stress. On the other hand, each of us also needs a deep, caring relationship with one or more special persons, such as a close friend, lover, or spouse. Sharing our deepest thoughts and feelings with an understanding partner who accepts us despite our faults is one of life's most satisfying experiences. It makes us feel at home in the world despite the usual ups and downs in everyday life. Those who lack such close relationships experience emotional isolation and loneliness, regardless of their network of social ties.

At the same time, individuals differ in their respective needs for social relationships. Some people prefer a variety of relationships that satisfy different needs, often with little emotional depth. Others value the closeness that comes with more intense emotional involvement with fewer people, such as a circle of close friends or a lover. Then, too, the same person's need for companionship fluctuates according to the mood of the moment. Most of us like to share happy occasions such as a birthday or a promotion at work. But we prefer to be alone when physically tired or embarrassed about something. To get a better idea of your own affiliative needs, complete the Interpersonal Orientation Scale in Figure 7–1.

FIGURE 7–1

INTERPERSONAL ORIENTATION SCALE

This scale focuses on four dimensions of affiliative needs or potential sources of gratification that come from interpersonal relationships: (1) positive cognitive stimulation, which helps to prevent boredom; (2) attention, which enhances our feelings of importance; (3) social comparison, which reduces ambiguity by providing information about social reality; and (4) emotional support and sympathy.

As you read the following statements, indicate how true or descriptive each is of you by placing the appropriate number before each item. Then consult the scoring key at the end of this chapter.

1—not at all true

2—slightly true

3—somewhat true

4—mostly true

5—completely true

_____ 1. One of my greatest sources of comfort when things get rough is being with other people.

_____ 2. I prefer to participate in activities alongside other people rather than by myself because I like to see how I am doing on the activity.

_____ 3. The main thing I like about being around other people is the warm glow I get from contact with them.

_____ 4. It seems like whenever something bad or disturbing happens to me I often just want to be with a close, reliable friend.

_____ 5. I mainly like people who seem strongly drawn to me and who seem infatuated with me.

_____ 6. I think I get satisfaction out of contact with others more than most people realize.

_____ 7. When I am not certain about how well I am doing at something, I usually like to be around others so I can compare myself to them.

_____ 8. I like to be around people when I can be the center of attention.

_____ 9. When I have not done very well on something that is very important to me, I can get to feeling better simply by being around other people.

_____ 10. Just being around others and finding out about them is one of the most interesting things I can think of doing.

_____ 11. I seem to get satisfaction from being with others more than a lot of other people do.

_____ 12. If I am uncertain about what is expected of me, such as on a task or in a social situation, I usually like to be able to look to certain others for cues.

_____ 13. I feel like I have really accomplished something valuable when I am able to get close to someone.

_____ 14. I find that I often have the desire to be around other people who are experiencing the same thing I am when I am unsure of what is going on.

_____ 15. During times when I have to go through something painful, I usually find having someone with me makes it less painful.

_____ 16. I often have a strong need to be around people who are impressed with what I am like and what I do.

_____ 17. If I feel unhappy or kind of depressed, I usually try to be around other people to make me feel better.

_____ 18. I find that I often look to certain other people to see how I compare to others.

_____ 19. I mainly like to be around others who think I am an important, exciting person.

_____ 20. I think it would be satisfying if I could have very close friendships with quite a few people.

_____ 21. I often have a strong desire to get people I am around to notice me and appreciate what I am like.

_____ 22. I don't like being with people who may give me less than positive feedback about myself.

_____ 23. I usually have the greatest need to have other people around me when I feel upset about something.

_____ 24. I think being close to others, listening to them, and relating to them on a one-to-one level is one of my favorite and most satisfying pastimes.

_____ 25. I would find it very satisfying to be able to form new friendships with whomever I liked.

_____ 26. One of the most enjoyable things I can think of that I like to do is just watching people and seeing what they are like.

SOURCE: C. A. Hill, "Affiliation Motivation: People Who Need People . . . But in Different Ways," *Journal of Personality and Social Psychology, 52,* 5 (1987), 1008–1018. Copyright © 1987 American Psychological Association. Reprinted with permission.

FIRST IMPRESSIONS

When Gale first observed Anita, Anita seemed very bright and was absolutely engaging, but Anita wondered if a woman so senior to her would ever be friendly. From the beginning, they were busy forming **first impressions** of one another. All of us do this. But why?

Perhaps we're curious. We're intrigued by the unknown. Another reason has to do with anxiety and the need for understanding people around us, especially if we think we may have to respond to them. Furthermore, the more fearful we are about people, the more likely we are to misjudge them. Whatever the reasons, the basic principle of person perception is this: We tend to form extensive impressions of others on the basis of very little information. One other generalization has also been demonstrated, that first impressions probably are most important. How are these first impressions formed?

At first, when people meet, such as Anita and Gale, they have surface contact. That is, they see each other and perhaps exchange greetings at most. After this stage, though, people need to decide whether to continue the interaction. What factors determine whether we indeed will continue?

Physical attractiveness. A person's physical appearance makes a strong first impression. Someone's height, weight, sex, facial features, and dress all affect our senses and feelings. We're influenced a lot by a person's physical attractiveness. In fact, much research has concluded that physical appearance may be one of the most powerful determinants of our impressions of others even though we won't often admit this. The more physically attractive someone is, the more positively we judge that person. When people have been asked to give their impressions of others, they attribute all sorts of positive qualities to attractive people. Many of these qualities actually have little or nothing to do with a person's physical appearance (Johnstone, Frame, & Bouman, 1992). Attractive people are judged to be more interesting, intelligent, compassionate, sociable, and better adjusted than less attractive people (e.g., Diener, Wolsic, & Fujita, 1995; Eagly & Makhijani, 1991). They are regarded as more successful in their careers and happy in their personal lives. Physical attractiveness is also associated with such diverse accomplishments as getting good grades, better jobs, and faster promotions, as well as having less serious psychological disorders than others (e.g., Jackson, Hunter, & Hodge, 1995). But we're not always so favorably impressed. Handsome men and beautiful women are apt to be viewed as more egotistical and less sincere (e.g., Cash & Duncan, 1984). As a result, they are often rejected by their same-sex peers, partly because of jealousy.

People in our society are considered attractive if they have an appropriate waist to hip ratio with the waist circumference about 70 percent or 80 percent of the hip circumference (Singh, 1995) and are fairly thin (Henss, 1995). Some of these same effects are often found in other cultures. D. Jones (1995) found that Americans, Brazilians, and Russians preferred large eyes, small noses, and full lips. And Hatfield and Sprecher (1995) gathered data from college students in the United States, Russia, and Japan on preferences for marital partners. In all three countries men cared very much about physical attractiveness, that is men cared more than women about appearance. The most likely explanation is that because of cultural conditioning, many women may be less likely to initiate opposite-sex relationships. These generalities are true up to a point. Individuals within various ethnic and racial groups tend to show some degree of ethnocentrism when judging the attractiveness of others. That is, they find members of their own group more attractive than members of other groups (Liu, Campbell, & Condie, 1995). Another caveat is this: These standards are the typical "White" standards in our society. When standards of this group are used as ideal reference points by other groups such as African Americans for judging their own attractiveness, a slow but definite form of erosion of self-esteem can occur (Hall, 1995).

As you look around, it is obvious that few people of either sex have such an ideal face or figure. Most of us have some attractive features as well as others we'd like to change. At the same time, each of us manages to modify the cultural expectations

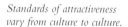

Standards of attractiveness vary from culture to culture.

regarding physical attractiveness to fit ourselves and our partners. For example, the better we like someone, the more we modify our subjective evaluation of that person's physical attractiveness. Thus, you may find someone attractive regardless of others' opinions. Because beauty is partly, at least, in the eye of the beholder, there are many people in the world who would probably consider each one of us highly attractive, which is a good thing to keep in mind.

Each of us might fantasize about having a highly attractive opposite-sex partner. But when it comes to choosing a date or romantic partner, we usually settle for someone like ourselves, at least in regard to physical attractiveness. This tendency has been labeled the **matching hypothesis.** For example, 67 couples who were introduced by a dating service in Los Angeles were later judged in terms of their attractiveness and romantic attachment. Not surprisingly, there was a positive association between the similarity of physical attractiveness and increasingly deeper romantic involvement (Folkes, 1982).

People sometimes turn to dating services or to personal ads to find romantic partners. One person might advertise that he is a handsome professional and seeks "same" for sharing entertainment and romance. To learn more about personal ads, read Box 7–1, "Meeting People Through Personal Ads."

If you're going steady with someone or are married, to what degree does the matching hypothesis apply to your relationship? Can you think of couples who are exceptions to this rule? All things considered, how important do you think physical attractiveness is in love and marriage?

People we regard as physically unattractive are typically judged unfavorably. Like beauty, ugliness is mostly in the eye of the beholder. For some, fatness or homely facial features appear to be ugly, as do, for others, irregular features such as a large nose, discolored skin, or physical handicap (Crandall, 1994). Whatever the case, unattractive people may be discriminated against for no good reason. One young man who was confined to a wheelchair since an automobile accident observed, "Even when people hold the door open for me, they avoid touching me or looking me in the eye." Yet those who've gotten to know this man look past his handicap at the person himself. Individuals such as this young man still need friends and lovers. For further exploration of this issue, please read Box 7–2, "Unattractive People Also Need Love."

Reputations.   Someone's reputation also affects our impression of that person. Suppose Gale is your friend and says, "I can't wait for you to meet Anita." Chances are you will like her. Even before you meet Anita, you'll probably find yourself forming a positive image of her based on what Gale tells you. Should you later discover Anita has some unfavorable qualities Gale didn't tell you about, chances are you'll give her the benefit of the doubt. Of course, it works the other way, too. If someone says, "I hear that professor named Gale is a terrible teacher," you may find yourself forming a negative impression of that teacher, rightly or wrongly (Graziano, Jensen-Campbell, Shebilske, & Lundgren, 1993). Such is the power of reputation.

Similarity.   One other reason that we initially notice and like others is because they seem similar to us. Anita and Gale probably quickly came to realize that they both liked Tex-Mex food and rhythm and blues. Even if people are not really similar, we often assume that they are. Research has shown there is a very strong correlation between liking and similarity. People with the same attitudes are attracted to one another. In other words, "birds of a feather do flock together." How does this happen? When people interact, they cannot help but notice each other's age, sex, height, and other physical features. Shortly after, they begin to disclose attitudes and values to each other. Research has shown that the *proportion* of similar attitudes, not the raw number of similar attitudes that are expressed, is most important.

For example, Gale and Anita share attitudes toward school, education, and dating. But they disagree on matters such as the definition of psychology, religion, and how to create better race relations. The proportion of similar attitudes here is 50 percent, though the number of items is three. Yet they would like each other less than another set of

---

BOX 7–1

MEETING PEOPLE THROUGH PERSONAL ADS

Have you ever considered seeking a romantic partner through a personal ad? Apparently, more people are resorting to such devices in the hopes of meeting that special person in their lives. Personal ads are no longer relegated to underground newspapers and sex magazines. Today, they are a booming business and have become a popular and reputable way of meeting people in our mobile, urban society.

Composing an ad with oneself as the product is itself an interesting exercise, requiring a blend of self-confidence and humor. Interpreting these ads is equally demanding. One must first decipher the codes used, such as DWF (divorced White female) and SBM (single Black male). Then, too, one must make due allowance for exaggeration. For instance, *slim* and *attractive* are not taken literally. Similarly, *sensuous* is likely to mean *sexual, discreet* often implies a married person seeking an affair, and words like *sincere* are often counterproductive. If you write "Sincere young woman 32 would like to meet sincere man," you're apt to receive a dozen boring letters (Foxman, 1983). However, humor almost always helps.

The more responses the ad draws, the more choices the advertiser has of various types of people to meet. In one simple study, Jeff Rubin (Raven & Rubin, 1983) found that the most successful ads generally highlighted the author's needs and trust of the reader, did not stress the importance of the reader's qualities, and/or were placed by women. One of the most successful ads was the following:

> Lonely WF, 22 seeks WM 22–28 for companionship, dating, fun times, and possible love making. No promises of deep involvement. Sincerity necessary. Please write. I need you.

In contrast, most unsuccessful ads imposed various demands or restrictions on the reader and emphasized the services that the author would provide rather than what the author needed. The following ad yielded no response at all:

> Complete satisfaction and gratification guaranteed by experienced WM. Discretion assured! By appointment only, of course, because of the tremendous demand for my services. Big, medium to heavy, strong sexy women preferred, and all of their demands will be completely met.

Perhaps the biggest surprise of all is that many of the ads reflect traditional values. It seems that many people are seeking romance, love, and long-term relationships rather than sex (Morrow, 1985).

BOX 7–2

Unattractive People Also Need Love

Physically unattractive people—for example, the facially disfigured, obese, and surgically scarred—who make up the bottom 10 percent in terms of appearance (or 24 million Americans) are victims of countless acts of discrimination in our society. Ugly people have a harder time getting jobs. Homely waitresses receive lower tips. Teachers think unattractive students are dumber than attractive students. And strangers perceive unsightly people as cold, insensitive, and unhappy.

The constant insults and humiliation faced by ugly people cause them to have negative self-images and feelings of worthlessness; they grow up thinking they are not as "good" as attractive people.

Uglies Unlimited—with headquarters in Garland, Texas—strives to prevent discrimination because of physical appearance. It was founded to protest a major airline's requirement that prospective flight attendants be physically attractive. The first Uglies Unlimited members picketed the airline's offices with signs that read "Ugly ducklings can fly, too." Since then, the organization has devoted much of its efforts to raising the public's consciousness about ugly people's plight throughout society.

When people first hear about Uglies Unlimited, they think it's some kind of joke. But it's not. The discrimination against ugliness is serious. We must realize that just as *attractive* doesn't automatically mean *good, ugly* doesn't necessarily mean *bad.* Instead, we need to accept people—all people—for what they *are* rather than what they *look* like.

friends sharing similar attitudes in just two areas but disagreeing on only one. In the latter case, the couple agrees in 66 percent of attitudes, though the number of items is only two. That is, it is the proportion of shared attitudes rather than the absolute number of them that makes for attraction. For instance, one study of attitude similarity and attraction compared couples with no attitudes in common, similarity in half of their attitudes, and similarity in all of their attitudes. As expected, the results showed that the attraction between partners increased directly according to the proportion of their similar attitudes (Gonzales, Davis, Loney, Lukens, & Junghans, 1983). (See Figure 7–2.)

There is less agreement about the importance of similarity in needs and personal traits. According to one view, people with similar needs and personalities are attracted to each other; the other view is that people who are complementary (opposite but compatible) in their needs and traits are attracted. Actually, the theory of complementary needs tends to apply mostly to specific traits rather than to the meshing of two personalities as a whole. That is, a talkative person may become attracted to someone who is quiet; a dominant individual might seek out a more dependent partner. Also, complementarity probably isn't important in the early stages of attraction, though it may become more important in a long-term relationship like marriage. Nevertheless, even among married couples, the weight of evidence seems to favor similarity. For example, a study of 108 married couples showed that couples with similar needs had greater marital happiness and adjustment than those with dissimilar needs (Antill, 1983).

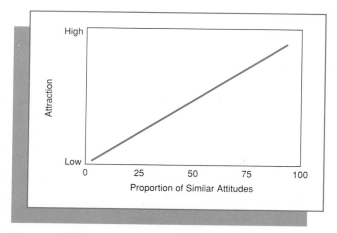

FIGURE 7–2

Attitude similarity and friendship. The more similar the proportion of attitudes between two people, the more they like each other.

Propinquity.   Chances are that at some time your friends lived nearby, attended the same school, or worked at the same place just as Gale and Anita did. Nearness is especially important in the early stages of attraction. First, the more you come into contact with people, the more opportunities you have for getting to know them better. This factor is called proximity or propinquity. **Propinquity** means physical closeness. Many studies (e.g., Hays, 1985) have demonstrated that the farther away a person lives or sits (in class, for example) the less likely he or she is to become a friend. Being in close proximity also exposes us more often to an individual. Again, ample research has demonstrated that "the more I see you, the more I like you" (Moreland & Beach, 1992). There's also a strong association between interaction and liking. That is, the more you get to know someone, the more you like that person. And it works the other way, too: The more you like someone, the more you associate with him or her. We also tend to emphasize the positive qualities and minimize the negative qualities of people we associate with every day. Otherwise, you feel you're stuck with an unpleasant coworker or roommate and feel a lot of resentment. Then, too, our social norms imply cooperative relationships with others, so that we make a special effort to get along with people we live or work with. Otherwise, life might be just too miserable.

If it's true that the more you associate with someone, the more you like that person, then the longer couples are married the happier they should be—right? Because this is obviously not the case for many couples, other factors, such as compatibility, are involved. As a result, when there are serious differences or basic incompatibilities between two individuals, close contact may lead to overt conflict, resentment, and alienation. In such cases, "familiarity breeds contempt." It is well known among those who work in the justice system that in assault and murder cases, the leading suspects are likely to be lovers, spouses, or ex-spouses.

Nonverbal signals.   Our impressions of others are also shaped by a variety of nonverbal signals. A person's posture, facial expressions, and gestures definitely affect our impressions. Those who stand erect or walk youthfully (Montepare & Zebrowitz-McArthur, 1988) while talking to us make a more favorable impression than those who slouch. Also, people who point, glare, and interrupt a lot make a more negative impression than those who are attentive to what we say. Similarly, we are more favorably impressed with people who smile and look us in the eye. People who make eye contact with us are apt to be seen as more trustworthy and likable (Kleinke, 1986) unless they gaze into our eyes for an uncomfortably long time. Those who avoid our gaze, whether from shyness or deceit, may strike us less favorably.

There are also differences in the verbal communication patterns that people use, not the words but other features of verbal communication such as the rate of speech, pauses, and so forth. These unspoken but nonetheless important features of spoken communications are called **paralinguistics.** There are large differences between men and women. You can read more about paralinguistics and spoken communications in Box 7–3, "Did You Know That . . ."

MISTAKEN IMPRESSIONS

Anita initially assumed that Gale would not be interested in being friends with her because of their age difference. Anita was mistaken. The biggest single reason we misjudge others is the lack of sufficient information about them, as first happened when Anita met Gale. Nor should this be surprising, given our tendency to "size up" people so hastily. When we quickly assess someone, we generally use **heuristics** or mental shortcuts for making complex decisions. One such shortcut or heuristic is the **false consensus effect,** where we assume that others feel as we do (Alicke & Largo, 1995). We

---

BOX 7–3

Did You Know That . . .

When a man and a woman converse with each other,

Men do most of the talking and women do most of the listening?

Women tend to carry the greater burden in keeping the conversation going?

Women raise more topics, ask more questions, and vary the pitch and tone of their voices more than men do?

Men are much more likely to interrupt women than women are to interrupt men?

Women are more likely to make "retrievals," that is, attempts to resume the line of communication from the point where they were interrupted?

Women are more adept in decoding nonverbal cues, such as the meaning behind voice tones and facial expressions?

Men who work with people—psychiatrists, psychologists, teachers, and social workers—tend to listen better than other men?

Good listeners of either sex make a better impression on others than those who do most of the talking?

might guess, then, that if Gale initially liked Anita, she also assumed that Anita liked her in return. We also form a **mistaken impression** of others because of false cues, stereotypes, global judgments, and underestimating the importance of their circumstances.

False cues consist of various signals and indirect suggestions that unconsciously trigger certain associations in our minds. Signs of money and status are often misleading, especially to the unsuspecting. Because people who are successful and financially well off often live in large, impressive houses and drive expensive cars, we may assume, mistakenly, that anyone who indulges in expensive cars and clothes is rich. Thus, some unscrupulous individuals deliberately take prestigious addresses and entertain at lavish parties to impress others. One man and his wife, who were living on social security at the time, transformed themselves into jet-setters by displaying the signs of wealth. They let it be known that they were soon to inherit millions from a rich uncle. Then they ran up huge charge accounts against their anticipated fortune. In due time, however, their unpaid creditors became suspicious and the couple was brought to justice. Because this couple *acted* rich, most people assumed they were.

We also misjudge people because of **stereotypes**—widespread generalizations that have little, if any, basis in fact. Whenever people begin statements with such phrases as "all teachers" or "all women drivers," they're slipping into stereotypic thinking. A stereotype held by many is that people who wear glasses are smarter than those who don't (Terry & Macy, 1991). The unspoken assumption is that such people need glasses because they've strained their eyes so much from reading. The truth of the matter is that the need for glasses depends more on hereditary weakness than on one's study habits. Here are some other stereotypes: Men with beards, mustaches, and an abundance of body hair are regarded as more masculine and virile than those with less hair. Brunette women are seen as more intelligent and responsible than blondes—the latter as more fun and sexier than brunettes. Redheads of both sexes are seen as more "hot-tempered" than people with other hair colors. All Whites are prejudiced against Blacks. Do you sometimes feel misunderstood because of stereotypes? If so, which ones?

We also tend to label people good or bad because they possess a few good or bad characteristics. This is called the **halo effect** or **devil effect.** In the former case, it's as if the person we like wears a halo (ring of light) over his or her head, like an angel, and can do no wrong. We're especially likely to attach this label in regard to such important qualities as warmth and sociableness. When we regard people as warm and outgoing, we're apt to attribute all sorts of other positive qualities to them, such as intelligence and industriousness. Conversely, if we see others as cold and withdrawn, we tend to attribute other negative qualities to them as well. In reality, of course, few individuals are all good or all bad. Instead, it's well to bear in mind that each of us is a complex mixture of traits, some desirable and others not so desirable.

We frequently misjudge people by not taking sufficient account of situational influences on their behavior. That is, we assume that people are always acting in character, so to speak. For example, if Anita dropped her coffee, Gale might think of her as clumsy rather than attribute the spill to the coffee's being hot. The truth is that people are often constrained by their immediate situations. The tendency to overattribute people's behavior to their personalities rather than to their circumstances is so pervasive and of such importance to social perception that it has been called the **fundamental attribution error** (e.g., Burger, 1991). Here is another example: One day Gale and Anita had a verbal skirmish. Anita was angry with Gale because she thought her friend was too hot-tempered. Little did Anita know that Gale simply was exhausted from staying up late to grade her students' papers. To avoid misjudging people, we must take account of the powerful and changing influences of their situation. Thus, it is wise to observe someone in a variety of different situations across time in order to know what that person is really like.

SHYNESS

"Everyone but me was having such a good time laughing and talking," said Anita after the faculty reception. "My boyfriend was moving around the room greeting friends. And there I was trying to think of something to say to this woman I was talking to. She must have felt sorry for me. I couldn't wait until the party was over."

This sounds familiar, doesn't it? **Shyness**—the tendency to avoid contact or familiarity with others—afflicts people of all ages, but especially the young. According to a study of shyness by Zimbardo (1986), about 80 percent of college students report they have been shy at some point in their lives and that almost half of Americans have a chronic problem with shyness (Carducci & Zimbardo, 1995). Shyness is typically consistent across situations and over time (Briggs, Cheek, & Jones, 1986). Contrary to the myth of the shy female, men and women reported shyness with equal frequency.

Shyness means different things for different people and covers a wide range of feelings and behaviors. At one end of the spectrum are those who are not especially apprehensive about meeting people when necessary. When they are alone, it is because they prefer being in nature or working with ideas or things rather than with people. In the middle range are those who are sometimes embarrassed and occasionally lack self-confidence and social skills. Such individuals hesitate to ask for a date or a favor from others. At the other extreme are individuals whose shyness has become a sad form of self-imprisonment. These people judge themselves with impossible rules that result in avoiding unfamiliar people and situations, thus minimizing the possibility of rejection.

Almost all of us tend to be shy in some situations, such as meeting strangers, dealing with people of the opposite sex, and being in large groups. But people who are habitually shy are different: They see shyness as something within themselves, that is, as a personal trait. Yet they dislike being shy. Shyness also creates many problems for them: feeling lonely, being overly self-conscious and unassertive, having difficulty making

Shy people are often perceived as aloof and condescending.

friends (Bruch, Hamer, & Heimberg, 1995), being unable to think clearly in the presence of others, or freezing up in the middle of a conversation (Carducci & Zimbardo, 1995). Shy people are also often misunderstood by others. They are apt to be regarded as aloof, condescending, emotionally "cold," and egocentric.

In American culture we value freedom and independence and celebrate bravado. This is not true in all cultures. In many Asian cultures, the Chinese and Japanese cultures for example, reticent individuals might be construed as more socially sensitive than extroverted individuals and therefore be more accepted by their peers (Carducci & Zimbardo, 1995; X. Chen, Rubin, & Sun, 1992). People in Japan and Taiwan report being the most shy (60 percent), whereas Israelis tend to be the least shy (about 30 percent) (Carducci & Zimbardo).

Where does shyness originate? Although some shyness can be traced to biology, most psychologists assume it is learned in childhood. The cause may be related to the process of **attribution**. In forming attributions, we search for the reasons for a behavior. In Japan, for example, when children succeed, parents get the credit. In Israel, a child who tries gets rewarded regardless of the child's success. In other words, the child gets the credit. Israeli but not Japanese children take chances and do things that make them stand out or seem extroverted. Not so in Japan (Carducci & Zimbardo, 1995).

If you or someone you know suffers from shyness, rest assured that shyness can be reduced by learning to modify shyness when it creates problems (Scholing & Emmelkamp, 1990). First and foremost, strive to reduce the inner monitoring of your thoughts, feelings, and actions, especially the concern for how people see you. Instead, focus on your participation in the activities and people around you. Second, identify those aspects of situations that elicit shyness, such as meeting new people, as well as the social skills you may be lacking. Third, develop your social skills, such as how to initiate and carry on a conversation and how to assert yourself. In other words, allow yourself some successes on the interpersonal front. Fourth, keep in mind that shyness subsides when you step out of your usual identity, as in role playing, or when you become totally absorbed in something or when you are helping others. Fifth, try to stop being so self-critical and perfectionistic. If shyness has become too disabling, seek counseling or therapy. One young woman said, "I was so shy I couldn't even tell the guy I was going with how I felt about him." After counseling she was considerably less shy. Finally, remember that shyness is widespread. When a stranger at a party doesn't look at you or speak to you, do not assume you are being rejected. Perhaps this other individual is just as shy as you are. Why not introduce yourself? If you feel up to it, for an entire day make it a point to say "Hi" or "Hello" to everyone you meet. See what response you get. You may be pleasantly surprised.

Interestingly, shyness is on the rise in America. The advent of technology, for example, electronic communication in the form of e-mail, voice mail, and other devices, has reduced the need for us to meet face-to-face. Most of us even pump our own gasoline and can therefore avoid talking to the station attendant. This reduces the opportunities for shy people to practice their interpersonal skills. Organized sports where coaches and referees talk to youngsters but where the youngsters do not practice talking to each other have reduced opportunities for children to learn interpersonal skills (Carducci & Zimbardo, 1995). On the other hand, if face-to-face interaction is so feared that individuals are lonely and isolated from others, technology affords new opportunities for meeting others. Probably a balance of electronic and interpersonal communication is best.

Interpersonal Attraction

The desire for human connectedness and attachment is a fundamental human motive (Baumeister & Leary, 1995). Perhaps it was simply Gale and Anita's desire to have a good friend that brought them together in the first place. Think about how you've met your friends. Can you recall what attracted you to one another? Frequently, we're attracted to people with whom we have a lot in common, as mentioned earlier. We may be interested in the same career goals or taking the same course. In some instances, we're attracted to people who are different from us; perhaps they complement us in some way. Then, too, a lot depends on the "chemistry," or subjective factors, when people meet. We seem to get along with some people better than others almost from the start.

FRIENDSHIP

After we have formed our first impressions and decided whether we want to continue the interaction, the more we get to know someone, especially when we're mutually attracted, the more likely our relationship will ripen into friendship as did Gale and Anita's. **Friendship** can be defined as the affectionate attachment between two or more people. We usually think of a friend as someone we've known a long time, which is often true. Yet friendship has more to do with the quality of the relationship than with the frequency of association. Friendships provide a warmth and closeness that are often missing in daily transactions. As society becomes more complex and mobile, and thus more impersonal, we cherish close friendships even more. Youths growing up in our rapidly

Friendship is defined as the affectionate attachment between two or more people.

changing, competitive society place a high priority on close relationships. When asked what would bring them the most happiness, almost 7 out of 10 American youths (69 percent) selected "love" and "close relationships," far above "good career," "family," and "helping others" ("What the World's Teenagers," 1986).

WHEN FRIENDS GET TOGETHER

Not surprisingly, one of the most common activities among friends is having an intimate talk. This is one of the most frequently mentioned activities by both men and women. Just as Anita and Gale might, you may call up a friend to tell her about an incident that happened to you at work. Or your friend may want to talk about the trouble he's having with his girlfriend or wife. In both instances, sharing your feelings and getting someone else's reaction on the subject may be extremely helpful. Another frequently mentioned activity, especially for men, is doing a favor for a friend. Perhaps you ask your friend to write a letter of reference for you. Or your friend may want you to witness a legal document for her. Asking or doing a favor for someone else presupposes a great deal of trust as well as give and take in a relationship, both important qualities of friendship. (See Box 7–4.)

As mentioned in the chapter on stress, one of the greatest favors friends can do for each other is to lend a listening ear. Although people who report general well-being have only a few close friends, they often report high levels of sharing of intimate and personal information to those friends (McDonough & Munz, 1994). Sometimes a casual friend becomes a close friend because that person listens sympathetically to some personal problem of yours. Faced with such crises, many people will turn to a friend

---

BOX 7–4

To WHOM CAN YOU TURN?

There's an old saying—"A friend in need is a friend indeed." With this in mind, think of all the people you call your friends. Now list the names of those

> Who would really listen to you when you need to talk
> With whom you can share your innermost feelings
> To whom you can turn when you're very upset
> With whom you can be totally yourself
> Whom you can count on to help during a personal crisis

If you can name only two or three people, your personal support system may be too narrow. Perhaps your name isn't on enough other people's lists. After all, friendship is a two-way affair.

Young adults are more apt to turn to their peers than their families when in need. People who are middle-aged or older are more inclined to seek out members of their families, perhaps because the current generation of older people has been socialized in this way. With a growing population of elderly and the development of adult communities, perhaps future generations of older people will be more peer oriented.

before talking about it with their families. A friend may serve as a sounding board and provide needed support without the conflict of kinship loyalties. Do you have friends you could turn to in a personal crisis? If so, who are they? At the same time, people who ask their friends to share serious problems that are more properly discussed with a professional may be asking too much. In these instances, it's often best to refer a friend to the appropriate help, while remaining supportive.

MUTUAL SELF-DISCLOSURE

As the relationship between two people changes from strangers to acquaintances to close friends, individuals disclose a greater breadth and depth of information about themselves. **Self-disclosure** is the sharing of intimate or personal information with others. For example, Anita and Gale shared an apartment for a month when Anita's new apartment was being painted, so Anita met Gale's husband, Rick. Rick and Anita talked about common, benign topics such as their favorite movies, baseball teams, and foods. By the end of Anita's stay, they felt more comfortable talking about a greater variety of subjects, such as their career goals, leisure activities, and more intimate matters like health concerns, families, religious beliefs, and political preferences. As Rick and Anita became good friends, they developed greater trust in each other and shared matters that might threaten a weaker relationship.

Increasing levels of self-disclosure do not always lead to greater *intimacy* between two people. Ordinarily, the more you disclose about yourself, the more your friend will do likewise. Otherwise, your friend would hold a power advantage over you, knowing intimate details about you not ordinarily shared with others. However, if your friend does not feel sufficiently comfortable or trustful in the relationship, he or she would not reciprocate in such intimate self-disclosure. Eventually, you'd back off and restrict your communication to more superficial matters. In other instances, someone may share information that presents a conflict in the relationship, so that both partners may retreat to more superficial levels of sharing. For example, a young man in his late 30s told his wife about a brief sexual affair he'd had while out of town on business a few months earlier. He reassured his wife that he felt no affection for this other woman and promised never to see her again. The young man also said he felt better for having told her and hoped it would bring them closer together. He was wrong. His wife became extremely resentful and suspicious. Ever since then, she has doubted that he loves her and is worried about what he's doing while he's out of town. Both partners have become more guarded, a reversal of intimacy.

Gale and Anita were fortunate in that they each shared intimate information with the other. Other individuals, however, differ in their willingness to share personal information for several reasons. Those who enjoy high self-esteem feel not only more comfortable sharing personal information about themselves but also greater security that comes with close relationships. Those with low esteem are more apt to withhold personal information and thereby fail to learn about themselves through closeness with others. Then, too, men and women often differ in their willingness to share personal matters. Pairs of women characteristically engage in more intimate disclosure than do pairs of men (Dolgin, Meyer, & Schwartz, 1991). In fact, female-female friendship pairs seem particularly close (Dolgin & Kim, 1994). Disclosure with men is less reciprocal; that means men disclose less than is disclosed to them (Parker & deVries, 1993).

There are also significant cultural differences in how acceptable self-disclosure is. Wheeler, Reis, and Bond (1989) found that Americans have many more social interactions each day than those in other countries, but American interactions are shorter in duration. Similarly, Americans (especially men) disclose very little intimate information in their interactions compared to the Chinese. Another study suggested that American compared to Taiwanese college students disclose more than the Chinese on rather superficial topics, such as interests, work, and finances, but Americans show substantially higher degrees of self-disclosure to strangers (G. M. Chen, 1995).

All things considered, the association between liking and mutual self-disclosure depends a lot on the particular individuals—how compatible they are and how comfortable they feel sharing intimate matters. Also, with the influence of diminishing gender-role stereotypes, we can expect men to engage in more self-disclosure than has been the case in the past, especially with their friends and lovers.

SAME-SEX, OPPOSITE-SEX FRIENDS

Friendship is not necessarily more important to one sex than to the other, but it does tend to have different meanings for men and women. More specifically, intimacy plays a more central role among women friends, so the case of Anita and Gale in this chapter fits the topic well. Women generally are more physically and emotionally expressive in their friendships than men. Also, as we've already seen, women are more apt to share intimate details about their lives, such as their worries, joys, and secrets. At the same time, women experience greater anxiety over close relationships. Tensions, jealousies, and rejections are more common in friendships between women, whereas men are apt to engage in outright disputes over money, property, and dominance. Usually, men are not as emotionally close in their friendships with other men. They are more apt to seek out a male friend for a particular activity, like tennis or hunting, or to ask a favor. Yet, when in the throes of a personal problem, men are more inclined to seek out and put greater confidence in the advice of a close woman friend than a male friend. In contrast, half the married women in one survey felt more comfortable talking with their best woman friend about certain topics—doubts about themselves, rocky spots in their marriage, and problems with the children—than with their husbands (Sherman, 1987).

Men and women prefer different characteristics in their friends. Likewise, same-sex friends often interact differently than opposite-sex friends.

At the same time, with changing gender roles, neither the "activity friend" nor the "all-purpose friend" friendship style is distinctively male or female. Women, whose active lives now include everything from working lunches to health-club workouts, are discovering the pleasure of activity friends, who may be rarely seen otherwise. And men, realizing the importance of a personal support system, are discovering the value of an all-purpose friend with whom they share their deeper feelings and concerns. Furthermore, neither friendship style gives an advantage in mental health, achievement, or the enjoyment of life. Most of us are better off with a mixture of both types of friends among people of both sexes. Each type of friend brings out different aspects of ourselves.

Can you be a close friend with someone of the opposite sex without being romantically or sexually involved with this person? Some people remain skeptical; but now that men and women are working side by side just about everywhere, more people of both sexes are choosing friends of the opposite sex. At the same time, most people feel that opposite-sex friendships are different, in that they may easily turn into erotic relationships. Although this change strengthens some friendships, it may jeopardize others, especially when one or both friends are married to someone else. Do you think married people can have close friends of the opposite sex? Would you agree that a lot depends on how happily married the respective couples are? Then, too, a lot depends on whether both friends respect the marriage commitments of one or both partners.

STAYING FRIENDS OR BREAKING UP

"There's no friend like an old friend," goes the time-honored saying. With old friends we can relax and be ourselves without fear of rejection. We're familiar with each other's mannerisms and make allowances for each other's weaknesses. Staying friends depends more on the special quality of the relationship than the frequency of contact between two people. Most of us have some friends we don't see very often, but we still consider them friends. We may keep in touch by calling up occasionally or exchanging cards or letters. Class reunions and vacations also afford additional opportunities for renewing old ties. At the same time, physical separation often exacts a toll on friendship. When people are asked why friendships cool off, the most frequently given reason is that one person has moved away. In fact, the most common reason people cite for the breakup of friendships is simply life transitions; 77 percent of American adults said that their friendships ended because of life changes (S. Davis, 1996). One person's life situation changes and the other person's does not. Specific life changes that affect friendships include marriage, childbirth, and new jobs and schedules.

Apart from life transitions, the most common reason for ending a friendship is feeling betrayed by a friend; in other words, trust is broken. **Trust** can be defined as people's abstractive positive expectations that they can count on friends and partners to care for them and be responsive to their needs, now and in the future (Berscheid, 1994). The importance of trust and the ability to keep a confidence in friendship cannot be overestimated. In one study, about one-third of the people said that their basic expectations in friendship had been violated by a best or close friend. In some instances, there were minor infringements, such as using a personal item without asking permission. But other cases involved more serious offenses, such as "repeating things I said in confidence" or "trying to seduce my wife." In some instances, people still claimed someone as a friend but with such qualifications as "You have to watch what you tell her; she gossips a lot" or "You just can't trust him" (K. E. Davis, 1985). Box 7–5, "How Trusting Are You of Your Friends?," presents more information on trust and close relationships.

BOX 7–5

How Trusting Are You of Your Friends?

Trust is one of the most important aspects of close relationships. Many people regard "keeps confidence" and "loyalty"—two aspects of trust—as the top two qualities of a friend. And feeling betrayed by a friend is one of the most common reasons for ending a friendship.

John Rempel and John Holmes (1986) found that people's characteristic level of trust, in turn, vitally affects their friendships, including the extent to which they can rely on others, how much they will tell others, and how they will handle conflict and disagreement in their relationships.

People who describe themselves as very trusting approach interactions with others in a positive manner. And they expect a partner to behave in a similar way toward them. Even when faced with disagreement, they anticipate that their partner will respond in an accepting, considerate manner. As you might expect, trusting people generally have their expectations confirmed. It appears that trust keeps them from attaching too much importance to any particular negative event. That is, because they have faith in a person, they're more willing to give that person the benefit of the doubt when things don't go well. And on the whole, trusting people enjoy relatively secure and comforting relationships.

People who characterize themselves as having low levels of trust also have difficulty trusting others. They express less affection for their partners and are less inclined to see their relationships as those of mutual giving. Their emotional attachments remain fragile, mostly because they fear becoming close to and dependent on others. When it comes to disagreement, they generally predict that their partner will act in an angry and defensive manner. And they, too, often have their expectations confirmed. It's as if people who are initially reluctant to express trust are in no position to risk giving their partner the benefit of the doubt when necessary. Not surprisingly, these people report being the least satisfied in their relationships with others.

The irony is that once trust has been violated, a vicious cycle often ensues, so that trust becomes even more difficult to establish. Yet, as Rempel and Holmes (1986) point out, the paradox of close relationships remains: To be able to trust, you must take the risk of trusting. If you see new signs of caring in your partner, you risk being wrong. But if you don't try, you may never be right.

SOURCE: Rempel, J. K., & Holmes, J. G. (1986, February). "How Do I Trust Thee?" *Psychology Today.* Reprinted with permission from Psychology Today Magazine. Copyright © 1986 (Sussex Publishers, Inc.).

There are yet other reasons friendships cool. Friendships may also cool off or break up because the individuals discover they have very different views on matters that are important to them. Not surprisingly, this is the third most frequently cited reason for ending a friendship. Curiously, in some cases, increasing intimacy between friends, such as may be occasioned by taking a vacation together, may make them even more aware of their differences or they find they have less in common than originally believed. But friendship is such a deeply satisfying experience that each of us will continue making new friends throughout life, while cherishing the special closeness that comes with a long-lasting friendship.

LONELINESS

Anita was so fortunate to have someone like Gale meet her, watch over her, and befriend her. On the other hand, some people have trouble forming or keeping close friendships, and they become lonely. Essentially, **loneliness** is a subjective state reflecting the fact that the quality and quantity of relationships wanted is lower than the quality and quantity of relationships available (Archibald, Bartholomew, & Marx, 1995). It is not to be confused with solitude, which is a more objective and often desired state denoting the absence of people. Thus, people may feel lonely despite being surrounded by others if they don't feel close to those people. On the other hand, people with many friends may deliberately seek brief periods of solitude to sort out what's happening in their lives, without feeling lonely. Thus, it appears that loneliness is largely a state of mind that results from the gap between our desire for closeness and the failure to find it. Loneliness, then, is often associated with depression, anxiety, unhappiness, and shyness (Neto, 1992). Interestingly, the duration of loneliness may be related more to reported psychological and somatic stress symptoms than the intensity of loneliness (DeBerard & Kleinknecht, 1995).

Sharon Brehm (1985) found that the experience of loneliness varies somewhat depending on which aspects of our lives are most affected. People who feel lonely because they lack a network of social ties and acquaintances suffer mostly from social isolation. That is, they may not be close to other members of their family or participate enough in community activities. Other people may be dissatisfied because they lack closeness in their intimate relationships, and they suffer more from emotional isolation. They may lack close friendships or a romantic or sexual relationship. Other studies have shown that married women report greater loneliness than married men, probably because of the greater importance of close relationships for women. However, among separated and divorced people, men report greater loneliness than women, most likely because men's main source of closeness is their romantic partners (Brehm).

Ironically, college students suffer more from loneliness than any other age group. Having loosened the ties with their parents, people this age are actively seeking intimacy with their peers, especially those of the opposite sex. The idealism of youth, plus the desire for intimacy and a happy marriage, makes them especially sensitive to the discrepancy between their expectations of intimacy and their actual relationships.

Loneliness tends to decline over the years, leveling off throughout middle-age, though less so among women than men. Although older adults spend much of their time alone, most of them are less prone to loneliness than popularly depicted, probably because they have learned to put their need for companionship in better perspective. However, loneliness appears to increase again among those in their 80s, reflecting, in part, the greater sense of disengagement from life among those at an advanced age (Perlman, 1991).

How often do you feel lonely—sometimes or often? Which areas of your life are most affected—your social life or your love life? To assess your loneliness, you might complete the sample questions from the Revised UCLA Loneliness Scale in Figure 7–3.

Many factors contribute to loneliness. People who have grown up with warm and helpful parents are less likely to report loneliness in adulthood than those who describe their parents as disagreeable and unhelpful. Some of the loneliest people are those whose parents divorced when they were younger than 6 years old, partly because young chil-

FIGURE 7–3

UCLA LONELINESS SCALE

Here are some sample items from this well-known scale:

Statement	Never	Rarely	Sometimes	Often
a. I lack companionship	1	2	3	4
b. There is no one I can turn to	1	2	3	4
c. I am no longer close to anyone	1	2	3	4
d. No one really knows me well	1	2	3	4

SCORING KEY: Add the sum of the four items to get your total score. Remember that you did not take the whole scale, so if you have a high score (maximum = 16), the score does not necessarily indicate a high degree of loneliness on your part.

dren often misperceive parental divorce as abandonment. In contrast, people who have lost a parent through death experience no corresponding increase in loneliness, probably because they realize that their loss was not intentional (Rubinstein, Shaver, & Peplau, 1982). People with low self-esteem tend to experience loneliness more than people who have high esteem. Individuals with low esteem are often lonely because their own beliefs in their unworthiness limit their recognition of positive feedback from others. This keeps them from taking steps to reduce their loneliness. Another reason people are rejected by others is because they have poor social skills; they are especially vulnerable to loneliness (Braza, Braza, Careeras, & Muñoz, 1993). Children who lack appropriate social skills are sometimes rejected by their friends because they are aggressive, withdrawn, or fail to show appropriate responses to others' needs. On the other hand, individuals who are high in empathy, aware of their own emotions, and cooperative tend to be very popular (Goleman, 1995). The ability to regulate one's own emotions and to be empathic for others is called **emotional intelligence** or EQ. People with high EQ are often very socially skilled and popular. Finally, research has shown that individuals who have a negative or cynical world view are more likely to be rejected by others (Crandall & Cohen, 1994).

Culture affects loneliness, too. The emphasis on personal fulfillment, often at the expense of stable relationships and commitment to others, is thought to make Americans especially prone to loneliness (De jong-Gierveld, 1987). Immigrants and long-term visitors to the United States are likely to report feeling very lonely (Nah, 1993). In one study of international students, cultural distance predicted mood disturbance or adjustment (C. Ward & Searle, 1991). The further the student's culture was sociologically from American culture, the more lonely and depressed was the student. Canadian students, for example, are less lonely than students from Japan. Befriending international students and helping them adjust by assisting them with understanding our culture would be very considerate. At the same time, you would have the interesting opportunity to learn about their culture.

How well we cope with loneliness depends largely on how we interpret its causes. People who suffer the most from loneliness tend to exaggerate its internal aspects and minimize its external ones. Thus, people who blame their loneliness on their personal inadequacies ("I'm lonely because I'm unlovable" or "My lover and I have split up, but that's the way my relationships go") make themselves even more lonely and depressed. Cognitive therapy to change the self-schema would be very useful in this instance (Hope, Holt, & Heimberg, 1995). In contrast, people are more likely to overcome their loneliness when they focus on the external, situational factors involved ("It's hard to meet people in large classes") and their own efforts ("I'll stop working so much and get out and meet more people"). Similarly, people who react to loneliness in passive ways—watching television, crying, sleeping—feel even lonelier. Those who adopt more active or behavioral strategies—reading, writing a letter, calling up a friend—are more likely to alleviate their loneliness. Social-skills training can help change behaviors (Hope et al., 1995). The best course is to continue developing our interpersonal skills, so that we always have access to a network of social ties as well as a circle of close friends.

SUMMARY

MEETING PEOPLE

We began the chapter by pointing out that each of us tends to have both a network of social ties with which to fulfill a variety of needs and a smaller circle of close friends with whom we can be more intimate. We begin acquaintances with surface contacts; then, based upon first impressions, we decide whether to continue the interaction.

We're attracted to people for a variety of reasons, including such factors as familiarity, physical attraction, and similar backgrounds and interests. The more we interact with someone, the more we tend to like that person, unless we discover serious differences or basic incompatibilities. Also, we tend to judge physically attractive people more favorably than others, even on matters that have little or nothing to do with physical appearance. Furthermore, we're attracted to people with similar attitudes and interests as ourselves. However, in long-term relationships, we're often attracted to someone on the basis of a mixture of similar and complementary needs.

When meeting people, we tend to form erroneous impressions of others on the basis of limited information, usually judging by such factors as a person's physical appearance, especially his or her attractiveness, speech, and nonverbal behavior. Not surprisingly, the most common reason for misjudging people is the lack of sufficient information, causing reliance instead on false cues and stereotypes, and the failure to account for the situational influences on people's behavior. Shy people, in particular, tend to be misperceived as aloof and disinterested, largely because of their silence and lack of eye contact. Shyness can be overcome.

INTERPERSONAL ATTRACTION

As society becomes more complex and impersonal, we value close friends even more. At the same time, we're choosing friends from a wider diversity of people than in the past, including more opposite-sex friends. Close friends frequently get together for good talk and companionship, in addition to sharing a variety of other activities. There's a close link between friendship and mutual self-disclosure, so that the emotional sharing strengthens the bond of friendship. Generally, opposite-sex friends tend to supplement rather than displace our same-sex friends and may or may not involve a sexual relationship. Staying friends with someone depends more on the special quality of the relationship than on the frequency of contact. The two most common reasons friendships break up are that one person moves away or one feels betrayed by the other.

Essentially, loneliness is a state of mind that results from the gap between our desire for closeness and the failure to find it. Ironically, youths in their teens and 20s suffer more from loneliness than any other age group, and loneliness decreases as people age. People who suffer the most from loneliness tend to blame themselves for their plight or resort to passive strategies, such as watching television or sleeping. In contrast, those who cope the best with loneliness tend to recognize the situational factors involved and take more active steps to alleviate them, such as calling up a friend. Sojourners or international visitors often have problems adjusting to their new culture and therefore feel lonely.

SCORING KEY FOR THE INTERPERSONAL ORIENTATION SCALE

Compute your score for each of the four dimensions of the affiliative need. Add up the numbers in each category as follows: (1) Positive cognitive stimulation is assessed by items 3, 6, 10, 11, 13, 20, 24, 25, and 26. (2) Attention is assessed by items 5, 8, 16, 19, 21, and 22. (3) Social comparison is assessed by items 2, 7, 12, 14, and 18. (4) Emotional support is assessed by items 1, 4, 9, 15, 17, and 23. The average or mean scores for male and female undergraduate students are

	Male	Female
1. Positive cognitive stimulation	30.16	33.02
2. Attention	17.64	17.45
3. Social comparison	16.50	16.63
4. Emotional support	18.63	21.01

SELF-TEST

1. Our initial impressions of people are generally based on
   a. their family backgrounds
   b. negative stereotypes
   c. very little information
   d. their body language

2. We often misjudge people when we fail to consider how their behavior is affected by
   a. situational influences
   b. social status
   c. moral principles
   d. unconscious motives

3. Shy people are especially apt to be misjudged as
   a. intelligent
   b. cold
   c. aggressive
   d. undersexed

4. The more familiar we become with a person, the more we tend to
   - a. envy that person
   - b. dislike that person
   - c. criticize that person
   - d. like that person

5. We're attracted to people directly according to the proportion of shared
   - a. attitudes
   - b. interests
   - c. motives
   - d. traits

6. According to the fundamental attribution error, we often blame _____ rather than _____.
   - a. traits/situations
   - b. friends/family
   - c. strangers/friends
   - d. situations/traits

7. One of the most common activities among same-sex and opposite-sex friends is
   - a. taking a vacation
   - b. having an intimate talk
   - c. sharing a meal
   - d. going shopping

8. The process of revealing intimate information about ourselves is called
   - a. self-disclosure
   - b. bragging
   - c. attribution
   - d. all of these

9. Almost half of Americans report that they feel
   - a. bravery
   - b. chronic shyness
   - c. in love
   - d. closer to opposite-sex friends than same-sex friends

10. The most frequently given reason for friendships breaking up is that one person has
    - a. moved away
    - b. borrowed money
    - c. been promoted at work
    - d. gotten married

EXERCISES

1. *First impressions.* Look around in your classes and select someone you haven't met. Jot down your impressions of this person. Then make it a point to introduce yourself and become better acquainted. To what extent was your initial impression accurate or inaccurate?

2. *Do you ever suffer from shyness?* If so, in which situations? How has shyness affected your life? What steps have you taken to overcome it?

3. *Write a personal ad about yourself.* Suppose you were writing a personal ad for the classified section of a magazine devoted to introducing singles. How would you describe yourself? How would you describe the type of person you're looking for? Write a short paragraph for this purpose.

4. *Self-disclosure.* Write a paragraph or two including your thoughts on the following matters: How comfortable do you feel sharing personal information with friends? With whom do you share the most? Which topics? If married, do you share more with your spouse or friends? Would you agree that the rewards of mutual self-disclosure outweigh the risks?

5. *Who can you turn to?* If you were experiencing a personal crisis, who would you turn to for help—your family or friends? Which person would you seek out first? Explain the reasons for your answers.

6. *Intimacy and growth.* Think of a close friendship or love relationship. Then describe your relationship in a page or so, including your thoughts on the following points: Do you both maintain other friendships? If lovers, are you also friends? Can each of you experience closeness without giving up your individuality? To what extent does this relationship encourage each of you to grow as a person?

QUESTIONS FOR SELF-REFLECTION

1. How much do you judge by first impressions?
2. Do you make a good first impression on others?
3. Are you ever bothered by shyness?
4. Do you usually find that the more you know someone, the better you like the person?
5. How important are good looks in being attracted to someone of the opposite sex?
6. Do some of your friends have interests and personalities quite different from yours?
7. Who is your best friend? With which people do you feel most comfortable sharing secrets?
8. Do you have a close friend of the opposite sex?
9. Have you ever been betrayed by a close friend?
10. Have you ever befriended an international student? How was that person's culture similar to yours? How was it different?

FOR FURTHER INFORMATION

RECOMMENDED READINGS

BRINKMAN, R., & KIRSCHNER, R. (1994). *Dealing with people you can't stand: How to bring out the best in people at their worst.* New York: McGraw-Hill. We sometimes have to interact with people we don't like or who have weak social skills. Here is a how-to book designed to make these interactions easier.

FEHR, B. A. (1996). *Friendship processes.* New York: Sage. A guide to friendship, intimacy, and man-woman relationships.

GOLEMAN, D. (1995). *Emotional intelligence.* New York: Bantam Books. Learn all about EQ and why it is just as or more important than IQ.

HOPSON, D. S. (1994). *Friends, lovers, and soul mates: A guide to better relationships between Black men and women.* New York: Simon & Schuster. A book about close relationships written especially for African Americans from which we can all learn.

LEARY, M. (1995). *Social anxiety.* New York: Guilford. A book for people with social phobias or fear of meeting and interacting with others.

WEBSITES AND THE INTERNET

http://www.epix.net/~tlizotte/date1.html: A site to find friends. Individuals can find links to all sorts of sites for finding friends and lovers. Take caution, though. Anyone, including some unscrupulous and strange people, can surf and post to the Web.

usenet:alt.personals.intercultural: An interesting website where people around the world post to find friends. An opportunity to learn about culture through cyberspace.

http://w3.com/date/: A personals service where the postings are somewhat moderated by the webmaster. You can post anonymously to feel safer using the site.

Usenet:alt.support.shyness: A site for people who are shy to meet other shy people and discuss their shyness.

Usenet:alt.support.social-phobia: Another site for those who are uncomfortable in public or when interacting with other people.

http://208.14.0.131/empo/empo.html: A chat room with lots of possibilities. Several languages and many topics are available so that you can link up with other interesting people in cyberspace.

CHAPTER 8

Being Part of a Group

Learning Objectives

After completing this chapter, you should be able to

1. Name and describe various kinds of groups.
2. Discuss how groups form and reform.
3. Cite reasons why people join groups.
4. Describe how groups communicate and how the shape and size of groups affect communication.
5. Understand various types of social influence such as conformity.
6. Describe how individuals become leaders.
7. Know how groups go wrong, recognize the symptoms of group dysfunction, and describe some of the cures for group problems.

Roy grew up in the cornfields of Iowa. His father, Harry, inherited the family farm and soon married Sara, Roy's mother. Sara and Harry were so excited and proud the day their baby boy, Roy, was born. Sara and Harry developed great plans for their child from the moment of his arrival. Sara and Harry hoped that Roy would attend college and become an engineer or a lawyer so that he would not have to lead the hard farming life they had.

Sara and Harry pushed hard for Roy to achieve in school. High grades, they thought, were Roy's ticket out of the cornfields. Although Roy was resistant at first, much like any child who enjoyed playing rather than studying, Roy soon settled into his studies and was near the top of his class. Upon graduation, Roy was accepted to a large university in the East and even landed a good scholarship, thus relieving his parents of a huge financial burden.

September 5, 1990, was a day his parents were never to forget. Roy left for college and never again returned to the cornfields. What happened to Roy? While at college, Roy soon became fascinated with a local group called the Akaries, a group that worshipped the sun, moon, and stars and believed that soon the world would end. Once Roy became fully initiated into this group, a well-known cult in the same city as the university, Sara and Harry never heard from him again.

How do such groups as the Akaries form? Why do some individuals such as Roy become followers whereas others become the cherished leaders? Do all groups function the same; is there such a thing as a dysfunctional group? These questions and others are the focus of this chapter on being part of a group.

◆ Kinds of Groups

Groups are all around us. Everywhere we look we see people in groups. People congregate in their places of worship, families can often be seen in restaurants around America, college classrooms are filled to the brim with eager students. Football fans collectively cheer for their favorite teams, and sororities and fraternities hold their deliberations on new members in the privacy of their houses. Everywhere—groups.

What kinds of groups are there and how do they differ? There are many different kinds of groups, each with its own characteristics, but only a few of them will be reviewed here.

PRIMARY GROUPS

Perhaps the most immediately important groups in our lives are our **primary groups.** These groups are important because they are small and intimate. For these and other reasons primary groups have much influence on us. Of course, in turn, we can have great impact on them. Primary groups typically function through face-to-face interaction such as do families and roommates in residence halls. A nuclear family, for example, has great impact on its members. The parents instill in their children the same values, dreams, and culture as the parents. Children often adopt their parents' religion, political views, and

Primary groups, such as families, are small and communicate face-to-face.

Secondary groups are larger and communication is more formalized.

Collectives are so large that interpersonal communication is often impossible.

other likes and dislikes. College roommates sometimes become more like each other the more they interact. Happy husbands and wives often influence each other; they share the same friends, the same preferences for politicians, music, and television programs. The Akaries, although somewhat large with 22 members, perhaps could be classified as a primary group because they were so close-knit and interdependent on one another.

SECONDARY GROUPS

Another type of group is a **secondary group.** These groups are usually larger than primary groups, have a formal or contractual reason for coming together, often disband when the reason for their existence evaporates, and are less likely to engage in regular face-to-face interaction. An example of this type of group would be your class, the one for which you are reading this book. The class has a formal reason for coming together (to learn about adjustment and personal growth) but probably does not exclusively engage in face-to-face interaction. Other examples would be a church congregation or a social club such as the psychology club. Secondary groups, then, often configure in an audience rather than in a face-to-face, interactional pattern.

COLLECTIVES

Very large groups exist in our society. The cheering football spectators mentioned earlier can number in the tens of thousands if the stadium is large enough. Fans at a rock concert offer another example. A crowd gathering to watch a spontaneous event such as a fire at an office building is a third example. These groups, called **collectives,** tend to be very large and are less likely to have a leader or clear rules compared to primary and secondary groups. Collectives often form and disband for no readily apparent reasons. Because collectives are large and without clear-cut rules, they can often be disorderly. Americans have historically witnessed the tragedy of this disorderliness, especially at rock concerts where a crowd distressed over the long wait spreads rumors that there are too few seats. Pushing and shoving begin and fans are trampled in the ensuing stampede. Other instances come to us from the sports world where crowds have rioted when their favorite teams have lost; fights start in the stands and spread throughout the stadium.

IN-GROUPS AND OUT-GROUPS

There are two other very important groups that influence our social selves. One is the group with which we identify, the **in-group.** The in-group can be contrasted with the **out-group,** the group that we perceive as being different from our own group. In-group perceptions can develop based on **ethnicity,** gender, age, religion, occupation, and income level among other factors. To the locals around Roy's campus, the Akaries in their strange wardrobes and weird haircuts were clearly the out-group; to the Akaries, the rest of the world was the out-group. Their own respective group was the in-group.

What is perhaps most important about the distinctions we make between our own group and the out-group is that these discriminations often result in prejudice against the out-group. **Prejudice** is an attitude toward another person or group based solely on group membership. Prejudice is sometimes accompanied by behavior whereby the group against which the prejudice is held is discriminated against or treated worse than our own group. This behavioral component is called **discrimination.** Although the two usually occur together, prejudice can occur without discrimination and discrimination can occur without prejudice. For example, a restaurant owner could harbor negative attitudes toward Native Americans but still serve them in his restaurant because of the laws against discrimination.

Psychologists are concerned about prejudice and discrimination because prejudice leads to negative evaluations of individuals in the outgroup (Bodenhausen, 1990) as well as causes damage to the self-esteem of the target of prejudice (Baron & Byrne, 1997). Interestingly, one reason biased individuals tend to hold prejudices is that they seek to enhance their own self-esteem by viewing their own group as superior to the outgroup (Meindl & Lerner, 1984).

 ## How Groups Form

Think about a fairly new group that you recently joined. How and why did the group form? Why did you join? The group probably was one from your campus and was a secondary group. Suppose that the group was initiated by a group of disgruntled commuter students who feel there are insufficient numbers of parking spaces and too few evening classes to accommodate their busy schedules.

The first process in group development is **forming.** When Roy became entranced by the Akaries, the group was already well-formed. In other groups, in the forming stage, members sometimes do not know each other as well as they will later in the developmental process; they are simply coming together as a group. In the commuter group, one concerned individual may call the meeting, which is initially attended by many strangers. Even in a new marriage, where the couple has dated for months, the new wife may not know that her new husband squeezes the toothpaste in the middle when she prefers to squeeze neatly from the end. Neither does she know that her new husband prefers to watch game shows rather than the political debates she favors. If enough of these differences exist, friction can build and squabbles might begin in any group. Initially, though, most group members step forward with their best and most cooperative foot while the group forms and people jockey for positions.

When group members learn more about each other's attitudes and predilections, differences among individuals lead to the second stage, **storming.** In this stage, which can follow quickly on the heels of the first, individuals disagree and often openly argue. In the commuter group, some individuals may prefer a university-sponsored bus service whereas others argue for more parking spaces.

This stage is a troublesome one. Members may decide there exists too much friction so thus leave the group. Some individuals initially attracted to the Akaries did not remain long. Other members may decide that it is best to remain passive rather than be pulled into the fray, and others are so vociferous and aggressive about promoting their agendas that the remaining members intensely dislike them. At this point it may seem that the group will never start functioning. However, if group members recognize that this is a normal group stage, they can move beyond this difficult stage to the next, more productive one.

When roles become more sharply defined, when groups finally come to terms with how they will function, when rules by which they will function are clear, the group is said to be **norming.** That is, through discourse and debate the group eventually comes to consensus about the rules under which it will operate. As just mentioned, roles start to emerge in groups in the storming and norming stages. A **role** is a set of rules that defines how an individual in a particular post in a group will behave. As just mentioned,

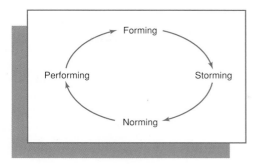

FIGURE 8–1
Cycle of group formation.

each group also develops its own idiosyncratic **norms** *or* unwritten rules by which it will function and by which it will exert pressure on nonconforming members. For example, the married couple may agree that the husband will squeeze the toothpaste from the end because it creates less waste. The wife may agree that every other night they will watch what her husband prefers and on off nights the couple will watch what she likes. Suite mates in residence halls may ultimately decide that the one suite mate who stays up late watching television has to go to the downstairs lounge to do so; otherwise, she disturbs her suite mates with early morning classes. The Akari group had very strange norms to outsiders. In his posh bedroom, the leader, Otu, was allowed to have sex with any woman in the group, except married women and young girls. The husbands and other men had to remain in their collective bunk room.

Once a group has formed, worked through its initial disagreements, and developed norms, the group is ready to perform. **Performing** is the final stage of group development. It is during this stage that the group functions better and actually gets down to its business, whether it be the rearing of children in a marriage, or developing a strategic plan for a work team. Once this developmental pattern has been played out by a group, new issues can arise or new members can be added. The group then cycles through these stages again. (See Figure 8–1.)

 Why Join a Group?

Why would individuals follow a cult leader such as Otu? What would draw intelligent men and women to the Akaries? What would attract any individual to a group? What makes you join some clubs and teams at college and resist others?

Social psychologists have identified a multitude of reasons for people's joining groups. People sometimes connect with groups because groups offer possibilities not available to us as individuals. One possibility that groups offer is the chance to **affiliate,** to be with others who often are similar to us or whom we like. Sororities and fraternities fill this need by attracting new members who generally are very similar to existing members. Synagogues and temples offer more than religious support; they also offer the chance to socialize with members of the same faith. The Akaries afforded the opportunity to individuals with the same religious and political attitudes to be with similar others and test out their attitudes.

Groups also offer us information we might not otherwise possess. Although most people in America have access to the media, some do not avail themselves of television and newspapers because they do not have the time, do not speak English, or cannot afford televisions. Groups to which we belong can keep us informed about important as well as mundane events. Groups, however, offer us more than mere facts. Groups help us understand whether we harbor attitudes that represent a minority position in a group. Groups also help us understand our position in the social order. For example, you do not know whether you are short until you stand next to many individuals to whom you have to look up. When you receive examinations back in a college class, you may think that a score of 37 is terrible until you see that the classmates around you received 25, 19, and 32. Now the 37 feels better, doesn't it? Groups, then, allow us to compare ourselves to others and understand who we are relative to them. This is the process of **social comparison.**

The concept of **social support,** introduced elsewhere in the book, is important to groups. Recall that social support is a process whereby one individual or group offers psychological and sometimes physical aid to another individual or group. Groups, especially of friends and family, can offer us much needed social support. When something goes wrong in our lives, when we have difficult decisions to make, and even when something wonderful has happened (for instance, receiving a promotion), groups can give us a needed boost. Coworkers can help us ponder the advantages and disadvantages of various alternatives that confront us when we have to make an important decision. Friends can give us affection and sympathy when we suffer the loss of a loved one. Our families can enhance our joy when we have succeeded. Groups, therefore, offer social support that research has repeatedly demonstrated is important to our mental health (e.g., Helgeson & Cohen, 1996).

Groups also give us more collective power. There may be needs we have that we alone cannot meet. For example, the Akaries may have been comprised of individuals who for one reason or another were failures elsewhere. By joining, they realized their collective power. One such individual was John, Roy's friend, who was educated in journalism but who joined the Akaries shortly after applying and being rejected by graduate schools.

Labor unions offer another example. Unions can collectively negotiate better raises and working conditions than any individual member can. Alliances and coalitions can better lobby governments for needed legislation. And student groups, such as your student government, possess consolidated power compared to each individual student. The student government with the force of hundreds or thousands of students behind it can better approach the administration to advance student causes on your campus.

 Group Processes

You have already been introduced to two group processes, development of roles and development of norms. There are other processes that are unique to groups that would rarely be discussed with regard to individuals. These processes include communication, social influence, social loafing, and polarization, which are all important to decision making and performance in groups.

COMMUNICATION IN GROUPS

One of the most important group processes is communication. Intragroup communication is important to all the other processes discussed next. Communication within a group allows group members to coordinate their actions, share information, and express emotions and ideas, all of which are important to decision making and performance.

Networks.   Some of the earliest research on group communication concerned communication networks within groups (K. Davis & Newstrom, 1985). There are **centralized communication networks** in which one or two individuals control the flow of information. One such network is the wheel in which there is a centralized individual or node with spokes or channels extending outward to other individuals or nodes. The wheel is similar to a university where department chairs go to a dean who makes funding, personnel, and other decisions. Certainly, Otu was the important focal point or the center of the group known as the Akaries. The wheel and other networks are depicted in Figure 8–2.

Centralized networks can be contrasted to decentralized communication networks. In **decentralized communication networks** individuals can communicate more freely with one another. An example of a decentralized network is the circle, also shown in Figure 8–2. Rumors that pass from one person to another, then to yet another, and back to the original source offer an example of the circle. Of course, there are other centralized and decentralized systems. Can you think of concrete examples for all of the networks represented in Figure 8–2?

Centralized and decentralized networks result in different types of performance in groups. Centralized networks are much more efficient so thus work capably and efficiently on simple tasks or simple decisions. When tasks are complicated or decisions require complex input and deliberation, decentralized networks are best.

Group size.   One other group factor that affects quality of communication and therefore quality of the group's work is the size of the group. Groups vary in their size depending on the situation. Juries are usually comprised of 12 individuals, university academic departments can be as small as 2 people or as large as 60, and families average about 4 or 5 members in the United States. A group with many members has more resources available so may be able to generate more ideas. However, the number of ideas generated is not directly proportionate to group size (Moorhead & Griffin, 1995). As the size of the group increases, the number of ideas increases at a slower rate. Interactions and communications are also more likely to be formalized in a larger group. For instance, large groups are more likely to set agendas and to follow Roberts' Rules of Order to control discussions. Finally, some individuals may be shy about participating in large groups but not in small groups, so participation is uneven (Moorhead & Griffin, 1995).

Electronic communication.   As groups turn more and more to electronic technology, it will be interesting to determine whether the above principles still hold true. For

FIGURE 8–2
Examples of various communication networks. "O" represents an individual and the dash represents the communication links between individuals.

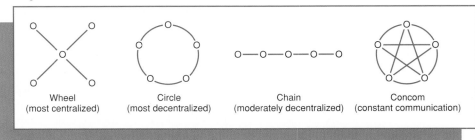

| Wheel (most centralized) | Circle (most decentralized) | Chain (moderately decentralized) | Concom (constant communication) |

example, in electronic communication such as e-mail, the impact of nonverbal communication is lessened. However, Finholt and Sproull (1990) analyzed incoming and outgoing electronic messages of 96 employees and found that most of the employee groups behaved like real social groups. This was true despite that the groups did not share physical space and that their members were essentially invisible. McGuire, Kiesler, and Siegel (1987) also found that computer-mediated groups are less vulnerable to problems such as groupthink and group polarization (discussed later). Other research has established that status inequalities are reduced with electronic participation (Dubrovsky, Kiesler, & Sethna, 1991). This is important because in face-to-face groups often the highest status members do the most communicating. Dubrovsky and colleagues' research shows that with electronic communication each group member has a greater likelihood of participating. Given this, the group has a better chance of maximizing the potential of all its members.

SOCIAL INFLUENCE

What is **social influence?** Social influence involves efforts on the part of one person to alter the behavior or attitudes of one or more others. Otu and other cult leaders have immense social influence over their followers. Other groups and leaders have such influence, too, although not to the extremes of the Akaries and Otu. Social influence can occur at three different levels. We can publicly go along with others but refuse to change our private beliefs. An example of this would be that you are seated in the snack bar between classes and three friends all declare that they are voting for a political candidate whom you detest. In a hurry to make your next class, you do not want to debate with them so nod your head in agreement. Another level of social influence is when you behave like others or are influenced by others because you are attracted to them. Very often when you steadily date a new person, you adopt the new date's tastes for food and music. If you and your date then part company, you return to your own tastes in cuisine and melody. The third level is one where someone has truly influenced you in that you change forever. At this level, an individual or group convinces you that you should adopt their ideas, behaviors, and tastes. This third and most important type of influence is the one possessed by Otu over his followers.

How and why do people gain influence over others? Three processes—conformity, compliance, and obedience—shed light on the mechanisms.

Conformity.   **Conformity** is a change in behavior due to the real or imagined influence of other people. When American youths started wearing backward baseball caps, they were conforming to age-mate pressure to conform, to be like others their age. No one issued orders or laws proclaiming that youths needed to wear their caps backwards.

Conformity has been well examined since the seminal research of Solomon Asch. Asch (1951) requested subjects to come to an experimental room one at a time. When the subject entered the room, the subject was confronted by what appeared to be other subjects. These other subjects actually were **confederates** or friends of the experimenter who were told by the experimenter how to behave. The subject and confederates were asked to judge lines similar to those in Figure 8–3. One at a time each was to say aloud which line of the three, B, C, or D, was closest in length to the standard line A.

At first, confederates gave correct answers. Then confederates gave wrong answers. Asch reasoned that the real subject would stand his or her ground and give the correct answer or not go along with the crowd. Asch, to his surprise, found that many subjects

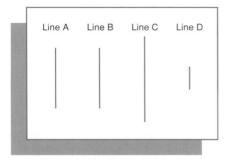

| Line A | Line B | Line C | Line D |

FIGURE 8–3

The Asch conformity experiment. Subjects sat with confederates and looked at the following lines. The subject and confederates were to compare line A with lines B, C, and D and state which of the three was closest in length to line A. Confederates often gave the wrong answer; results indicated that many subjects simply conformed to the confederates' wrong answers.

conformed to the apparently wrong answer. Specifically, Asch found that of 123 subjects, 94 or 76 percent gave the wrong answer at least once. On average, subjects gave the same wrong answer as did the confederates on 4 of 12 trials. Asch concluded that the tendency to conform in our society is strong, even on obviously easy tasks and even when no one forces conformity.

Since Asch's initial research, scientists have discovered factors that enhance or reduce conformity. We are most likely to conform when we are in optimally sized groups of approximately four people (Tanford & Penrod, 1984) and when there are no other nonconformists (Asch, 1956). Not all groups function exactly according to these findings on conformity. Interestingly, the Akaries group was large but still exerted much influence over its members.

It is also important to comment on cultural differences in conformity. Despite Asch's results, most Americans espouse independence and autonomy so eschew conformity. There exist, however, cultures that emphasize **interdependence;** thus, conformity is

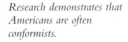

Research demonstrates that Americans are often conformists.

an integral part of the social fabric of that culture. Some examples of these more inter-dependent cultures where conformity to group norms is expected include the Japanese, Zimbabwean, and Lebanese cultures (P. B. Smith & Bond, 1993).

Compliance.   Another process of social influence is compliance. **Compliance** may be defined as a change in behavior in response to a direct request from another person to do so. Compliance, like conformity, is an everyday phenomenon. When your professor requests that you take your seats so that she can begin lecturing, you sit down, thus complying with the entreaty. When your mother calls you to the dinner table, you usually come in response to her request. And when you ask to borrow your roommate's extra umbrella, she usually loans it in a demonstration of compliance. Note that we may comply publicly but disagree with the request privately just as is true for conformity.

There are conditions under which we are more likely to comply. In mainstream American society there exists a **norm of reciprocity.** This unwritten rule guides reciprocal behavior related to the granting of favors. If someone does you a favor, you are compelled to return the favor. For example, when you borrow your roommate's umbrella, you are obligated to let her borrow something of yours, or when food companies give free samples, there is some feeling of obligation to buy the product after the sampling.

Another method to induce compliance is **ingratiation,** which involves managing the impressions you leave on others so that they will like you more and comply with your requests. *Flattery* is a form of ingratiation in which the flatterer hopes that the flattered individual might later give in to a certain request. Another form of ingratiation is opinion conformity, where one individual publicly agrees with a speaker so that the speaker will like the agreer. *Opinion conformity* then occurs when one individual repeatedly agrees with another's viewpoint. The agreer can later ask the speaker for a favor because now the speaker better likes the person in agreement.

Sometimes a two-step approach to compliance increases its likelihood. There are several two-step approaches, one of which will suffice here. In the **door-in-the-face effect,** the requester first issues a large, unreasonable request (Cialdini, 1988). When the respondent answers no, the requester asks for the truly desired but smaller and more reasonable demand. Not wanting to appear difficult or stubborn, the respondent often answers yes to the second, smaller request. For example, a friend may ask to borrow your new, expensive car to impress his new date. Not having driven the car much yourself, you readily say no. The friend then asks to borrow $20 for the same date, to which you are more likely to agree.

There is yet another way to ensure compliance, complaining. Research demonstrates that complaining is a moderately successful method for gaining others' compliance. Alicke et al. (1992) asked college students to keep diaries about their complaints. Recorded complaints fell into three general categories. The desire to vent frustrations was by far the most common type of complaint; followed by complaints designed to seek advice, sympathy, or information; finally followed by complaints tailored to alter others' attitudes or behaviors. Overall, complaining did get compliance from listeners about 25 percent of the time, with indirect complaints being the most successful.

As you can see, both ingratiation and the door-in-the-face technique are rather manipulative ways to bring about compliance. You can also ascertain that complaining does not always work. We are not suggesting here that you utilize manipulation or complaining to obtain what you desire. Rather, we are hoping you will be able to identify these techniques when they are used on you and thus be able to make better decisions about when to comply with others' requests.

Obedience.   **Obedience** involves following a direct order or command. The command typically comes from someone who has the capacity to enforce the order if it is not followed. You probably think of an army officer issuing an order that soldiers follow. Otu's followers were surely obedient to him, but are other individuals so servile? Surprisingly, many Americans are obedient to different authority figures. A classic series of studies on obedience demonstrates this propensity to obey.

In 1974, Stanley Milgram published his dramatic *Obedience to Authority*. In this book he detailed a series of studies on obedience to authority figures that stirred the psychological world. Imagine that you are in the following prototype of Milgram's experiment. You are led to a room and introduced to Mr. Wallace, a kindly older man who is to be the learner in the study. You are going to be the teacher. Mr. Wallace is to learn a list of words. Each time he errs, you are to give him an electric shock that you are both told will be painful but will cause no permanent tissue damage. For each error, you are to proceed up the shock generator one step. The first step is 15 volts and labeled "slight shock." The other end is 450 volts and labeled only with XXX. As the teacher you are not aware that the experiment is fixed such that you are not really administering shocks and that Mr. Wallace is really a *confederate* (the experimenter's assistant) and told how to act.

As you proceed up the shock generator, you hear Mr. Wallace's groans. Eventually, Mr. Wallace refuses to continue and states that he has a heart problem. Finally, Mr. Wallace becomes silent. Each time you query the experimenter (the authority figure) about Mr. Wallace's condition, the experimenter urges you to continue. The experimenter reminds you that although the shocks may be painful, they cause no permanent damage. The experimenter requests that you continue.

The most dramatic and disconcerting part of these studies was that 65 percent of the American subjects went all the way up the shock generator to 450 volts at the urging of the experimenter. It would be easy to explain away these results by suggesting that the subjects were disturbed or that they were all aggressive men. Milgram assures us that all subjects were mentally healthy and that even women shocked the learner at about the same rate.

What contributes to this dismaying and blind obedience? What diminishes it? Milgram and others (e.g., Stone, Lederer, & Christie, 1993) suggest that a certain personality factor contributes, authoritarianism. **Authoritarians** are submissive to authority figures but are aggressive to subordinates. They are also rigid, dogmatic, conservative, punitive, and ethnocentric. There are situations, however, that diminish the effects of obedience to authorities. If the authority figure appears less official (i.e., removes the lab coat) and is not proximal to the teacher, and if the learner is close to or touching the teacher, the teacher will shock the learner less intensely.

SOCIAL LOAFING

Another process that occurs in groups is social loafing. **Social loafing** means that individuals contribute less to a group effort than they would contribute to an individual effort (Weldon & Gargano, 1988). For example, if individuals are asked one at a time to paint a mural or to clap for an athlete, they put more effort into the performance than they would if asked to perform as a group. In fact, the larger the group, the less individual effort everyone puts into his or her accomplishment.

Certain factors reduce the amount of social loafing (Karau & Williams, 1993). When people believe their performance will be evaluated, when the task is important or meaningful, when failure is possible if loafing occurs, or when the group is valued by individual members, loafing is minimized. There also exist cultural differences in amounts

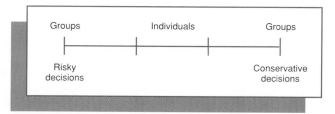

FIGURE 8–4
The group polarization effect. Groups often make more extreme decisions (conservative or risky) than individuals.

of social loafing. As mentioned elsewhere, American society is an *individualistic society;* individuals are expected to be independent and autonomous, so they contribute less to group efforts. In more **collective societies** where group effort is valued, social loafing is less likely to occur. These collective societies are generally Eastern cultures such as the Chinese, Japanese, and Taiwanese cultures.

GROUP POLARIZATION

People often work in groups that make decisions where consensus is needed. In 1964 Kogan and Wallach compared how individuals versus groups make decisions. In their study, participants were given a series of social dilemmas and asked to select a solution for the dilemma. The solutions varied on amount of risk. For example, participants were asked to decide whether a risky experimental drug should be administered to a dying patient. What Kogan and Wallach determined is that groups make riskier decisions than individuals. They labeled this phenomenon **risky shift.** The researchers explained that individuals in groups feel less responsible for the risk so are willing to make riskier decisions in groups; feeling less responsible in a group is known as **responsibility diffusion.**

Subsequent research (Myers & Arenson, 1972) demonstrated that some groups tend to make more conservative decisions than individuals. That is, if individuals in the group made fairly conservative decisions, as a group they tend to make even more conservative decisions. In other words, groups are likely to shift to either a more conservative or a riskier decision than individuals alone make. This newer phenomenon is the **group polarization effect** depicted in Figure 8–4. One factor that predicts whether individuals in a group will press for caution or for risk is culture. In African cultures, for example, caution is valued over risk. In American culture, risk and bravado are valued over caution (Gologor, 1977). Given that you, too, spend so much time in groups, you should be aware of these effects so that you can make the best possible decisions.

 Leaders and Followers

In almost all groups, someone rises as leader. Committees elect their leaders, corporations retain presidents appointed by the board of directors, some countries are governed by a self-appointed dictator. Research has demonstrated that groups with leaders outperform groups without leaders (De-Souza & Klein, 1995). How do leaders emerge and what qualities make for good leadership? The answers to these questions are difficult

Scientists are unsure why one person becomes a great leader and another individual does not. Not all leaders share the same characteristics.

because each situation is so different from the next. We can merely summarize here some of the literature. Let us first examine from where leaders come.

THE GREAT MAN THEORY

Did Otu possess certain traits that set him on the path to leadership? The earliest theory of leadership was the **great man theory.** This theory suggests that a great leader is born with a certain set of traits. If an individual possesses these traits, then he or she will become a leader. If not, the individual is out of luck. Researchers supposed that they ought to be able to assess great leaders and find common features. Simonton (1987) did just that. Simonton gathered information from a variety of sources about the presidents of the United States. Information collected included personality attributes as well as demographic and educational factors. Out of 100 characteristics, only 3 correlated with how effective each president was in office. For example, one factor was family size; another was height; and the third was number of books published. Presidents are more likely to have been born into small families and to be tall. There were no personality factors that consistently correlated with performance in office. The great man theory has essentially been abandoned in favor of other notions of leadership.

SITUATIONAL EXPLANATIONS

Other explanations for leader emergence involve the situation people find themselves in. In other words, perhaps being in the right place at the right time means that you are likely to become a leader. For example, if you sit at the head of the table with everyone else seated at the sides, you might be appointed to lead the group. This indeed can happen, but depending on the individual, it is not always likely. Curiously, research has demonstrated that women who sit at the head of the table in mixed-sex groups do not become the heads of the group (Porter, Geis, Cooper, & Newman, 1985). It is only in all-female groups that women at the head of the table become the leader.

CONTINGENCY THEORY

The most popular theory of leadership at present is one that combines trait or personal factors with situational factors. In other words, the theory suggests that you have to be the right person in the right situation. The theory is Fiedler's (1978) **contingency theory of leadership.** Fiedler identifies two attributes or styles of leaders known as people-oriented or task-oriented, as measured by the scale in Figure 8–5. **People-** or **relationship-oriented leaders** concern themselves with members' feelings and relationships. **Task-oriented leaders** are primarily concerned with getting the job done well and in a timely fashion. Fiedler measures these two styles by asking leaders to rate their least-preferred coworker. Interestingly and not unpredictably, the people-oriented leader sees the good in this coworker even though he or she is not preferred. The task leader, interested more in performance than people, has stronger negative feelings toward those coworkers who do not do their jobs well. Figure 8–5 presents Fiedler's leadership style scale.

The situations under which each of these leaders is most effective differ. Surely you know social situations where the task to be done is clear and members of the group have good relationships. This is what Fiedler calls a high control situation as compared to a low or medium control situation. Results of research demonstrate that task-oriented leaders are most effective in high or low control situations. On the other hand, people-oriented leaders are most effective in medium control situations. Fiedler strongly suggests that leader style should match the situation, as suggested by Figure 8–6.

Is there support for contingency theory? Chemers, Hays, Rhodewalt, and Wysocki (1985) surveyed college administrators to determine both their leadership style and their level of situational control. The styles, of course, were people- or task-oriented. The levels of control were classified as low, moderate, or high. As predicted, those administrators whose style was mismatched to the situation reported the most job stress, a higher number of days absent, and the most health problems.

GENDER AND LEADERSHIP

There are at least two other well-researched factors related to leadership: gender and culture. We'll examine issues related to gender first. Alice Eagly and her colleagues are some of the leading scientists in this area. Eagly has performed meta-analyses of many studies and determined that there are differences in the way men and women lead and whether these styles are accepted by followers. A **meta-analysis** is a statistical technique whereby the effects of a variable or factor can be measured across many studies. In this case, the variable is gender.

In one meta-analysis, Eagly and Johnson (1990) found that men and women tend to lead differently; that is, women are more democratic than men. Women also tend to consult more with subordinates, utilize more extensive networks, and share more information and power with colleagues than do men (Helgeson, 1990). Eagly and Johnson as well as Wheelan and Verdi (1992) contend that women are every bit as task-oriented as men especially because this is a criterion by which organizations select and train leaders.

FIGURE 8–5

FIEDLER'S SCALE FOR DETERMINING LEADERSHIP STYLE

INSTRUCTIONS: Rate your least-preferred coworker on the following dimensions by placing an "X" in the appropriate space. First impressions are best.

pleasant	____	____	____	____	____	____	____	unpleasant
unfriendly	____	____	____	____	____	____	____	friendly
close	____	____	____	____	____	____	____	distant
rejecting	____	____	____	____	____	____	____	accepting
brave	____	____	____	____	____	____	____	cowardly
unattractive	____	____	____	____	____	____	____	attractive
strong	____	____	____	____	____	____	____	weak
uncooperative	____	____	____	____	____	____	____	cooperative
relaxed	____	____	____	____	____	____	____	tense
impolite	____	____	____	____	____	____	____	polite
honest	____	____	____	____	____	____	____	dishonest
simple	____	____	____	____	____	____	____	complex
active	____	____	____	____	____	____	____	passive
bad	____	____	____	____	____	____	____	good
unaggressive	____	____	____	____	____	____	____	aggressive

Rate your most-preferred coworker on the following scale by placing an "X" in the appropriate space. First impressions are best. Try not to let your ratings of the least-preferred worker influence these ratings (i.e., don't use comparisons).

pleasant	____	____	____	____	____	____	____	unpleasant
unfriendly	____	____	____	____	____	____	____	friendly
close	____	____	____	____	____	____	____	distant
rejecting	____	____	____	____	____	____	____	accepting
brave	____	____	____	____	____	____	____	cowardly
unattractive	____	____	____	____	____	____	____	attractive
strong	____	____	____	____	____	____	____	weak
uncooperative	____	____	____	____	____	____	____	cooperative
relaxed	____	____	____	____	____	____	____	tense
impolite	____	____	____	____	____	____	____	polite
honest	____	____	____	____	____	____	____	dishonest
simple	____	____	____	____	____	____	____	complex
active	____	____	____	____	____	____	____	passive
bad	____	____	____	____	____	____	____	good
unaggressive	____	____	____	____	____	____	____	aggressive

SOURCE: Fiedler, F. (1967). *A theory of leadership effectiveness.* New York: McGraw-Hill.

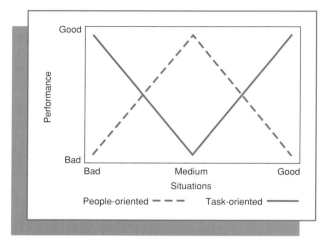

FIGURE 8–6

Graph of the effects of people-oriented versus task-oriented leaders on group performance. SOURCE: Adapted from Fiedler, F. (1967). *A theory of leadership effectiveness.* New York: McGraw-Hill.

If women are equally as effective as men, why are there so few women leaders? At least two factors help explain this societal phenomenon. Eagly, Makhijani, and Klonsky (1992) in another literature review found that women leaders tend to be slightly less positively evaluated than men. D. Butler and Geis (1990) found that this is especially true when men are doing the evaluating. It also appears to be true when a woman leader is perceived as leading in a masculine manner, for example, in a task-oriented and autocratic manner (Eagly et al., 1992). Another reason fewer women achieve top leadership positions may be that they are conflicted about mixing career and family (Crosby, 1991) because of societal pressure. For example, although most women work outside the home, it is still relatively common to see television portray women as homemakers (Jewell, 1993), and women's magazines are more likely to carry articles about cooking and home products than careers (French, 1992).

CULTURE AND LEADERSHIP

The literature on culture and leadership is ever increasing first because the American work force is diversifying and second because different leadership expectations and styles have been noted in different cultures (Moorhead & Griffin, 1995). One extremely important dimension of leader or managerial style is **power distance,** which is the idea that people in groups accept the idea that people in an organization rightfully have different levels of power and authority. In a high power distance culture, the leader makes decisions because he or she has the authority to do so. That is, the subordinates accept large distances in the distribution of power and expect leaders to behave autocratically, be somewhat paternalistic, be subject to different rules than subordinates, and enjoy privileges not available to subordinates. Examples of high power distance cultures are Mexico and India. In medium power distance cultures such as the United States and Italy, subordinates expect to be consulted but will sometimes accept some autocratic behavior. Subordinates also expect rules and policies to apply to all; however, they will accept some status differences between superiors and subordinates. In low power distance cultures subordinates expect to be consulted on most issues, prefer a participative democratic style of leadership, and often rebel if superiors appear to be stepping outside their authority or possess status symbols. Rules are seen as applicable to all. Examples of such cultures are those of Denmark and Israel (Adler, Dokter, & Redding, 1986).

 # When Groups Go Wrong

On May 24, 1995, Sara and Harry received the sad news that their son Roy was dead. The Akaries had committed mass suicide the day after their predicted doomsday when the world did not end. The Akaries functioned in a peculiar and dysfunctional manner. Other examples of dysfunctional groups are unfortunately replete in world history. John Kennedy's disaster at the Bay of Pigs in Cuba, the Mai Lai massacre in Vietnam, and the explosion of the Space Shuttle (Moorhead, Ference, & Neck, 1991) offer other poignant instances of poor group processes. Fortunately, many other groups function well. Thankfully, most U.S. presidents' cabinets operate successfully. Committees on college campuses are often very productive. Community groups holding charity events often raise phenomenal amounts of money. We will examine next some processes that result in poor decisions or poor performance in social settings.

GROUPTHINK

John Kennedy's administration was thought by many Americans to be the Camelot administration, but the first years of Kennedy's presidency actually were shaky. One egregious error of this administration was the invasion of the Bay of Pigs in Cuba. Young Kennedy was fully aware of the connections of Fidel Castro to the communist Soviet Union. Kennedy and his advisors considered Castro and Cuba a threat to America. This close-knit group sequestered itself and eventually decided to invade Cuba. The CIA trained a small cadre of Cuban exiles and landed them on the Cuban coast (the Bay of Pigs) where they were to instigate a mass uprising against Castro. Castro's forces quickly defeated, captured, or killed most of these insurgents. Latin American neighbors expressed outrage and dismay that the United States would take upon itself the invasion of Cuba. Unfortunately, the disaster also served to bring Cuba even closer to the Soviet Union.

"Where had Kennedy and his advisors gone wrong?" asked historians. Psychologist Irving Janis (1982) answered with the concept of **groupthink.** Groupthink occurs when a group becomes more concerned with maintaining consensus and cohesion than with developing good ideas. This concept has been somewhat modified by Neck and Moorhead (1995); they suggest, for example, that within the same group, groupthink can occur during one decision-making situation and not another.

Antecedents of groupthink. Groupthink begins when a group is close-knit and the members view the group as attractive. In other words, people strive to be members of the group. Certainly, the cabinet of advisors to the young, popular Kennedy was prestigious. The group becomes somewhat isolated, as was true for the Kennedy group, which for national security reasons wanted to keep the invasion a secret as long as possible. The leader is usually directive, that is, controls the discussion. It was no secret to his advisors that Kennedy favored an invasion. The cabinet was also new so had not developed any standard procedures for discussing such important matters. The Akaries also kept outside influences to a minimum; Otu himself was also very directive, especially about the planned suicide the day after the doomsday failure.

Symptoms of groupthink. Janis has detailed symptoms of groupthink for us. Knowing these symptoms, you should be able to sense groupthink occurring and stop it before poor decisions are made. Kennedy and his advisors unfortunately were unaware of this process so did not recognize that they were experiencing groupthink.

One symptom of this phenomenon is the illusion of invulnerability. The group is so close-knit and in agreement that the members believe they are invincible; they can do no wrong. This occurs because no one in the group wants to dissent and break the cohesiveness. In fact, dissenters are quickly dismissed or pressured to conform to the group's sentiments. In the Akaries, individuals were physically punished with spanking or dumped in a pit of raw sewage. The individuals who take it upon themselves to censor dissenters Janis labeled **mindguards.** When Sara and Harry investigated this strange cult to which their son had belonged, the authorities told them that the Akaries had had special lieutenants who saw to the punishment of errant group members. In any group-think group, members eventually censor their own behavior; thus, it appears that there is little to no disagreement. Because dissension then ceases, the group comes to think that it is morally correct. The group also believes that there is eventual unanimity. What makes the process of unanimity and self-righteousness likely is that the group also stereo-types the outgroup (the opposition). Members may view the outgroup as lazy, stupid, or incapable. In the Bay of Pigs case the stereotyped group was the Cubans. For the Akaries it was citizens of the outside world.

Consequences of groupthink. You are aware by now that groupthink results in defective decision making. The deficient decision making is a consequence of several other processes. The group generally discusses only one or two ideas, because the members fail to survey all possible alternative solutions. For the favored solution, the group commits the blunder of not looking at all possible risks. That is, the group avoids discussing the downside of its chosen alternative. The group therefore never develops any contingency plans in case something goes wrong. For Kennedy and his advisors, this meant they had no way of retrieving the insurgents when the invasion started to sour. Groupthink therefore is an insidious and pernicious process that should be avoided by groups.

Preventing groupthink. Fortunately, groupthink can be averted. One means to prevent groupthink is to promote open inquiry and skepticism. Perhaps the group can appoint an official devil's advocate, or the group leader can invite criticism and open debate about each alternative. To ensure that a number of alternatives are generated, subgroups can be formed. Each group should produce its own solutions; consequently, several alternatives result. Once an alternative has been selected, a second chance meeting should occur. In this way the group has the opportunity to rethink its position and to express any remaining doubts. The leader also should refrain from expressing his or her opinion at the outset so as to foster the generation of options. One last recommendation is to call upon outside experts so that the group does not remain isolated and so that more informed decisions can be made by group members. This information on groupthink is summarized in Table 8–1.

CONFLICT

We would hope that groups are free of conflict; however, all of us probably can recall instances of intragroup and intergroup conflict. When Roy called his parents to tell them that he had joined the Akaries, his parents were shocked. They threatened to cut off any

TABLE 8–1
GROUPTHINK: ITS SYMPTOMS AND CURES

Symptoms	Consequences	Cures
Illusion of invulnerability	Defective decision making	Appoint a devil's advocate
The group can do no wrong	Discussion of only one or two ideas	Use subgroups
Mindguards	No examination of risks	Discuss every alternative fully
False sense of unanimity	No contingency plans developed in event of disaster	Leader should refrain from giving opinion
Stereotyping of the outgroup	Little contact with the outgroup	Call in outside experts
		Hold a second chance meeting

SOURCE: Adapted from Janis, Irving, *Victims of Groupthink,* Copyright © 1972 by Houghton Mifflin Company. Used with permission.

financial support to him and to disinherit him so that he would not inherit the family farm. This open conflict between Roy and his parents offers a poignant example of the first intragroup conflict. As for intergroup conflict, the taunting of the Akaries that some of the university students did offers an example.

The good side of conflict.   Conflict need not always be deleterious (Worchel & Lundgren, 1991). Conflict can be useful in terms of testing and assessing ourselves, others, and the issues facing us. Conflict challenges us to develop creative responses and solutions. Conflict can also result in much positive social change. Witness, for example, how the civil unrest of the 1950s resulted in advances for African Americans and other people of color. Conflict can also increase cohesiveness within a group. Conflict, then, is not always bad.

The down side of conflict.   Most of us frown on conflict. One reason we dislike conflict is that it often results in a **non-zero sum** in which one person or group wins something and loses something as does the other side. For example, in an international war one country is usually declared the winner and another country the loser. However, both countries suffer the loss of economy, and both sides also lose citizens' lives.

Conflicts typically are the result of complex **mixed motives.** In other words, a number of divergent motives fuel the conflict. Individuals and groups generally want more than just to win the conflict. Sometimes they also hope to inflict pain, humiliation, or punishment on the other side or to make the other side suffer a greater loss than they themselves. Besides being unpleasant, then, conflicts are complex and often difficult. One other major problem with conflict is that it often seems to escalate out of control. In other words, a little shove goes a long way (Worchel & Lundgren, 1991).

Many factors contribute to conflict escalation (Rubin, Pruitt, & Kim, 1994). Threats are one such factor. When one group or party threatens another, the other side often responds with a like threat. For example, in international conflict, if one country threatens invasion, the threatened country often responds with a counterattack or threat of retaliation. In fact, classic research by Morton Deutsch and Robert Krauss (1960) found that people often use coercive means and threats even if they also result in damage to their own outcomes. This may be true because threats at first appear to offer quick resolution to the conflict and are easy to use. Deutsch and Krauss used the Acme

While conflict can sometimes be productive, it often escalates because of the use of threat. When conflict heightens, it is more difficult to manage.

Trucking Game to study this phenomenon. (See Figure 8–7.) In the trucking game, as in real life, the players had gates (or threats) that they could use at will. Once the gate was closed (the threat), the player's partner could not move his or her truck through the one-lane road (the short route). The point of the game was to move the truck from start to destination as quickly as possible. What Deutsch and Krauss found is that the game was strongly influenced by the introduction of the gates or threats; that is, the threats dramatically reduced cooperativeness.

Back in his junior year of college when Roy informed his parents that he had joined the Akaries, Sara and Harry threatened him as mentioned earlier. Roy threatened back that he would break all contact with his parents. As threats from each side increased and promises were broken, trust decreased. It is no wonder that the conflict finally spiraled out of control, and Sara and Harry never heard from their son until they were notified of his suicide.

Perceptions of others such as stereotypes and prejudice also fuel conflict escalation. Such perceptions divide conflicting groups into "us" versus "them" or ingroup and outgroup quite easily. The *fundamental attribution* error in part accounts for this division. When you fall prey to the fundamental attribution error, you make trait or person-centered attributions rather than situational attributions. If a divorcing spouse does something negative such as threaten the other spouse with stopping child support, the threatened spouse imagines that the threatener is inherently bad rather than that something in the situation (such as a bad day at work or fatigue) accounts for the threat. Once this negative image is established, the **self-fulfilling prophecy** sustains it. The self-fulfilling prophecy occurs when people's expectations become a reality by virtue of their own behavior. Once the spouse threatens to stop payments, the other spouse becomes embittered and counterthreatens. The counterthreat induces more threats and negative behaviors from the first spouse. The conflict escalates often out of control.

One other reason conflict escalates is that once we are committed to a position, we continue to devote time and energy to the effort. People interestingly do not seem to cut their losses when they begin to lose. This process of throwing more time, energy, or

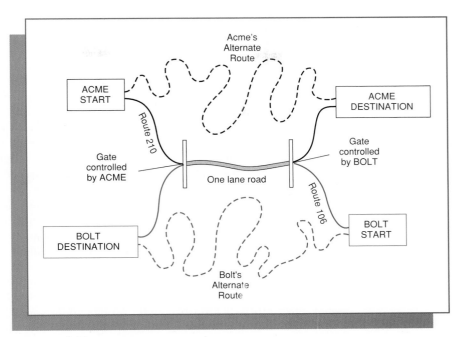

FIGURE 8–7

The Acme Trucking Game used to study the effects of threat on the development of cooperation. SOURCE: Deutsch, M., & Krauss, R. M. (1960). The effect of threat upon interpersonal bargaining. *Journal of Abnormal and Social Psychology, 61,* 181–189.

money into a bad situation is called **entrapment** (Brockner & Rubin, 1985). Entrapment occurs when commitments to a failing course of action are increased to justify investments already made. Entrapment contributes to conflict escalation by motivating the losers to keep trying to win.

Culture and conflict.   International conflict was mentioned earlier. However, much conflict can also occur within a culture. Psychologists, sociologists, and anthropologists have noted that different cultures manage conflict differently. Specifically, the distinction between collectivistic cultures and individualistic cultures becomes important. Recall that collectivist societies value group efforts over individual efforts, but the converse is true for individualistic cultures. Many Asian cultures are far more collectivistic than American and European cultures. Ting-Toomey (1988) has suggested that in collectivistic cultures, face saving of others is more important so the self-respect and image of the other disputant is maintained. In many collectivistic cultures opponents would not try to humiliate each other. In individualistic societies individuals are more concerned with saving their own images so might well humiliate or denigrate their opponent.

Ting-Toomey et al. (1991) examined other differences in conflict between these two types of cultures. Ting-Toomey thought that the strategies individuals in these two cultures utilize for managing conflict might also differ. By means of surveys, thousands of individuals from various cultures answered questions about their preferred methods for conflict resolution. Participants from the United States preferred domination of others as their mode of resolution, whereas participants from Asian countries preferred giving in or avoiding conflict. Knowing this, you should not assume that your opponents' methods and desires during conflict are the same as yours.

Conflict resolution.   Luckily, experts in conflictology have developed several tools for dealing with conflict. When conflict is completely settled, the experts say that conflict resolution has occurred. At other times, conflict can at best be managed; that is, conflict cannot be settled but rather contained or kept from escalating. The latter is especially true for competing groups. Groups are more likely to be competitive with each other than are two individuals in conflict (Insko, Schopler, Hoyle, Dardis, & Graetz, 1990).

Because most conflicts are mixed-motive conflicts, it is not always true that because one side wins, the other must lose. Groups and individuals in conflict can look for integrative solutions. **Integrative solutions** are those that take into account the needs of both sides such that both sides can win something. At first, it may sound as if integrative solutions involve compromise. In compromise, though, each side must also lose a little to win a little. Integrative solutions go beyond compromise. Thompson (1991) examined compromise versus integrative solutions in a study where she asked students to play the role of buyer or seller of a car. As you know, selling or buying a car involves financial arrangements, warranties, delivery dates, and so forth. The parties, buyer or seller, could negotiate almost anything they wanted. To the buyer, warranty was most important. To the seller, finance rate was most important. What Thompson found was that the students simply compromised or split everything down the middle (between highest and lowest bid). It was not until specifically told to ask the other party exactly what he or she wanted that integrative solutions were found where the buyer was pleased with the warranty period and the seller was pleased with the finance rate. The lesson here is that when in conflict, it is important to know exactly what the other party is after. If one side does not ask, that party may make mistaken assumptions.

Charles Osgood (1962) introduced another negotiating technique designed to end or lower the level of conflict. The technique is known as GRIT or **graduated and reciprocated initiatives in tension-reduction.** With this technique each side gradually concedes something to the other side. For example, in international conflict, one side might concede a small piece of disputed territory. Because of the norm of reciprocity, there exists pressure on the other side to concede something as well, perhaps a partial troop retreat in an international conflict. Often these concessions are made public so as to keep the pressure to reciprocate on both sides. The key here, then, is communication with the public as well as with the other side. There is always a danger with GRIT that one side will not reciprocate and in fact take advantage of the other conceding side. Should this happen, the side that made the concession needs to respond with a like competitive action so that the other side knows the first will not be taken advantage of.

There are other possibilities for conflict management and resolution. One final method to be addressed here is the intervention of a third party. Third parties are usually mediators or arbitrators. **Mediators** are neutral third parties who intervene in conflict and who help the two disputing parties come to common agreements via communication, creative problem solving, and other techniques. **Arbitrators** are similar to mediators in that they are neutral third parties who, using the same techniques, assist the parties with the conflict, hope that the parties can resolve their differences, but if they cannot, render a binding decision upon the parties (Duffy, Grosch, & Olczak, 1991). Every state in the United States houses mediation or neighborhood justice centers as alternatives to the courts. The typical case is a two-party dispute over property, but some centers handle felonies such as rape where the rapist and victim meet face to

A neutral person can often help to defuse a conflict. Mediators are specially trained in conflict management techniques.

face. Mediators and arbitrators are used in many different arenas to facilitate the resolution of conflict. Mediators, in particular, have been utilized in international, environmental, business, family, neighborhood, and other conflicts with a high degree of success (Duffy et al., 1991). Empirical research has also demonstrated that mediation is a humanistic process. Individuals who mediate function at a higher level on Maslow's need hierarchy after mediation (Duffy & Thomson, 1992).

As you can determine from this chapter, you do not operate in isolation. Most humans are social beings; for that reason, groups affect us daily. Understanding how groups form and function, comprehending why people join groups, recognizing detrimental group processes when they first develop, and knowing how to correct dysfunctional group behaviors are valuable skills.

SUMMARY

KINDS OF GROUPS

There are several different types of groups to which we can belong. The most important group is our primary group, the small, close-knit, face-to-face groups formed by family or friends. Secondary groups are larger and less intimate whereas collectives are very large. We usually also distinguish our own group or ingroup from other outside groups or outgroups. Ingroups are our reference points for our feelings about ourselves.

HOW GROUPS FORM

Groups go through a developmental process just as do humans. Groups come together in the forming stage and then usually move quickly to the storming stage where friction exists. Once the storming is over, the group agrees on norms or rules by which it functions and then moves to the performing or productive stage. Groups sometimes slide back to one of these stages and the process recycles.

WHY JOIN A GROUP?

There exist a variety of reasons individuals join groups. One reason is that groups furnish us with the opportunity to affiliate or to be with similar others; groups also provide us with social support or psychological aid. Groups often possess more information and more collective power than a single individual would, too.

GROUP PROCESSES

Several processes operate no matter what the type of group. Various centralized or non-centralized communication systems typically develop. Individuals in groups also try to influence one another through pressures to conform, comply, or obey. Some individuals feel they do not have to work as hard in a group where their individual efforts are less likely to be noticed, a phenomenon known as social loafing. Groups can often become polarized in their decision making, another influence process by which groups make more extreme decisions than individuals.

Psychologists are unsure exactly why someone in a group emerges as leader. Traits, the situation (i.e., someone being in the right place at the right time), or some combination of the two may account for leader evolution.

WHEN GROUPS GO WRONG

There are negative group processes. One is groupthink, where groups value cohesiveness or "sticking together" over sound decision making. Another is conflict. Although conflict is not always bad, conflict can sometimes keep a group from performing well. There are known techniques for overcoming both of these phenomena. For example, appointing a devil's advocate who criticizes the group's decisions is helpful in preventing groupthink. For conflict, integrative solutions provide the opportunity for the parties in conflict to come to some mutual understanding.

SELF-TEST

1. Our family represents which type of group?
   - a. primary
   - b. secondary
   - c. a collective
   - d. out-group

2. The group with which we identify is known as our
   - a. in-group
   - b. out-group
   - c. norming group
   - d. secondary group

3. The second stage of group formation is the _____ stage.
   - a. forming
   - b. storming
   - c. norming
   - d. performing

4. For what reasons do members usually join groups?
   a. affiliation   c. social comparison
   b. collective power   d. all of these

5. An example of a centralized group communication network is
   a. circle   c. wheel
   b. chain   d. hierarchy

6. When people issue a request for us to do something, they are actually requesting that we
   a. obey   c. comply
   b. conform   d. collectivize

7. Tony realizes that during class the class is large so he need not contribute often. This is an example of
   a. social loafing   c. norm of reciprocity
   b. authoritarianism   d. group polarization

8. People-oriented leaders are most effective in
   a. all situations
   b. poor situations
   c. moderately good situations
   d. good situations

9. The phenomenon in which groups value cohesiveness over sound decision making is known as
   a. groupthink   c. norming
   b. conformity   d. responsibility diffusion

10. Most conflicts are characterized by
   a. mixed motives
   b. the fundamental attribution error
   c. the self-fulfilling prophecy
   d. all of these

EXERCISES

1. *Think about the primary and secondary groups to which you belong.* Do the characteristics of your groups fit the descriptions in the book? If not, why not?

2. *Watch a newly formed committee or some other group.* Did the group go through the stages of group development as outlined in this chapter?

3. *Ask a number of people why they join the groups they choose.* Do the reasons conform to those cited in the book?

4. *Make a list of occasions on which someone offered you social support in the last two months.* Do the occasions have anything in common? What kinds of support were offered?

5. *Have you ever used electronic communication in a group of which you are a member?* Write a few paragraphs about how these communications differed from face-to-face communications in other groups.

6. *Observe a group coming to consensus about some issue.* Do you see any signs of group-think? How could the group have avoided this phenomenon?

7. *For the groups of which you are a member, think about how the leader was selected.* Can you add anything to the literature on leader emergence based on your experience?

QUESTIONS FOR SELF-REFLECTION

1. Why did you join the groups you did? Why did you leave any of the groups?

2. Who is a member of your ingroup? Do you think that your ingroup will remain the same over a lifetime? Why not?

3. When groups are storming, have you contributed to the storming or tried to move the group toward norming and performing? What were your motives for doing what you did?

4. Are you as likely to offer social support to someone in need as others are to offer you support?

5. What do you enjoy more, face-to-face communication with others or electronic (phone, e-mail, etc.) communication? Why?

6. Are you a conformist or a nonconformist? Is one better than the other for you given your life circumstances? Could you change if you want to?

7. Do you do your fair share of work in the groups of which you are a member?

8. Are you a leader of any groups? If you are a leader in one but not another group, why? If you do not lead any groups, why not? Are you comfortable being a leader or nonleader?

9. Reflect on your life; have you ever experienced groupthink? What were the results of the groupthink process? Can you reverse any poor decisions?

FOR FURTHER INFORMATION

RECOMMENDED READINGS

CASTELLAN, N. J., JR. (Ed.). (1993). *Individual and group decision making: Current issues.* Hillsdale, NJ: Erlbaum. A book about how people make decisions and the group effects on decision making.

CIALDINI, R. B. (1993). *Influence: Science and practice* (3rd ed.). New York: Harper Collins. A very readable book about conformity and other influence processes with an eye to practical applications in everyday life.

JANUS, I. L. (1982). *Groupthink: Psychological studies of policy decisions and fiascoes.* Boston: Houghton Mifflin. The lead book on groupthink as a process and how to overcome it.

MINDELL, A. (1995). *Sitting in the fire: Large group transformation using conflict and diversity.* Portland, OR: Lao Tse Press. An interesting book about group conflict and how to overcome it.

SIMONTON, D. K. (1994). *Greatness: Who makes history and why.* New York: Guilford Press. Written by a social psychologist, this book is about great leaders and how these leaders became powerful.

WEBSITES AND THE INTERNET

http://www.yakima.net/selcarim/: Selcarim Youth Leadership Exercises. A website about exercises that involve students working in small groups for the purpose of teaching human relations skills leading toward leadership development.

http://www.can.ibm.com/edu/course/S6332.html: Information about a 2-day program focused on effective group facilitation skills or skills that help groups set their own values and goals, maintain commitment toward those goals, and use all of their resources to achieve these goals.

http://www.altika.com/leadership/: A monthly on-line magazine developed with the mission to provide insights into new ways of leadership.

http://www.uwyo.edu/A&S/comm/donaghy/measures.html: Presents brief descriptions of studies and measures as well as the leadership behaviors that have been identified.

http:www.tc.cornell.edu/edu/artsocgateway: A site that provides many links to all types of social science information for the reader who wants to browse all sorts of topics related to social psychology and other social sciences.

CHAPTER 9

Marriage and Intimate Relationships

After completing this chapter, you should be able to

1. Describe several theories about the nature of love.
2. Discuss the influence of cohabitation on marriage and divorce.
3. Discuss the factors that make for a happy and lasting marriage.
4. Identify several different ways couples attempt to manage marital conflict.
5. Describe the typical changes that occur in marriages over time.
6. Describe the various aspects of the divorce experience.
7. Discuss the challenges faced by single-parent and stepparent families.

David and Diane, both in their mid 20s, have been going together for two years. They met at their community college in their freshman biology class. They're deeply in love with each other and have discussed the possibility of living together as well as of marriage. Both left home and took apartments with their high school friends who are attending the same college. However, they realized that they could share an apartment with each other and still save money.

Having worked through many of the differences in their interests, they enjoy spending as much time together as their busy schedules permit. Because they attend some of the same classes, they could also study together. Both want a close, rewarding relationship, in which they're best friends as well as lovers. But they're having difficulty achieving it. Diane complains that David is preoccupied with his part-time job. She also complains that when they are together, all he wants to do is watch sports events on television. Although Diane likes basketball, she detests football. David argues that he is too tired to go out to a movie or elsewhere after attending classes, studying, and working. Even when they're together, Diane says David doesn't share his feelings enough. This trait has become especially troublesome when he's moody and won't explain why. In David's view, Diane doesn't understand that this is a critical stage in his planned career and that Diane is more concerned about getting married than about him. Also, David feels Diane is too possessive at times, for example, her recent jealousy over his casual friendship with a woman at the office. David readily admits that talk of marriage at this point in his life makes him feel "trapped." Diane explains that David's feelings have been shaped, at least in part, by his older brother's recent, messy divorce. Consequently, she worries about how committed David is to their relationship and about their future together.

Love, Intimacy, and Marriage

Like so many other couples their age, David and Diane want a great deal of closeness in their relationship. At the same time, they're having difficulty developing it partly because they've both grown up in families lacking warmth and intimacy. Consequently, David feels uneasy when people get too close to him, and Diane worries about loved ones leaving her, resulting in an anxious, ambivalent relationship. Some couples grow in love and understanding and eventually achieve a satisfying relationship despite their different backgrounds and shortcomings. Other couples are not so fortunate. Faced with frustration and disillusionment, many of them simply get divorced. Countless others continue in conflict-laden marriages or the more familiar "empty marriage."

We'll begin the chapter by exploring the essentials of love as well as the different ways people approach intimate relationships. We'll also look at the practice of unmarried couples living together and the process by which couples move toward marriage. We'll discuss some of the major areas of marital adjustment, including sharing marital responsibilities, communication and conflict, marital sex, and changes in marriage over time. Finally, we'll describe divorce, along with single-parent families and remarriage.

THE ESSENTIALS OF LOVE

Psychologists recognize that **intimate relationships** and friendships overlap to a considerable extent. Both lovers and friends initially seek out others who are similar to them (Whitbeck & Hoyt, 1994). Both types of couples enjoy each other's company, despite occasional disappointments. Individuals in both types of relationships generally accept each other as they are, without trying to make their partner over into a different person. That is, we want friends and lovers who can validate our self-concept (Swann, De

Romantic relationships are both more rewarding and more volatile than friendships.

LaRonde, & Hixon, 1994). Both friends and lovers know they can count on each other in times of need. Also, they can confide in each other without fear of betrayal. Finally, friends and lovers understand each other and make allowances when the other person occasionally acts in an unexpected or annoying manner.

At the same time, love relationships are distinctively different from friendships. Essentially, it appears that **love** heightens the potential for both positive and negative aspects of close relationships, making love relationships more rewarding and more frustrating. Love relationships include characteristics such as fascination, sexual desire, and exclusiveness, so that lovers tend to be preoccupied with their partners in an exclusive sexual relationship (Simpson & Gangestad, 1992). There is also more intense caring for each other in love relationships, for example, being a champion or advocate and giving of oneself, with the result that lovers are willing to give their utmost to their partners, even more so than in friendships. However, because of the greater exclusiveness and emotional involvement between them, lovers also experience greater ambivalence, conflict, distress, and mutual criticism in their relationships than do friends. In its extreme form this can result in physical abuse, something that is rare in friendships (Sugarman & Hotaling, 1989). In sum, love relationships are both more rewarding and more volatile than friendships.

The intensely satisfying but unstable nature of love relationships is often attributed to a special variety of love, that is, **romantic love**—the strong, emotional attachment to a person of the opposite sex and on occasion the same sex. The faith in romantic love is widespread and has prompted the development of several theories regarding love. One such theory has been advanced by psychologist Elaine Hatfield (1988). Passionate and companionate love are the two types of love she has identified. **Passionate love** perhaps best fits our notion of romantic love. Passionate love is an intense emotional reaction to a potential romantic partner who might not even love you in return. This is the "head over heels" reaction some of us experience when we first realize we are in love. This type of love is what David and Diane first experienced. They sat in the same row of their biology class where David first noticed Diane. He thought she was very pretty so when he saw her in the cafeteria, he walked over and introduced himself, stating that he, too, was in the biology class. Diane invited him to join her and her friend for lunch. They walked to the class after lunch and became acquainted. Within days, David was head over heels with this gentle, pretty young woman whom he asked for a date. Diane soon "fell" for David, too. As is true of passionate love, they were initially blind to each other's foibles and faults (Murray & Holmes, 1994).

Hatfield claims that three conditions must be met in order for individuals to feel they have fallen madly in love. First, the individuals must be exposed to romantic images and role models that lead to the expectation that love is possible. Second, the individual must come into contact with an appropriate person to love. "Appropriate," of course, is culturally defined. We will consider cultural variations in notions of love soon. Finally, Hatfield states that an intense arousal must be present. For example, fear, sexual excitement, even drunkenness can all change our arousal level, and we can confuse them with perceptions that we are in love.

Another type of love identified by Hatfield is **companionate love,** defined as an affection for those with whom our lives are deeply entwined. This is a practical kind of love that involves trust, caring, and tolerance for the partner's flaws. Emotionally, companionate love is more moderate; it also takes longer to develop than passionate love. Companionate love tends to be more characteristic of long-term relationships, including many happy marriages. Perhaps this kind of love had not yet developed between Diane and David, causing them to be more critical of one another as their relationship evolved over time.

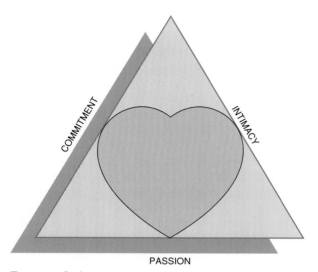

FIGURE 9–1

The three components of love. SOURCE: Robert J. Trotter, "The Three Faces of Love," *Psychology Today* (September 1986), p. 47. Reprinted with permission from Psychology Today Magazine. Copyright © 1986 (Sussex Publishers, Inc.).

A **triangular theory of love,** a theory that suggests there are three components to love, has also been developed. After studying various types of relationships to figure out what differentiates romantic relationships from other types of love, Robert Sternberg and Susan Grajek (1984) developed their triangular theory built around the three components of love—intimacy, passion, and commitment. (See Figure 9–1.) **Intimacy** is the emotional aspect of love and includes closeness, sharing, communication, and support. Intimacy tends to develop slowly in the beginning, then progress more steadily until it levels off and later declines. An apparent lack of intimacy may mean that the relationship is dying. Or intimacy may be present but taken for granted, requiring some disruption such as a family crisis or separation to make people more aware of how close they really are.

Passion, the motivational aspect of love, involves physiological arousal and an intense desire to be united with the loved one. Unlike intimacy, sexual desire blossoms quickly. But after a while, you get used to it, or "habituated," so that increased exposure to the person no longer brings the arousal and satisfaction it once did. Worse still, when you break up with the person, you may experience withdrawal symptoms—depression, irritability, and loss of desire.

Commitment, the cognitive aspect of love, includes both the short-term affirmation of your love for the person as well as the long-term commitment to maintain that love. Commitment usually develops in a more straightforward manner than does intimacy or passion. In long-lasting relationships, commitment increases gradually at first and then more rapidly. As the relationship continues, the amount of commitment levels off. If the relationship begins to weaken, the level of commitment will decline. And if the relationship falls apart, commitment falls back to zero. In contrast to romantic love, the love of a parent for a child usually is marked by a high and unconditional level of commitment. The triangular theory of love is not the only theory. Figure 9–2 introduces another manner for categorizing love.

As mentioned earlier, the perception of love is influenced by **culture.** Many social scientists are discovering that love is a universal phenomenon (Hatfield & Rapson, 1993);

FIGURE 9–2

PORTRAITS OF THE LOVE STYLES

EROS—Higher self-esteem, more disclosure, related to relationship satisfaction, important to both women and men

LUDUS—Less disclosure, more sensation seeking, less relationship satisfaction, more tolerated by men than by women

STORGE—Greater endorsement by women, involves greater contentment

PRAGMA—Many commonalities with Storge, but less quietly contented. Endorsed by pragmatic individuals

MANIA—More endorsed by women, related to less relationship satisfaction for women but related to less relationship satisfaction for them. Lower self-esteem, greater relationship communication, greater relationship turbulence

AGAPE—More characteristic of persons who are religious and/or who are in long-term relationships; more agapic women have more satisfied relationship partners; related to greater relationship stability and contentment

SOURCE: Hendrick, S. S., and Hendrick, C. (1992). *Romantic love.* Newbury Park, CA: Sage Publications. Copyright © 1992 by Sage Publications. Reprinted by permission of Sage Publications.

---

however, its importance in selecting appropriate others to marry varies by culture. Elsewhere in this book we have discussed two main types of cultures: individualistic and collectivistic societies. In individualistic societies the goals of the individual are more important than the goals of the collective (or of society), and in collective societies the goals of society or the collective are more important than the goals of the individual. The United States harbors a decidedly individualistic culture, wheras India, Japan, and other Asian countries promulgate collectivism. Dion and Dion (1993) in their literature review propose that romantic love is more likely to be an important basis for marriage in individualistic than in collectivistic societies. Similarly, psychological intimacy in marriage is more important for marital satisfaction in individual than in collective societies. Finally, although intimacy is important in individualistic marriages, intimacy can be more problematic because of individualism in such societies than in collective societies. Recent research supports some of these contentions. Levine, Sato, Hashimoto, and Verma (1995) studied attitudes about love and marriage in college students from 11 different countries. They found that for college students from Western or individualistic cultures such as the United States as compared to collectivistic or Asian societies there was more emphasis placed on love as a basis for establishing a marriage. Love was also a stronger reason for establishing a marriage in individualistic cultures than for dissolving a marriage. Those students who assigned greater importance to love, came from countries with higher economic standards than those who did not do so. This means that the students from the United States assign the highest worth to love, whereas students from India, a country whose economy is Third World, emphasize love the least in selecting marriage partners. In Japan, a collectivistic society with a good economy, the ratings of the value of love by college students fall somewhere between those of the other two countries. Interestingly, countries that do not emphasize romance in mate selection have lower divorce rates.

In the United States, as we have repeatedly mentioned, there are a variety of subcultures. Contreras, Hendrick, and Hendrick (1996) conducted research on Hispanic Americans and Anglo Americans to determine whether each group differentially values love in marital relationships. They found that Hispanic respondents were more pragmatic about love and less idealistic about sex than Anglo Americans. In both subcultures, the researchers also found that passionate love was also correlated with marital satisfaction. That is, the higher the passion, the higher the marital satisfaction. We might conclude from all of these cross-cultural studies what others have concluded. That is, many cultural groups in today's world believe in and value romantic love; in this regard they are more similar than dissimilar in their views about love and intimacy (Hatfield & Rapson, 1993).

LOVE AND CLOSE RELATIONSHIPS

Diane sometimes accused David of being "just like his father," whom she judged to be lazy—a couch potato who would rather watch sports on TV than attend community events with his wife or help with housework. The way people approach close relationships as well as their view of love can be a reflection of their personal development. That is, their characteristic styles of attachment to their parents probably also influence their **attachment style** to their romantic partners. Early attachments often give children a working model of relationships (Hazan & Shaver, 1994).

A series of studies by Cindy Hazan and Phillip Shaver (1994) show an interesting similarity between people's romantic relationships and beliefs about love and the kind of attachment they formed with their parents during childhood. The researchers polled 620 adults and 108 college students, asking them how they typically approach close relationships, their important romantic experiences, their beliefs about love, and their childhood relationships with their parents. Based on the responses, Hazan and Shaver classified each person into one of three groups.

Securely attached people believe it's easy to get close to others, and they report happy and trusting love relationships. Their romances last the longest and end in divorce least often. Many of them feel that romantic love never fades. People in this group saw their parents as especially loving, responsive, and warm.

Those who form **avoidant** attachments feel uneasy when people get too close to them. Because they fear intimacy, they have trouble trusting and depending on others and are prone to jealousy. They hold a cynical picture of love, feeling that the head-over-heels romantic love depicted in movies and novels does not exist in real life. Instead, it is rare to find someone to fall in love with, and even then romantic love seldom lasts. Avoidant adults generally rated their parents rather harshly, seeing their mothers as not very likable, if not rejecting, and their fathers as uncaring. Although the college students often rated their parents more positively than the older adults, the researchers speculated that the unduly rosy picture of their childhood is destined to become more realistic, and hence more negative, as they get older.

The third group, called **anxious/ambivalent,** includes people who desire a level of closeness many partners don't seem willing to give. Yet they also worry a lot about loved ones leaving them. Accordingly, these people experience more emotional extremes and jealousy in their relationships. They find it easy to "fall in love" but difficult to find "true love." They generally gave more mixed reports about their parents than did those in the other two groups.

Is there evidence that we do attach to our romantic partners as we did to our parents? Waters, Merrik, Albersheim, and Treboux (1995) followed individuals across the lifespan and found strong evidence for the constancy of attachment style over time. Most participants had the same style as young adults that they had as infants. These data suggest the answer is likely yes. Another question pertains to whether we marry someone with the same or different attachment style. Research does suggest that people with certain styles are unattracted to each other. Kirkpatrick and Davis (1994) found that avoidant types are not attracted to each other. On the other hand, securely attached adults tend to have more satisfactory and close relationships than avoidant and anxious individuals (Shaver & Hazan, 1993).

It is important to point out that although childhood attachments influence adult relationships, they do not necessarily repeat themselves. For instance, parents may change their initial behavior toward their child. Or a child might form a close, stable relationship with a friend or another family member as David did with his older brother. David was much closer to his brother than he was to his father, so his brother served as his role model for attachment. Then, too, some people manage to resolve the problems caused by early relationships and establish better ones as adults, especially now that intimacy has become more important to their happiness.

Some researchers question the assumption that men have less need for intimacy than do women. Emotional intimacy is of almost equal importance for the happiness of both sexes. However, men and women often differ in *how* they experience intimacy. For women, emotional intimacy generally leads to happiness in their relationships as wives and mothers. But for men, a sense of closeness is not as strongly related to their satisfaction with personal relationships as it is to their sense of certainty about the world. Accordingly, intimacy at home provides men with a sense of confidence and resilience that leads to achievement in the world. At the same time, these differences between men and women may help explain marital tensions. For instance, women tend to share their feelings more readily than men, with such emotional disclosure giving them a satisfying intimacy with their partners. Yet many men get a sense of closeness by simply sharing enjoyable activities with their partner without necessarily talking about their feelings (Goleman, 1987).

COHABITATION

Couples who begin living together as did Diane and David often experience greater intimacy than other dating couples their same age, at least in the short run. Although people of varying ages and prior marital statuses engage in **cohabitation,** the largest proportion are unmarried singles in their 20s to 40s. Some drift into this type of arrangement, often keeping a place of their own. Others deliberately set up a joint household from the outset as did Diane and David. Table 9–1 presents data on unmarried couples and their status.

Drawing on a national sample of 2,536 unmarried individuals aged 35 years or younger, Nock (1995) compared participants who had never divorced or cohabited with those who had. He found that individuals who had experienced divorce and cohabitation expressed consistently different preferences in their willingness to marry others. The existence of these differences seems reflected in the "marriage markets" for those who have and have not experienced divorce or cohabitation. For example, 40 percent of the men and 43 percent of the women who are currently living together were previously married. Many of these individuals are between 25 and 44, so they are older individuals who may have tried singles bars and found them unsuitable; yet they also do not want to remarry right away.

Because cohabitation is often viewed as a first step toward marriage, many researchers have explored its impact on marital happiness and the divorce rate. However,

Table 9–1
Unmarried Couples, by Marital Status

Marital status of male	Marital status of female				
	Total	Never Married	Divorced	Widowed	Married, husband absent
Total 1991	3,039[a]	1,658	1,022	184	175
Never married	1,682	1,219	337	53	75
Divorced	1,075	357	593	73	53
Widowed	95	19	25	48	4
Married, wife absent	185	63	67	9	45

[a]Numbers of couples are in thousands.

Source: U.S. Bureau of the Census, *Statistical Abstract of the United States: 1992* (112th ed.) (Washington, DC: U.S. Government Printing Office, 1992), p. 45.

the evidence is conflicting and inconclusive. There is substantial evidence that couples who live together before marriage are more likely to get divorced within 10 years than couples who married before living together, as shown in a series of studies reported on by Jean Marbella (1989). For instance, 38 percent of couples who lived together before marriage were divorced within 10 years, as compared with only 27 percent of couples who married without cohabiting first. However, such a negative outcome may have less to do with the act of cohabitation. Many people who cohabit have a different set of values, believing that relationships are breakable if they're not personally satisfying. As a result, they are more likely to divorce than to stay in a less than satisfying marriage. Many of these individuals tend to be independent minded, and they believe that their right to personal happiness takes precedence over a marital relationship. At the same time, much of this evidence reflects the increasing economic status of women, who may have less financial need to marry. Also, there is a greater acceptance of sex outside of marriage and a greater emphasis on personal satisfaction in close relationships than on working together. As a result, in most instances, cohabitation is not a lifelong relationship. Only about one-half of cohabiting couples eventually marry. Figure 9–3 presents a pie chart for outcomes for unmarried couples living together.

Getting Married

Although **marriage** as an institution is being challenged by alternative arrangements such as cohabitation, it is not going out of style. Most people in the United States still want to marry, though they won't condemn someone who isn't married. Also, most Americans still think children should be reared within a marriage. Consequently, more than 9 out of 10 people eventually marry, most of them during their 20s and 30s. The median age for marriage of women is now over 23 years of age; for men it is over 25 (U.S. Bureau of the Census, 1995). Couples today tend to wait a bit longer to marry, and the median age of first marriages rises slightly each year. But because about half of all marriages performed each year involve remarriage for one or both partners, who are typically in their 30s, the median age of *all* marriages has risen even more (U.S. Bureau of the Census, 1995).

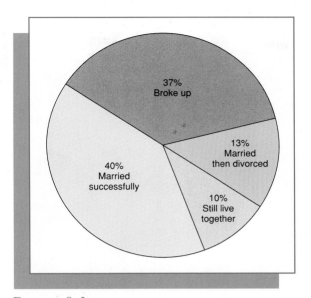

For the most part, people tend to marry partners of similar age, education, ethnic and social background, race, and religion (U.S. Bureau of the Census, 1995). Much of this tendency reflects the ways we have been socialized as well as the opportunities for meeting people, with physical proximity and interaction increasing the chances for attraction. However, as our society becomes more mobile and diverse, people are marrying across many of these familiar boundaries, and such factors as similar values play a more important role.

People tend to marry out of mixed motives, many of them unclear even to themselves. The tradition of marriage along with the social and legal advantages of marriage play a larger role than is commonly realized. Yet, when asked, people characteristically say they marry mostly because they are in love. Now that marriage is no longer necessary for economic survival, the satisfaction of sexual needs, or for that matter the rearing of children, love has become the major rationale for getting and staying married. Even upper-class couples and royalty, who have traditionally married for social reasons, prefer marriages based on love.

However, most American couples who marry believe in **voluntary marriage**— with the assumption that they will remain married only as long as they are in love. When they are no longer in love, it's mutually understood they will get divorced. When people marry on the basis of romantic love—with its emphasis on emotional and physical intimacy—it's no surprise so many marriages fail. The longer a couple lives together, especially in a satisfying marriage, the more both partners come to value companionate love, as discussed earlier, with a greater emphasis on personal intimacy and commitment than physical attraction.

The alarming divorce rate, higher than 50 percent for some groups, has prompted social scientists to turn their attention to successful marriages and what makes them

How couples manage conflict makes a crucial difference in their marriages.

work. Until recently, marital "success" meant longevity, that is, how long a couple's marriage lasted. Divorce was universally regarded as a failure on the part of both partners. However, the changes in values in recent years have shifted the emphasis to the quality of the marital relationship rather than its duration. Success in marriage is interpreted more in terms of **marital satisfaction,** especially in the relationship aspects of marriage—mature love, intimacy, and companionship. Divorce is often taken to be the price one may have to pay to end a dead or destructive relationship, presumably in order to seek a more satisfying one. Such changes pose some nagging questions. Must marital happiness exact such a high price? Can't people live in long-lasting relationships without becoming bored or having a devitalized relationship? In other words, is it possible to have marriages that are both happy and enduring? To test your attitudes about marriage, take the Marital Myths survey provided in Figure 9–4.

Let's first look at new marriages to see what they are like. M. P. Johnson, Huston, Gaines, and Levinger (1992) asked newly marrieds (married 2 years or less) to describe their daily lives, that is, to describe their leisure, conversational, conflictual, and other activities. Based on these descriptions, the researchers were able to identify four different marital patterns. **Symmetrical marriages** were characterized by both spouses working outside of the home and holding egalitarian ideas about gender roles. This was a very common pattern. They therefore divided household tasks; one reason may be that they have little leisure time. A second type of marriage was the **parallel marriage,** where the husband is the primary wage earner. Housework is divided in a sex-typed manner, and the spouses spend little time together. A higher number of these marriages have children.

A third type of marriage was the **differentiated marriage.** In this type of marriage both partners work, but the husband's job is emphasized. The housework is again divided in a sex-typed fashion, but the couple spends their leisure time together. These couples are also likely to have children. The fourth type of marriage was **reversed,** in which the wife's job is emphasized. The household tasks are not segregated by gender; half of these marriages have children. This type of marriage tends to be

---

FIGURE 9–4

MARITAL MYTHS

Some truisms about marriage follow. Indicate which of them you think are true and which are false. Then check your responses by consulting the correct answers at the end of the chapter.

1. More than 9 out of 10 Americans eventually marry.
2. Partners who live together before marriage are less apt to get divorced than those who did not do so.
3. Marriage should be a 50-50 partnership.
4. Husbands and wives should be best friends.
5. Differences and incompatibilities between partners are the major causes of marital dissatisfaction.
6. Having a child will improve an unhappy marriage.
7. Most divorces are initiated by women.
8. Extramarital affairs will destroy a marriage.
9. Children are damaged more by a legal divorce than by remaining in an intact but unhappy home.
10. Married people tend to live longer than unmarried people.

---

highly companionate. Despite these patterns, all couples reported equal satisfaction with their marriages.

An important question, then, is what characterizes long-term, satisfactory marriages. Although there is no foolproof recipe for long-lasting happy marriages, an overview (Marano, 1992) of numerous marital studies provides some valuable clues. First, a major factor that turns up in almost every longitudinal study of marriage is "joint problem-solving ability." This factor is mentioned by over two-thirds of the highly satisfied couples but barely one-third of the unsatisfied couples. Second, when asked specifically to cite the factors they believe contribute to the longevity of their marriage, almost half of the satisfied couples say they "have fun" together and cherish such experiences. Yet fun, humor, and playfulness are not even mentioned by the mildly satisfied and unsatisfied couples. Third, one of the best predictors of marital success is the quality of the couple's communication *before* marriage, presumably because it is more important *how* differences and problems are handled than their occurrence, especially early in the marriage. Fourth, one of the strongest predictors of marital success is "affective affirmation"—the communication of loving, accepting attitudes or the unconditional approval of one's mate. That is, if a partner is accepted as he is, he's more apt to do things her way, and she moves toward his way. We would predict that Diane and David would need to improve the quality of their communications and better solve joint problems if they want a long and happy relationship.

Such findings support the importance of companionate love in long-term happy marriages. That is, such couples are more apt to place importance on interpersonal intimacy and commitment to marriage as a lasting relationship than on physical satisfaction. Couples who are fortunate enough to sustain a vital sex life, more often because of the quality of their sex life than the frequency of intercourse, may experience **consummate love**—the balanced combination of intimacy, commitment, and passion. But this remains more of an ideal than a reality for most couples in lasting relationships.

 ## Marital Adjustment

Whether or not couples achieve a lasting happy marriage depends to a large extent on what happens after they marry, over and above how well matched they are in such matters as compatibility. Of great importance is each partner's flexibility and willingness to change, especially in a rapidly changing society. A major difference between today's couples and those of the past is the lack of clearly defined roles for each partner, as seen in the Johnson team's research on early marriage patterns. The changing nature of gender roles creates problems for all types of couples as they settle down to live together. Even the most mundane tasks may become a problem. Who cooks? Who takes out the trash? Who writes the checks? Yet such tasks are only a part of a much larger issue, namely, how men and women relate to each other. Getting along in marriage involves the larger questions of authority, fairness, and respective fulfillment of needs. In this section, we'll discuss several important areas of **marital adjustment,** including the sharing of marriage responsibilities, communication and conflict, marital sex, and the changes in the relationship over time.

SHARING MARITAL RESPONSIBILITIES

Marriage partners are sharing marital responsibilities to a greater degree today than in the past. As a result, the respective role expectations between husbands and wives are becoming more flexible and functional. More wives are sharing the provider role by working outside the home. Husbands are expected to provide greater emotional support in the marriage, including help with child rearing. Decision making has become more democratic, especially among dual-income couples.

A major area of marital adjustment for many couples concerns the wife's employment outside the home. More than 50 percent of the U.S. women in the labor force are married and living with their husbands (U.S. Department of Labor, 1994). Most married women like the option of working outside the home and feel it helps their marriage and family. However, the household tasks and the amount of time needed to complete them is constant whether both individuals in the marriage work outside the home or not. In American families, women overall perform between 65 percent and 75 percent of the household chores. Diane, for example, complained to David that after they started living together, she did 150 percent of the daily chores! David argued back that this was fair. He was going to school and working; she, on the other hand, was only attending school.

If women do work outside of the home, does this mean that they will do fewer chores or that their mates will assist with housework? Several studies demonstrate that women still do more housework than men even when the women work outside of the home (Matlin, 1996). How do the wives feel about this? Interestingly, many wives report feeling guilty that they cannot spend even more time on household jobs (Biernat & Worthman, 1991). Another typical response, particularly from working women, might be exhaustion. Besides her anger with David, this feeling will likely be one Diane experiences if and when she obtains a job.

About one in five families is headed by a single parent.

Although egalitarian marriages might seem to be the ideal, one difficulty that comes with the increased sharing of marital responsibilities is the issue of fairness. More specifically, there is a tendency for each partner to want greater rewards at no additional costs. For example, a husband may want his wife to work to help pay the bills but will still expect her to continue doing all the things she did around the house before taking the job. In turn, a working wife may want to keep most of her earnings but expect her husband to help out more around the house. Couples need to learn means to resolve these conflicts before they destroy the marriage.

COMMUNICATION AND CONFLICT

The ongoing change in marital responsibilities makes communication and conflict management even more important in marriage. Only 1.2 percent of married couples say they never disagree (McGonagle, Kessler, & Schilling, 1992). Although many couples argue, the priorities of particular problems vary somewhat from couple to couple. For instance, some couples see conflicts over money as one of the leading problems in marriage. Many couples regard sexual incompatibilities as the major problem in marriage. In fact, marital well-being is closely associated with sexual satisfaction for both men and women (Henderson-King & Veroff, 1994). Other couples complain of unrealistic expectations of marriage and spouse, lack of affection, and power struggles. Other problems include problems related to child rearing; with the birth of a child comes a decline in passionate love (P. Tucker & Aron, 1993). Other issues that create conflict are in-laws and extramarital affairs (Yarab & Allgeier, 1997). However, the most common problem, appearing at the top or next to the top of almost every list, is difficulty in communication. Again and again, husbands and wives complain, "We just can't talk to each other."

Why can't couples communicate? Married people talk to each other all the time. They say such things as "What are we having for dinner?" and "I'll be home later than usual tonight." This type of communication is easy enough. The failure in communication tends to occur at a deeper level of sharing feelings, expectations, intentions, and personal needs. It's in these areas that partners have trouble getting through to each other. In most instances both partners long for intimacy and tenderness. But the price is being open and vulnerable. Accordingly, each tends to hold back, settling into a kind of guarded communication. Aaron Beck (1988) in his book *Love Is Never Enough* says that we assume our spouse can understand our hints and our indirect complaints. Often a spouse cannot detect these fine nuances, which leaves the communicator feeling as if the listener does not care. Even when feelings are expressed, they're likely to be the "safer" negative feelings like anger. Individuals are sometimes more reluctant or embarrassed to express their positive feelings of love and tenderness.

These difficulties in communication are further compounded as couples try to mesh their lives more closely. As they become involved with each other, some areas of disagreement are inevitable. As they struggle to resolve their disagreements, the sparks begin to fly. Irritation, frustration, exasperation, and hostility accumulate. The harder they try to resolve their disagreements, the more anger they generate. Each partner wants closeness; yet each feels cheated. Their love is blocked by anger. So instead of loving each other, they find themselves hating each other or arguing constantly. When one negative emotion is the catalyst for more conflict and more intensely negative emotions such as anger, psychologists label the phenomenon **conflict spiral.** Figure 9–5 provides a scale for measuring how solid your relationship is, that is, how well you communicate. Both you and your partner should take it independently of each other.

How couples manage conflict makes the crucial difference in marriage. When one partner is clearly dominant in the relationship, that person often resorts to the "hammer" approach. The person may get angry and demand that his or her partner give in. The person may even threaten to leave if the partner doesn't agree. Stability is achieved because one partner is dominant and the other submissive. The more controlling a partner is in the relationship, the more inclined he or she is to use "hard tactics" of anger, threat, and domination (Kipnis & Schmidt, 1985).

Other solutions more commonly seen among partners committed to companionship are emotional alienation or avoidance. The sharing of power allows a democratic, two-vote system. Yet this approach is difficult to operate successfully when the partners disagree over a matter they both feel strongly about. Conflicts are not resolved because neither is willing to give ground or because one partner will not discuss (avoids) the conflict. A clash of conflicting wills can generate increasing tension and resentment. Such a state becomes so intolerable that the partners withdraw emotionally from their relationship. Conflicts are not resolved, but an uneasy peace is achieved at a price—an "emotional" divorce. Unfortunately, this is probably the most familiar type of marriage, with the partners drifting apart, experiencing fewer conflicts, to be sure, but also less satisfaction in an "empty" marriage. Those who avoid communicating or avoid conflict also feel that the marriage is empty or in trouble but will not commit to doing anything about it. Men are more likely than women to avoid conflicts or to avoid communicating about conflicts (Oggins, Veroff, & Leber, 1993).

Another approach to conflict management, usually advocated by marriage and family counselors, is based on rational problem-solving and negotiation skills. The assumption here is that conflict is not all bad. Indeed, conflict is an inevitable part of vital, close relationships; it may help individuals learn more about themselves and each other and may deepen their relationship. But most couples need to improve their negotiating skills and adopt mutual guidelines. Not surprisingly, couples who rely mainly on such ratio-

FIGURE 9–5

COMMUNICATION AND RELATIONSHIPS

The following test assesses how much love and respect you and your partner communicate to each other. If you mostly agree with the statement, circle *yes*. If you mostly disagree, circle *no*. Be sure to have your partner take the test, too.

1.	My partner seeks out my opinion.	yes	no
2.	My partner cares about my feelings.	yes	no
3.	I don't feel ignored very often.	yes	no
4.	We touch each other a lot.	yes	no
5.	We listen to each other.	yes	no
6.	We respect each other's ideas.	yes	no
7.	We are affectionate toward one another.	yes	no
8.	I feel my partner takes good care of me.	yes	no
9.	What I say counts.	yes	no
10.	I am important in our decisions.	yes	no
11.	There's lots of love in our relationship.	yes	no
12.	We are genuinely interested in one another.	yes	no
13.	I love spending time with my partner.	yes	no
14.	We are very good friends.	yes	no
15.	Even during rough times, we can be empathetic.	yes	no
16.	My partner is considerate of my viewpoint.	yes	no
17.	My partner finds me physically attractive.	yes	no
18.	My partner expresses warmth toward me.	yes	no
19.	I feel included in my partner's life.	yes	no
20.	My partner admires me.	yes	no

If you or your partner answered no more than seven times, chances are you or your partner does not feel loved or respected in this relationship. You need to communicate about these feelings and reestablish these bonds.

SOURCE: Gottman, J. (1994). *Why marriages succeed or fail.* New York: Simon & Schuster.

nal tactics and compromise tend to be the most satisfied with their relationship (Kipnis & Schmidt, 1985). Also, couples who are similar in their coping strategies are more satisfied with their marriages than those whose strategies differ (Ptacek & Dodge, 1995).

For those couples who cannot alter their own relationship, marriage therapy might be a viable solution. A review of the marriage therapy literature demonstrates that couples of younger ages, low levels of depression, nonrigidity regarding gender roles (Bray & Jouriles, 1995), and wife dominant couples and egalitarian couples (Gray-Little, Baucom, & Hamby, 1996) leave therapy with the most marital satisfaction.

SEX IN MARRIAGE

Newlyweds bring greater sexual knowledge and experience to their marriages today than in the past. But they're also more likely to judge their sex lives by higher standards. In one study of newlyweds (Arond & Pauker, 1988), more than three-fourths of them had had sex with their partners before marriage, and half of them had lived together before marriage. A surprising 1 out of 4 couples experienced sexual problems during their first year of marriage. About 1 in 5 wives and 1 in 10 husbands suffer from a lack of sexual desire. By the end of their first year of marriage, almost half of them aren't having sex as frequently as they wish. In other words, they might be bored with each other; passionate love seems to decrease with time (P. Tucker & Aron, 1993). Nevertheless, married couples today are engaging in sexual intercourse more frequently than couples did in the past, with an average of two to three times a week for couples in their 20s and 30s. They're also open to a wide array of sexual practices, use a greater variety of positions in intercourse, and engage in intercourse for a longer time than the 2-minute average reported in the 1950s.

The longer couples, unmarried and married alike, live together, the less frequently they have sexual intercourse. Reasons usually cited include the lack of time or physical energy. Perhaps a more important factor is the decline of sexual ardor because the partners have become "accustomed to each other." The decrease in physical vigor associated with aging is also a related factor, especially among couples in middle and late adulthood. Couples with children also complain about the lack of privacy. Actually, the longer couples are married, the more attention they pay to the quality of sex than to its frequency, though these two are related. Yet it's almost impossible to distinguish cause and effect. Do couples have sex more frequently because they are happy in their marriage and sex lives? Or does the frequency of sex serve to strengthen a couple's love? It's hard to tell. One point is clear: For most couples, though not necessarily all, a good sex life and a happy marriage go together.

Most couples aspire to the ideal of sexual monogamy, whether they adhere to it or not. But when asked if they've ever had sex outside of marriage it's a different story. Traditionally, the double standard in sex has permitted husbands to engage in extramarital sex more than wives (Masters, Johnson, & Kolodny, 1995), but this too is changing. Today about 15 percent of the women and 25 percent of the men are engaging in extramarital sex (Laumann, Gagnon, Michael, & Michaels, 1994). Men report having extramarital affairs to find more sexual excitement, to counteract boredom, to provide better sex, and to have greater sexual frequency (Masters et al., 1995). On the other hand, marital infidelity is somewhat common among women who have engaged in sex before marriage or who work outside the home (South & Lloyd, 1995). Women in the workplace are about twice as likely as full-time homemakers to have sex outside of marriage. Although women who engage in extramarital sex are often dissatisfied with their marriages, this is not always the case. Some women who engage in extramarital affairs do so out of curiosity or the desire for personal growth rather than marital unhappiness.

CHANGES IN MARRIAGE OVER TIME

Let's suppose two couples with similar backgrounds get married. For example, David and Diane marry and two of their friends from the same college marry each other. Then after a few years of marital bliss, Diane and David's marriage goes steadily downhill. One squabble leads to another; within a few years they are headed to divorce court. On the other hand, their friends report that their marriage has become happier with each passing year, and they are saddened to learn that their friends, David and Diane, are divorcing.

How do these patterns develop? What makes them persist? Is there any hope that unhappy marriages can be saved? Couples who are happy tend to make relationship-enhancing attributions. Couples who are unhappy tend to make distress-enhancing attributions (Bradbury & Fincham, 1990). To make an attribution means to seek the cause of another person's behavior. We can attribute cause to the person, such as blaming a person's traits, or to something external, such as to fate or to the situation. If a husband does something negative such as forget his wife's birthday, the wife can attribute the forgetfulness to the fact that her husband is unreliable and uncaring or so busy at work that he simply and unintentionally forgot. In happy couples, the wife makes the attribution that the husband is just plain busy. In unhappy couples, the wife makes the attribution that the husband is uncaring.

On the other hand, if a wife does something positive for her husband, such as surprise him at work with a birthday party, the attributions are the reverse. In the happy couple, the husband attributes the surprise to his wife's kind heart. In the unhappy couple, the husband assumes his wife merely wants to impress his coworkers. If it were not for the coworkers, he wouldn't have had the surprise party.

The lesson here is that couples need to monitor the attributions they make toward each other early in their relationships. If they find themselves in the distress-maintaining attributional model, they should talk about why they are making these attributions, decide what they can do to reverse the types of attributions they are making, and take appropriate measures. In their early marriage, Diane and David had unfortunately developed this negative attributional style. Let's see what happens to them next.

 ## Divorce and Remarriage

Unfortunately, as we all know, many marriages now end in **divorce,** the legal dissolution of marriage. The divorce rate among Americans has more than doubled in the past 25 years, with one out of every two marriages now ending in divorce (U.S. Bureau of the Census, 1995). Each year over 1 million couples get divorced, most of them within the first 10 years of their marriage. Interestingly, White Americans have the highest divorce rate among all racial groups (U.S. Bureau of the Census, 1995), although they probably have easier lifestyles due to their higher social class standing and suffer the fewest indignities of racial prejudice.

Why the dramatic rise in the divorce rate in America? Many different reasons have been put forth, ranging from the lack of preparation for marriage to the fading of religious values. A major factor has been the gradual shift away from the traditional notion that marriage is forever to the idea that the primary goal of marriage is happiness and fulfillment. This shift in values has also been accompanied by changes in the laws that make it easier for couples to get divorced.

THE DIVORCE EXPERIENCE

The decision to divorce usually comes after a long period of mutual alienation, often accompanied by a separation, in which both partners suffer from hurt, damaged self-esteem, and loneliness. In many instances, the couple may have sought help from professionals such as marriage counselors and family therapists. Studies by psychologists and sociologists indicate that the wife is the key player in divorce and adjusting to it (Crane, Soderquist, & Gardner, 1995). As is true for dating relationships, women are more likely to initiate the breakup (Helgeson, 1994). In fact, women make more specific plans and are more likely to implement the plans for divorce. Women also think more about divorce and talk to their friends during the decision making (Crane et al., 1995).

When women work outside the home, many men do not necessarily assume more household responsibilities; thus by his increased involvement in housework, this modern man is somewhat unique.

No matter how good or bad the marriage has been, the process of getting divorced is almost always painful. Divorce is also a complex experience because so many things are happening at once. The partners tend to withdraw emotionally from each other or coexist with a great deal of mutual antagonism. The legal aspects of divorce are not only expensive but emotionally draining as well; for example, the settlement of property, money, and custody/visitation issues drains both parties. Disapproval and rejection by friends, family members, and coworkers can also be agonizing. Separating oneself from the influence of a former partner and becoming an autonomous social being again might be difficult. For example, David and Diane divorced after 7 years of marriage. They both found it hard to reenter the world of dating. These changes may be quite frightening at first, but some are potentially the most constructive aspects of divorce in that the individual may experience considerable personal growth. Nevertheless, it takes most people 2 or 3 years to recover fully from the distress of a divorce. The increasing number of divorces as well as the support groups available for divorced people help to alleviate much of the loneliness and emotional pain that inevitably accompanies divorce.

A divorce involving parents can be particularly painful for the parents and for the children. The courts tend to follow the principle of "the best interests of the child," which traditionally has meant that custody was generally given to the wife. But today there is a tendency to award joint custody (which usually means joint decision making about the child's care) and in some cases custody to the father. The partner who is not granted residential and legal custody of the children is usually granted certain visitation rights.

SINGLE-PARENT FAMILIES

Divorce generally takes a toll on the children as well as on the divorcing couple. The number of children affected by divorce is on the increase. In 1970 the rate of affected children was 12.5 children out of every 1,000; in the 1990s, the rate is 16.8 out of every 1,000 children (U.S. Bureau of the Census, 1995). Figure 9–6 presents another pie chart of children and with whom they reside.

How children are affected by their parents' divorce varies considerably, depending on such factors as the intensity of the parental conflict, the child's personality, the age and sex of the child, whether the child is uprooted from familiar friends in the process, and the custodial parent-child relationship. Some psychologists argue that divorce makes children vulnerable to depression and other psychological disorders. On the other hand, studies show that parental discord before and after a divorce influences children's adjustment more powerfully than does the actual divorce itself (Derdeyn, 1994). Grandparents also suffer when their adult children divorce, because they might not be able to see their grandchildren as frequently or at all (Gray & Geron, 1995).

Following a parental divorce, about 9 out of 10 children live with their mothers, with single-mother families making up about one-fifth of all families. The absence of the father and/or his diminished support becomes an important factor, as shown in Amato's (1987) study of children and adolescents in single-parent, stepparent, and intact families. Compared to their counterparts in intact families, children and adolescents in single-parent families generally report less father support, less family cohesion, more sibling conflict, and more household responsibility. Boys tend to be more adversely affected by the absence of the father than girls, and boys in single-mother families show a higher rate of aggression and other problem behaviors.

FIGURE 9–6

Children under 18 years old and presence of parents.
SOURCE: U.S. Bureau of the Census. (1992). *Statistical abstract of the United States, 1992* (112th ed.). Washington, DC: U.S. Government Printing Office, p. 55. Cherlin, A., & McCarthy, J. (1985, February). Remarried couple households. *Journal of Marriage and the Family, 47,* 23–30.

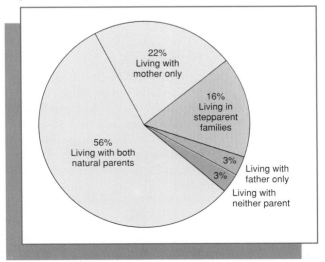

Divorce typically provides children with a double dose of stress. Immediately after their parents' divorce, many children feel resentful and depressed. Older children and adolescents are especially apt to exhibit heightened aggression. However, within a few years, children generally adjust to the new living arrangements. Then, about 3 to 5 years after the divorce, there is a second dose of stress associated with the custodial parent's remarriage. Because about three-fourths of divorced mothers and fathers remarry, most children of divorce will gain a stepparent. In fact, more than 2 million people have been married more than three times (G. H. Brody, Neubaum, & Forehand, 1988). The stepparent's intrusion into the home may be initially an unwelcome event, disrupting the single mother's relationship with her children, especially her daughters. All of this turmoil necessitates another period of readjustment (Hetherington, Stanley-Hagan, & Anderson, 1989).

Children and adolescents of African American backgrounds are especially likely to grow up in single-parent families. Almost half of all African Americans under 18 live in single-mother families. The most widely cited reason is the increase in out-of-wedlock births, many of them attributable to teenage pregnancies. The high rate of out-of-wedlock births combined with the greater proportion of women who never marry and those who remain single after divorce all contribute to the increase in female-headed homes among African Americans.

However, this is an integral part of a larger, more complex pattern attributable to a combination of social, economic, and cultural factors (M. P. Tucker & Taylor, 1989). A major factor is the high rate of unemployment among African American males, rendering many unable to assume the responsibilities of husband and father. In addition, faced with such circumstances, many African American women strive to be independent, thereby encouraging the trend toward single-parent families. At the same time, many African American women are in dead-end jobs, lack alimony and child support, and require public assistance. In contrast, African American families who have achieved middle- or upper-class standards may derive even greater satisfaction from family than from their jobs. Children and adolescents in these homes are much more likely to be living with two parents and share many of the opportunities and values of their Caucasian counterparts. Meanwhile, an even larger number of African American children and teenagers are growing up in father-absent, economically deprived homes, thereby setting the stage for problem behaviors such as dropping out of school, delinquency, alcohol and drug abuse, and teenage pregnancy. Male teenagers are especially at risk.

REMARRIAGE

Despite the painful experience of divorce, most divorced people remarry, one-fourth within 1 year of their divorce. Half of them remarry within 3 years after the divorce, and three-fourths of them within 9 years. Men remarry at an average age of 36, women at an average age of 33 years (U.S. Bureau of the Census, 1992). In most instances, a divorced person marries another divorced person, probably because they share similar experiences. Then, too, participation in various support groups which have been recently formed such as Parents Without Partners increases the likelihood of meeting and marrying someone like themselves.

Interested people often ask, "How successful are second marriages?" And to be frank, it's difficult to answer because the record is mixed. Statistically, second marriages are even more likely to end in divorce. But we should hastily add that there are a small number of "repeaters" who marry and divorce several times, thus inflating the overall figures. Many second marriages are quite successful, both in terms of marital happiness and longevity. When the divorce repeaters are removed from consideration, the outlook for second marriages may be even better than previously thought. At least 6 out of 10 second marriages last until death, which is higher than first marriages. Also, the remarriage of divorced people over 35 years of age further enhances their chances for a successful marriage (U.S. Bureau of the Census, 1995). Partners in a second marriage often benefit from their mistakes in an earlier marriage. They know full well the value of give and take in a close relationship like marriage. Age and maturity also help. Most of all, remarried people usually realize the value of commitment and often work harder at their second marriage.

An increasing number of remarriages now involve children. About half of these children have stepparents, mostly stepfathers because of the tendency for children to live with their mothers. The remaining children are born after the remarriage of the partners. The majority of remarried couples have children from the previous marriage of just one spouse. A much smaller number of families have children from the previous marriages of both spouses. And only a very small number of remarried couples have children of their own in addition to children from previous marriages of both partners (Cherlin & McCarthy, 1985). Such families are called **blended families.**

Remarriages involving children pose special demands on both the adults as well as the children. In addition to learning how to live with a new person, one or both partners must also become accustomed to a ready-made family. When the children are young, the stepparent has more opportunity to develop rapport and trust with the children. But when adolescents are involved, it's more difficult for everyone. If a stepfather too quickly assumes the authority of a parent, especially in matters of discipline, the children may resent it. Both parents must make allowances for the children's initial suspicion and resistance. Part of the problem is that the role of stepparent is not well defined. This problem is often compounded by the child's continued interaction with the remaining biological parent. Yet when both parents in the home develop a good working relationship, talking things out and cooperating on parental issues, stepparent families may do at least as well as intact families, if not better in many cases. Furthermore, as nontraditional families become a more substantial proportion of all families, both generations may assume their respective roles more easily.

FAMILY MEDIATION

Before David and Diane divorced, they attempted to reconcile following a short separation. In an attempt to work through their problems, they visited a family mediation center. Mediation is the intervention in a conflict by a neutral third party who assists the conflicting parties in managing or resolving their disputes (Duffy, 1991). Mediators, the neutral individuals, can manage more than family disputes; for example, they are often used to intercede in neighborhood, school, consumer, and other disputes. But here our focus is families and marriage. In family mediation, the mediator would listen to both sides tell their stories and then try to help them find concrete solutions to their problems. For example, Diane complained that David did little housework and David defended himself that he was tired from work. The mediator worked out an agreement that Diane would cook dinner and David would do the dishes each night. On evenings when they were too tired to prepare dinner and do the dishes, they would go out to a restaurant and each split the bill. Unfortunately, the process did not work well for David and Diane, but for other couples, family mediation has a remarkable success rate, varying from 80 percent to 90 percent agreement and 80 percent to 90 percent satisfaction with the process and compliance with the mediated agreements (Duffy, 1991). There are family mediators and mediation centers in every state in the United States; most large cities have their own centers.

SUMMARY

LOVE, INTIMACY, AND MARRIAGE

We began the chapter by discussing the intensely satisfying but often unstable nature of love relationships. Although most people retain a stubborn faith in romantic love, they regard it as only the first stage of love, from which a more mature love may grow. Individuals from most Western (individualized societies) have been exposed to romantic images in the media, have come in contact with someone to love, and have experienced the strong emotional arousal they label as love. Thus, they report the experience of passionate or romantic love. A second type of love, companionate love, where the company and friendship of the lover is enjoyed, can develop later. A second view is Sternberg's view where the ideal love includes equal and generous amounts of the three essential components of love—intimacy, passion, and commitment.

Couples who live together before marriage may enjoy greater intimacy than other dating couples, but they may be more likely to get divorced within 10 years, mostly because of the attitudes and values they brought to the marriage. More than 9 out of 10 Americans will eventually marry, most of them in their 20s and 30s. People who marry, especially those from individualized societies, hold the view of voluntary marriage, the assumption that they will remain married only as long as they are in love. When they are no longer in love, it's mutually understood they will divorce. In contrast, one of the keys to lasting, happy marriages is the couple's commitment to marriage as a long-term relationship and their willingness to communicate and work through their conflicts.

MARITAL ADJUSTMENT

A major change in marriage is the lack of fixed roles for husbands and wives, with a greater sharing of marital responsibilities between partners than in the past. Difficulty in personal communication continues to be a major problem for many couples. In contrast, good communication is necessary for resolving the inevitable differences and conflicts that surface in any close relationship. A satisfying sex life is also an important part of marriage, with a strong association between a satisfying sex life and satisfaction in the marriage relationship itself. Although the average marriage tends to devitalize over time, partners who remain open to each other and continue growing in their relationship report increasing happiness in their marriage.

DIVORCE AND REMARRIAGE

The divorce rate has more than doubled in the past 25 years, with one out of every two marriages now ending in divorce. Getting a divorce involves overlapping and painful experiences, including the emotional, legal, economic, parental, and community aspects. How children are affected by divorce depends on a variety of factors, such as the age and sex of the child and custody arrangements. Almost half of the children under 18 years of age are now growing up in single-parent or stepparent families. Most divorced people eventually remarry, many of them achieving happy marriages. Remarriages involving children from a previous marriage pose special demands on the adults as well as the children. Yet, when both parents in the home develop a good working relationship, talking things out and cooperating on parenting issues, stepparent families may do at least as well as intact families, if not better in some cases. For families troubled by conflict, family mediation and family therapy offer effective solutions.

SCORING KEY FOR THE MARITAL MYTHS QUIZ

1. True. Although the marriage rate has declined somewhat, more than 9 out of 10 Americans do eventually marry, most of them in their 20s and 30s.

2. False. As discussed in the text, couples who live together before marriage are even more apt to divorce than other couples, mostly because of the attitudes and values they bring to the marriage.

3. False. Changing circumstances often trigger differing ratios of input among marital partners. For instance, a 30-70 ratio of husband to wife might be characteristic of a newly married couple in which the man is busy starting a new business, though the ratio might well be reversed (70-30) later in the marriage if the wife works and assumes more responsibilities at home because her husband has a life-threatening illness.

4. True. This factor is mostly true in that love and friendship are overlapping relationships. Sexuality adds a special dimension to marriage and love relationships that is not found in friendships.

5. False. It is the lack of good communication in discussing their differences rather than the differences themselves that is a major cause of marital dissatisfaction.

6. True. Studies show that married individuals report being healthier and happier than single individuals (Steinhauer, 1995).

7. True. In contrast to the past, most divorces are now initiated by women. One reason may be women's greater concern with the quality of the marriage relationship, with divorcing women reporting more dissatisfaction with their marriages than do divorcing men.

8. False. This factor varies. Extramarital affairs may rejuvenate some marriages, make no differences to others, and prove downright destructive of still others. A lot depends on how both partners deal with an extramarital affair.

9. False. Although studies vary, there is mounting evidence that children are damaged more by the conflict-ridden atmosphere of an intact home, especially when it is long-standing, than by the legal divorce itself.

10. True. On the average, married people, not simply happily married couples, live longer than unmarried people. One reason may be the need to look after someone else; another may be the emotional support people receive from their partners.

SELF-TEST

1. Compared to close friendships, romantic relationships are characterized by greater
   a. stability
   b. trust
   c. volatility
   d. acceptance

2. Couples in long-term relationships characterized by intimacy and commitment but little or no passion exhibit
   a. romantic love
   b. companionate love
   c. consummate love
   d. empty love

3. Compared to other married couples in the United States, couples who have cohabited before marriage
   a. are happier than other married couples
   b. are more likely to get divorced
   c. have greater problems than other married couples
   d. are more apt to remain married

4. Couples with happy and enduring marriages attribute their success to belief in marriage as a long-term relationship and
   a. a highly satisfying sex life
   b. their similarity in ages
   c. liking their spouse as a person
   d. sharing similar social backgrounds

5. Most married women are most concerned about
   a. taking separate vacations
   b. preparing meals
   c. doing household chores
   d. working outside the home

6. The most common problem among married couples is
   a. sharing household chores
   b. difficulties in personal communication
   c. problems with in-laws
   d. who earns the most money

7. The longer a couple stays married, the more the marriage tends to become
   a. devitalized
   b. less stable
   c. happier
   d. more vital

8. About one in five families is headed by
   a. a single mother
   b. a single father
   c. a stepparent
   d. both natural parents

9. Most divorced people tend to
   a. never marry again
   b. remarry another divorced person
   c. remarry someone who has never been married
   d. remarry within 1 year of their divorce

10. What process attempts to bring divorced families in conflict together with a neutral third person to come to agreements about how they will behave to reduce the level of conflict in the future?
    a. family mediation
    b. cohabitation
    c. blending
    d. family therapy

EXERCISES

1. *Qualities desired in a mate.* Make a list of some personal qualities you would like in a marriage partner. You might list a dozen such qualities; then go back and check the three most important ones. Write a short paragraph telling why you think these three qualities are the most important. You might do the same for personal qualities you would not like in a marriage partner. Again, list a dozen such qualities, and then check the three most important ones. Why do you think these qualities are undesirable?

2. *Qualities you offer to a prospective mate.* Make a list of the major personal strengths and weaknesses you would bring to a marriage relationship. What are the three most desirable qualities you have to offer? What are some of your less desirable qualities that might affect the marriage? If you are going steady with someone or if you are married, you might ask your partner to add to your list. Try to list more desirable qualities than undesirable ones.

3. *Cohabitation.* If you are currently living with someone of the opposite sex or have had such an experience, write a page or so telling what you learned from this experience. To what extent is your experience similar to that of cohabiting couples described in this chapter? Did cohabitation include serious plans for marriage? What are some of the values of cohabitation? The hazards? Would you recommend this experience to others?

4. *The marriage relationship.* If you are going steady, are living with someone, or are married, describe the type of relationship you have with your partner. If lovers, are you also friends? Do you and your partner return each other's love? Or is one of you more emotionally involved in the relationship than the other? To what extent are both of you relationship-oriented?

5. *Marital adjustment.* If you're living with someone or married, what has been your major adjustment in learning to live together? Has it involved learning how to communicate and handle conflict? Or has it had to do with specific problems involving money and sex? Select one or two of the most difficult adjustments you've had in marriage, or your current relationship, and write a page or so about it.

6. *The divorce experience.* If you have gone through a separation or divorce, write about your experience in a page or so. How has the divorce experience influenced your desire to remarry? If you came from a home with divorced parents, you might write about your experience, telling how you have been affected by your parents' divorce. How has your experience influenced your outlook on marriage? On divorce?

QUESTIONS FOR SELF-REFLECTION

1. Can you be in love with more than one person at a time?
2. How can you tell whether your partner loves you?
3. Are you and your partner equally involved emotionally in your relationship?
4. Do you believe that living together before marriage ensures a happier marriage?

5. If you are living together with someone or are married, to what extent are the household chores shared?

6. Do you and your partner "fight fair" so that you can disagree without undermining your relationship?

7. To what extent do you feel that sexual satisfaction and marital happiness go together?

8. If you or your parents have gone through a divorce, what was the hardest part for you?

9. As a single person or single parent, which characteristics do you most desire in a mate?

10. If you're happily remarried, what makes this marriage better than your earlier one?

FOR FURTHER INFORMATION

RECOMMENDED READINGS

BROWN, P. (1995). *The death of intimacy: Barriers to meaningful interpersonal relations.* New York: Haworth Press. A book designed to improve close personal relationships.

EVERETT, C. A., & EVERETT, S. V. (1994). *Healthy divorce.* San Francisco: Jossey-Bass. A book about diminishing the negative effects of divorce on all who are involved.

GOTTMAN, J. (1994). *Why marriages succeed or fail.* New York: Simon & Schuster. A practical book designed to help couples understand why their marriage is satisfactory or not.

MARKMAN, H., STANLEY, S., & BLUMBERG, S. L. (1994). *Fighting for your marriage: Positive steps for preventing divorce and preserving a lasting love.* San Francisco: Jossey-Bass. A guide designed for those whose marriages are not quite in trouble but who think they might need an assist in preserving their quality.

STERNBERG, R. (with WHITNEY, C.). (1991). *Love the way you want it: Using your head in matters of heart.* New York: Bantam Books. A consideration of how unattainable expectations sabotage love and how to build satisfying, long-lasting relationships.

WEBSITES AND THE INTERNET

http://einet.net/galaxy/Community/Family.html: A website for the whole family. Topics include parenting, teenagers, and marriage.

http:www.autonomy.com/luv.htm: A website for romantics. Although there is information for people who are dating, the site also includes material for married couples who want to keep the spark in their romance.

Usenet:soc.couples: A location for couples who want to share the ups and downs of their relationship.

Usenet:alt.romance.unhappy: A site for individuals whose romances have gone bad and need social support.

http://hughson.com/: Named one of the top 5 percent websites, this is an address for individuals contemplating or involved in a divorce.

CHAPTER

10

Sexuality

Learning Objectives

After completing this chapter, you should be able to

1. Discuss the changing views of sexuality.
2. Discuss the importance of sexual communication for a mutually satisfying sex life.
3. Describe the human sexual response cycle for males and females.
4. Identify various sexual dysfunctions.
5. List the most effective birth-control methods.
6. List ways to reduce your risk of getting AIDS.
7. Discuss the psychological aspects of sexual abuse of children and rape in American society.

After taking a test during their evening class, Carol and Kim stood in the hallway discussing some of the questions. Both felt tense and agreed they needed some time to unwind. They decided to visit a bar near the campus. Because the bar was crowded, they had to share a table with two male students whom they didn't know. Striking up a conversation, they soon discovered several areas of mutual interest. Carol found that Steve was also a psychology major and began sharing her career aspirations with him. And Kim soon discovered that she and Bob, Steve's friend, liked the same musical group. Initially, the four of them enjoyed talking and relaxing. However, as the evening wore on, the men began drinking more heavily and telling offensive stories. The women felt uncomfortable. Furthermore, Carol and Kim became aware that what they intended as friendliness was being perceived by the men as a sexual invitation. Sensing that an awkward situation was imminent, the women excused themselves and left.

 Male and Female

CHANGING VIEWS OF SEXUALITY

As depicted in the opening vignette, do men and women misunderstand each other sexually? This question has intrigued poets, philosophers, songwriters, and psychologists for decades. The experience of Kim and Carol and Steve and Bob demonstrates how our understanding of sex continues to be hampered by **gender stereotypes**—widespread generalities about the characteristics and behaviors of males and females. Stereotypes exaggerate the real differences between men and women, thereby setting the stage for misunderstanding and frustration between the sexes. In this section, we'll examine several gender stereotypes and their implications for men's and women's sexual behavior. Then we'll look at a healthier view of sexuality that is emerging along with the extensive changes in gender roles in our society.

There's a long-standing but mistaken belief that men have a stronger sex drive than women and that they enjoy sex more than women do. Although this stereotype is beginning to diminish as younger generations are socialized differently than those in the past, many men and women still subscribe to it in varying degrees. Even "normal" women, it is assumed, don't enjoy sex as much as men do. Sex is something women do mostly to please the men they love. In contrast, men are regarded as innately "sexual animals," ever in search of sexual variety, and inclined to play around with other women even after marriage. Once acquired, such beliefs function as self-fulfilling prophecies in the lives of both men and women.

There is no convincing evidence that the female sex drive is any less intense or animalistic than the male's. The main difference appears to be that women, especially in the past, have been taught greater restraint in expressing their sexuality. As women affirm their sexuality and enjoy satisfying relationships with men, as more and more women are doing, they enjoy sex as much as men do. In some instances a woman's sexual responsiveness may surpass that of a man, though it varies more widely among women than men and within a particular woman at a particular time (Masters, Johnson, & Kolodny, 1995).

There's also the mistaken notion that men are inherently sexual "predators" and women are natural "controllers." Thus, a man tends to regard a woman as a challenge, to see "how far" he can go with her. But having been taught that men are lustful creatures with "sex on the brain," a woman feels she must assume the role of controller. Instead of enjoying cuddling and kissing, she may be thinking about how to keep his hands off her breasts or genitals. Several recent studies support the conclusion that men and women often misperceive each other's intentions. For example, Cowan and Campbell (1995) studied high school students and found that girls rated male pathology as the most likely cause of rape, whereas boys rated female precipitation ("coming on to a guy") as the major cause of rape. Another study found that although there were differences in seventh and eighth grade boys and girls regarding whether they were sexually experienced (with boys more likely to have experience), there were no differences in recency or frequency of sexual encounters (DeGaston, Weed, & Jensen, 1996). Regarding adults, Robinson, Ziss, Ganza, and Katz (1991) report that 80 percent of the men and 63 percent of the women report having engaged in premarital sex. Males and females are not as different as stereotypes suggest.

Still another stereotype is that *masculinity* and *femininity* are polar opposites, inherent in the biological makeup of men and women, respectively. Thus, certain behaviors such as initiating sex or expressing affection are thought to be the natural prerogative of one sex or the other. However, behavioral scientists, armed with research findings in this area, find few people are 100 percent masculine or feminine. Instead, such characteristics are thought to coexist in varying degrees in individuals of both sexes, mostly because of important learned gender-role influences on behavior as well as individual differences. Interestingly, a survey was conducted in 1976 and again in 1984. The earlier results showed that men and women held very different views on the role of love in marriage with men regarding love as more important. By the 1980s, both men and women in high frequencies were endorsing the notion that love is important to marriage (Simpson, Campbell, & Berscheid, 1986). There are interesting cultural differences also in whether love is expected in a relationship. See Table 10–1 for more information.

Furthermore, considerable attention has been given to the concept of psychological **androgyny**—the combination of desirable masculine and feminine characteristics in one person. Carol and Kim and Steve and Bob are probably traditionally sex-typed.

TABLE 10–1
PASSIONATE LOVE AND SEXUAL DESIRE:
A CROSS-CULTURAL PERSPECTIVE

Percent of individuals in various countries that answered yes, no, or undecided to the question, "Would you marry someone you didn't love?"

	Responses (Percentage)		
Cultural Group	*Yes*	*Undecided*	*No*
Australia	4.8%	15.2%	80.0%
Brazil	4.3	10.0	85.7
England	7.3	9.1	83.6
Hong Kong	5.8	16.7	77.6
India	49.0	26.9	24.0
Japan	2.3	35.7	62.0
Mexico	10.2	9.3	80.5
Pakistan	50.4	10.4	39.1
Philippines	11.4	25.0	63.6
Thailand	18.8	47.5	33.8
United States	3.5	10.6	85.9

SOURCE: Hatfield, Elaine. (1994). *Passionate love and sexual desire: A cross-cultural perspective.* Paper presented at the Annual Meeting, Society for the Scientific Study of Sexuality, Miami.

That is, Steve and Bob are masculine and Carol and Kim are feminine, so they played the typical roles respectively of initiators and controllers. On the other hand, an androgynous woman might initiate sexual activity (traditionally a masculine role) but do so in a way that is both warm and sensitive to her partner (a traditionally feminine role). Social scientists disagree over the desirability of androgyny for men's and women's optimal adjustment, because an individual who is androgynous in one situation might not behave androgynously in another context. Similarly, the concept of androgyny leads us to believe that the solution to gender bias lies in changing individuals to become less gender-role stereotyped when the real solution might lie in social rather than individual change (Matlin, 1996). There exists research, however, that indicates that androgynous individuals are more comfortable with same- and opposite-sex touching (Crawford, 1994) and that androgyny is the preferred sex-role orientation in various types of relationships (Green & Kenrick, 1994). Whatever your personal view in this matter, one thing seems clear: Traits labeled masculine and feminine are mostly learned and coexist to some extent within each of us.

The ongoing changes in gender roles taking place in our society are giving rise to a new, healthier view of sexuality. As Masters et al. (1995) point out, many men and women are discovering that they cannot achieve the satisfaction they want until they realize sex is not something a man does to or for a woman, or vice versa. Instead, they are learning that sex is something a man and a woman do together as equal participants. The woman who affirms her sexuality learns that she can, when she so chooses, express the full range of her excitement and involvement without feeling guilty and not primarily to please the man. Similarly, the man who appreciates his sex partner may not always feel compelled to take the initiative nor assume total responsibility for satisfying her. Instead, each partner can appreciate the other's emotional needs and sexual urges—

which vary with mood, time, and place—without labeling them as masculine or feminine. When sexual needs conflict, as sometimes happens with most couples, they can negotiate a solution, less as adversaries than as two separate partners united by a common concern.

The Masters and Johnson team has also discovered that at least half the potential pleasure of sexual experience comes from the partner's response. If one partner is critical, unresponsive, or even at best passive, the emotional vitality of the couple's sex life steadily weakens and eventually withers away. However, when both partners are actively involved, each person's feelings spontaneously communicated heighten the other person's excitement and responsiveness. What he gives returns to him, and what she gives him comes back to her. All too often the relationship between the sexes is marred by a misleading image—two people on a seesaw, with power as the pivot. If one sex goes up, the other goes down. What women gain, men must lose. The sexual relationship among couples with a satisfying sex life shows this image to be false. What men and women achieve together benefits both. The quality of a couple's sex life, along with their overall relationship, is greatly enriched by a *fully shared partnership.*

SEXUAL COMMUNICATION

The extent to which we share our desires and feelings about sex with a partner is an integral part of our communication pattern, especially in regard to intimate matters. Carol and Kim obviously were not interested in having a sexual relationship with Bob and Steve that night but were afraid to openly express it. When we know someone better than Carol and Kim knew these two men, it is sometimes but not always easier to express our sexual desires. How easily can you communicate with your partner your sexual needs and wants? To assess your own level of communication in intimate relationships, you and your partner might complete Figure 10–1 and then discuss the results.

One of the most astounding things about sexual behavior is the reluctance of most people to talk about sex with their lovers or spouses. It's as if talking about sex would spoil the spontaneity—which might be only partly true. A lot depends on how you talk about your sex life. Sex therapists discover over and over again that one person doesn't

Sexual communication is mostly nonverbal.

FIGURE 10–1

How Well Do You Communicate With Your Partner or Close Friend?

This exercise is designed to give you some indication of your level of communication in intimate relationships.

With your partner or a particular person in mind, respond to each of the following questions by answering yes or no. Then consult the scoring key at the end of the chapter to determine your score and its meaning for you.

_____ 1. Do you feel that your partner does not understand you?

_____ 2. Do you know how to dress to please your partner?

_____ 3. Are you able to give constructive criticism to each other?

_____ 4. In appropriate places, do you openly show your affection?

_____ 5. When you disagree, does the same person usually give in?

_____ 6. Are you able to discuss money matters with each other?

_____ 7. Are you able to discuss religion and politics without arguing?

_____ 8. Do you often know what your partner is going to say before he/she says it?

_____ 9. Are you afraid of your partner?

_____ 10. Do you know where your partner wants to be in 5 years?

_____ 11. Is your sense of humor basically the same as your partner's?

_____ 12. Do you have the persistent feeling you do not really know each other?

_____ 13. Would you be able to relate an accurate biography of your partner?

_____ 14. Do you know your partner's secret fantasy?

_____ 15. Do you feel you have to avoid discussion of many topics with your partner?

_____ 16. Does your partner know your biggest flaw?

_____ 17. Does your partner know what you are most afraid of?

_____ 18. Do you both take a genuine interest in each other's work?

_____ 19. Can you judge your partner's mood accurately by watching his/her body language?

_____ 20. Do you know who your partner's favorite relatives are and why?

_____ 21. Do you know what it takes to hurt your partner's feelings deeply?

_____ 22. Do you know the number of children your partner would like to have after getting married?

SOURCE: Robert F. Valois & Sandra Kammermann, *Your Sexuality: A Self-Assessment* 2nd ed. (New York: McGraw-Hill, 1992), pp. 96–97. Copyright © 1992. Reproduced with permission of McGraw-Hill.

---

have the foggiest notion of his or her lover's or spouse's sexual likes or dislikes. Consequently, the person's well-intentioned caresses are not fully appreciated because they're either too heavy-handed, too quick, or too far off the mark—all matters that could be easily corrected by a few words murmured at the right time. Better yet, couples might set aside some time to share their feelings about sex—what was most satisfying and what might be improved. However, it's best to avoid discussing sex in a calculating or clinical way. Many couples avoid talking about sex immediately before or after, lest it put their partner on the defensive.

Communication in sexual matters, as with almost all other aspects of life, is most successful when it is two-sided, with both partners expressing themselves clearly and actively listening to each other. It is unfortunate that the taboo against doing this is so strong that Carol and Kim could not express their reluctance to continue talking to Steve and Bob. Perhaps sex wasn't really on the young men's minds. Maybe they just wanted company and friendly chatter. The most important part of sexual communication is the attitude you and your partner have toward each other. Especially crucial is the sense of trust and mutual empathy—the sense that each cares for the other and knows this feeling is reciprocated. A lot depends on the spirit and tone of voice in which you say something and your partner's willingness to discuss it in good faith. For instance, in making a request, you might say something like "I'd prefer doing something together before we have sex, such as taking a stroll on the beach." Such personal sharing tends to elicit a similar disclosure from your partner. You may also want to use questions to discover your partner's preferences. You might ask a yes-or-no question, such as "Did you enjoy that?" Or you could ask an open-ended question, such as "What part of our sexuality would you most like to change?" Some individuals prefer either-or questions such as "Do you want to talk about this now or at a later time?" Open-ended and either-or questions encourage more participation from your partner than simple yes-or-no questions. It's also important to use questions selectively and, most important, as a means to the end of really listening to what your partner is saying to you.

Giving and receiving criticism regarding sexuality is a touchy but important matter. In fact, some highly destructive patterns have been identified (Gottman, 1994). One pattern is **criticism** which entails attacking the partner's character, for example, calling the partner "selfish." Another pattern is **contempt,** where insults are used to denigrate the partner's sexuality. A third damaging type of communication is **defensiveness,** in which we make excuses or refuse to take responsibility or use some other self-protective defense. Finally, **withdrawal** is lethal to sexual relationships. In withdrawal we ignore our partners by watching TV or turning our backs on them. There are much better means to communicate our sexual feelings.

When you feel the urge to criticize, ask yourself, "What's the reason for my saying this?" If there's no good reason, perhaps it's better not to say it. Also, wait for the most appropriate time and place to offer criticism. When you feel you must criticize, express your remarks in a nonjudgmental way—using "I" messages, as discussed in Chapter 3. Whenever possible, demonstrate what you mean. If a woman feels her partner has been too rough in stimulating her, she might place his hand on hers and show him how she'd prefer to be stroked and say, "This is what I like." When receiving criticism, try not to overreact. Remember that criticism is often how your partner shows that he or she cares for you. Look beyond the words to what your partner is trying to tell you. Ask what the person would prefer you to do; then try to take it to heart.

Finally, remember that much of our communication is nonverbal, especially in sex. How close your partner sits next to you or the way your partner touches and caresses you reveals a lot about his or her attitude at the moment. Then, too, your partner's facial expressions and sounds communicate a lot. Most individuals find rapid breathing, moans, groans, and orgasmic cries very arousing. The absence of such sounds can be very frustrating.

INITIATING AND REFUSING SEX

Nowhere is sexual communication put to the test more than in initiating and refusing sex, as Carol and Kim discovered. Some couples don't communicate very well in this area and expect their partners to be mind readers. Others have developed nonverbal cues or elaborate rituals to signal their interest in sex. One woman says, "When John gets out the champagne and suggests we watch a movie on TV, I know what he's thinking."

Love enhances sex.

Men have traditionally taken the initiative in sexual intercourse. But nowadays men and women are moving away from such restricted notions of what "men must do" or what "women must not do." We might expect that individuals of both sexes are learning to share the roles of initiator and refuser equally. It is probably true that the more emotionally expressive the partner, regardless of gender, the more he or she initiates lovemaking. This pattern holds true among married couples, cohabiting couples, and gay and lesbian couples alike. Men and women who express their feelings readily tend

Men have traditionally taken the initiative in sexual encounters; however, modern men and women are moving away from such restricted notions.

to feel comfortable making the first move because they are sensitive about how to approach their partner. The more they succeed, the more they inherit the role. Also, the more expressive partner is less likely to refuse sex. In contrast, the more powerful partner of the two, usually the person who is less emotionally involved in the relationship or less in love, is more likely to refuse sex. By refusing sex, a partner can become a force to be reckoned with.

The more couples can initiate and refuse sex on an equal basis, the more satisfied they are with their sex lives. Not surprisingly, they also engage in sex more frequently than other couples. Among married and cohabiting couples alike, most of the couples who share the initiator and refuser roles equally are satisfied with the quality of their sex life, compared to couples for whom sexual initiation is not equal.

 ## Human Sexual Response

Let's assume that a week later, Carol is again in a bar with another girlfriend and Steve is also there. They immediately recognize each other. He comes over to her and starts talking about college life. They soon find that they went to high schools in the same city, enjoy basketball, country music, and pizza. Carol and Steve leave to go for pizza, spend the night talking, and eventually agree to begin dating one another. Their dating soon leads to a sexual relationship.

Much of sexual behavior, especially intercourse, takes place in private, so that it's difficult to know what occurs. Even the participants themselves are so emotionally involved that their recall is often inaccurate. For years people simply filled in the gaps of their sexual knowledge with jokes and stories, obscuring their understanding of sex with half-truths and myths. For example, when Bob discovered that Carol and Steve were dating, Bob called Steve "Strike-out Steve" because Steve didn't score with Carol on the first night they met. Steve did not care much for Bob's teasing. Despite people's reluctance to discuss their sex lives, researchers have been able to better understand human sexuality due to the pioneering work of William Masters and Virginia Johnson.

THE SEXUAL RESPONSE CYCLE

Through an extensive series of interviews and controlled observations of volunteers masturbating and engaging in **sexual intercourse,** Masters and Johnson have identified the basic sexual response patterns of men and women. These patterns consist of certain common physiological changes that occur in a predictable sequence and are collectively labeled the **sexual response cycle.** What follows is a modified version of the cycle, incorporating some of the recent changes suggested by other authorities in the field. We'll describe five phases of the sexual response cycle: (1) transition, (2) excitement, (3) plateau, (4) orgasm, and (5) resolution. Before reading the following, it is important for you to know that although Masters and Johnson's work is seminal work in the field of human sexuality, it is not without criticism. Tiefer (1991), for example, claims that their studies are replete with experimenter and methodological biases as well as subject-selection biases. For example, most Americans simply would not allow scientists to observe them having sex.

Transition (or desire).   In the sexual response cycle, *transition* is the gradual shift from a nonsexual to a sexual state of being, and it includes the awakening of sexual desire and a readiness for sexual arousal. We're all familiar with the importance of "getting ready" for a special evening out. The same is true with sex. Although individuals vary widely in regard to what puts them in the mood for sex, some things commonly facilitate the transition. Anything that induces relaxation, with a shift from a goal-centered to a more process-centered awareness, almost always helps. Some people enjoy a relaxed meal, including a small to moderate amount of alcohol. Others may prefer dancing, listening to music, or watching a romantic or erotic movie. Physical touching, massage, or relaxing in moving hot water, such as in hot tubs and Jacuzzis, are favorite ways to get into the mood for sex. It is quite possible that the lack of sexual desire stems from one partner's *unreadiness* for sex. Men in particular tend to be more impatient and less in tune or interested in the need for transition than women. Many women prefer a more gradual transition, accompanied by emotional sharing and tender caressing.

Interestingly, most of the erotica produced in the United States is designed to stimulate interest in sex in men (Hyde & DeLameter, 1997). For example, M. L. Ward (1995) conducted a content analysis of 12 prime-time television programs preferred by adolescents. Three different installments of each program were analyzed. Findings indicated that discussions about sexuality were common. The most frequent discussions depicted sexual relations as a form of competition between men who commented on women's bodies and appearance. In other words, masculinity was equated with sexuality. A corresponding assumption found in erotic media is that women are not interested in eroticism. However, research demonstrates few differences between men and women. Both men and women find explicit heterosexual erotica very arousing, and both men and women find female-initiated sex to be more arousing than male-initiated sex. Interestingly, though, women are sometimes not aware of their own arousal. When women are physically aroused, they sometimes cannot make a self-report of it, so this is one of the few differences (C. M. Davis & Bauserman, 1993).

Excitement.   Sexual arousal, or *excitement,* involves a combination of mental and sensory stimulation. Each partner's anticipation of sex is an important part of getting in the mood. Sexual desire is also heightened through the stimulation of the senses. Although individual preferences vary widely, sights and sounds, the sense of smell, and even taste all combine to heighten the mood. Mutual caressing of various parts of the body, especially the erogenous zones, almost always intensifies sexual arousal, even when sexual desire is initially low in one partner. As Carol once said, "Sometimes in the beginning I'm not much in the mood for sex, but I rarely end up feeling indifferent."

Sexual arousal activates two types of body changes. First, there is an increased muscle tension (myotonia) throughout each partner's body, which builds until the eventual release in the involuntary contractions of orgasm. There is also an increased heart rate, blood pressure, and engorgement (vasocongestion) of blood vessels throughout the sexual parts of our anatomy. The man's penis may become erect and subside several times during this phase. The woman's breasts enlarge, and her nipples become erect. Her clitoris and vaginal opening swell in size. The inner two-thirds of the vagina also lengthens and becomes lubricated.

Sexual arousal also depends greatly on psychological changes in the central nervous system, such as thoughts and feelings about a specific partner or the sexual act. As you might suspect, men and women are often aroused by different stimuli, thereby setting the stage for misunderstanding between the sexes. At the same time, individual differences tend to outweigh gender differences, so that each person needs to be appreciated in terms of his or her own preferences.

Many people become aroused more readily through erotic fantasies covering a wide range of situations. For some, fantasy provides an initial boost to sexual arousal. Others use a treasured fantasy to move them from the plateau phase of arousal to orgasm. Some can't experience orgasm without it. Erotic fantasy serves a variety of functions, ranging from the reduction of anxiety to the focusing of our thoughts and feelings, thereby avoiding distraction. Sexual fantasies are especially helpful in counteracting boredom, a common obstacle in long-term relationships like marriage. The fantasies of men and women are often similar. Common fantasies include reliving a past experience or activity with another attractive or famous partner.

There are some gender differences in fantasies (Leitenberg & Henning, 1995). Men fantasize about women's bodies and sexual activity whereas women fantasize about their own attractiveness to men. Men are likely to fantasize about being dominant, and women fantasize about the emotional or romantic context of the sexual activity. Men and women, though, seem equally likely to fantasize. Interestingly, research on the fantasies of gay men and lesbians has found similar gender effects except that the fantasized partner is of the same sex (Leitenberg & Henning, 1995).

Plateau.   The *plateau* phase is usually quite brief, lasting anywhere from a few seconds to several minutes. It's difficult to define the onset of this phase because there is no clear outward sign, such as erection of the man's penis or lubrication of the woman's vagina. Actually, the usual signs of sexual arousal become more pronounced as the individuals approach orgasm. The heart beats faster and breathing grows more rapid. Increasing muscle tension and blood pressure lead to engorgement of the sex organs, promoting the partners' readiness for orgasm. Men rarely lose their erection at this phase. Women also experience a marked increase in the swelling of the outer third of the vagina, or the "orgasmic platform," making stimulation by the male even more pleasurable. At this point, the partner who is moving faster toward orgasm, often the man, may need to slow down or vary the stimulation from time to time, so that both partners may reach orgasm at the same time if they so desire.

Orgasm.   As the climax of sexual excitement approaches, the partners may sense that *orgasm* is inevitable. Men usually realize orgasm once they reach the plateau, or charge, phase of arousal. However, women may reach the heightened sexual tension of the plateau phase without necessarily experiencing orgasm, as scientists have observed. This is the case during penile-vaginal intercourse when the man reaches orgasm first or when he replaces manual or oral stimulation with penetration as the female approaches orgasm.

In both sexes, orgasm is experienced as a highly pleasurable release from tension, accompanied by tingling muscle spasms throughout the body and uncontrollable cries and moans. Muscles in and around the man's penis contract rhythmically, causing the forcible ejaculation of semen. Similarly, the outer third of the woman's vagina contracts rhythmically along with the pulsation of her uterus. For both sexes, the first few contractions are the most intense and pleasurable, followed by weaker and slower contractions. Individuals of both sexes vary considerably in their subjective reports of orgasm. Interestingly, the underlying physiological processes are basically the same. Similarly, the physiological process of orgasm in females seems to be the same, regardless of the method of stimulation.

Resolution.   When no further stimulation occurs, orgasm is immediately followed by the *resolution* phase. The body returns to the normal, nonexcited phase. Heart rate, blood pressure, and breathing quickly subside. Muscle tension usually dissipates within 5 minutes after orgasm. Men lose about 50 percent of their erection within a minute or so after orgasm, and the remainder in the next several minutes. Men also enter into a **refractory period**—a time when no added stimulation will result in orgasm. The length of time varies widely, from a few minutes to several days, depending on such factors as the man's age, health, and frequency of previous sexual activity as well as his sexual desire for his partner. Women experience no equivalent refractory period. Most women are physically capable of another orgasm, though they may not desire it. Ordinarily, the woman's clitoris descends to its usually overhanging position within a few seconds, though the engorgement of the shaft and glans dissipates more slowly. Nipple erection also subsides. Women who have not experienced orgasm after high levels of arousal usually experience a slow resolution. However, when both partners have reached orgasm, they generally find this a pleasant and relaxed time.

INDIVIDUAL AND GENDER DIFFERENCES

We've stressed the similarity in men's and women's sexual response in accordance with the more recent knowledge of the sexual response cycle. This knowledge helps to dispel the old notion that men and women are worlds apart in their experience of sex, encouraging better communication between them. Yet there are some important differences between men's and women's experience of sex in addition to the refractory period in males just noted.

First, there are marked differences in sexual arousal in men and women. In their review of relevant research findings, Robert Valois and Sandra Kammermann (1992) point out that certain characteristics are more of a turn-on for men than for women, and vice versa. For instance, when asked which characteristics people most desire in a partner, men generally report physical attractiveness and erotic ability, as seen in women wearing hip-hugging jeans or tight skirts and having long legs and small, firm breasts. In contrast, women are more apt to mention the personality of the man or his achievements. Women tend to be attracted to men who have a good sense of humor; are intelligent, thoughtful, and supportive; and are romantic and sexy. (See Table 10–2.)

Much of the difference in sexual activity may be due to cultural factors, especially those that restrict women's sexuality more than men's. One of the clearest examples is the double standard in sex, which implies that the same sexual behavior is evaluated differently, depending on whether a male or female engages in it. At the same time, there are other factors not easily classified as biological or cultural that may contribute to the differences in sexual arousal among men and women. For instance, when asked, "What has prevented you from freely expressing your sexuality?" women are more likely than men to report being affected by the fear of pregnancy, guilt, lack of desire, and social disapproval. The fact that women can become pregnant and men do not remains a factor even in this era of more effective contraceptives.

Also, as Helen Singer Kaplan (1983), a leading sexuality expert, observes, the differences between male and female sexuality tend to change across the lifespan. That is, the teenage male's sexuality is very intense and almost exclusively genitally focused. But as he ages, his refractory period becomes longer, he becomes satisfied with fewer orgasms a week, and his focus of sexuality is not so completely genital. Sex becomes a more sensuously diffuse experience, including a greater emotional component in relation to his partner. In women, the process is often quite different. Their sexual awakening may occur much later. While they are in their teens and 20s, their arousal and orgasmic response may

TABLE 10–2
GENDER DIFFERENCES IN SEXUAL AROUSAL

Characteristics that are ranked as the most and least likely to arouse men and women sexually:

Highest	Lowest
Men	
1. Tight jeans and T-shirts	40. A woman in sunglasses
2. A see-through blouse	39. A crowded elevator
3. Long legs	38. A pantyhose commercial on television
4. Erotic talk	37. A woman driving a powerful car
5. Small, firm breasts	36. A pleasingly plump woman
6. A woman in a tight skirt	
Women	
1. A good sense of humor	40. A man wearing a wedding band
2. A thoughtful and supportive man	39. A vampire story
3. Flirtation	38. Watching a space launch
4. Knowing that I look good	37. A men's underwear commercial on television
5. A really smart man	36. Spending his money
6. A sexy passage in a romantic novel	35. A man in dark glasses

SOURCE: Robert F. Valois & Sandra Kammermann, *Your Sexuality: A Self-Assessment* 2nd ed. (New York: McGraw-Hill, 1992), p. 119. Copyright © 1992. Reproduced with permission of McGraw-Hill.

be slow and inconsistent. However, by the time they reach their 30s, women's sexual response has become quicker and more intense, especially among sexually experienced women. In sum, men seem to begin with an intense, genitally focused sexuality and only later develop an appreciation for the sensuous and emotional aspects of sex. In contrast, women have an earlier awareness of the sensuous and emotional aspects of sex and tend to develop the capacity for intense genital response later. Put somewhat differently, adolescent male sexuality is body-centered, and the person-centered aspects are incorporated only later. Adolescent female sexuality is more person-centered, and the body-centered aspects of sex tend to be added later in women's development (Hyde & DeLameter, 1997). Thus, the differences in sexual arousal between men and women tend to diminish with greater maturity and sexual experience by individuals of both sexes, often aided by social and cultural changes that encourage equality between the sexes.

A major difference between the sexes is the greater orgasmic variation among women compared to men, both in the physiology of orgasm and in the individual's subjective awareness of sexual climax. Masters, Johnson, and Kolodny (1988b) have identified three basic patterns of the sexual response cycle in women, though only one for men. (See Figures 10–2 and 10–3.) Pattern A most resembles the male pattern and differs mainly in the woman's capacity for additional orgasm. Pattern B shows a prolonged, fluctuating plateau phase, with small surges toward orgasm, followed by a gradual resolution. This is sometimes referred to as "skimming" because of the lack of a single, intense climax and is most often reported by young or sexually inexperienced women. Pattern C shows a rapid rise in sexual excitement leading to a single, intense orgasm and quick resolution. Masters et al. (1988b) suggest that after many experiences of intercourse, some women gradually change their sexual response patterns. The developmental sequence begins with the minor orgasm pattern (B), changes to the intense orgasm pattern (C), and finally to multiple orgasmic responses in (A).

Although men exhibit fewer variations, it would be a mistake to assume that all men experience the sexual response cycle in the same way. Some men have reported ex-

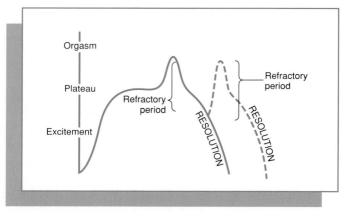

FIGURE 10–2

The male sexual response cycle. Masters and Johnson identified one typical male response pattern, though men have reported considerable variation in their response patterns. SOURCE: William H. Masters and Virginia E. Johnson, *Human Sexual Response* (Boston: Little, Brown, 1966). © 1966 by William H. Masters and Virginia E. Johnson.

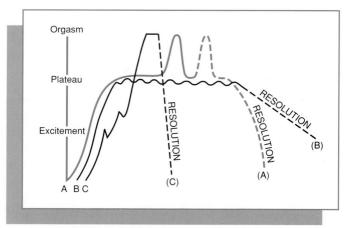

FIGURE 10–3

The female sexual response cycle. Masters and Johnson identified three basic patterns in the female's sexual response. Pattern A most resembles the typical male pattern, except for the lack of a refractory period between orgasms. Variations include an extended plateau phase with no orgasm (B), or a rapid rise to orgasm (C) with no definitive plateau and a very brief resolution. SOURCE: William H. Masters and Virginia E. Johnson, *Human Sexual Response* (Boston: Little, Brown, 1966). © 1966 by William H. Masters and Virginia E. Johnson.

tended periods of intense sexual stimulation before reaching orgasm. Others have experienced several mild sexual climaxes, finally leading to an expulsion of semen. Still others have prolonged pelvic contractions after ejaculation. A marked difference between the sexes is the ability to experience **multiple orgasms**—two or more sexual climaxes within a short period of time.

Although it is not at all uncommon for women to have several orgasms in quick succession, multiple orgasms are the exception rather than the rule for men. Multiple orgasm is best seen as a potential area to be explored by some rather than an ultimate goal for all. Women's greater capacity for multiple orgasms should not be construed to mean that they "must" have more than one climax to be satisfied. Many women prefer to have one orgasm or perhaps none at all. Similarly, the infrequency with which men report multiple orgasms does not mean that they cannot have them. Much depends on the particular person, with individual differences often exceeding those between the sexes. Finally, the more relaxed the partners are about sex, the more opportunities they will have to experience the full range of their sexual potential.

Another individual difference relates to preference for sex partners. Some individuals prefer opposite-sex partners and are considered to be **heterosexual.** Others prefer same-sex partners and are referred to as **homosexual.** Homosexual men often prefer to call themselves gay, whereas homosexual women refer to themselves as lesbian. In the early study of human sexuality, sexologist Alfred Kinsey (Kinsey, Pomeroy, & Martin, 1948) determined that men and women are not always exclusively heterosexual or homosexual. Rather, there are gradations of sexual preference, which include, for example, bisexuality. **Bisexuality** means that the individual prefers sex with either same- or opposite-sex partners.

No one knows how many heterosexuals, homosexuals, and bisexuals live in the United States. These numbers are extremely difficult to ascertain because homosexuality in particular carries a social stigma that keeps some homosexuals "closeted" or secretive about their sexual orientation. In fact, homosexuality was so stigmatized in the past that the American Psychiatric Association in its early history considered homosexuality to be a mental disorder. This is no longer the case. Unfortunately, the AIDS epidemic among homosexuals has done little recently to lessen the social stigma against homosexuality. Furthermore, there are heterosexual individuals who are **homophobic;** that is, they are afraid of homosexuals or hold negative attitudes toward homosexuals for various reasons. Interestingly, one reason, according to Freudian analysts, might be that homophobics unconsciously fear they, themselves, are homosexual.

Pioneering sex researchers Masters and Johnson (1966, 1979) compared the actual sexual behaviors of male and female heterosexuals and homosexuals. The physiological responses of the genitals of heterosexuals and homosexuals were nearly identical. In other words, Masters and Johnson found the very same sexual response cycles in homosexual men and women as they did in heterosexual men and women. These cycles were described previously in this chapter. Masters and Johnson (1979) also reported that for homosexual men and women, there was more communication about preferred sexual activities and these preferred activities were engaged in for longer periods of time than between heterosexual partners.

There is a question in the adjustment literature about whether homosexuals cope well in the face of the strong stigma against their sexual orientation. Edwards (1996a, 1996b) found in two different studies that homosexual youths cope as well as or are as well adjusted as heterosexual youths. This seems especially true when the homosexual individual accepts his or her sexual orientation (Dupras, 1994) and when the family is supportive of the individual when disclosure about homosexuality is made (Saltzburg, 1996).

LOVE AND SEX

So far we've been emphasizing the physical aspects of sex. But what about the attitudes of and relationship between the partners? For example, if Carol and Kim had become sexually involved with Steve and Bob on the first night, should they have experienced guilt and shame? Must people be in love to enjoy sex? Must people be in love to not feel guilty about sex? Not necessarily. Healthy, guilt-free people *can* function well sexually and derive pleasure from sex without being in love. Masters and Johnson observe that there is nothing inherently bad about sex without love, especially if it is consented to by both parties. Under certain circumstances for some people, sex without love may be enjoyable in its own right (Masters et al., 1995). A great deal depends on the individuals involved, especially their value systems. For example, Carol did not want to have sex with Steve the first night she met him. Another woman might have reacted quite differently and have seen the opportunity that night to be an exciting challenge. Carol wanted to get to know Steve better and feel that he acknowledged some commitment toward her before engaging in sex with him.

For some individuals, such as Carol, sexuality without commitment or love signals problems. As Godfrey Cobliner (1988) points out, all too often casual encounters between individuals are formed for the primary purpose of sexual gratification without shared intimacy or commitment. Such relationships are meant to be transient, and the partners are expected to suppress deliberately any feelings of closeness. As one male college student said, "I stay cool. If any feelings well up in me, I check them at once. I am afraid of strong feelings of passion" (p. 103). Similarly, in explaining how easy it is to get hurt when you become emotionally involved, a female college student said, "You can become the victim of your own strong feelings. I have to always be on guard. I have to curb my feelings" (p. 104). Cobliner points out that the inhibition of feelings leads to *depersonalization,* the separation of oneself from one's feelings. Thus, casual sex can tend to involve manipulative relationships that eventually undermine the meaning and satisfaction of sex.

Consequently, it is possibly worth emphasizing that love tends sometimes to enrich sex, especially in a long-term relationship like marriage. The affection and commitment two people enjoy in their relationship may enhance their overall pleasure, compensating somewhat for the loss of sensual excitement that can occur after years of marriage. In contrast, couples who have sex mechanically, especially when one or both partners have little or no affection for the other, soon discover that sex itself is no longer satisfying. But it is erotic love—including a healthy acceptance of sex and sensuality—that might make for better sex.

Romantic love, which consists of intimacy or closeness and passion, may lead to satisfying sex, at least for a while, though it may soon diminish as romantic ardor cools. In contrast, among couples in a long-term relationship like marriage, romantic love often matures into companionate love, consisting of intimacy and commitment, but often with diminished or little or no passion or sex. Indeed, Masters and Johnson have worked with hundreds of couples with a loving, committed relationship (companionate love) whose sex life is disappointing. The ideal type of love remains that of consummate love, which includes intimacy, commitment, *and* passion—or sex. It is worth noting that marital happiness and a satisfying sex life are positively correlated, though it is almost impossible to distinguish between cause and effect. Thus, for most couples, though not necessarily all, a good sex life and happy relationship go together. Consummate love not only strengthens the closeness and commitment between a man and woman but also engenders better sex. It is no coincidence that most couples refer to sexual intercourse by the phrase "making love"; sex and love seem to go together.

 Practical Issues

The emphasis on sexual fulfillment in recent years has had many beneficial effects. There is more objective information about sex, increased sexual communication between partners, and less anxiety and guilt over harmless sexual practices like masturbation. At the same time, such changes have been accompanied by new anxieties. Many sexually normal men worry about their sexual performance. Women who are not orgasmic may suffer the same loss of self-esteem as the man who has a fairly flaccid erection. Then, too, increasing sexual activity outside of marriage has accentuated the perennial problems of birth control, unwanted pregnancies, and sexually transmitted diseases such as AIDS. Most disturbing of all is the increasing occurrence of sexual victimization in our society, as seen in the sexual abuse of children and rape.

SEXUAL DISORDERS

Even sexually experienced couples discover that each time they experience sex, it is different. Sometimes sex is highly pleasurable for both partners; at other times it is less satisfying for one or both of them. Such occasional problems are usually not serious; often they are caused simply by excessive alcohol, fatigue, or stress. Alcohol consumption, a particular inclination of college students, can be specially troublesome in terms of interfering with sexual activity (Fahrner, 1995). When sexual problems persist or become distressful to the individuals involved, they may be classified as **sexual dysfunctions.** Unfortunately, because sexual performance is sometimes associated with a loss of self-esteem and may result in stigmatization within certain cultures, individuals may resist seeking help. Fortunately, this situation is changing with the greater openness about sex and the general availability of sex therapists.

Sexual dysfunctions may be grouped according to the phase of the sexual response cycle in which they occur. They include difficulties of desire, arousal, and orgasm. **Hypoactive sexual desire,** sometimes called **inhibited sexual desire,** refers to the lack of interest in sex. There is a higher incidence of this disorder in women than in men (Rosen & Leiblum, 1995). In some instances, the lack of desire may be a realistic response, such as with a partner who practices poor hygiene or is verbally abusive. In many cases, it reflects the individual's preoccupation with a life problem such as divorce, a death in the family, or a problem at work. Emotional factors are often involved, and boredom is a frequent cause of inhibited sexual desire. So is anger, especially buried anger. Other factors are anxiety, guilt, low self-esteem, depression, and the fear of intimacy. Prolonged frustration from the lack of arousal or orgasm may result in low sexual desire. And a person who feels pressured into sex or feels guilty about saying no may become less and less interested in sex. Some people may be so fearful of sexual pleasure or closeness that they unconsciously prevent themselves from feeling sexual desire by developing a "turn-off" mechanism. By becoming angry, fearful, or distracted, they draw on the natural inhibiting mechanisms that suppress sexual desire, and the lack of desire appears to emerge automatically.

We do not necessarily mean to emphasize psychological causes of this disorder because the cause can also be physiological. For example, in women who have experienced menopause, low estrogen levels or lack of vaginal lubrication can reduce sexual feelings or make sex painful. In fact, the literature seems to be moving away from the emphasis mainly on psychological causes as promoted by Masters and Johnson toward biomedical and organic causes of sexual disorders (Rosen & Leiblum, 1995). Similarly, the issue of low sex desire often stems from the fact that one partner simply has a higher level of sex desire so thus defines the partner with lower desire as having a disorder.

Aversion to sex refers to anxiety, disgust, repulsion, and other negative emotions toward sex. Although both men and women experience sexual aversion, it is more common among women. Individuals who are repelled by sex often have a history of **childhood sexual abuse,** such as incest, or have been a victim of sexual assault. In some instances, such individuals have been subject to constant pressuring or bargaining for sex in a relationship. Also, repeated but unsuccessful attempts to please a sexual partner may eventually lead to the avoidance of sex. Finally, anxiety about sexual conflicts in one's sexual identity or orientation may also create fear of sex (Masters et al., 1995).

Another type of sexual dysfunction is **inhibited sexual arousal,** which occurs most often as **erectile inhibition** (impotency) and **inhibited vaginal lubrication.** Men who suffer from this problem usually have **secondary erectile inhibition**—that is, they've previously experienced erections but are consistently unable to have an erection of sufficient firmness to penetrate the woman's vagina. Most men have occasional difficulties with erections, usually because of fatigue or stress. It's only when this difficulty continues to occur or becomes distressful to the man or his partner that it should come to the attention of a professional. Many factors may contribute to erectile failure.

Physiological factors of erectile inhibition include severe diabetes and the effect of certain drugs, especially alcohol, narcotics, amphetamines, and some prescribed medications. Worry and criticism from a partner may also lead to an erectile failure. In most instances, erectile inhibition is only a passing problem. But sometimes these experiences may generate such concern and anxiety that they develop into a pattern. The man's anxiety assumes the form of a "spectator's role." That is, instead of relaxing and letting his erection occur spontaneously, he watches and judges his own performance. Thus, his crucial attitude and tenseness contribute to the erectile failure. Treatment consists of helping the man learn how to relax and let things happen. It's especially important not to overreact to the temporary loss of erection. After all, men usually have and lose several erections during the excitement phase, without even noticing it.

Inhibited vaginal lubrication in the woman is similar to the man's lack of erection because in both cases insufficient vasocongestion occurs. Normally, during sexual stimulation the massive congestion of blood vessels in the vaginal walls secrete droplets of fluid, which eventually form a shiny film on the walls of the vagina. Lack of lubrication doesn't always mean something is wrong. Frequently, the woman is not sufficiently stimulated; or apathy, boredom, anger, or fear may inhibit her arousal. Also, during prolonged intercourse with lengthy plateau periods the woman may have a decrease in vaginal lubrication. In such instances, increased stimulation of the woman's clitoris or other parts of her body may help to increase vaginal lubrication. Older women who have passed the menopause age sometimes supplement their vaginal lubrication by adding small amounts of vaginal jelly purchased from the local pharmacy.

The most common difficulty of the orgasm phase in the sexual response cycle is **premature** or **retarded ejaculation** on the man's part and delay or absence of orgasm for the woman known as **female orgasmic disorder.** Premature ejaculation consists of experiencing orgasm so quickly that the man's enjoyment of sex is significantly lessened and/or his partner is not satisfied. It is a common problem for men. As many as half of the cases of erectile disorder may be due to organic factors (Richardson, 1991). Another common reason is that men have become accustomed to experiencing orgasm quickly, to allay their anxiety, demonstrate their sexual prowess, or avoid discovery. Fortunately, this condition is readily treatable through such measures as the stop-start technique. The man, usually with the aid of his partner, practices recognizing the sensations of impending orgasm and momentarily stops stimulation until he gradually learns to delay ejaculation.

The most common problems for women are slowness or inability to reach orgasm. Because orgasm is a reflex, an involuntary reaction, and differs considerably from one individual to another, it may help to see this problem in the context of women's overall sexual response. Clinically, female orgasm seems to be distributed more or less along a bell-shaped curve. On one extreme are the women who have never climaxed at all. Next are women who require intense clitoral stimulation when they are alone. Women who need direct clitoral stimulation but are able to climax with their partners fall in the middle range. Also near the middle are women who can climax during sex but only after lengthy and vigorous stimulation. Near the upper range are women who require only brief penetration to reach their climax, and, at the very extreme are the women who can experience orgasm via fantasy and/or breast stimulation alone.

Women who have never experienced orgasm often lack knowledge of their own sexual response cycle which is often learned through masturbation. These women may become orgasmic by minimizing their inhibitions and by maximizing their sexual stimulation through masturbation. A more common complaint is slowness or failure to reach orgasm through intercourse with a partner. This problem is not surprising, considering that orgasm is usually triggered through sensory stimulation of the clitoral area, which is accomplished only indirectly during intercourse. Consequently, only about one-half of women experience orgasm regularly through intercourse (Masters et al., 1995). Those who prefer vaginal orgasm and are unable to experience vaginal orgasm often need more lengthy thrusting on the man's part.

But there are many more women who need direct clitoral stimulation, either by manual or oral stimulation from the man or self-stimulation, in addition to the penile-vagina thrusting during intercourse to reach climax. Women frequently complain that men don't know how to provide clitoral stimulation. Men tend to be impatient, rubbing the clitoris directly or too long, thereby irritating it. Women usually prefer a more indirect, playful approach, which may include caressing one side of the clitoral shaft or use of an indirect, circular motion of the whole clitoral area. Occasionally, women have difficulty experiencing an orgasm even with adequate clitoral stimulation. In some instances, women may be experiencing anxiety, anger, or guilt. Or they may be ambivalent about their relationship with their partner. We should also keep in mind that even healthy, sexually experienced women do not always reach orgasm, either because of fatigue or temporary, situational factors. Nor is this necessarily a problem.

BIRTH CONTROL

The availability and use of reliable birth-control methods has become increasingly important in recent years for several reasons. Most unmarried couples want to avoid an unwanted pregnancy. Although Carol liked Steve very much, she knew she was not ready to have his children or to marry him. Even among married couples, there's a growing tendency to have planned and wanted children. Many couples wait several years or more

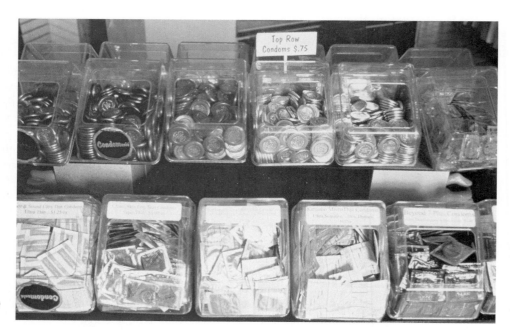

Access to birth control has become easier in the last two decades.

after marriage to strengthen their relationship and acquire financial stability before having their first child. Men and women who want to combine a career with parenthood often can accomplish their career goals better by using dependable birth-control methods and timing their pregnancies.

American women are not particularly happy with the contraceptive choices available to them. They also are not happy that the burden of birth control typically falls on them because there are few methods available to men. As their relationship progressed, Carol and Steve had several discussions about birth control. Steve wanted Carol to start using birth control pills; she replied that she did not want to do so and that he should just buy condoms. Unlike Carol, most women have tried several contraceptive methods in the search for one that suits them best, but they feel that every method requires trade-offs between safety, convenience, and effectiveness. What women want are birth-control methods that do not require them to make trade-offs.

The effectiveness of the various contraceptives, along with their advantages and disadvantages, is shown in Table 10–3. Generally, the condom and the birth-control pill are most popular among young people in their teens and 20s. Those over 30 favor methods that combine high effectiveness with maximum safety, such as vasectomy for men and tubal ligation for women. It is important for couples to choose the method of birth control that suits them best. The primary concern is that the method be effective without jeopardizing either partner's health and the spontaneity of sex.

Shared responsibility for birth control can enhance a relationship. When the man takes an active interest in contraception, the woman is less likely to feel resentment over assuming all the responsibility. Men may share responsibility for birth control in several ways. An important step is discussing the matter of birth control before first engaging in intercourse. This initial step is rarely taken, however, mostly because of the fear of spoiling the spontaneity of sex. In long-term relationships, men can share the expense of any medical exams or the cost of contraceptives. In addition, the man might help by

TABLE 10–3
COMPARATIVE EFFECTIVENESS OF BIRTH-CONTROL METHODS

Method	Effectiveness rating	Advantages	Disadvantages
Tubal ligation (female)	Excellent	Extremely reliable and permanent	Initial expense; not considered reversible
Vasectomy (male)	Excellent	Extremely reliable and permanent	Initial expense; not considered reversible
Combined birth-control pills	Excellent	Highly effective; not used at time of coitus	Cost; must be taken daily; possible side effects
Progestin-only pill	Excellent	Fewer potential side effects than combination pill	—
IUD	Excellent	Effective; little attention after insertion	Side effects; may be expelled
Condom	Very good	Easy to use; protects from STDs	Interrupts sexual activity; reduces sensation
Diaphragm, with cream or jelly	Good	Effective; inexpensive	Interrupts sexual activity
Cervical cap with spermicide	Good	Inexpensive; few side effects	May be difficult to obtain
Vaginal foam	Fair	Easy to use; wide availability	Messy; unreliable when used improperly
Sponge	Poor to fair	Easy to use; minor side effects	Unreliable when not used properly
Withdrawal	Poor to fair	No cost	Requires high motivation; interrupts sexual activity
Rhythm	Poor to fair	No cost or side effects; acceptable to Roman Catholic church	Requires high motivation and periods of abstinence
Douching	Poor	Low cost	Unreliable; can encourage infection
Unprotected intercourse	Very poor	Requires no effort or planning	High risk of unintended pregnancy and STDs

SOURCE: Adapted from data in Robert A. Hatcher et al. (1994). *Contraceptive Technology* (16th ed.). (New York: Irvington Publishers).

inserting the diaphragm into his partner's vagina before intercourse or by using a male-only method such as a condom.

Just as individuals in the United States have different ideas about birth control, especially about abortion as a means of birth control, there are differences worldwide in what methods are most popular or acceptable. Likewise, various medical practices, education levels, and gender-role expectations affect what methods are utilized if at all. Table 10–4 compares the use of various methods in different countries. We should realize that various medical, religious, folkloric, and cultural practices and beliefs influence different individuals.

SEXUALLY TRANSMITTED DISEASES

When Steve and Carol first started having sex, they did not discuss whether each of them was healthy. Carol, in particular, did not know that Steve had had a variety of other sex partners, each of whom could have been a risk to Carol as well as Steve. A variety of diseases may be contracted through sexual interaction. These are called **sexually transmitted diseases (STDs),** a broader and less value-laden term than venereal disease. Although many of these diseases can be treated successfully, many are on the increase,

TABLE 10–4
CONTRACEPTION AROUND THE WORLD AS REPORTED BY MARRIED WOMEN

Region, Country	Voluntary Sterilization		Pill	IUD	Condom	Injectables[a]	Vaginal Methods[b]	Rhythm
	Male	Female						
North America								
United States	11	25	28	2	13	NA	7	2
Europe								
Netherlands	11	8	38	10	7	NA	NA	NA
Italy	NA	1	14	2	13	NA	2	9
Norway	2	4	13	28	16	NA	2	3
Africa								
Botswana	0	4	16	6	1	6	0	0
Nigeria	0	0	1	1	0	1	0	1
Asia								
Korea	11	37	3	7	10	NA	2	NA
Thailand	6	22	20	7	1	9	0	1
Latin America								
El Salvador	1	30	8	2	2	1	0	2
Mexico	1	18	11	11	2	3	1	5
Middle East and North Africa								
Egypt	0	1	16	17	3	0	0	1
Jordan	0	6	5	15	1	0	1	4

Percentage Using Contraceptive Method

NA: Statistics not available.
[a]Includes injections such as Depo-Provera and implants such as Norplant.
[b]Includes diaphragm, cervical cap, and spermicides.

SOURCES: Bryant Robey et al. (1992). The reproductive revolution: New survey findings. *Population Reports,* Series M, Number 11. Baltimore: Johns Hopkins University, Population Information Program. Kathy A. London et al. (1985). Fertility and family planning surveys: An update. *Population Reports,* Series M, Number 8, M-291-M-348. Baltimore: Johns Hopkins University, Population Information Program. Robert Hatcher et al. (1994). *Contraceptive Technology.* 16th ed. New York: Irvington.

because of increased sexual activity and a tendency to have more than one sexual partner, especially during one's youth. The incidence of STDs is highest among those in the 20- to 24-year-old group, with the next highest incidence among those in the 15- to 19-year-old group and then among the 25- to 29-year-olds.

Chlamydia—a bacterium that is spread by sexual contact and that affects both males and females—has rapidly become one of the most common sexually transmitted diseases. The Center for Disease Control estimates that there are approximately 4.4 million new cases a year, making chlamydia one of the most common STDs (Cates & Wasserheit, 1991). An estimated 10 percent of all college students are affected by this disease. A condom can help prevent the spread of chlamydia.

Men who contract the infection have symptoms similar to gonorrhea, such as a discharge from the penis and a mild burning sensation during urination. Women with chlamydia infections show little or no symptoms and are often unaware of the disease until they are informed by an infected partner. Yet a woman may have the infection for a long time, during which period she may pass it on to her sexual partners. If left untreated in women, it may result in cervical inflammation or pelvic inflammatory disease and, if she is pregnant, may cause eye damage to infants at birth. In men, it may spread to the prostate. It is important that an infected person get laboratory diagnosis before receiving treatment because the symptoms are often confused with those of gonorrhea, though the disease is usually treated with a different drug, tetracycline, rather than penicillin as is used in gonorrhea.

Gonorrhea continues to be another common sexually transmitted disease. Gonorrhea increased dramatically through the 1960s and 1970s, mostly because of the rising use of the birth-control pill. In the 1990s an estimated 700,000 new cases a year develop (Hatcher, 1994). A condom may help prevent the transmission of gonorrhea during intercourse, but it doesn't guarantee immunity. Early symptoms in men include a bad-smelling, cloudy discharge from the penis and a burning sensation during urination. Many women fail to seek treatment because they have so few early symptoms that they don't realize they are infected. Untreated gonorrhea is the single most common cause of sterility among men. Women with untreated gonorrhea may experience inflammation of the fallopian tubes, infertility, birth malformations, or menstrual disorders. Fortunately, in most cases, when it is discovered, gonorrhea is easily treated with penicillin.

Genital herpes, one of several herpes viral infections, has increased dramatically in recent years, with about 200,000 new cases each year and over 30 million infected Americans (Hatcher, 1994). Genital herpes appears to be transmitted primarily through sexual contact. Symptoms usually appear within several days after sexual contact with an infected partner: one or more small, red, painful bumps (papules) in the genital area, such as on the man's penis and the woman's labia and inner vaginal walls. These bumps change into blisters, which eventually rupture into painful open sores. The person continues to be contagious throughout this time. In addition to the periodic discomfort, genital herpes can have serious complications. Pregnant women may require a Caesarean section if active herpes is in the birth canal at the time of delivery. Furthermore, women infected with genital herpes are more likely to contract cervical cancer than others. So far there is no real cure for genital herpes, but medical researchers are pursuing an effective treatment on many fronts. Current treatment consists of the drug acyclovir, which reduces discomfort and assists healing during an outbreak of herpes.

Syphilis, though less common than herpes and gonorrhea, is a far more serious disease. Syphilis is caused by a spiral-shaped bacterium or spirochete. Although fewer than 60,000 new cases of syphilis are recorded each year, the actual incidence is thought to be much higher. In fact, the numbers recently have been rising due to the exchange of sex for drugs in our society (Hyde & DeLameter, 1997). Syphilis is caused when the spiral-shaped bacteria are transmitted through sexual contact. It is not exclusively transmitted by vaginal sex. Other organs of the body can be the site of entry. The early signs of syphilis are painless sores at the place of sexual contact, usually the man's penis and the inner walls of the woman's vagina or cervix in heterosexual couples. Although the sores usually disappear within a month or two, a skin rash and other sores may appear, along with sores on other parts of the body, in a later stage. These symptoms eventually disappear, but if the disease is left untreated it may progress to an advanced stage, causing brain damage, heart failure, blindness, or paralysis. Fortunately, syphilis is readily detected through a blood test, and there is a highly effective treatment when it is detected in its early stages.

Compared to other STDs, **AIDS** (Acquired Immune Deficiency Syndrome) is a fairly new disease in humans that has achieved national and worldwide prominence in recent years because of its growing threat. By 1995 more than a half million persons in the United States had been diagnosed with the AIDS virus and more than half of them had died (Hyde & DeLameter, 1997). In addition, 50,000 Americans now get the AIDS virus each year (Eckholm, 1992). Public health officials believe that the numbers are even greater than this; a large number of people have AIDS but do not yet know it. Knowing about AIDS, then, might literally save your life. To test your knowledge, take the AIDS Quiz found in Figure 10–4.

People who are initially infected generally show no symptoms and have no antibodies to the disease, so blood tests may come back negative. Individuals can carry this disease and be asymptomatic for long periods of time, years in fact. Because the AIDS virus destroys the T-helper cells in the body's immune system, diseases that would ordinarily be less harmful to a person with a normal immune system can produce devastating, ultimately lethal diseases in the person with AIDS, for example, a common cold. This is often when it becomes apparent that the individual has AIDS. By this time it may be too late for the infected individual's sex partners; they may have already contracted the illness.

Although AIDS is classified as a sexually transmitted disease, it is communicated through blood or blood products containing the virus. By all indications, the AIDS virus does not readily penetrate intact body surfaces, so that there is no danger of getting it through a kiss, a sneeze, a handshake, or a toilet seat. Instead, the AIDS virus is acquired by direct exposure of one's bloodstream to the virus, which is carried by body fluids—notably blood and semen. Among homosexually active men, who make up the largest fraction of AIDS patients in the United States, the main source of transmission has been

---

FIGURE 10–4

AIDS QUIZ

Which of the following statements are true?

1. You can tell by looking that someone has the AIDS virus.
2. People cannot become infected with the HIV virus by donating blood.
3. The AIDS virus can enter the body through the vagina, penis, rectum, or mouth.
4. It's possible to get the AIDS virus from hugging, kissing, or a toilet seat.
5. Condoms are an effective but not a foolproof way to prevent the spread of the AIDS virus.
6. The AIDS virus may live in the human body for years before symptoms actually appear.
7. The AIDS virus may be spread through sneezing and coughing.
8. Any person can become infected with the AIDS virus through sexual intercourse.
9. If you think you've been exposed to the AIDS virus, you should get an AIDS test.
10. Presently, there is no cure for AIDS.

Answers: Numbers 1, 4, and 7 are false. The others are true.

SOURCE: *Understanding AIDS* (1988). (HHS Publication No. 88–8404). Washington, DC: U.S. Government Printing Office.

The public has increasing awareness and knowledge about AIDS and other sexually transmitted diseases.

anal intercourse. The risk of intravenous drug users, who are likely to share needles, comes through direct exposure of the bloodstream to someone else's infected blood. In the United States where needles are purchased by prescription, about one-fourth of AIDS patients have been intravenous drug users. In Canada, where needles are sold over the counter, the figure is only 0.5 percent (*Harvard Medical School Health Letter,* 1985). The virus can also be transmitted through vaginal intercourse, from men to women or, less commonly, from women to men. Although heterosexual infection has accounted for only a small number of AIDS victims in the United States so far, this proportion is rising rapidly. The risk of catching AIDS through blood transfusions has diminished considerably because of more careful screening of blood donors.

No single pattern of symptoms fits all cases of AIDS. Some common symptoms include a progressive, unexplained weight loss; persistent fever (often accompanied by night sweats); swollen lymph nodes in the neck, armpits, and groin; reddish purple spots on the skin; chronic fatigue; and unexplained diarrhea or bloody stools. Symptoms may remain unchanged for months or may be quickly followed by additional infections. People afflicted with the AIDS syndrome tend to have one overwhelming infection after another until their immune system gives out. AIDS is usually fatal within a matter of several years, though for unexplained reasons some individuals survive longer than 3 years (Masters et al., 1995). Presently, screening tests can identify people with antibodies to the AIDS virus, meaning they have been infected.

People can reduce their risk for AIDS by following some practical guidelines, such as those shown in Box 10–1. Using condoms is a good start. Research has demonstrated that although college students and others seem to possess much knowledge about the transmission of AIDS (Spears, Abraham, Sheeran, & Abrams, 1995), their behaviors such as engaging in casual sex leave them at risk for AIDS (Winslow, Franzini, & Hwang, 1992). Behaviors do not always follow from attitudes. Ultimately, of course, the surest way to prevent the infection will be the development of a vaccine. Although research efforts are being intensified, there are no guarantees, and a vaccine may very well take a long time. Meanwhile, the threat of AIDS will be a major influence on people's sexual habits and lifestyles for the foreseeable future.

BOX 10–1

How to Reduce Your Risk of Getting AIDS

You can reduce your risk of getting AIDS by following these guidelines:

1. Avoid sexual contact with people known to have AIDS or suspected of having AIDS.
2. If you use intravenous drugs, do not share needles or syringes (boiling does not guarantee sterility).
3. Do not have sex with people who use intravenous drugs.
4. Avoid anal intercourse, with or without use of condoms.
5. Avoid oral contact with semen.
6. Do not have sex with prostitutes.
7. Have sex with someone you know well, preferably a person who has not had multiple sex partners.
8. Use condoms during sexual intercourse. Condoms are an effective, though by no means foolproof, way of preventing the spread of AIDS.

SEXUAL VICTIMIZATION

Another issue that attracts public concern is **sexual victimization.** To go back to our opening vignette, Carol was fortunate that she found Steve, who turned out to be a loving, sensitive man. Other people are not so fortunate; they become victims of **sexual exploitation** when they are forced to comply with sexual acts under duress. Sexual victimization may take many forms, ranging from the sexual abuse of a child by a parent, relative, or family friend to an adult who feels coerced to engage in offensive sexual acts by his or her partner. In this section, we'll focus on two particularly exploitative forms of sexual victimization: sexual abuse of children and rape.

Sexual abuse of children.   About 17 percent of American women and 12 percent of American men have had sexual contact as a child with an adolescent or an adult (Laumann et al., 1994). Most often the abuser is a family member, close relative, or friend—usually a man. Women can also sexually abuse children, and their abuse can be just as severe (Rudin, Zalewski, & Bodmer-Turner, 1995). Not uncommonly, the abuser has been a victim of sexual abuse as a child (Boney-McCoy & Finkelhor, 1995). In many instances, sexual abuse is not limited to a single episode and does not involve physical force. Sexual interactions generally consist of touching and fondling the genitals of the child, though some child molesters may engage in intercourse. Sexual abuse is most likely to involve prepubescent children between 9 and 12 years of age.

The immediate effects of child sexual abuse include increased anxiety, anger, eating and sleeping disturbances, guilt, withdrawal, and other psychological problems of adjustment (Jumper, 1995). Abused children are sometimes preoccupied with sex, as seen in an unusual interest in the sex organs, sex play, and nudity. They're also likely to exhibit a host of physical complaints, such as rashes, headaches, and vomiting, all without medical explanation. The child's emotional trauma can be magnified when parents overreact to the discovery of sexual abuse. It is important, however, that parents show sufficient concern, such as making certain the child is not left alone with the suspected abuser as well as reporting incidents of sexual abuse to the police. Above all, the child needs to know that the parents will protect the child from other abuse and that the parents still love the child.

In adulthood, even when there are no serious psychological problems, which is the norm, victims of sexual abuse often have other problems, such as difficulty becoming involved with the opposite sex or compulsively engaging in sex. Also, abused women may feel isolated and distrustful of men. They're likely to feel anxious, depressed, and guilt-ridden. One of the most disturbing findings is the effect childhood sexual abuse has on the next generation. Boys who are abused are at increased risk of becoming child molesters, and girls are more likely to produce children who are abused. In addition, as many as two-thirds of childhood sexual abuse victims later become victims of rape or attempted rape in adulthood. Fortunately, most victims of childhood sexual abuse—and molesters—may benefit from psychotherapy.

Rape. Rape—sexual intercourse under conditions of actual or threatened force that overcomes the victim's resistance—has become an increasing problem in American society. Although the rape of males has increased in recent years, the overwhelming majority of rapes involve male rapists and female victims. According to a federally funded survey by the National Victim Center, 683,000 women were forcibly raped in the United States in 1990. One out of every eight adult women (13 percent), or 12 million American women, has been the victim of a forcible rape (*Rape in America,* 1992).

One of the most disturbing findings is that almost two-thirds of rape victims are younger than 18 at the time of the attack. (See Figure 10–5.) Equally unsettling is the fact that only one in six rapes (16 percent) is ever reported to the police. Most cases are reported within 24 hours after the rape, although a substantial minority (25 percent) are reported later. Half of all rape victims say that they would be much more likely to report rapes to the police if there were a law prohibiting the news media from disclosing their names and addresses. Another significant finding is that most rapes are committed

FIGURE 10–5

Rape victim's age. SOURCE: Adapted from data in *Rape in America,* National Victim Center, Crime Victims' Research and Treatment Center, Fort Worth, TX, April 23, 1992.

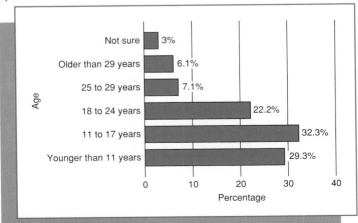

by someone known to the victim. Only about one-fifth of all rapes are committed by strangers (*Rape in America,* 1992). (See Figure 10–6.)

Date rape—coercive sexual activity that occurs during a date—has become a widespread problem on many college campuses. However, victims of date rape are often reluctant to so label such assaults, mostly because of the common misconception that rape must be committed by a stranger under conditions of extreme violence. In one survey, Struckman-Johnson (1988) found that 22 percent of college women and 16 percent of college men had been forced to engage in sexual intercourse at least once. However, *force* means something different to each sex. Women tend to say they were physically coerced to have sex, whereas men are more apt to feel they were responding to psychological pressures. Such gender differences are also reflected in the long-term effects of rape. The majority of women feel that the date rape has had a long-term impact on them, whereas most men deny such effects.

Studies of rape victims show that rape usually has a devastating effect on the woman's mental health. Almost one-third of all rape victims develop rape-related posttraumatic stress disorder (RR-PTSD) sometime during their lives. In turn, RR-PTSD dramatically increases a woman's risk for major alcohol and drug abuse problems. Compared to women who have never been raped, rape victims with RR-PTSD are 13 times more likely to have major alcohol problems and 26 times more likely to have two or more major drug abuse problems (*Rape in America,* 1992).

Rape survivors may experience a variety of emotional repercussions in two phases. The *acute phase* begins immediately after the assault and may continue for hours, days, or weeks. During the first few hours after being assaulted, the woman may react in an expressive manner, crying and being very upset. Or in some instances, a woman may maintain a controlled, subdued manner and only later become aware of her feelings. Victims commonly report anxiety, shame, anger, guilt, self-blame, and a sense of powerlessness. Physical symptoms include headaches, nausea, and sleeplessness.

FIGURE 10–6
Rape victim's relationship to rapist. SOURCE: Adapted from data in *Rape in America,* National Victim Center, Crime Victims' Research and Treatment Center, Fort Worth, TX, April 23, 1992.

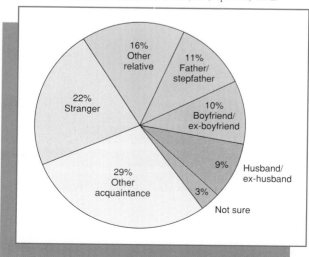

Nervousness and fear may continue into the second, *reorganization phase,* which may last for years. Women often fear retaliation by the rapist. They might also harbor negative feelings about sex. Most of the others greatly reduce the frequency of their sexual activity or discover that they have sexual problems such as sexual disorders. Rape, therefore, is usually a very traumatic experience, which interferes more with the psychological aspects of sexual activity than the physiological response. Fortunately, the passage of time, combined with support from others and psychotherapy, can help to alleviate the effects of rape for most victims. Furthermore, improvements in the police and court system, which make them more sensitive and supportive of rape victims, along with the establishment of rape victim advocate programs, not only increase the likelihood that victims will report the crime but also help them in making an effective recovery.

SUMMARY

MALE AND FEMALE

At the outset, we noted how the understanding of sex is often distorted by gender stereotypes. At the same time, the ongoing changes in gender roles taking place in our society are giving rise to a healthier sexuality; for example, sexual intercourse is understood as something a man and a woman do together as equal participants. Personal communication about sexual matters tends to be more effective when both partners express themselves clearly and listen to each other. Nowhere is sexual communication put to the test more than in initiating and refusing sex. Although the more emotionally expressive partner tends to initiate sex most of the time, couples whose partners share the initiator and refuser role equally tend to have a more satisfactory sex life than other couples.

HUMAN SEXUAL RESPONSE

We described five phases of the sexual response cycle: transition, excitement, plateau, orgasm, and resolution. A major difference between the sexes is the greater variation among women in the physiology and subjective awareness of orgasm, especially in the woman's ability to have several orgasms in quick succession. At the same time, individual differences tend to outweigh gender differences, so that each person needs to be understood and appreciated in terms of his or her own preferences. Although many people now feel it is not necessary to be in love to enjoy sex, love tends to enrich sex, especially in long-term relationships like marriage.

PRACTICAL ISSUES

Common sexual dysfunctions include the lack of sexual desire, erectile inhibition and premature ejaculation in men, and inhibited vaginal lubrication and female orgasmic disorder in women. Each method of birth control has its advantages and disadvantages, the final choice often involving a trade-off between the safety, convenience, and effectiveness of a given method. Sexually transmitted diseases, such as chlamydia, gonorrhea, genital herpes, and syphilis, continue to present a health hazard, though they can be effectively treated. In contrast, AIDS is a deadly disease that poses a growing threat.

Although the majority of AIDS victims in the United States have been homosexual and intravenous drug users, the risk of AIDS from heterosexual intercourse is increasing. Another problem that has attracted public concern is sexual victimization, such as sexual abuse of children and rape. One of the most disturbing findings is that most rape victims are younger than 18, and the rapist is known by the victim. Although coercive sex continues to be a problem, improvements in the justice system, along with the establishment of sex victim advocate programs, increase the likelihood that victims will report the crime and be helped in making an effective recovery.

SCORING KEY FOR THE LEVEL OF COMMUNICATION EXERCISE

Scoring: To determine your score, give yourself one point for each yes response for questions 2, 3, 4, 6, 7, 8, 10, 11, 13, and 14, and one point for each no response to questions 1, 5, 9, 12, and 15.

Interpreting your score:

If you scored

1–5:   There is little communication between you and your partner. Perhaps the two of you simply need to develop better communication.

6–9:   Your relationship is lacking in communication, but you are trying to improve it.

10–14: There are weak areas in your relationship, which you may already be aware of. Just keep working to develop open and honest communication.

15–18: You have a great relationship, but you do have your differences. Learning to deal with your differences will strengthen the relationship.

19–22: You tend to have a great understanding of what it takes to make a relationship continue to grow and endure.

SELF-TEST

1. Traits such as masculine and feminine are best understood as
   a. mostly inborn
   b. polar opposites
   c. largely learned
   d. biological terms

2. The most important part of sexual communication is the partners'
   a. persuasive skills
   b. use of questions
   c. factual knowledge of sex
   d. attitudes toward each other

3. Married and unmarried couples alike tend to be more satisfied with their sex lives when the initiative for sexual intercourse is
   a. taken mostly by the man
   b. shared equally by both partners
   c. taken mostly by the woman
   d. always taken by the man

4. The sex fantasies of men and women
   a. are exactly the same
   b. are somewhat different
   c. occur only in the excitement phase of the sexual response cycle
   d. occur only in the resolution phase of the sexual response cycle

5. Multiple orgasms are
   a. more common in women
   b. experienced by all men
   c. more common in men
   d. experienced by all women

6. Is love necessary to a sexual relationship?
   a. love is necessary to enjoy sex
   b. sex without love is wrong
   c. love enriches sex
   d. love interferes with the enjoyment of sex

7. The most common sexual dysfunction among men during the orgasm phase of the sexual response cycle is
   a. premature or retarded ejaculation
   b. inhibited sexual desire
   c. difficulty keeping an erection
   d. inhibited sexual arousal

8. Which of the following birth-control techniques has an excellent effectiveness rating?
   a. cervical cap
   b. condom
   c. combined birth-control pills
   d. diaphragm

9. The most common sexually transmitted disease in the United States is
   a. gonorrhea
   b. genital herpes
   c. AIDS
   d. chlamydia

10. Victims of childhood sexual abuse are most likely to be
    a. boys 13 to 15
    b. children 9 to 12
    c. girls 3 to 7
    d. children under 7

EXERCISES

1. *Gender stereotypes.* Select a specific gender stereotype you disagree with, whether discussed in this chapter or not. Then write a page or more telling why you feel so strongly about it. Is there any truth to this stereotype? What is the evidence against it? Why do you think this stereotype persists?

2. *Sexual communication.* What has been the most difficult part of sexual communication for you? Have you discovered your partner's sexual likes and dislikes? Do you have difficulty initiating sex? How well can you refuse an unwanted sexual invitation or accept rejection?

3. *How important is love for sex?* Do you feel two people can enjoy sex without being in love? Or do you feel people must be in love to have good sex? Write a short paragraph explaining your views about sex and love.

4. *Sharing sexual fantasies.* If you're married or sexually active in a secure relationship, share some of your sexual fantasies with your partner. Such sharing is usually more helpful when it is mutual. It may be wise to begin with mild fantasies that can help desensitize fears and embarrassment and enable you to judge the impact of such sharing on your partner as well as yourself. It's also best to avoid sharing fantasies that would shock your partner or threaten the relationship.

5. *Shared responsibility for birth control.* How do you feel about men sharing the responsibility for birth control? What are some of the pros and cons? Does it present any special problems for the woman?

6. *Sexual victimization.* Suppose you were asked to suggest ways to decrease the incidence of sexual victimization, for example, childhood sexual abuse and rape, in our society. Write a page or more describing the changes you would propose.

QUESTIONS FOR SELF-REFLECTION

1. When was the last time you read a book about sex by a recognized authority in the field?
2. How well do you and your partner communicate about sex?
3. Do you and your partner share the initiative for sex? Or does one of you usually initiate sex?
4. Must physical hugging and touching always lead to sexual intercourse?
5. Are you aware of what is sexually arousing for your partner?
6. Do you and your partner agree about the relationship between sex and love?
7. Are you aware that an occasional sexual dysfunction may be due to emotional stress?
8. How safe is your method of birth control?
9. Can you recognize the symptoms of prevalent STDs?
10. Are you familiar with the practical guidelines for avoiding AIDS?

FOR FURTHER INFORMATION

RECOMMENDED READINGS

BASS, E., & DAVIS, L. (1988). *The courage to heal.* New York: Harper & Row. A comprehensive guide for women survivors of childhood sexual abuse.

ENGEL, B. (1995). *Raising your sexual self-esteem: How to feel better about your sexuality and yourself.* For individuals who want to feel more comfortable with their sexuality.

HASTINGS, A. S. (1996). *Body and soul: Sexuality on the brink of change.* New York: Insight Books. All about sexuality and your sexual being and how to bring the two into harmony.

MASTERS, W. H., JOHNSON, V. E., & KOLODNY, R. C. (1994). *Heterosexuality.* New York: Harper Collins. Up-to-date research on heterosexuality.

REINISCH, J. M. (1990). *The Kinsey Institute new report on sex.* New York: St. Martin's Press. Informed answers to the most frequently asked questions about sexuality.

WEBSITES AND THE INTERNET

http://www.tatertot. come/agenda/: A good place to start surfing the Web for information on gay and lesbian issues.

http://www.safersex.org/: A site where you can find out the do's and don'ts of sexual safety.

http://www.wavefront.com/~raphael/raq/raq.html: Learn about androgyny on this interesting connection.

http://english-www.hss.cmu.edu/gender/: A site designed to inform you about a variety of issues related to gender.

http://gladstone.uroregon.edu/~service/: A place where you can learn more about the traumatic experience of sexual assault, date rape, and other forms of sexual victimization.

Work and Leisure

Learning Objectives

•••••••••••

After completing this chapter, you should be able to

1. Explain the importance of self-assessment in career choice.
2. Discuss the process of identifying a compatible career.
3. Describe Holland's six personality-occupational types.
4. Describe the changing demographic picture of the labor force.
5. Identify several major issues facing women and minorities in the workplace.
6. List several of the fastest-growing careers requiring a college degree.
7. Discuss work and leisure patterns for various groups.

Kristin was thrilled. She had just marched down the aisle of the stadium at her university to celebrate her graduation. Her parents and her grandmother were there with flashbulbs popping. Of course, Kristin was saddened to be leaving her good friends. "There is always e-mail and the phone," she thought to herself.

The next day was Sunday so Kristin rested. In fact, she continued this routine for about 10 days. She lazed her time away watching TV, talking on the phone, and helping her parents around the house. In the third week after her graduation, her father asked, "Krissy, do you have a resume?" "Sure, Dad," she answered, "the university career center helped me assemble it." "Krissy, tomorrow we are getting in the car and we are going to drop off your resume in downtown Manhattan." Kristin was startled by her father's abrupt candidness, but she agreed to accompany him. She took her resume and cover letter to over 45 different businesses during the next week. Nothing happened. The phone did not ring; no one asked for interviews. Kristin was disheartened. Her parents kept insisting that she get out of the house and find a job. She finally landed a job waiting on tables at the local country club. "Sure, I am earning money," she thought. "But I had hoped for a job that would better utilize my skills and training." Kristin was a psychology major with a business minor and had hoped to work in a big firm in the human resources department, the modern name for the personnel department. Specifically, Kristin hoped to be a recruiter for new employees or a trainer for new hires. None of this was coming true.

Kristin kept sending her resumes and cover letters. She was determined that waitressing was only a means to pay bills until something better came along. One day her dream really came true. A large department store in New York City called and requested an interview. The store was interested in Kristin because she had completed an internship in a human resources

291

department for a smaller store near her university. Kristin landed the job of her dreams. She was indeed to be a recruiter, but not just any recruiter. Her job was to hire celebrities for big publicity functions at the large Manhattan store.

 ## Choosing a Career

Kristin's experience illustrates some of the perils and promises of finding your own niche in the American **workplace.** On the minus side, you can see that no matter how well educated you are, you can still end up without a **job.** A major reason is the lack of a system for matching people with careers and jobs. As a result, in addition to millions of unemployed people, it has been estimated that more than three-fourths of the people in the United States are *underemployed*—working in a job beneath their abilities and/or education.

On the plus side, Kristin's success story shows what you can do when you take the initiative and make the most of your opportunities. Notice that in reassessing her **career**—one's purposeful life pattern of work, as seen in the sequence of jobs held throughout one's life—Kristin needed to take stock of what she had to offer and what she really wanted. One of the keys to Kristin's success was her eventual emphasis on a positive, take-charge attitude, as opposed to the conventional image of the job applicant as a panhandler cowering before employers. All of these points are relevant for our own lives as we, too, face the challenges of choosing a compatible career and finding a job that uses our talents, as we'll see in the rest of this chapter.

TAKING STOCK OF YOURSELF

When choosing a career goal, it's best to begin by taking stock of yourself. Such self-assessment should include a consideration of your interests, abilities, personality, and personal values. What are your interests? Which school subjects do you like the most? The least? Which hobbies do you enjoy? Which recreational and sports activities do you play or follow? In each case, try to determine what it is that most interests you, whether it's the activity itself or the people you're doing it with. Generally, the intrinsic or internal enjoyment of the activity is your best guide to the choice of a career.

What are you good at? People often balk at this question. They say, "I haven't done anything but go to school" or "I've been busy raising three kids." The implication of such remarks is that these people don't have any marketable skills. But when they are confronted with a checklist of things they can do, the picture brightens. For example, a woman who has organized a mothers' cooperative day care, planned field trips for children, and managed the family budget has had considerable experience with management skills, a very important ability for a variety of jobs. Another way to find out what you're good at is to reflect upon your achievements, including those in school. Better yet, select several achievements in each of the 5-year periods of your life. What do these achievements have in common?

Your personality also offers valuable clues for choosing a compatible career. Each of us possesses a unique combination of traits, needs, and motives that make some

Homemakers possess more marketable skills than they are aware of.

work environments more compatible for us than others. For example, a meticulous homemaker may be good working with computers, a field that requires the ability to manage details with precision. A young man who has never cared much for school may like working with his hands, such as rebuilding car engines. Many times our experience in part-time and summer jobs helps us to see which type of work environments we like the most. For example, after spending a summer working with a tree service, one young woman realized how much she enjoyed working outside. Kristin loved her position in the human resources department at the store, in part because it matched her training, including her business skills and her desire as a psychology major to work with others.

Your values are also an important consideration, especially your **work values**— what brings you the most enjoyment or satisfaction in a career or job. All too often, we take our work values for granted, becoming aware of them only when faced with job dissatisfaction, changing jobs, or deciding among several jobs. An example is the choice between a job we enjoy that doesn't pay well and one that we don't especially like that does. However, the sooner we clarify our work values, the easier it will be to make a satisfying decision regarding a career or job. (To learn more about your work values, see Figure 11–1.)

IDENTIFYING COMPATIBLE CAREERS

Once you have a better understanding of your interests and abilities, you're ready to match yourself with a compatible career. With more than 20,000 different careers to choose from, this can be a formidable task. Fortunately, there are many helpful resources, such as the *Occupational Outlook Handbook* (OOH), published by the United States Department of Labor Statistics. This handbook contains more than 20 basic career

FIGURE 11–1

WHAT ARE YOUR WORK VALUES?

The list below includes typical work values, that is, reasons people say they like the work they do. After reading each definition, place a check mark next to the items you would like to have as part of your ideal job.

Next, review all the items you've checked and circle the 10 items you want most.

Finally, rank-order your list of 10 items in the order of importance, from 1—the most important—to 10—the least important.

———— *Help society.* Do something to contribute to the betterment of the world.

———— *Help others.* Be involved in helping other people in a direct way, either individually or in a small group.

———— *Have public contact.* Have a lot of daily contact with people.

———— *Work with others.* Have close working relationships with a group as a result of my work activities.

———— *Compete.* Engage in activities that pit my abilities against others where there are clear win-and-lose outcomes.

———— *Make decisions.* Have the power to decide courses of action.

———— *Hold power and authority.* Control other people's work activities.

———— *Influence people.* Be in a position to change the attitudes and opinions of other people.

———— *Work alone.* Do projects by myself, without any significant amount of contact with others.

———— *Seek knowledge.* Engage myself in the pursuit of knowledge, truth, and understanding.

———— *Hold intellectual status.* Be regarded as a person of high intellectual prowess, an acknowledged "expert."

———— *Create.* Create new ideas and programs, not following an established format.

———— *Supervise.* Have a job in which I'm directly responsible for the work done by others.

———— *Experience change and variety.* Have work responsibilities that frequently change content and setting.

———— *Be stable.* Have a work routine that is largely predictable.

———— *Be secure.* Be assured of keeping my job and a reasonable financial reward.

———— *Live at a fast pace.* Work in circumstances where there is a high pace of activity and work must be done rapidly.

———— *Gain recognition.* Be recognized for the quality of my work.

———— *Feel excitement.* Experience frequent excitement in the course of my work.

———— *Find adventure.* Have work duties that involve frequent risk taking.

———— *Profit materially.* Have a strong likelihood of accumulating large amounts of money or other material gain.

———— *Be independent.* Determine the nature of my work myself; not have to do what others tell me to.

———— *Be in the right location.* Find a place to live (town, geographical area) that allows me to do the things I enjoy most.

———— *Control my own time.* Have work responsibilities that I can accomplish on my own schedule.

SOURCE: List adapted from H. E. Figler, *Path: A Career Workbook for Liberal Arts Students* (Cranston, RI: Carroll Press, 1993). Copyright 1993 by Carroll Press.

groups, each with dozens of related **occupations.** For example, health-related careers include physicians, physician's assistants, registered nurses, practical nurses, medical technologists, and the like. For each career, the handbook provides information on the type of work involved, places of employment, entrance requirements, working conditions, and employment outlook. The OOH also has an introductory section with helpful information on such topics as how to find a job and employment opportunities. The OOH, revised every 2 years, is available in most libraries and job counseling centers and can also be purchased from any of the regional centers of the Bureau of Labor Statistics. Other books that you may find helpful are the *Careers Encyclopedia* from VGM Career Horizons and *College to Career: The Guide to Job Opportunities* from the College Board. These books are often available in libraries as well as university career development and career planning offices.

In identifying compatible careers, it's often advisable to talk over your plans with an interested teacher, school counselor, or someone in your field of interest. Professionals in school counseling centers and career development centers spend a good part of their time assisting people with their career planning. They also have access to a wide assortment of inventories for this purpose. These inventories may furnish valuable leads to compatible careers for someone with your interests, especially when discussed with a counselor.

John Holland's Self-Directed Search (SDS) may be completed by yourself or taken under the supervision of a counselor. When taking the SDS, you indicate choices in regard to your career daydreams, activities, abilities, preferences, and self-estimates. The results are then tabulated to indicate which three personality-occupational types you most resemble and in which order. See Box 11–1 for descriptions of Holland's six

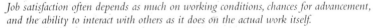

Job satisfaction often depends as much on working conditions, chances for advancement, and the ability to interact with others as it does on the actual work itself.

BOX 11–1

HOLLAND'S SIX PERSONALITY-OCCUPATIONAL TYPES

The following are descriptions of Holland's six personality-occupational types. These descriptions are, most emphatically, only generalizations. None will fit any one person exactly. In fact, most people's interests combine all six themes or types to some degree. Even if you rate high on a given theme, you will find that some of the statements used to characterize it do not apply to you.

The archetypal models of Holland's six types can be described as follows:

Realistic: Persons of this type are robust, rugged, practical, physically strong, and often athletic; have good motor coordination and skills but lack verbal and interpersonal skills, and are therefore somewhat uncomfortable in social settings; usually perceive themselves as mechanically inclined; are direct, stable, natural, and persistent; prefer concrete to abstract problems; see themselves as aggressive; have conventional political and economic goals; and rarely perform creatively in the arts or sciences, but do like to build things with tools. Realistic types prefer such occupations as mechanic, engineer, electrician, fish and wildlife specialist, crane operator, and tool designer.

Investigative: This category includes those with a strong scientific orientation; they are usually task-oriented, introspective, and asocial; prefer to think through rather than act out problems; have a great need to understand the physical world; enjoy ambiguous tasks; prefer to work independently; have unconventional values and attitudes; usually perceive themselves as lacking in leadership or persuasive abilities, but are confident of their scholarly and intellectual abilities; describe themselves as analytical, curious, independent, and reserved; and especially dislike repetitive activities. Vocational preferences include astronomer, biologist, chemist, technical writer, zoologist, and psychologist.

Artistic: Persons of the artistic type prefer free unstructured situations with maximum opportunity for self-expression; resemble investigative types in being introspective and asocial but differ in having less ego strength, greater need for individual expression, and greater tendency to impulsive behavior; they are creative, especially in artistic and musical media; avoid problems that are highly structured or require gross physical skills; prefer dealing with problems through self-expression in artistic media; perform well on standard measures of creativity, and value aesthetic qualities; see themselves as expressive, original, intuitive, creative, nonconforming, introspective, and independent. Vocational preferences include artist, author, composer, writer, musician, stage director, and symphony conductor.

Social: Persons of this type are sociable, responsible, humanistic, and often religious; like to work in groups, and enjoy being central in the group; have good verbal and interpersonal skills; avoid intellectual problem-solving, physical exertion, and highly ordered activities; prefer to solve problems through feelings and interpersonal manipulation of others; enjoy activities that involve informing, training, developing, curing, or enlightening others; perceive themselves as understanding, responsible, idealistic, and helpful. Vocational preferences include social worker, missionary, high school teacher, marriage counselor, and speech therapist.

Enterprising: Persons of this type have verbal skills suited to selling, dominating, and leading; are strong leaders; have a strong drive to attain organizational goals or economic aims; tend to avoid work situations requiring long periods of intellectual effort; differ from conventional types in having a greater preference for ambiguous social tasks and an even greater concern for power, status, and leadership; see themselves as aggressive, popular, self-confident, cheerful, and sociable; generally have a high energy level; and show an aversion to scientific activities. Vocational preferences include business executive, political campaign manager, real estate sales, stock and bond sales, television producer, and retail merchandising.

Conventional: Conventional people prefer well-ordered environments and like systematic verbal and numerical activities; are usually conforming and prefer subordinate roles; are effective at well-structured tasks, but avoid ambiguous situations and problems involving interpersonal relationships or physical skills; describe themselves as conscientious, efficient, obedient, calm, orderly, and practical; identify with power, and value material possessions and status. Vocational preferences include bank examiner, bookkeeper, clerical worker, financial analyst, quality control expert, statistician, and traffic manager.

SOURCE: David P. Campbell and Jo-Ida C. Hansen, *Manual for the Strong-Campbell Interest Inventory.* Form T325 of the *Strong Vocational Interest Blank,* 3rd ed., with the permission of the distributors. Consulting Psychologists Press Inc., for the publisher, Stanford University Press. © 1974, 1977, 1981, by the Board of Trustees of the Leland Stanford Junior University.

personality-occupational types. Using a separate occupational-finder booklet, you match your preferred personality-occupational types with representative compatible careers.

There is also the System of Interactive Guidance and Information (SIGI), published by the Educational Testing Service (Princeton, New Jersey), and similar programs such as Discover for Colleges and Adults (1995), published by Educational Technology Center (Hunt Valley, Maryland). College career development centers often house these programs. You sit at a terminal and enter into a dialogue with the computer, examining your values, exploring career options, and making tentative career choices that can be tested realistically and revised. In this way, you may better appreciate the decision-making strategies involved in the choice of a career. Kristin used Discover, which revealed her interest in both business and psychology. Before she utilized this system, Kristin was aware of her interest in human behavior but not her interest in business.

The Strong Interest Inventory probably dominates the field of career assessment as the most popular instrument (Watkins, 1993) and has been demonstrated to be very effective in dealing with the complexities of career interests (Donnay & Borgen, 1996). This same inventory has also been used in research with college freshmen. Freshmen with "flat" profiles (that is, students with less differentiated interests) have more difficulty in selecting a major, less career certainty during college, and are more likely to change jobs than those freshmen with well-developed interests (Sackett & Hansen, 1995).

The Strong Interest Inventory is usually administered by a professional counselor and is also widely used for career guidance. Using this inventory, you indicate your preferences (like, dislike, or indifferent) for various careers, school subjects, activities, amusements, and types of people as well as something about your own personal characteristics. Computer-scored printouts organize the results around Holland's six categories. The results include information on general career themes, basic interests, and specific careers with which you are most compatible. Discussion of the results with a counselor usually provides valuable leads to the most compatible careers for you. To help you prepare to see a career counselor, use Figure 11–2.

How helpful are these inventories? A lot depends on how they are used. If you take them in hopes that they'll tell you which career you *should* choose—a common misunderstanding—you'll probably be disappointed. Nor will the results predict how

FIGURE 11–2

WHICH PERSONALITY-OCCUPATIONAL TYPES ARE YOU MOST LIKE?

Look over the descriptions (Box 11–1) of Holland's personality-occupational categories. Which category most accurately describes you? Now review the other categories in regard to which most nearly fit you. Write down your second and third choices. Then list your three preferred categories, along with the typical careers associated with each.

1. _____

2. _____

3. _____

Example:

1. *Social.* Social worker, missionary, high school teacher, marriage counselor, and speech therapist

2. *Investigative.* Astronomer, biologist, chemist, technical writer, zoologist, and psychologist

3. *Artistic.* Artist, author, composer, writer, musician, stage director, and symphony conductor

Have you thought of choosing any of the careers, or similar careers, listed in your first category? How about the careers included in your second and third categories? If you care to delve into this process more extensively, you could go to the counseling or career center on your campus and ask to take Holland's Self-Directed Search (SDS), a self-scoring inventory that helps you to arrive at your three preferred categories in a more systematic manner. Then match your three preferred categories—social, investigative, and artistic (SIA) in the above example—with a more extensive listing of compatible careers in the separate occupational-finder booklet. Customarily, you rotate the preferred categories—for example, SIA, ISA, and SAI—so that you get a more extensive list of compatible careers.

successful or happy you'll be in a given career inasmuch as these factors depend on your abilities, personal motivation, and so on. Instead, these inventories are best used as an *aid* in making an informed career choice. For instance, the results of the Strong Interest Inventory have proven quite useful in predicting which people will remain in a given field (Sackett & Hansen, 1995). Those who choose careers very similar to their career profiles tend to remain in their careers, whereas those who enter careers highly dissimilar to their profiles eventually tend to drop out of them. When you consider all the time and money invested in preparing for a career, this information can be extremely helpful to you.

ARRIVING AT A DECISION

If you're like most people, you'll end up with not just one but a number of potentially compatible careers. Ultimately, you must make a decision about which is the best career for you. The process of decision making is so important that we've devoted the better part of a chapter to it—Chapter 12, " Personal Control and Decision Making." You might pay close attention to the steps in decision making—especially the balance sheet procedure. This step consists of listing all the pluses and minuses involved in a given course of action, such as the choice of a career goal. Such an approach helps you to make a comprehensive appraisal of what is involved. It also promotes contingency planning, that is, figuring out what to do if one or more of the unfavorable consequences in the minus column were to materialize.

In the process of deciding on a career, there are certain pitfalls to guard against. One is the accidental choice, which consists of choosing a career mostly because of one's first job. People who fall into this trap may discover later, to their regret, that they would have been happier or more successful in another line of work. Another pitfall is the choice of a career or job because of its external trappings, like money, prestige, power, or security. In the long run, it's better to choose a work activity that is enjoyable in itself, as long as the financial rewards are adequate. A major mistake is not exploring your career options sufficiently. Kristin, for example, knew she did not want to be a waitress all of her life. She was not so sure what she did want to do. Just as Kristin did, you must take the initiative and engage in an active process of finding a compatible career, as we've already discussed. Still another pitfall has to do with the timing of your decision, with the risk of making a premature decision or undue delay. People who make strong career commitments in their 20s, before they are fully informed about careers, often regret their choices later. On the other hand, those who delay making a career commitment until their 30s usually deprive themselves of the necessary work experience to make a wise choice. Thus, we need to choose a career goal but be willing to modify that choice in light of our subsequent experience and growth.

PREPARING FOR YOUR CAREER

Once you've determined your career goal, you'll need to know how to prepare for it. Kristin was only partly prepared in that she had only developed a resume. She had no further strategies for finding her first professional-level job until her father told her to drop off her resume at various businesses. As you might expect, there are many ways to prepare for a career. Some careers are entered through an apprenticeship, vocational-technical school, internships, or on-the-job training programs. Others require a 2-year or 4-year college degree. In addition, careers such as teaching, accounting, and nursing also require a state license or some type of certification. Professions such as medicine and law also require an advanced degree, supervised training, and a state license. Because most of you are already enrolled in some sort of post–high school education, you may have begun the appropriate education for your career. Others of you, especially those in a liberal arts program, may not have arrived at a firm career goal. But in either case, an integral part of career planning is finding out the appropriate educational requirements of your chosen career.

As you may know, more people are choosing to attend college today than in the past. Whereas only one-third of the high school graduates went on to college in the 1960s, more than half of them do so today. In turn, this ratio raises the educational attainment of people in the workplace, as well as the value of a college education.

College is supposed to make you a better-informed person and provide access to higher status and better-paying careers. Admittedly, college graduates continue to have higher lifetime earnings and lower unemployment rates than high school graduates. For instance, people with a 4-year college degree earn about 75 percent more than high school graduates the same age. Those with graduate or professional degrees enjoy an even greater advantage. Of course, people's salaries vary considerably depending on many factors, such as the field of study and actual position held. Given the rapid changes in the job market and the fact that one in nine persons changes careers every year, some of the most valuable but often overlooked advantages of a college education are the abilities for critical thinking, appreciation of lifelong learning, and enhanced adaptation to continuing change.

Career Outlook

How promising your job is often depends on the outlook for your field. Do you know the outlook for your chosen career? Are the job openings in your field expected to remain stable? Or is a rapid growth of jobs projected? Kristin based her career choice of wanting to work in human resource management on her love of psychology and the results of the Strong Interest Inventory, which indicated she was also attracted to business environments. Although it's difficult to answer all possible questions about specific jobs, the Bureau of Labor Statistics periodically makes informed projections of jobs in the various careers. Because employment projections, by their nature, are somewhat imprecise, you should not use them as the sole basis of a career decision. But such projections can help you assess future opportunities in the careers that interest you.

PROJECTED GROWTH

The number and types of jobs available in the years ahead depend on the interaction of many factors, especially economic, demographic, and technological. By analyzing changes in the economy and the factors involved, the Bureau of Labor Statistics develops projections of future demands for many careers. To make these projections, authorities must make some assumptions about the growth of the labor force, inflation, and unemployment.

Although a projected slowdown in employment growth is expected, certain jobs will grow. For example, service-producing industries will account for most new jobs. Business, health, education, and social services are projected to grow whereas manufacturing and mining industries are expected to decline. In fact, business, health, and education will account for 70 percent of the new growth or about 9.2 million jobs (U.S. Department of Labor, Bureau of Labor Statistics, 1996). The health-care industry in particular will experience dramatic growth because of the aging baby boomers, because of innovative medical technology for diagnosis and treatment, and because more individuals will receive outpatient rather than inpatient treatment. Thus, jobs requiring the most education and training will be the fastest growing and highest paying. Specifically, occupations that require a bachelor's degree or above will average 23 percent growth, almost double the 12 percent growth projected for occupations that require less education and training. As far as the goods-producing sector or manufacturing is concerned, only employment opportunities in construction and agriculture are expected to increase. Table 11–1 lists fast-growing jobs by the higher education degrees they generally require.

CHANGING JOBS OR CAREERS

Looking over the job projections and alternative career patterns may start you thinking about your own career goal. Perhaps many of you already have firm career goals and are busily preparing for them. Others may have doubts or reservations. Either way,

TABLE 11–1
FASTEST GROWING JOBS BY LEVEL OF EDUCATION

Master's degree

Operations research analysts
Speech-language pathologists and audiologists
Management analysts
Counselors
Urban and regional planners

Bachelor's degree

Systems analysts
Computer engineers
Occupational therapists
Physical therapists
Special education teachers

Associate's degree

Paralegals
Medical records technicians
Dental hygienists
Respiratory therapists
Radiological technicians

SOURCE: Adapted from U.S. Department of Labor, Bureau of Labor Statistics. (1996). *Occupational Outlook Handbook, 1996–1997.* Washington, DC: U.S. Government Printing Office.

remember that it's perfectly natural to modify your career goal with experience and with greater knowledge of career opportunities. Students are often reluctant to change their career goals for many reasons. Sometimes they would rather keep to their original goal than risk disappointing their parents, spouses, or peers. They forget they are choosing for themselves. Switching career goals may also be regarded as an admission of failure. But to continue in a direction you have misgivings about will only make matters worse. Then, too, individuals may overestimate the price of changing career goals. After gathering all the facts, the penalties may not be as great as expected. The longer you delay changing career goals or careers, the more difficult it is. More often than not, the positive gains outweigh the costs.

People are changing jobs more frequently than in the past. The time a worker keeps a job has steadily declined to an average of 3.5 years. The typical American worker has more jobs (or employers) in his or her lifetime than workers during the 1950s. The typical pattern is that an individual tends to hold several brief jobs in the first few years after graduation, then settles into a position that lasts several years. Workers in their 30s who stay with the same employer for 5 years or more are likely to remain in that job for a long time. As men and women get older, they make fewer job changes. By the age of 40, workers will make about two more job changes; at 50, only one more. Few people change jobs in their 60s, and most of them are probably moving into second careers because of retirement. At the same time, there are exceptions to this pattern. A small number of workers exhibit extremely stable job patterns throughout their careers. Others change jobs every few years until they reach retirement. For yet others, as many as 1 in 10, a career crisis exists for a long time before a change is made. These individuals, particularly women, ponder career change for a long time before actually changing careers (Hutri, 1996).

 Getting Along on the Job

During our teens and 20s, most of us gain considerable work experience through a variety of part-time and summer jobs and, in many cases, full-time jobs. Although these jobs may not have been especially interesting or related to our career goals, they do provide practical knowledge. Experience in the workplace teaches us how to budget our time; take responsibility for a job; and most important, get along with other people. However, getting and holding our first satisfying full-time job in our chosen career is much more involved and important. Figure 11–3 introduces you to some of the com-

---

FIGURE 11–3

THE JOB INTERVIEW

Securing a job usually involves one or more formal interviews. Your major goal is to convince the employer that you are the person for the job, that is, that you have the necessary qualifications and personal qualities for the job and would fit into the organization. It's best to create a favorable impression. Be confident and ambitious, emphasizing your strengths. If asked about your weaknesses, admit a minor one such as "At times I'm too conscientious." Also, it's generally best not to furnish more information than requested by the employer. Finally, a crucial part of a successful job interview is preparing for the interview. Consider the following job interview tips:

Preparation

- Learn about the organization.
- Have a specific job or jobs in mind.
- Review your qualifications for the job.
- Prepare to answer broad questions about yourself.
- Review your resume.
- Arrive before the scheduled time of your interview.

Personal appearance

- Be well groomed.
- Dress appropriately.
- Do not chew gum or smoke.

The interview

- Listen carefully to the questions.
- Respond specifically to each question.

- Use good manners.
- Use proper English and avoid slang.
- Convey a sense of cooperation and enthusiasm.
- Ask questions about the job and the organization.
- Avoid discussing salary until an offer has been made.

Test (if one is given)

- Listen carefully to instructions.
- Read each question carefully.
- Write legibly and clearly.
- Budget your time wisely, not dwelling on one question.

Information to bring to an interview

- Social security number
- Driver's license
- Resume
- Three references (usually). Get people's permission before using their names. For each reference, provide the following information: Name, address, telephone number, and occupation.

SOURCE: Adapted from U.S. Department of Labor, Bureau of Labor Statistics. (1992). *Occupational Outlook Handbook, 1992–1993*. Washington, DC: U.S. Government Printing Office, p. 6.

plexities of obtaining a job. This figure explores one of the first steps, the job interview and preparing for it.

JOB SATISFACTION

Job satisfaction is people's feelings about different aspects of their jobs (Spector, 1996). People who are satisfied with their jobs not only are less susceptible to stress-related illnesses but also visit the doctor less frequently and live longer than those who are dissatisfied in their jobs—all important considerations.

Despite all the griping you hear on the job (as well as your own choice comments), a substantial majority of people—87 percent—are satisfied with their jobs overall (Hugick & Leonard, 1991). Many of these same individuals say they would continue to work even if they didn't need the money. This does not mean, though, that these same individuals are happy with all aspects of their jobs. College-educated workers, especially those in the professions and executive positions, are generally more satisfied with their jobs than those with less education. Workers in the unskilled and service jobs tend to be less satisfied. Sales personnel tend to fall below the norm in job satisfaction, despite being well compensated.

Satisfaction on the job depends heavily on the work activity itself. People generally prefer work that involves contact with others, is interesting, offers the opportunity to learn new skills, and allows them some independence (Hugick & Leonard, 1991). How well you feel you perform on the job is also important. Authorities now believe that there's a greater probability of job satisfaction resulting from job performance than the opposite, which is contrary to findings in the 1960s and 1970s, when job satisfaction was regarded as the major "cause" of job performance. Thus, workers who feel competent at their jobs and are properly recognized and rewarded for their performance tend to be more satisfied with their jobs (Halloran & Benton, 1987).

Job satisfaction also depends to a great extent on the working conditions of the job. In addition to a rewarding job, workers generally prefer having a job that provides opportunities for advancement, good pay, job security, and good working hours (Hugick & Leonard, 1991). They also want friendly, cooperative coworkers and considerate supervisors. Workers are also happier with work that allows them to make decisions on their own without checking everything with their supervisors. Pay has generally risen in importance in recent years, so that it now appears close to the top of workers' priorities—often second or third in the list of things most desired in a job (Stark, 1988). Money is not only a major means of recognizing job performance or success; it also may be used to purchase other items we want. For the majority of people in the middle and working classes who are caught between materialistic aspirations and economic pressures, pay has become an increasingly important part of job satisfaction.

Many other variables affect satisfaction on the job. Age and years on the job continue to be important considerations. Recent graduates initially enjoy high job satisfaction, as did Kristin. But as soon as the novelty of the work wears off and reality sets in, job satisfaction drops sharply. The drop occurred for Kristin when she realized that another employee doing much the same job but with more experience was earning almost 25 percent more than she was. Unrealistic ideas about work may be due to the fact that colleges and universities create expectations that are often not realistic. However, after 5 years on the job, satisfaction tends to rise steadily with age and years on the job. A major reason is greater job security as well as more realistic expectations. Thus, the rising level of education among younger workers often helps to account for the relative dissatisfaction among younger, better-educated workers. The major exception is for workers with professional and graduate degrees, such as doctors and lawyers, who generally are happy in their work. However, unlike blue-collar workers, who reach a plateau in earnings relatively early, college-educated workers generally reap the rewards of greater education in their 30s and the later years of their careers (Halloran & Benton, 1987).

Workers who are not promoted often complain of favoritism, suggesting that getting ahead on the job depends more on "who you know" rather than on what you know. Yet as Halloran and Benton (1987) point out, surveys of larger samples of workers provide a more balanced view. When asked about the ways to get ahead in the job, most workers emphasize the importance of performing the job well (60 percent), working extra hours (53 percent), and being willing to accept responsibility (52 percent). At the same time, almost half of them realize the importance of knowing the "right people" (49 percent) and having highly visible work assignments (45 percent).

These findings suggest the importance of knowing how promotions are made in the organization you work for. Many companies make their policies on promotion clear in the employment interview or at the time of hiring. If not, you should inquire about them. You should know to what extent promotions are based on such factors as education, work experience, job performance, and seniority. For example, Kristin was hired by the department store to bolster sagging sales. She did so in record time. She initiated an innovative advertising campaign based on celebrity appearances and never hesitated to take work home during evening hours or over weekends. As a result, Kristin believed she was responsible for the increase in sales. Kristin hoped for a promotion when her supervisor was promoted, but no promotion was forthcoming. Someone from the outside was brought in to become the new manager. When Kristin asked why, she was told that coworkers and a few celebrities had complained of her aggressive, high-handed style. Kristin had expected to be promoted primarily because of the sales results, but her superiors had judged her by a broader standard, including how well she related to people. Such misunderstanding could have been avoided if either Kristin or her boss had clarified the policy on promotion at the outset.

MINORITIES IN THE WORKPLACE

One of the major shifts in the workplace between now and 2005 will be the changing demographic picture of the labor force. Although Whites will continue to account for the vast majority of workers, as they did in 1990, their share will decline. (See Figure 11–4.) In contrast, both the number and proportion of minority workers will increase. The number of African Americans will increase faster than the number of Whites because the birthrate for African Americans declined more slowly than for Whites during the 1970s. At the same time, the proportion of Hispanics and Asian Americans will grow even faster. The number of Hispanics will increase because of a higher historic birthrate and immigration from Spanish-speaking countries such as Mexico, so that by 2005 they will be approaching the number of African Americans in the workplace. For Asian Americans, growth will be due primarily to immigration from countries such as Vietnam and Korea. Also, smaller minority groups, such as the Pacific Islanders, Native Americans, and Alaskan natives, are expected to enter the workplace in greater numbers.

As a result of these changes, about 4 out of 10 entrants into the workplace will be non-White, many of whom will have only a limited education especially if they are

FIGURE 11–4

Distribution of the labor force by race, 1994 and projected 2005 (in percentages). SOURCE: U.S. Department of Labor, Bureau of Labor Statistics. (1996). *Occupational Outlook Handbook, 1996–1997*. Washington, DC: U.S. Government Printing Office, p. 6.

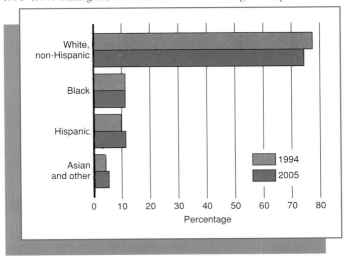

immigrants. A majority of new jobs will require some form of postsecondary or college education. For instance, the U.S. Labor Department forecasts that growth in future jobs will occur largely in high-skill areas, such as information processing, and there will be a decline in jobs in manufacturing, mining, and other industries in which unskilled workers have traditionally found entry-level jobs as laborers. This gap between the limited educational level of many immigrants and the rising demand for educated workers will make it difficult for some minorities to find a job or, once hired, to find job satisfaction and advancement.

A key factor is improving the educational level of minority students. Although high school graduation rates have improved among minority groups in the past 20 years, especially among African Americans, they still lag compared to Whites. For instance, fewer than two-thirds of Hispanics graduate from high school versus more than three-fourths of African Americans and more than 80 percent of Caucasians. For most minorities, the proportion of high school graduates enrolling in college continues to be smaller than that of Whites. Furthermore, very few minority students are transferring from 2-year community colleges to 4-year institutions, where they could earn bachelor's degrees. As a result, more than three-fourths of all undergraduate degrees are awarded to Whites, and only about 3.6 percent are awarded to Asian Americans, 5.2 percent to Hispanics, and 9.2 to African Americans. An even smaller proportion of master's and doctorate degrees are earned by minority groups. Consequently, unless colleges attract more minority students, minority group members will lack the necessary skills to enter the workplace. In turn, this lack will not only add to the existing frustration and poverty of minorities but also create labor shortages and jeopardize our nation's economy (Rendon, 1992).

Research on job satisfaction in multicultural organizations has just begun. In some studies Black Americans report lower job satisfaction than Whites (e.g., Tuch & Martin, 1991). One study also revealed that Hispanic Americans are particularly likely to feel that their Chicano culture is threatened by integration into the mainstream American work force (Segura, 1992). Other studies show few to no race or ethnic differences (Greenhaus, Parasuraman, & Wormley, 1990). One reason for these findings may be differences in the kinds of jobs and organizations analyzed. In any event, White Americans will face the same problems as minorities because American corporations are internationalizing and sending Americans to other countries. We are indeed facing increasing numbers of multicultural organizations in the near future.

WOMEN'S ISSUES IN THE WORKPLACE

More than 9 out of 10 women work outside the home sometime during their lives, and over half participate in the workplace at any given time. The case of Kristin, then, is typical. Actually, the participation rate of women in the workplace varies, depending on such factors as age and marital status. For instance, over two-thirds of married women 25 to 44 years of age work outside the home, with an even higher rate among women the same age who are single, divorced, or widowed (U.S. Bureau of the Census, 1992). Figure 11–5 reveals how the labor force changed historically as more women began to work outside the home.

Women usually work to support themselves or to help with the family income. Although Kristin was not married and without children, she wanted to work to support herself and to be able to buy some of the goods that she deprived herself of when she was in college. The excitement of living on her own, without her parents, also attracted

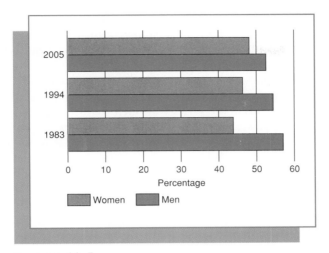

FIGURE 11–5

Past and predicted changes by sex in the U.S. work force. SOURCE: U.S. Department of Labor, Bureau of Labor Statistics, (1996). *Occupational Outlook Handbook, 1996–1997.* Washington, DC: U.S. Government Printing Office, p. 5.

Working women face role conflict and lower wages than men. Nonetheless women often report job satisfaction as high as men's.

her to the job market. Even if women have the means to maintain their current standard of living without working, most young women workers say they would continue to work. Jobs provide women with a sense of competence and a chance to apply talents not used in their roles as mother and homemaker.

The most notable inequity between men and women in the workplace is the earnings gap. Women on the average earn only about one-half to two-thirds of what men earn. Actually, this figure varies with such factors as age and education, with younger, better-educated women earning about three-fourths of what men do (U.S. Bureau of the Census, 1992). A major reason for the earnings gap is that many women enter lower-paying service jobs such as secretarial positions. Until recently, most women have been crowded into less than 10 percent of the Labor Department's job categories. Women are overrepresented in careers such as secretaries, nurses, and librarians; they are underrepresented in careers such as engineers, dentists, and physicians. Fortunately, an increasing number of careers have a more equitable distribution of the sexes. (See Table 11–2.) Another reason for the discrepancy in pay between the sexes is that women workers have had less education and work experience. But this factor, too, is changing. Entering college classes now contain slightly more women than men—a relatively recent phenomenon. Although the proportion of women in the traditional male careers remains small, the rate of increase has been dramatic. For instance, in the past 25 years the percentage of college professors who are women has increased; more than one-fourth of all professors are women (S. H. Russell, Fairweather, Hendrickson, & Zimbler, 1991). There are now more women physicians, women in the life and physical sciences, women engineers, lawyers, and judges. Research shows, however, that traditionally feminine women

TABLE 11–2
GENDER DISTRIBUTION IN SELECTED CAREERS

Male-dominated careers	Percentage men	
Auto mechanics	99.2	
Engineers	91.8	
Clergy	90.7	
Dentists	89.9	
Physicians	79.9	
Female-dominated careers	**Percentage women**	
Secretaries	98.5	
Registered nurses	94.8	
Speech therapists	88.2	
Elementary school teachers	85.9	
Librarians	83.0	
Evenly distributed careers	**Percentage men**	**Percentage women**
Management positions	53.7	46.3
Secondary school teachers	45.3	54.7
Real estate sales	48.5	51.5
Designers	46.6	53.4
Accountants	48.5	51.5

SOURCE: U.S. Bureau of the Census. (1992). *Statistical Abstract of the United States, 1992* (112th ed.). Washington, DC: U.S. Government Printing Office, pp. 392–394.

are still more likely to seek traditionally female employment whereas nontraditional women are more career-minded (Morinaga, Frieze, & Ferligoj, 1993). Unfortunately, these pioneering, nontraditional women in the work force are more susceptible than men or traditional sex-typed women to physical illnesses, stress, and other psychological outcomes (Gerdes, 1995).

Among the other issues that concern women in the workplace are role conflicts between home and work, opportunities for advancement, sexual harassment, and child care. For example, working women report spending more time on various chores both at work and at home than do men (Chebat & Zuccaro, 1995). And although few studies report sex differences in job satisfaction (Spector, 1996), women are less happy about opportunities for advancement. Admittedly, some companies offer better opportunities for women than others. Yet ambitious women often feel that their careers are hindered by a glass ceiling, which they can't see and can't pass beyond, mostly because of stereotyped attitudes and expectations in the workplace. For example, only 2 to 4 percent of the top management jobs are held by women (Snyder, Verderber, Langmeyer, & Myers, 1992). Similarly, women who are promoted into better managerial positions are likely to have salaries that lag behind their male colleagues (Stroh, Brett, & Reilly, 1992).

Sexual harassment—any unwanted attention of a sexual nature occurring in the workplace that interferes with a person's ability to work—is now illegal. Sexual harassment includes but is not limited to unwelcome sexual advances, physical contact, offensive language, and threats of punishment for rejection of these acts. Instances of sexual harassment still abound in many places. For example, a woman might have been having an affair with the head of her division. She notifies him that she wants to break it off, and he retaliates by saying she will not get the promotion she has been expecting. In order to reduce such instances, the Equal Employment Opportunity Commission (EEOC) has issued guidelines for preventing sexual harassment. These guidelines suggest that employers should raise the consciousness of employees about the subject of sexual harassment, express strong disapproval of such behavior, inform all workers of their right to raise the spectre of sexual harassment, explain the appropriate procedures for making a complaint, and sensitize everyone concerned (Halloran & Benton, 1987). Box 11–2 discusses further how you can better cope with sexual harassment.

Still another issue for women as well as for men is child care. Today, most married women in the workplace have children; over half have preschool-age children. Yet high-quality day care is hard to find, difficult to afford, and still not fully tax deductible in most cases. Presently, only a small proportion of employers provide child-care facilities for their workers. As an increasing proportion of women enter the workplace, issues such as maternity leaves and subsidized day care may become valued fringe benefits.

 Leisure

No matter how much you like your job, it's important to have sufficient time off to do many of the other things you enjoy in life. Yet most Americans feel that they are working more and playing less—a perception now being confirmed in fact. In 1987 Lou Harris pointed out that in little more than a decade, the number of hours Americans work would increase from about 40 hours per week to 48 hours. That time has arrived; thus, the amount of **leisure** time available to the average person has dropped by a whole working day.

This dramatic change can be accounted for in several ways. A major factor is the growing practice of businesses and other organizations to employ fewer workers, often

BOX 11–2

COPING WITH SEXUAL HARASSMENT ON THE JOB

At a workshop on this topic, when women were asked to share their experiences, a recently hired college graduate said, "My boss hinted I'd get a raise faster if I went out with him." A young married woman complained, "One man makes these suggestive remarks like 'You look happy today—it was that kind of night, eh?'" A middle-aged woman said, "A male colleague can't keep his hands off me."

Sexual harassment in the workplace takes many forms. A familiar practice is directing catcalls, whistles, and demeaning words like *doll* at women. Another one is recurring, offensive flirtation. Although most sexual harassment is verbal, physical patting, pawing, or sexual advances are not uncommon. Soliciting sexual favors for promotion at work is often cited in lawsuits against large companies.

Although each situation is different, some suggested strategies are usually helpful in dealing with sexual harassment on the job.

1. Make it clear when you disapprove. Say directly but tactfully something such as, "I find that remark offensive."
2. Jot down the time, place, and manner of such incidents. Who are the biggest offenders? Under what circumstances?
3. Talk about the incident to other workers. Find out how many other women (or in some instances, men) have been harassed.
4. Take positive steps in raising the awareness of male workers. Report offensive incidents to supervisors. Discuss problems of sexual harassment at staff meetings. Encourage workshops on the subject.
5. If necessary, make an official complaint to your employer, either orally or in writing, depending on the situation. As a last resort, contact federal agencies, like the Equal Employment Opportunity Commission.

assigning them additional responsibilities, rather than more full-time workers. The stated aim is to increase productivity. But the average worker feels overworked. As more than one worker has said, "I find that I'm working harder just to stay even." Administrators and managers are most apt to put in the longest work week. Many baby boomers, perhaps your parents, work over 50 hours a week. Small-business people also work over 50 hours a week. Although women in dual-income families work almost the same number of hours as men do, they have less leisure time, mostly because they do many more chores at home, as mentioned earlier. Ironically, the most affluent sectors of society—college graduates, professionals, and those with incomes of $50,000 or more—work the longest hours and have the least time for leisure. This trend runs counter to predictions 20 years ago, when it was assumed that automation and technology would shorten the work week and give us more leisure time. Actually, the opposite has occurred, perhaps because computer owners are determined to perfect and reperfect their work.

The growing commitment to work has heightened the nation's productivity, helping the United States to compete in the global market. But by the same token, the precarious balance of work and play has become even more threatened. Many people are becoming so absorbed with work that they aren't giving the loving care needed to make marriage work or providing growing children with enough attention or taking part in community endeavors. Also, as Juliet Schor (1992) points out in *The Overworked American,* work now contributes to a host of problems, including stress, physical ailments, marital discord, child neglect, and lack of sleep. Americans have become locked into a vicious work-and-spend cycle in a culture obsessed with possessions. Meanwhile, time has become a premium in our society, making leisure time an even more precious commodity. People must now think carefully about the most desirable way to spend their leisure hours.

WHAT IS LEISURE?

Leisure ordinarily refers to "free time" apart from work. There are many things we do outside of work that are anything but leisure, for example, cleaning up after meals, lawn work, studying, and visits to the dentist. Such activities are usually labeled **maintenance activities.** In contrast, leisure has to do with the *way* we use our free time, our motivation for doing it, the meaning it has for us, and how it affects our lives. The purpose of leisure, Aristotle believed, is the cultivation of the self and the pursuit of the higher things of life. **Leisure** may be defined as any activity we've freely chosen to do, excluding work and maintenance activities. Playing a musical instrument primarily for the enjoyment of it or bicycling for pleasure are examples of **unconditional leisure.** Many forms of leisure—such as vacations—involve planning and, to a certain degree, prescribed activities. When you're so tired you feel like "doing nothing," you're probably

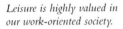
Leisure is highly valued in our work-oriented society.

recuperating from work, which is more of a maintenance activity. People who have a satisfying leisure life, such as Kristin who played tennis in her spare time, often find they must acquire certain skills and play often enough to keep up their game. At the same time, individuals who are highly competitive or perfectionistic may become so concerned about their performance that the pleasure in their leisure activities is lost. Leisure also implies the absence of monetary reward; that is, we do something primarily for the enjoyment we get out of it. (See Figure 11–6).

WORK AND LEISURE

Many people regard their work and leisure activities as separate—and perhaps unrelated—parts of their lives. When Kristin was disappointed that she did not receive her promotion after her supervisor was promoted, she nonetheless enjoyed her friends and recreational life, especially tennis. Another person may have a very satisfying career, with

FIGURE 11–6

The 10 most popular sports activities, by sex: 1990. SOURCE: U.S. Bureau of the Census. (1992). *Statistical Abstract of the United States, 1992* (112th ed.). Washington, DC: U.S. Government Printing Office, p. 230.

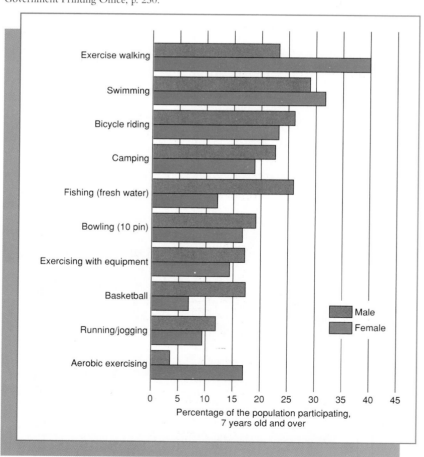

little or no time for play. In each instance, a person's involvement and satisfaction in work and leisure are related to personal characteristics, needs, and values.

Researchers have identified various leisure patterns based on sex, race, and age. Stanley and Freysinger (1995) conducted a survey on leisure activities of over 1,000 Americans over 16 years. They found that negative health changes had a greater impact on the leisure activities of men than on women. Men's participation in all categories of activities declined over time (or with age), whereas women maintained their involvement in various activities. Other studies have found that African Americans have lower levels of leisure time physical activity than Whites (Airhihenbuwa, Kumanyika, Agurs, & Love, 1995) and that this difference might be accounted for by differences in attitudes about control over personal health or in the efficacy of preventive health behavior (Broman, 1995).

Not everyone fits neatly into these patterns. What pattern describes your involvement and satisfaction in work and play? In what ways would you like to change your pattern? These are just as important to your mental health as are notions about what career you think is best for you.

USING LEISURE POSITIVELY

By the time people have driven home after a hard day's work and eaten dinner, they're often too tired to do anything else. When asked their favorite way to spend an evening, the majority say watching television. Adults now watch television an average of 3 to 4 hours a day, most of it in the evening. Although people watch television primarily for entertainment and to a lesser extent for the news, watching television is also a time to relax and unwind, or to recuperate, which is mostly a maintenance activity, as described earlier. The ease with which someone may push a button and be entertained hours on end remains a great temptation. At the same time, individuals who have curtailed their TV habits are usually amazed at how many other interesting things there are to do in life.

In contrast, the positive use of leisure requires a certain degree of choice and planning. Ideally, you should select activities that are compatible with your interests and lifestyle rather than simply doing whatever is convenient at the time or what your friends want to do. Kristin was fortunate to have friends who also enjoyed tennis. They typically played every other Saturday morning. Kristin knew, however, that there were Saturdays she would be too tired to play and preferred instead to sleep late. She would call her friends on Friday night to inform them of her decision.

To enjoy an activity to the fullest, you usually have to acquire the necessary skills. You must also budget your time and money to keep up the activity. For example, people who take pride in their tennis game tend to play regularly and probably derive greater satisfaction than those who play only occasionally.

A favorite American form of leisure is taking a vacation. About half the population takes some type of vacation each year, typically a 1- or 2-week vacation. Most people feel little or no guilt taking time off for a vacation. But when asked the main reasons for taking a vacation, their responses reflect a variety of motives. The most common motive is to relax. Other motives are intellectual stimulation, family togetherness, adventure, self-discovery, and escape. After the vacation, most people are glad to be back home and look forward to returning to work. Only a few feel depressed at facing the familiar routine. Most people feel that work is more important than leisure, and they seek not so much a leisure-filled life as a better balance of the two. Now that more women are working outside the home, leisure has become even more important for families.

Furthermore, more flexible work schedules enable people to take more long weekends, which promises to make vacations a regular event rather than a once-a-year affair.

Leisure becomes increasingly important from midlife on because of all the changes in people's lives. By this time, people are reassessing their needs and values and what they want out of life. Also, people this age tend to have more job security, more discretionary money, more free time, and more paid vacation time than younger adults. For many, this may be the first time they've been able to follow their own inclinations without having to worry about the productivity of their efforts. Now they can take up interests and express abilities not previously used in career and family responsibilities. In short, leisure becomes a means of personal growth.

Constructive leisure activities are also an important way to prepare for retirement. People who have developed rewarding leisure activities as well as a network of social and family relationships are more able to make the crucial shift from full-time work to a satisfying retirement.

SUMMARY

CHOOSING A CAREER

We began the chapter by discussing the process of choosing a career, one's overall or life pattern of work. In choosing a career goal, it's best to begin by taking stock of yourself, including your interests, abilities, personality, and work values. Then you're ready to explore the career options available to you, realizing that there are a variety of career inventories that may help to identify the most compatible careers for someone like yourself. The most revered scale is the Strong Interest Inventory. You should also be aware of certain pitfalls in decision making, such as arriving at a career goal prematurely or unduly delaying the choice of a career. It's best to keep your career goal somewhat flexible and to be willing to modify it in light of subsequent experience, especially while you are in college.

CAREER OUTLOOK

Career outlook depends on the interaction of many factors, especially the makeup of the labor force and the growth of the various careers as well as one's own career choice. Major changes in the labor force include the increase of minority and women workers. Because jobs for college-educated workers will grow faster than average, college graduates will continue to have higher rates of employment and lifetime earnings. In contrast, people with less than a high school education will find it difficult to get good jobs with good pay and chances for advancement. There is also more mobility in the workplace today, with the typical American worker now having more jobs in his or her lifetime.

GETTING ALONG ON THE JOB

Satisfaction on the job depends heavily on how interesting and meaningful the work activity itself is as well as the conditions on the job itself. A major shift now taking place in the workplace is the increase in the number and proportion of minority workers. Our workplaces are indeed becoming multicultural. However, because of the gap between the limited educational level of many of these individuals such as recent immigrants and the rising demand for educated workers, it will be difficult for some minorities to find a suitable job, much less achieve job satisfaction and advancement. Also, now more women work outside the home, with over half of them participating in the workplace at any given time. Among the many issues that especially concern women are the earnings gap between the sexes; opportunities for advancement; sexual harassment; role conflicts between home and work; and child care, an issue for the entire family.

LEISURE

No matter how much you like your job, it's important to have time off for things you enjoy. Most Americans are working more hours per week and having fewer hours for leisure than they did in the past. Consequently, leisure—time free from work that may be spent in meaningful activities—becomes more important in our society. The value of leisure and whether we engage in leisure activities varies with gender and race. A favorite form of leisure is taking a vacation, and half the population takes some type of vacation each year. The positive use of leisure becomes increasingly important from midlife on as we reassess what we want out of life.

SELF-TEST

1. In choosing a career goal, it's best to begin by
   a. taking a test
   b. seeking counseling
   c. taking stock of yourself
   d. getting parental advice

2. Inventories such as Holland's Self-Directed Search and the Strong Interest Inventory help to predict which careers you
   a. are most compatible with
   b. will succeed in
   c. should choose
   d. will be happy in

3. Which of the following is widely regarded as the major advantage of a college education?
   a. greater social skills
   b. better job opportunities
   c. more thinking ability
   d. a lot of knowledge

4. Above all, most people are looking for a job that provides
   a. an interesting job
   b. contact with other people
   c. a feeling of accomplishment
   d. all of the above

5. Which of the following groups will have a smaller proportion of people in the workplace by the year 2000?
   a. Whites
   b. Asian Americans
   c. Hispanics
   d. African Americans

6. The greatest inequity between men and women in the workplace is the gap between their
   a. earnings
   b. job productivity
   c. education
   d. job qualifications

7. In the future, which jobs are expected to have the biggest numerical increase of workers?
   a. health care
   b. mining
   c. manufacturing
   d. agriculture

8. Which statement is true about American workers changing their careers?
   a. Americans seek jobs and then keep them a long time.
   b. Job changes are more common late in life rather than early in life.
   c. Americans are prone to changing jobs.
   d. In the 1950s Americans changed jobs more frequently than now.

9. Compared to people in the 1970s, the average American now
   a. works more hours a week
   b. has more leisure time
   c. works fewer hours a week
   d. has the same amount of leisure time

10. The most common reason for taking a vacation is
    a. self-discovery
    b. relaxation
    c. family togetherness
    d. escape

EXERCISES

1. *Exploring your career interests.* Make an extensive list of all the activities you've enjoyed, including school courses, extracurricular activities, full- and part-time jobs, hobbies, and sports. Then select a dozen of the most satisfying activities and rank them from the most enjoyable down. Ask yourself what made each activity satisfying. Was it the activity itself? Or was it mostly the people you did it with or the recognition or money involved? Activities that are intrinsically enjoyable are usually the best indications of the types of careers you'll enjoy.

2. *Identifying compatible careers.* Go to your campus career development center or career guidance center and take some type of career inventory like Holland's Self-Directed Search or one that requires professional supervision, like the Strong Interest Inventory. Then review the results with a trained counselor.

3. *Become better informed about your career goal.* How much do you know about your chosen career? You might find it helpful to look up some basic information about it in a resource like the *Occupational Outlook Handbook.* Look up your chosen career or one you're interested in. Then write down information on the following: (1) description of the work, (2) typical places of employment, (3) educational and entry requirements, and (4) employment outlook. This exercise should give you a more realistic view of your career goal and how to prepare for it.

4. *Write about your experience finding jobs.* If you've held part- or full-time jobs, how have you found out about them? Did a friend tell you about the job? Or did you use the want ads or see a notice posted? How much luck was involved? Would you agree that in finding a job you need to use as many different resources as you can?

5. *Describe your experience as a woman or minority in the workplace.* If these categories don't fit you, interview someone whom they do fit. Describe your or their experience in part-time and full-time jobs, paying special attention to the working conditions on the job, such as pay, supervision, and promotion. If you're married and have chil-

dren, has your family been supportive? If you're a single parent, what special problems has this presented for you?

6. *Think about your work and leisure pattern.* In what ways would you like to change your pattern at work or play? How would you keep your patterns the same? Why?

QUESTIONS FOR SELF-REFLECTION

1. Do you have a specific career goal?
2. If not, are you actively engaged in choosing a career—or are you "waiting for things to happen"?
3. Do you believe that hard work eventually pays off?
4. What are the three most important things you look for in a job?
5. If you won a million dollars in the state lottery, would you continue to work?
6. What is the projected outlook for your chosen career?
7. If you were to change careers, what would your alternate career choice be?
8. Have you ever been unemployed? What did it feel like? How did you overcome these feelings?
9. What is the most important thing you've learned from your part-time jobs?
10. What is your favorite leisure activity?

FOR FURTHER INFORMATION

RECOMMENDED READINGS

KRANNICH, R. L., & KRANNICH, C. R. (1995). *The best jobs for the 1990s and into the 21st century.* Manassas Park, VA: Impact Publications. A good guide to what careers are projected to be hot sellers in the near future.

REARDON, K. K. (1995). *They don't get it, do they?: Communication in the workplace—Closing the gap between women and men.* Boston: Little, Brown. A good book about gender issues in the workplace.

ROSENBERG, H. G. (1994). *How to succeed without a career path: Jobs for people with no corporate ladder.* Manassas Park, VA: Impact Publications. A source for individuals who are either entry level or who lack much higher education.

SCHWARTZ, J. A. (1993). *Successful recareering: When changing jobs just isn't enough.* Hawthorne, NJ.: Career Press. Thinking of changing jobs? This is the book for you.

TRACY, D. M. (1994). *Take this job and love it: A personal guide to career empowerment.* New York: McGraw-Hill. How to make the best of any job.

WEBSITES AND THE INTERNET

http://www.aboutwork.com/: A site for anyone who wants work, is working, or has retired from work. Something for everyone.

http://www.ajb.dni.us/: A website to help you find a job anywhere in the country. This is a free service from the U.S. Department of Labor.

http://www.careers.org/: Another site that can help you find jobs and information about work, including information about working in other countries.

http://www.collegegrad.com/: A job site designed specially for recent college graduates.

leisurenet: A list serve designed to help those interested in leisure studies, the study of recreation, and how people spend their leisure time. To subscribe send a message to *listproc@gu.edu.au.*

Personal Control and Decision Making

After completing this chapter, you should be able to

1. Discuss the importance of perceived control.
2. Describe the cognitive explanatory style associated with learned optimism.
3. Identify the five stages of decision making.
4. List several suggestions for improving decision-making skills.
5. Explain how group decisions differ from individual decisions.
6. Describe the suggestions for applying the principles of decision therapy to your life.
7. Give an example of someone who has experienced significant growth because of a decision he or she has made.

Stan, a 46-year-old married student, had an important choice he was facing. It seems he had lost his job as a foreman in a steel plant during the past year. Then, after months of unsuccessful job hunting and agonizing over his future, Stan had decided to enroll in college to become an engineer. Recently and unexpectedly, Stan's former employer called and offered him a chance to return to work. "It's a tempting offer," Stan said. "But I'm not sure I want to go back." Stan explained that by taking back his old job he would be able to support his wife and two small children more adequately. "But then I'd always worry about when the next layoff was coming," he said. At the same time, Stan was under great stress attending school full time while supporting his family. He was having a difficult time paying bills, and he was constantly tired. Nor was there any assurance he would get a good job as an engineer once he got his degree.

Personal Control

Stan, like many of us, is striving to attain a greater degree of mastery, or **personal control,** over his life. He resents being at the mercy of a large corporation and having a job that is so vulnerable to the ups and downs of the economy. Also, he realizes that acquiring greater control over his life means facing up to important life choices. It's not simply a matter of whether to accept his old job or to remain in school, as hard a choice as this is. It goes deeper than that. Such decisions also involve important value choices in regard to what he wants out of life, what he's willing to settle for, and how hard he's willing to work to get what he wants. It's no surprise that this has been a trying time in Stan's life, with many sleepless nights and numerous heart-to-heart talks with his wife, who supports his decision to attend college. You may be interested to know that eventually Stan refused the offer of his old job and continued his education.

Stan's experience reminds us of the importance of personal control and of the crucial role of decision making in our lives. We'll begin the chapter by exploring the topic of personal control and its implications for personal adjustment and growth. Then we'll devote the rest of the chapter to the process of decision making, including how we may improve our decision-making skills to facilitate our personal growth.

Personal control has become a very important issue today for many reasons. First, our lives are increasingly shaped by large, impersonal bureaucracies, such as the government and business corporations, which often have more impact on the economy, and thus on our personal lives, than what we do as individuals. Then, too, there is greater awareness that our lives are at the mercy of events or conditions beyond our immediate control, such as economic recession, terrorism, or the continuing pollution of the earth. At the same time, the civil rights movement and the other movements that have followed in its wake have taught us that individuals can gain greater control over their lives by active participation in the democratic process, like demonstrations, social action, and legislation. In a democratic society that nourishes **independence** and freedom of choice, it is well to remember that each of us has considerable power to shape our destinies through personal decisions, such as the choice of a career, where to live, and a marriage partner, as well as through our lifestyles and values.

The idea of personal control, or self-mastery, is not new. It has been around since antiquity but is usually expressed in other terms, for example, stoical self-control or philosophical self-determination. However, in an era oriented to scientific explanations, newer theories that highlight the psychological and social factors in personal control, such as Seligman's view of learned helplessness, have been put forth in recent years. Convinced that these theories have much in common, Christopher Peterson and Albert Stunkard (1988) have developed a generic theory of personal control, which includes the following points.

- First, individuals differ considerably in the degree of personal control they believe they exercise over their lives.
- Second, personal control resides in the interaction or relationship between the individual and his or her world. Accordingly, personal control depends on both dispositional factors within us as well as characteristics of the environment.
- Third, a major factor in personal control is the belief that we can affect actual outcomes, choose among them, cope with the consequences, and/or understand them.
- Fourth, in many environments, a high degree of personal control is desirable in that it encourages us to persist, adapt, and thrive in the face of challenge and adversity.
- Fifth, personal control may be encouraged by success and thwarted by failure, but it does not necessarily bear a one-to-one relationship to past patterns of success and failure (Bandura, 1997). Thus, it's possible for individuals growing up in a supportive environment to feel that they have little control over their lives. And, conversely, it is possible for those in an indifferent or hostile environment eventually to acquire a high degree of personal control over their lives despite their circumstances.

PERCEIVED CONTROL

The aspect of personal control that has received the most attention, primarily because it is the most accessible to empirical investigation, is **perceived control**—the belief that we can influence the occurrence of events in our environment that affect our lives. An individual like Stan who believed college would lead to a better job and a better life has an internal **locus of control** and therefore would apparently have high perceived control. A different individual with an external locus of control would perceive less personal control. Perceived control is also very similar to a concept introduced in other chapters, **self-efficacy,** the belief in one's capabilities to organize and execute the courses of action required to produce given attainments (Bandura, 1997).

Psychologists have identified *two sources* of perceived control. One is an **internal locus of control** where the individual believes he or she has control over life events. The other is an **external locus of control** where the individual believes that something outside of him- or herself such as other individuals, fate, or various external situations control life events. Individuals with an internal locus of control adjust better to college (Martin & Dixon, 1994), are more likely to take advantage of programs such as career development programs designed to enhance their adjustment (Pugh, 1993), and cope better with illness, even life-threatening ones such as AIDS (Reed, Taylor, & Kemeny, 1993). There are cultures, however, where external control is more valued. For example, Weisz, Rothbaum, and Blackburn (1984) found that in Japan most individuals place less value and emphasis on what the researchers called "primary control," which is very much like personal or internal control. The Japanese instead accommodate to others' needs and to fitting in, which the authors labeled "secondary control." In other words, the Japanese do not find their rewards by trying to directly influence other people and external events. They are more tolerant of others trying to influence them. Given these cultural differences, for most people, research demonstrates that optimal adjustment is achieved when the amount of actual control matches the desired need for control (Conway, Vickers, & French, 1992).

Research also demonstrates that individuals high in external control can learn to develop a sense of internal locus of control. Cone and Owens (1991), for example, enrolled freshmen at risk for failing or dropping out in a study skills and college adjustment course. At the end of the semester, these students' grade point averages were compared to students who were also at risk but who were not enrolled in the special course. Compared to students not in the class, the students who were registered had higher grades and had shifted to more internalized loci of control.

How much control would you say you have over your personal life? To check on your perception, complete the classic Locus of Control Scale, a widely used measure of personal control. (See Figure 12–1.)

Research has shown that the presence or absence of perceived control has important consequences in our lives, over and above the actual control available to us in a given situation. When we believe we can affect actual outcomes in our lives, choose among them, cope with the consequences, and/or understand them, we behave in a significantly different way than when we don't share this belief. Stan, for example, sincerely believed that if he studied hard he would earn a college degree which would eventually garner his family and him a better standard of living. Thus, Stan studied hard in college and persisted at his studies even though at times he was discouraged by a below-average grade.

People who possess a high degree of perceived control tend to exhibit certain characteristics. First and foremost, they are likely to seek knowledge and information about the events that affect their lives. Feeling they are in control of their lives, they make greater efforts to acquire information about themselves and their environment. For instance, when facing surgery or a serious illness, patients with a high degree of perceived control are especially likely to seek information about their condition, to ask questions of the doctors and nurses, and to make use of the resources available to them. This is one of the most consistent findings in studies of perceived control. Second, people high in perceived control are likely to attribute responsibility to themselves and to their abil-

FIGURE 12–1

THE LOCUS OF CONTROL SCALE

This scale measures the extent to which you believe you retain a high degree of personal control within yourself (internal locus of control) or whether your life is controlled largely by forces in the environment or fate (external locus of control).

Write yes or no before each of the following statements. Then check your responses with the scoring key at the end of this chapter.

_____ 1. Do you believe that most problems will solve themselves if you just don't fool with them?

_____ 2. Do you believe that you can stop yourself from catching a cold?

_____ 3. Are some people just born lucky?

_____ 4. Most of the time do you feel that getting good grades meant a great deal to you?

_____ 5. Are you often blamed for things that just aren't your fault?

_____ 6. Do you believe that if somebody studies hard enough he or she can pass any subject?

_____ 7. Do you feel that most of the time it doesn't pay to try hard because things never turn out right anyway?

_____ 8. Do you feel that if things start out well in the morning it's going to be a good day no matter what you do?

_____ 9. Do you feel that most of the time parents listen to what their children have to say?

_____ 10. Do you believe that wishing can make good things happen?

_____ 11. When you get punished does it usually seem it's for no good reason at all?

_____ 12. Most of the time do you find it hard to change a friend's opinion?

_____ 13. Do you think cheering more than luck helps a team win?

_____ 14. Did you feel that it was nearly impossible to change your parents' minds about anything?

_____ 15. Do you believe that parents should allow children to make most of their own decisions?

_____ 16. Do you feel that when you do something wrong there's very little you can do to make it right?

_____ 17. Do you believe that most people are just born good at sports?

_____ 18. Are most other people your age stronger than you are?

_____ 19. Do you feel that one of the best ways to handle most problems is just not to think about them?

_____ 20. Do you feel that you have a lot of choice in deciding who your friends are?

_____ 21. If you find a four-leaf clover, do you believe that it might bring you good luck?

_____ 22. Did you often feel that whether or not you did your homework had much to do with what kind of grades you got?

_____ 23. Do you feel that when a person your age is angry with you, there's little you can do to stop him or her?

_____ 24. Have you ever had a good-luck charm?

_____ 25. Do you believe that whether or not people like you depends on how you act?

_____ 26. Did your parents usually help you if you asked them to?

_____ 27. Have you ever felt that when people were angry with you it was usually for no reason at all?

_____ 28. Most of the time, do you feel that you can change what might happen tomorrow by what you do today?

_____ 29. Do you believe that when bad things are going to happen they are just going to happen no matter what you try to do to stop them?

_____ 30. Do you think that people can get their own way if they just keep trying?

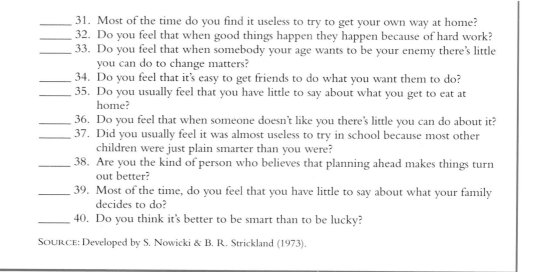

_____ 31. Most of the time do you find it useless to try to get your own way at home?

_____ 32. Do you feel that when good things happen they happen because of hard work?

_____ 33. Do you feel that when somebody your age wants to be your enemy there's little you can do to change matters?

_____ 34. Do you feel that it's easy to get friends to do what you want them to do?

_____ 35. Do you usually feel that you have little to say about what you get to eat at home?

_____ 36. Do you feel that when someone doesn't like you there's little you can do about it?

_____ 37. Did you usually feel it was almost useless to try in school because most other children were just plain smarter than you were?

_____ 38. Are you the kind of person who believes that planning ahead makes things turn out better?

_____ 39. Most of the time, do you feel that you have little to say about what your family decides to do?

_____ 40. Do you think it's better to be smart than to be lucky?

SOURCE: Developed by S. Nowicki & B. R. Strickland (1973).

ities and efforts rather than to luck or the environment, at least in regard to desirable outcomes. When Stan received high grades in college, he readily attributed them to his hard work and intelligence. Third, people high in perceived control are resistant to social influence and are especially likely to take part in social action that helps others. Stan, for example, ignored his brother's chuckles when his brother teased him about returning to college only to look at the young coeds. Stan also found time to volunteer at the Special Olympics held each year on the college campus. And finally, individuals high in perceived control are strongly achievement oriented such as Stan. They appear to work harder at intellectual and performance tasks, and their efforts are rewarded with better grades than those with less perceived control.

As you might expect, there is a strong positive relationship between perceived control and personal adjustment. Individuals high in perceived control tend to be less anxious, better adjusted, and less likely to be classified with psychiatric labels than those with less perceived control. Perhaps the active, self-reliant qualities of those high in perceived control lead to the kinds of successes that promote adjustment and growth. Or it may be that simply believing that one is in charge of one's destiny results in less anxiety and better adjustment. Actually, it's hard to disentangle cause from effect in these matters because most of the data are correlational.

People high in perceived control use more effective strategies for coping with stress. For example, individuals high in perceived control tend to use positive coping strategies, such as making a plan of action and sticking to it, taking one step at a time, and getting professional help and doing what is recommended (e.g., Cooper, Okamura, & McNeil, 1995). In contrast, people low in perceived control are more apt to use maladaptive strategies, such as wishing the problem would go away; blaming themselves; and seeking relief through overreacting, drinking, or abusing drugs. Yet in the long run, the use of more effective coping strategies promotes better adjustment and growth (e.g., Aspinwall & Taylor, 1992).

People high in perceived control also are more likely to take steps that will maximize their health and well-being and minimize the risk of illness. Such individuals are especially apt to seek information about health maintenance, engage in preventive health practices, adopt more positive attitudes about physical exercise, and participate in physical exercise more regularly. Stan, for example, realized that his college studies and his part-time job were creating stress, so he often went for what he called "stress management walks" when he came home from his day's classes. People who believe they are in charge of their lives are also likely to refrain from or give up the habit of smoking, to successfully complete weight-reduction programs, and to cooperate with prescribed treatment for medical problems. In regard to substance abuse, perceived self-control is a reliable predictor of who will complete the program and who will drop out. High perceived control also helps to predict who will succeed in overcoming eating disorders and successfully recover from the trauma of heart attacks.

Finally, people who feel empowered in their personal lives also demonstrate a relatively high level of happiness. For instance, before the reunification of Germany, Gabriel Oettingen and Martin Seligman (1990) observed the body language of working-class men in East and West Berlin bars. They found that compared to their counterparts in East Berlin, those in West Berlin were more apt to sit upright than to slump in their seats and to smile and laugh more often.

MISPERCEPTION AND MALADJUSTMENT

Unfortunately, the misperception of personal control usually tends to have negative consequences. For instance, some individuals habitually believe they have even less control over their lives than they do, and thus they prematurely surrender the potential control available to them. Others, even in the same situation, may go to the opposite extreme: Believing they exercise greater control than they actually do, they set themselves up for frustration and eventual disappointment. In both cases, as we will see, such mistaken beliefs about personal control lead to maladaptive behavior.

When people repeatedly encounter bad outcomes regardless of what they do, such as losing a job because of a company layoff, they tend to experience a diminished sense of personal control, thereby attributing *too little control* to themselves. Suppose that no matter how hard Stan studied when he first matriculated at college, he failed every test. Stan might come to think that he could not succeed in college no matter what he did.

Martin Seligman (1981), who has studied this problem extensively, refers to this phenomenon as **learned helplessness**—a maladaptive passivity that frequently follows an individual's experience with uncontrollable events. In a series of now classic studies, Seligman exposed animals to a sequence of uncontrollable shocks. Then, 24 hours later, the animals were tested in a shuttle box. Animals could turn off the shocks by moving from one end of the box to another, that is, by "shuttling." Most animals learned how to shuttle with little difficulty. However, animals previously exposed to *uncontrollable* shocks failed to learn how to escape. They just sat there passively absorbing the shocks. They had learned to be helpless. In contrast, animals exposed to similar shocks they could control had no trouble learning how to escape.

Seligman (1988) points out that learned helplessness also occurs among people. Studies have shown that a host of psychological and physical difficulties follow a series of bad events outside a person's control, like unemployment, accidents, illnesses, death of a spouse, and victimization. However, uncontrollable events in themselves do not necessarily produce learned helplessness. The crucial matter consists of *how* people explain these events. To the extent they offer a *permanent* ("It's going to last forever"), *universal* ("This screws up everything"), and *internal* ("It's me") explanation for bad events, people tend to surrender control over their lives prematurely and respond poorly to such events when they occur. Accordingly, learned helplessness is associated with a variety of ills, including depression, academic failure, bureaucratic apathy, and premature death.

At the other extreme are people who believe they exercise more control over their lives than they actually do. In some cases, people *exaggerate* the degree of control they possess when outcomes are positive. That is, they take more credit for good outcomes than they probably deserve, perhaps as a way of enhancing their self-regard. In other cases, people subscribe to the **illusion of control,** believing they exert control over what is really a chance-determined event—such as winning a lottery. People with a strong desire to control events are especially susceptible to the illusion of control, which is an inversion of learned helplessness.

For instance, a key element in the Type A stress syndrome introduced elsewhere in this book is thought to be the *perceived lack* of control. That is, Type A individuals feel a strong need to exert control. Their active, dynamic style makes them look as if they are in control of situations regardless of whether they are or not. Therefore, much of Type A behavior may be seen as people's chronic attempt to regain the control they continually feel is slipping away from them. It's almost as if they have a mental set to control everything, followed by an inevitable frustration-hostility reaction when events in their lives elude their grandiose plans. Thus, Type A individuals set themselves up for greater disappointment in themselves, needless frustration, and pessimism—all because of their *undue* need to control events (Strube, Lott, Heilizer, & Gregg, 1986). People who are equally competent but without the exaggerated need for control may accomplish just as much but with considerably less stress and the attendant health problems.

LEARNED OPTIMISM

A helpful way of achieving optimal but realistic perceived control can be seen in what Martin Seligman (1992) calls **learned optimism.** Optimism is another personality dimension that has been linked to good adjustment. Optimism is related to good problem solving under stress (Amirkhan, Risinger, & Swickert, 1995), ego-resiliency (Klohnen, 1996), better physical health (Chang, 1996), active coping and seeking of social support when appropriate (Aspinwall & Taylor, 1992), and overall psychological well-being (Scheier & Carver, 1993).

As mentioned earlier, Seligman, along with other cognitive theorists, holds that it is not life events in themselves that overwhelm us. Rather, it is our beliefs and interpretations about them and, in turn, our subsequent responses that most affect our lives. Consequently, in learned optimism, the emphasis is on interpreting life events in a reasonably accurate way to enhance our perceived control and, thus, our adaptive responses. This goal is accomplished primarily by modifying our explanatory style, that is, the way we explain life events to ourselves. The term *learned* precedes the word *optimism* because optimism can be learned. Parents can teach their children optimism by instructing them in problem-solving skills and adaptive coping skills and by modeling optimistic thinking for their children (Scheier & Carver, 1993).

The three main categories of explanatory style are permanence, pervasiveness, and personalization. However, there are two polar meanings within each category; one meaning is preferable to the other, depending on whether you are dealing with a negative or positive life event. For instance, suppose Stan's best friend hasn't returned his phone calls all day, which is understandably a negative event. If Stan interprets this situation as something that is *permanent* ("I guess he isn't going to call back"), *universal*

A sense of optimism not only fights off discouragement, it helps us achieve our personal goals.

("Well, there goes my whole day"), and *internal* ("No wonder he doesn't call back, I'm so selfish and inconsiderate"), Stan would tend to feel depressed all day. However, if this situation were viewed differently, it might not bother Stan, for example, if he interprets the same event as *temporary* ("He may be especially busy today"), *specific* ("Not having my phone call returned doesn't make or break my entire day"), and *external* ("Not re-turning my calls probably has more to do with his schedule than his attitude toward me"). See Table 12–1 for a summary of these phenomena.

In contrast, the preferred way of explaining positive or good events is the opposite of that used for negative events. You interpret positive events in terms of that which is permanent, universal, and internal, that is, more attributable to your own efforts than to circumstances. For instance, suppose Stan did exceptionally well on an essay exam. Regarding his performance as *temporary* ("It was my lucky day"), *specific* ("It happened to be an easy test, nothing more"), and *external* ("The professor liked me") would tend to undermine Stan's self-confidence by attributing his success mostly to circumstances. However, if Stan regarded his success as *permanent* ("I can take advantage of good luck"), *universal* ("A good essay is one of the many things I do well"), and *internal* ("I think and write well"), his self-esteem would be enhanced and he would perceive control by giv-ing himself sufficient credit for his success. (See Table 12–2.)

TABLE 12–1

OPTIMISTIC VS. PESSIMISTIC STYLE OF EXPLAINING BAD EVENTS

Event: Your best friend hasn't returned your phone calls all day.

Category	Optimistic	Pessimistic
Permanence (time)	Temporary ("She may be especially busy today.")	Permanent ("I guess she isn't going to call back.")
Pervasiveness (space)	Specific ("Not having my phone calls returned doesn't make or break my day.")	Universal ("Well, there goes my day.")
Personalization (locus of self-esteem)	External ("Not returning my calls has more to do with her schedule than her attitude toward me.")	Internal ("No wonder she doesn't call back. I'm so selfish and inconsiderate.")

SOURCE: From *Learned Optimism* by Martin E. P. Seligman. Copyright © 1991 by Martin E. P. Seligman. Reprinted by permission of Alfred A. Knopf, Inc.

TABLE 12–2

OPTIMISTIC VS. PESSIMISTIC STYLE OF EXPLAINING GOOD EVENTS

Event: You do exceptionally well in a job interview.

Category	Optimistic	Pessimistic
Permanence (time)	Permanent ("I can take advantage of good luck.")	Temporary ("It was my lucky day.")
Pervasiveness (space)	Universal ("A successful interview is one of the many things I do well.")	Specific ("It happened to be a good interview, nothing more.")
Personalization (locus of self-esteem)	Internal ("I interview well.")	External ("The interviewer liked me.")

SOURCE: From *Learned Optimism* by Martin E. P. Seligman. Copyright © 1991 by Martin E. P. Seligman. Reprinted by permission of Alfred A. Knopf, Inc.

Although there are clear benefits to learned optimism, there is also a danger, namely, whether or not changing beliefs about failure from internal to external ("It wasn't my fault . . . it was bad luck") will undermine personal responsibility. As a result, Seligman (1992) does not advocate changing beliefs from internal to external in a wholesale manner, although there is one condition under which it is best to do so, namely, depression. When people become depressed, they tend to assume more responsibility, or more accurately, self-blame, for bad events than is warranted. Thus, if people are to change, the internal dimension is less crucial than that of permanence. If you believe the cause of your trouble is permanent, such as the lack of intelligence or talent, you will not act to change it. But if you believe the cause is temporary, such as too little effort or a bad mood, you can act to effect a change.

Furthermore, Seligman (1992) emphasizes that learned optimism is not an absolute, unconditional optimism to be blindly applied to all situations. Instead, it is a *flexible* optimism that is more appropriate in some situations than in others. An optimistic explanatory style tends to be appropriate in the following situations:

• If you're in a situation that involves achievement, such as writing a paper, getting a promotion, or winning a game, it helps to be optimistic. If you're concerned about how you will feel, that is, about keeping up your morale or fighting off discouragement and depression, emphasize the positive.

• If you're under chronic stress and your physical health is an issue, an optimistic outlook becomes crucial.

• If you want to lead, inspire others, or gain people's confidence, it's better to use optimism.

However, there are also times when optimism is not appropriate:

• If your goal involves planning for a risky and uncertain future, do not use optimism.

• If your goal is to counsel others whose future is dim, do not use optimism initially.

• If you want to appear sympathetic to people's troubles, do not start with optimism, although once confidence and empathy are established, optimism may help.

The basic guideline for not choosing optimism is to ask what the cost of failure is in the particular situation. When the cost of failure is high, optimism is the wrong strategy, for example, the party goer deciding whether to drive home after drinking. When the cost of failure is low, optimism is more appropriate, for example, the sales agent who decides to make one more call at the risk only of losing some time.

 ## Decision Making

As we stated earlier, a major means of exercising personal control is through the decisions we make—the basic life choices as well as everyday decisions. From the moment we awake until we go to sleep at night, we must make decisions. Fortunately, many of our day-to-day decisions, such as when to get up and what to eat for breakfast, are made with little effort, mostly because of our habits and daily routines. It is mainly when we encounter a new problem or face an important life choice, as did Stan when he had to decide between his old job or college, that we become acutely aware of the need to make a decision. Then we may become so overwhelmed by the alternatives or so caught up in the mental anguish of considering the consequences of our choice that we put off making the decision. Worse still, we may make a hasty decision to "get it over with," thereby increasing the risk of a poor decision. In both instances, we lose sight of the overall procedure of making decisions we can live with.

In this section we'll explain the process of **decision making** along with some valuable aids for making sound decisions.

THE PROCESS OF DECISION MAKING

Psychologists have formulated a system for making wise decisions—the kind of decisions we can live with. They recommend that we proceed systematically through several stages:

1. *Accept the challenge.* This stage involves recognizing a problem or challenge for what it is, guarding against such hazards as faulty assumptions and oversimplifying a

complex problem. Key question: "What are the risks of doing nothing, or not changing?"

2. *Search for alternatives.* What is most needed at this stage is an attitude of openness and flexibility, with a concern for information about all possible alternatives, obvious or not. Key question: "Have I considered all the alternatives?"

3. *Evaluate the alternatives.* All the options should be evaluated concerning their practicality and consequences. Here you weigh various risks, costs, and possible gains. Key question: "Which is the best alternative?"

4. *Make a commitment.* Ordinarily, it's best to choose the alternative that gives maximum benefits at minimum costs. Yet there's the danger of acting impulsively to "get it over with." Key question: "When do I implement the best alternative and let others know my decision?"

5. *Follow through with your decision.* Because every decision involves some risk, it is important not to overreact in disappointment, criticism, and self-blame. The danger here is often changing your mind prematurely or justifying your choice, thus shutting out valuable feedback. Key questions: "Are the risks serious if I don't change? Are they more serious if I do change?"

A critical element in the decision-making process, especially in the earlier stages, is vigorous information processing. That is, we need to seek out sources of information, take time to read and understand them, and talk to people who are in a position to help us. Gathering information takes time and energy, disrupting our routines and building tension and conflict, all of which can be unpleasant. Consequently, we're usually more willing to look for new information when we expect the benefits of a decision to outweigh the costs. Unfortunately, in making important life choices, such as that of a career, we tend to underestimate the benefits of information gathering and often pay a high price for it. There's nothing so agonizing as discovering an ideal choice *after* we've already committed ourselves to a less desirable course of action—right? Fortunately for Stan, before he paid his first semester of tuition, a major expense for him, he visited the college's career development center to examine career projections for the next decade. These projections estimated the number of jobs in various fields and forecasted future salaries. Armed with this information, Stan was firmly convinced he had made the right decision to enroll in college.

Another element in decision making of which to be mindful is postdecisional regret. It is quite normal after we have made a decision to feel that we may have made an incorrect or poor decision. In other words, we all tend to suffer from the "grass is greener on the other side of the fence" phenomenon. Psychologists call this uncomfortable feeling **cognitive dissonance.** Most people can live with dissonance, especially if they have carefully planned the decision by adequate information gathering. Eventually, the dissonance goes away as we determine that we really did make a good decision or that the unselected alternatives really are less desirable. For Stan, the support of his wife confirmed for him that not returning to his old job but rather staying in college was wise. Postdecisional dissonance or regret did not last a long time for Stan.

There are other processes that essentially take decision making out of our hands. When this happens, we often feel uncomfortable, as we like to control our own decisions and our own actions. One manipulative strategy that others use to influence our decision making is known as **reactance** by social psychologists. Reactance occurs when others limit our **personal freedom** by getting us to do what they want rather than what we want. In other words, we lose some control over our decision making. Box 12–1 reveals more about this social psychological process.

When another individual restricts our freedom (for example, when someone tailgates us to make us drive faster), we experience reactance.

BOX 12–1

Reactance

Reactance is a negative reaction to efforts by others to limit our personal freedom. Others limit our freedom by getting us to behave or decide things in accord with their wishes rather than our wishes. For example, while out driving, you may decide that it is a nice sunny, spring day and that you are not in a hurry. Another car suddenly zooms up behind you and tailgates you. This other driver is nudging you to go faster against your wishes. Although you were previously content to drive at the moderate speed you had selected before the tailgating, you might now decide to drive even more slowly in reaction to this other driver's insistence that you go faster.

Try this little demonstration of reactance. Buy a small bag of potato chips and try to give it to a stranger. The stranger will probably refuse. Perhaps the stranger wanted some chips just before you made the offer, but now you have limited the stranger's ability to decide for him- or herself whether chips are wanted. On the other hand, leave the unopened chips on a table as if they were accidentally left behind by an unfortunate diner. The chips, which appear to be waiting for their rightful owner, will probably quickly disappear because they are not supposed to be taken by anyone else.

Reactance can make us want things we did not previously want and avoid things that we really do want. When was the last time reactance altered your decision or sense of control?

AIDS IN MAKING DECISIONS

Keep in mind that the purpose of making a decision is to bring about desired results and avoid undesirable ones. In this sense, what constitutes a "good" or "bad" decision varies with the individual and his or her situation. At the same time, decision making is often complicated by personal matters, such as our attitudes, values, and tolerance for anxiety. With such factors in mind, we can improve our decision-making skills by following these suggestions.

- *Use sounder judgment.* Judgment, the raw material of decision making, involves drawing inferences from data. Many decisions are doomed from the start because of poor judgment, often involving the human tendency to simplify complex matters into familiar ideas, especially stereotypes. Replace simplistic, intuitive strategies with the more empirical probability orientation that guides scientists, asking yourself such questions as these: What are the facts? How representative are they? What do the alternatives look like? How much is due to situational and chance factors? Sounder judgments may lead to better decisions.

- *Draw up a balance sheet.* This step consists of listing the various advantages and disadvantages of a given course of action. The sample balance sheet in Table 12–3 represents Stan's situation before he made his decision. Students like Stan as well as adults of all ages have found that the balance sheet procedure helps them to make a comprehensive appraisal of a situation requiring a decision and promotes contingency planning, that is, figuring out what to do if something in the minus column materializes. People who use this procedure are more likely to stick to their decisions and express fewer regrets about the options not taken.

- *Clarify your values and objectives.* Many conflicts arise from confusion over values rather than the conflicting alternatives. Because values are neither "good" nor "bad" in themselves, this step requires a personal examination. Once you have clarified your values, they can be translated into tangible objectives that guide your decisions. For example, students are sometimes torn between the need to study, work, socialize, or play, often vacillating in their decisions. Yet

TABLE 12–3
STAN'S BALANCE SHEET: ATTENDING COLLEGE

Projected Consequences	Positive Anticipations	Negative Anticipations
Tangible gains and losses for me	1. Better job prospects 2. Better income 3. More challenging career	1. Hard courses 2. Financial difficulties 3. Need to start over in new job and career
Tangible gains and losses for others	1. Family proud of me 2. Substantial emotional support from family 3. Positive role model for my children	1. Fewer toys and clothes for children and parents 2. Wife will need to work and care for children—more stress for her
Self-approval or disapproval	1. Confidence in mastering challenge 2. Pride in new opportunities	1. Lingering doubts about my academic abilities
Social approval or disapproval	1. Admiration from others for making a midlife change	1. Will be unemployed and perhaps stigmatized due to this

Many New Year's resolutions are made and then soon abandoned.

those who have made a clear choice about what they hope to gain from college will be more likely to resolve their daily decisions effectively.

- *Accept reasonable results.* Nothing is so devastating to decision making as the wish for an "ideal" solution. People with perfectionist tendencies are especially susceptible, although constant striving for perfection guarantees failure. It is usually wiser to accept the most reasonable results under the circumstances. Among the methods of combating perfectionism are recognizing the advantages and disadvantages of perfectionism and comparing how perfectly you did something with how much you enjoyed it. For example, you may feel that you didn't play tennis very well, but you enjoyed the game nevertheless because of the exercise and companionship.

- *Make the best of faulty decisions.* Despite your best efforts, not every decision will turn out to be a wise one. Some common reasons are the limitations in circumstances, unforeseen events, and the difficulty of anticipating how differently you'll view things 10 to 20 years down the road. Yet many people waste time berating themselves or trying to justify their poor decisions. It may be wiser to realize that more often than not they made the best decision possible under the circumstances. It's better to learn from your mistakes and, whenever possible, to modify your decisions to achieve a more desirable result. If all else fails, take heart in the fact that no one makes perfect decisions. Box 12–2 shares some interesting facts about successful as well as failed decision making.

GROUP DECISIONS

Many matters are decided through a process of shared decision making, either informally, as when Stan and his wife pondered his return to college, or through a more formalized process of decision making, such as the deliberations of a jury. We have already

- Half the people who make New Year's resolutions give up within 3 months? Nearly one-quarter give up the first week?
- Those who put their resolutions in writing or reveal them openly are more likely to achieve them?
- Indecisive people who exercise regularly for a few months become more decisive during this period?
- It's easier to choose between two desirable outcomes, such as attaining better health or more money, than between two undesirable ones, such as being ill or poor?
- Our decisions are affected by whether the outcome is presented positively or negatively; for example, more people elect to have surgery when told they have a 90 percent chance of living than when told they have a 10 percent chance of dying?
- When we freely choose an activity, we become more involved in it and enjoy it more than when we feel it is something "expected" of us?

discussed group decision making at length in the chapter on group processes but can add some relevant information here.

Group decisions *can* be superior to those made by individuals, especially when people can creatively use differences of opinion and conflict. Some guidelines for achieving creative consensus in groups are:

1. Realize that differences of opinion are natural and may lead to better solutions.
2. Present your views, but listen to those of others.
3. Don't feel that someone has to win and someone has to lose.
4. Explore the reasons for the various views, yielding only to those that have objective and logically sound foundations.
5. Strive for the best possible decision or solution.

 ## Decisions and Personal Growth

Decisions are especially crucial in regard to personal growth, including overcoming problem behaviors. All too often, people become stuck in self-defeating behaviors because they've never made a decision to change their ways. Change may be resisted because of the inertia of past habits, psychological laziness, or simply fear. When confronted with the need for change, people become defensive, although they may promise to change if threatened with the loss of their jobs or their family's love. However, many of those who enter psychotherapy or a treatment program drop out prematurely, mostly because they haven't made a firm decision to change. For instance, while talking with a classmate who works with alcoholics and people who are drug dependent, Stan asked at what point in the program clients begin making significant progress. "It's hard to say,"

Better that a few hundred people risk ulcers negotiating peace than thousands lose their lives on the battlefield.

he said, "because so much depends on when a person makes up his or her mind to change. In fact, we won't even admit people into our program until they have made some sort of commitment to change."

A similar realization led Harold Greenwald (1973, 1984) to adopt a new approach to treating clients, which eventually was called **direct decision therapy.** Greenwald was convinced that the main occurrence in therapy, regardless of the techniques used, is that the client is helped to make a decision to change and then is supported in carrying out that decision. Direct decision therapy is aimed at helping people to see their problems in terms of their past decisions, to examine the consequences of such decisions, and then to choose a more satisfying alternative. Greenwald readily admits that this approach has been helpful in his own personal life, including his earlier decision to become a psychologist. He has also found that many people who have never participated in therapy have benefited from applying the principles of decision therapy to their personal lives. (See Figure 12–2.)

IDENTIFYING THE BASIC DECISIONS IN YOUR LIFE

According to Greenwald, a good beginning point is to find the basic decisions underlying our everyday behavior, especially problem behavior. Although we may be aware that our behavior is a reaction to people and situations, on closer examination we may find that we have *chosen* to act in a certain way. Greenwald speaks of the "decision behind the decision," referring to basic life choices involving our needs and motivation, which we're only dimly aware of, if at all. Yet once such decisions are made,

FIGURE 12–2

USING DECISION MAKING FOR PERSONAL GROWTH

Greenwald has outlined the following suggestions for applying the principles of decision therapy to yourself:

1. State your problem as clearly and completely as you can. Your problem need not be acute or a crisis, just something you would like to deal with. You may even find it helpful to put it in writing.

2. See each problem not as something that just happened to you but as the consequence of a decision you have made. Such a problem could be something you decided to do, something you decided to be, or some way you decided to regard other people.

3. Look for the basic decision behind the decision. Did you decide to have the problem to avoid something? If so, what were you avoiding?

4. List the advantages and payoffs of the decision. These may be actual positive gains or may include the avoidance of anxiety. In either case, they are still payoffs.

5. What was the context in which you made the original decision? Were you very young? What was the situation then? Was your decision a sound one, given the circumstances?

6. Ask yourself if the context is different now that you're older. Maybe the payoffs are not so important or have become more trouble than they are worth.

7. List the alternatives to each decision you've made. Examine them in terms of the advantages and disadvantages of each.

8. Now choose one of the alternatives and decide to put it into practice. Revealing your decision to friends or colleagues may help you carry it out.

9. If you have trouble putting the decision into practice, go back to the first suggestion to see if you're still operating under an old decision. Remember that what you actually do is the best clue to the decision you've made, not what you'd like or wish to do.

10. Remember that it's not enough to make your decision only once. You must reaffirm your decision repeatedly. For example, if you decide to lose weight, each time you sit down to eat you must reaffirm your decision.

11. If you fail occasionally in carrying out your decision, that doesn't mean that you have to give up altogether. Because most of us are not infallible, we must be able to accept an occasional failure, pick ourselves up, and continue with our decision.

SOURCE: Adapted from Harold Greenwald, *Direct Decision Therapy* (San Diego, CA: Edits Publishers, 1973). Reprinted with permission.

we usually organize our lives around them and our perceptions as well, so that we understand everything that happens to us in a certain way. Some practical examples illustrate that point.

Take Stan's wife, Susan, for example. Before Stan decided that he wanted to return to college, Susan was unsure what she wanted to do. After high school and before marriage, she had gone to secretarial school and had worked as a secretary until she met Stan and had their first child. For the next 10 years Susan talked, but only talked, about returning for a college degree. Have you ever wondered why people procrastinate or fail to put forth their best efforts on important matters? Often such behavior is the outgrowth of a basic life choice to protect themselves from failure or hurt, though they may not be aware of it. Perhaps Susan was afraid that she would not succeed in college, but once Stan decided to return to college and give up his job, she had no choice. She had to return to secretarial work to help supplement the family income. College was out of the question for her. Another example is a young man who waits until August to apply for college admission. In both instances, these individuals have a face-saving excuse if they fail—"I was too late." Somewhere in the dim past, each has made a basic decision to play it safe because of a fear of failure or of getting hurt. Only when they change that decision will they put forth their best efforts and have a greater chance of success.

Much negative behavior, such as rebelliousness and defiance, is also the result of a basic life decision, though again not in the person's awareness. For example, Stan's neighbor's son, Bobby, left home in his late teens because of constant fights with his father whom he considered overly strict. Nevertheless, even after leaving home, he was still known to be "touchy" and "hard to get along with," even by his friends. He was always doing the opposite of what people expected of him, often with disappointing results. Bobby had made a choice in opposition to what he believed was coercive parental authority: He had decided "No!" Until this rebellion, he was an appendage of his parents. But after rebelling, he felt more in charge of his life. Nor should that surprise us because the defiance of the young child or adolescent is often the initial step toward autonomy. However, as long as this young man remained stuck in this initial but negative stage of independence, his life was destined to be controlled more by what he was against than what he was for.

MAKING NEW DECISIONS

It is only when a *wish* to change leads to a *decision* to change that we really change and grow. For example, many smokers dislike their smoking habit. They say things such as "I'd *like* to stop smoking" and "I *hope* to give it up soon" and "I *plan* to cut down on my smoking." But until they *decide* to stop smoking and learn how to implement that decision, nothing happens.

So far we have assumed that people will automatically decide to change for the better, but this is not always the case. In some instances, people may become so overwhelmed with the anxiety and risks of change or fear postdecisional regret so much that they decide to remain the way they are, however unsatisfying or painful that may be. Nor can someone be forced into growth, especially by therapists who are militant about people living up to their human potential. However well-intentioned such therapists may be, they can make the same mistakes that parents and spouses are prone to make—namely, trying to tell someone else what he or she ought to decide. Rather, the therapist's task is to help the client first to discover what he or she wants to do and then to make a personal decision to do it. As most of us have discovered, once you know what you want to do and really decide to do it, you're well on your way.

SOME PRACTICAL APPLICATIONS

One of the most common examples of decision making is decision by default. Putting things off, whether temporarily or indefinitely, is itself a decision. An example that comes to mind is a young man who was having considerable difficulty completing his doctoral dissertation, partly because of emotional blocks in writing and partly because of conflicts with his advisor. This young man became so frustrated that he simply turned his efforts elsewhere. He took an administrative post at the university ("while I finish my degree") and spent more time painting ("to take my mind off my problems"). Several years later, when asked how his degree program was progressing, he said he had finally "decided" to give it up. Actually, he had made that decision earlier. The failure to make a positive decision is itself a decision with fateful consequences.

Overcoming negative, self-defeating behavior usually involves making a positive decision at a basic level of motivation. For example, when Stan's sister, Janet, was 24, she was bothered by depression and a poor relationship with her supervisor. She reported that she was constantly complaining at work and was especially critical of her boss, often without an apparent reason. During some counseling Janet discovered that earlier in her life she had learned to suppress her anger for fear of parental disapproval. She had become a passive, "good" little girl but resented those on whom she remained dependent. Gradually, she learned to take more initiative, to show her anger more directly, but as an expression of her feelings rather than as judgmental remarks that might put others on the defensive. As Janet became more assertive, she felt less depressed and enjoyed a more satisfying relationship with those in authority. She also returned to school for a master's degree and later assumed a supervisory position.

Sometimes it is wise to make a decision that counters or reverses an earlier commitment that has led to undesirable consequences. For example, Stan's brother-in-law was a 45-year-old lawyer who married the daughter of a senior partner in his firm. He admits having married out of "mixed motives." That is, although he had been genuinely attracted to his wife, he had also hoped that his "connections" would enhance his career. He soon discovered that conflicts with his father-in-law complicated his life both at work and at home. Consultation with a specialist about his asthma attacks, which seemed worse during joint vacations at his in-laws' summer house, suggested that they were brought on by emotional conflicts concerning his in-laws. Gradually, Stan's brother-in-law realized that it had not been a good idea to marry the "boss's daughter," and eventually he decided to start his own firm. Although he went through a few lean years, he soon had a flourishing law practice and was much happier in his marriage as well. Failure to make such a courageous decision often results in feeling trapped in one's career, drinking problems, or extramarital affairs.

Sometimes dramatic improvements involve group decision making. In one instance, the quality of work had gotten so bad that Stan's former company was considering simply closing several divisions. As a final gesture, the manager suggested that officials inform the workers of the situation and ask for their suggestions. They discovered that the workers themselves were well aware of their poor work, although they justified it because of poor working conditions. Nevertheless, they wanted to improve the situation just as much as the company officials did. A group decision was reached to save the plant, involving concessions from both management and labor. During a 6-month probationary period, a new policy was adopted involving workers' suggestions to improve assembly-line production, to improve treatment of workers, and to make the work more meaningful. Each team of workers followed a product through the assembly line and became responsible for the acceptance of the final product. The improvement in productivity and quality of work was so dramatic that the plant not only survived but also became a model for the rest of the plants in the parent company.

SUMMARY

PERSONAL CONTROL

We began by discussing the importance of personal control in our lives. Emphasis has been placed on attaining greater *perceived control*—the belief that we can influence the occurrence of events in our environment that determine our lives. People who underestimate the control they have over their lives exhibit learned helplessness; those who exaggerate their personal control exhibit the illusion of control. In both cases, the misperception of control leads to maladaptive behavior. In contrast, people who are high in realistically perceived control tend to be less anxious and better adjusted. A way to achieve optimal perceived control is through what Martin Seligman calls learned optimism—interpreting life events in a reasonably accurate way that enhances our perceived control and, thus, our adaptive response to events.

DECISION MAKING

A major way of exercising personal control is through our life choices and everyday decisions. Guidelines for making sound decisions include five stages: Accept the challenge, search for alternatives, evaluate the alternatives, make a commitment, and follow through with the decision. We may improve our decision-making skills by better judgment, the balance sheet procedure, clarifying our objectives, accepting reasonable results, and making the best of a poor decision. Group decisions may be inferior or superior to individual decisions, depending largely on whether the group suppresses differences of opinion or encourages the expression of differences as a way of reaching the best decision, as in the more desirable decision-making process.

DECISIONS AND PERSONAL GROWTH

We can promote personal growth by applying the principles of Harold Greenwald's direct decision therapy to our personal lives. This approach is aimed at helping people to see their problems in terms of their past decisions, to examine the consequences of such decisions, and then to choose a more satisfying alternative. In this way, we learn to view our problems and unfulfilled potential more in terms of our decisions than as the result of events and circumstances that simply happen. However, it's only when a wish to change leads to a personal decision to change that our personal lives begin to improve. Also, we must reaffirm our decision to change repeatedly, accepting an occasional failure and picking ourselves up and continuing our commitment to personal growth.

SCORING KEY FOR THE LOCUS OF CONTROL SCALE

Give yourself one point each time your response agrees with the answer in the scoring key. Your overall score is the sum of all your points.

1. Yes	21. Yes
2. No	22. No
3. Yes	23. Yes
4. No	24. Yes
5. Yes	25. No
6. No	26. No
7. Yes	27. Yes
8. Yes	28. No
9. No	29. Yes
10. Yes	30. No
11. Yes	31. Yes
12. Yes	32. No
13. No	33. Yes
14. Yes	34. No
15. No	35. Yes
16. Yes	36. Yes
17. Yes	37. Yes
18. Yes	38. No
19. Yes	39. Yes
20. No	40. No

Low scorers (0–8). About one-third of those who complete the scale attain a score of 0 to 8. These people tend to have an internal locus of control; that is, they perceive themselves as being largely responsible for their successes and failures in life.

Average scorers (9–16). Most people score in the 9 to 16 range. Such people see themselves as having partial control over their lives, such as being in control at work but less so in their social relationships.

High scorers (17–40). About 15 percent of respondents earn scores of 17 or above. Such high scorers tend to have an external locus of control, believing that success or failure in life is more a matter of luck or other people's generosity than their own efforts.

SELF-TEST

1. The belief that you can influence events in your environment that affect your life is known as
   a. perceived control
   b. external control
   c. the illusion of control
   d. a psychological delusion

2. The maladaptive passivity that frequently follows people's experience with uncontrollable events is called
   a. the Type A syndrome
   b. learned helplessness
   c. the illusion of control
   d. shuttling

3. People who exhibit high perceived control tend to
   a. exhibit high anxiety about themselves
   b. make only average grades in school
   c. attribute their successes to good luck
   d. use effective strategies for coping with stress

4. Explaining negative events in temporary, specific, and external terms is a way of increasing which outlook?
   a. learned helplessness
   b. the illusion of control
   c. learned optimism
   d. external locus of control

5. The first stage of decision making is to
   a. evaluate the alternatives
   b. make a commitment
   c. accept the challenge
   d. search for alternatives

6. The final stage of the decision-making process consists of
   a. following through with the decision
   b. making a commitment
   c. evaluating the alternatives
   d. accepting the challenge

7. One way to improve your decision-making skills is to
   a. make decisions more quickly
   b. accept only the best decisions
   c. use sounder judgment
   d. put aside your values

8. A common phenomenon after a decision has been made is the experience of
   a. a feeling of external control
   b. elation
   c. pessimism
   d. cognitive dissonance

9. Following the principles of direct decision therapy, we would initially state our problems
   a. as something that happened to us
   b. in terms of changes we'd like to make
   c. as the consequences of decisions we've made
   d. in terms of our value conflicts

10. Once we've made a decision to change our behavior in some way, we
    a. must reaffirm this decision repeatedly
    b. automatically begin to change our behavior
    c. should never share this decision with others
    d. should never accept even occasional failures

EXERCISES

1. *Personal control.* To what extent do you believe you can influence the occurrence of events in your environment that affect your life? In a page or so, discuss the degree of personal control you have over your life, emphasizing perceived control, or the

belief you can control your life. How does your belief affect specific aspects of your life, such as your work, intimate relationships, fitness, and health?

2. *Understanding bad outcomes.* Select some negative event that has happened to you over which you had little control, such as losing your job because of a layoff at work. Then explain this event in terms of the three categories of causal explanation discussed in the chapter, that is, permanence, pervasiveness, and personalization. To what extent do you now understand this event in temporary, specific, and external terms?

3. *Stages in decision making.* Review the five stages of decision making discussed in the chapter. Select an important decision you're about to make or one you've already made. Then analyze it in terms of the five stages of the decision-making process. How well did you follow these five stages? What do you find to be the most difficult part of making decisions?

4. *Aids in making decisions.* Reread the section on aids in making sounder decisions. Then select one of the poorer decisions you've made, and review this decision in light of these aids. What do you think you need to do to make better decisions in the future?

5. *Group decisions.* Select some group to which you belong, such as a couple, family, work group, or some other organization. Then in a page or so, explain the extent to which this group usually suppresses differences of opinion in order to arrive at a decision, any decision, or encourages differences of opinion as a way of making the best possible decision.

6. *Decision making and personal growth.* Select some aspect of your life, such as a habit or problem behavior, that you would like to change. Then apply Greenwald's principles of direct decision therapy. Do you consider the problem behavior to be partly the result of some other decisions you've made? Have you made a deliberate decision to change your behavior, or do you merely wish to?

QUESTIONS FOR SELF-REFLECTION

1. How much control do you believe you have over your life?
2. Are you inclined to underestimate your level of personal control?
3. Or do you suffer from the illusion of control?
4. When there appears to be no choice in a situation, what do you do?
5. How do you go about making important decisions?
6. Do you often "decide" things by *not* deciding?
7. Are you willing to take calculated risks?
8. What was the best decision you ever made? Why was your decision process successful?
9. What was your worst decision? What would you do differently now?
10. How much truth is there in the saying that "life is what happens to us while we're making other plans"?

FOR FURTHER INFORMATION

RECOMMENDED READINGS

BANDURA, A. (1997). *Self-efficacy: The exercise of control.* New York: W. H. Freeman. The leading authority on self-agency writes about its development and its uses.

LOGUE, A. W. (1995). *Self-control: Waiting until tomorrow for what you want today.* Englewood Cliffs, NJ: Prentice Hall. A book for those who think they have little self-control but would like to develop it.

MILIOS, R. (1992). *Discovering positive thinking.* New York: Rosen Publishing Group. An interesting book about optimism and self-esteem.

SELIGMAN, M. E. P. (1992). *Learned optimism.* New York: Pocket Books. Shows how we can acquire an optimistic outlook by altering the way we explain disappointments and failure to ourselves.

SNYDER, C. R. (1994). *The psychology of hope: You can get there from here.* New York: Free Press. A book for those who feel hopeless and want to reverse this trend.

WEBSITES AND THE INTERNET

http://www.calabrese.com/decision/: Tips on decision making and useful products for sale such as a self-help checklist to improve decision making.

http:drum.reference.be/wo-mancracy/network.html: A website for women involved in decision making, especially in political decisions.

http//.www.demon.co.uklmindtool/apprecn.html: A site that provides what it calls mind maps to help sharpen your analytical skills.

alt.society.civil-liberty: A world-wide website discussion group for all civil liberties and freedoms.

http://orpheus.ucsd.edu/sdm/shared/htm: For those who are involved in joint or group decision making and designed to enhance such decisions.

CHAPTER 13

Psychological Disorders

After completing this chapter, you should be able to

1. Describe the four characteristic features of a psychological disorder.
2. Identify the *DSM-IV.*
3. Describe several anxiety disorders.
4. Distinguish between a major depression and bipolar disorder.
5. List the warning signs of suicide.
6. Describe the characteristic features of anorexia and bulimia.
7. Explain the diathesis-stress hypothesis of schizophrenia.

Lisa, age 28, was a happy young adult with a good job in the loan department of a bank. She began working for the bank immediately upon her graduation from college and slowly worked her way up through the ranks such that she held a good mid-level management job. She was engaged to Joseph, a nice looking man who worked in a different department of the bank. Lisa recently moved back home to live with her elderly, widowed mother who was having some health problems. Although Lisa was not very happy about this arrangement, as it restricted her freedom after work and the time she could spend with Joe, she nonetheless felt it was her duty as a good daughter, as the only child of her parents, to care for her ailing mother. Just when Lisa thought her mother was improving, her mother suddenly died. The surprise of this event deepened Lisa's grief. At the same time, her mother's health care left Lisa and her mother's estate with some large unpaid bills. Lisa became more depressed as she tried to manage the aftermath of her mother's death. After about 2 months of working on her mother's estate, Joe greeted Lisa with another unpleasant surprise. He announced that he wanted to break their engagement. In the time that Lisa had been caring for her mother, Joe had met another woman and wanted to date her. Again, Lisa was stunned and saddened. As if this weren't enough to worry her, there were rumors at the bank that the work force would soon be downsized. Lisa soon found that she had difficulty getting out of bed. She would stand in her closet for a long time trying to decide what to wear each morning before work. In fact, she began missing work; she would call in sick even though she really felt she was just tired. Eventually, Lisa's coworkers began noticing that she seemed somewhat disheveled, not the old meticulous Lisa. Lisa's hair was uncut and not well combed.

Sometimes she wore the same clothes all week only to have the same garments reappear the following week. Lisa's coworkers also noticed that she was losing weight. One day Lisa did not appear for work but neither did she call in sick. After this happened 3 more days in a row, one of the coworkers went to Lisa's house to find her in bed alternately staring at the ceiling and sobbing. Lisa appeared normal, at least she was able to carry on a normal conversation, but she did not want to get out of bed or to eat anything. The coworker also found that the house was a mess. There was garbage overflowing the trash cans, newspapers and clothing were strewn everywhere, the mail was unopened, and empty food cans littered the kitchen. "What was wrong with Lisa?" wondered her coworker.

 Understanding Psychological Disorders

Among themselves, Lisa's coworkers and friends might call her "neurotic" or "nuts." Others might refer to her as a "flake" or a "weirdo." Upon hearing of her admission to the hospital, they might say Lisa was having a "nervous breakdown." Psychologists and other mental health workers generally avoid such terms because they are negative. Instead, these professionals tend to focus on more relevant matters, such as Lisa's intense personal distress and the degree of impairment in her everyday behavior. In short, mental health workers would be concerned about the type and severity of Lisa's disorder and, thus, how best to help her. As it turned out, Lisa was suffering from a depressive disorder, one of the most common and potentially disabling disorders, as we'll explain later in this chapter.

The study of psychological disorders is often associated with abnormal behavior because many disorders involve thoughts, feelings, or actions that are not considered normal. Yet abnormal behavior and psychological disorders are not synonymous. For instance, some forms of depression are too common to be labeled abnormal or statistically out of the normal but are nevertheless classified as a psychological disorder. Other behaviors may be considered socially deviant, such as bathing nude at a public beach, without being a psychological disorder. Consequently, we'll begin by looking at some of the common standards used in defining psychological disorders, the incidence of such disorders, and how they are classified.

WHAT ARE PSYCHOLOGICAL DISORDERS?

You may be surprised to discover that there is no precise and universally agreed on standard that distinguishes between abnormal and normal behavior or, for that matter, between the presence of a **psychological disorder** and no disorder. Probably the best guide in these matters is the authoritative *Diagnostic and Statistical Manual of Mental*

Disorders, fourth edition, published by the American Psychiatric Association. This manual is popularly referred to as the *DSM-IV* (American Psychiatric Association, 1994). At the outset, the authors acknowledge the difficulties in defining a psychological disorder, much less specifying precise boundaries to particular disorders. Thus, they define a psychological disorder as a clinically significant behavioral or psychological pattern that is associated with (1) present distress (a painful symptom); (2) disability or impairment in one or more important areas of functioning; (3) significantly increased risk of suffering disability, pain, or death; and (4) an important loss of freedom or personal control (p. xxi).

A major factor is the individual's level of **personal distress,** or *discomfort.* Someone with a chronic fear of heights or a marked change in mood as in severe depression would be diagnosed as having a psychological disorder. Yet people who behave in an unusual or eccentric way but are otherwise happy would not be so diagnosed. Many professionals have adopted the concept of level of personal distress in their view of homosexuality. That is, homosexual behavior itself is not considered a disorder. It is only when individuals are seriously distressed by their homosexual orientation that it is considered a psychological disorder.

As useful as this standard of "personal distress" is, it isn't sufficiently comprehensive by itself. We need to consider other factors. What about the aggressive behavior of a domineering person who feels no remorse for the distress inflicted on others? Such behavior may fall into the category of *personality disorders,* a group of disorders that gives less discomfort to the people who have them than to those who have to deal with them—their coworkers and families.

Another important factor in defining a disorder is **maladaptive behavior.** People with psychological disorders usually suffer from a significant impairment in one or more areas of psychological functioning, especially in their inability to work, to care for themselves, or to get along with family and friends. This is a practical approach because it focuses on behavior that is relative to life circumstances. Accordingly, expected behavior like intense grief in response to a friend's death would not be considered a disorder. Also, atypical behavior motivated by political or religious dissent or conflicts that are primarily between the individual and society are not considered psychological disorders, unless the atypicality or conflict is a *symptom* of a dysfunction within the person.

Still another important consideration involves the violation of **social norms.** People in every studied society live by certain rules of what is acceptable and unacceptable behavior. For instance, it may be acceptable to eat food at a rock concert but not at a symphony concert. Yet acceptable eating behavior varies around the world. In most societies, people commonly eat in public but urinate in private, though just the reverse occurs in some societies. Consequently, what is considered abnormal varies somewhat from one culture to another, as do the rates of the various psychological disorders. For instance, the prevalence of depression is low in China and many parts of Africa—just the opposite of its occurrence in the United States. One explanation is that in "Western" societies, individuals are more likely to be held personally responsible for their failures and misfortunes and are thus susceptible to depression.

As you can see, there is no simple way of determining when someone has a psychological disorder. In practice, mental health professionals rely on a combination of standards to determine whether a given behavior is normal or not or is classified as disordered. Personal distress, significant impairment in one or more areas of functioning, the social acceptability of the individual's behavior, and an important loss of personal control are all taken into account, though in varying degrees.

THE OCCURRENCE OF DISORDERS

Much of our information about the extent of psychological disorders comes from in-depth surveys of representative samples of the population, along with admission figures to various mental health facilities such as psychiatric hospitals and community mental health clinics. Two frequently used terms are *incidence* and *prevalence*. **Incidence** refers to the number of new cases of disorders reported during a given period. This term is usually distinguished from **prevalence,** which refers to the total number of active cases that can be identified in a given population at a particular time.

During any 6-month period, mental health experts estimate that one in five adults will suffer from some type of psychological disorder, according to surveys conducted by the National Institute of Mental Health (Robins & Regier, 1991). Overall, about one out of every three persons will experience at least one significant psychological problem in his or her lifetime. Fortunately for you, college graduates generally report fewer such ailments than noncollege graduates. This then makes Lisa's case a bit unusual.

People who have a psychological disorder usually have their first symptoms by early adulthood; three-fourths of those surveyed reporting their first symptoms by age 24. In this case, Lisa is more typical. However, symptoms of alcohol abuse, obsessive-compulsive behavior, bipolar disorder, and schizophrenia appear somewhat earlier, at a median age near 20. Table 13–1 shows the relative prevalence of selected disorders among Americans.

There's a popular notion that more women than men are emotionally disturbed. Is there any truth to this view? Apparently not. When all disorders are taken into account, men and women are equally likely to suffer from psychological disorders. However, the patterns of disorders differ somewhat between the sexes. Women suffer more from phobias (intense and irrational **fear**) and depression (a sense of hopelessness and lack of pleasure in life much as that experienced by Lisa), and men are more apt to abuse alcohol and drugs and exhibit long-term antisocial behavior. At the same time, women are twice as likely as men to seek help, which may have given the mistaken impression in the past that women were more troubled than men.

Figures regarding the prevalence or *total* number of active cases in the population are even more alarming. According to conservative estimates, there are about 30 million people who suffer from anxiety disorders, 4.5 million people with schizophrenia, and 17.5 million people with personality disorders, all of which are discussed in this

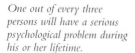

One out of every three persons will have a serious psychological problem during his or her lifetime.

TABLE 13–1
OCCURRENCE OF SELECTED PSYCHOLOGICAL DISORDERS

	Ethnicity			Sex		
	Caucasian	African American	Hispanic	Men	Women	Total
Alcohol abuse or dependence	13.6%	13.8%	16.7%	23.8%	4.6%	13.8%
Generalized anxiety	3.4	6.1	3.7	2.4	5.0	3.8
Phobic disorder	9.7	23.4	12.2	10.4	17.7	14.3
Obsessive-compulsive	2.6	2.3	1.8	2.0	3.0	2.6
Mood disorder	8.0	6.3	7.8	5.2	10.2	7.8
Schizophrenic disorders	1.4	2.1	0.8	1.2	1.7	1.5
Antisocial personality	2.6	2.3	3.4	4.5	0.8	2.6

SOURCE: Adapted with permission of The Free Press, a Division of Simon & Schuster, from *Psychiatric Disorders in America: The Epidemiologic Catchment Area Study* by Lee N. Robins and Darrel A. Regier. Copyright © 1991 by Lee N. Robins and Darrel A. Regier.

chapter. Although mood disorders are so widespread that it's difficult to estimate the total number of clinically depressed people who are like Lisa, at least 1 million suffer from severe mood disorders with psychotic features. In addition, it is estimated that between 10 and 15 percent of school-age children are clinically maladjusted, and about 5 percent of the aged population suffers from several emotional disturbances caused by organic factors, usually destruction of brain tissue or biochemical imbalances in the brain.

CLASSIFYING DISORDERS

Because there are no sharp boundaries between the various psychological disorders, as well as between a psychological disorder and no disorder, you can readily appreciate the difficulty of classifying the various disorders. Lisa's coworker was fairly sure there was something amiss with Lisa the day she visited Lisa's home, but she was not certain what it was. So, too, might a psychologist or psychiatrist be puzzled at first about the type and extent of Lisa's disorder. However, within the limitations mentioned earlier, the *DSM-IV* classifies, defines, and describes over 200 psychological disorders, using practical criteria as the basis of classification. To arrive at a diagnosis—in which the problem is classified within a set of recognized categories of abnormal behavior—the clinician compares the behavior of the patient with the description in the manual and then selects the label of the description that best fits the problem. The purpose is to provide an accurate description of the person's overall problem and functioning, along with a prediction of the course of the disorder, which helps during treatment.

Throughout the *DSM-IV,* the emphasis is on classifying *behavior* patterns, not people, as is often thought. Thus, the manual refers to "people who exhibit the symptoms of schizophrenia" rather than to "schizophrenics." Also, the terminology refers to "mental health professionals" and "clinicians" instead of "psychiatrists,'" thereby acknowledging the broader range of workers who deal with people with psychological disorders. Finally, the emphasis is on *describing* rather than interpreting psychological disorders, especially when the causal factors are unknown. Thus, the *DSM-IV* gives clinicians a practical, behavioral approach to dealing with people exhibiting symptoms of psychological disorders.

TABLE 13–2
SELECTED CATEGORIES OF PSYCHOLOGICAL DISORDERS IN THE *DSM-IV*

Organic mental disorders	Psychological or behavioral abnormalities associated with a temporary or permanent brain dysfunction	Senile dementia[a]
Disorders arising in childhood or adolescence	Disorders that are first evident in these stages of development	Anorexia[a] Bulimia[a] Mental retardation
Personality disorders	Long-standing patterns of thought and behavior that are maladaptive	Narcissistic personality[a] Antisocial personality[a]
Mood disorders	Disturbances of mood that pervade one's entire life	Depression[a] Bipolar disorder[a] Panic attacks[a]
Anxiety disorders	Disorders in which the main symptom is anxiety or attempts to escape from anxiety	Phobias[a] Obsessive-compulsive disorder[a]
Somatoform disorders	Disorders involving physical symptoms with no known physical cause, often associated with stress	Psychogenic pain disorder
Dissociative disorders	Sudden loss or alteration in the integrative functions of consciousness	Amnesia (not caused by organic mental disorder) Multiple personality
Sexual disorders	Disorders of sexual functioning or identity caused by psychological factors	Sexual dysfunctions, e.g., erectile dysfunctions, inhibited orgasm[a]
Factitious disorders	Physical or psychological symptoms voluntarily produced by the individual, often involving deliberate deceit	Factitious disorder with psychological symptoms
Disorders of impulse control	Difficulties controlling one's emotions or behavior	Pathological gambling
Adjustment disorder	Impaired functioning due to identifiable life stresses, such as family or economic crises	Adjustment disorder with academic inhibition Adjustment disorder with depressed mood
Schizophrenic disorders	Serious alterations of thought and behavior that represent a split from reality	Disorganized, paranoid, catatonic, and undifferentiated types of schizophrenia[a]
Substance use disorders	Undesirable behavioral changes associated with the use of drugs that affect the central nervous system	Alcohol abuse or dependence[a] Amphetamine abuse or dependence

[a]Denote disorders that are discussed in this chapter or another chapter of this book.

SOURCE: Reprinted with permission from *Diagnostic and Statistical Manual of Mental Disorders,* Fourth Edition. Copyright 1994 American Psychiatric Association.

We'll describe several of the more common or serious disorders, such as the anxiety disorders, affective or mood disorders, personality disorders, and schizophrenia, in the body of this chapter. In addition, some of the other disorders will be highlighted in separate boxed items. An overall list of many of the major categories of disorders described in the *DSM-IV* is shown in Table 13–2.

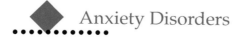

Anxiety Disorders

As you may recall from the chapter on emotions, a mild to moderate level of anxiety may be helpful in mobilizing us to meet a threat, such as studying for an important exam. However, an excessive level of anxiety becomes disruptive, making it difficult to concentrate and to perform well. Although our anxiety level fluctuates somewhat, depending largely on the situation, individuals also differ from one another.

In an **anxiety disorder,** the anxiety is all out of proportion to the stressful situation or may occur in the absence of any specific danger. Anxiety may be experienced in several ways. In a **generalized anxiety disorder,** the anxiety itself becomes the predominant disturbance. Either the person is anxious most of the time or suffers from periodical panic attacks, as in the closely related panic disorder. However, in a **phobic disorder,** the anxiety is evoked by some dreaded object or situation, such as flying in an airplane. In the **obsessive-compulsive disorder,** anxiety occurs if the people do *not* engage in a particular thought or avoidance behavior, for example, repeatedly rechecking a door they have already locked, which may be senseless and often embarrassing even to the individuals themselves.

GENERALIZED ANXIETY DISORDER

The main characteristic of generalized anxiety disorder is a persistent sense of "free-floating" anxiety. People who are chronically anxious can't say what they are afraid of. All they know is that they feel on edge all the time. They generally worry a lot and anticipate the occurrence of something bad. Lisa, for example, felt this way when her mother was ill, but the anxiety did not incapacitate her. For example, she did not feel the symptoms associated with anxiety, such as cold sweat, pounding heart, and dry mouth as do people with generalized anxiety disorder. Lisa also knew the cause of her anxiety. Anxiety may disrupt the everyday functioning of individuals with generalized anxiety disorder, so that they may find it hard to concentrate and make decisions. People with this disorder may also develop headaches, muscular tension, indigestion, a strained face, and fidgeting. Frequently they become apprehensive about their anxiety, fearing their condition will give them ulcers or a heart attack or make them go crazy.

Chronically anxious people may also suffer from **panic attacks,** attacks that occur in the absence of a feared situation. In many instances, the attack occurs in response to a specific phobic situation, such as driving in city traffic or speaking publicly. In a panic attack, anxiety increases to an almost intolerable level. The people break out in a cold sweat, feel dizzy, and may have difficulty breathing. Almost always they have a feeling of inescapable doom, as if they won't make it to safety or will die. Panic attacks may last only a few minutes or continue for hours. Afterward, the victims feel exhausted. Because panic attacks are unpredictable, they often create additional anxiety, and the victims avoid certain situations in which they fear losing control or being helpless.

For example, Cynthia, a young woman who graduated from the same university as Lisa, suffered from periodic panic attacks while at college. She couldn't concentrate on her studies, had difficulty sleeping, and complained of stomach pains. The college counselor observed that these attacks occurred toward the end of a semester, usually before a long holiday. Cynthia said she loved her parents and looked forward to going home. Yet as the end of the semester approached, she became more susceptible to panic attacks. In her discussions with the counselor, Cynthia discovered that her anxiety was precipitated by problems at home. She felt caught in a conflict between her parents, who were separated. Because she was unable to cope with the pressure to side with her mother or father, the prospect of going home for the holidays evoked intense anxiety.

To determine your general level of anxiety, try the scale in Figure 13–1.

FIGURE 13–1

Self-Rating Anxiety Scale (SAS)

Put a check in the column indicating how often each of the following statements has applied to you during the past 2 weeks.

A—None or little of the time
B—Some of the time
C—A good part of the time
D—Most or all of the time

Statement	A	B	C	D
1. I feel more nervous and anxious than usual.	—	—	—	—
2. I feel afraid for no reason at all.	—	—	—	—
3. I get upset easily or feel panicky.	—	—	—	—
4. I feel like I'm falling apart and going to pieces.	—	—	—	—
5. I feel that everything is all right and nothing bad will happen.	—	—	—	—
6. My arms and legs shake and tremble.	—	—	—	—
7. I am bothered by headaches, neck and back pains.	—	—	—	—
8. I feel weak and get tired easily.	—	—	—	—
9. I feel calm and can sit still easily.	—	—	—	—
10. I can feel my heart beating fast.	—	—	—	—
11. I am bothered by dizzy spells.	—	—	—	—
12. I have fainting spells or feel like it.	—	—	—	—
13. I can breathe in and out easily.	—	—	—	—
14. I get feelings of numbness and tingling in my fingers and toes.	—	—	—	—
15. I am bothered by stomachaches or indigestion.	—	—	—	—
16. I have to empty my bladder often.	—	—	—	—
17. My hands are usually dry and warm.	—	—	—	—
18. My face gets hot and blushes.	—	—	—	—
19. I fall asleep easily and get a good night's rest.	—	—	—	—
20. I have nightmares.	—	—	—	—

SCORING: All but statements 5, 9, 13, 17, and 19 indicate positive symptoms of anxiety. For positive statements score A as 1, B as 2, C as 3, and D as 4. On the five negative statements, reverse the scoring (A as 4, B as 3, C as 2, and D as 1). Add them up. If your total score is below 36 you are within the normal range, no anxiety present. Scores of 36 to 47 indicate minimal to moderate anxiety, while scores between 48 and 59 point to marked or severe anxiety, and 60 and over indicate extreme anxiety. If you have signs of anxiety, consult your physician or a psychotherapist and take the self-rating scale with you.

PHOBIAS

Phobic disorders are characterized by a persistent and irrational fear of a specific object or activity, accompanied by a compelling desire to avoid it. Most of us experience an irrational avoidance of selected objects, like spiders or snakes, but it usually has no major impact on our lives. In contrast, when the avoidance behavior or fear becomes a significant source of distress to the individual and interferes with his or her everyday behavior, the diagnosis of a phobic disorder is warranted. There are several major types of phobic disorders: simple phobias, social phobias, and agoraphobia, which involves an intense fear of unfamiliar situations.

Simple phobias are the most common type in the general population, though not necessarily among those seeking treatment. Objects commonly feared include animals, particularly dogs, snakes, insects, and mice. Other simple phobias are **acrophobia,** the fear of heights, and **claustrophobia,** the fear of closed places. Most simple phobias originate in childhood and disappear without treatment. However, the more intense fears that persist into adulthood generally don't disappear without treatment.

Social phobias involve a chronic, irrational fear of and a compelling desire to avoid situations in which the individual may be scrutinized by others. If confronted with the necessity of entering such a situation, the individual experiences marked anxiety and attempts to avoid it. Examples are an intense fear of speaking or performing in public, eating in public, using public lavatories, and writing in the presence of others. Although this type of disorder itself is rarely incapacitating, it does result in considerable inconvenience, such as avoiding a trip that involves the use of a public lavatory. Also, in an effort to relieve their anxiety, individuals with this disorder often abuse alcohol, barbiturates, and other antianxiety medications.

Agoraphobia, classically known as "fear of open spaces," is typically the most severe phobic reaction and the one for which people often seek treatment. Agoraphobia is a cluster of different fears, all of which evoke intense anxiety about crowds, such as in a crowded store, in elevators or tunnels, or on public transportation or bridges. This type of phobia tends to occur in the late teens or early 20s, though it can occur later in life and is often precipitated by separation anxiety in childhood or a sudden loss of significant objects or persons. During the outbreak of this phobia, the victims are often

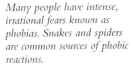

Many people have intense, irrational fears known as phobias. Snakes and spiders are common sources of phobic reactions.

BOX 13-1

SELECTED PHOBIAS

Acrophobia—fear of heights

Androphobia—fear of men

Arachitbutyrophobia—fear of peanut butter sticking to the roof of your mouth

Autophobia—fear of oneself

Decidophobia—fear of making decisions

Ergophobia—fear of work

Gamophobia—fear of marriage

Gynephobia—fear of women

Hypergiaphobia—fear of responsibility

Monophobia—fear of being alone

Mysophobia—fear of dirt

Nyctophobia—fear of darkness

Ophidiophobia—fear of snakes

Sophophobia—fear of learning

Topophobia—fear of performing (stage fright)

Triskaidekaphobia—fear of the number 13

Tropophobia—fear of moving or making changes

Zoophobia—fear of animals

---

housebound. Or if they go out, they take great care to avoid certain situations, such as being in an elevator. Box 13–1 presents the names and descriptions of various types of phobias.

OBSESSIVE-COMPULSIVE DISORDER

The essential features of obsessive-compulsive disorder are recurrent obsessions or compulsions or, as is usually the case, both. An **obsession** is a thought or image that keeps recurring to the mind, despite the individual's attempts to ignore or resist it. Similarly, a **compulsion** is an act that the individual feels compelled to repeat again and again, usually in a ritualistic fashion or according to certain rules. The act is performed with a sense of compulsion, coupled with a desire to resist such action, at least initially. The individual usually realizes that the behavior is senseless and does not derive pleasure from carrying it out, though doing so provides a release of tension.

Most of us experience mild obsessions from time to time. For example, Lisa sometimes found herself humming a tune she heard recently. For others, their thoughts might keep going back to an article they read in the daily newspaper about a tragic accident. But these minor obsessions are temporary and do not interfere with everyday activities. In contrast, pathological obsessions reoccur day after day. They also tend to involve thoughts of lust and violence, partly because of their association with the individual's anxiety and guilt, which makes them even more demoralizing. Examples are the fear of being contaminated by germs, the fear that one will kill one's child or spouse, or the temptation to have sex with a forbidden partner.

Pathological compulsions tend to fall into two categories. The first group includes checking rituals, such as making certain the windows are closed, the doors are locked, or the stove is turned off. For instance, one young man habitually spent about an hour checking his car each time he started it. The second group involves cleaning rituals, such as cleaning floors, keeping the bathroom immaculate at all times, and changing clothes several times a day to ensure that they are spotless. Lisa had a friend who used to make her giggle; every time they went to lunch in a restaurant, the friend had to jump up from the table to straighten any crooked pictures in the restaurant. The friend also arranged books, bottles, and other similar items in descending order of height. Whatever their routine, individuals afflicted with this disorder become very anxious if they are unable to engage in it. Accordingly, this disorder can be disabling, usurping much time and energy.

 Depression and Suicide

Most of us go through periods of time when nothing seems to go right. For example, when Lisa's mother became ill and Lisa decided to move in with her, Lisa's car was also giving her trouble and her old landlord informed her that she would not receive all of her security deposit for her apartment. Other individuals are overdrawn at the bank and have problems in their close relationships all at the same time. We may say we're "depressed." But we're usually not suffering from a psychological disorder. Our mood is one of mild dejection that generally passes within a matter of days. In contrast, when the disturbance of one's mood is more severe and persistent as Lisa's became, it may be classified as a **depression,** one of the mood disorders. Without counting normal dejection, depression is one of the most common disorders in our society. It is sometimes referred to as "the common cold of mental illness." But whereas the common cold never killed anyone, clinical depression often does. Many suicides in the United States are committed by people suffering from depression.

THE RANGE OF DEPRESSION

Depression may assume a variety of forms, some of which are more severe and chronic than others. In many instances, people experience the symptoms of depression only to a mild or moderate degree, so that they may continue their everyday activities. They may suffer from any number of the common symptoms of depression, including decreased energy, loss of interest in everyday activities such as eating, feelings of inadequacy, periods of crying, and a pessimistic attitude. You may have recognized some of these symptoms in the case of Lisa, the young woman in the opening vignette.

It is estimated that three-quarters of all college students suffer some symptoms of depression during college, one-quarter of them at any one time. In almost half of these students, the depression is serious enough to require professional help. Depression may be triggered by the stress of student life, academic pressures, and the felt need to make a career decision. Yet depression is often brought on by cognitive distortions, such as exaggerating the importance of getting good grades or the loss of a love relationship. When students confront their actual problems instead of dwelling on their distorted

Famous individuals can develop mental disorders such as manic depression.

self-perceptions, they tend to have more success in breaking out of their depression (Beck & Young, 1985).

People who suffer from **major depression** experience many of the same symptoms, except in a more severe and chronic way. In some cases, a major depression includes psychotic features such as delusions and hallucinations. This condition almost always interferes with everyday functioning, and in many instances, periods of hospitalization may be necessary. Contrary to popular belief, a major depression may occur at any age. The age of onset is fairly evenly distributed throughout adult life. It is estimated that 5 to 12 percent of men and 9 to 26 percent of women will experience a major depression at some point in their lives. This last finding is so well-known that it has triggered much literature on the cause. Box 13–2 discusses in some detail the suggested causes. More than half of those who experience one episode of major depression will eventually have another within 2 years. However, recovery is more apt to be enduring the longer people stay well, the less stress they experience, and the more social support they have (Belsher & Costello, 1988).

Some people are more vulnerable to depression at certain times of the year, especially the winter months. They may suffer from a peculiar mood disorder commonly labeled **SAD—seasonal affective disorder.** The causes of this recently recognized disorder remain unclear. Because more than two-thirds of those with this syndrome have a close relative with a mood disorder, genetic factors are suspected (Toufexis, 1988). Another theory is that winter weather disturbs the body's natural clock, affecting the production of chemicals such as serotonin and melatonin. The presence or absence of light is thought to be a major factor. During darkness, the pineal gland in the brain secretes larger amounts of the hormone melatonin, associated with drowsiness and lethargy. Light suppresses the secretion of this chemical. Although the extra melatonin

BOX 13–2

MEN, WOMEN, AND DEPRESSION

Depression has been called the common cold of mental disorders. In other words, depression is very common. Women are more prone to depression than men, at least that is what is believed by American psychologists and psychiatrists. Let's look a little closer at this issue.

Why are women more depressed? Or are they? One might readily assume that there are biochemical differences, for example, hormonal differences, between men and women which leave women more vulnerable to depression. This notion has pretty generally been dismissed by knowledgeable mental health professionals (A. Schwartz & Schwartz, 1993). It was also once believed that women were simply more likely to seek professional help for depression compared to men, thus inflating the figures for women. Again, studies have demonstrated that this is not true (A. C. Petersen et al., 1993).

There are instead other viable explanations for the higher rates of depression in women than in men. One is that there is generally more discrimination against women than men, especially in the workplace. Discrimination is a difficult burden to bear. Furthermore, women are more likely to live in poverty than men, for example, single mothers. Women also do more housework than men; few people report liking such chores. In fact, one study demonstrated that there is a relationship between amount of household strain, housework performed, and depressive symptoms (Golding, 1990). These and other factors, then, are likely to contribute to higher rates of depression in women than in men (Matlin, 1996).

secreted in winter doesn't disturb the body's chemical balance in most people, those with SAD suffer from an overdose of this hormone (Bootzin & Acocella, 1988).

So far, people with SAD are finding relief with light therapy. During the winter months, they spend time each day in front of a sun-box, a device fitted with powerful fluorescent lights that emit the full spectrum of natural daylight. One young woman, who suffered from near suicidal depression and weight gains up to 30 pounds, found light therapy liberating. "It's given me more energy and a sense of well-being—something I haven't had during winter."

Depression has been attributed to a variety of causes, ranging from biological factors such as genes and biochemical processes to social and cultural influences. In recent years, cognitive theorists have pointed out that people can make themselves depressed by negative thinking. For instance, Beck, Brown, Steer, Eidelson, and Riskind (1987) found that depressed people tend to focus on themes of loss, self-deprecation, and negative attitudes toward themselves and the future. In this view, distorted thinking is experienced as "automatic thoughts," which pop into people's minds spontaneously and are accepted as statements of fact rather than habitual ways of thinking. You might identify some of your own cognitive distortions and negative automatic thoughts by completing the Inventory of Negative Thoughts in Figure 13–2.

FIGURE 13–2

INVENTORY OF NEGATIVE THOUGHTS

Many of the negative thoughts that are commonly linked with depression are listed below. How many of them have you thought in recent weeks and months? Do you regard them as accurate and appropriate to the situation? Or do you recognize them as distorted and negative thoughts that need to be modified?

Before each statement write a number from 1 to 4, using the code below to indicate how often you have a particular thought. Pay special attention to the content of the thought rather than the wording. The greater the number of negative thoughts you have often or very often, the more vulnerable to depression you may become in the face of stressful life events.

1—Never
2—Seldom
3—Often
4—Very often

_____ 1. It seems such an effort to do anything.
_____ 2. I feel pessimistic about the future.
_____ 3. I have too many bad things in my life.
_____ 4. I have very little to look forward to.
_____ 5. I'm drained of energy, worn out.
_____ 6. I'm not as successful as other people.
_____ 7. Everything seems futile and pointless.
_____ 8. I just want to curl up and go to sleep.
_____ 9. There are things about me that I don't like.
_____ 10. It's too much effort even to move.
_____ 11. I'm absolutely exhausted.
_____ 12. The future seems just one string of problems.
_____ 13. My thoughts keep drifting away.
_____ 14. I get no satisfaction from the things I do.
_____ 15. I've made so many mistakes in the past.
_____ 16. I've got to really concentrate just to keep my eyes open.
_____ 17. Everything I do turns out badly.
_____ 18. My whole body has slowed down.
_____ 19. I regret some of the things I've done.
_____ 20. I can't make the effort to liven up myself.
_____ 21. I feel depressed with the way things are going.
_____ 22. I haven't any real friends anymore.
_____ 23. I do have a number of problems.
_____ 24. There's no one I can feel really close to.
_____ 25. I wish I were someone else.
_____ 26. I'm annoyed at myself for being bad at making decisions.
_____ 27. I don't make a good impression on other people.
_____ 28. The future looks hopeless.
_____ 29. I don't get the same satisfaction out of things these days.
_____ 30. I wish something would happen to make me feel better.

SOURCE: Adapted with the permission of The Free Press, a Division of Simon & Schuster, from *The Psychological Treatment of Depression: A Guide to the Theory and Practice of Cognitive-Behavior Theory* by J. Mark Williams. Copyright © 1984 by J. Mark Williams.

BIPOLAR DISORDER

In some instances, people may experience an alternation of elated and depressive moods. Popularly known as manic-depression, this condition is now termed **bipolar disorder.** Usually, this disorder first appears in the form of a manic episode, in which the individual exhibits such symptoms as an expansive mood, increased social activity, talkativeness, sleeplessness, and reckless behavior. For example, a different college classmate of Lisa's had his first manic episode at the age of 20. His speech and behavior became frenetic and fast paced. At first his close friends thought he was taking drugs or "uppers." The young man stayed up all night one night and moved all of the lounge furniture from every lounge in the dormitory into the main lounge. The next morning he awoke all of his friends and invited them to his new "breakfast club," designed just for them so that they could eat breakfast in their pajamas rather than dress to go to the dining hall.

The subsequent episodes may occur in any one of several patterns. The initial manic episode may be followed by periods of normal activity, followed by a depressed episode and then another normal period. Or one mood may be followed immediately by its opposite, with normal intervals occurring between the manic-depressive pairs. In rare forms, the person's mood may alternate between manic and depressive episodes, with no intervals of normal functioning. In another rare form, the mixed type, the individual may experience symptoms of both moods simultaneously, that is, being expansive and yet weeping and threatening suicide. Box 13–3 lists some famous individuals who you will be surprised to learn were manic-depressive.

In addition to the manic episodes, there are other characteristics that distinguish bipolar disorder from major depression. First, bipolar disorder is much less common than major depression, affecting between 0.4 and 1.2 percent of the population. Second, bipolar disorder is equally prevalent among men and women. Third, unlike major depression, which occurs more frequently among the lower socioeconomic classes, bipolar disorder is more prevalent among the upper classes. Fourth, although married people are less susceptible to major depression, they enjoy no such advantage in regard to bipolar disorder. Fifth, although major depression can occur at any time in life, bipolar disorder usually appears before the age of 30. Sixth, bipolar episodes tend to be briefer and more frequent than those in major depression. Finally, bipolar disorder is more likely to run in families.

SUICIDE

People who take their own lives, or attempt to do so, are often depressed. Accurate figures on **suicide** are even more difficult to obtain than those on depression. One reason is that many people who commit suicide prefer to make their deaths look accidental, thereby enabling their survivors to collect insurance or be spared the stigma associated with suicide. Also, if the truth were known, as many as one out of six single-car accidents could actually be a suicide. Despite incomplete statistics, official figures indicate that about 30,000 people commit suicide each year in the United States (U.S. Bureau of the Census, 1992). However, most authorities estimate the actual cases of suicide to be two or three times that number. Thus, about every 5 minutes someone takes his or her life. If all the suicide attempts were included, someone is contemplating self-destruction every *minute.*

Especially alarming is the fact that the suicide rate for youths in the 15- to 24-year-old group has tripled in the last 30 years. As a result, suicide now ranks as the third high-

BOX 13-3

FAMOUS MANIC-DEPRESSIVES

King Saul of Israel—*I Samuel* records his plight. Uncontrollable outbursts of irritability and suspiciousness alternated with a depressed state. While manic he tried to kill David and later his own son, Jonathan. On another occasion he stripped off his clothes and lay down naked all that day and night. When in a depressed state he committed suicide.

Ernest Hemingway—The novelist experienced manic phases of activity—fishing, hunting, writing, fighting, loving—that alternated with depressions. When manic he believed he was immortal, which may partially explain his frequent accidents and automobile collisions. Committed suicide in 1961.

George III of England—The "mad monarch" asked rapid fire questions while waiting for answers, bolted his food, rode his horse to death, and had episodes of sleep-depriving energy.

Theodore Roosevelt—Irrepressible, all action and energy, he could work for days with little sleep; he was constantly occupied with talking, telephoning, and writing. During his governorship and presidency, he wrote 150,000 letters and wrote an estimated 18 million words in his lifetime.

Winston Churchill—Brilliant, impulsive, and domineering, Britain's Prime Minister had high periods when he talked nonstop and said whatever came to mind, alternating with bouts of deep depression that he called his "Black Dog."

Robert Schumann—The peak years of his musical output occurred during his manic phase; while depressed he created nothing. He tried to drown himself in the Rhine, and spent the last 2 years of his life in a mental hospital.

SOURCE: J. Ingram Walker, *Everybody's Guide to Emotional Well-being* (San Francisco: Harbor Publishing, 1982). © 1982 by J. Ingram Walker, p. 41.

est cause of death among males and females in this age group. However, suicide rates generally increase with age before decreasing for everyone except male Caucasians. (See Table 13–3.) Men are more likely than women to commit suicide, and Whites are more likely than Blacks to do so. What other trends do you see in this table? Men are more successful than women partly because men tend to use swifter and more violent means, such as a gun. In contrast, women are more likely to take pills or turn on the gas, which often permits intervention. As a result, many of these unsuccessful suicide attempts are regarded as a cry for help.

Why do people commit suicide? Surprisingly, suicide is more prevalent in affluent societies, so much so that it has been described as a disease of civilization. At the level of individual behavior, many possible motives have been suggested: escaping from pain or stress, trying to eliminate unacceptable feelings, turning aggression inward, punishing others by making them feel guilty, and acting impulsively on momentary feelings of desperation. Suicidal people often suffer from "tunnel vision"—the misperception that suicide is the only alternative to seemingly unsolvable problems in living. The tragedy is that such problems are often transitory, whereas the solution of suicide is permanent.

TABLE 13-3
SUICIDE RATES BY SEX AND RACE

Age in years	Males		Females	
	White	Black	White	Black
10–14	2.6	2.0	1.1	a
15–19	18.4	14.8	3.7	1.9
20–24	26.6	21.2	4.0	2.4
25–34	25.1	20.7	5.4	3.3
35–44	25.2	16.9	7.2	3.3
45–54	24.0	12.4	7.9	3.0
55–64	26.0	10.1	7.2	2.0
65–74	32.0	11.8	6.3	a
75–84	53.0	18.5	6.6	a
85 and older	67.6	a	6.3	a
Total—All Ages	21.2	12.0	5.1	2.0

[a]Base figure too small to meet statistical standards for reliability.

SOURCE: U.S. Bureau of the Census. (1995). *Statistical Abstract of the United States, 199* (115th ed.). Washington, DC: U.S. Government Printing Office, p. 100.

Suicide is also related to psychological disorders, especially depression. A study of adolescents attempting suicide found that compared to nonattempters, attempters were more likely to report a past suicide attempt, report suicidal ideation, and to be depressed (Rotheram-Borus, Walker, & Ferns, 1996). Curiously, severely depressed people are more likely to take their lives as their situations improve. When they are most depressed, they may not have sufficient energy to take their own lives, as was fortunately true for Lisa, the young woman introduced at the opening of the chapter. Usually, it's when they start to feel better and get their energy back that they commit suicide. At the same time, autopsies of suicide victims have found abnormally low levels of serotonin—a neurotransmitter that has been linked to depression—suggesting that biochemical deficiencies may play a role in suicide. Box 13–4 alerts you to these and some of the other warning signs of suicide.

The *prevention of suicide* has received greater attention in recent years. One approach is to make it more difficult to commit suicide by having tighter control over the prescription of sedatives, more gun-control legislation, and protective measures (such as putting a wire fence around the observation platform of the Empire State Building in New York City). Another approach is to increase community awareness and resources for dealing with suicide. Many communities now have suicide and crisis intervention hotlines available 24 hours a day. Volunteers usually have specific goals, such as determining the seriousness of the suicide threat, establishing contact, conveying empathy and understanding of the caller's problems, describing available resources, and getting some sort of agreement that the caller will seek help.

Contrary to the myth that people who threaten to kill themselves seldom do so, most people who commit suicide express some suicidal intent, directly or indirectly, within several months before their deaths. It helps to recognize the warning signs, as noted in Box 13–4. Perhaps you've heard that questioning depressed people about their suicidal ideas will give such thoughts greater force. But this isn't true. Providing an opportunity to talk about suicidal thoughts often helps these people to overcome such

BOX 13-4

Warning Signs

Here are some warning signals of suicide:

- Expression of suicidal thoughts or a preoccupation with death
- Prior suicide attempt
- Giving away prized possessions
- Depression over a broken love relationship
- Despair over a chronic illness or a situation at school or work
- Change in eating habits
- Change in sleeping habits
- Marked personality changes
- Abuse of alcohol or drugs
- Sense of hopelessness

wishes and to know where to turn for help. If you notice the warning signals of suicide in a family member or friend, do your best to see that he or she gets professional help.

Selected Disorders

Many other psychological disorders are described in the *DSM-IV,* covering almost every conceivable complaint, from compulsive gambling to delusional (paranoid) disorder. Here we'll describe three types of disorders that are of special interest: eating disorders; two personality disorders—narcissistic and antisocial personalities; and schizophrenia, one of the most disabling of all disorders.

EATING DISORDERS

Pam, 5 feet, 5 inches tall, is a 17-year-old who is slightly overweight for her age but suffers from an intense fear of getting fat. Her fears, coupled with a desire to become socially attractive, have led her to experiment with stricter diets. She blames much of her troubles on her mother, who constantly urges her to eat more, and her boyfriend, who threatens to break off their relationship if she gets any skinnier. But the more Pam is pressured to eat, the more she resists. As a result, her weight has dropped from 145 pounds to 95 pounds in less than a year.

Pam is diagnosed as having **anorexia nervosa.** The essential features of this eating disorder are a fear of becoming fat along with a disturbance in body image and a refusal to maintain normal weight. (See Figure 13–3.) Being 85 percent of normal body weight, along with other physical signs such as the suspension of menstrual periods, is usually sufficient for this diagnosis. The weight loss is usually accomplished by a reduction in total food intake, especially foods high in carbohydrates and fats; self-induced vomiting; use of laxatives or diuretics; and sometimes extensive exercise.

FIGURE 13-3

THE FEAR OF FAT SCALE

This scale may help to identify individuals who are at greater risk of developing an eating disorder, especially anorexia or bulimia.

As you read each of the following statements, write the number that best represents your own beliefs and feelings. Then check your responses with the scoring key at the end of the chapter.

1—very untrue

2—somewhat untrue

3—somewhat true

4—very true

_____ 1. My biggest fear is of becoming fat.

_____ 2. I am afraid to gain even a little weight.

_____ 3. I believe there is a real risk that I will become overweight someday.

_____ 4. I don't understand how overweight people can live with themselves.

_____ 5. Becoming fat would be the worst thing that could happen to me.

_____ 6. If I stopped concentrating on controlling my weight, chances are I would become very fat.

_____ 7. There is nothing that I can do to make the thought of gaining weight less painful and frightening.

_____ 8. I feel like all my energy goes into controlling my weight.

_____ 9. If I eat even a little, I may lose control and not stop eating.

_____ 10. Staying hungry is the only way I can guard against losing control and becoming fat.

SOURCE: Goldfarb, L. A, Dykens, E. M, & Gerrard, M. (1985). "The Goldfarb Fear of Fat Scale." *Journal of Personality Assessment, 49,* 329–332.

Anorexic adolescent girls (about 1 percent of that population) may have emotional conflicts caused by growing up in strict families. Typically, they have been "model" children and are quiet, obedient, or perfectionistic (Thornton, Leo, & Alberg, 1991). But they often lack a firm sense of personal identity and autonomy. They also suffer from a disturbed body image, so that they do not realize they are getting dangerously thin, even when they view themselves in the mirror. Dangerously thin is not a misstatement; up to 10 percent of all anorexics die from this disorder. It is also conjectured that the eating habits of these girls may have been so regulated by their parents that they have not learned to interpret the inner cues signaling the need for food. Instead, they have an obsessional need to control their lives primarily through their eating habits, often engaging in elaborate rituals to ensure they will not eat too much. For example, one anorexic was observed to push her food around her plate a number of times before nibbling on it. It appeared that she was eating because of all the motion. In actual fact, she was eating very little. Other authors regard other parts of the anorexic's family system as being dysfunctional, for example, that sexual abuse has occurred by a family member (Kinzl, Traweger, Guenther, & Biebl, 1994).

Cheryl lives in the same city as Lisa but does not know her. Cheryl is 5 feet, 10 inches tall, is 20 years old, and has always been somewhat chubby for her age. However, for the past several years, she has begun to indulge in binge and purge cycles. For instance, she will eat a quart of ice cream and a box of brownies, gobbling the food down quite rapidly, with little chewing. Once she has started to eat, she feels a loss of control. Later, in secret, she induces vomiting by sticking her finger down her throat. The vomiting decreases the physical pain of overeating, thereby allowing either continued eating or termination of the binge. The entire cycle is followed by disparaging self-criticism and depression.

Cheryl's condition is **bulimia nervosa,** a disorder that is closely related to but different from anorexia, which is more common. Whereas the aim of the anorexic is to lose weight, the bulimic attempts to eat without gaining weight. The essential features of this disorder are episodic eating sprees, or binges, accompanied by an awareness that the eating pattern is abnormal; a fear of not being able to stop eating voluntarily; and the depressed mood and self-disparaging thoughts that follow the eating binges. The bulimic is also unhappy with her body image, as is the anorexic (Joiner, Wonderlich, Metalsky, & Schmidt, 1995). The bulimic sometimes diets excessively between binges. Like anorexia, bulimia is more common among girls, especially those in the middle and upper socioeconomic groups. Although the estimated frequency of the disorder varies considerably, about one in five college-age women are involved in bulimic behavior (Muuss, 1986). New research is also indicating that gay men are prone to eating disorders because they, too, hope to please male partners. On the other hand, lesbians and heterosexual men are less prone to eating disorders (Siever, 1994). Similarly, Black women seem less prone to be critical of their bodies than White women (A. D. Powell & Kahn, 1995).

Recently, compulsive overeating has attracted greater attention among clinicians. Compulsive or binge eaters constitute a distinct subgroup among the obese. Whereas most overweight people consume more calories than they expend and eat normal amounts of food most of the time, compulsive overeaters consume large amounts of food in a very short time without the subsequent use of purgatives or exercise. It is estimated that about one-third or more of all individuals in weight-control programs report frequent episodes of compulsive overeating. Compulsive overeaters exhibit a higher than average incidence of psychological problems, especially depression. They also tend to experience greater mood fluctuations during the course of the day, eating more often in response to positive and negative emotional arousal. Binge eating is commonly triggered by tension, hunger, consumption of any food, boredom, craving for specific foods, and solitude or loneliness.

One of the most useful approaches to compulsive overeating is to set a goal weight that is more consistent with one's weight history than that obtainable from a normative chart. Thus, a 5-foot, 5-inch woman whose weight was 160 pounds before binge eating and subsequent weight gain would be better off striving for a weight in the 155- to 160-pound range than trying to get down to 125 pounds. Such an approach reduces the need for stricter diets, which in turn set up additional binges (Bartlett, 1992).

PERSONALITY DISORDERS

Personality traits are enduring patterns of thinking, feeling, acting, and relating to others that we exhibit in a wide range of situations. However, when personality traits are so inflexible and maladaptive that they cause marked impairment in an individual's social and occupational life, he or she may have one of the **personality disorders.** Such disorders are unique in that they tend to cause less distress to the individuals themselves than to others who live and work with them. As a result, these individuals resist getting professional help. Two personality disorders of special interest are the narcissistic personality disorder and the antisocial personality disorder.

The **narcissistic personality** is thought to be the characteristic personality disorder of our time, mainly because so many otherwise normal individuals in our society exhibit undue self-interest. Whereas a certain degree of self-interest may shield us from the effects of criticism or failure, excessive self-interest can be maladaptive, especially when the cravings for affection and reassurance become insatiable. (See Figure 13–4.) People with this disorder generally exhibit a grandiose sense of self-importance in behavior or fantasy, often accompanied by a sense of inferiority. They exaggerate their talents and accomplishments and expect to be treated as special without the appropriate achievements. Yet they are hypersensitive to others' evaluation and react to criticism with arrogance and contempt. They believe they are unique and can be understood only by special people.

Clinicians differ about the causes of this disorder. Psychodynamic theorists believe narcissistic personalities compensate for the inadequate affection and approval they received in childhood. Lacking parental support, these children often fail to develop an adequate sense of self-esteem. Instead, they construct grandiose self-images as a way of avoiding perceived shortcomings and need constant reassurance to maintain their inflated self-esteem. In contrast, cognitive and social learning theorists see narcissistic people as the products of exaggerated expectations during childhood of what they will achieve in adulthood. Whatever the primary cause, narcissism may be fostered by many forces in today's society, such as the preoccupation with self-fulfillment, the "overvaluing" of children, the heightened expectations and entitlements among youths, the prominence of television, and our pervasive consumer orientation.

FIGURE 13-4

NORMAL AND NARCISSISTIC SELF-INTEREST

Normal self-interest	Narcissistic self-interest
1. Feels good about oneself without compliments.	Requires constant attention; fishes for compliments.
2. May be temporarily hurt by criticism.	Feels enraged and humiliated when criticized.
3. Feels specially talented in some way.	Feels incomparably better than others and insists on their acknowledgment of this.
4. Retains a sense of self-respect without special treatment.	Has a sense of entitlement, for example, assumes he or she does not have to stand in line.
5. Respects the needs and rights of others.	Takes advantage of others to achieve his or her ends.
6. Is empathic and caring about others.	Lacks empathy and sensitivity to others' feelings.
7. Aspires to self-improvement and success.	Holds fantasies of unlimited success, power, brilliance, or ideal love.
8. Appreciates others' success without feeling inferior.	Is preoccupied with feelings of envy.

SOURCE: Reprined with permission from the *Diagnostic and Statistical Manual of Mental Disorders,* Fourth Edition. Copyright 1994 American Psychiatric Association.

One of the most unsettling personality disorders is the **antisocial personality**— formerly called the psychopath or sociopath. These people have a history of chronic antisocial behavior, usually starting before mid-adolescence. They tend to get in trouble with the law because of their predatory attitude toward people and their disregard for others' rights. They may act in an impulsive manner, such as stealing a pack of cigarettes or a car, depending on what seems easier at the moment. Also, they are irresponsible, often walking out on their jobs or spouses. Antisocial personalities lack a normal conscience and, with little or no guilt, are manipulative toward others. An example is the man who courted and married 105 women, some of them more than once, but all without benefit of a divorce. Then there is the individual who spent his entire life as an impostor, passing himself off at various times as a minister, teacher, zoologist, prison warden, psychologist, college dean, Trappist monk, and surgeon. When such individuals are prone to violence, they are dangerous and can kill with little or no remorse.

How can people get away with such outrageous behavior? One explanation may be their superficial charm, poise, and intelligence, all of which disarm their victims. Also, lacking a sense of responsibility, these individuals can engage in spontaneous behavior, giving the appearance of being free-spirited. In many cases, they have grown up in families in which they have been undersocialized, with one or more of their parents exhibiting antisocial behavior. For instance, Western society may encourage antisocial tendencies by glamorizing fame and success, so that superficial charm and lack of concern for others may help antisocial people get ahead.

SCHIZOPHRENIA

Most of us can understand what it's like to be panic stricken or depressed, but the bizarre behavior of the schizophrenic individual is strange to us. At least 1 out of every 100 people will suffer from a schizophrenic episode sometime during his or her life. Schizophrenia is so disabling that it often results in hospitalization.

Because **schizophrenia** is a label given to a group of related disorders, it's impossible to describe the "typical" patient. The essential features of these disorders include **psychotic symptoms,** such as hearing voices during the active phase of the disorder; marked impairment in work, self-care, and social relationships; and continuous signs of the disturbance for at least 6 months, including an active phase of at least 1 week, or less if the symptoms have been successfully treated (American Psychiatric Association, 1994). Here are other symptoms:

1. *Disorders of speech.* One of the most striking features of individuals suffering from schizophrenia is their peculiar use of language—both in the form and content of thought and speech. There is a loosening of associations of thought and rambling, disjointed speech. Words that have no association beyond the fact that they sound alike, such as *clang* and *fang,* may be juxtaposed with each other.

2. *Distorted beliefs.* The major disturbance of the content of thought involves **delusions**—beliefs that have no basis in reality. For example, individuals may feel they are being spied on or plotted against by their families.

3. *Distorted perception.* Individuals suffering from schizophrenia seem to perceive the world differently from other people. They have difficulty focusing on certain aspects of their environment while screening out other data. Instead, their inner world is flooded with an undifferentiated mass of sensory data, resulting in odd

associations, inner confusion, and bizarre speech. In addition, many of them experience hallucinations—sensory perceptions that occur in the absence of any appropriate external stimulus. The most common hallucination is hearing voices, which characteristically order these people to commit some forbidden act or accuse them of having done some terrible misdeed.

4. *Blunted or inappropriate emotions.* Schizophrenia is characterized by a blunted affect, or in more severe cases, a lack of emotions. Schizophrenic individuals may stare with a blank expression or speak in a flat, monotone voice. Or they may display inappropriate emotions, such as giggling when talking about some painful experience.

5. *Social withdrawal.* People who eventually have a schizophrenic episode tend to be loners, often preferring animals, nature, or inanimate objects to human company. Perhaps they are preoccupied with their inner world. Or having learned that they are often misunderstood, they may prefer to keep to themselves. But they also exhibit a marked avoidance of people. They avoid eye contact and tend to stand or sit at a greater distance from people than others do. They are also emotionally distant, making it difficult to establish satisfying close relationships with them.

Despite extensive research, the causes of schizophrenia are not fully understood. For a long while, a dysfunctional family environment was regarded as a major cause of this disorder, although in recent years there has been increasing evidence that genetic, neurological,

Many street people suffer from severe emotional disturbances.

and biochemical factors may play an even greater role. Nevertheless, about half of the identical twins who share the same genes with a schizophrenic twin do not develop this disorder (Gottesman, 1991). Thus, a predisposition by itself is not sufficient for the development of schizophrenia. The **diathesis–stress hypothesis** views schizophrenia as the interaction of a genetic vulnerability (the diathesis or predisposition) with environmental stressors. That is, schizophrenic individuals tend to inherit a lower threshold to certain types of stress, which if exceeded may precipitate an acute episode of the disorder. However, if an individual manages to keep the level of environmental stress well below his or her particular threshold, he or she may never experience an acute episode of schizophrenia.

The initial onset of schizophrenia usually occurs in adolescence or early adulthood. We might think that Lisa would be a candidate for schizophrenia, then, but instead she developed depression. It may occur abruptly, with marked changes in behavior in a matter of days or weeks, or there may be a gradual, insidious deterioration in functioning over many years. During this initial phase, individuals are socially withdrawn. They display blunted or shallow emotions and have trouble communicating with others. They may neglect personal hygiene, schoolwork, or jobs. By this time, such individuals may have begun to exhibit the bizarre behavior and psychotic symptoms signaling the onset of the active phase.

The active phase of the disorder is often precipitated by intense psychological stress, such as the loss of a job, rejection in love, or the death of a parent. During this period

---

FIGURE 13–5

OUTLOOK FOR RECOVERY

How well an individual recovers from the active phase of schizophrenia depends on a variety of factors, especially the following:

1. *Premorbid adjustment.* The more adequately the person functioned before the illness, the better the outcome.
2. *Triggering event.* If the illness is triggered by a specific event, such as the death of a loved one, the possibility of recovery is more favorable.
3. *Sudden onset.* The more quickly the disorder develops, the more favorable the outcome.
4. *Age of onset.* The later in life the initial episode of schizophrenia appears, the better. Men are more at risk before the age of 25; women are more at risk after 25.
5. *Affective behavior.* Symptoms of anxiety and other emotions, including depression, are favorable signs. A state of hopelessness not accompanied by depression is a poor sign.
6. *Content of delusions and hallucinations.* The more delusions involve feelings of guilt and responsibility, the better the outlook. Conversely, the more the delusions and hallucinations blame others and exonerate the individual, the more severe the illness.
7. *Type of schizophrenia.* Paranoid schizophrenia, the most common type, has a better outlook, mostly because the individual's cognitive functioning remains relatively intact compared to other types of schizophrenia.
8. *Response to the illness and treatment.* The more insight individuals have concerning what makes them ill, the more responsive they are to the medication; and the more cooperative they are with their therapists, the better their chances of recovery.
9. *Family support.* The more understanding and supportive these individuals' families are, the better their chances of a good recovery.

the psychotic symptoms become prominent. Schizophrenic individuals begin to hallucinate, hold delusions, and exhibit the incoherent and illogical thought and bizarre behavior characteristic of the disorder. However, no one patient manifests all these symptoms; each individual exhibits a somewhat different pattern.

In the residual phase, individuals may recover from the acute episode in a matter of weeks or months. Some of the psychotic symptoms, such as hallucinations or delusions, may persist, although no longer accompanied by intense emotion. These individuals may continue to exhibit eccentric behavior and odd thoughts, for example, believing they are able to control events through magical thinking. As a result, many of them are not ready to fully resume everyday responsibilities, such as holding a job or running a household.

There is a considerable difference of opinion about the outlook for individuals who have suffered an acute schizophrenic episode. Traditionally, clinicians adhered to the principle of thirds; that is, about one-third of the people who have experienced a schizophrenic episode make a good recovery, another one-third make a partial recovery with occasional relapses, and still another one-third remain chronically impaired. However, with improved methods of treatment, including powerful antipsychotic drugs, more favorable attitudes toward those afflicted with this disorder, and more sophisticated research strategies, a larger proportion of schizophrenic individuals are making at least a partial recovery. How well an individual recovers from an acute schizophrenic episode depends on many factors. (See Figure 13–5.)

SUMMARY

UNDERSTANDING PSYCHOLOGICAL DISORDERS

We began the chapter by noting that there is no simple way to determine when someone has a psychological disorder. In practice, professionals rely on a combination of standards, such as the presence of personal distress, significant impairment in behavior, the social acceptability of the behavior, and an important loss of personal control. During any 6-month period, one in five adults will suffer from some type of psychological disorder, ranging from the mildly disabling anxiety disorders to severe ones like schizophrenia. In the *DSM-IV,* an authoritative guide for the various disorders, the emphasis is on describing the characteristic behavior patterns of the various disorders rather than interpreting the possible causes, which are often unknown.

ANXIETY DISORDERS

In an anxiety disorder, the level of anxiety is all out of proportion to the stressful situation or may occur in the absence of a specific danger. Anxiety may be experienced in different ways in the various disorders. In the general anxiety disorder a chronic sense of diffuse or free-floating anxiety becomes the predominant disturbance, and the person is anxious most of the time. In contrast, the phobic disorders are characterized by a chronic, irrational fear of a specific object or activity, together with a compelling desire to avoid it, that is, avoidance behaviors. The essential features of the obsessive-compulsive disorder are recurrent obsessions or compulsions or both, as seen in people preoccupied with various checking and cleaning rituals.

DEPRESSION AND SUICIDE

The mood disorders cover different types of mood disturbances, including extreme elation and depression. Depression may range from mild despondency to a major depressive disorder that is so disabling it requires hospitalization. Contrary to popular belief, the onset of a major depression is evenly distributed throughout the lifespan. In contrast, bipolar disorder, popularly known as manic-depression, involves an alternation between moods of extreme elation and depression and usually appears before age 30.

Almost half of the suicides in the United States involve people suffering from depression. Suicide now ranks as the third-highest cause of death among males and females in the 15- to 24-year-old group. However, the incidence of suicide among White males continues to rise with age, the highest incidence at 75 years and older.

SELECTED DISORDERS

Anorexia is an eating disorder of adolescent girls that is characterized by a disturbance in body image and eating habits and results in a loss of normal body weight. Bulimia, a related eating disorder, is more common among older girls and involves episodic eating binges accompanied by a fear of not being able to stop eating voluntarily, eventually followed by a depressive mood. Recently, attention has been given to compulsive or binge eaters, those who consume large amounts of food in a very short time without the subsequent use of purgatives or exercise.

People with personality disorders are characterized by maladaptive behavior patterns that impair their social and occupational lives. Those with a narcissistic personality disorder have an exaggerated sense of self-importance and need constant reassurance to maintain their inflated esteem. In contrast, those with an antisocial personality disorder get into trouble because of their predatory attitude toward people and their disregard for others' rights.

Schizophrenia, one of the most severely disabling of all the psychological disorders, affects about 1 percent of the American population sometime during their lives. Symptoms include disordered thought, imaginary voices, blunted emotions, and social withdrawal. Although the causes of schizophrenia are not fully understood, it is thought that it results from an interaction of a genetic predisposition and environmental stress.

SCORING KEY FOR THE FEAR OF FAT SCALE

Add up the numbers on the 10 items to get your total score. Comparable scores are available for women only. You may compare your score with those obtained by the following groups:

Group	N	Mean
Nondieting college women (those satisfied with their weight)	49	17.30
General female college population	73	18.33
College women who are dissatisfied with their weight and have been on three or more diets during the past year	40	23.90
Bulimic college women (actively bingeing and purging)	32	30.00
Anorexic women in treatment	7	35.00

A word of caution. As you interpret your scores, remember that (1) the samples in the Goldfarb study are quite small, and (2) a score at a certain level does not necessarily place you in that group. Instead, it means that you report an equivalent fear of fat. For instance, a score of 33.00 does not indicate that you are bulimic or anorexic. It simply means that your self-reported fear of fat score approximates the scores reported by bulimic and anorexic women in Goldfarb's study.

SELF-TEST

1. A major factor in determining whether or not someone has a psychological disorder is the presence of
    a. interpersonal conflicts
    b. personal distress
    c. unusual behavior
    d. anxiety

2. The most common groups of psychological disorders in the United States are the
    a. anxiety disorders
    b. personality disorders
    c. schizophrenic disorders
    d. mood disorders

3. A chronic state of free-floating anxiety is often the main symptom in which one of the following disorders?
    a. phobic disorder
    b. generalized anxiety disorder
    c. bipolar disorder
    d. personality disorder

4. An example of a social phobia is someone with an intense fear of
    a. closed places
    b. crowded stores
    c. public speaking
    d. being in elevators

5. The person who reenters the house several times to make certain the stove has been turned off before leaving for work probably has a
    a. mood disorder
    b. simple phobia
    c. personality disorder
    d. obsessive-compulsive disorder

6. In contrast to major depression, the bipolar, or manic-depressive, disorder
    a. usually occurs before age 30
    b. affects more women than men
    c. is more common after age 50
    d. is less likely to run in families

7. Which of the following age groups exhibits the highest suicide rates?
    a. women 15 to 24
    b. men 45 to 54
    c. women 65 to 74
    d. men over 75

8. The eating disorder characterized by episodic eating binges and purges is called
    a. anorexia
    b. fasting disorder
    c. bulimia
    d. compulsive overeating

9. People who have a history of chronic deviant behavior with little or no regard for the rights of others probably have
    a. a schizophrenic disorder
    b. an antisocial personality disorder
    c. a bipolar disorder
    d. a multiple personality disorder

10. Which of the following factors generally indicates a favorable sign for recovery for someone experiencing an acute schizophrenic episode?
    a. sudden onset
    b. resigned to being sick
    c. lack of emotion
    d. onset by adolescence

EXERCISES

1. *Have you ever experienced a panic attack?* Even if you've experienced only intense anxiety, write a page or so describing what it was like. Be sure to include what occasioned the anxiety and how it affected you. Also, how well do you cope with similar situations today?

2. *Are you bothered by an intense fear or phobia?* If you were to list your worst fears, which ones would you include? Do you share some of the more common fears, such as the fear of snakes or spiders? Or are you bothered by other fears? What are you doing to overcome your fears?

3. *Managing the "blues."* Most of us have times when we feel down. The important thing is knowing how to handle ourselves so that we can snap out of such low moments. Write a page or so describing how you cope with discouragement and depression. How effective is your approach?

4. *Have you known someone who committed suicide?* To what extent did this person exhibit the characteristics discussed in the chapter? Also, in retrospect, did the person display any of the warning signs of suicide? At this point, do you think you're better able to recognize individuals with a high risk for suicide?

5. *Psychological disorders in the family.* Do you have relatives who have suffered from a psychological disorder? If so, which ones? Are any of these disorders those that tend to run in families, for example, alcoholism, schizophrenia, and major depression? What steps, if any, are you taking to avoid such problems?

6. *Distinguishing schizophrenia and multiple personality disorder.* People tend to confuse these two disorders. Do you know the difference between them? To test yourself, you might write a paragraph or so explaining how they are different from each other. Ask your instructor to check your answer to make certain you really understand the differences.

QUESTIONS FOR SELF-REFLECTION

1. What are the advantages and disadvantages of tolerating greater deviance in today's society?
2. When you become very anxious about something, how does this affect your behavior?
3. How do you cope with occasional feelings of despondency?
4. Why do you think women are more apt to seek help for their depression than men?
5. Would you agree that depression among males is often masked by drinking or drug problems?
6. Why do you think the suicide rate is rising among youths?
7. How would you account for the high suicide rate among older White men?
8. What are some of the *chronic* self-destructive behaviors people engage in?
9. Are you aware that some individuals who have experienced acute schizophrenic episodes resume normal lives?

FOR FURTHER INFORMATION

RECOMMENDED READINGS

AMERICAN PSYCHIATRIC ASSOCIATION. (1994). *Diagnostic and statistical manual of mental disorders (DSM-IV)* (4th ed.). Washington, DC: Author. An authoritative guide that describes and classifies the various psychological disorders.

COHEN, D. B. (1994). *Out of the blue: Depression and human nature.* New York: W. W. Norton. An interesting book about a common problem of our day—depression. This book emphasizes severe depression.

HESS-BIBER, S. J. (1996). *Am I thin enough yet?: The cult of thinness and the commercialization of identity.* New York: Oxford University Press. A book about how American women's images of the typical woman are too thin because of media portrayals of the ideal woman.

STYRON, W. (1990). *Darkness visible: A memoir of madness.* New York: Random House. A well-known author uses his writing skills to reveal the personal experience of depression.

TORREY, E. F. (1995). *Surviving schizophrenia: A manual for families, consumers, and providers.* New York: Harper Perennial. A handy book for families of schizophrenics and others touched by this baffling illness.

WEBSITES AND THE INTERNET

http://www.psycom.net/depression.central.html: A site provided by a psychiatrist about depression in all ages and groups of people with information on genetics and other causes of depression. The site also contains information on other mood disorders and links to other sites.

http://www.save.org/: A valuable site on suicide, its warning signs, misconceptions about suicide, and how a forgotten group, survivors, can better cope with their loss.

http://www.mentalhealth.com/p.20.html: Contains information about all types of mental disorders with good information on a large variety of personality disorders and phobias. The information includes symptoms, treatments, and relevant research on each.

http://www.appi.org/schizo.html: Provides general information on schizophrenia for the general public. The site is provided by the American Psychiatric Association, author of *DSM-IV.*

http://www.hebs.scot.nhs.uk/menus/publics/phobia/phob21.htm: Discusses phobias, what they are, and how to treat them. This site also provides links to other sites as well as quotes from phobics.

CHAPTER

14

Therapy

After completing this chapter, you should be able to

1. Define the terms *psychotherapy* and *therapist*.
2. Describe the main features of insight therapy.
3. Explain the cognitive-behavioral approach to therapy.
4. Describe the three major categories of psychoactive drugs used in biomedical therapy.
5. Discuss the importance of community-based services for comprehensive mental health care.
6. Discuss the effectiveness of psychotherapy.
7. List the five questions to consider in seeking professional help.

Since moving back home 3 months ago, Sergei, age 24, has been at odds with his parents who immigrated with him from Russia when Sergei was 10. Sergei admits he's going through a difficult time in his life. He recently lost his job, again, and is having trouble making the payments for his car. To make matters worse, he has just asked his father for another small loan to help him through the present financial crisis. But Sergei's parents see things differently. They feel that Sergei is floundering and has no sense of direction in his life. Also, they sense that he is depressed, as seen in his constant complaints, fatigue, and boredom. Since the recent breakup with his girlfriend, Sergei has been staying out late and drinking heavily several evenings each week. Sergei's friends are also concerned and insist he get therapy. Sergei agrees reluctantly. "But I'll see the shrink just *once,*" he says, "mostly to satisfy you I'm not crazy." His parents are immigrants and do not want Sergei sharing their family problems with a stranger. They remember all too well when secrets shared with strangers in Russia resulted in the informant's disappearance. Sergei's friends insist that he should give the therapist a chance. "Okay, okay, I'll give it a try. But I'm not making any promises."

Insight Therapies

Why are people like Sergei so reluctant to get professional help? The answers probably vary from one person to another. Some individuals, especially those with little education, resist getting help because of the stigma associated with it. In the popular mind, **psychotherapy** is for people who are "crazy." Yet in practice, therapy is more likely to be used by people with the milder disturbances, who seek it as a means of personal growth as well as for the relief of symptoms. Then, too, in a society that puts a high value on self-sufficiency, getting help may be seen as an admission of weakness. This is probably the major reason men are less likely than women to seek professional help for psychological problems. It's more acceptable for women to express their emotions and admit weakness. Men are expected to cope on their own and, as a result, often mask their problems with alcohol and drugs as Sergei is doing. In many instances, people don't know how to go about getting help, or they may feel that therapy is too costly. In any event, only about one in five adults with a serious psychological problem will seek help from a mental health professional such as a psychiatrist or psychologist. Many of the others will be seen by family physicians, the clergy, and other types of counselors (Robins & Regier, 1991).

What is your attitude toward getting professional help? Are you reluctant? Or do you admit that professional help can be useful? Would you benefit from additional information regarding the therapeutic process? To assess your view in this matter, complete Attitudes Toward Seeking Professional Help in Figure 14–1. Then check your responses with the scoring key at the end of the chapter. Cultivating a more positive attitude toward therapy will affect not only whether you will seek help but also the effectiveness of your therapy. Success in therapy requires a certain degree of trust both in the therapeutic process and in the therapist.

FIGURE 14–1

ATTITUDES TOWARD SEEKING PROFESSIONAL HELP

Read each statement carefully and indicate your agreement or disagreement by using the scale below. Please express your honest opinion or feeling about each statement.

0—Disagreement
1—Probable disagreement
2—Probable agreement
3—Agreement

_____ 1. Although there are clinics for people with mental troubles, I would not have much faith in them.

_____ 2. If a good friend asked my advice about a mental health problem, I might recommend that he or she see a psychiatrist.

_____ 3. I would feel uneasy going to a psychiatrist because of what some people think.

_____ 4. A person with a strong character can get over mental conflicts by himself or herself and would have little need of a psychiatrist.

_____ 5. There are times when I have felt completely lost and would have welcomed professional advice for a personal or emotional problem.

_____ 6. Considering the time and expense involved in psychotherapy, it would have doubtful value for a person like me.

_____ 7. I would willingly confide intimate matters to an appropriate person if I thought it might help me or a member of my family.

_____ 8. I would rather live with certain mental conflicts than go through the ordeal of getting psychiatric treatment.

_____ 9. Emotional difficulties, like many things, tend to work out by themselves.

_____ 10. There are certain problems that should not be discussed outside of one's immediate family.

_____ 11. A person with a serious emotional disturbance would probably feel most secure in a good mental hospital.

_____ 12. If I believed I was having a mental breakdown, my first inclination would be to get professional attention.

_____ 13. Keeping one's mind on a job is a good solution for avoiding personal worries and concerns.

_____ 14. Having been a psychiatric patient is a blot on a person's life.

_____ 15. I would rather be advised by a close friend than by a psychologist, even for an emotional problem.

_____ 16. A person with an emotional problem is not likely to solve it alone; he or she is likely to solve it with professional help.

_____ 17. I resent a person—professionally trained or not—who wants to know about my personal difficulties.

_____ 18. I would want to get psychiatric attention if I were worried or upset for a long period of time.

_____ 19. The idea of talking about problems with a psychologist strikes me as a poor way to get rid of emotional conflicts.

_____ 20. Having been mentally ill carries with it a burden of shame.

_____ 21. There are experiences in my life I would not discuss with anyone.

_____ 22. It is probably best not to know everything about oneself.

_____ 23. If I were experiencing a serious emotional crisis at this point in my life, I would be confident that I could find relief in psychotherapy.

_____ 24. There is something admirable in the attitude of a person who is willing to cope with his or her conflicts and fears without resorting to professional help.

_____ 25. At some future time I might want to have psychological counseling.

_____ 26. A person should work out his or her own problems; getting psychological counseling would be a last resort.

_____ 27. Had I received treatment in a mental hospital, I would not feel that it had to be covered up.

_____ 28. If I thought I needed psychiatric help, I would get it no matter who knew about it.

_____ 29. It is difficult to talk about personal affairs with highly educated people such as doctors, teachers, and the clergy.

To determine your total score, use the scoring key at the end of the chapter. Then interpret the meaning of your score by comparing it with the norms presented there.

SOURCE: E. Fischer & J. Turner, "Orientations to Seeking Professional Help: Development and Research Utility of an Attitude Scale," *Journal of Consulting and Clinical Psychology, 35* (1970), 82–83. Copyright © 1970 by the American Psychological Association. Reprinted by permission.

A major problem in choosing a **therapist**—a person trained to help people with psychological problems—is sorting through the various approaches to therapy. There are now more than 250 different schools of therapy, including various insight therapies as well as many types of behavioral and group therapies. Despite their differences, most therapies share certain common goals. All of them afford clients relief from their symptoms, such as intolerable anxiety or depression. Many of them afford clients better understanding of their thoughts, feelings, motives, and relationships. They also help clients to modify their problem behaviors, such as excessive fear. In addition, many therapies help clients to improve their relationships at home and work. Different schools of therapy emphasize some of these goals more than others; some may put more emphasis on adjustment, whereas others may emphasize growth.

We'll begin with the **insight therapies**—those that bring change by increasing self-understanding.

PSYCHOANALYSIS

According to Sigmund Freud (1965), the founder of **psychoanalysis,** psychological disturbances are due to anxiety that we feel about hidden conflicts among the different parts of our unconscious personality. If not expressed directly, these unconscious impulses and conflicts seek indirect release in all kinds of symptoms. The therapist's purpose is to help the individual gain insight or conscious awareness of these unconscious desires or conflicts, thereby gaining emotional release and eventual mastery of them.

The core of the psychoanalytic approach is the analysis of **transference**—the unconscious tendency of clients to project onto the therapist their feelings and fantasies, both positive and negative, about significant others in their childhood. Therapists deliberately foster the development of the transference relationship through their own neutrality and relative passivity. Then, as the therapy proceeds, the therapist analyzes or explains the transference process as a way of helping clients achieve insight into the influence of the past on their present behavior.

"Working through" the transference relationship involves an exploration of unconscious material and defenses and includes a variety of techniques. One of the earliest of these was **free association.** The client is usually asked to lie down on a couch, relax, clear his or her mind of everyday thoughts, and then say whatever comes to mind regardless of how trivial it sounds. Sometimes clients are encouraged to talk about their dreams. Though these recollections might appear irrelevant, the well-trained analyst may use *dream interpretation* to shed light on the clients' problems. When an individual hesitates or is reluctant to talk about some painful experience, this is seen as a sign of **resistance.** For example, if Sergei had elected to see a psychoanalyst, he may have been reluctant to discuss his immigrant background. The therapist would have viewed this as important simply because Sergei would not talk about it. The therapist may simply wait or may use another approach to the area of resistance, so that eventually this problem can be overcome. By *analyzing the resistances,* the therapist helps the clients see how they handle anxiety-provoking material.

Traditionally, psychoanalysis involved hour-long sessions 3 to 5 times a week, often lasting several years. But at the level of current fees, this schedule would make psychoanalysis prohibitively expensive for all but the privileged few who could afford it. As a result, there have been many changes in this approach. Now psychoanalytic therapy may involve only 1 or 2 sessions a week and often lasts only 20 or 30 sessions. The therapist sits facing the client and takes a more active role in therapy than the impenetrable "mirror" role advocated by Freud. Psychoanalytic therapists are also likely to be more eclectic than in the past, using techniques from other approaches when appropriate. At the same time, the emphasis remains on gaining insight and self-mastery of the unconscious forces affecting one's behavior.

THE PERSON-CENTERED APPROACH

One of the major alternatives to psychoanalysis is Carl Rogers's humanistic approach to therapy. Toward the end of his career, Rogers (1980) changed the name of his approach from client-centered therapy to **person-centered therapy,** as a way of indicating that the same principles apply to a variety of fields of human interaction as well as to psychotherapy. According to this view, the helper's genuineness, acceptance, and empathetic understanding of the client are necessary and sufficient conditions for producing therapeutic change.

Rogers developed his view of therapy out of his own experience as a therapist. Early in his career he was counseling a mother about her son, who was having problems. No matter what strategy he tried, he got nowhere. Finally, he admitted his failure. As the mother walked toward the door, she turned and asked Rogers if he ever saw adult clients. Then the woman returned to her seat and began pouring out her own problems. She spoke of her own sense of confusion and failure and her despair about her marriage, all of which were more pertinent to her son's problems than the sterile case history approach they had followed before. After many more interviews, the woman felt better about her marriage, and her son's problem behavior dropped away as well. Rogers felt the improvement had come because he had followed her lead, because he had listened and understood rather than imposed his diagnostic understanding on her. This was the first of many experiences that gradually led Rogers to the view that therapeutic progress comes mostly from respecting and responding to the client's own frame of reference and his or her inherent potential for growth.

Therapists using this approach believe that all of us have within ourselves vast resources for self-understanding and for altering our behavior and that these resources can be tapped if the proper climate for change can be provided. According to Rogers (1980), three conditions must be present for a therapeutic climate to be growth producing. All of them pertain to the client-therapist relationship. First, the therapist must be genuine, or "congruent," in the relationship, rather than maintaining a detached professional façade. That is, there is a congruence, or close matching, between what the therapist experiences at the gut level and what is expressed to the clients. The second essential is an attitude of acceptance and caring. When the therapist is accepting of and caring toward the clients at the moment, therapeutic change is more likely to occur. But such caring is nonpossessive. The therapist accepts the clients unconditionally, so that they are free to feel what is going on within themselves at the moment—whether confusion, resentment, fear, or love. The third aspect of the therapeutic relationship is empathetic understanding. That is, the therapist accurately senses the feelings and personal meanings the clients are experiencing and communicates this understanding to them. Rogers holds that as clients are understood and accepted, they accept themselves more fully and listen more accurately to the flow of their inner experience. They also become increasingly self-directed and feel greater freedom to become the true, whole person they would like to be. During the early stages of therapy, one young woman said that whenever she looked within herself she felt nothing but emptiness:"There was just a cavern." Later, speaking about the change in her life, the same woman said,

> It's real: I am in a very dynamic process of becoming. I'm not on top of the world yet (maybe, as Joe suggests, I'm somewhere around five on the process scale), but now I know I will be. The cavern is filling with experiencing, and feeling—and I'm in there—ME—A PERSON. (Rogers, 1980, p. 218)

A VARIETY OF APPROACHES

New forms of insight therapy continue to appear and take their place alongside the more established ones just described. Many of these newer approaches are attempts to add or emphasize aspects of therapy thought to be missing in existing therapies. For instance, in contrast to the so-called value-neutral approach to therapy, two other therapies—**existential therapy,** as practiced by Rollo May, and **logotherapy,** developed by Viktor Frankl—stress the importance of clarifying those values that give personal meaning and purpose to one's life. Thus, individuals must have the courage to make choices, break away from restrictive lifestyles, and take responsibility for their lives. Similarly, Greenwald's direct decision therapy, described in Chapter 12 on personal control and decision making, emphasizes the importance of taking responsibility for one's life, especially in terms of the decisions one has made or needs to make. **Gestalt therapy,** founded by Fritz Perls, also puts great value on the individual's responsibility in therapy but makes more use of the here-and-now nonverbal behavior in the therapy session as a way of helping clients to unify their feelings and actions. **Actualization therapy,** developed by Everett Shostrom, combines elements of the person-centered approach, gestalt therapy, and rational-emotive therapy as a way of maximizing the individual's growth, or self-actualization.

There are, as always, many therapists who continue to practice the type of therapy in which they have been trained, modifying their orientation somewhat with experience. But an increasing number of therapists would characterize themselves as eclectic in the sense of having been exposed to more than one theoretical orientation in their training and continuing to add new techniques to their repertoire of therapeutic strategies. They seem more intent on being able to use the most appropriate treatment strategy for a given client's problems than remaining within a particular school of therapy. As a result, in practice, many therapists incorporate aspects of more than one insight therapy as well as different behavioral techniques (Norcross & Prochaska, 1988).

 Cognitive-Behavioral Therapies

Today, there is a large and diverse group of therapists who characterize their orientation as either behavioral or cognitive, or, as is increasingly the case, cognitive-behavioral. Having developed from research psychology, both approaches focus on the problems themselves and how to modify them rather than on what caused them. Although we'll describe the behavioral and cognitive approaches separately, keep in mind that the trend is toward combining elements of each into a more inclusive alliance labeled **cognitive-behavioral therapies.**

BEHAVIORAL THERAPIES

Instead of searching for the underlying causes of the client's difficulties, as in many insight therapies, behavioral therapists focus directly on the problem behaviors involved. For example, instead of focusing on Sergei's Russian childhood, behavioral therapists would focus on his present problems of drinking too much, being unemployed, and being adversarial with his well-intentioned parents. Their aim would be to help Sergei replace these maladaptive behaviors with more appropriate and satisfying ones. Typically, **behavioral therapy** involves discovering the factors that trigger and reinforce the problem behavior; specifying a target behavior to replace it; and then, by manipulating these factors, bringing out the desired behavior. In the process, behavioral therapists help clients to develop the necessary skills to cope more effectively with their life situations.

Behavioral therapists draw on a repertoire of behavioral methods of proven effectiveness, for example, desensitization, aversive counterconditioning, token economies, modeling, and social-skills training such as assertiveness training. For instance, many of our fears are acquired through the process of conditioned responses, based on the principles of classical conditioning. **Desensitization,** developed by Joseph Wolpe, aims at reversing this process by inculcating a new response that is incompatible with the fear. By linking the feared object or situation to something pleasant, like relaxation, the client becomes "desensitized" to the fearful situation. (See Figure 14–2.)

Desensitization is especially effective with fears and phobias. Wolpe (1973) tells of a 24-year-old art student who came for treatment because of her fear of taking

---

FIGURE 14–2

OVERCOMING YOUR FEARS

Although desensitization is ordinarily done under professional supervision, it can also be used on a do-it-yourself basis with mild fears.

There are four steps in desensitizing yourself.

First, on separate 3 × 5 inch cards, write down each situation you associate with a given fear or apprehension. Include at least 10 but no more than 25 items in your stack of cards.

Next, arrange these cards in a hierarchy from the least to the most threatening situation, preferably with small steps of anxiety arousal between each. For example, suppose you are afraid of riding in a crowded elevator. You might construct a hierarchy that includes imagined situations such as the following:

1. You're entering a building that has an elevator.
2. You're walking down the hall toward the elevator.
3. You're standing alone in front of the elevator.

The next step is to train yourself in relaxation techniques. Sit in a comfortable chair or lie on a couch or bed. Then, beginning with your forehead and scalp, practice relaxing and letting your muscles go limp. Then progress to your jaw muscles, your neck, and so on. You may vary this technique by alternately tensing and relaxing each set of muscles. Or you can combine it with deep breathing, as described in the chapter on stress. Whichever method you use, spend two or three sessions practicing your relaxation techniques until you can become reasonably relaxed.

Now you're ready for the fourth step. Take the top card from the pile and look at it. Then close your eyes and visualize the situation as vividly as you can. As soon as you experience any anxiety, stop imagining the scene and go back to your relaxation techniques. When you are completely relaxed, look at the card again. Repeat this process until you can look at the card without feeling anxious. Then progress to the next card. You can heighten the realism of the imagined scenes by using such aids as pictures, recordings, slides, and videotapes.

It is important not to rush. Don't be upset if you can visualize only a few scenes in the hierarchy in each session. Each person has his or her own rate of progress. It's also a good idea to begin each new session with the last hierarchy scene that didn't arouse anxiety in the previous session.

examinations, which had resulted in repeated failures. Wolpe began by making up a hierarchy of imagined situations that made her anxious, culminating with the day of the examination. Then he taught her how to relax her body muscles and gradually associate the relaxed state with each of the feared situations. After 17 sessions, the art student felt free from anxiety at the highest level of the hierarchy. Four months later she took and successfully passed her examinations without any disruptive anxiety.

In addition to confronting the client with imagined scenes, as in systematic desensitization, therapists may also use variations of this technique. In behavior rehearsal, for example, the client role-plays the feared situation. In real-life, or "in vivo," desensitization, the individual gradually approaches the feared situation directly, an approach often used in treating agoraphobia.

COGNITIVE THERAPIES

Cognitive therapists, drawing on a different set of principles, focus on faulty cognitive processes as the crucial element in maladaptive behavior. A major reason is their belief that cognitive processes—such as attention, perception, thoughts, and beliefs—may affect behavior independently of the stimulus events traditionally emphasized by behaviorists. Indeed, cognitive therapists claim that people's actions are often shaped more by their own interpretation and reaction to external events than the events themselves. Albert Ellis's rational-emotive therapy (Ellis & Dryden, 1987), Aaron Beck's cognitive therapy (1979), and Donald Meichenbaum's (1985) stress-inoculation training are all well-known **cognitive therapies.** Although these therapies differ in emphasis and tone, they share a common approach. The central assumption is that the emotional and behavioral problems result from the individual's distorted thoughts and reactions to external events rather than from the events themselves.

Ellis's (Ellis & Harper, 1975) A-B-C theory of personality is central to his rational-emotive therapy. (See Figure 14–3.) The activating event (A) triggers the behavior. The emotional, behavioral reactions to the event (C) may be either appropriate or inappropriate. However, Ellis points out that it is the person's beliefs (B) about the activating event rather than the event itself that causes his or her emotional, behavioral reactions. Therefore, rational-emotive therapists focus on changing the clients' thoughts and beliefs as a way of changing their behavior. Some of the irrational ideas that commonly lead to maladaptive behavior are listed in Figure 14–4.

FIGURE 14–3

The a–b–c theory of personality. SOURCE: Albert Ellis and Robert A. Harper, *A New Guide to Rational Living* (Englewood Cliffs, NJ: Prentice Hall, and Hollywood, CA: Wilshire Books, 1975). Reprinted by permission of the publishers and the authors.

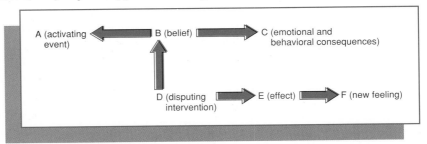

FIGURE 14–4

SOME COMMONLY HELD IRRATIONAL IDEAS

Albert Ellis has identified a dozen irrational ideas or assumptions that are widespread in our society and when believed tend to lead to self-defeating behavior.

1. The idea that you must—yes, must—have sincere love and approval almost all the time from all the people you find significant.
2. The idea that you must prove yourself thoroughly competent, adequate, and achieving, or that you must at least have real competence or talent at something important.
3. The idea that people who harm you or commit misdeeds rate as generally bad, wicked, or villainous individuals and that you should severely blame, damn, and punish them for their sins.
4. The idea that life proves awful, terrible, horrible, or catastrophic when things do not go the way you would like them to go.
5. The idea that emotional misery comes from external pressures and that you have little ability to control your feelings or rid yourself of depression and hostility.
6. The idea that if something seems dangerous or fearsome, you must become terribly occupied with and upset about it.
7. The idea that you will find it easier to avoid facing many of life's difficulties and self-responsibilities than to undertake more rewarding forms of self-discipline.
8. The idea that your past remains all-important and that because something once strongly influenced your life, it has to keep determining your feelings and behavior today.
9. The idea that people and things should turn out better than they do and that you have to view it as awful and horrible if you do not quickly find good solutions to life's hassles.
10. The idea that you can achieve happiness by inertia and inaction or by passively and uncommittedly "enjoying yourself."
11. The idea that you must have a high degree of order or certainty to feel comfortable, or that you need some supernatural power on which to rely.
12. The idea that you can give yourself a global rating as a human being, and that your general worth and self-acceptance depend upon the goodness of your performances and the degree that people approve of you.

SOURCE: Albert Ellis and Robert A. Harper, *A New Guide to Rational Living* (Englewood Cliffs, NJ: Prentice Hall, and Hollywood, CA: Wilshire Books, 1975), pp. 83–85. Reprinted by permission of the publishers and the authors.

For example, Melissa, a friend of Sergei's, has just discovered that she earned a low grade on her first test in psychology. She feels discouraged and engages in self-defeating thinking: "How stupid can I be! I'll never make a good grade in this course. I might as well drop it." A therapist trained in rational-emotive therapy might point out that Melissa is "awfulizing," that is, overreacting to her poor performance. The therapist would point out the irrationality of Melissa's thinking and model a more realistic evaluation of her situation, for example: "This was just the first test, not the final exam." Then the therapist would help Melissa take positive steps to improve her performance, such as talking to the teacher to discover the particular reasons why she did poorly on the test, getting suggestions for improving her performance on the next test, and finding out what her chances are for eventually earning a good grade in the course. The therapist might instruct Melissa in self-monitoring and correcting her thinking and how to begin preparing more effectively for the next test now.

Cognitive therapists differ from insight therapists in that they do not probe for deep-seated causes of the client's problems. For example, they would not be as likely as a psychoanalyst to explore Sergei's Russian childhood. Instead, their goal is to identify faulty assumptions and thought patterns and then rely on established behavioral procedures such as relaxation training and behavioral rehearsal to alter the overall behavior.

MULTIMODAL THERAPY

Multimodal therapy, developed by Arnold Lazarus (1981), is a comprehensive and flexible approach to behavior therapy that in many ways incorporates the trend toward the cognitive-behavioral alliance. Lazarus holds that because human behavior is complex and people's problems are multidimensional in nature, it is essential to attend to these different dimensions for lasting changes to occur. Accordingly, multimodal therapy begins with a systematic assessment of the BASIC-ID, an acronym for the various aspects of personality and behavior. Following is a modified version of this assessment process and the questions used.

- *Behavior.* How active are you? What specific behaviors would you like to start doing? What would you like to stop doing?
- *Affect.* How emotional are you? What makes you laugh? What emotions are a problem for you?
- *Sensation.* How much do you focus on the pleasures and pains derived from the senses?
- *Imagery.* How would you describe your self-image? How would you like to see yourself in the future?
- *Cognition.* What are the main shoulds, oughts, and musts in your life? How do they get in the way of effective living?
- *Interpersonal relationships.* To what degree do you desire closeness with others? Are there any relationships with others you would like to change?
- *Drugs/Biology.* What are your concerns about health? Do you take any prescribed drugs? What are your eating and exercise habits?

The preliminary questioning is followed by a detailed life-history questionnaire. Throughout assessment and treatment, special attention is given to both the deficits and the excesses that arise within each of these dimensions. For instance, shyness would represent a deficit that might be treated with social-skills training, such as assertiveness training. Compulsive drinking of alcohol as in Sergei's case would be an excess that needs to be reduced or eliminated, perhaps through a combination of procedures aimed at achieving greater control over one's diet and how one socializes. Also, multimodal therapists are encouraged to borrow techniques of proven effectiveness from other approaches to therapy, thereby giving them greater flexibility in the treatment process. The aim is to find the most appropriate treatment for each client's problems rather than to fit all clients into the same therapeutic mold.

Selected Approaches to Treatment

In addition to the individual therapies discussed so far, there is a wide variety of other types of treatment. For instance, group therapies have mushroomed in number and variety in the past several decades. Groups not only offer opportunities for people to interact with others with similar problems, but are also more cost efficient, saving time and money—an important consideration today. We'll look at family therapy in particular because the disruption of marriages and families has become a major source of stress in our society. Also, the gains in medicine and technology have produced more powerful drugs and sophisticated biomedical therapies, which have become an integral part of many treatment programs. Finally, one of the most dramatic changes in regard to treating the emotionally disturbed is the shift away from prolonged stays in large institutions to the use of community-based services, as we'll explain shortly. Before you read further about professionally led groups, read Box 14–1 about mutual-help or self-help groups where laypersons assist one another.

BOX 14–1

MUTUAL-HELP GROUPS

Today, more than 12 million people participate in an estimated 500,000 self-help or mutual-help groups—groups whose members share a common problem and meet regularly to discuss their concerns without the guidance of professionals.

Although these groups frequently have multiple functions, such as fostering self-help and lobbying for reform, most have the same underlying purpose—to provide social support as well as practical help in dealing with a problem common to all members. A major assumption is that no one understands you or may help you better than someone who has the same problem, whether it's obesity, depression, or alcoholism. New members may approach their first meeting with apprehension, wondering what the group can do for them or what it will ask in return. Experienced members, well aware of these mixed emotions, encourage new members to feel relaxed and welcome. In an atmosphere that is friendly and compassionate, new members soon realize that their participation is voluntary, with no strings attached. There is usually an unwritten code of confidentiality within the group. Even when there is a series of steps to recovery, as in the various "Anonymous" groups, members can proceed at their own pace. Some groups, especially those that deal with addictive behavior or emotional disorders, may use a "buddy" system so that a new member can count on a familiar person for encouragement and support. All in all, mutual-help groups provide an atmosphere of acceptance and support that encourages their members to communicate more openly, view their problems more objectively, and find more effective coping strategies.

Numerous agencies and clearinghouses provide information on mutual-help groups. If you fail to find the mutual-help groups of interest in your phone book, phone American Self-Help Clearing House [(201)-625-7101], which publishes a directory of national self-help groups.

MARITAL, FAMILY, AND RELATIONSHIP THERAPY

Married and unmarried couples alike usually come to relationship therapy because of some crisis, such as infidelity on the part of one partner or a breakdown in communication. A common problem encountered by therapists is the case in which one partner, usually the more dominant person in the relationship, threatens to leave, and the other partner wants to keep the marriage or relationship intact. Although each person tends to blame his or her partner for the predicament, therapists tend to focus more on the partners' interaction and relationship. For instance, if one person has engaged in an extramarital affair, instead of joining in the blame, the therapist may ask each partner what he or she thinks caused this situation. Perhaps the offending partner sought to fill a void in an empty marriage or wanted to get back at the other partner. Either way, the therapist helps both of them become more aware of how they treat each other; how they may unwittingly hurt each other; and most important, how they may nurture each other. The therapist often has to help the couple clarify the extent to which they really want to work at the marriage and, if so, how to proceed.

Family therapy, as the name implies, involves the larger family unit, including children and adolescents. There are now dozens of different types of family therapy, which vary in their theoretical approaches, range of techniques, and procedures. Some therapists prefer to see the entire family from beginning to end. Others may see the identified client or parents for a couple of sessions and the identified client with his or her parents and siblings in the remaining sessions. Still others, such as *contextual* therapists, who adhere to an intergenerational approach, may involve members of the extended family in therapy. In Sergei's case, perhaps even his grandparents would participate if they were available. However, implicit in all such therapies is the assump-

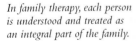

In family therapy, each person is understood and treated as an integral part of the family.

tion that families function as systems, so that the individual's problems are best understood and treated as an integral part of the family unit. In Sergei's case, his parents would also be involved in Sergei's therapy so that they could learn to interact more effectively with one another.

Suppose a teenager is having trouble in school or is doing something that indicates a problem. The usual course of events is to make the teenager the client, leaving untouched the larger web of problems at home. However, helpers oriented to family therapy may discover, upon further investigation, that the identified client is actually the most sensitive and vulnerable person in the family and has become the scapegoat of a troubled family. When this is the case, it may be necessary to see other members of the family to get a better understanding of the family dynamics in order to help the identified client. For example, Brad, another friend of Sergei's, reluctantly consulted a therapist because of parental pressure to do so. He was running around with a group that was into drugs and serious delinquency. The therapist soon discovered that Brad's problems were fueled in part by his parents' serious marital problem, and Brad was suffering from "split loyalty." His mother was resentful of the long hours her husband spent at work, along with numerous alleged extramarital affairs, and went to great efforts to make certain Brad knew about his father's disloyalty to the family. As a result, Brad felt pressured, mostly subconsciously, to take his mother's side in the family feud. However, in doing so, he felt cut off from his father's positive influence and support. Brad responded by withdrawing from both parents, pretending he "didn't care" about his parents' marital problems and spending all his time with his friends. The therapist asked both parents to come in and gradually helped them to see how their marital problems were contributing to their son's problems. Once the parents became aware of what they were doing to their son, both of them made greater efforts to cooperate, at least as far as their son's welfare was concerned. Brad, in turn, felt less divided in his loyalty to his parents and spent his energy on resolving his own problems. In fact, Brad's therapy was so successful that he was one of the friends who encouraged Sergei to see a mental health professional.

BIOMEDICAL THERAPIES

In contrast to the various forms of verbal therapy, **biomedical therapies** use direct physiological intervention to treat the symptoms of psychological disorders. In recent years, there has been a rapid accumulation of evidence that many disorders are related to biochemical abnormalities, especially neurotransmitters—chemical messengers that travel across the synapses in the brain. As a result, psychoactive drugs in particular have become an indispensable part of treatment. Many of those with severe disorders like schizophrenia may be treated primarily with drugs. Those with less severe disorders may also be treated with medication, but often in conjunction with the other therapies discussed so far.

Drug therapies continue to be the most widely used biomedical therapies. The three major categories are antianxiety, antidepressant, and antipsychotic drugs. Sergei would be an unlikely candidate for such therapies. These medications do not mix with alcohol well.

Antianxiety drugs, or minor tranquilizers, are the most commonly prescribed psychoactive drugs in the United States. Each year, about 1 out of 10 adults will use a tranquilizer at some time or another (Bootzin & Acocella, 1988). In most cases, family physicians prescribe a tranquilizer for people going through a difficult time, but these drugs are also used in the treatment of anxiety disorders, stress-related disorders, and withdrawal from alcohol and other drugs. As useful as these drugs are, they are not without their side effects. The most common are fatigue, drowsiness, and impaired motor coordination. Also, when used in combination with alcohol or other central nervous system depressants, these drugs can be dangerous or even fatal. Finally, the most common criticism of tranquilizers is that they may provide such prompt alleviation of symptoms that people may avoid solving their problems. Consequently, they are most useful on a short-term basis.

Antidepressant drugs are used to elevate mood, usually by increasing the level of certain neurotransmitters, especially norepinephrine and serotonin. These drugs help to relieve many of the typical symptoms of depression, such as sleeplessness or excessive sleepiness, chronic fatigue, loss of appetite, loss of sex drive, sadness, and feelings of worthlessness. A significant disadvantage of these drugs is that they do not begin to take effect for about 2 to 4 weeks—which can be a long time for seriously depressed people waiting for relief. Newer, quicker-acting antidepressants have been introduced, but it remains to be seen whether they will be as effective.

Lithium—a natural mineral salt—is used to treat people with bipolar disorder. Lithium is capable of terminating three-fourths of all manic episodes (unduly elevated moods) and some cases of depression. When taken regularly, in maintenance doses, lithium eliminates or at least diminishes mood swings in bipolar disorder. However, because the effective dosage is close to the toxic dosage, it is difficult to prescribe the proper maintenance dosage of lithium. Furthermore, many patients stop taking their medication because lithium takes away the sense of well-being they feel in their mildly excited state. However, the interruption of lithium treatment usually leaves patients just as vulnerable to the disabling manic episodes as they were before treatment began.

Antipsychotic drugs, as the name suggests, are used to treat the symptoms of severe disorders such as schizophrenia. As mentioned earlier, the use of antipsychotic drugs is often the primary treatment for schizophrenic patients, especially the chronically impaired. These drugs are thought to work by blocking the activity of dopamine— a neurotransmitter intimately involved in schizophrenia—thereby reducing such symptoms as hallucinations, delusions, and bizarre behavior. However, they do not cure the apathy, social withdrawal, or interpersonal difficulties found in people with schizophrenia, for which psychotherapy is usually needed. Antipsychotic drugs also have several side effects. In producing calm, they may produce apathy as well, reducing the patient to a zombielike state. Also, a small proportion of patients develop *tardive dyskinesia,* characterized by jerking movements around the neck and face and involuntary protrusions of the tongue. Despite these disadvantages and the criticisms surrounding

The number of psychoactive drugs has increased dramatically since the 1960s.

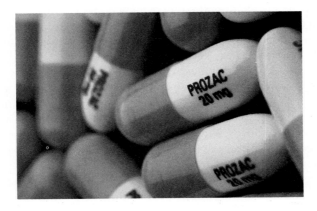

the use of such drugs, antipsychotic drugs have been the single biggest factor in reducing the institutionalized patient population in the United States from over half a million in the 1950s to about one-third that number today. Over two-thirds of schizophrenic individuals who take their medication regularly can remain out of the hospital. Consequently, most professionals who work with schizophrenic patients believe the value of these drugs outweighs their potential abuse.

Electroconvulsive therapy (ECT), for reasons that are not completely understood, helps to relieve severe depression in some patients. Although people often bristle at the mention of the name, ECT has been refined and is done in a more humane manner than in the past. It usually involves 6 to 10 treatments, spaced over a period of several weeks. The patient is usually given general anesthesia and a muscle relaxant. Then an electric current of approximately 70 to 130 volts is administered to the temple area for a fraction of a second, causing convulsions for a minute or so. Within half an hour, the patient awakens and remembers nothing of the treatment. The most common side effects are memory loss, especially the recall of events before the treatment, though this tends to be recovered within 7 months. Despite the controversy over ECT, a 1985 National Institute of Mental Health Consensus Conference concluded that it is an effective treatment for people suffering from severe depression with delusions and should be used with such patients when other treatments, such as antidepressants, have failed (Bootzin & Acocella, 1988).

Psychosurgery is an even more drastic procedure, so much so that Sergei certainly would not be a candidate for it. Psychosurgery is aimed at reducing abnormal behavior. In the earlier prefrontal lobotomies, the surgeon severed the nerves connecting the frontal lobes of the brain with the emotion-controlling centers. Although many severely disturbed patients became calm, others emerged from surgery in a vegetative state. As a result, professionals welcomed the introduction of antipsychotic drugs, which produce similar results in a safer, reversible manner. Since then, the surgical procedure has been refined. However, lobotomies are still the treatment of last resort and are used only rarely, mostly for severely depressed, suicidal patients who have not responded to other treatments.

After reading these passages on biopsychological approaches to treatment of mental disorders, you may be wondering whether we can use less intrusive physiological methods for improving our mental status. After all, each of the techniques just described can have serious side effects. The answer is yes, as you will see in Box 14–2.

COMMUNITY-BASED SERVICES

The introduction of antipsychotic drugs, along with convincing evidence that custody care in large mental hospitals is detrimental, has led to the release of large numbers of ex-patients into the community in the past 35 years. Because most of these patients require some type of treatment, as do others in the community who wish to avoid hospitalization, mental health professionals have responded by providing more **community-based services.** The passage of the Community Mental Health Centers Act in 1963 aimed to create a **community mental health center** for every 50,000 people in the United States. Everyone in the *catchment* area, an area of geographical coverage, would have access to the needed psychological services at affordable fees without having to leave the community. Although the actual services provided by these centers have fallen far short of the initial vision, they have been a major factor in the nationwide shift to community-based mental health care.

As you might expect, the outpatient services are the most heavily used services of local mental health centers. The goal of outpatient services is to provide help for indi-

BOX 14–2

ALLEVIATING DEPRESSION THROUGH EXERCISE

Dozens of studies link regular physical exercise with lower levels of depression and anxiety. People who exercise regularly are less depressed. But researchers realize it might work the other way around, namely, that people who are more depressed simply exercise less.

To demonstrate a causal link between exercise and depression, psychologists Lisa McCann and David Holmes (1984) performed an experiment with women students at the University of Kansas. Students were randomly assigned either to an exercise group, involving running and aerobic exercise, or to a control group, which involved no exercise program. Before the experiment began, the women were tested to measure the degree of their depression. Later, they were retested after 5 weeks of the exercise program and again after 10 weeks. Results showed that only the students in the exercise group became markedly less depressed.

It is not clear how or why exercise affects depression. Some explanations focus on the changes in body and brain chemistry, resulting in rising levels of endorphins in the blood during exercise (Hopson, 1988). Other explanations suggest that the sense of mastery over one's body gained through exercise may contribute to a greater sense of personal control over other aspects of one's life as well, thereby alleviating the passivity and helplessness often found in depressed people (C. Peterson & Seligman, 1984). Because the more severe types of depression often result from a complex interaction of genetic, physiological, and psychological factors, exercise is best seen as only one factor in the overall treatment of depression—but one that should not be overlooked.

viduals without disrupting their normal routine. Most mental health centers offer short-term therapy for individuals in the community with a variety of problems, ranging from domestic disputes to severe emotional disturbances.

The more comprehensive centers also provide alternatives to hospital care, such as day hospitals, halfway houses, and emergency or crisis services. Over 1,000 **day hospitals** have been established throughout the United States. These hospitals provide the needed therapeutic care to patients from 9:00 A.M. to 5:00 P.M. and then allow them to return to their families in the evening. Another agency that has proliferated in recent years is the **halfway house**—a residence in which newly released patients and ex-addicts can live under supervision for a short period of time while they make a crucial transition in their lives. Halfway houses are also called group homes and board-and-care homes. The best halfway houses are small residences that are staffed by paraprofessionals who help the residents learn to live together and acquire the appropriate skills for returning to community life. **Crisis intervention** has also emerged in response to a widespread need for immediate help for individuals and families confronted with stressful situations. Most people who come for short-term crisis therapy do not continue in treatment for more than one to six sessions. In addition, a variety of hotlines is now available in many communities.

Community-based services often fall short of what is needed, mostly because of insufficient funding and the resultant inadequacies in facilities, staffing, and carefully thought-out and coordinated programs that address the needs of the community (Duffy & Wong, 1996). Because of these inadequacies, the return of patients to the community has slowed significantly. Even when patients return to the community, they lack the necessary supervision and support to stay there. In the large cities, many of them become "street people" before returning to the hospital. As a result, in many regions, the number of admissions to mental hospitals has *increased* rather than decreased, leading to a "revolving-door" syndrome or **transinstitutionalization** (Duffy & Wong, 1996). The revolving-door syndrome and the presence of so many former mental patients in jails, on the streets, and in nursing homes remind us that although comprehensive community-based care is an excellent idea, it is far from achieving its original goals (Duffy & Wong, 1996).

How Well Does Therapy Work?

For many years, hardly anyone bothered to ask such a question. Therapists and clients alike held a kind of blind faith that therapy does work. Then after reviewing various studies on the subject, Hans Eysenck (1966) shocked the world of therapy by concluding that as many clients with neurotic complaints improved with the mere passage of time as did clients in psychotherapy. Eysenck's claims were hotly contested and challenged by other studies. Researchers have typically asked three major questions about the effectiveness of therapy. Is therapy or treatment better than no therapy? Is one particular type of therapy more effective than others? And are certain disorders more amenable to certain therapies? Let's answer these questions in order of presentation.

Is psychotherapy effective? Extensive studies have confirmed that therapy tends to have modest positive effects. In a comprehensive review of 475 studies, one investigation has shown that the average client receiving therapy is generally better off than 80 percent of those who do not receive therapy. And the improvement rate is even higher for the alleviation of anxiety and fear. Equally important, the researchers found that the different types of therapy—psychodynamic, humanist, and behavioral therapies—do not differ significantly in their overall rates of effectiveness (M. L. Smith, Glass, & Miller, 1980). (See Figure 14–5.)

Most other research on the question of the efficacy of psychotherapy also suggests that Eysenck was incorrect. Another investigation (Howard, Kopta, Krause, & Orlinsky, 1986), including 2,431 clients in 15 studies, found a positive relationship between the length of treatment and client improvement. About one-third of the clients had improved within the first 3 sessions, regardless of the ultimate duration of treatment. Similarly, half of them had improved by 8 sessions, and approximately three-fourths by 28 sessions. At the same time, the rate of improvement varied considerably among different types of clients. Depressed clients generally showed improvement after the first few sessions, clients with anxiety disorders usually needed somewhat more sessions before showing improvement, and the more severely disturbed psychotic clients required the most sessions. Also, a comparison of subjective and objective improvement measures showed that early in treatment clients begin to feel better before they appear better to their therapists. But later in therapy, clients' own perceptions of change lag behind improvement in their clinical condition. Although such findings do not prove that time-limited therapy is as effective as time-unlimited therapy, 26 sessions could be used as a

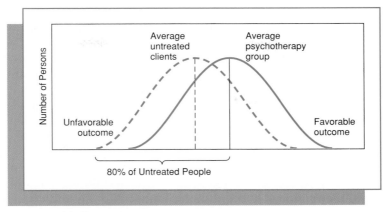

FIGURE 14–5

**The improvment of clients receiving psychotherapy versus
untreated clients.** SOURCE: Smith, M. L., Glass G. V., & Miller R. L. (1980).
The benefits of psychotherapy. Baltimore: Johns Hopkins University Press, 1980. ©1980
Johns Hopkins University Press. Reproduced with permission.

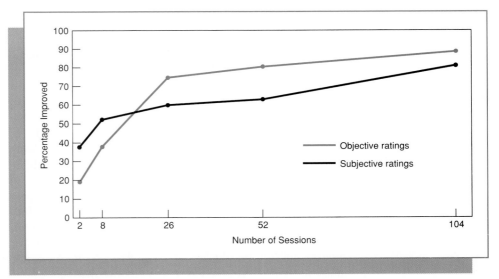

FIGURE 14–6

**Relation of number of sessions of psychotherapy and percentage of patients
improved.** SOURCE: Kenneth I. Howard, S. Mark Kopta, Merton S. Krause, and David E. Orlinsky, "The
Dose-Effect Relationship in Psychotherapy," *American Psychologist* (February 1986), p. 160. Copyright 1986 by the
American Psychological Association. Reprinted by permission.

point in the treatment process at which cases that have not shown any measurable improvement would be subjected to a clinical review. (See Figure 14–6.) And finally, other
studies have demonstrated that the effects of psychotherapy are usually well-maintained
over time (Nietzel, Bernstein, & Milich, 1991).

Subsequent research has also derived some notions about what ingredients make
therapy effective, no matter what type. One important aspect found over and over again

is the match between the client and the therapist. For example, directive treatments are more effective than nondirective or person-centered ones with low-resistance clients (Beutler, Mohr, Grawe, Engle, & MacDonald, 1991).

This leads us to our second question: Is one type of psychotherapy more effective than another? The answer the scientific literature gives is that there is little difference among types of therapy. What the literature again shows is that the therapeutic alliance and match between client and therapist is of utmost importance. And because most successful therapies include individualized attention, a credible rationale for the client's problems, experiences with mastery, and higher expectations for improvement, most therapies are effective (G. E. Powell & Lindsay, 1987). In fact, behavior therapists who traditionally have slighted the curative power of the therapeutic relationship are now emphasizing it to a far greater extent than in the past (Glass & Arnkoff, 1992). You might be wondering if laypersons can ever serve as effective therapists. Some of them, friends for example, can sometimes offer a distressed person these same benefits. Box 14–3 discusses this possibility.

BOX 14–3

INFORMAL HELPERS

Surveys have shown that about 22 percent of the people who need psychological help receive no treatment (Walker, 1982). However, there is increasing recognition that many of these people get informal help from a variety of sources, including neighbors, work supervisors, and cab drivers.

One study (Cowen, 1982) focused on four groups engaged in informal helping: hairdressers, divorce lawyers, personnel supervisors, and bartenders. As expected, the kinds of problems discussed and the help received varied from one group to another. The investigators found that the problems discussed with hairdressers usually involved children, health, and marriage. Divorce lawyers dealt more with anger at a spouse, depression, and problems contacting a spouse, whereas supervisors dealt mainly with relationships with other workers, problems in advancement, and restlessness on the job. Bartenders tended to hear job, marriage, and money problems.

The most common helping strategy in all four groups was listening and offering support. In addition, the lawyers tended to ask questions, point out consequences of faulty ideas, and propose alternatives. More than any other group, the hairdressers used the questionable technique of changing the topic or telling people to count their blessings. Both hairdressers and bartenders were more apt to use a lighthearted approach, including humor.

People in all four groups felt comfortable with their roles as informal helpers. Furthermore, most of them viewed their efforts as moderately effective. Obviously, they provide a useful service by simply listening because it is often helpful to "talk out" our problems. Beyond that, there may be some risk in giving advice or making light of serious problems, especially with those who are depressed and suicidal. Also, there is added risk that some troubled people may feel such informal help is all they need, when in fact they need professional guidance.

According to this research, then, Sergei would be well served by psychotherapy. His disorder is probably depression; what type of therapy works best in this case?

This leads to our last question. Is one type of therapy better or worse for any particular disorder? Although more research is merited on all of these issues, the answer to this third question at this point seems to be yes. Behavior therapies appear to be effective for phobic disorders (Bowers & Clum, 1988; Wilson, 1990). Psychoactive drugs are most effective for treating schizophrenic disorders, whereas cognitive-behavioral therapies in conjunction with medication are most effective for depression (Beck, 1991; Dobson, 1989). As more answers become available, psychotherapists may increasingly offer specific treatments for particular problems or integrate different approaches that may be more effective than a single approach with certain individuals (Wilson).

Remember, too, that therapy is not exclusively dependent on the therapist's skills, the disorder, and the type of therapy. The client's traits are also important. The type of person likely to benefit most from psychotherapy is someone who is articulate, motivated, anxious to change, capable of becoming personally involved in therapy, and believes in psychological processes as explanations of behavior (Nietzel et al., 1991). Another client characteristic that affects efficacy of therapy is ethnic background. Recall that Sergei's Russian parents wanted to keep their family problems to themselves and not share them with a stranger, in this case his therapist. Some research has suggested that Asian and Hispanic Americans tend to underutilize mental health care services (Bui & Takeuchi, 1992; Sue, Fujino, Hu, Takeuchi, & Zane, 1991). Sue and his colleagues argue that even when ethnic minorities seek mental health care, they tend to have higher dropout rates than Whites. What they suggest is that mental health care professionals share the ethnic background as their clients.

Getting Help

Being knowledgeable about psychotherapy is one thing. Knowing how to get professional help for yourself or others is another matter. Should you or someone like Sergei have the occasion to seek professional help, you might consider the following questions.

1. *When should you seek professional help?* As you might expect, there is no simple answer to this question as so much depends on the particular person and his or her situation. However, a rule of thumb is this: Whenever your problems begin to interfere with your work and personal life, it's time to seek professional help. Also, when your present methods of coping with your problems no longer work, that's another sign that you may need help, especially when your family or friends are tired of being used as therapists and become openly concerned about you. Most important, whenever you feel overwhelmed and desperate and don't know what to do, it's best to seek help.

   However, you don't have to have a serious problem, much less a psychological disorder, to benefit from therapy. As mentioned earlier, more and more people are seeking therapy as a means of personal growth, to improve their coping skills and to get more out of life.

2. *Where do you find help?* Help is available in a wide variety of settings. A large proportion of therapists work in the comprehensive mental health centers now

available in most communities. Staffed by a combination of psychiatrists, psychologists, social workers, and counselors, these centers offer a variety of services, including emergency help, all at a nominal fee that depends on income and ability to pay. See Figure 14–7 for a description of the various types of mental health professionals.

Many therapists work in private practice, either in a group or individual setting. They are usually listed in the yellow pages by their respective professions, for example, psychiatrists, psychologists, social workers, or family therapists. Although they are relatively expensive, you may be reimbursed for part of the fee, depending on the type of insurance you have.

In addition, many private social service or human service agencies provide short-term counseling and support for such matters as family problems, drug problems, and career counseling. Also, many private and mental hospitals offer emergency help for psychological problems. Then, too, most high schools and

---

FIGURE 14–7

WHO ARE THE THERAPISTS?

Unlike law or medicine, in which there is a single path to professional practice, there are many routes to becoming a psychotherapist. Because few states regulate the practice of psychotherapy as such, the question of who may legitimately conduct psychotherapy is governed by state law or professional boards within the respective professions.

- Psychiatrists are medical doctors who specialize in the treatment of mental illness. They usually spend 3 to 4 years training in a clinical setting following their medical degree and can treat the psychological disorders requiring drugs and hospitalization.

- Psychoanalysts are psychiatrists or other mental health professionals who have received several years of additional training in personality theory and the therapeutic methods of one of the founding analysts, such as Freud, Jung, Adler, or Sullivan.

- Psychologists receive clinical training in the methods of psychological assessment and treatment as part of a program in clinical, counseling, or school psychology. They may have a Ph.D., Ed.D., or Psy.D. degree.

- Psychiatric social workers receive supervised clinical training as part of their master's degree program in the field of social work, and some earn a doctorate as well. They tend to be community oriented and usually work as part of a clinical team, though many now enter private practice.

- Counselors receive training in personality theory and counseling skills, usually at the master's degree level. Their counseling emphasis tends to reflect their respective professional affiliations, depending on whether they are doing marriage counseling, career counseling, pastoral counseling (clergy), or some other type.

- Paraprofessionals (*para* meaning "akin to") have two- or four-year degrees (or sometimes no degree at all) and work in the mental health field. Sometimes as many as half the staff members of a community mental health center work at the paraprofessional level, assisting in the helping process in a variety of ways.

colleges have counseling centers, which may provide psychological help as well as academic guidance and career counseling.

3. *What should you look for in a therapist?* Among the major considerations for choosing a therapist should be (1) whether the therapist is professionally trained and certified and (2) how comfortable you feel with this person. Ordinarily, people must be properly qualified to list themselves as psychiatrists, psychologists, or social workers in the telephone directory. Also, professionals are encouraged to display their state license and other certificates in a prominent place in their office. But you will also want to feel comfortable talking to the therapist. Does this

---

BOX 14–4

COMPUTERS AND THERAPY: WAVE OF THE FUTURE?

An increasing number of psychotherapists are offering on-line help. Many are setting up World Wide Web pages accessible to millions of Americans with credit cards and computers. Most computer therapists provide the caveat that cybertherapy does not allow for as detailed probing as does face-to-face intervention. For example, it is impossible to get a complete family history in a short, typed message. There is little research on cybertherapy as of yet, but at present it appears best for those individuals who can clearly identify their own dilemmas. Critics of cybertherapy argue that confidentiality may be betrayed if the wrong person receives the electronic message either to or from the therapist. Critics also argue that the client may know little about the on-line therapist's qualifications because of the geographic distance between client and therapist.

Other means for finding help on-line are currently and rapidly developing. For example, social support is offered in the form of chat lines, bulletin boards, and newsgroups for individuals with specific disorders. Similarly, some psychological journals have gone on-line so that mental health consumers can do their own literature searches. One rich website is PsychNET offered by the American Psychological Association.

Another new use for computers in therapy is virtual therapy. Virtual therapy employs the high-tech tools of virtual reality, which essentially is often a computer-generated fantasy world which can be controlled by the client. Virtual therapy has been used to distract burn victims from their pain as well as to engulf phobics with harmless but feared virtual stimuli such as spiders and snakes. Research on this type of therapy is just beginning, but one disadvantage is already well-known—the expense of the hardware and software.

Researchers are hoping to adapt virtual reality for use on PCs, which, if successful, would make this therapy much more accessible to patients not living near large research universities. These same researchers recommend virtual therapy only for those clients for whom traditional forms of therapy have not been effective.

SOURCE: Adapted from Salyer, S. (1997, July 18–20). The dawn of "virtual therapy." *USA Weekend;* and Hannon, K. (1996, May 13). Upset? Try cybertherapy. *U.S. News & World Report.*

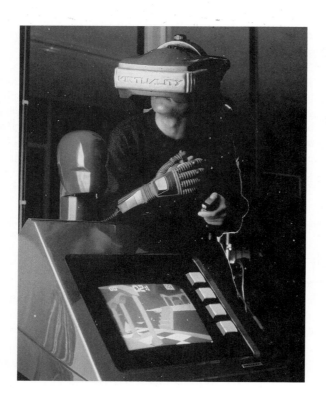

Virtual reality offers an exciting possibility as a form of therapy.

person really listen to you? Is he or she warm and empathic without being condescending? Does this person understand and/or appreciate your point of view? Box 14–4 discusses therapy via computers which have yet to be shown to be warm and empathic, among other disadvantages.

Once you've selected a therapist, it's appropriate to inquire in the initial session about such matters as his or her approach to therapy as well as fees. You may be interested to know that the therapist's theoretical orientation is less important than his or her personal characteristics, professional experience, and skills. The relative influence of other matters, such as the therapist's age, gender, and ethnic background, depend largely on their importance to you. Finally, you will also want to discuss fees. Fees vary widely among private practitioners with clinical psychologists and psychiatrists being the most expensive. The extent to which you will be reimbursed for a given type of treatment depends largely on your health insurance policy.

4. *What can you expect from therapy?* Most therapies provide certain common benefits, such as an empathic, caring, and trusting relationship; hope for the demoralized; and a new way of understanding yourself and the world (Strupp, 1986). Beyond this, a lot depends on the goals and progress made in your particular therapy. People seeking relatively short-term therapy usually acquire a better understanding of their problems as well as the necessary skills to cope with a personal or family crisis. Those undergoing relatively long-term therapy, such as psychodynamic therapy, aspire for more fundamental changes in their personality and may remain in therapy for a year or longer.

5. *How long must you go?* In the past, the lack of objective guidelines made it difficult for therapists and clients alike to know how long therapy should last. However, the recent trend toward short-term therapies and the increased concern for containing health-care costs have made the length of therapy a major issue. At the same time, as the studies by Howard et al. (1986) remind us, the rate of improvement varies considerably among different types of clients. Consequently, the appropriate length of treatment often becomes an empirical issue to be decided by clients and their therapists.

As a practical guide for deciding when to terminate therapy, Luborsky and his colleagues (1988) suggest that you consider two key issues: First, is the crisis or problem that brought you to therapy under control? You need not have resolved all of your difficulties, but you should have more understanding and control over your life so that your difficulties do not interfere with your work and personal activities. Second, can you maintain the gains acquired in therapy on your own? It's best to discuss these two issues with your therapist before deciding to terminate therapy. At the same time, bear in mind that in therapy, as in all close relationships, there will be unsettling as well as gratifying occasions. Therapy can become so uncomfortable that you may want to quit. However, if you put yourself into it and keep going, you'll eventually find it's a very rewarding experience.

SUMMARY

INSIGHT THERAPIES

At the outset, we stated that only about one out of five people suffering from a psychological disorder will get help from a mental health professional, such as a psychologist. Many of the others will be seen by their family physician or a counselor. Traditionally, many clients have sought out insight-oriented therapies, which aim at bringing about change by increasing self-understanding.

Modern psychoanalytic therapists use a modified version of Freud's ideas and techniques to help clients achieve insight into and self-mastery of the unconscious forces in their lives. In contrast, Rogers's person-centered approach assumes that individuals have within themselves vast resources for self-understanding and growth, which may be actualized within a caring and empathic relationship conducive to change. In addition, a variety of other insight therapies emphasize aspects of therapy thought to be missing in existing therapies, such as existential therapy, gestalt therapy, and actualization therapy.

COGNITIVE-BEHAVIORAL THERAPIES

Cognitive-behavioral approaches developed out of research and experimental psychology and tend to focus on the maladaptive thoughts and behaviors themselves rather than on their causes. Behavioral therapists focus directly on the client's problem behaviors, with the aim of replacing maladaptive behaviors with more appropriate and satisfying ones. For instance, in desensitization, the client learns to substitute a new response, such as relaxation, for an old, maladaptive response, such as anxiety or fear. Cognitive therapies tend to focus on the irrational thoughts and beliefs that contribute to problem behaviors, as seen in Ellis's A-B-C theory of personality.

Today, there is an increasing alliance between behavioral and cognitive therapies. As a result, more therapists characterize their orientation as cognitive-behavioral, with the goal of modifying faulty assumptions and thought patterns and then relying on established behavioral procedures like relaxation training to help modify the problem behavior. In many ways this trend is incorporated in multimodal therapy, a comprehensive approach that uses a wide variety of cognitive and behavioral techniques with the aim of finding the most appropriate treatment for each client's problems.

SELECTED APPROACHES TO TREATMENT

The various group therapies, including family therapy, deal with the individual as a function of group dynamics or family structure and utilize the group process to help members achieve mutually satisfying solutions. Biomedical therapies treat the symptoms of psychological problems with direct physical intervention, including drugs—antianxiety, antidepressant, and antipsychotic drugs; electroconvulsive therapy; and psychosurgery.

One of the most dramatic changes in mental health care has been the marked shift from a prolonged stay in large institutions to the use of community-based services. Although the latter have expanded to include a variety of services, such as day hospitals and halfway houses, outpatient services continue to be the most widely used.

HOW WELL DOES THERAPY WORK?

Studies show that psychotherapy generally works better than no therapy, and clients who have had therapy are better off than untreated clients. Much of the current research focuses on specific, measurable factors that make therapy effective, like the length of treatment and client improvement. Also, some approaches appear to be especially well suited to certain problems, such as the behavioral approach for people suffering from phobias and compulsions and the cognitive approach for those suffering from mild to moderate depression.

GETTING HELP

Individuals who are considering professional help might benefit from asking the following questions: (1) When should I seek professional help? (2) Where can I find it? (3) What should I look for in a therapist? (4) What can I expect from therapy? and (5) How long must I stay in therapy?

SCORING KEY FOR ATTITUDES TOWARD PROFESSIONAL HELP

First, use reverse scoring on the following items: 1, 3, 4, 6, 8, 9, 10, 13, 14, 15, 17, 19, 20, 21, 22, 24, 26, and 29. That is, 0 = 3, 1 = 2, 2 = 1, and 3 = 0. Then add up all the numbers for each statement. This is your total score.

This questionnaire measures your attitude toward getting professional psychological help. Low scorers (0–49) tend to have a negative attitude toward seeking professional help for themselves or their friends. Medium scorers (50–63) realize that professional help may be useful, but they are somewhat reluctant to seek it. High scorers (64–87) have a positive attitude toward therapy. Ironically, they regard professional help during times of distress as a means of gaining more control over their lives.

SELF-TEST

1. The process of helping clients gain insight into their unconscious conflicts through such techniques as the analysis of transference is called
   a. behavior therapy
   b. logotherapy
   c. psychoanalysis
   d. multimodal therapy

2. To establish the proper climate for change, a person-centered therapist strives to be accepting, empathetic, and
   a. genuine
   b. patient
   c. objective
   d. compassionate

3. Which one of the following therapies places central importance on clients' finding meaning and purpose in their lives?
   a. gestalt therapy
   b. psychoanalysis
   c. actualization therapy
   d. existential therapy

4. Which of the following techniques is especially effective in treating fears and phobias?
   a. transference
   b. desensitization
   c. logotherapy
   d. gestalt therapy

5. The therapeutic approach of modifying clients' behavior by changing their irrational thoughts is called
   a. cognitive therapy
   b. existential therapy
   c. desensitization
   d. actualization therapy

6. Which of the following approaches assumes that people's problems are best understood and treated as an integral part of the groups to which they belong?
   a. existential therapy
   b. logotherapy
   c. family therapy
   d. psychoanalysis

7. Which of the following groups of psychoactive drugs are the most widely prescribed in the United States?
   a. antianxiety drugs
   b. antidepressants
   c. lithium derivatives
   d. antipsychotic drugs

8. The most commonly used community-based services are the
   a. day hospitals
   b. halfway houses
   c. state hospitals
   d. outpatient services

9. Comparative studies have shown that by eight sessions of therapy, improvement is seen in what proportion of clients?
   a. one-fourth
   b. one-third
   c. one-half
   d. two-thirds

10. Therapists who receive clinical training in clinical, counseling, or school psychology are called
    a. psychiatrists
    b. psychologists
    c. social workers
    d. counselors

EXERCISES

1. *How do you feel about getting help?* Write a paragraph or so describing your attitude toward getting help for a psychological problem. To what extent do you feel that psychological help is a sign of personal weakness? How severe would the problem have to be before you sought help? Be honest.

2. *To whom would you turn for help?* Suppose you needed psychological help immediately: Who would you turn to? Write down the name, address, and telephone number of the person or agency. If you're unable to do so from memory, you might ask for appropriate referrals. Regardless of whom you select, also write down the name, address, and phone number of the nearest mental health center or similar agency for your local community.

3. *Distinguishing between psychiatrists and psychologists.* People often confuse these two professionals. Reread Figure 14–7. Then write a paragraph or so describing the differences between these two types of professionals. What services are usually reserved for psychiatrists? What types of problems or psychological disorders are most appropriate for psychiatrists and for psychologists? You might ask your instructor to comment.

4. *First-person account of therapy.* If you've participated in counseling or therapy, write a page or so describing your experience. In what ways was it beneficial? Do you have any misgivings about it? On the basis of your experience, what suggestions would you make to those considering therapy?

5. *Desensitization.* Reread Figure 14–2. Then apply the material to one of your mild to moderate fears, such as test anxiety or the fear of riding in a crowded elevator. If you're unsure of how to proceed, check with your instructor or an experienced counselor.

6. *Mutual-help groups.* Perhaps you've participated in a group like Parents Without Partners or Toughlove. If so, write a page or so describing your experience. If not, which type of mutual-help group would you be most interested in joining and why? You might call the American Self-Help Clearing House to get a list of such groups (201-625-7101).

7. *Cognitive therapy.* Reread Albert Ellis's list of irrational ideas (in Figure 14–4) that foster self-defeating behavior. Now think about how you would recast each idea so that it represents a more rational view of life, which in turn leads to competent, gratifying behavior. For instance, the first idea might be rephrased as follows: "At one time or another, the important people in my life are going to disapprove of something I'm doing. But I refuse to let that get me down." Choose any six of these ideas, and in a page or so rewrite them as explained here.

QUESTIONS FOR SELF-REFLECTION

1. Do you believe that friends can be good medicine?
2. If you were looking for a therapist, either for yourself or someone else, whose recommendation would you seek?
3. What are some personal qualities you would look for in a therapist?
4. Have you ever considered using desensitization to reduce your own anxieties or fears?
5. Can you recall aggravating a problem by irrational expectations or thoughts?
6. Do you think some of your limitations or problems might be related to your family patterns, either present or past?
7. Have you ever belonged to a mutual-help group?
8. Would you agree that people have to want to change in order to benefit fully from therapy?
9. Do you realize that asking for help when you need it is itself a mark of maturity?
10. Are you aware that many people experience personal growth as well as the relief of symptoms in psychotherapy?

FOR FURTHER INFORMATION

RECOMMENDED READINGS

ANUNDSEN, K. (1995). *Nobody's victim: Freedom from therapy and recovery.* New York: C. Potter Publishers. Another lay guide for persons interested in therapy and who may be skeptical of it.

CORSINI, R. J. (Ed.). (1991). *Five therapists and one client.* Itasca, IL: Peacock. Therapists representing five different approaches describe how they might work in therapy with the same client.

HAMSTRA, B. (1994). *How therapists diagnose: Seeing through the psychiatric eye.* New York: St. Martin's Press. A book for laypeople about how mental health experts diagnose others. It is meant as a source of consumer education.

SELIGMAN, M. E. (1994). *What you can change and what you can't: The complete guide to successful self-improvement.* New York: Knopf. By examining the scientific literature, Seligman offers a realistic picture of what we can and cannot change so that the average person does not waste time nor become discouraged with self-improvement efforts.

WARD, J. H. (1992). *Therapy?* Tarrytown, NY: Wynwood Press. A layperson's guide about what to expect in therapy.

WEBSITES AND THE INTERNET

listproc@solar.rtd.utk.edu: Sign up here for on-line information about Al-Anon and Alateen, for people whose lives are affected by alcoholics.

Usenet: alt.support: Provides information on a variety of support groups.

http://www.psychcrawler.com: The American Psychological Association's website that offers scientific and practical information on a variety of topics related to therapy and other psychological issues.

Usenet: alt.psychology.help: Another place to find groups wanting to discuss their problems rather anonymously.

http://www.nami.org: The website for the National Alliance for the Mentally Ill, an advocacy group for the mentally ill and their families.

CHAPTER
15

Older and Still Growing

After completing this chapter, you should be able to

1. Describe the internal and external aspects of leaving home.
2. Explain the importance of a secure sense of identity for forming close relationships.
3. Explain Erikson's midlife developmental task of generativity versus stagnation.
4. Describe the characteristic physical and cognitive changes accompanying late adulthood.
5. Identify the different notions of successful aging.
6. Discuss differences between men and women with regard to the process of aging.
7. Describe how individuals cope with retirement.

Zena sat on the edge of her bed. She felt stiff this morning and did not know why. She thought, "The funny thing about aging is the way it sneaks up on you. One minute you're 30 or 40. Before you know it, you're 64, like I am." She continued her thoughts as she rubbed her sore, stiff hands. "I don't feel 64, but my birthdays betray me. So do my grandkids and my arthritic hands," she thought.

It seems that at least unconsciously, each of us remains the same age throughout our lives. That is, we pick the age we like best and seem to stay there no matter what our chronological age. Some people have a mental image of themselves as still in their 20s. Others don't seem comfortable with themselves until they are older. However, there are some people who never find their optimum age. As teenagers, they can't wait to grow up; in middle age, they want all the privileges of adults but not the responsibilities; and in old age, they regret what they feel they missed in their youth. Zena continued to think of herself as someone in her late 40s, though she was reminded otherwise each time she looked in the mirror. It usually came as a surprise when her body rebelled. She didn't feel older, except in those rash moments when she overexerted herself, such as walking too quickly up a steep hill, or when she awoke to morning stiffness. As had Zena at times in her life, virtually all of us have been hit with the admonishment "Act your age." "But what if your chronological age isn't the age you feel?" Zena wondered as she sat on her bed.

Adult Development

Fortunately, our attitudes toward aging are being reexamined. Until recently, **adulthood** was believed to be a period of stability between the growth of childhood and youth and the decline of old age. An adult was a person who had completed his or her growth, compared to youth, and was marking time, so to speak, until the end of life. But this image of adulthood is being challenged by a new view that **development** is a lifelong process, which begins at conception and continues until death and includes psychosocial and physical growth. Our capabilities and behaviors continue to change as we grow older not only because of the biological growth process but also because of our understanding and the way we interact with our environment. New tasks, different challenges, and new sources of frustration and happiness mark each new period of our lives into adulthood. The process of personal growth, therefore, continues throughout our life span as we will see in this chapter. Before you read further, take the quiz in Box 15–1 to examine how much knowledge you have about the aging process.

A central theme of development concerns continuity and change in our coping skills. On the one hand, extensive studies by Bernice Neugarten (1986) have shown that the individual's coping style remains relatively consistent throughout his or her adult life. For example, people who have been relatively successful in their earlier stages of development also seem to cope well with the critical stages of adult life, such as marriage, parenthood, and retirement. And, interestingly, there is new research that demonstrates that time (age) heals. A trauma earlier in childhood has relatively little impact on people's psychological well-being at 60 (Sheehy, 1995). The good news, then, is that aging can help us heal.

BOX 15–1

How Much Do You Know About Aging?

Write either true or false by each of the following statements. Then check your responses with the answers at the end of this chapter.

_____ 1. All five senses tend to decline in old age.
_____ 2. People lose about one-third of their brain cells or neurons by late adulthood.
_____ 3. Drivers over 65 years of age have fewer traffic accidents per person than those under 30.
_____ 4. Most older people are pretty much alike.
_____ 5. Older adults become less susceptible to short-term illnesses, such as the common cold.
_____ 6. Recognition memory declines sharply with old age.
_____ 7. Reaction time generally becomes slower with age.
_____ 8. About one-fourth of those over 65 live in nursing homes.
_____ 9. People become more fearful of death as they grow older.
_____ 10. Widows outnumber widowers about three to one.

The answers may be found at the end of the chapter.

Seeing three generations in a family is not unusual today.

Why? People are dynamic organisms who continue striving to master their environment; thus, they also change and grow as they get older. This striving and change is another dominant theme in the developmental literature. Perhaps more than ever before, people are deliberately trying to change themselves, so that with age and experience they have greater coping skills and self-mastery. Consequently, as Carl Rogers (1980)—one of the pioneers of personal growth—grew older, he became convinced that the phrase "older but still growing" is a more apt description of adult development than the conventional cliché "growing old." Zena, our gracefully aging woman in the opening vignette, would heartily agree.

Another theme of development concerns the emergent individuality or uniqueness that often comes with maturity. Up through adolescence, much of our development is associated with **age-related changes**—those that occur at a given age, such as puberty and high school graduation. In contrast, adult development depends more on **non-age-related changes,** or events and influences that are unique to each of us and may occur at any age or not at all, such as divorce or the decision to change careers. Also with advanced age, individual differences in development become more pronounced. For example, Zena met her school classmates later in life at a high school reunion and discovered that they were even more different from each other at 35 or 40 years of age than they were at 18. With age, we all develop our own individual identities to a greater extent, feel more confidence in ourselves, and achieve greater personal control and mastery over our lives. Thus, with age and experience, each of us tends to become his or her "own" person to a greater extent than in our formative years. If anything, the emphasis on individuality and uniqueness is even more pronounced in our later years.

Because of the increased importance of individual differences with age, some social scientists prefer to discuss adulthood without regard to any *stages* at all. However, the self-perceptions and social circumstances of a 25-year-old are likely to differ from those of a

45-year-old, and both are likely to differ from those of a 65-year-old. Consequently, as is customary, we'll examine adult adjustment and growth in terms of three broad stages: early, middle, and late adulthood. Author Gail Sheehy (1995) prefers the terms *provisional adulthood* (from about 18 to 30), *first adulthood* (from about 30 to 45), and *second adulthood* (from 45 to 85 and beyond). She divides the last stage into two other stages, the Age of Mastery and the Age of Integrity, which we will introduce later in the chapter. At the same time, keep in mind that the age boundaries between these stages are fuzzy and that people differ considerably in their own individual patterns of development.

Early Adulthood

In their classic longitudinal study of adult development, Levinson, Darrow, Klein, Levinson, and McKee (1978) discovered what parents and young people themselves have long suspected, namely, that the transition to adulthood is more complex and strung out than ordinarily understood. In their view, **early adulthood** begins with an "early adult transition," roughly from the late teens until the early 20s and lasts well into a person's 30s. The major developmental tasks of this period are leaving home, choosing and preparing for a career, establishing close relationships like friendship and marriage, and starting a family of one's own.

LEAVING HOME

Essentially, this stage concerns coming to see ourselves as autonomous adults separate from our families of origin. Because the separation from our families is never complete, it may be more accurate to understand leaving home in terms of the transformation of

Youths often have conflicting feelings about leaving home.

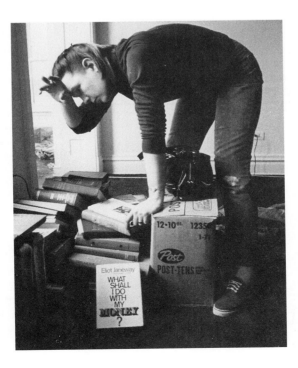

emotional ties between young persons and their families that takes place during this period. The external aspects include moving out of the family home, becoming less dependent financially on our parents, and entering new roles and responsibilities. The internal aspects include increasing differentiation of ourselves from parents and more autonomous decision making. It is this psychosocial transition, however, that is most essential for entering adulthood. That is, some youths may run away from an unhappy home at an early age but take a long time before growing up emotionally. Others, mostly because of a lengthy education, may remain home well into their 20s, choosing to achieve self-sufficiency in other ways. In both cases, it is the "symbolic" leaving home that is so crucial to attaining emotional autonomy.

Maladjustments at this stage may reflect problems in separating both from home and from the dynamics of the family itself. Separation troubles can take many forms, including drug addiction, delinquent behavior, emotional disturbances, paralyzing apathy, or suicide. In the case of Zena's second son, his separation problems showed up in problems with his grades at college. In many instances, young people have difficulty leaving home because of their parents' unwillingness to "let go." Such parents may complain of a young person's problems at school or with drugs, while deriving an unconscious satisfaction from knowing they are still needed as parents. Young people themselves also experience conflicts over leaving home. On the one hand, they may feel impatient and resentful toward their parents for their attempts to control them, but on the other hand, they may also feel anxious about their ability to be successful on their own.

At the same time, a curious thing has been happening in the last decade. Like birds flying back to the nest, more young adults are moving in with their parents after years of absence from home. (See Table 15–1.) The increase in "nesters," as some social service workers call them, is partly due to the increase of this age group in our society. For example, Zena's only daughter, Jonelle, moved back with Zena after her divorce to "regroup," as Jonelle called it. Demographers estimate today that up to 5 percent of American grandparents are raising their grandchildren. An even larger percent of elderly have grown children with their own young children living with them. Much of

TABLE 15–1
LIVING ARRANGEMENTS OF PERSONS 15 YEARS OLD AND OVER BY AGE AND SEX

Age and Sex	Total (1,000)	Percent living			
		Alone	With spouse	With parents/relatives	With nonrelatives
Male					
15–19 years	9,008	1	1	95	4
20–24 years	9,221	6	17	60	17
25–34 years	20,873	11	51	23	15
Female					
15–19 years	8,722	1	3	91	5
20–24 years	9,338	5	28	52	51
25–34 years	21,073	7	58	26	9

SOURCE: U.S. Bureau of the Census. (1995). *Statistical Abstract of the United States, 1995* (115th ed.). Washington, DC: U.S. Government Printing Office, p. 56.

this, however, is the result of economic pressures of the past few years. The economy has made it difficult for young people to maintain their own apartments or homes. Many college graduates, as well as high school graduates, are having a hard time finding a suitable job.

As you might expect, there are pros and cons to such an arrangement. The increased food bills are sometimes incredible, though some young people pay board to offset these expenses. Also, parents may find it natural to ask, "Where were you last night?" as Zena asked of Jonelle, who deeply resented this questioning. However, individuals and their parents often find that this is a satisfying time for sharing and strengthening their ties before a son or daughter leaves home again, usually for good.

CHOOSING A CAREER

A major developmental task during this period is the choice of a career, along with the appropriate preparation for it. In choosing a career, people this age must strike a balance between two somewhat contradictory tasks. One task is to explore the possibilities in the adult world, keeping their options open. The other task is to create a stable life structure with the aim of making something of themselves. Young adults often agonize over the important decisions they must make at this stage, whether they are making the right choice and, if not, how difficult it will be to change. If you experience some distress about career options as you progress through college, this is perfectly normal to an extent. Because of this distress, many college-bound youths are delaying their entry into college several years or more. Once in school they are less hesitant than youths in the past to drop out of college to return later or not at all, largely out of a need to clarify their career goals as much as from financial need. Even after graduation from school, early adulthood continues to be a time of change and experimentation for many people, the typical worker this age holding several brief jobs before settling into a more promising position.

Young men often grow up expecting to work and provide for their families. On the other hand, women are still less likely to grow up believing they *must* support their families. However, those who do work, and many do, may experience the conflicting priorities of marriage and work. Unlike in Zena's adolescence and young adulthood, today's young women are working before marriage, delaying marriage, combining work with marriage, and returning to work after the birth of their children. They are also enrolling in colleges, graduate schools, and professional schools in greater numbers than ever before. College-educated women are especially likely to combine career and marriage. When the woman works outside the home, couples often tend to share power more equally, and we might assume, therefore, that they would be happier with their marriages. Although some studies show no differences between working wives and homemakers, one study did indicate that women who have to work but wish they could stay home tend to be unhappy (Perry-Jenkins, Seery, & Crowter, 1992).

Careers and financial security have become more important considerations for many of today's young adults compared to their parents. This development can be seen in the marked shift in values among college students in the past 25 years (Dey, Astin, & Korn, 1991). For instance, in 1967 more than 80 percent of entering college students felt that developing a "meaningful philosophy of life" was a major life goal, and less than half that number felt that "being well off financially" was equally important. However, 25 years later these values have become reversed, as indicated in Figure 15–1. Many students now plan to major in biology (for medical school), business, or economics, almost double

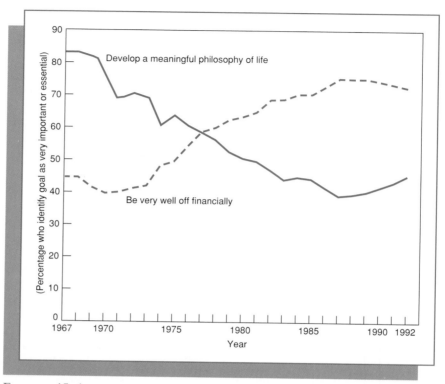

FIGURE 15–1

Life goals among first-year college students: 1967–1992. SOURCE: Adapted
from data in Dey, E. L., Astin, A. W., & Korn, W. S. (1991, September). *The American Freshman: Twenty
Year Trends.* Los Angeles: Higher Education Research Institute and University of California; Dey, E. L.,
Astin, A. W., Korn, W. S., & Riggs, E. R. (1991, December; 1992, December). *The American Freshman:
National Norms for Fall 1991 and 1992.* Los Angeles: Higher Education Research Institute, University
of California.

the number 20 years ago. Also, fewer students major in the humanities and social sciences. As a result, many young adults decide to delay or to give up starting a family for
the benefit of their careers because they want to start earning a good salary and building their careers as soon as possible. However, not everyone fits this pattern. Many students and young adults do plan to have families and want to do more with their lives
than make money. Many are concerned about social issues, such as the environment,
and reject the crass materialism of today (Gross & Scott, 1990).

ESTABLISHING CLOSE RELATIONSHIPS

A major developmental task during the period of early or provisional adulthood is forming close relationships with one's peers. Developmental psychologist Erik Erikson
(1974), who was introduced in Chapter 2, contends that young adults' success in this
venture depends largely on how well they have resolved the earlier issue of identity exploration in adolescence. Individuals who are unsure of themselves or what they want
to be may be so fearful of losing themselves in a close relationship that they enter into

only superficial, dependent, or unstable relationships. Those with more self-assurance and clearer life goals are freer to engage in the emotional give and take of a close relationship such as marriage. At least one study has examined young adults of both sexes with a firm sense of identity and quality of later married life (Kahn, Zimmerman, Csikszentmihalyi, & Getzels, 1985). They found that identity resolution in young adulthood predicted the establishment and stability of marital relationships at midlife. For example, young men with good identity resolution were more likely to marry, whereas those with low levels of identity tended to remain bachelors. Young women with a strong sense of identity were later less likely to divorce.

How well two people get along as a couple also depends largely on their emotional involvement and commitment to the relationship. For most couples, there is at least one partner who is primarily committed to the relationship. Yet the person who is more emotionally involved is also the more vulnerable and unhappy partner. Furthermore, relationships with uneven emotional involvement are not only less satisfying but also less stable.

STARTING A FAMILY

Early adulthood is also the time for starting a family. However, couples are giving more thought to whether they want children and, if so, when to have them. One result is more voluntary childlessness. Few couples resolve this issue directly. Usually, couples decide to postpone having children until they eventually make the postponement permanent. Those who decide to have children tend to wait longer before doing so than did couples during the 1950s. When Zena and her husband married in their early 20s, they decided they wanted children right away and that Zena would delay her education and her career until the youngest began school. Today many couples do not have their first child until they are in their late 20s or early 30s.

Couples who have their children early as did Zena and her husband point to the advantages of growing up with their children and then being free of their children at a relatively early age. A major disadvantage for Zena and her husband was missing the freedom to do things on their own early in the marriage. On the other hand, couples who wait to have their children cite the advantages of having a chance to strengthen their marriage, advance their careers, and generally grow up before having children. A common disadvantage is the conflict over balancing the claims of careers and child rearing. Figure 15–2 highlights how child-care arrangements have changed in the last few decades because more mothers are working outside the home. Because so many mothers work, society has had to offer alternate arrangements to in-home care.

For Zena and her husband, having children was not questioned. Married couples in those days were expected to have children—ideally a boy and a girl, with the boy born first. Today, having children may affect a couple's marriage in several ways. On the positive side, many couples report that having children makes them feel more responsible and adult. They also report increased satisfaction in sharing affection and learning experiences with their children, which enhances their sense of purpose in life. On the minus side, taking care of small children is an added stress on the marriage, leaving less time for the parents to do things on their own. Even without children, there can be a great deal of marital stress as people question their marriages and their relationships with their mates.

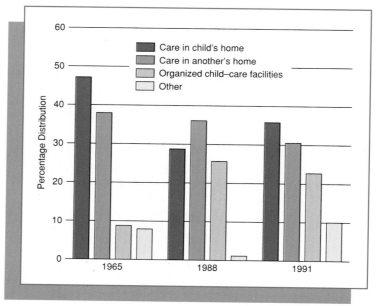

FIGURE 15–2

Changing child–care arrangements of children under 5 years of age of employed mothers, 1965, 1988, and 1991. SOURCE: U.S. Bureau of the Census. (1987). *Statistical Abstract of the United States, 1988* (108th ed.). Washington, DC: U.S. Government Printing Office, p. 357; U.S. Bureau of the Census. (1995). *Statistical Abstract of the United States, 1995* (115th ed.). Washington, DC: U.S. Government Printing Office, p. 390.

 Middle Adulthood

Sometime between the late 30s and mid 40s, people must make the transition from early or provisional adulthood to **middle adulthood** (Sheehy, 1995), often called midlife by many developmental psychologists. Both men and women begin to see themselves differently, with new opportunities and tasks as well as limitations. They are going through the **midlife transition.**

MIDLIFE TRANSITION

Essentially, this is a period of personal evaluation that comes sometimes with the realization that one's life is about half over. The individual gradually pays less attention to the "time since birth" and starts thinking more in terms of "time I have left." Some people at this age may hide some of the more obvious changes of age or compensate by trying harder to appear young. For example, in 1990 Americans spent between $3 to $4 billion on cosmetic surgery in an attempt to obtain a more youthful or pleasing appearance (*Consumer Reports,* 1992). It is sometimes difficult for middle-aged individuals to ignore other fundamental changes. For one thing, their parents retire, become ill, and die during these years. More of their friends and acquaintances are also lost through death, with death from all causes rising sharply at this time of life. Children grow up and leave home, and middle-aged parents feel more aware of the mistakes they have made raising their children than in earlier years. For Zena, these middle adult years were particularly trying times; not only did her mother die, but her father was infirm, and her beloved husband died from cancer. As a result, the midlife transition can become an uncomfortable time for some people, who may develop a sense of regret over the loss of their youth. This need not be so, as recent research has discovered. Box 15–2 discusses well-being in adulthood with the surprising information that middle-aged people are remarkably happy.

In Erikson's (1968) view, the main life task at this stage is achieving a sense of generativity, which involves becoming less self-absorbed and more caring about others and future generations. The realization that life is half over prompts people to ask themselves what they would like to do with the rest of their lives. Such self-questioning may lead to changes in their careers, marriages, or personal relationships. It often leads them to take up new interests or become active in community or national affairs as a way of making their world a better place in which to live. It's a time for becoming aware of the "opposite," unrealized side of one's personality. For example, a hard-driving businessperson may take more of an interest in helping others, or a mother may go back to school to develop her skills as a research scientist. Middle age is a time for shifting gears and developing new interests and values. Not to do so may result in undue self-absorption or stagnation or even physical illness. In fact, research has shown that developing multiple identities or interests is a great buffer against mental and physical illness in adults. People with more than one sense of self can draw upon other sources of self-esteem while they regroup (Sheehy, 1995).

Box 15–2

Well-Being Throughout Adulthood

Many people believe that life will become less satisfying as they move away from their 20s and 30s. They view midlife as an unstable period and old age as the worst of times. Yet such a negative image of aging is at odds with the self-reports of older people.

Surprisingly, middle-aged people and those 60 or older report levels of happiness and satisfaction similar to people in their 20s and 30s. Although individuals vary, very little of the variation in the sense of well-being is due to age. Interviews with people in 16 countries, including 10 European nations, demonstrate that age differences are somewhat trivial in regard to life satisfaction (Inglehart, 1990).

At the same time, the remarkable stability of well-being across the lifespan may be partly due to age-related emotional differences. Costa and others (1987) have found that as people age their feelings tend to mellow. They find themselves less often getting excited and being on top of the world, but also less often becoming depressed. Their highs become less high, and their lows become less low. Typically, youths may come down from euphoria or up from gloom in less than an hour. In contrast, older adults' moods are less extreme but more stable. Thus, old age may bring less intense happiness but more contentment.

PHYSICAL AND COGNITIVE CHANGES

The most obvious signs of middle age are certain physical changes in appearance. People tend to gain weight around the waist, especially after 40, and their hair may turn gray. Men's hairlines may begin to recede around the temples. All these changes reflect a gradual slowing down in the overall physical system, which results in less physical energy and stamina. People get tired more easily and take more time to bounce back from fatigue or illness.

There is actually some improvement in general health in the sense that middle-aged adults get fewer colds, allergies, or minor illnesses, and they may experience fewer accidents. But they become more susceptible to chronic and serious illnesses, such as diabetes, heart attacks, strokes, and cancer. Recall that Zena's husband died of cancer in midlife. As a result, there is increasing concern over health and sometimes more attention placed on keeping fit.

Cognitive abilities also change depending on the person and the cognitive activity. Starting around the age of 50, people begin to differ more and more from one another. In other words, people's cognitive capacities decrease at different rates. And some cognitive capacities seem to drop while others remain steady or might actually rise (Schrof, 1994). If any, one of the first abilities that declines is the ability to make sense of spatial relationships. Spatial capability helps us navigate through three-dimensional space. For example, it allows us to remember where we parked our cars at the airport. Another ability that may decline is abstract reasoning ability. This is the ability that helps us solve the following puzzle: apple is to pear as dog is to which of the following: (1) movie, (2) tree, (3) moon, (4) cat. Finally, in midlife, the ability to remember things after some delay might also decline (Schrof, 1994). For example, in their middle age, Zena and her husband were likely to forget punch lines to jokes a few days after they heard them.

CAREER CHANGES

How people's work is affected by the midlife transition depends on many factors, such as their earlier successes and failures, satisfaction on the job, and unfulfilled aspirations. Men and women who have been successful run the risk of going stale unless they continue to grow. Sometimes the needed challenge comes from a promotion at work or a more rewarding job. For people who have not realized their ambitions, this may be a time for now-or-never decisions. They may redouble their efforts to achieve their career goals at this age—which ironically increases their stress and susceptibility to heart attacks. Or if they sense that they are in a dead-end job, they may switch jobs or careers.

Jorge, a friend to both Zena and her husband, was middle-aged and worked in a bank. Jorge began selling cleaning supplies on the side to supplement his income as his children approached college age. After his long-awaited promotion to a management position was denied, Jorge decided to go into business for himself full time. He worked extra hard to add new customers and expand his line of cleaning products. His wife, Anna, supported his decision and did the accounting and inventory work. "It was rough for the first few years," Jorge said. "But now that we've built up the business, I'm happier than ever. There's nothing like being your own boss."

Women sometimes react to their midlife transitions somewhat differently than men, depending largely on whether their primary involvement has been in a career or the home. Professional women who have considered having children may realize that the biological clock is running down, and they may decide to have a child at this age. Single-mother adoptions also tend to increase. The common pattern is seen among women who married in their 20s as Zena did. Their children are in school, and their husbands are working longer hours. Having spent much of their married lives caring for their husbands and children, these women often feel the need to fulfill themselves in other ways. Many women return to school at this age, take a job outside the home, or do both simultaneously.

Zena married soon after leaving high school and enjoyed being a wife and mother. But as her three children approached college age, she began rethinking what she wanted to do with her life. Initially, she joined a paramedic team and began taking one course each semester at the local community college. She quickly gained confidence in her ability to do the work and decided to fulfill her ambition to become a nurse. By the time her youngest son graduated from college, Zena received her 4-year degree and became a registered nurse. "I feel lucky," she said upon landing her first job. "My husband has been supportive all the way. And I really enjoy nursing."

SEXUAL CHANGES

The biological and psychological changes that accompany the loss of reproductive powers contribute to the midlife transition in both sexes. Although these changes can pose new anxieties for men and women, they also present new opportunities for personal growth.

The most significant physical change in women is **menopause,** or cessation of menstruation, which signals the loss of childbearing capacities. Menopause tends to occur sometime between 45 and 55 years of age in American women. The physical effects vary from a certain degree of atrophy in the uterus, vagina, and breasts to a variety of other changes such as hot flashes. Some women find menopause mostly a negative experience, with adverse effects on their appearance and their physical, emotional, and sexual lives. Other women feel little or none of these effects. Some positive changes also occur during this period. The lessened fear of pregnancy often leads to increased sexual responsiveness for many women. Other events of middle adulthood, such as changes in the marriage relationship, freedom from child-care responsibilities, and return to work outside the home are more important to women than the physical changes.

Although men are not subject to menopause, they do go through a male **climacteric,** defined technically as the loss of reproductive capacity. There is a gradual reduction in fertile sperm, a diminution of testosterone, and reduced sexual vigor sometimes with increasing impotency in some men. However, men tend to reach their climacteric 5 to 10 years later than women and do so in a much more gradual way, with fewer physiological consequences.

Men and women who take these changes in stride often find their lives even more satisfying than before, including the sexual aspects of their lives. For one thing, the changes and anxieties of this period may make each individual more aware of his or her need for a spouse and the security of marriage. Nothing helps a man or woman through the turmoil of this stage as much as an understanding and supportive partner. Actually, there is a rise in marital happiness among many couples at this period, with individuals in their late 40s and 50s reporting levels of marital happiness surpassing couples in their 20s. The fact that men and women tend to become more like each other also brings each a new sense of freedom and "settling down" in sex and marriage. As Carl Jung said,

The other sex has lost its magic power over us, for we have come to know its essential traits in the depths of our own psyche. We shall not easily "fall in love," for we can no longer lose ourselves in someone else, but we shall be capable of a deeper love, a conscious devotion to the other. (Quoted in Jacobi, 1973, pp. 282–283)

◆ Late Adulthood

What is it like to be old? Zena was just beginning to find out. If you are a traditionally aged college student, this might be hard to imagine. If you are daring, you might do what Patricia Brown (1985) did. With the help of a theatrical makeup artist, she transformed herself into an 85-year-old woman. She altered the shape and texture of her face with a mask and makeup and tinted her hair gray. She inserted clouded lenses into her eyes; taped her fingers together; and swathed herself in splints, bandages, and corsets to restrict her body movements. Then off and on for the next 3 years she experienced life as a person would in **late adulthood.** She discovered that old people don't fit into our society. Bottle caps are too hard to get off. The print on medicine labels is so small older people can't read it. During a period of turbulence on an airplane flight, the cabin attendant spilled coffee all over her but pretended not to notice. Had the cabin attendant spilled coffee on a businessman's pants, it probably would have been a different story, wouldn't it?

Such experiences have led gerontologists to coin the term **ageism,** which refers to negative attitudes and treatment of older Americans. Ageism can be seen in the readiness with which people attribute all sorts of negative qualities to the elderly, mostly because of their age. For example, many younger people assume that the typical older person is helpless and infirm and resides in a nursing home (Levin, 1988), despite the fact that over 95 percent of older adults are not in need of custodial care (McLean, 1988). Such instances of ageism perpetuate stereotypes—false generalizations—about the elderly, thereby restricting their opportunities, undermining their personal dignity, and

An individual changes with age; the changes go far beyond physical appearance.

alienating them from the larger society. We need to become more sensitive to ageism because the American population will continue to age as the largest cohort group, the baby boomers, moves through historic time. Box 15–3 presents the results of an interesting study on the attitudes of college students toward various age groups.

Let's look at some statistics on the aging of America. Today, about 30 million men and women are 65 years of age or older. By the year 2080, the elderly proportion of the population will almost double, making for an older and more diverse society. By the year 2050, 1 in 20 Americans will be over 85 (McLean, 1988). The "graying of America" will alter every aspect of society—business, education, government spending, housing, medical care, and leisure. We need to develop a better understanding of the aging process and what it's like to grow old.

PHYSICAL AND COGNITIVE CHANGES

The literature on aging has identified two distinct groups of elderly: one group aged 65 to 74, known as the young elderly, and another group aged 75 and beyond, known as the old elderly. At age 64, Zena is about to become one of the young elderly. These two groups differ psychologically and physically. Many of the young elderly are free of

---

BOX 15–3

AGE STEREOTYPES AND COLLEGE STUDENT ATTITUDES

William Levin (1988) performed an interesting experiment with college students to detect their attitudes toward individuals of various ages. Levin obtained three photographs of the same individual when he was 25, 52, and 73 years of age. The photographs, although showing the individual at various ages, were identical in other respects. For example, the individual wore similar clothing, held the same head position, and was lit from the same angle. In other words, the only thing that varied was his appearance based on age-related changes.

Using a 7-point scale, groups of college students were asked to rate one of the pictures on such dimensions as activity, competence, intelligence, creativity, attractiveness, flexibility, memory, and other factors. Male and female students from three different geographic locations across the United States participated.

On almost all dimensions there were significant differences in the way the individual was rated depending on whether the students received the picture that represented him as young, middle-aged, or elderly. In almost all cases, when students received the photograph of the individual at age 73, their ratings were significantly more negative. Levin suggests that these results indicate strong and consistent age stereotypes by college students, no matter what the students' gender or where they lived.

What else is remarkable about this experiment is that the students thought it was reasonable to evaluate a total stranger on the basis of a photograph and a little bit of other information.

SOURCE: Adapted from W. C. Levin (1988, March). "Age Stereotyping: College Student Evaluations," *Aging*, pp. 134–148. Reproduced with permission.

infirmity, whereas those in the old elderly experience more disability. For example, among the young elderly, 11 percent have cataracts; among the old elderly, that number jumps to 23 percent (Crispell & Frey, 1993). **Alzheimer's disease,** a debilitating mental disorder, strikes 1 in 12 young elderly but 1 in 3 old elderly (Brownlee, 1991).

Aging can involve a progressive slowing down of bodily processes. However, these changes do not necessarily result in disability, especially in the young elderly and those older elderly who continue to exercise ("Exercise Isn't Just for Fun," 1991). Contrary to stereotypes, two-thirds of America's elderly are free of serious chronic health problems (Crispell & Frey, 1993). With age, the skin wrinkles and becomes thinner, the hair grays, there is a reduction in sharpness of vision and hearing, and the reflexes slow down (A. Brown, 1991). Some older people eat less, exercise less, and have less physical energy for life. They also sleep less restfully, though they spend more time in bed compensating for this lack of sleep. The old elderly sometimes have more trouble maintaining their sense of balance. Deaths from falls occur twice as frequently as those from other accidents. Deaths from high blood pressure, cancer, and heart disease are also more common among the old elderly.

Fortunately for Zena and others like her, with improved understanding of aging and the importance of health care and supportive environments, we are discovering that older people can remain in reasonably good health and function better at the same age than their parents and grandparents did (A. Brown, 1991). We're also learning that many of the negative changes associated with aging are due to stress and disease rather than to the aging process itself. Box 15–4 discusses ways we can approach aging as healthy individuals.

Cognitive functions can also continue to be affected by the aging process, though rarely to the extent justifying the stereotype of the absent-minded old person. **Fluid intelligence,** which refers to those mental abilities most affected by aging of the nervous system, such as mental agility and visualizing an old problem in new ways, does decline somewhat in middle age and more sharply in late adulthood. As a result, older people exhibit slower mental reactions and are often less adept in processing new information. But **crystallized intelligence,** which refers to those abilities most affected by learning, such as verbal skills and vocabulary usage, remains the same and in many instances continues to improve with age.

It is also thought that individuals can maintain their creativity well into late adulthood, depending on their type of work. Artists hit their peak in their 40s, scientists maintain their creativity well into their 60s, and those in the humanities (e.g., historians and philosophers) may show a steady increase in creativity through their 70s. For example, Benjamin Franklin invented the bifocal lens at age 78, and actress Jessica Tandy won acting awards well into her 80s. It may be that any decreased creativity ordinarily seen among older people is due more to their restricted environments than to aging. For example, about 16 percent of America's elderly have some mobility limitations, especially elderly women who are more prone to osteoarthritis than men. Such limitations restrict the types of environments in which the elderly find themselves. Box 15–5 showcases other individuals who seemed at their peak of achievement in their old age.

PERSONAL AND SOCIAL ADJUSTMENT

Gail Sheehy (1995), who often writes about stages of adult development, suggests that there are two distinct stages of personal adjustment for older Americans. The stages of adjustment are the Age of Mastery, from midlife through age 65, and the Age of Integrity,

BOX 15–4

Healthy Aging

For traditionally aged college students, old age may seem far away. For less traditional students, old age may be approaching. Each of us can start NOW practicing healthy techniques that can ensure a healthier old age. The sooner we start, the longer our life is likely to be and the better the quality of our health as we age.

- *Exercise, exercise, exercise.* Study after study shows the benefits even for the very old. Exercise lowers the risk of heart attacks, results in fewer hip fractures, and promotes better mental health ("Exercise Isn't Just for Fun," 1991).
- *Stop smoking.* No matter how long you have smoked, when you stop your health improves. Avoid the use of drugs (other than medications), and if you drink alcohol, drink only in moderation.
- *Eat well.* In the chapter on health, the food pyramid was reviewed. Refer to this pyramid daily. Avoiding sugars and fats also improves overall health and helps ward off diabetes and atherosclerosis (McLean, 1988).
- *Avoid stress.* This is easier said than done in today's modern world. If stress is overtaking your life, refer to Chapter 4 on stress and stress management.
- *Develop and maintain outside interests.* In one observational study in the Bahamas, the elderly were found to have more meaningful work and a strong sense of community compared to individuals in more complex societies. The elderly in the Bahamas enjoyed higher levels of respect and intimacy and did not suffer from forced retirement, nursing homes, or age segregation (Savishinsky, 1991).
- *See a physician regularly.* Some of the infirmities of aging are silent, such as high blood pressure. Preventive checkups earlier in life can ensure healthier aging later in life.
- *Find and maintain a social support system.* Social support for the elderly increases their morale, buffers the effects of the loss of loved ones, and enhances their self-esteem (Duffy & Wong, 1996).

beyond age 65. Erik Erikson also referred to late adulthood as the age of integrity (versus despair). In this stage the individual looks back on his or her life as a whole. To the extent that the individual has achieved a satisfying life, he or she will feel happy with the self in old age.

Age of Mastery.   Whereas young adulthood and early midlife are all about "ourselves" (our own advancement), the Age of Mastery for midlife to older adults is a stage in which we begin to control what happens to us rather than to react to what happens to us. The Age of Mastery takes us beyond our self-preoccupation. This stage also brings with it emotional and social license, according to Sheehy (1995). Individuals become more outspoken and less self-conscious.

Age of Integrity.   Sheehy (1995) claims that the 60s, 70s, and beyond are serene years, particularly if the elderly are not passive about aging. That is, if the elderly are resilient and motivated rather than bitter and passive, aging is more successful. Integrity, then, brings successful aging. The elderly who can concentrate on what they can do rather

---

BOX 15–5

A FEW OF THE LATE, GREAT ACHIEVERS

Sophocles wrote *Oedipus Rex* when he was 70 and *Electra* when he was 90.

Michelangelo began work on St. Peter's Basilica at age 70.

Anna Mary Robertson ("Grandma") Moses took up painting as a hobby at 76 and later staged 15 one-woman shows throughout Europe.

Pablo Picasso married for the second time at 77 and completed three series of drawings between 85 and 90.

Laura Ingalls Wilder didn't publish her first book until age 65 and wrote some of her best children's stories during her 70s.

Benjamin Franklin helped to write the Declaration of Independence at age 70 and was named chief executive of the state of Pennsylvania at 79.

Mother Teresa continued her missionary work around the clock, helping less fortunate people throughout the world, until her death at age 87.

Artur Rubinstein gave one of his greatest piano performances at New York's Carnegie Hall at age 89.

Golda Meir was named prime minister of Israel at age 71 and held that office for 5 years.

Mahatma Gandhi led India's opposition to British rule when he was 77.

Frank Lloyd Wright completed New York's Guggenheim Museum at 89 and continued teaching until his death.

---

than on what they cannot do age more gracefully and experience less anxiety about aging. One of the most important ingredients to successful aging is the ability to maintain internal control or a sense of autonomy, as discussed in the chapter on Personal Control and Decision Making. When the elderly feel that they have control over their fates, they tend to live longer, healthier lives. Due to losses that older individuals experience, in Zena's case the loss of her husband, her parents, and her children who left home to be on their own, the elderly often perceive less control than younger adults (Mirowsky, 1995; J. C. Weiss, 1995). Older adults who cope with loss of control by maintaining or enhancing their competencies (Schulz & Heckhausen, 1996) or by shifting the subjective importance of their personal goals (Brandstadter & Rothermund, 1994) adjust better to the aging process.

An important area of psychosocial change and therefore control involves living arrangements for the elderly. The young elderly, those individuals from 65 to 74 years of age, are more likely to live at home, be in better health, and be more financially comfortable than the old elderly. Many elderly prefer to stay in their own homes, but a small number (less than 20 percent) find themselves unable to care for themselves (Crispell & Frey, 1993). These individuals generally are the old elderly. Contrary to stereotypes, however, only a small portion of these individuals will reside in nursing homes. Zena, as she faces her 65th birthday, is pleased that she is able to live in the same charming home that she shared with her husband and her children. She is somewhat typical in that about twice as many women as men are still living alone, and conversely, more than twice as many men as women are living with their spouses. (See Figure 15–3.)

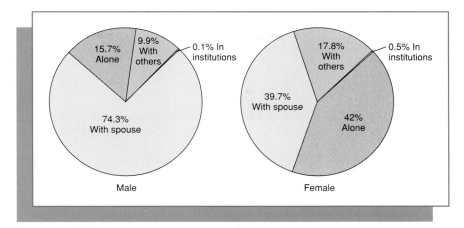

FIGURE 15–3
Living arrangements of people age 65 or over by sex. SOURCE: U.S. Bureau of the Census. (1992). *Statistical Abstract of the United States, 1992* (112th ed.). Washington, DC: U.S. Government Printing Office, p. 38.

By the age of 85 only about one-half of all the old elderly live alone; and unfortunately, a significant proportion is at or below the poverty level, making any living arrangement difficult. Poverty is a special problem for elderly women, especially for elderly women of color (F. Leonard & Loeb, 1992). A much smaller proportion of old elderly lives with others, although only about one in eight lives with a grown child because of the mutual desire for independence (i.e., autonomy or control) and privacy. Other older people live near a grown child and visit frequently. In some instances, as mentioned earlier, elderly parents can assist their children with child care, and the latter can help their parents with finances and emotional support in times of illness. Thus, as previously mentioned, only a small number of old elderly live in nursing homes. Others opt for retirement homes or assisted-living facilities for the elderly.

Because most married women will outlive their husbands, there are more widows like Zena than widowers among the elderly. About half of the women in the United States are widowed by their early 60s, and 80 percent by their early 70s. Among those over 65, widows outnumber widowers three to one. Women tend to adjust to the loss of their spouse more readily than men. Although, as mentioned earlier, older men are usually better off financially than older women, they tend to have more difficulty coping with routine household tasks, are lonelier, and are less happy than widows and older women. People who have remained single throughout their lives often feel more satisfied in late adulthood than do widows or widowers the same age, possibly because they have chosen a single lifestyle and have become better adjusted to it.

Women often have an easier time making and keeping friends in their old age, partly because of the way they have been socialized and partly because of the disproportionate number of older women. Yet with the reduction of social contacts at this age, friends become even more important to both sexes. People who continue to live in the same neighborhood as they get older, an increasing phenomenon, may keep in touch with their friends from the past. Other friends may be deceased, so the social networks of the old elderly are smaller but just as close as those of younger people (Lang & Cartensen, 1994). Those who move elsewhere must make new friends. In both instances, friends can play as important a role as relatives in preventing loneliness among the elderly. This is perhaps why some people, to have more friends the same age, prefer to live in a retirement home or community, often in the sunbelt of the South (Crispell & Frey, 1993).

RETIREMENT

At one point in history, Congress extended the compulsory retirement age from 65 to 70 in business and industry, and some executives worried that corporate mobility would be adversely affected. But such fears have not materialized, and mandatory retirement has generally been set aside altogether (McLean, 1988). Most workers, however, continue to retire in their mid 60s, although a previous trend toward retirement at even earlier ages is beginning to reverse as companies realize the benefits of luring older workers back into the work force (Olivero, 1989).

The retirement experience, which varies considerably from one person to another, usually depends on several factors. First and foremost is the person's attitude toward retirement. In general, the more voluntary the retirement, the better the adjustment. Second, reasonably good health is also an important predictor for a satisfying retirement as well as age of retirement, as some retired people's complaints are related to poor health. Third, an adequate income is also very important at this age. It is the "perceived adequacy" of one's income rather than actual income that is the most crucial factor. Although retired people usually have a reduced income, they also have fewer major expenses such as mortgage payments, so that their income may be sufficient for their present lifestyle. Zena, for example, was glad that she, her husband, and ultimately her husband's life insurance had paid off their mortgage when she was in her mid 60s. At the same time, people from upper-level careers generally report a more favorable retirement experience, partly because they have ample income.

As the population of older adults swells, there is increasing concern for a more humane policy toward the elderly. Individuals from a variety of fields—academia, business, government, and medicine—have begun discussing key issues such as the importance of preretirement planning, alternative work patterns for the elderly (such as part-time or slower-paced jobs), and phased-in retirement. Both Zena and her husband were fortunate to have good pension plans; other elderly are not so fortunate. There is a growing realization that as more and more older adults view their later years as productive and satisfying, everyone in society will benefit.

SUCCESSFUL AGING

Which person does a better job of growing old gracefully—the individual who continues to work actively as a lawyer and keeps up an active social life or the person who retires to a rocking chair on the porch? Authorities who favor the activity theory of aging suggest that the more active a person remains, the more satisfied and better adjusted that person is likely to be, regardless of age. Those who adhere to the disengagement theory of aging point out that individuals tend to disengage from society with advancing age, psychological disengagement usually preceding social withdrawal by about 10 years. Zena, for example, was content to sit in a chair and read and also to do volunteer work at her former place of employment, the community hospital. She was both active and disengaged, depending on the day.

As Zena's retirement demonstrates, there is no single way to age successfully, and different people adapt to old age in their own way. Bernice Neugarten (1986) found

Older Americans function better at the same age than did their parents and grandparents.

that each person tends to select a style of aging that best suits his or her personality, needs, and interests. Thus, an energetic, hard-working person will continue to tackle new projects, whereas a more contemplative person will probably do more reading. Neugarten found that some older people tend to benefit from activity more than others. For example, although those with a well-integrated personality generally adjusted better to old age regardless of how active they were, the less well integrated exhibited better adjustment with higher levels of activity.

It's also important for individuals to feel an inner satisfaction with their lives as they grow older. Recall that in Erikson's theory (1968), the developmental task of older people is to establish a sense of integrity—a sense that one's life as a whole has been meaningful and satisfying. Those who have experienced a great deal of frustration and suffering may have more misgivings than satisfactions, experiencing despair and depression. Actually, people ordinarily experience both ego integrity and despair, but the healthier the person, the more self-acceptance and satisfaction will prevail.

Older people also obtain a sense of their lives as a whole by engaging in the **life review**—a naturally occurring process prompted by the realization that life is approaching an end. Although such a process can lead to wisdom and serenity, it may also evoke some negative aspects, such as regret, anger, guilt, depression, or obsessional rumination about past events. The process consists of **reminiscence**—thinking about oneself and reconsideration of past events and their meanings. Some older people prefer to reminisce in private, whereas others may enjoy doing it more publicly, such as by making a family tree or telling their children and grandchildren about the significant aspects of their family history. Such reminiscing serves to give them a final perspective of their lives while leaving a record of the past to their family and friends.

SUMMARY

ADULT DEVELOPMENT

We began by pointing out that human development is now viewed as a lifelong process that includes psychological growth as well as biological changes, so that individuals tend to acquire greater coping skills and individuality with age and experience. Although we've followed the common practice of describing adult development in terms of three broad stages—early, middle, and late adulthood—the age boundaries are often fuzzy, and individual patterns of development vary considerably within each stage.

EARLY ADULTHOOD

The transition to adulthood is more complex and prolonged than is ordinarily understood, especially now that a lengthy education often postpones financial independence. Leaving home involves achieving emotional and psychological independence as well as moving out of the family home; going away to college is a natural transition for many people at this age. Close relationships are an important consideration for men and women at this age, and couples in which both partners put their relationship first seem happiest. Couples are giving more thought to whether they want children and, if so, when to have them. Many couples are waiting until their late 20s or early 30s to have their first child.

MIDDLE ADULTHOOD

Sometime in between the late 30s and the mid 40s, people experience the midlife transition, a time of personal evaluation that comes with the realization that life is half over. The most obvious signs of middle age are certain physical changes such as graying hair and perhaps slower mental reactions. Midlife sometimes brings changes in careers for both sexes, with both women and men changing jobs or careers to fulfill their aspirations, and many traditional women taking a job outside the home or returning to school. The biological and psychological changes that accompany the loss of reproductive powers pose both new anxieties and new opportunities for both sexes, and men and women may experience a new stability in their marriages as they enter their 50s.

LATE ADULTHOOD

About 30 million men and women, or 12 percent of the American population, are now 65 years of age or older. The literature on aging now recognizes the young elderly and the old elderly, with the old elderly being more infirm and less active. As people get older, their body functions progressively slow down. Yet crystallized intelligence, or those cognitive functions that depend mostly on learning, may continue to improve with age. People's basic adaptive abilities tend to remain remarkably stable throughout adulthood. Satisfaction in retirement depends on a variety of factors, such as one's attitude toward retirement, health, income, and involvement in meaningful activities. However, there is no single best way to age successfully, and each individual adapts to old age in his or her own way. Aging is an individualized process. Successful aging depends on one's social network, maintaining a sense of control, and positive reminiscing.

ANSWERS TO AGING QUIZ

1. True. Various aspects of hearing, vision, and touch decline in old age. In many cases, taste and smell also become less sensitive.

2. False. People lose very little of their neurons (perhaps 7 percent). The loss starts at about the age of 30 rather than in later adulthood.

3. True. Aged drivers have fewer accidents than those under 30 but more accidents than middle-aged people.

4. False. There are at least as many, if not more, differences among older individuals as among people at other age levels.

5. True. Because of the accumulation of antigens, older people suffer less from short-term ailments such as the common cold. However, the weakening of the immune system makes them more susceptible to life-threatening ailments, such as cancer and pneumonia.

6. False. Recognition memory shows little or no decline with age, in contrast to the marked decline in recall memory.

7. True. Slower reaction time is one of the best-documented facts about older people.

8. False. Only about 5 percent of the population over 65 lives in a nursing home during a given year.

9. False. Although older people become more aware of death, they tend to have less fear of it than other age groups.

10. True. There are about three times as many widows as widowers.

SELF-TEST

1. Which of the following is a developmental task of young adulthood?
   a. leaving home
   b. choosing a career
   c. establishing close relationships
   d. all of the above

2. Which young couples are least happy in their marriage?
   a. both partners are work centered
   b. the man is immersed in his career
   c. the woman is a full-time homemaker
   d. the woman works but prefers to be a homemaker

3. Compared to couples in the past, married couples are
   a. starting their families later
   b. having more children
   c. more likely to include a working husband and a stay-at-home wife
   d. having more girl babies

4. According to Erikson, the main developmental task of middle-aged people is
   a. identity versus confusion
   b. generativity versus stagnation
   c. intimacy versus isolation
   d. integrity versus despair

5. The most obvious signs of middle age are
   a. more colds and allergies
   b. significant memory losses
   c. fewer chronic illnesses
   d. changes in physical appearance

6. The correct term for the reduction in fertile sperm and lessened sexual vigor among middle-aged men is
   a. the climacteric
   b. menopause
   c. male menopause
   d. sexual senility

7. Midlife has been typified as a stage of
   a. self-absorption
   b. despair
   c. integrity
   d. generativity

8. By 65 years of age,
   a. half the men are widowed
   b. three-fourths of the women live alone
   c. half the women are widowed
   d. one-fourth of the men are divorced

9. What factor is most important in determining how people will adjust to retirement?
   a. health
   b. whether the retirement was voluntary
   c. income
   d. all of these are important

10. The study of aging by Bernice Neugarten showed that
   a. retired people need to keep busy
   b. those disengaging from society are the happiest
   c. there is no single way to age successfully
   d. reflecting on one's life is unhealthy

EXERCISES

1. *How have you grown as an adult?* Write a brief paragraph describing your personal developments since adolescence. In what ways has your personality changed or remained the same? Comment on the factors that have contributed to your personal growth, such as success at school, disappointment in love, or new responsibilities at work.

2. *Leaving home.* Describe your experience with leaving home. If you're already living on your own, how peaceful or stormy was your departure? If you're still living at home or are away at college part of the year, how well are you coming to terms with this developmental task? How helpful are your parents in this matter?

3. *Mentors.* List all the people who have influenced your career development from your high school years and up. Have any of these people served as your mentor, that is,

encouraged or sponsored your career? What effect has this person had on your career? Would you recommend mentors for others? Do you think there are sex differences in the likelihood of being mentored?

4. *The midlife transition.* If you're going through the midlife transition or have completed this stage, write a page or so describing your experience. To what extent has this been a stressful time or crisis for you? In what ways have you reevaluated your life situation and grown as a person?

5. *Widows and widowers.* Select an older person you know well who has outlived his or her spouse, including yourself if this applies to you, and comment on how well this person has adjusted to living alone. What has been the most difficult adjustment? Has the experience of loss also brought about personal growth?

6. *Successful aging.* Select someone in your family who has reached late adulthood, such as an aunt, uncle, or grandparent. Or perhaps this applies to you. Then comment on how successfully the person has aged. To what extent has the person kept active or become disengaged from his or her environment? Has this person also grown old in his or her own distinctive way? How has your relationship with this person affected your understanding of aging?

QUESTIONS FOR SELF-REFLECTION

1. In what ways have you mellowed with age and experience?
2. Would you agree that leaving home involves more than moving out of the family home?
3. What were your parents like at your age?
4. At what stage of adulthood are you now? Does this differ from your perceived or favorite age?
5. Are you aware that the midlife transition doesn't have to be a crisis? How so?
6. Do you realize that people in middle and late adulthood are more active for their age than in the past? How are they more active?
7. What kind of older people were you familiar with as a child? Did these experiences fashion your stereotypes of the elderly? If not, what did fashion your stereotypes?
8. What would you like to do when you retire?
9. Are you aware that our personal traits become more pronounced with age?
10. What do you think it would be like to live in a nursing home? At home?

FOR FURTHER INFORMATION

RECOMMENDED READINGS

COLARUSSO, C. (1994). *Fulfillment in adulthood: Paths to the pinnacle of life.* New York: Plenum Press. Offers an uplifting look at the various ways to achieve a rewarding adulthood.

ESKIN, B. A. (1995). *Mid-life can wait: How to stay young and healthy after 35.* New York: Ballantine Books. As the title suggests, this book advises those about to enter midlife how to stay healthy.

GARROD, A., SMULYAN, L., POWERS, S. I., & KILKENNY, R. (1992). *Adolescent portraits: Identity, relationships, and challenges.* Boston: Allyn & Bacon. College students from varied backgrounds describe their transition to adulthood and how they have dealt with the major challenges and problems of our era.

PIFER, A., & BRONTE, L. (Eds.). (1986). *Our aging society.* New York: W. W. Norton. A fresh look at the meaning of aging in American society by leading authorities in the field.

SHEEHY, G. (1995). *New passages: Mapping your life across time.* A lifespan look at the various changes or passages we make as we make the transition from one life era to another.

WEBSITES AND THE INTERNET

http://www.cweb.com/resources/resource.html: A rich source of information on careers, internships, how to network, resume development, and other useful information for job seekers.

http://www.alz.org: This is the website for the Alzheimer's Association with lots of good information for patients and families about this disabling disease.

http://www.caregiving.com/: The site for finding out about eldercare. A good place to find information for those caring for a frail elderly family member.

http://www.aarp.org/: The website for the largest advocacy group for the elderly, the American Association for Retired Persons. Contains information on the association's advocacy programs, information on retirement and aging, and the benefits of membership.

http://www.podi.com/appwp/: The website for the Association of Private Pension and Welfare Plans. This group advocates for fair public policy on retirement issues, for example, that pensions should be portable from one job to another.

CHAPTER 16

Death and Bereavement

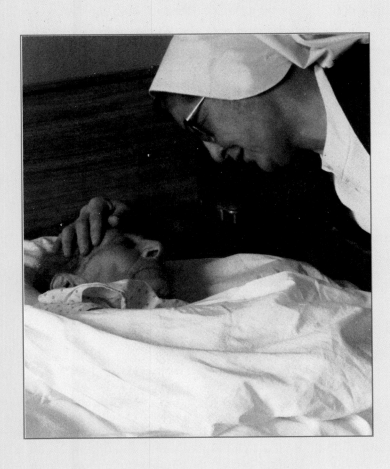

- ◆ **Death and Dying**
    - Risks of dying
    - Awareness of death
    - Near-death experiences
    - The experience of dying

- ◆ **Bereavement and Grief**
    - Grief work
    - Unresolved grief
    - Good grief

- ◆ **Life And Death in Perspective**
    - The right to die
    - A natural death
    - Funerals and other services
    - Death and growth

SUMMARY
RANKINGS OF HEALTH RISKS
SCORING KEY
SELF-TEST
EXERCISES
QUESTIONS FOR SELF-REFLECTION
FOR FURTHER INFORMATION

Learning Objectives

....

After completing this chapter, you should be able to

1. List some of the hazards and risks that result in dying.
2. Describe the near-death experience.
3. Identify and describe several models of the experience of death.
4. Explain the importance of grief work for bereavement.
5. Describe the experience of unresolved grief.
6. Distinguish between a living will and powers of attorney.
7. Discuss how the awareness of death may help to give new meaning to one's life.

Two people have sharply contrasting attitudes toward death. Mark, who is in his late 40s, bristles at the mention of the word *death*. Those who know him well say this reaction may have something to do with the tragic loss of his older brother in a car accident when Mark was a young adult. In any event, Mark refuses to attend funerals, even for his closest friends. One can only speculate how Mark would react if his wife or children should die before he does. For years, Mark has boasted that the only way he'll ever go to a cemetery is "feet first"—when he's carried there for burial.

Joanna, a widow in her mid 80s, has a more realistic attitude toward death. She is grieving over the recent loss of her husband, to whom she was happily married for 50 years. She talks openly with her friends about how much she misses him. Also, she regularly tends to the plants at the family grave. Knowing that her husband never liked being alone, she sometimes pauses by his grave to talk to him. "Don't worry," she says, "I'll be with you one day." Then she glances at the unused gravesite adjacent to her husband's, together with the stone containing her name—"Joanna C. Hunzinger, 1913– ." How does she feel about seeing her own tombstone? "Well, you see," she replies, "we saved a little money by getting both at the same time."

Death and Dying

....

With which of these people's attitudes toward **death** do you most identify? Many of us would prefer to think we're like Joanna, with her open and matter-of-fact attitude toward death. But we probably realize also that we may be more like Mark, with his characteristic denial of death. Perhaps most of us fall somewhere in between these two extremes.

Actually, some denial of death as Mark holds is necessary to function effectively. Mark's denial was extreme, though. Death, especially the possibility of our own death,

432

is such a harsh reality that few people can face it directly. Denial helps to keep our anxiety level over the threat of nonexistence at a low, manageable level. Denial also helps us to avoid thoughts of being separated from loved ones, whose relationship to us is essential to our self-esteem and well-being. Then, too, there's another reason for not thinking about death—the idea that it's futile to think about the inevitable. Because we aren't certain what comes after death, though we suspect it's nothingness, death is a most unpleasant thought. As Ben Franklin said, "In this world nothing can be said to be certain, except death and taxes." Or as we might say, "Since there's nothing I can do about my death, why bother to think about it?" (Worden & Proctor, 1988). Interestingly, both Joanna and Mark, with their individual styles of coping with the prospect of death, agree with this thought.

An excessive or inappropriate denial of death tends to be counterproductive. For instance, people who constantly reassure themselves that "It can't happen to me" or who insist "I don't want to think about it" may continue to smoke, drink alcohol, eat junk food, and drive fast, all of which increases their vulnerability. Similarly, the denial of death makes us avoid the aged or the seriously ill, who may remind us of our own mortality. Joanna, being more comfortable with death than Mark, was able to stay at her dying husband's side and support him through this passage. Then, too, as long as we mistakenly assume we are going to live forever, we tend to postpone doing the things that really matter to us, which results in a superficial life. For example, throughout his prime years John, Mark's deceased brother, spent most of his waking hours trying to increase his income and buy a bigger house rather than getting to know his children.

Accordingly, we'll begin this chapter by considering some of the realities of death, such as the everyday risks of dying, death anxiety, and the experience of dying. In the middle section we'll describe the process of grief and the importance of working through the emotions associated with personal loss. Then in the final section, we'll examine some of the ethical and practical issues associated with dying, such as the right to die, a living will, funerals, and how the awareness of our mortality and experiences of loss may enrich the meaning of life itself.

RISKS OF DYING

Every day each of us risks dying as a consequence of engaging in certain activities and the use of various technologies. To become more aware of these risk factors, you might complete Figure 16–1 before reading further. Then compare your answers with those of the public and experts given at the end of this chapter.

People tend to *over*estimate the risk of death from sensational causes such as accidents and homicides. But they *under*estimate the risk of death from nonspectacular causes such as heart attacks, strokes, and diabetes. Such misjudgments arise from our tendency to believe an event is likely to occur if we can easily imagine or recall it, which is further compounded by the media's practice of overreporting dramatic, negative events like accidents and homicides. For example, newspapers carry three times as many articles about death from homicide as about death from disease, although disease takes 100 lives to every 1 homicide. Because most of these deaths are noted in the obituary columns rather than the headlines, we underestimate the risk of death from familiar hazards such as smoking, X-rays, surgery, and food preservatives. However, these are the very things over which each of us has a great deal of control (Allman, 1985).

As you might suspect, the risk of dying varies greatly from one person to another, depending on such factors as lifestyle, heredity, and gender. (See Table 16–1.) Health

FIGURE 16–1

RATING HEALTH RISKS

Rank the risks of dying in the general population in any year from the following activities and technologies. Rank each health risk on a scale from 1 to 30, putting the most hazardous first and the least hazardous last. Then compare your rankings with those obtained from the public and experts at the end of this chapter.

_____ handguns
_____ smoking
_____ spray cans
_____ mountain climbing
_____ X-rays
_____ high school/college football
_____ vaccinations
_____ swimming
_____ food coloring
_____ nuclear power
_____ fire fighting
_____ railroads
_____ prescription antibiotics
_____ pesticides
_____ police work
_____ motor vehicles
_____ alcoholic beverages
_____ home appliances
_____ surgery
_____ commercial aviation
_____ motorcycles
_____ food preservatives
_____ bicycles
_____ large construction
_____ general (private) aviation
_____ hunting
_____ power mowers
_____ electric power (nonnuclear)
_____ contraceptives
_____ skiing

SOURCE: Adapted from a similar table in Allman, W. (1985, October). Staying Alive in the 20th Century. _Science, 85,_ 31–41.

habits and lifestyles, as mentioned elsewhere in this book, are especially important. People who smoke a pack or more of cigarettes a day can expect to die 5 or 6 years sooner than those who don't smoke. Similarly, those who are overweight by 50 pounds or more die many years sooner than those closer to their ideal weights.

People who have healthy eating and exercise habits not only keep themselves more fit but also tend to live longer than those with less healthy habits. Personality and stress management are also important. Whereas individuals who are intense, hostile, and eas-

TABLE 16–1
THE THREE LEADING CAUSES OF DEATH BY AGE GROUP AND SEX IN THE UNITED STATES

Age		1	2	3
All ages	M	Heart disease	Cancer	Cerebrovascular disease
	F	Heart disease	Cancer	Cerebrovascular disease
Under 15 years	M	Accidents	Cancer	Homicide
	F	Accidents	Cancer	Homicide
15–24	M	Accidents	Cancer	Homicide
	F	Accidents	Homicide	Cancer
25–44	M	Accidents	Heart disease	Cancer
	F	Cancer	Accidents	Heart disease
45–64	M	Heart disease	Cancer	Accidents
	F	Cancer	Heart disease	Cerebrovascular disease
65 and over	M	Heart disease	Cancer	Cerebrovascular disease
	F	Heart disease	Cancer	Cerebrovascular disease

SOURCE: U.S. Bureau of the Census. (1995). *Statistical Abstract of the United States, 1995* (115th ed). Washington, DC: U.S. Government Printing Office, p. 93.

ily angered tend to die sooner than average, those who are relaxed and easygoing live longer than average (Dolnick, 1995).

Heredity also affects our life expectancy. It is well known that people with long-lived parents and grandparents tend to live longer than those whose close relatives die before 50. However, if your relatives are not noted for their longevity, you need not become fatalistic. Instead, you might make even greater efforts to adopt healthier eating and exercise habits. For instance, because most of the men in Mark's family died before the age of 50, he continued his "eat, drink, and be merry" outlook, believing he would be dead by middle age anyway. But at the insistence of his doctor and wife, he underwent a coronary bypass operation and began eating healthier foods and exercising regularly, all of which have given him a somewhat more positive outlook on life as well as a longer life expectancy.

Health habits and lifestyles affect life expectancy, but unpredictable events also alter longevity.

AWARENESS OF DEATH

Despite attempts at denial, each of us has some awareness of our own mortality. For instance, suppose you were asked, "How often do you think about your own death?" If your reply is "once in a while," you've got a lot of company. About half the people asked this question answer "occasionally." Another fourth say "frequently" or "very frequently," whereas another fourth claim they rarely have thoughts about their own death.

Actually, our personal awareness of death fluctuates somewhat every day. Most of the time, we have very little awareness of death. We avoid thinking about the possibility of our death and deny that someday our lives must end. And the more intense the denial, the lower our awareness of death. Other days, we're more aware that our life span is limited. Perhaps we've just seen a gory automobile accident, or someone we know has discovered he or she has a serious illness. People who investigate such matters have found that when individuals are questioned directly about death, they rarely admit being fearful of it. But when more indirect methods are used, such as fantasy and imagery, people express greater fears of death.

The personal awareness of death also varies somewhat by age. Interestingly, youths in their late 20s are the most fearful of all, perhaps partly because they have most of their lives ahead of them. Then, too, the leading causes of death for youths—accidents, homicide, and suicide—imply that death often comes violently. At the same time, some studies indicate that youths who have acquired a sense of meaning and purpose in life have less fear of death than those who are still struggling to find themselves (Hughes & Noppe, 1985). As individuals reach late adulthood, they generally think about death more often and talk about it more openly. The increase in chronic illnesses and the death of close friends at this age are all reminders that death is the natural end of life. Finally, older people are usually less fearful of death than other age groups. After all, they've already lived a reasonably long life and may have less to look forward to. Also, those with

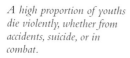

A high proportion of youths die violently, whether from accidents, suicide, or in combat.

a deep religious faith, including a belief in some kind of afterlife, are generally less fearful of death. Such a belief may provide an important mechanism for dealing with the anxieties of aging and death. When Joanna was asked if she feared death, she replied, "I'm more worried about ending up in a nursing home and becoming a burden to my children than I am of dying. I've made my peace with death."

NEAR-DEATH EXPERIENCES

Suppose you're knocked unconscious in an automobile accident and taken to the hospital. Critically injured, you're put on a life-support system that keeps you alive. After a couple of days you regain consciousness, only to discover that you almost died. There's a good chance you would have had a **near-death experience**—the distinctive state of recall associated with being brought back to life from the verge of death.

Various accounts of such experiences show striking similarities. Initially, individuals experience a detachment from their bodies and are pulled through a dark tunnel. Then they find themselves in another kind of "spiritual body," in which physical objects present no barrier and movement from one place to another is almost instantaneous. While in this state they may have a reunion with long-lost friends and loved ones. One of the most incredible elements is the appearance of a brilliant light, perceived as a warm, loving "being of light," which fosters a kind of life review in a nonjudgmental way. Finally, people report being drawn back through the dark tunnel and undergoing a rapid reentry into their bodies. For most people, the near-death experience brings a profound change in attitudes. They not only become less fearful of death but are also more concerned with learning and loving and valuing the life they have (Koerner, 1997).

Of the nearly 18 percent of Americans who claim to have been on the verge of dying, perhaps as many as a third or up to 15 million may have had a near-death experience. No matter what their age, race, sex, or education level, the experience seems transforming. Alcoholics find themselves unable to imbibe; hardened criminals opt for a life of helping others. Atheists embrace religion or report feeling welcome in any church temple or synagogue. Although many who have had near-death experiences prefer to view them as spiritual encounters, recent researchers are taking the mysticism out of such occurrences by claiming that they are physiological events or hallucinations created by the nervous system (Koerner, 1997). However, others such as Elisabeth Kübler-Ross (1987) believe that the near-death phenomena are an integral part of the more inclusive experience of dying, including the physical level (loss of consciousness), psychic level (out-of-body awareness), and spiritual level (glimpse of nonjudgmental light or the realm of God).

THE EXPERIENCE OF DYING

Now that people are likely to die in a hospital, often sedated and isolated from all but their immediate family and hospital personnel, the **experience of dying** has become something of a mystery for the average person. Many people have never been in the presence of someone who is dying. Even people who have sat with a loved one or friend who is dying have only a limited awareness of the dying person's inner world or how to communicate with that person. For those who are heavily sedated, as was Joanna's husband when he died of cancer, perhaps the final moments are meaningless. But some people with a terminal illness remain alert up to the end and have expressed their thoughts and feelings about dying, giving us a more accurate understanding of it.

One of the best-known pioneers in this field is Elisabeth Kübler-Ross. She and her colleagues interviewed more than 500 terminally ill people at the University of Chicago hospital. She also started a course on the dynamics of death and dying. Kübler-Ross (1975) found that even when patients were not told of the seriousness of their illness, they usually sensed that fact as well as the approximate time of their death. Hence, there is a growing realization that when persons indicate a willingness to know the truth about their impending death, it may be wiser to give the relevant information than to protect them with a conspiracy of concealment. This also provides them with some time to get their affairs in order, for example, write a will if they do not have one. How the knowledge of impending death is conveyed is more important than the particular facts communicated. Furthermore, dying people have benefited from the opportunity to face death openly and to talk about it, removing much of the fear, sense of isolation, and mystery.

Kübler-Ross (1993) noted that individuals tend to go through several stages in dying, although there is considerable overlap between these stages. The first stage consists of a **denial** of death, with people characteristically feeling, "No, not me." Such denial protects them from the deep emotions associated with death and provides time to cope with the disturbing facts. Later, individuals tend to show small signs that they are now willing to talk about death, but at this stage friends or professionals should talk about it only for a few minutes at a time, allowing the dying time to make the needed adjustment. In the second stage, denial eventually gives way to the emotions of *anger* and **resentment.** "Why me?" people ask. The sight of others enjoying their health evokes envy, jealousy, and anger. The dying often take their feelings out on those closest to them, mostly because of what these people represent—life and health. Consequently, it is important for those nearby not to take these remarks personally but to help the dying express their feelings.

The third stage characteristically consists of attempts to **bargain for time.** Individuals at this stage often say, "I know I'm dying *but . . .*" Then they indulge in a bit of magical thinking, "If I cooperate with the doctor or my family, maybe God will let me live till my daughter graduates or my son gets married." When individuals tend to drop the *but* and admit, "Yes, I'm dying," they enter the fourth stage, **depression.** In a sense this is a natural response to the threat of losing their life, and it is very important to allow people to grieve and express their sadness. One of the worst things a friend can do is deny these feelings and say, "Cheer up." Thus, it is important for family and friends as well as professionals to learn to accept their own feelings about death so that they can help dying people accept their own impending death without dwelling on it unduly.

The final stage is the **acceptance** of death, though not all dying persons reach this stage. By this time, most people who are dying have pretty much disengaged themselves from others and ask for fewer visitors, but they don't want to die alone. Although most people prefer to die at home, they are more likely to die in a hospital. In fact, much of the pain of dying comes from mental anguish, especially the fear of being separated from loved ones.

Elisabeth Kübler-Ross (1975, 1993) was the first to point out that the experience of dying is not a fixed, inevitable process and that many people do not follow these stages. For some, anger remains the dominant mood throughout, whereas others are depressed until the end as was Joanna's husband, although he died quickly. Many authorities go even further and hold that individual differences are more pronounced in the experience of dying than are any stages (e.g., Corr, 1993). Consequently, each person experiences the dying process in a unique way because of such factors as age, sex, and personality differences as well as cultural backgrounds and the nature of various types of illnesses.

Another classic model of dying is that of E. Mansell Pattison (1977), who describes the dying process in terms of three broad phases that each individual experiences differently. Initially, individuals build up a **life trajectory,** which consists of their anticipated life span and how they will live it. However, when a serious injury or illness disrupts the life trajectory, people realize that they are likely to die sooner than they had anticipated. The interval between the time they discover they will die sooner than they had thought and the time they die is called the *living-dying interval,* which consists of three phases of development.

1. **The acute phase.** The awareness of impending death creates considerable anxiety and stress. Individuals usually need a great deal of emotional support and assistance in dealing rationally with their imminent death.
2. **The chronic phase.** As individuals begin to confront their fear of death, many other emotions surface, such as fear of the unknown, loneliness, suffering, and loss of identity, which is closely associated with family and friends.
3. **The terminal phase.** As the hope for getting better is replaced by the realization that one's condition will probably get worse, individuals withdraw from people and resign themselves to the finality of death.

How people experience the living-dying interval is vitally affected by the **dying trajectory**—the duration and form of the dying process. Pattison (1977) has identified four major dying trajectories. First, someone is told that the end of life is near, for example, "You have only a few more months to live." Second, death may be imminent, but the precise time remains unknown. Third, it is unclear whether or not the person will die, depending on the success of surgery or some other type of treatment. Fourth, death may also remain uncertain if the person has some chronic condition, such as a heart problem. In each case, *how* the person faces his or her death and goes about the experience of dying depends on a variety of factors, such as one's personality as well as the dying trajectory. Although family and friends, as well as those who work with the dying person, may not be able to resolve the ultimate problem of imminent death, they may give considerable support to the dying person, thereby helping to alleviate the emotional suffering associated with dying.

 ## Bereavement and Grief

To lose a loved one or friend through death is to lose part of ourselves. It's a very painful experience that is labeled variously as bereavement, grief, or mourning. **Bereavement** ("to be deprived of") is the general term for the overall experience of loss. **Grief** refers to the intense emotional suffering that accompanies our experience of loss, and **mourning** refers to the outward expressions of bereavement and grief.

Because death is one of the universal rites of passage, most societies have mourning customs to facilitate the experience of grief. Until recently in mainstream American culture, widows dressed in black and widowers wore black armbands. Such dress excused any show of grief on the part of the bereaved and afforded them an opportunity to talk about their loss and to receive the needed sympathy. However, many of these customs have been modified or given up in recent years. Wakes and visitations have been replaced by brief funerals and memorial services. Ordinarily, the bereaved are expected to resume their usual dress and activities as soon as possible.

GRIEF WORK

Our modern customs sometimes get in the way of grief work—the healthy process of working through the emotions associated with loss. **Grief work** consists of freeing ourselves emotionally from the deceased, readjusting to life without that person, resuming ordinary activities, and forming new relationships. The grief process parallels the experience of dying and involves many of the same emotions. There are many individual differences in how people grieve (see Box 16–1), but we will describe the typical experience.

After the initial shock wears off, we're likely to be bothered by memories of the deceased. This was the stage most bothersome for Mark when his brother died. He was very close emotionally to his brother. As may be the case, Mark did not feel like socializing with his friends, especially in activities that reminded him of his deceased brother. He missed a whole season of football games, sold a car they enjoyed riding in, and cut off his otherwise friendly relationship with his brother's girlfriend. Negative emotions such as anger and guilt are likely to surface at this stage. We may blame God, fate, or those who've been taking care of the deceased. It's not uncommon to blame the deceased person for having abandoned us, especially if that person committed suicide.

BOX 16–1

SAYING GOOD-BYE

The two women were very similar. Both were in their late 50s and had grown children, and, like Joanna, both had recently lost their husbands through death, but they were quite different in one important way. One woman was devastated and felt sorry for herself. The other woman, though sad, began building a new life for herself, filling her days with friends and activities. The second woman had learned how to say good-bye.

Actually, life is a series of separations, with death the most significant good-bye of all. Parents who can comfortably say good-bye when their children go off to school and college or get married are better prepared to survive the death of a loved one. Those who handle separation best have a firm sense of self-identity and other interests and don't think of themselves solely in terms of their roles as parents or spouses. By the time their children reach their 20s, healthy parents learn how to "let go." Similarly, a healthy spouse is able to say, "I can make it on my own if I have to."

How have you handled separations, such as leaving home or breaking up with a friend or spouse? Have you learned how to say good-bye?

Mark's brother did not commit suicide; he died in a car accident. Nonetheless, it is apparent that Mark had and still has a difficult time coping with his brother's death. Also, we may have feelings of guilt because of something we said or did or feel we should have done while the person was still alive. Some of our guilt may be "survivor's guilt," that is, feeling guilty simply because we're still alive and the other person is not.

The emotional intensity of grief often appears in the disguise of physical symptoms, especially among older adults. In the early months of bereavement, the most common symptoms of grief are crying, depressed feelings, lack of appetite, and difficulties concentrating at work or at home. Fortunately for Joanna, these symptoms did not last long. Many people rely on sleeping pills and tranquilizers at some point during their bereavement. However, an understanding family physician may realize that such symptoms are a normal part of the grief process.

In the final stage of grief, we usually come to terms with our loss and resume ordinary activities. This stage may occur anytime from a few months to a year or more after the initial loss, depending on how close we were to the person and the circumstances surrounding his or her death. Recent research has shown that about 1 year is the norm for normal grief work (Lindstrom, 1995). From this time on, we're likely to recall the deceased person with pleasant memories. In some ways we never fully get over the death of a loved one, such as a parent, child, or spouse. But the more fully we work through our grief, the more likely we'll be able to get on with our lives. People who are unable to do so may delay the grief process.

UNRESOLVED GRIEF

Psychological reactions. **Unresolved grief** may assume a variety of forms, from unexplained physical complaints to psychological symptoms. In some instances, the psychological reactions are obviously related to the loss. For example, some people can't bring themselves to return to the house, hospital, or room where a person has died because of unresolved grief. In other cases, unresolved grief may be more disguised. A friend of Mark's complained that when her father died, she did not really experience any grief. She recalled that she never cried or experienced the usual grief reactions. It was later found that she was left out of the family bereavement process; that is, no one in the family had talked to her about her father's death, and she had not been allowed to accompany them when they attended the funeral or burial. Years later, this woman discovered that much of her resentment toward her mother and her apprehensiveness over her husband's traveling were related to unresolved grief over her father's death. As she expressed the pent-up tears and anger, she gradually worked out her grief, which resulted in more satisfying relationships with her mother and husband.

On the other hand, some individuals do just the opposite. Instead of thinking too little about their loved one or the death, they think too much about their grief and the loss of their loved one. Studies have also shown that rumination about the death, that is, preoccupation with the death, can be bad. Individuals who ruminate or constantly rehash details of the death, especially when they have few social supports and other stressors, experience more depression and are more pessimistic than those who don't rely on rumination (Nolen-Hoeksema, Parker, & Larson, 1994).

Physical reactions. People who live alone, especially those without close friends, are the most likely to have difficulty working through their grief. They may be more prone to a variety of illnesses like heart disease, strokes, cirrhosis of the liver, hypertension, and

Women often outlive their spouses.

cancer, as well as premature death. For example, heart disease, depending on the age of the individual, is anywhere from two to five times higher among the divorced, single, and widowed than among the married. Men are likely to die within a few years after the death of their spouse, although women's chances of dying are less affected by their husband's death. Although there is little difference in the death rates between people who have lost a spouse in the past year and married people the same age, in the ensuing years widowed men suffer a much greater mortality rate than their married counterparts. Widowed men between the ages of 55 and 65 die at a 60 percent higher rate than married men the same age. The most likely explanation is that the quality of life changes more drastically for men than for women, possibly because of their greater reliance on wives for their emotional and daily needs. Women tend to have a better support system for coping with their grief. However, when widowers remarry, they have an even lower mortality rate than their married counterparts who have never lost a spouse.

GOOD GRIEF

So far, we've seen that it is better to go through the full experience of bereavement, however painful it may be, than to get over it too quickly or too intently as in rumination. In this regard, Joanna was coping better with her loss than was Mark, even years later. There are some positive aspects of grief. That is, grief may be a learning experience that helps us grow. It is sometimes said that we don't fully appreciate something until we have lost it, which is especially applicable to human relationships. While people are still with us, we often have ambivalent feelings toward them. One moment we love them, another we're angry with them. In retrospect, however, grief helps us appreciate loved ones and friends more fully despite their shortcomings. Grief also helps us value our relationships with those still living. In short, **good grief** means that we have learned and grown in our bereavement.

People who share their grief are better able to work through the emotions associated with loss.

There are several ways to make the experience of bereavement more effective: talking it out, feeling it out, and acting it out. Even though it may be very difficult to talk about the death of a loved one for the first several weeks, this is exactly when talking it out can be most helpful. The main thing to remember is that the focus is on the feelings of the bereaved. Some things may sound trivial or hollow, such as "at least he is out of his misery," but whatever it takes, a friend should attempt to listen and help the bereaved person to talk out his or her feelings as much as possible.

Encouraging and empowering the bereaved to express their feelings may also be cathartic. People tend to feel less embarrassed when they can do so in the company of a few close friends, especially those who consider themselves "private" people. Men usually have more difficulty expressing bereavement, largely because society considers a show of emotions by men to be a sign of weakness. It is also important to realize that each person's characteristic way of expressing his or her emotions differs somewhat from one person to another. For some, moistened eyes and a warm handclasp are about as close as they ever come to expressing grief. Others may cry openly and unashamedly. Still others seem to be inclined toward more dramatic and at times hysterical expressions of grief, such as screaming and tearing their hair and clothes.

Another way of resolving grief is to express it in appropriate ways. Sometimes just sheer physical activity helps to alleviate the tension and sadness of bereavement, at least temporarily. Funeral rituals may afford an outlet for grief. Also, taking care of the affairs of the deceased may be therapeutic as well as helpful. As the executor of her husband's estate, Joanna found herself faced with a great deal of correspondence and many legal transactions. Initially she regarded it as a burden but soon realized it was one of the few tangible things she could do for her deceased husband and their grown children. It became her way of showing her love and respect for him and of helping her express her grief. Research supports this. Individuals who are resilient or hardy, utilize problem-focused rather than emotion-focused coping, and have adequate social support are far less likely to be depressed and tend to recover from their grief faster (Caserta & Lund, 1992; Nolen-Hoeksema et al., 1994).

 ## Life and Death in Perspective

In 1900 more than half the deaths were of children (Fulton, 1987). The children died from disease and hunger. Now that the average life expectancy is over 75 years, more people are apt to suffer from chronic diseases such as many forms of cancer, heart disease, and kidney failure. As a result, death comes more slowly and usually occurs in the hospital. Hospitals tend to be large and impersonal institutions, however, geared more to the treatment of acute illnesses and the prolonging of life. Consequently, the change in the context of death presents new ethical issues, such as the use of lifesaving machines and the right to die in a dignified way. Examining such issues may help us put life and death in better perspective.

THE RIGHT TO DIE

Joanna remembers what her husband was like in the early years of their marriage. He was a fun-loving, hard-working, out-of-doors kind of person. Then, 6 months ago, Joanna's husband was diagnosed with cancer, which eventually left him in a coma. His health disintegrated so quickly that he was unable to tell Joanna what his last wishes were. He was sustained in the end by a feeding tube and intravenous pain killers at the hospital, as there was no hospice nearby. At that point, Joanna, together with her grown children, wanted to have the feeding tube removed. All of them believed that her husband would not want to continue existing in this way.

Patients like Joanna's husband—there are about 10,000 such Americans—pose an ethical dilemma for their families and doctors regarding the **right to die.** Family members are torn between their desire to be loyal to their loved one and the emotional and financial realities of supporting someone in a permanent vegetative state. Doctors also face the conflict between their duty to sustain life and their obligation to relieve suffering. Doctors often continue treatment because of their moral commitments or the fear of legal consequences of doing otherwise. In recent years, however, the American Medical Association's Council on Ethical and Judicial Affairs has provided some guidelines for doctors in such situations. After struggling with the issue for 2 years, the seven-member panel affirmed that it is not unethical for doctors to discontinue all life-support systems for patients who are in an irreversible coma as was Joanna's husband, even if death is not imminent. A more controversial provision includes food and water on the list of treatments that might be withheld. In each case, the patient's wishes, as well as can be determined, should be respected and his or her dignity maintained. The council's decision reflects growing public support on such issues. According to national surveys, more than 8 out of 10 adults think terminally ill patients ought to be able to tell their doctors to let them die and the doctor should be able to remove feeding tubes if this is the patient's wish. Because the council's decision is not binding, doctors are free to follow their consciences, but such guidelines may make it easier for them to comply with a patient's or family's request to end treatment (Wallis, 1986). Box 16–2 shares with you the results of a survey of doctors about their sentiments regarding life support.

All too often, family members and physicians ignore their elderly or ailing patients' desire to be allowed to die. One study (Cohn, 1984) found that although 1 in 3 patients

---

DOCTORS POLLED ON LIFE SUPPORT

Almost 80 percent of randomly selected American doctors favor withdrawing life-support systems from terminally ill patients or patients in irreversible comas if the patients or their families request it. Doctors in the poll included male and female doctors of various ages and specialties.

More specifically, when doctors were asked "Would you favor or oppose withdrawing life-support systems, including food and water, from hopelessly ill or comatose patients" if requested, 58 percent answered that they strongly favored this alternative. Another 20 percent answered that they were favorably disposed. Only 5 percent answered that they opposed this option with another 10 percent strongly opposed. Interestingly, nearly 70 percent of the doctors polled revealed that they had been directly involved in such cases.

A majority of the doctors also acknowledged that they were uncertain of the legal aspects. Finally, a very large majority (90 percent) said that doctors should discuss these options with patients and their families.

SOURCE: Adapted from Larue, G. A. (1988/1989, Winter). Euthanasia: The time is now. *Free Inquiry*, 4–6. Reproduced with permission.

---

would reject any medical intervention if he or she were about to die, patients were seldom asked their wishes in the matter. In a review of 154 cases in which physicians tried to restart a patient's heart, only 30 patients had been asked in advance. Yet, of the 24 patients who managed to survive in a mentally competent state, 8 said they would have preferred to die. The study suggested that doctors often assumed they knew what their patients wanted, even though they had not asked. Only 1 doctor in 10 had actually discussed resuscitation with his or her patients. And only 1 in 5 consulted family members rather than the patient, even when the patient was fully competent. Such evidence suggests an overprotectiveness that is ill founded. Most patients, whether they are well or seriously ill, wish to be well informed and to participate in medical decisions.

A president's commission on this subject, including doctors, lawyers, theologians, and others, has concluded that a competent patient who is able to understand treatment choices and their consequences has an all but absolute right to decide his or her fate. When a person is incompetent, a surrogate, usually a family member, should be given the authority to make these decisions. Such thinking has led to a growing use of instruments like the so-called **living will,** in which a person instructs doctors and family members to stop using life-sustaining procedures in the event of a terminal condition. To date only about 15 percent of Americans have made out living wills. To encourage more people to do so, a new law requires all federally funded hospitals, nursing homes, and hospices to tell incoming patients of their right to write a living will. (See the sample living will in Box 16–3.)

Some right-to-die laws attempt to make these directives binding on doctors, who may then transfer medical responsibility for the patient if they disagree with the patient's wishes. Because such documents may not cover the precise circumstances that occur, many authorities prefer the **power of attorney,** which empowers anyone—

relative, friend, or adviser—to make any medical, financial, and other decisions when the signee becomes incompetent. At least three-fourths of the states already have laws authorizing the power of attorney in such situations. Both the living will and power of attorney may be revoked by a rational person, but the power of attorney is probably more adaptable.

BOX 16–3

MY LIVING WILL TO MY FAMILY, MY PHYSICIAN, MY LAWYER, AND ALL OTHERS WHOM IT MAY CONCERN

Death is as much a reality as birth, growth, maturity, and old age—it is the one certainty of life. If the time comes when I can no longer take part in decisions for my own future, let this statement stand as an expression of my wishes and directions, while I am still of sound mind.

If at such time the situation should arise in which there is no reasonable expectation of my recovery from extreme physical or mental disability, I direct that I be allowed to die and not be kept alive by medications, artificial means, or "heroic measures." I do, however, ask that medication be mercifully administered to me to alleviate suffering even though this may shorten my remaining life.

This statement is made after careful consideration and is in accordance with my strong convictions and beliefs. I want the wishes and directions here expressed carried out to the extent permitted by law. Insofar as they are legally enforceable, I hope that those to whom this Will is addressed will regard themselves as morally bound by these provisions.

(Optional specific provisions to be made in this space)

Durable Power of Attorney (optional)

I hereby designate _____ to serve as my attorney-in-fact for the purpose of making medical treatment decisions. This power of attorney shall remain effective in the event that I become incompetent or otherwise unable to make such decisions for myself.

Optional Notarization:
"Sworn and subscribed to before me this ____ day of ___, 19 ___."
_____
Notary Public (seal)
Signed _____
Date_____
Witness _____
Address _____
Witness _____
Address _____
Copies of this request have been given to _____

Another form you might think about is an organ donation card. Many individuals die suddenly, as did Mark's brother, in a traumatic accident. Their brains become incapacitated, but other organs such as their hearts, livers, and eyes remain unharmed. These individuals perhaps are candidates for organ donations, which involve the immediate transplantation of a vital organ from someone who has essentially died to an otherwise healthy individual. Most states have means by which you can ensure that your healthy organs are donated; the forms look very much like the one in Box 16–4.

A NATURAL DEATH

One of the dangers of the right-to-die movement is that it may unwittingly program people to die quickly. It is often said that death is more of a problem for the survivors than for the dying. For this reason, sudden death from a heart attack or an automobile accident is often less stressful for the survivors than death from a drawn-out illness. On the surface, the dying are supposed to have been spared the suffering of a terminal illness, but also the survivors have been saved from the burden of taking care of an invalid or having to watch someone die slowly. A fast death also helps us to avoid our social responsibilities, such as caring for the lingering convalescent and the aged. Ironically, the revolt against needless prolongation of life may incline us toward an equally "unnatural" hastening of death. A quick, induced death, however, does not answer the key

---

BOX 16–4

UNIFORM DONOR CARD

_____
(print or type name of donor)
In the hope that I may help others, I hereby make this anatomical gift, if medically acceptable, to take effect upon my death. The words and marks below indicate I give:
a) _____ any needed organs or parts
b) _____ only the following organs or parts

_____
(specify the organs or parts)
for the purposes of transplantation, therapy, medical research, or education:
c) _____ my body for anatomical study if needed. Limitations or special wishes, if any: _____
(specify limitations here)
Signed by the donor and the following two witnesses in the presence of each other:

_____   _____
Signature of donor   Date of birth of donor

_____   _____
Date signed   City and State

_____   _____
Witness   Witness

questions: How old is old? How ill is ill? At what point should a person on the heart-lung machine be allowed to die? When does a life cease to have meaning?

Perhaps the nearest we come to a natural death is helping people to die at their own pace and style. For example, if a young person has been an active, outdoor type as was Mark's brother and doesn't have the desire to adjust to an invalid state, perhaps that person should be allowed to die a dignified death. Others who may suffer from equally disabling handicaps but who prefer making the adjustment to their diminished capacities should be encouraged and supported in their efforts to go on living.

The hospice movement for the terminally ill represents a giant step toward the kind of humane and supportive community needed for a dignified death. In the Middle Ages the hospice was a shelter for travelers who had nowhere else to go. Today the **hospice** is a place to take care of those approaching the end of their lives. As we mentioned earlier, much of the suffering of the terminally ill consists of the treatments, the impersonal atmosphere, and the sense of isolation experienced in hospitals. In contrast, the hospice is a community that helps people to *live,* not merely exist, while they are dying.

The term *hospice* generally refers to a *system* of care that integrates a physical facility for the terminally ill with the patient's family and home. In some cases, patients may spend their final days at home being taken care of by loved ones and trained volunteers. In addition to helping with such practical matters as pain control and preparing meals, hospice personnel also give emotional support and guidance to family members. The aim throughout is to provide a humane and supportive community in which the patient may die with dignity. Begun in England, the hospice movement has since spread to other countries, including several thousand hospice programs in the United States and Canada. The increasing population of elderly people and rising costs of hospitalization are such that the hospice movement is likely to expand during the years ahead. Caution must be made in assuming that hospice care is for everyone, though. Talamantes, Lawler, and Espino (1995) have found that Hispanic Americans, for example, are unlikely to use hospice care as they are better connected to their communities, have different cultural values, and perceive a language barrier.

There are many individuals who prefer to die at home, so many families, friends, and others in the community also provide care to the dying. Box 16–5 discusses who these caregivers are and how caregivers can take care of themselves, too.

FUNERALS AND OTHER SERVICES

When death finally comes, it is a rite of passage to be recognized by the family and community alike. In most societies, parting with the dead is recognized by some kind of **funeral**—the ceremonies and rituals associated with the burial or cremation of the dead. Such rites may enable people to maintain order and defend themselves against lack of closure.

In earlier eras, when belief in an afterlife was a more dominant influence in human affairs, funerals were held primarily for the benefit of the dead. Death was seen as a passage to heaven or eternal life. Hence, some ancients not only buried the corpse but also included personal items of the deceased to be used on the "journey." Perhaps you have heard about the pyramids of Egypt where items were buried with the deceased to make their journey to and life in the afterworld easier. In today's secularized American society, however, the emphasis tends to be humanistic and materialistic. Although it is the dead who are remembered at funerals, the ceremony is more for the benefit of the survivors. Funerals may become the occasion for according the dead the recognition and honor they may not have achieved in life. Families sometimes get caught in a status game, selecting expensive bronze caskets, ornate headstones, and choice burial sites to maintain their position in society. Consequently, funerals have become increasingly lavish and expensive. The funeral industry has been criticized for exploiting people in their bereavement, but its defenders point out that bereaved family members themselves are

---

BOX 16–5

GUARDIAN ANGELS: CAREGIVERS

Older Americans, those dying from AIDS and cancer, the disabled, and others often need help from caregivers. Some require permanent care; others need assistance during convalescence. Friends and families wanting to assist become the caregivers. They are not professional caregivers such as home health aides, yet they are often expected to perform some of the very same duties. Today nearly 34 million elderly alone cannot do their own shopping, bathing, or cooking. Caregivers also act as chauffeurs, fill out insurance forms, give medications, take care of financial arrangements, and act as therapists among other duties. One reason the number of caregivers has skyrocketed is because more Americans want to die in their own homes. Doing this would not be possible without the assistance of voluntary caregivers.

Who are these guardian angels who step in to help? Over 22.4 million American households report that their homes include someone who cannot care for him- or herself. Caregivers are frequently family members, but not all caregivers. Caregivers may be neighbors, friends, church members, Kiwanis members, or anyone else. In fact, there are more nonpaid caregivers in the United States than paid or professional caregivers. The primary recipients of care are often families, but some caregivers are assisting neighbors, friends, and, in some cases, individuals who are almost strangers, such as homeless or runaway children.

Some caregivers are full-time or nearly full-time caregivers. Often this task falls on the eldest daughter when a family member is involved. With more women working outside the home, though, the stress placed on such women by their families is immense. Men need to and often do help with the caregiving. Children are called on more and more to assist as well.

Caregivers often need help themselves. They may need some medical training as well as emotional and social support. Caregivers also need respite from their many duties. Caregiving is both emotionally and physically exhausting. To assist the caregiver, local support groups are springing up all around the country. Such groups offer advice, emotional support, and often respite care where another member fills in for a few hours a week. There are also nationwide organizations that publish newsletters, sell useful products, and provide other insightful information. If you are a caregiver or expect to be, you can join the National Family Caregivers Association. Their address is 9621 E. Bexhill Dr., Kensinton, MD 20895. There are also specialized national groups for individuals caring for those with AIDS, Alzheimer's, physical disabilities, the elderly, and others requiring specialized assistance in living. Most of these organizations maintain easily accessible websites.

SOURCE: Adapted from France, D. (1997, May/June). The new compassion. *Modern Maturity*, 33–40, 80. Used with permission of the author.

partly to blame because they choose on the basis of their emotions rather than reason. Thus, whether out of respect for the dead, guilt, or vanity, many expensive funeral practices continue.

Funerals are sometimes the fourth largest consumer purchase, following a house, car, and wedding. The average cost of a funeral is now about $5,000, although you can easily pay more. One of Joanna's friends was shocked when confronted by a funeral bill of more than $8,000 for her husband's funeral. Like many, she didn't think to ask about all the extras, such as the use of the chapel, visitation room, and parking lot. And like many, she paid the bill, feeling she had no other option. However, under a "truth-in-funerals" ruling, funeral directors must now send itemized bills and provide information regarding the cost of coffins and other burial procedures. They must also offer embalming as an option where it isn't required by state law. In cases of cremation, funeral directors must also notify a customer that a casket is not necessary and present the option of buying a plain wood box or alternate container for use in burial. Most important of all, we need to realize that the decisions made at such a time are our decisions, and we must be sure that we are not being pressured into anything against our will.

The movement toward simpler funerals can also be seen in the nonprofit funeral and memorial societies springing up all around the country. Members have access to expert guidance and can specify what they want done with their bodies and what kind of service they want. All of this information helps people to end their lives in a way that reflects their lifestyle and values, while sparing their relatives the worry of how best to carry out their wishes. For example, Charles Lindbergh requested that he be buried without embalming or eulogies within 8 hours of his death in a tiny church cemetery in Hawaii. The only mourners present were his wife and one son.

DEATH AND GROWTH

It may seem strange relating death to growth. Ordinarily, death is seen as the end of growth and existence. Yet in the larger scheme of things, death is an integral part of life that gives meaning to human existence. It sets a limit on our lives, reminding us to spend our days on the things that matter most. Those who are fortunate enough to have some warning of their end often find it a time of personal growth. Similarly, grieving over the loss of a loved one may help us relate more deeply to those who remain.

Whether you are young or old, if you can begin to see death as an inevitable companion of life, it may help you to live your life fully rather than passively. Not that you should rush out and begin doing all those things people fantasize about. Instead, the awareness that you have only so much time to live may help you make the most of your life—the disappointments and pains as well as the joy. As Joanna said, "I've begun to take time to smell the roses." Usually, it is those who have not lived their lives fully who are the most reluctant to die. Haunted by broken relationships and unfulfilled dreams, they grow ever more anxious and fearful in the face of death.

Far from being morbid, thinking about your own death may give you a new perspective on life. For instance, if you were told you had only a limited time to live, how would you spend the time? What unfinished business would you be most concerned about? Which people would you most want to be with? Pondering the answers to such questions may help you to clarify what is really important to you. We should plan to do these things before it's too late. As Elisabeth Kübler-Ross (1975) reminds us, the greatest lesson we may learn from the dying is simply "LIVE, so you do not have to look back and say, 'God, how I wasted my life'" (p. xix).

SUMMARY

DEATH AND DYING

The prospect of our own death is sometimes so frightening that some denial of death is necessary for us to function effectively. However, people tend to underestimate the risk of death from nonspectacular causes, such as heart attacks, stress, and diabetes, and over-estimate the risk of death from sensational causes, such as accidents and homicides. Although most people think about their own deaths occasionally, older people think about death more often but are less fearful of it. Also, near-death experiences, often associated with the use of life-saving machines, tend to make people less fearful of death and more appreciative of life. Terminally ill people tend to go through several stages of dying—denial, anger, bargaining, depression, and acceptance—with considerable over-lapping between the stages. However, each person experiences the dying process some-what differently, depending on such factors as personality and type of illness.

BEREAVEMENT AND GRIEF

It is important for the bereaved to engage actively in grief work, a process that parallels the experience of dying and involves many of the same emotions. People who have not been able to resolve their grief exhibit various symptoms, ranging from physical com-plaints to more persistent psychological symptoms. Those who live alone are especially likely to have difficulty working through their grief. Healthy grief consists of talking about our grief, sharing our feelings, and taking part in suitable rituals and activities that may eventually alleviate grief. Resilient individuals who use problem-focused coping and have social support are most likely to resolve their grief work in positive ways.

LIFE AND DEATH IN PERSPECTIVE

Now that people live longer they are more apt to suffer from chronic and life-threatening illnesses and often die in a hospital. Also, the increased use of life-saving technology poses critical questions about prolonging life or letting someone die rather than suffer unduly. As a result, patients are being encouraged to express their own wishes through such in-struments as the living will and the power of attorney. The importance of providing ter-minally ill people with a humane and supportive community has led to the hospice movement, which is likely to expand in the coming years. Criticism of the funeral in-dustry has spurred a movement toward simpler and less expensive funerals. It appears that a more realistic awareness of death as an inevitable companion of life, far from being mor-bid, may help each of us to put our lives in better perspective and to live more fully.

Rankings of Health Risks by the Public and Experts (to accompany Figure 16–1)

Activity/technology	Public	Experts
handguns	3	4
smoking	4	2
spray cans	14	26
mountain climbing	15	29
X-rays	22	7
high school and college football	23	27
vaccinations	30	25
swimming	19	10
food coloring	26	21
nuclear power	1	20
fire fighting	11	18
railroads	24	19
prescription antibiotics	28	24
pesticides	9	8
police work	8	17
motor vehicles	2	1
alcoholic beverages	6	3
home appliances	29	22
surgery	10	5
commercial aviation	17	16
motorcycles	5	6
food preservatives	25	14
bicycles	15	16
large construction	12	13
general (private) aviation	7	12
hunting	13	23
power mowers	27	28
electric power (nonnuclear)	18	9
contraceptives	20	11
skiing	21	30

Notice that the estimates of the public and experts are similar in some respects. Both groups judge motorcycles, smoking, and handguns to be quite risky, and power mowers and football as less risky. Yet in other respects their assessments vary greatly. The biggest difference concerns nuclear power, which is ranked first by the public and twentieth by the experts. In contrast, medical X-rays are thought to be far less risky by laypeople than by the experts.

SELF-TEST

1. Compared to young adults, older adults tend to
   a. become more fearful of death
   b. think of death more often
   c. become less religious
   d. think of death less often

2. Near-death experiences are generally
   a. more frequent among churchgoers
   b. more common among college graduates
   c. more common among men than women
   d. equally common among churchgoers and atheists

3. According to Elisabeth Kübler-Ross, the second stage of dying consists of
   a. depression
   b. bargaining for time
   c. anger
   d. denial

4. The emotional intensity of grief is especially apt to appear in the disguise of physical symptoms among
   a. older adults
   b. young adults
   c. adolescents
   d. middle-aged people

5. The group with a higher-than-average rate of death compared with others their age is
   a. widows over 55
   b. married people
   c. college graduates
   d. widowed men over 55

6. Good grief, or the constructive use of grief, involves
   a. repressing one's grief
   b. avoiding thoughts of death
   c. talking out one's grief
   d. trying to forget one's loss

7. Although as many as one in three patients would reject any medical intervention if they were terminally ill, patients
   a. seldom are asked their wishes
   b. usually change their minds
   c. seldom express their wishes
   d. do not have such a legal right

8. The hospice is a supportive community that helps patients to
   a. exist as long as possible
   b. live and die with dignity
   c. remain in the hospital to the end
   d. die as quickly as possible

9. Today's American funeral ceremony is primarily for the benefit of the
   a. survivors
   b. undertaker
   c. larger community
   d. deceased

10. The realization that death is an inevitable companion of life
   a. usually hastens one's death
   b. is a morbid idea
   c. may give life new meaning
   d. generally leads to depression

EXERCISES

1. *Subjective life expectancy★.* Simply knowing a person's age does not tell you how that person feels about his or her future. To discover this information, try the following exercise in subjective life expectancy. You may want your friends or other individuals to try it as well.

   1. I expect to live to age (circle your answer)
      25 30 35 40 45 50 55 60 65 70 75 80 85 90 95 100
   2. I want to live to age (circle your answer)
      25 30 35 40 45 50 55 60 65 70 75 80 85 90 95 100

   Are there discrepancies between the expressed desire and expectation? If so, what are the possible reasons? Are there differences in desires with increasing age? Usually findings have shown that those past middle age expect and wish to live to a later age than younger subjects do. Did you find this to be true? When people expect to live less than the average life expectancy for their age, do they have a good reason? Did you find that some people were afraid to specify an age for fear it would somehow make death occur at that time?

2. *Your attitude toward death.* Analyze your attitudes toward death. First, write down your actual experiences with death, such as the loss of a friend or loved one, the age at which it occurred, and so forth. Then describe some of your feelings and attitudes toward death. Include your own responses to the subjective life expectancy exercise as well.

3. *Death as an altered state of consciousness.* Some people have observed a similarity between dying and the marginal state of awareness experienced just before sleep. Try to catch yourself in this state some night and make a mental note of your reactions. Was it a peaceful state? Did you find yourself naturally giving into it? How did you feel after the loss of control or power?

4. *Reflections on the experience of bereavement.* Recall a personal experience of bereavement, whether the loss of a loved one or friend. Then describe your experience in a page or so. To what extent did your experience include the grief work process described in the chapter? In what ways was your experience unique? Finally, how has your experience of grief affected your life? Has it made you more cautious and, perhaps, bitter toward life? Or has it eventually become a "good grief," leading you to make the most of life and to reach out to others in a more meaningful way?

5. *Disposing of your body.* If you had a choice, how would you want your body disposed of? Do you want to be embalmed and buried? Or would you rather be cremated? If

★R. J. Kastenbaum, *Death, Society, and Human Experience,* 2nd ed. (St. Louis: C. V. Mosby, 1981).

so, what do you want done with your ashes? Some people want their ashes to be scattered over water or a favorite spot on land; others prefer their ashes to be left in a mausoleum or buried in a cemetery. People sometimes write down such preferences and leave them with their families or a memorial society. Have you thought about donating organs from your body? If so, which ones? Are you interested in leaving your body for medical science?

6. *Write your own obituary.* This isn't as strange as it may seem. Major newspapers have a file of obituaries written while celebrities and national figures are still alive, and then they update these accounts at the time of death. Try writing your own obituary in two or three paragraphs. In addition to giving the standard information, such as your name, age, and position at work, point out some of your major accomplishments. Which community activities would you mention? Who are your survivors? In addition, list your funeral and burial plans. What day and time do you prefer to be buried? Where is your service being held? Do you have any preferences regarding financial contributions to charities in lieu of flowers? Where do you want to be buried or have your ashes deposited?

QUESTIONS FOR SELF-REFLECTION

1. Do you occasionally think about the possibility of your own death?
2. Have you ever had a close brush with death?
3. Are you afraid of dying?
4. How often do you think of someone who is dead?
5. Is there something you would especially like to do before you die? Why have you not done this thing?
6. Can you recall your first experience of grief? Whose death was it?
7. Have you ever experienced good grief?
8. Have you made a will?
9. What kind of after-death service would you like?
10. What do you believe happens to us after death?

FOR FURTHER INFORMATION

RECOMMENDED READINGS

BLACKMORE, S. J. (1993). *Dying to live: Near-death experiences.* Buffalo, NY: Prometheus Books. An examination of whether a phenomenon such as near-death does indeed exist.

KRAMER, H., & KRAMER, K. (1993). *Conversations at midnight: Coming to terms with dying and death.* New York: W. Morrow and Co. A book about the psychological aspects of death for the terminally ill and the survivors.

KÜBLER-ROSS, E. (1993). *On death and dying.* New York: Collier Books. Kübler-Ross's classic on the stages of death.

MOOREY, J. (1995). *Living with grief and mourning.* New York: St. Martin's Press. A book for the bereaved and survivors on how to cope with grief and mourning.

WEENOLSEN, P. (1996). *The art of dying: How to leave this world with dignity and grace, at peace with yourself and your loved ones.* New York: St. Martin's Press. A book for those who are dying which addresses many topics related to how to die without anger and depression.

WEBSITES AND THE INTERNET

http://www.funeral.net/info/brvres.html: A site that contains all types of resources for the bereaved with information on coping with grief, social support networks, suicide, and other important topics.

http://www.ca-probate.com/links.htm: Designed to assist people with financial estate planning but also contains links to other resources related to death and dying.

http://www.soros.org/death.html: A link to an agency funded by the Soros Foundation. The agency researches death and dying in America.

http://www.newciv.org/gibinatdeath/ndhbook-html: A site maintained by the Natural Death Center in England. The center supports the concept that there are better ways to die and grieve than what we have traditionally done. Includes information on living wills, euthanasia, how to organize a funeral, and so forth.

http://www.funeral.net/info/fninfo.html: The site for the Funeral Information Page which provides information on funerals and their costs, death with dignity, and bereavement and other relevant topics.

Answers to the Self-Tests

Chapter					Questions					
	1	2	3	4	5	6	7	8	9	10
1	C	B	A	D	A	A	C	B	A	C
2	A	B	A	D	B	D	C	A	C	B
3	D	A	A	D	A	C	B	D	C	D
4	A	B	D	C	B	C	A	D	C	A
5	C	A	B	D	A	B	A	C	A	D
6	B	C	A	D	C	B	C	B	D	A
7	C	A	B	D	A	A	B	A	B	A
8	A	A	B	D	C	C	A	C	A	D
9	C	B	B	C	D	B	A	A	B	A
10	C	D	B	B	A	C	A	C	D	B
11	C	A	B	D	A	A	A	C	A	B
12	A	B	D	C	C	A	C	D	C	A
13	B	A	B	C	D	A	D	C	B	A
14	C	A	D	B	A	C	A	D	C	B
15	D	D	A	B	D	A	D	C	B	C
16	B	D	C	A	D	C	A	B	A	C

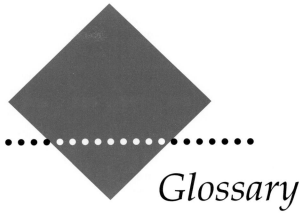

Glossary

acceptance. The final stage of death and dying in which dying people have somewhat disengaged themselves from others and are more accepting of their impending death.

achievement motivation. The striving to maintain or increase our competence or effectiveness, usually as a mixture of inner motives and environmental incentives.

acrophobia. An irrational fear of heights.

actualization therapy. An approach that stresses self-actualization rather than adjustment as the goal of therapy.

acute phase (of dying). The awareness of impending death which creates considerable stress and anxiety.

adjustment. The psychosocial process by which we manage the demands of everyday life, through modifying ourselves and/or our environment.

adulthood. The period of life from physical maturity on; consisting of a sequence of physical and psychosocial changes throughout early, middle, and late adulthood.

affiliate. To be with others who are often similar to us or whom we like.

African Americans. Americans descended from ethnic and racial groups indigenous to Africa.

age-related changes. Changes that tend to occur at a given age, such as puberty.

ageism. Negative attitudes and discrimination toward older Americans because of their age.

aging. A decline in the biological processes that comes with advancing years, increasing the risk of illness and death and usually accompanied by appropriate psychosocial changes.

agoraphobia. A cluster of irrational fears about open spaces.

AIDS. Acquired Immune Deficiency Syndrome caused by HIV and which is transmitted through body fluids.

alarm reaction. Part of Selye's notion of the general adaptation syndrome of stress when the body attempts to restore its normal functioning.

alcohol and drug abuse. Misuse or dependence on a psychoactive substance like alcohol; see the symptoms of substance abuse disorder.

altruism. A desire to help others at a cost to the helper.

Alzheimer's disease. A brain disorder that usually occurs after 60 years of age and is characterized by progressive deterioration of the mind until death.

anal stage. According to Freud, the stage that occurs during the second year of life when the child's major source of physical pleasure becomes the releasing or retention of feces.

androgyny (psychological). The combination of desirable traits from both male and female sex roles, in contrast to traditional sex roles.

anger. The feeling of extreme displeasure, usually brought about by frustration or mistreatment.

anorexia nervosa. An eating disorder characterized by a severe loss of appetite and weight.

antianxiety drugs. Drugs that are used primarily for alleviating anxiety; minor tranquilizers.

antidepressant drugs. Drugs that are used primarily to relieve depression and elevate mood.

antipsychotic drugs. Drugs that are used primarily to relieve symptoms such as extreme agitation, hyperactivity, and hallucinations and delusions in psychotic patients; major tranquilizers.

antisocial personality. A personality disorder characterized by long-standing habits of maladaptive thought and behavior that violate the rights of others; formerly called psychopath or sociopath.

anxiety. A vague, unpleasant feeling warning of impending threat or danger.

anxiety disorder. A group of disorders characterized by symptoms of excessive or inappropriate anxiety or attempts to escape from such anxiety.

anxious attachment. An attachment style in which the individual experiences emotional extremes such as jealousy but in which the individual also desires extreme closeness.

arbitrators. Third parties who remain neutral in a conflict but render a binding decision.

assertiveness. The expression of one's rights and feelings in a direct way without violating the rights of others.

attachment style.   Our typical style of becoming involved with others. This includes the secure attachment style in which individuals find it easy to trust and love others, the avoidant style in which individuals feel uneasy about getting close to others, and the anxious/ambivalent style which involves individuals who want to be attached but find it difficult to commit to others.

attribution.   Finding the cause of a certain action.

authoritarian (personality).   Someone who is submissive to authority figures but is aggressive to subordinates.

aversion to sex.   Anxiety, disgust, repulsion, and other negative emotions toward sex.

avoidance.   A pattern an individual utilizes to minimize or deny that there are symptoms of illness to notice.

avoidant/ambivalent attachment.   An attachment style that results in the individual feeling uneasy when other people get too close.

bargain for time.   The third stage of death and dying in which individuals attempt to negotiate with others who might help them live longer.

basic needs.   Needs that have a clear physiological basis and that are related to survival.

behavioral therapy.   The application of learning principles and other proven methods to modify maladaptive behavior directly.

behaviorism.   The view that psychology is an objective science that studies overt or external behavior.

bereavement.   The process of adjusting to the experience of loss, especially the death of friends or loved ones.

biological perspective.   The view that emphasizes the influence of genetic and physiological factors in human behavior.

biomedical therapies.   Therapeutic strategies that rely on direct physiological intervention to treat the symptoms of psychological disorders.

bipolar disorder.   An emotional disorder characterized by both manic and depressed episodes; formerly called manic-depressive disorder.

bisexuality.   Preference for sexual activity with partners of either sex.

blended families.   When remarried couples have children of their own in addition to children from previous marriages.

body ideal.   One's image of the ideal body.

body image.   The part of the self-concept that is based on the perception of one's own body and feelings of satisfaction with it.

body leakage.   When body postures rather than the face leak the true emotion.

bulimia nervosa.   An eating disorder characterized by excessive overeating or uncontrolled binge eating followed by self-induced vomiting.

career.   The purposeful life pattern of work, as seen in the sequence of jobs and occupations held throughout life.

centralized communication networks.   Communication in groups where one or two individuals control the flow of information.

child sexual abuse.   Coercive touching and fondling of a child's body and genitals, sometimes involving sexual intercourse.

chlamydia.   A bacterium spread by sexual contact that affects males and females. One of the most common STDs.

chronic phase (of dying).   The second stage in dying in which the individual begins to confront the fear of death.

claustrophobia.   An irrational fear of closed places.

climacteric.   Physiological changes in reproductive abilities that accompany the aging process, as seen in the menopause in women and the more gradual reduction of fertile sperm in older men.

cognition.   A general term for information processing, including a variety of processes such as attention, perception, and memory.

cognitive-behavioral therapies.   The combined use of cognitive and behavioral therapeutic strategies to modify people's faulty thinking and maladaptive behavior.

cognitive dissonance.   An uncomfortable feeling caused when one's actions do not match one's attitudes or when one has made the wrong decision.

cognitive therapies.   Therapies based on the view that people's maladaptive behavior is caused more by their own thinking and reaction to external events than the events themselves; encourage people to think more rationally about themselves and their problems.

cohabitation.   Unmarried persons living together, sharing bed and board.

collectives.   A large group that is unlikely to have a leader or clear rules.

collectivist cultures/collective societies.   A culture or society in which collective or societal gain is cherished over individual advancement.

commitment.   The pledge or promise to make something work, as in committing ourselves to a career or relationship. In love relationships, commitment is the cognitive aspect of love, which includes both a short-term assurance of love as well as a long-term assurance to maintain love.

community-based service.   The general term for a variety of mental health services located in the patient's own community, such as a community mental health center.

community mental health center.   A center designed to provide a variety of psychological services for people living within a specific area.

companionate love.   A loving but practical relationship based primarily on emotional closeness and commitment rather than physical, sexual intimacy.

compliance. A change in behavior in response to a direct request from another person to do so.

compromise. An adjustment brought about by modifying opposing ideas or behaviors.

compulsion. An act that the individual feels obliged to repeat again and again, usually in ritualistic fashion or according to certain rules.

confederates. Friends of the experimenter who have been told by the experimenter how to behave.

conflict spiral. When one negative emotion is the catalyst for more conflict and more intensely negative emotions between two or more individuals.

conformity. A change in behavior due to the real or imagined influence of other people.

confrontation. A pattern an individual utilizes to directly note that there are symptoms of illness present.

consummate love. Complete and balanced love characterized by emotional closeness, sexual intimacy, and commitment between the partners.

contempt (in sexual relationships). A tactic where insults are used to denigrate a partner's sexuality.

contingency theory of leadership. A theory that suggests there are two types of leaders, person and task leaders, who are effective at leading in different situations.

correlational studies. Studies aimed at demonstrating a statistical relationship between two or more variables or sets of data.

crisis intervention. A treatment for those who are in a state of acute crisis but do not need treatment for many sessions. Many cities possess these in the form of telephone hotlines.

criticism (in sexual relationships). A response pattern related to human sexuality in which one partner attacks or criticizes the other partner's character.

crystallized intelligence. The ability to use accumulated knowledge to make judgments and solve problems.

cultural diversity. The cultural pattern by which people from different cultural and ethnic backgrounds maintain in varying degrees both their national and their ethnic identities.

culture. The ideas, customs, arts, and skills that characterize a group of people during a given period of history.

date rape. Coercive sexual intercourse that occurs during a social date.

day hospitals. Hospitals that provide the needed therapeutic care to patients during regular working hours and then allow them to return to their families in the evening.

death. The cessation of biological life, as measured by the absence of breathing, heartbeat, and electrical activity of the brain.

decentralized communication networks. Communication in groups where individuals can communicate relatively freely with one another.

decidophobia. The fear of making the more important decisions in our life.

decision making. The process of gathering information and relevant alternatives and making an appropriate choice.

defense mechanisms. Automatic unconscious mechanisms that protect us from the awareness of anxiety, thereby helping us to maintain a sense of self-worth in the face of threat.

defenses. A shortened term for defense mechanisms.

defensiveness (in sexual relationships). A tactic in which we make excuses or refuse to take responsibility or use some other self-protective defense.

delusions. Beliefs that have no basis in reality.

denial. The first stage of death and dying in which people characteristically feel that death cannot happen to them.

depersonalization. The sense of not being intimately attached to one's body.

depression. An emotional state characterized by intense and unrealistic sadness that may assume a variety of forms, some more severe and chronic than others.

desensitization. The method of controlling anxiety by learning to associate an incompatible response, like relaxation, with the fear-provoking stimulus.

development. The relatively enduring changes in people's capacities and behavior as they grow older because of biological growth processes and people's interaction with their environment.

development of personality. In Freud's view, the process by which the psyche develops through a sequence of psychosexual stages, culminating in the adult personality.

devil effect. Inferring uniformly negative traits from an appearance of a few negative traits.

diathesis–stress hypothesis. A proposal that views schizophrenia as the interaction between a genetic vulnerability and environmental factors.

differentiated marriage. A marriage in which both partners work but the husband's job is emphasized. Housework is divided in a sex-typed manner, but the couple spends free time together.

direct decision therapy. The view that therapy is best aimed at helping clients see their problems in terms of their previous decisions that may no longer be appropriate and then choosing a more satisfying alternative.

discrimination. Negative or unfair treatment of people in groups on the basis of such features as age, sex, or race. Often these groups are different from our own groups.

disease-prone personalities. Individuals who seem insecure and neurotic and who some psychologists believe are less resistant to illness.

desire for success. The urge to succeed.

distress. Stress that has a harmful effect.

divorce. The legal and formal dissolution of a marriage.

door-in-the-face effect.   When someone issuing a request asks first for a large, unreasonable request and then asks for what is really desired.

downward comparison.   A pattern of behavior an individual utilizes to compare his or her own situation to others who are worse off.

dying trajectory.   The individual's anticipated length of life before death and the manner of facing the end of life.

early adulthood.   The initial stage of adult development, from the late teens or early 20s through the 30s, characterized by the establishment of personal and economic independence.

ego.   The executive agency of the psyche, which manages the various components of personality in accordance to the reality principle.

electroconvulsive therapy (ECT).   The administration of an electric current to the patient's brain to produce a convulsion; sometimes used in the treatment of severe depression.

emotion.   A complex state of awareness, including bodily changes, subjective experiences, outward expressions of our experiences, and reactions to events.

emotional intelligence (EQ).   The ability to regulate one's own emotions and to be empathic for others' emotions.

entrapment.   Throwing time, energy, and money into an already bad situation.

environment.   All the conditions and influences surrounding and affecting human development and behavior.

erectile inhibition disorder.   In sexuality, this is known as impotence or the inability of the man to experience erection.

ethnicity.   Socially distinguished by a combination of different features, such as a common geographic origin, race, language, or customs.

eustress.   Stress that has a beneficial effect.

excitement (stage in the sexual response cycle).   When sexual arousal causes increased muscle tension, engorgement of the genitals with blood, and increased heart rate.

existential therapy.   An approach that emphasizes the client's capacity for growth through affirmation of his or her free choice and personal values.

experience of dying.   The sequence of physiological and psychological changes experienced by individuals who are dying, such as those with a terminal illness.

external locus of control.   When an individual believes that something outside of him- or herself controls events.

extroverts.   Individuals who tend to be warm, outgoing, and involved in life.

false consensus effect.   An assumption that others feel or believe as we do.

family therapy.   An approach that includes the entire family on the assumption that the disturbance of one family member reflects problems in the overall family patterns.

fear.   Apprehension about a specific and objective danger.

fear of failure.   Fear that we will fail and be humiliated by failure.

female orgasmic disorder.   Absence of orgasm in a woman.

first impression.   The initial perception we form of another person, in which we tend to judge others on the basis of very little information.

fixation.   When the personality becomes emotionally fixed at a particular anxiety-ridden stage and continues to act out symbolically the wishes that were overly inhibited or indulged.

fluid intelligence.   The ability to process new information based on perceptual skills and memory.

forming.   The initial stage of group development where the group simply comes together.

free association.   When a client is asked by the therapist to say whatever comes to mind regardless of how trivial it sounds.

friendship.   The affectionate attachment between friends of either sex.

fundamental attribution error.   The tendency to overattribute people's behavior to their personalities rather than to their present circumstances.

funerals.   The ceremonies and rituals associated with the burial or cremation of the dead.

gender.   Social and cultural distinctions between masculinity and femininity.

gender roles.   Social and cultural expectations about what is appropriate for males and females.

gender stereotypes.   Widely held generalizations about the characteristics of men and women that exaggerate the differences between the sexes.

general adaptation syndrome.   According to Selye, the body's reaction to stress, which includes three progressive stages—alarm reaction, resistance, and exhaustion.

generalized anxiety disorder.   A chronic state of diffuse or free-floating anxiety.

genes.   The biochemical units on the chromosomes by which hereditary characteristics are transmitted.

genital herpes.   A viral infection that is considered to be transmitted primarily through sexual contact.

genital stage.   The stage that begins with the onset of puberty and sexual maturation when the individual's sexual interests are reawakened.

gestalt therapy.   An approach that utilizes the here and now in therapy to facilitate the client's integration of personality.

giving/getting pact.   The unwritten rules governing what we give in our personal relationships, work, and community and what we expect in return.

gonorrhea.   A common STD that sometimes produces a cloudy, smelly discharge and a burning sensation upon urination.

good grief.   Grief that leads to learning and growth.

great man theory (of leadership).   A theory suggesting that great leaders all possess a certain set of traits.

grief.   The intense emotional suffering that accompanies our experience of loss.

grief work.   The healthy process of working through emotions associated with loss and death.

group polarization effect.   Groups are likely to shift to either riskier or more conservative decisions than individuals alone make.

groupthink.   The tendency for groups to reach a consensus prematurely because the desire for harmony overrides the process of critical thinking and the search for the best decision.

halfway house.   A residence in which newly released patients with a mental disorder and former drug addicts can live under supervision for a short period of time while they make a crucial transition in their lives.

halo effect.   Inferring uniformly positive traits from an appearance of a few positive traits.

happiness.   The state of well-being associated with a wide variety of experiences, including everyday pleasures, favorable circumstances, and a satisfying mental outlook on life.

health.   A state of complete physical, mental, and social well-being and not merely the absence of disease or infirmity.

heredity.   The transmission of traits from parents to offspring.

heterosexuality.   Emotional and sexual preference for opposite-sex partners.

heuristics.   Mental shortcuts or rules of thumb for making decisions.

hierarchy of needs.   According to Maslow, the hierarchical manner in which needs and motives function in relation to each other, so that the lowest level of unmet needs remains the most urgent.

Hispanic Americans.   Americans from different races and countries who speak the Spanish language, such as Mexico, Central and South America.

homophobic.   Individuals who are afraid of homosexuals or hold negative attitudes toward homosexuals.

homosexuality.   Emotional and sexual preference for partners of the same sex.

hospice.   A system of care that integrates a physical facility for the terminally ill with the patient's family and home to enable the patient to die with dignity.

human freedom.   The inherent capacity for free choice and self-determination.

humanistic perspective.   The view that emphasizes the holistic characteristics of human experience, including the capacity for choices and personal growth.

hyperstress.   An excessive amount of stress.

hypoactive sexual desire or **inhibited sexual desire.** Lack of interest in sex or desire for sexual intercourse.

hypochondriacs.   People who habitually complain of unfounded ailments or exhibit an undue fear of illness.

hypostress.   Insufficient stress.

hypothalamus.   A small but important structure at the core of the brain that governs many aspects of behavior, such as eating and hormonal activity.

id.   The unconscious reservoir of psychic energy that drives the personality.

ideal self.   The self we'd like to be.

illusion of control.   The mistaken belief that we can exercise control over chance-determined events.

"I" messages.   Honest but nonjudgmental expressions of emotions about someone whose behavior has become a problem.

immune system.   A complex surveillance system, including the brain and various blood cells, that defends our bodies by identifying and destroying foreign invaders.

incidence (of disorders).   The number of new cases of disorders reported during a given period.

independence.   The state of being autonomous or self-governing.

individualism.   The belief that individuals and basic human freedoms should not be restricted by social and government regulations.

individualistic societies.   Societies in which individual gain is more valued than general societal gain.

information age.   An era in which most industries are involved in the creating, processing, and distributing of information.

ingratiation.   Managing the impressions we leave on others so that they will like us and comply with our requests. An example is flattery.

ingroup.   The group with which we identify.

inhibited sexual arousal.   Insufficient sexual arousal, such as the male's difficulty in sustaining an erection of his penis or the female's difficulty in generating sufficient vaginal lubrication.

inhibited vaginal lubrication.   When insufficient vasocongestion occurs in the woman's vagina and there is insufficient lubrication.

insight therapies.   Any therapy that aims to bring about personal change primarily by increasing the client's self-understanding.

integrative solutions (for conflicts).   Solutions that take into account the needs of both sides in a conflict such that both sides can win something.

interdependence.   Mutual dependence among individuals in a given group or society.

internal locus of control.   When an individual believes that something within him- or herself controls life events.

intimacy.   The emotional aspect of love that includes closeness, sharing, communication, and support.

intimate relationships. Emotionally close relationships between two or more persons, such as friends or lovers, that may or may not include physical, sexual intimacy.

jealousy. A complex emotion evoked by the fear of losing a cherished relationship, including anger over betrayal and insecurity.

job. A position of employment; the set of work activities and responsibilities associated with a given position.

job satisfaction. People's feelings about different aspects of their jobs; how well one likes a given job, depending on such factors as pay and coworkers.

late adulthood. The final stage of adult development from mid 60s to death, characterized by adjustment to changing health, income, and social roles.

latency period. According to Freud, the period that takes place between 5 and 12 years of age during which the child's interests turn away from erogenous satisfactions. Sexual urges lie relatively dormant.

learned helplessness. Maladaptive passivity that is learned from a series of bad events outside a person's control.

learned optimism. A way of explaining both good and bad life events that in turn enhances our perceived control and adaptive responses to them.

learning theory. The systematic statement of principles that explains learning, defined as relatively permanent changes in behavior because of practice or experience.

leisure. Time free from work or duty that may be spent in recreational activities of one's choice.

libido. The psychic energy of the sex drive.

life review. A process of self-reflection among the aged, prompted by the realization that one's life is approaching an end.

life trajectory. The individual's anticipated life span and how he or she plans to live it.

living will. An instrument that instructs doctors and family members to stop using life-sustaining procedures in the event of a terminal condition.

locus of control. The source from where an individual believes control over life events originates, either from within (internal) or without (external).

logotherapy. Victor Frankl's approach for dealing with the spiritual aspects of psychopathology, such as confronting clients with their responsibility for finding personal meaning in life.

loneliness. Feelings of emptiness and isolation resulting from the absence of satisfying relationships.

longitudinal studies. Research in which the same people are studied over a long period of time.

love. Deep and tender feelings of affection for or attachment to one or more persons.

maintenance activities. Nonleisure and nonwork time spent in activities necessary for the maintenance of life, such as preparing meals and sleeping.

major depression. A prominent and relatively persistent state of depression manifested in poor appetite, insomnia, restlessness, apathy, fatigue, feelings of worthlessness, or recurrent thoughts of death.

maladaptive behavior. Significant impairment in one or more areas of psychological functioning, especially the ability to work and to get along with others.

marital adjustment. The changes and adjustments in a couple's relationship during the course of married life.

marital satisfaction. The sense of gratification and contentment in a marriage, especially in the personal relationship between the partners.

marital therapy. An approach that deals with the dynamics of the marriage relationship as well as the individual partners.

marriage. The state of being married; the legal union between a husband and wife.

matching hypothesis. The tendency to settle for someone like ourselves, especially someone similar in level of physical attractiveness.

mediators. Third parties who remain neutral in a conflict and help the parties in the conflict to come to a mutually acceptable solution via communication, creative problem solving, and other techniques.

menopause. The cessation of monthly menstrual cycles in a woman's life.

meta-analysis. A statistical technique whereby the effects of a factor can be measured across many studies.

microexpressions. Fleeting facial expressions that last only a fraction of a second.

middle adulthood. The middle stage of adult development, from the late 30s to the mid 60s, characterized by the fulfillment of career and family goals.

midlife transition. The period of self-assessment accompanying the realization that one's physical life is half over, beginning about the mid to late 30s.

mindguards. A situation in groupthink where individuals in the group take it upon themselves to censor dissenters in the group.

minority groups. Any ethnic, racial, religious, or political group smaller than and differing from the larger, controlling group in a community or nation.

mistaken impression. The mistaken perception of another person, often because of insufficient information.

mixed motives. A number of divergent motives are present.

moral anxiety. Anxiety caused when a person feels guilty about something he or she has done. The anxiety can be real or imagined.

motivation. A general term referring to the forces that energize and direct behavior toward particular goals.

motive. A specific goal-directed activity aroused by the deprivation of inner needs.

motive targets. The people toward whom our motives are directed.

mourning. The outward expressions of bereavement and grief, such as the wearing of black.

multimodal therapy. A comprehensive and flexible approach to behavior therapy that encourages the use of a wide variety of techniques.

multiple orgasms. Experiencing more than one orgasm within a short period of time.

narcissistic personality. A personality disorder characterized by an undue sense of self-importance, often accompanied by a sense of inferiority.

nature–nurture issue. The continuing debate over the relative contribution of heredity and of experience and the environment to the development of psychological traits and behaviors.

near-death experience. The distinctive state of recall associated with being brought back to life from the verge of death.

need. A state of tension or deprivation that arouses us to seek appropriate gratification.

negotiation. A cooperative approach to bargaining in which all parties make mutual concessions.

neurotic anxiety. Anxiety caused when the ego senses that some impulses of the id are threatening to get out of control and causes the individual to feel he or she will do something that will result in punishment.

neurotransmitter. A chemical substance involved in the transmission of neural impulses between neurons.

new rules. Changing guidelines and practices of human behavior associated with self-fulfillment values.

nicotine addiction. Difficulty giving up nicotine use, particularly cigarettes, because of the repeated effects of nicotine as well as the habit of smoking.

non-age-related changes. Events that may occur at any age or not at all, such as a specific illness.

non-zero sum. A situation in which one person or group both wins and loses something, as does the other side.

norm of reciprocity. An unwritten rule that guides reciprocal behavior related to the granting of favors.

norming. The third stage of group formation in which the group comes to consensus about the rules under which they will operate.

norms. Unwritten rules by which groups function and by which groups exert pressure on nonconforming members.

nutrition. Eating a proper, balanced diet to promote health.

obedience. Following a direct order or command.

obesity. An excessive amount of body fat, usually defined as exceeding the desirable weight for one's height, build, and age by 20 percent or more.

observational learning. The process in which people learn by observing other people and events without necessarily receiving any direct reward or reinforcement.

obsession. A thought or image that keeps recurring to the mind, despite the individual's attempts to ignore or resist it.

obsessive-compulsive disorder. The condition characterized by the involuntary dwelling on an unwelcome thought and/or the involuntary repetition of an unnecessary action.

occupation. The activities and responsibilities necessary to perform given work tasks in a line of work, such as the nursing occupation.

oral stage. According to Freud, the stage that occurs during the first few years of life when the mouth becomes the primary means of gratifying desires of the id.

organismic actualizing tendency. The human organism's inherent biological tendency to develop and fulfill itself.

orgasm (stage in the sexual response cycle). The climax of sexual excitement which is both pleasurable and a tension release.

outgroup. Any group we perceive as being different from our own group.

panic disorder and panic attacks. The type of anxiety disorder characterized by the occurrence of severe panic attacks.

paralinguistics. Unspoken but important features of spoken communications, such as gestures.

parallel marriage. A marriage in which the husband is the primary wage earner and housework is divided in a sex-typed manner.

passion. The motivational aspect of love that involves physiological arousal and an intense desire to be united with the loved one.

passionate love. An intense emotional reaction to a potential romantic partner.

people- or **relationship-oriented leaders.** Leaders who concern themselves with their group members' feelings and interpersonal relations.

perceived control. The belief that we can influence many of the events in our environment that affect our lives.

performing. The final stage of group development when the group functions better and performs its business.

personal control. Achieved control over our lives; mostly synonymous with perceived control.

personal distress. Intense or chronic negative self-awareness that interferes with one's sense of well-being or functioning.

personal freedom. The inherent capacity for free choice and self-determination.

personal growth. Personal change or development in a desirable direction, including the fulfillment of one's inborn potential.

personality. An individual's characteristic way of thinking, feeling, and behaving across different situations.

personality disorders. Inflexible and maladaptive behavior patterns that cause significant impairment in one's social and occupational functioning.

personality dynamics. Interaction between the different forces within the psyche, accompanied by anxiety, conflict, and defense mechanisms and the shifting of psychic energy among the various parts of the personality.

personality traits. Enduring patterns of thinking, feeling, acting, and relating to others that we exhibit in a wide range of situations.

person-centered therapy. According to Carl Rogers, the view that the therapist's genuineness, acceptance, and empathetic understanding of the client are necessary and sufficient conditions for producing therapeutic change in the client.

perspectives. Understanding ideas or events from different points of view.

phallic stage. According to Freud, the stage that extends from the third to the fifth or sixth year of life in which the child experiences sensual pleasure through handling of his or her genitals.

phenomenal self. The individual's overall self-concept that is available to conscious awareness.

phenomenology. The approach that describes human experiences apparent to the senses without any attempts at a metaphysical or causal analysis.

phobic disorders. The condition characterized by a persistent and irrational fear of a specific object or activity.

physical fitness. The entire human organism's ability to function efficiently and effectively, including both health-related and skill-related fitness components.

plateau (stage in the sexual response cycle). The stage just before orgasm in which sexual arousal becomes more pronounced.

pleasure principle. The principle by which the desires of the id automatically seek pleasurable gratification.

postindustrial society. A society characterized by the dominance of the service industries in contrast to the dominance of manufacturing and agriculture in the industrial society.

posttraumatic stress disorder. A severe anxiety disorder characterized by symptoms of anxiety and avoidance behavior; results from an unusually distressing event such as being assaulted.

power distance. The idea that people in organizations have about different levels of power and authority. The more status and privileges they ascribe to those in authority, the higher the power distance.

power of attorney. A document that empowers anyone—relative, friend, or advisor—to make any medical decision when the signer becomes incompetent to do so.

prejudice. An unjustifiable attitude, usually negative, based on group membership.

premature or **retarded ejaculation.** A delay or absence of orgasm in a man.

prevalence (of a disorder). The total number of active cases that can be identified in a given population at a particular time.

primary drives. Drives that have a clear physiological basis and that are related to survival.

primary emotions. The view that basic emotions such as disgust and sadness are frequently combined to form secondary emotions such as remorse, analogous to the mixing of primary colors to form other shades of color.

primary group. Small, intimate, face-to-face groups such as families.

propinquity. Physical closeness.

psychoanalysis. A form of psychotherapy developed by Sigmund Freud, aimed at helping the client gain insight and mastery over unconscious conflicts.

psychodynamic theory. The view that human behavior is based on the dynamics of interaction or the driving forces of personality, such as desires, anxiety, and conflicts.

psychological disorder. A clinically significant behavioral or psychological pattern that includes a painful symptom, impairment in one or more areas of functioning, increased risk of suffering or death, and a loss of personal control.

psychological hardiness. The attitude that allows individuals to make the most of what are often bad situations. A characteristic of individuals who cope successfully with stress.

psychosexual stages. According to Freud, the sequence of critical stages in the developmental process; the way in which individuals handle the conflicts among their pleasure-seeking impulses, inhibitions, and environmental restrictions becomes decisive for adult personality.

psychosurgery. A surgical procedure involving the destruction or disconnection of brain tissue in an attempt to regulate abnormal behavior.

psychotherapy. A helping process in which a trained, socially sanctioned therapist performs certain activities that will facilitate a change in the client's attitudes and behaviors.

psychotic symptoms. Symptoms that are signs of psychosis (e.g., schizophrenia) and that include hallucinations such as hearing voices, marked impairment in self-care and social relationships, and other signs of severe disturbance.

rape. Sexual intercourse that occurs without consent under conditions of actual or threatened force.

reactance. An oppositional response that occurs when our personal freedom is restricted.

reality principle. The rational orientation that guides the ego in its attempts to put the individual's well-being above the pleasure seeking of the id or moralistic control of the superego.

refractory period. The period of time following an orgasm when no added stimulation will result in another orgasm.

relapse. A return to a previous state; in psychology, return to a former problematic behavior.

reminiscence. Thinking about oneself and reconsidering past events and their meaning.

REM sleep. The rapid eye movement stage of sleep in which most dreaming occurs.

repression. The automatic, unconscious denial of a feeling to awareness, which if consciously admitted would be threatening.

resentment. The second stage of death and dying in which dying individuals resent those who are healthy.

resistance. In therapy, the hesitation or reluctance to talk about some painful experiences.

resolution (stage in the sexual response cycle). The stage immediately following orgasm in which the body returns to its normal, nonexcited phase.

responsibility diffusion. Individuals in groups feel less responsibility for risk than they do as individuals.

reversed marriage. A marriage in which the wife's job is emphasized; household tasks are not segregated by gender. A highly companionate marriage.

right to die. The ethical and legal view that competent individuals who are able to understand treatment choices and their consequences have the right to decide their own fate, such as the withholding of treatment that would delay death.

risky shift. When groups make riskier individuals than they did or would as individuals.

role. A set of rules that defines how an individual in a particular post in a group will behave.

romantic love. Strong emotional attachment to a person of the opposite sex, primarily on the basis of physical, sexual intimacy.

schizophrenia. A group of related psychotic disorders characterized by severe disorganization of thoughts, perceptions, and emotions; bizarre behavior; and social withdrawal.

seasonal affective disorder (SAD). A depression that is more likely to occur at certain times of the year, usually the winter months.

secondary erectile inhibition disorder. In sexuality, this is known as impotence or the inability of the man to experience erection after being able earlier to have an erection.

secondary group. Groups that are formal, have a contractual reason for coming together, and which disband when the reason for their existence disappears. They are less likely to engage in face-to-face interaction than primary groups.

securely attached. An attachment style by which people develop happy and trusting love relationships.

self-acceptance. Optimal awareness and affirmation of one's overall self as an experiencing organism; to like and believe in oneself.

self-actualization/self-actualized. The process of fulfilling our inborn potential, involving a biological growth tendency as well as self-conscious efforts at growth.

self-concept. The overall pattern of perceptions of "I" and "me," together with the feelings, beliefs, and values associated with them.

self-consistency. The tendency to perceive our experiences in a manner that is consistent with our self-concept; experiences that are not consistent with the self are distorted or denied to awareness.

self-direction. The need to learn more about ourselves and our world as a means of directing our lives more effectively.

self-disclosure. The sharing of intimate or personal information with others.

self-efficacy. The belief in one's capacity to organize and execute courses of action required to produce achievement.

self-enhancement. The tendency to seek favorable feedback about ourselves from others.

self-esteem. The sense of personal worth associated with one's self-concept.

self-fulfilling prophecy. A prophecy that is fulfilled when people's expectations become a reality by virtue of their own behavior.

self-fulfillment. The fulfillment of our deeper needs, including the need for self-actualization.

self-healing personalities. Individuals who seem illness resistant because they deal effectively with stress.

self-image. The self we see ourselves to be.

self-serving attributions. Attributions that glorify the self or conceive of the self as causing the good outcomes that come our way.

self-verification. The tendency to seek truthful feedback about ourselves from others.

sensation-seeking motive. The tendency to seek out stimulating and novel experiences, partly because of biological factors.

service industries. Industries that provide a service rather than a manufactured product, such as personal help, transportation, and education.

sexual abuse. When an individual is forced to make unwanted sexual contact.

sexual dysfunction. A persistent problem that prevents the individual from engaging in or enjoying sexual intercourse.

sexual exploitation. When an individual is forced to comply with sexual acts under duress.

sexual harassment. Any unwanted attention of a sexual nature occurring in the workplace that interferes with a person's ability to work.

sexual intercourse. The penetration of the vagina by the penis, characteristically accompanied by pelvic thrusting and orgasm for one or both partners.

sexual response cycle. The basic sexual response patterns of men and women, as in sexual intercourse.

sexual victimization. Being forced to comply with sexual acts under duress or force, such as rape.

sexually transmitted diseases (STDs). Infections transmitted primarily by sexual intercourse.

shyness.   The tendency to avoid contact or familiarity with others.

simple phobia.   A common disorder in which individuals are irrationally afraid of common objects such as dogs, snakes, insects, and mice.

social change.   Changes in the social patterns and institutions of society.

social-cognitive perspective.   The view that human learning and behavior necessarily involve higher cognitive abilities as well as environmental influences.

social comparison.   Using others to compare ourselves to in order to understand who we are relative to them.

social influence.   Efforts on the part of one person to alter the behavior or attitudes of one or more others.

social loafing.   When individuals contribute less to a group effort than they would contribute to an individual effort.

social norms.   The generalized expectations regarding appropriate behavior in a given situation or society.

social phobia.   A chronic, irrational fear of and a compelling desire to avoid situations in which the individual may be scrutinized by others.

social selves.   The impressions we think others have of us, derived from our social roles and interactions.

social support.   A process whereby one individual or group offers comfort and advice to others who can use it as a means of coping.

stage of exhaustion.   Stage of Selye's notion of the general adaptation syndrome response to stress in which the body is no longer able to continue secreting hormones at an increased rate, the body defenses break down, and physical symptoms of stress appear.

stage of resistance.   Stage of Selye's notion of the general adaptation syndrome response to stress in which increased resistance to the stressor develops.

stereotypes.   Widespread generalizations about people that have little if any basis in fact.

stimulus needs.   A psychosocial motive or need that has less to do with physical survival and more to do with our sense of well-being and competence in dealing with our environment. This need drives us to seek out stimulation.

storming.   The second stage in group formation where group members disagree or conflict when they learn about each other's attitudes.

stress.   The pattern of responses an individual makes to stimulus events that disturb his or her equilibrium or exceed coping abilities.

stress-related illness.   Any illness that is affected in an important way by one's emotions, lifestyle, or environment.

stress tolerance.   The degree and duration of stress we can tolerate without becoming irrational and disorganized.

stressor.   The collective label for the variety of external and internal stimuli that evoke stress.

structure of personality.   The basic components that make up the organization of personality.

substitution.   The pursuit of an alternative means or goal in place of the desired one.

suicide.   The act of intentionally taking one's own life.

superego.   The part of the psyche that has been shaped by the moral standards of society as transmitted by parental figures.

survival motives.   Motives that have a clear physiological basis and that are related to survival.

symmetrical marriage.   A marriage characterized by both spouses working outside of the home and holding egalitarian ideas about gender roles.

syphilis.   A sexually transmitted and serious disease caused by a spiral-shaped bacterium or spirochete.

task-oriented leaders.   Leaders who are primarily concerned with getting the job done well and in a timely fashion.

technological society.   A society that is dependent on and has high use of technology.

technophobia.   A fear of technology.

temperament.   The inherited disposition to behave in a particular way.

terminal phase (of dying).   When an individual realizes that all hope for recovery is gone, and the dying individual withdraws from people and resigns him- or herself to the finality of death.

therapist.   A trained, socially sanctioned healer who performs certain activities that will facilitate a change in the client's attitudes and behaviors.

third force in psychology.   The view that humanistic psychology is a major alternative to the deterministic outlook of psychodynamic and behavioral psychology.

tobacco abuse.   The use of tobacco to such an extent that heart, respiratory, and other health-related problems develop.

tokens.   Individuals who are distinctive in a group because they are not readily identified as members of the group.

transference.   The unconscious tendency of clients to project onto the therapist their feelings and fantasies, both positive and negative, about significant others in their childhoods.

transinstitutionalization.   The revolving door syndrome where mental patients find themselves housed in one institution after another, often including jails and prisons.

transition (stage in the sexual response cycle).   The gradual shift from a nonsexual state to a sexual state.

triangular theory of love.   A theory of love that suggests that there are three components to love—intimacy, passion, and commitment.

trust.   People's abstract but positive expectations that they can count on friends and partners to care for them and be responsive to their needs, now and in the future.

Type A individuals.   Competitive, hard-driving, and impatient individuals who are at increased risk of coronary heart disease.

Type B individuals.   Individuals who are relaxed rather than competitive and impatient.

unconditional leisure.   Any activity freely chosen, excluding work and maintenance activities.

unembodiment.   The sense of not being intimately attached to one's body.

unresolved grief.   A psychological state in which one's emotional reaction to loss remains repressed, often being manifested in unexplained physical or psychological symptoms.

voluntary marriage.   The assumption that two people will remain married only as long as they are in love.

wellness.   The positive ideal of health in which one strives to maintain and improve one's health.

withdrawal.   To remove oneself physically or emotionally from an activity, organization, or person. In sexual relationships, a response pattern in which one partner ignores the other.

work values.   Those values that bring you the most enjoyment and satisfaction on your job.

workplace.   Employment on a paid basis outside the home.

References

ACTON, R. G., & DURING, S. M. (1992). Preliminary results of aggression management training for aggressive parents. *Journal of Interpersonal Violence, 7,* 410–417.

ADELMANN, P. (1988, April). Possibly yours. *Psychology Today, 8,* 10.

ADLER, N. J., DOKTER, R., & REDDING, S. G. (1986). From the Atlantic to the Pacific century: Cross-cultural management reviewed. *Journal of Management, 12,* 295–318.

Aging in America: Trends and projections. (1991). Prepared by U.S. Senate Special Committee on Aging, The American Association of Retired Persons, The Federal Council on Aging, The U.S. Administration on Aging (DHHS Publ. No. 91-28001 [FCoA]). Washington, DC: U.S. Government Printing Office.

AIRHIHENBUWA, C. O., KUMANYIKA, S., AGURS, T. D., & LOVE, A. (1995). Perceptions and beliefs about exercise, rest, and health among African Americans. *American Journal of Health Promotion, 9,* 426–429.

AKAN, G. E., & GRILO, C. M. (1995). A comparison of African American, Asian American, and Caucasian college women. *International Journal of Eating Disorders, 18,* 181–187.

ALICKE, M. D., BRAUN, J. C., GLOR, J. E., KLOTZ, N. L., NAGEE, J., SEDERHOLD, H., & SIEGEL, R. (1992). Complaining behavior in social interaction. *Personality and Social Psychology Bulletin, 18,* 286–298.

ALICKE, M. D., & LARGO, E. (1995). The role of the self in the false consensus effect. *Journal of Experimental Social Psychology, 31,* 28–47.

ALLEN, B. P. (1997). *Personality theories: Development, growth and diversity.* Boston: Allyn & Bacon.

ALLMAN, W. (1985, October). Staying alive in the 20th century. *Science, 85,* 31–41.

ALTROCCHI, J. (1980). *Abnormal behavior.* New York: Harcourt Brace Jovanovich.

AMATO, P. R. (1987). Family processes in one-parent, stepparent and intact families: The child's point of view. *Journal of marriage and the family, 49,* 327–337.

AMERICAN CANCER SOCIETY. (1985). *Cancer facts and figures.* New York: Author.

AMERICAN PSYCHIATRIC ASSOCIATION. (1994). *Diagnostic and statistical manual of mental disorders (DSM-IV)* (4th ed.). Washington, DC: Author.

AMIRKHAN, J. H., RISINGER, R. T., & SWICKERT, R. J. (1995). Extroversion: A "hidden" personality factor in coping? *Journal of Personality, 63,* 189–212.

ANTILL, J. K. (1983). Sex-role complementarity versus similarity in married couples. *Journal of Personality and Social Psychology, 45,* 145–155.

ARCHIBALD, F. S., BARTHOLOMEW, K., & MARX, R. (1995). Loneliness in early adolescence: A test of the cognitive discrepancy model of loneliness. *Personality and Social Psychology Bulletin, 21,* 296–301.

AROND, M., & PAUKER, S. (1988). How marriage changes your sex life. In O. Pocs (Ed.), *Marriage and the family* (pp. 88–89). Guilford, CT: Dushkin Publishing Group.

ASCH, S. E. (1951). Effects of group pressure upon the modification and distortion of judgments. In H. Guetzkow (Ed.), *Groups, leadership, and men.* Pittsburgh, PA: Carnegie Press.

ASCH, S. E. (1956). Studies of independence and conformity: A minority of one against unanimous majority. *Psychological Monographs, 70* (Whole No. 416).

ASPINWALL, L. G., & TAYLOR, S. E. (1992). Modeling cognitive adaptation: A longitudinal investigation of the impact of individual differences and coping on college adjustment and performance. *Journal of Personality and Social Psychology, 63,* 989–1003.

ATWATER, E. (1992). *I hear you: A listening skills handbook.* New York: Walker & Company.

AUNE, K. S., & AUNE, R. K. (1996). Cultural differences in the self-reported experience and expression of emotions in relationships. *Journal of Cross Cultural Psychology, 27,* 67–81.

A very revealing picture: Psychology Today's 1997 body image survey find. (1997, January/February). *Psychology Today, 30,* 34–40.

BALAKRISHNAN, S. (1993). The new Russia: The challenge of psychological change. *Humanistic Psychology, 21,* 180–186.

BANDURA, A. (1973). *Aggression.* Englewood Cliffs, NJ: Prentice Hall.

BANDURA, A. (1986). *Social foundations of thought and action.* Englewood Cliffs, NJ: Prentice Hall.

BANDURA, A. (1997). *Self-efficacy: The exercise of control.* New York: W. H. Freeman.

BARNES, B. L., & SRINIVAS, R. (1993). Self-actualization in different sex subgroups. *Journal of Personality and Clinical Studies, 9,* 19–24.

BARON, R. A., & BYRNE, D. (1997). *Social Psychology.* Boston: Allyn & Bacon.

BARTLETT, S. J. (1992, Winter). Compulsive overeating—syndrome of the 90s. *Eating Disorders Bulletin,* 1–3.

BAUMEISTER, R. F., & LEARY, M. R. (1995). The need to belong: Desire for inter-personal attachments as a fundamental human motivation. *Psychological Bulletin, 117,* 497–529.

BAUMEISTER, R. F., TICE, D. M., & HUTTON, D. G. (1989). Self presentational motivations and personality differences in self-esteem. *Journal of Personality, 57,* 547–579.

BECK, A. T. (1979). *Cognitive therapy and emotional disorders.* New York: American Library.

BECK, A. T. (1988). *Love is never enough.* New York: Harper & Row.

BECK, A. T. (1991). Cognitive therapy: A 30-year retrospective. *American Psychologist, 46,* 368–375.

BECK, A. T., BROWN, G., STEER, R. A., EIDELSON, J. I., & RISKIND, J. H. (1987). Differentiating anxiety and depression: A test of the cognitive content-specificity hypothesis. *Journal of Abnormal Psychology, 96,* 179–183.

BECK, A. T., & YOUNG, J. E. (1985). Depression. In D. H. Barlow (Ed.), *Clinical handbook of psychological disorders* (pp. 206–244). New York: Guilford Press.

BELLAH, R. N., MADSEN, R., SULLIVAN, W. M., SWIDLER, A., & TIPTON, S. M. (1985). *Habits of the heart: Individualism and commitment in American life.* Berkeley: University of California Press.

BELSHER, G., & COSTELLO, C. G. (1988). Relapse after recovery from unipolar depression: A critical review. *Psychological Bulletin, 104,* 84–96.

BENNETT, W. I., GOLDFINGER, S. E., & JOHNSON, G. T. (Eds.). (1987). *Your good health: How to stay well and what to do when you're not.* Cambridge, MA: Harvard University Press.

BERSCHEID, E. (1994). Interpersonal relationships. *Annual Review of Psychology, 45,* 79–129.

BEUTLER, L. E., MOHR, D. C., GRAWE, K., ENGLE, D., & MACDONALD, R. (1991). Looking for differential treatment effects: Cross-cultural predictors of differential psychotherapy efficacy. *Journal of Psychotherapy Integration, 1,* 121–141.

BIENERT, H., & SCHNEIDER, B. H. (1993). Diagnosis-specific social skills training with peer-nominated aggressive-disruptive and sensitive-isolated preadolescents. *Journal of Applied Developmental Psychology, 26,* 182–199.

BISHOP, G. D. (1984). Gender, role, and illness behavior in a military population. *Health Psychology, 3,* 519–534.

BISHOP, G. D. (1994). *Health psychology.* Boston: Allyn & Bacon.

BLOOM, A. J. (1985). An anxiety management approach to computer phobia. *Training and Development Journal, 39,* 90–92.

BODENHAUSEN, G. V. (1990). Stereotypes as judgmental heuristics: Evidence of circadian variations in discrimination. *Psychological Science, 1,* 319–322.

BONEY-MCCOY, S., & FINKELHOR, D. (1995). Prior victimization: A risk factor for child sexual abuse and for PTSD-related symptomatology among sexually abused youth. *Child Abuse and Neglect, 19,* 1401–1421.

BOOTH-KEWLEY, S., & FRIEDMAN, H. S. (1987). Psychological predictors of heart disease: A quantitative review. *Psychological Bulletin, 101,* 343–362.

BOOTZIN, R. R., & ACOCELLA, J. R. (1988). *Abnormal psychology* (5th ed.). New York: Random House.

BOUCHARD, T. J., LYKKEN, D. T., MCGUE, M., SEGAL, N. L., & TELLEGEN, A. (1990). Sources of human psychological differences: The Minnesota study of twins reared apart. *Science, 250,* 223–228.

BOWERS, T. G., & CLUM, G. A. (1988). Relative contribution of specific and nonspecific treatment effects: Meta-analysis of placebo-controlled behavior therapy research. *Psychological Bulletin, 103,* 315–323.

BRADBURY, T. N., & FINCHAM, F. D. (1990). Attributions in marriage: Review and critique. *Psychological Bulletin, 107,* 3–33.

BRANDSTADTER, J., & ROTHERMUND, K. (1994). Self-percepts of control in middle and later adulthood: Buffering losses by rescaling goals. *Psychology and Aging, 9,* 265–273.

BRAY, J. H., & JOURILES, E. N. (1995). Treatment of marital conflict and prevention of divorce. Special Issue: The effectiveness of marital and family therapy. *Journal of Marital and Family Therapy, 21,* 461–473.

BRAZA, P., BRAZA, F., CAREERAS, M. R., & MUNOG, J. M. (1993). Measuring the social ability of preschool children. *Social Behavior and Personality, 21,* 145–158.

BREHM, S. (1985). *Intimate relationships.* New York: Random House.

BRIGGS, S. R., CHEEK, J. M., & JONES, W. H. (1986). Introduction in W. H. Jones, J. M. Cheek, & S. R. Briggs (Eds.), *Shyness: Perspectives on research and treatment* (pp. 1–14). New York: Plenum.

BRINGLE, R. G. (1991). Psychosocial aspects of jealousy: A transactional model. In P. Salovey (Ed.), *The psychology of jealousy and envy* (pp. 103–131). New York: Guilford Press.

BROCKNER, J., & RUBIN, J. Z. (1985). *Entrapment in escalating conflicts: A social psychological analysis.* New York: Springer-Verlag.

BRODY, G. H., NEUBAUM, E., & FOREHAND, R. (1988). Serial marriage: A heuristic analysis of an emerging family form. *Psychological Bulletin, 103,* 211–222.

BRODY, L. R., & HALL, J. A. (1993). Gender and emotion. In M. Lewis & J. M. Haviland (Eds.), *Handbook of emotion* (pp. 447–460). New York: Guilford Press.

BROMAN, C. L. (1995). Leisure-time physical activity in an African American population. *Journal of Behavioral Medicine, 18,* 341–353.

BROWN, A. (1991, December). How old is old? *Current Health, 2,* 4–10.

BROWN, J. D. (1991). Staying fit and staying well: Physical fitness as a moderator of life stress. *Journal of Personality and Social Psychology, 60,* 555–561.

BROWN, J. D., & GALLAGHER, F. M. (1992). Coming to terms with failure: Private self-enhancement and public self-effacement. *Journal of Experimental Social Psychology, 28,* 3–22.

BROWN, P. L. (1985, May 15). Disguised to learn the troubles of age. *Philadelphia Inquirer,* p. 1.

BROWNELL, K. D. (1989). Weight control and your health. In *World Book Encyclopedia* (pp. 369–384).

BROWNLEE, S. (1991, August 12). Alzheimer's: Is there hope? *U.S. News and World Report, 117,* 40–49.

BRUCH, M. A., HAMER, R. J., & HEIMBERG, R. G. (1995). Shyness and public consciousness: Additive or interactive relation with social interaction? *Journal of Personality, 63,* 47–63.

BRYSON, J. B. (1991). Modes of response to jealousy-evoking situations. In P. Salovey (Ed.), *The psychology of jealousy and envy* (pp. 178–207). New York: Guilford Press.

BUI, K., & TAKEUCHI, D. T. (1992). Ethnic minority adolescents and the use of community mental health care services. *American Journal of Community Psychology, 20,* 403–417.

BURGER, J. M. (1991). Change in attributions over time: The ephemeral fundamental attribution error. *Social Cognition, 9,* 182–193.

BUTLER, D., & GEIS, F. L. (1990). Nonverbal affect responses to male and female leaders: Implications for leadership evaluations. *Journal of Personality and Social Psychology, 58,* 48–59.

BUTLER, T., GIORDANO, S., & NEREN, S. (1985). Gender and sex-role attributes as predictors of utilization of natural support systems during personal stress events. *Sex Roles, 13,* 515–524.

Can you live longer? (1992, January). *Consumer Reports, 57,* 7–15.

CARDUCCI, B. J., & ZIMBARDO, P. G. (1995, November/December). Are you shy? *Psychology Today,* 34–40.

CAREY, K. B., & CAREY, M. P. (1993). Changes in self-efficacy resulting from unaided attempts to quit smoking. *Psychology of Addictive Behaviors, 7,* 219–224.

CASERTA, M. S., & LUND, D. A. (1992). Bereavement stress and coping among older adults: Expectations versus the actual experience. *Omega Journal of Death and Dying, 25,* 33–45.

CASH, T. F., & DUNCAN, N. C. (1984). Physical attractiveness stereotyping among Black American college students. *Journal of Social Psychology, 122,* 71–77.

CASPI, A., & HERBENER, E. S. (1990). Continuity and change: Assortative marriage and the consistency of personality in adulthood. *Journal of Personality and Social Psychology, 58,* 250–258.

CATES, W., & WASSERHEIT, J. N. (1991). Genital chlamydial infections: Epidemiology and reproductive sequelae. *American Journal of Obstetrics and Gynecology, 164,* 1771–1781.

CHANG, E. C. (1996). Cultural differences in optimism, pessimism, and coping: Predictions of subsequent adjustment. *Journal of Counseling Psychology, 43,* 113–123.

CHEBAT, J. C., & ZUCCARO, C. (1995). Attitudes toward items of time budgets as predictors of time uses: The case of men v. women. *Social Indicators Research, 36,* 75–89.

CHEN, G. M. (1995). Differences in self-disclosure patterns among Americans versus Chinese: A comparative study. *Journal of Cross-Cultural Psychology, 26,* 84–91.

CHEN, X., RUBIN, K. H., & SUN, Y. (1992). Social reputation and peer relationships in Chinese and Canadian children: A cross-cultural study. *Child Development, 63,* 1336–1343.

CHERLIN, A., & MCCARTHY, J. (1985, February). Remarried couple households: Data from the June 1980 current population survey. *Journal of Marriage and the Family, 47*(1), 23–30.

CHRISTENSEN, J. A., & ROBINSON, J. W. (1989). *Community development in perspective.* Ames: Iowa State University Press.

CIALDINI, R. B. (1988). *Influence: Science and practice* (2nd ed.). Glenview, IL: Scott, Foresman.

COBLINER, W. G. (1988). The exclusion of intimacy in the sexuality of the contemporary college-age population. *Adolescence, 23,* 99–113.

COHEN, S., & WILLIAMSON, G. M. (1988). Perceived stress in a probability sample of the United States. In S. Spacapan & S. Oskamp (Eds.), *The social psychology of health.* Newbury Park, CA: Sage.

COHEN, S., & WILLIAMSON, G. M. (1991). Stress and infectious disease in humans. *Psychological Bulletin, 109,* 5–24.

COHN, V. (1984, April 26). Last wish: Some patients would choose to die if asked, studies find. *Philadelphia Inquirer*, p. 11-A.

Coming to terms with obesity. (1994, November). *Harvard Women's Health Watch*, 4–5.

COMPAS, B. E. (1987). Coping with stress during childhood and adolescence. *Psychological Bulletin, 101,* 393–403.

CONE, A. L., & OWENS, S. K. (1991). Academic and locus of control enhancement in a freshman study skills and college adjustment course. *Psychological Reports, 68,* 1211–1217.

CONTRADA, R. S., LEVENTHAL, H., & O'LEARY, A. (1990). Personality and health. In L. A. Pervin (Ed.), *Handbook of personality: Theory and research* (pp. 638–669). New York : Guilford.

CONTRERAS, R., HENDRICK, S. S., & HENDRICK, C. (1996). Perspectives on marital love and satisfaction in Mexican American and Anglo American couples. *Journal of Counseling and Development, 74,* 408–415.

CONWAY, T. L., VICKERS, R. R., & FRENCH, J. R. (1992). An application of person-environment fit theory: Perceived versus desire control. *Journal of Social Issues, 48,* 95–107.

COOPER, H., OKAMURA, L., & MCNEIL, P. (1995). Situation and personality correlates of psychological well-being, social activity, and personal control. *Journal of Research in Personality, 29,* 395–417.

CORBIN, C. B., & LINDSEY, R. (1985). *Concepts of physical fitness with laboratories* (5th ed.). Dubuque, IA: Wm. C. Brown.

CORR, C. A. (1993). Coping with dying: Lessons that we should and should not learn from the work of Elisabeth Kübler-Ross. *Death Studies, 17,* 69–83.

COSTA, P. T., JR., & MCCRAE, R. R. (1989). Personality continuity and the changes of adult life. In M. Storandt & G. R. VandenBos (Eds.), *The adult years: Continuity and change* (pp. 41–77). Washington, DC: American Psychological Association.

COSTA, P. T., JR., ZONDERMAN, A. B., MCCRAE, R. R., CORNONI-HUNTLEY, J., LOCKE, B. Z., & BARRANO, H. E. (1987). Longitudinal analysis of psychological well-being in a national sample: Stability of mean levels. *Journal of Gerontology, 42,* 50–55.

COUCH, C. J. (1996). *Information technologies and social orders.* New York: Aldine DeGruyter.

COUSINS, N. (1989). *Head first: The biology of hope.* New York: Dutton.

COWAN, G., & CAMPBELL, R. R. (1995). Rape causal attitudes among adolescents. *Journal of Sex Research, 32,* 145–153.

COWEN, E. L. (1982, April). Help is where you find it: Four informal helping groups. *American Psychologist, 37,* 385–395.

CRAMER, P. (1991). *The development of defense mechanisms: Theory, research, and assessment.* New York: Springer-Verlag.

CRANDALL, C. S. (1994). Prejudice against fat people: Ideology and self-interest. *Journal of Personality and Social Psychology, 66,* 882–894.

CRANDALL, C. S., & COHEN, C. (1994). The personality of the stigmatizer: Cultural world view, conventionalism, and self-esteem. *Journal of Research in Personality, 28,* 461–480.

CRANE, R. D., SODERQUIST, J. N., & GARDNER, M. D. (1995). Gender differences in cognitive and behavioral steps toward divorce. *American Journal of Family Therapy, 23,* 99–105.

CRAWFORD, C. B. (1994). Effects of sex and sex roles on avoidance of same-and-opposite-sex touch. *Perceptual and Motor Skills, 79,* 107–112.

CREWS, D. J., & LANDERS, D. M. (1987). A meta-analytic review of aerobic fitness and reactivity to psychosocial stressors. *Medicine and Science in Sports and Exercise, 19,* 114–120.

CRISPELL, D., & FREY, W. H. (1993). American maturity. *American Demographics, 15,* 31–42.

CROCKER, J., & MAJOR, B. (1989). Social stigma and self-esteem: The self-protective properties of stigma. *Psychological Review, 96,* 608–630.

CROSBY, F. J. (1991). *Juggling.* New York: Free Press.

CUMMINS, R. C. (1988). Perceptions of social support, receipt of supportive behaviors, and locus of control as moderators of the effects of chronic stress. *American Journal of Community Psychology, 16,* 685–700.

DAVIS, C. M., & BAUSERMAN, R. (1993). Exposure to sexually explicit materials: An attitude change perspective. *Annual Review of Sex Research, 4,* 121–210.

DAVIS, K., & NEWSTROM, J. W. (1985). *Human behavior at work: Organizational Behavior.* New York: McGraw-Hill.

DAVIS, K. E. (1985, February). Near and dear: Friendship and love compared. *Psychology Today, 19,* 22–30.

DAVIS, S. (1996, July/August). The enduring power of friendship. *American Health,* pp. 60–63.

DeBERARD, M. S., & KLEINKNECHT, R. A. (1995). Loneliness, duration of loneliness and reported stress symptomatology. *Psychological Reports, 76,* 1363–1369.

DeGASTON, J. F., WEED, S., & JENSEN, L. (1996). Understanding gender differences in adolescent sexuality. *Adolescence, 31,* 217–231.

DE JONG-GIERVELD, J. (1987). Developing and testing a model of loneliness. *Journal of Personality and Social Psychology, 53,* 119–128.

DERDEYN, A. P. (1994). Parental separation, adolescent psychopathology, and problem behaviors: Comment. *Journal of the American Academy of Child and Adolescent Psychiatry, 33,* 1131–1133.

DE-SOUZA, G., & KLEIN, H. J. (1995). Emergent leadership in the group goal-setting process. *Small Groups Research, 26,* 475–496.

DE STEFANO, L. (1990, January 6). I'll be ok, you won't be ok. *Philadelphia Inquirer,* p. D1, 8.

DEUTSCH, M., & KRAUSS, R. M. (1960). The effect of threat upon interpersonal bargaining. *Journal of Abnormal and Social Psychology, 61,* 181–189.

DEY, E. L., ASTIN, A. W., & KORN, W. S. (1991, September). *The American freshman: Twenty-five year trends.* Los Angeles: Higher Education Research Institute, University of California.

DEY, E. L., ASTIN, A. W., KORN, W. S., & RIGGS, E. R. (1991, December; 1992, December). *The American freshman: National norms for fall 1991 and 1992.* Los Angeles: Higher Education Research Institute, University of California.

DIENER, E., SANDVIK, E., SEIDLITZ, L., & DIENER, M. (1993). The relationship between income and subjective well-being: Relative or absolute? *Social Indicators Research, 28,* 195–223.

DIENER, E., WOLSIC, B., & FUJITA, F. (1995). Physical attractiveness and subjective well-being. *Journal of Personality and Social Psychology, 69,* 120–129.

DION, K. K., & DION, K. L. (1993). Individualistic and collectivistic perspectives on gender and the cultural context of love and intimacy. *Journal of Social Issues, 49,* 53–69.

DOBSON, K. S. (1989). A meta-analysis of the efficiency of cognitive therapy for depression. *Journal of Consulting and Clinical Psychology, 57,* 414–419.

DOLGEN, K. G., & KIM, S. (1994). Adolescents' disclosure to best and good friends: The effects of gender and topic intimacy. *Social Development, 3,* 146–157.

DOLGEN, K. G., MEYER, L., & SCHWARTZ, J. (1991). Effects of gender, target's gender, topic, and self-esteem on disclosure to best and midling friends. *Sex Roles, 25,* 311–329.

DOLLARD, J., & MILLER, N. E. (1950). *Personality and psychotherapy: An analysis in terms of learning, thinking, and culture.* New York: McGraw-Hill.

DOLNICK, E. (1995, July/August). Hotheads and heart attacks. *Time,* pp. 58–64.

DONNAY, D. A. C., & BERGEN, F. H. (1996). Validity, structure, and content of the 1994 *Strong Interest Inventory. Journal of Counseling Psychology, 43,* 275–291.

DUBROVSKY, V. J., KIESLER, S., & SETHNA, B. N. (1991). The equalization phenomenon: Status effects in computer mediated and face-to-face decision-making groups. *Human Computer Interaction, 6,* 119–146.

DUFFY, K. (1991). Introduction to community mediation programs: Past, present, and future. In K. G. Duffy, J. W. Grosch, & P. V. Olczak (Eds.), *Community mediation: A handbook for practitioners and researchers* (pp. 21–34). New York: Guilford Press.

DUFFY, K. G., GROSCH, J., & OLCZAK, P. V. (1991). *Community mediation: A handbook for practitioners and researchers.* New York: Guilford Press.

DUFFY, K. G., & THOMSON, J. (1992). Community mediation centers: Humanistic alternatives to the court system, a pilot study. *Journal of Humanistic Psychology, 32,* 101–114.

DUFFY, K. G., & WONG, F. (1996). *Community psychology.* Boston: Allyn & Bacon.

DUPRAS, A. (1994). Internalized homophobia and psychosexual adjustment among gay men. *Psychological Reports, 75,* 23–28.

EAGLY, A. H., & JOHNSON, B. T. (1990). Gender and leadership style: A meta-analysis. *Psychological Bulletin, 108,* 233–256.

EAGLY, A. H., & MAKHIJANI, M. G. (1991). What is beautiful is good but . . .: A meta-analytic review of research on the physical attractiveness stereotype. *Psychological Bulletin, 110,* 109–128.

EAGLY, A. H., MAKHIJANI, M. G., & KLONSKY, B. G. (1992). Gender and the evaluation of leaders: A meta-analysis. *Psychological Bulletin, 11,* 3–22.

ECKHOLM, E. (1992, June 28). AIDS, fatally steady in the U.S., accelerates worldwide. *New York Times.*

EDWARDS, W. J. (1996a). A sociological analysis of an invisible minority group: Male adolescent homosexuals. *Youth and Society, 27,* 334–355.

EDWARDS, W. J. (1996b). Operating within the mainstream: Coping and adjustment among a sample of homosexual youths. *Deviant Behavior, 17,* 229–251.

EKMAN, P. (1985a). Expression and the nature of emotion. In K. R. Sherer & P. Ekman (Eds.), *Approaches to emotion.* Hillsdale, NJ: Erlbaum.

EKMAN, P. (1985b). *Telling lies.* New York: W. W. Norton.

EKMAN, P. (1993). Facial expression and emotion. *American Psychologist, 48,* 384–392.

ELLIS, A., & DRYDEN, W. (1987). *The practice of rational emotive therapy.* New York: Springer-Verlag.

ELLIS, A., & HARPER, R. A. (1975). *A new guide to rational living.* Englewood Cliffs, NJ: Prentice Hall.

ERBER, R., & THERRIAULT, N. (1993, October). *Sweating to the oldies: The mood-absorbing qualities of exercise.* Paper presented at the annual meeting of the Society for Experimental Social Psychology, San Diego, CA.

ERIKSON, E. H. (1963). *Childhood and society* (2nd ed.). New York: W. W. Norton.

ERIKSON, E. H. (1968). *Identity: Youth and crisis.* New York: W. W. Norton.

ERIKSON, E. H. (1974). *Dimensions of a new identity.* New York: W. W. Norton.

Exercise isn't just for fun. (1991). *Aging, 362,* 37–40.

EYSENCK, H. J. (1966). *The effects of psychotherapy.* New York: International Science Press.

FAHRNER, E. M. (1995). Sexual dysfunction and alcohol abuse. *Sexual and Marital Therapy, 10,* 5–8.

FALLON, A. E. (1990). Culture in the mirror: Sociocultural determinants of body image. In T. F. Cash & T. Pruzinsky (Eds.), *Body development, deviance, and change.* New York: Guilford Press.

FALLON, A. E., & ROZEN, P. (1985). Sex differences in perceptions of desirable body shape. *Journal of Abnormal Psychology, 94,* 102–105.

FARLEY, F. (1986, May). The big T in personality. *Psychology Today, 20,* 46–52.

FEIST, J. (1985). *Theories of personality.* New York: Holt, Rinehart & Winston.

FIEDLER, F. (1978). The contingency model and the dynamics of the leadership process. In L. Berkowitz (Ed.), *Advances in experimental social psychology* (Vol. 11). Orlando, FL: Academic Press.

FIGLER, H. E. (1993). *Path: A career workbook for liberal arts students.* Cranston, RI: Carroll Press.

FINHOLT, T., & SPROULL, L. S. (1990). Electronic groups at work. *Organization Science, 1,* 41–64.

FISCHER, E., & TURNER, J. (1970). Orientations to seeking professional help: Development and research utility of an attitude scale. *Journal of Consulting and Clinical Psychology, 35,* 82–83.

FLETT, G. L., HEWITT, P. L., BLANKSTEIN, K. R., & MOSHER, S. W. (1991). Perfectionism, self-actualization, and personal adjustment. Special Issue: Handbook of self-actualization. *Journal of Social Behavior and Personality, 6,* 147–160.

FOLKES, V. S. (1982). Forming relationships and the matching hypothesis. *Personality and Social Psychology Bulletin, 82,* 631–636.

FOXMAN, S. (1983). *Classified love.* New York: McGraw-Hill.

FRANCE, D. (1997, May/June). The new compassion. *Modern Maturity, 40,* 33–40.

FRANKL, V. (1978). *The unheard cry for meaning.* New York: Simon & Schuster.

FRENCH, M. (1992). *The war against women.* New York: Summit Books.

FREUD, S. (1933). *New introductory lectures on psycho-analysis.* New York: W. W. Norton. (First German edition, 1933).

FRIEDMAN, H. S., HAWLEY, P. H., & TUCKER, J. S. (1994). Personality, health, and longevity. *Current Directions in Psychological Science, 3,* 37–41.

FROMM, E. (1963). *Escape from freedom.* New York: Holt.

FULTON, R. (1987). The many faces of grief. *Death Studies, 11,* 243–256.

GALLUP, G., JR. (1991). *The Gallup poll: Public opinion 1990.* Wilmington, DE: Scholarly Resources, Inc.

GERDES, E. P. (1995). Women preparing for traditionally male professions: Physical and psychological symptoms associated with work and home stress. *Sex Roles, 32,* 787–807.

GLASS, C. R., & ARNKOFF, D. B. (1992). Behavior therapy. In D. K. Freedheim (Ed.), *History of psychotherapy: A century of change* (pp. 587–628). Washington, DC: American Psychological Association.

GLEICK, E. (1995, August 21). Out of the mouths of babes. *Time,* pp. 33–34.

GOLDFARB, L. A., DYKENS, E. M., & GERRARD, M. (1985). The Goldfarb Fear of Fat Scale. *Journal of Personality Assessment, 49,* 329–332.

GOLDING, J. M. (1990). Division of household labor, strain, and depressive symptoms among Mexican Americans and Non-Hispanic Whites. *Psychology of Women Quarterly, 14,* 103–117.

GOLEMAN, D. (1987, November 3). Worries about intimacy are rising, therapists find. *New York Times,* pp. Cl, C7.

GOLEMAN, D. (1988, November 1). Narcissism looming larger as root of personality woes. *New York Times, Science,* pp. C1, C16.

GOLEMAN, D. (1991, November 13). All too often, the doctor isn't listening, studies show. *New York Times,* pp. C1, C15.

GOLEMAN, D. (1995). *Emotional intelligence.* New York: Bantam.

GOLOGOR, E. (1977). Group polarization in a non-sick-taking culture. *Journal of Cross-Cultural Psychology, 8,* 331–346.

GONZALES, M. H., DAVIS, J. M., LONEY, G. L., LUKENS, C. K., & JUNGHANS, C. M. (1983). Interactional approach to interpersonal attraction. *Journal of Personality and Social Psychology, 44,* 1192–1197.

GORDON, T., & SANDS, J. S. (1978). *P.E.T. in action.* New York: Bantam Books.

GOTTESMAN, I. I. (1991). *Schizophrenia genesis: The origins of madness.* New York: Freeman.

GOTTMAN, J. M. (1994). *Why marriages succeed or fail.* New York: Simon & Schuster.

GRAY, C. A., & GERON, S. M. (1995). The other sorrow of divorce: The effects on grandparents when their adult children divorce. *Journal of Gerontological Social Work, 23,* 139–159.

GRAY-LITTLE, B., BAUCOM, D. H., & HAMBY, S. L. (1996). Marital power, marital adjustment, and therapy outcome. *Journal of Family Psychology, 10,* 292–303.

GRAZIANO, W. G., JENSEN-CAMPBELL, L. A., SHEBILSKE, L. J., & LUNDGREN, S. R. (1993). Social influence, sex differences, and judgment of beauty: Putting the interpersonal back in interpersonal attraction. *Journal of Personality and Social Psychology, 65,* 522–531.

GREEN, B. L., & KENRICK, D. T. (1994). The attractiveness of gender-typed traits at different relationship levels: Androgynous characteristics may be desirable after all. *Personality and Social Psychological Bulletin, 20,* 244–253.

GREENGLASS, E. S. (1995). Gender, work stress, and coping. *Journal of Social Behavior and Personality, 10,* 121–134.

GREENHAUS, J. H., PARASURAMAN, S., & WORMLEY, W. M. (1990). Effects of race on organizational experiences, job performance evaluations, and career outcomes. *Academy of Management Journal, 33,* 64–86.

GREENWALD, H. (1973). *Direct decision therapy.* San Diego, CA: Edits Publishers.

GREENWALD, H., & RICH, E. (1984). *The happy person.* New York: Avon Books.

GREENWOOD, M. R. C. (1989). Sexual dimorphism and obesity. In A. J. Stunkard & A. Baum (Eds.), *Perspective in behavior medicine: Eating, sleeping, and sex.* Hillsdale, NJ: Erlbaum.

GROSS, D. M., & SCOTT, S. (1990, July 16). Proceeding with caution. *Time, 142,* 56–62.

HALL, R. (1995). The bleaching syndrome: African Americans' response to cultural domination vis-à-vis skin color. *Journal of Black Studies, 26,* 172–184.

HALLORAN, J., & BENTON, D. (1987). *Applied human relations* (3rd ed.). Englewood Cliffs, NJ: Prentice Hall.

HANSEN, G. L. (1985). Dating jealousy among college students. *Sex roles, 12,* 713–721.

HARRINGTON, D. M., BLOCK, J. H., & BLOCK, J. (1987). Testing aspects of Carl Rogers's theory of creative environments: Child-reading antecedents of creative potential in young adolescents. *Journal of Personality and Social Psychology, 52,* 851–856.

HARRIS, L. (1987). *Inside America.* New York: Vintage Books.

HARVARD MEDICAL SCHOOL HEALTH LETTER. (1985, November). *AIDS: Update* (Part I), 1–4.

HATCHER, R. A. (1994). *Contraceptive technology* (16th ed.). New York: Irvington.

HATFIELD, E. (1988). Passionate and companionate love. In R. J. Sternberg & M. I. Barnes (Eds.), *The psychology of love* (pp. 191–217). New Haven, CT: Yale University Press.

HATFIELD, E., & RAPSON, R. L. (1993). Historical and cross-cultural perspectives on passionate love and sexual desire. *Annual Review of Sex Research, 4,* 67–97.

HATFIELD, E., & SPRECHER, S. (1995). Men's and women's preferences in marital partners in the United States, Russia, and Japan. *Journal of Cross-Cultural Psychology, 26,* 728–750.

HAYS, R. B. (1985). A longitudinal study of friendship development. *Journal of Personality and Social Psychology, 48,* 909–924.

HAZAN, C., & SHAVER, P. (1994). Attachment as an organizing framework for research on close relationships. *Psychological Inquiry, 5,* 1–22.

HEAROLD, S. (1986). A synthesis of 1,043 effects of television on social behavior. In G. Comstock (Ed.), *Public communication and behavior* (Vol. 1). Orlando, FL: Academic Press.

HEFT, L., THORESON, C. E., KIRMIL-GRAY, K., WIEDENFELD, S. A., EAGLESTON, J. R., BRACKE, P., & ARNOW, B. (1988). Emotional and temperamental correlates in Type A children and adolescents. *Journal of Youth and Adolescence, 17,* 461–475.

HELGESON, V. S. (1990). *The female advantage: Women's ways of leadership.* New York: Doubleday Currency.

HELGESON, V. S. (1994). Long-distance romantic relationships: Sex differences in adjustment and break-up. *Personality and Social Psychology Bulletin, 20,* 254–265.

HELGESON, V. S., & COHEN, S. (1996). Social support and adjustment to cancer: Reconciling descriptive, correlational, and intervention research. *Health Psychology, 15,* 135–148.

HENDERSON-KING, D. H., & VEROFF, J. (1994). Sexual satisfaction and marital well-being in the first years of marriage. *Journal of Social and Personal Relationships, 11,* 509–534.

HENSS, R. (1995). Waist-to-hip ratio and attractiveness. Replication and extension. *Personality and Individual Differences, 19,* 479–488.

HERBERT, T. B., & COHEN, S. (1993). Stress and immunity in humans: A meta-analytic review. *Psychosomatic Medicine, 55,* 364–379.

HETHERINGTON, E. M., STANLEY-HAGAN, M., & ANDERSON, E. R. (1989). Marital transitions: A child's perspective. *American Psychologist, 44,* 303–312.

HIGGINS, E. T., BOND, R. N., KLEIN, R., & STRAUMAN, T. (1986). Self-discrepancies and emotional vulnerability: How magnitude, accessibility, and type of discrepancy influence affect. *Journal of Personality and Social Psychology, 51,* 5–15.

HILL, C. A. (1987). Affiliation motivation: People who need people . . . but in different ways. *Journal of Personality and Social Psychology, 52,* 1008–1018.

HOBSON, J. A. (1988). *The dreaming brain.* New York: Basic Books.

HOLMES, T. H., & RAHE, R. H. (1967). The social readjustment rating scale. *Journal of Psychosomatic Research, 11,* 213–217.

HOPE, D. A., HOLT, C. S., HEIMBERG, R. G. (1995). Social phobia. In T. R. Giles (Ed.), *Handbook of effective psychotherapy.* New York: Plenum.

HOPSON, J. L. (1988, July/August). A pleasurable chemistry. *Psychology Today, 22,* 29–33.

HOUSE, J. S., LANDIS, K. R., & UMBERSON, D. (1988). Social relationships and health. *Science, 241,* 540–545.

HOWARD, K. I., KOPTA, M., KRAUSE, M. S., & ORLINSKY, D. E. (1986, February). The dose-effect relationship in psychotherapy. *American Psychologist, 41,* 159–164.

HUGHES, F. P., & NOPPE, L. D. (1985). *Human development across the life span.* St. Paul, MN: West Publishing Company.

HUGICK, L., & LEONARD, J. (1991). Job dissatisfaction grows; "moonlighting" on the rise. *The Gallup Poll News Service, 56,* 1–11.

HUTRI, M. (1996). When careers reach a dead end: Identification of occupational crisis states. *Journal of Psychology, 130,* 383–399.

HYDE, J. S., & DeLAMETER, J. (1997). *Understanding human sexuality.* New York: McGraw-Hill.

INGLEHART, R. (1990). *Culture shift in advanced industrial society.* Princeton, NJ: Princeton University Press.

INSEL, P. M., & ROTH, W. T. (1985). *Core concepts in health* (4th ed.). Palo Alto, CA: Mayfield.

INSKO, C. A., SCHOPLER, J., HOYLE, R. H., DARDIS, G. J., & GRAETZ, K. A. (1990). Individual-group discontinuity as a function of fear and greed. *Journal of Personality and Social Psychology, 58,* 68–79.

JACKSON, L. A., HUNTER, J., & HODGE, C. N. (1995). Physical attractiveness and intellectual competence: A meta-analytic review. *Social Psychology Quarterly, 58,* 108–122.

JACOBI, J. (1973). *The psychology of C. G. Jung.* New Haven, CT: Yale University Press.

JAMES, W. (1950). *The principles of psychology* (Vols. 1–2). New York: Dover. (Original work published in 1890.)

JANIS, I. L. (1982). *Groupthink* (2nd ed.). Boston: Houghton Mifflin.

JEMMETT, J. B., III, & MAGLOIRE, K. (1988). Academic stress, social support, and secretory immunoglobulin. *Journal of Personality and Social Psychology, 55,* 803–810.

JEWELL, K. S. (1993). *From Mammy to Miss America and beyond: Cultural images and the shaping of U. S. social policy.* London: Routledge.

JOHNSON, D. P., & SLANEY, R. B. (1996). Perfectionism: Scale development and a study of perfectionistic clients in counseling. *Journal of College Student Development, 37,* 29–41.

JOHNSON, M. P., HUSTON, T. L., GAINES, S. O., JR., & LEVINGER, G. (1992). Patterns of married life among young couples. *Journal of Social and Personal Relationships, 9,* 343–364.

JOHNSTONE, B., FRAME, C. L., & BOUMAN, D. (1992). Physical attractiveness and athletic and academic ability in controversial-aggressive and rejected-aggressive children. *Journal of Social and Clinical Psychology, 11,* 71–79.

JOINER, T. E., WONDERLICH, S. A., METOLSKY, G., SCHMIDT, N. B. (1995). Body dissatisfaction: A feature of bulimia, depression, or both? *Journal of Social and Clinical Psychology, 14,* 339–355.

JONES, A., & CRANDALL, R. (1986). Validation of a short index of self-actualization. *Personality and Social Psychology Bulletin, 12,* 63–73.

JONES, D. (1995). Sexual selection, physical attractiveness, and facial neoteny: Cross-cultural evidence and implication. *Current Anthropology, 36,* 723–748.

JONES, E. (1953). *The life and work of Sigmund Freud* (Vol. 1). New York: Basic Books.

JOURARD, S. M. (1975). Growing experience and the experience of growth. In A. Arkoff (Ed.), *Psychology and personal growth.* Boston: Allyn & Bacon.

JUMPER, S. A. (1995). A meta-analysis of the relationship of child sexual abuse to adult psychological adjustment. *Child Abuse and Neglect, 19,* 715–728.

KAGAN, J. (1989). *Unstable ideas: Temperament, cognition, and self.* Cambridge, MA: Harvard University Press.

KAHN, S., ZIMMERMAN, G., CSIKSZENTMIHALYI, M., & GETZELS, J. W. (1985). Relations between identity in young adulthood and intimacy at mid-life. *Journal of Personality and Social Psychology, 49,* 1316–1322.

KAPLAN, H. S. (1983). *The evaluation of sexual disorders.* New York: Brunner/Mazel.

KAPLAN, R., SALLIS, J. F., & PATTERSON, T. L. (1993). *Health and human behavior.* New York: McGraw-Hill.

KAPLAN, R. M., ANDERSON, J. P., & WINGARD, D. L. (1991). Gender differences in health-related quality of life. *Health Psychology, 10,* 86–93.

KARAU, S. J., & WILLIAMS, K. D. (1993). Social loafing: A meta-analytic review and theoretical integration. *Journal of Personality and Social Psychology, 65,* 681–706.

KASSER, T., & RYAN, R. M. (1996). Further examining the American dream: Differential correlates of intrinsic and extrinsic goals. *Personality and Social Psychology Bulletin, 22,* 280–287.

KATZ, I. M., & CAMPBELL, S. D. (1994). Ambivalence over emotional expression and well-being: Nomothetic and ideographic tests of the stress-buffering hypothesis. *Journal of Personality and Social Psychology, 67,* 513–523.

KAUFMANN, W. (1973, April). Do you crave life without a choice? *Psychology Today, 7.*

KEYS, C. B., & FRANK, S. (1987). Organizational perspectives in community psychology [Special issue]. *American Journal of Community Psychology, 15.*

KIECOLT-GLASER, J. K., & GLASER, R. (1995). Psychoneuroimmunology and health consequences: Data and shared mechanisms. *Psychosomatic Medicine, 57,* 269–274.

KINSEY, A. C., POMEROY, W. B., & MARTIN, C. E. (1948). *Sexual behavior in the human male.* Philadelphia: W. B. Saunders.

KINZL, J. F., TRAWEGER, C., GUENTHER, V., & BIEBL, W. (1994). Family background and sexual abuse associated with eating disorders. *American Journal of Psychiatry, 15,* 1127–1131.

KIPNIS, D., & SCHMIDT, S. (1985, April). The language of persuasion. *Psychology Today,* 40–46.

KIRKPATRICK, L. A., & DAVIS, K. E. (1994). Attachment style, gender, and relationship stability: A longitudinal analysis. *Journal of Personality and Social Psychology, 66,* 502–512.

KLEINKE, C. L. (1986). Gaze and eye contact: A research review. *Psychological Bulletin, 100,* 78–100.

KLOHNEN, E. C. (1996). Conceptual analysis and measurement of the construct of ego-resiliency. *Journal of Personality and Social Psychology, 70,* 1067–1079.

KOERNER, B. I. (1997, March 31). Life after death? *U. S. News & World Report, 123,* 61–64.

KOGAN, N., & WALLACH, M. A. (1964). *Risk-taking: A study in cognition and personality.* New York: Holt.

KRUPAT, E. (1986, November). A delicate imbalance. *Psychology Today, 20,* 22–26.

KÜBLER-ROSS, E. (1975). *Death.* Englewood Cliffs, NJ: Prentice Hall.

KÜBLER-ROSS, E. (1987). *Working it through.* New York: Macmillan.

KÜBLER-ROSS, E. (1993). *On death and dying.* New York: Collier Books.

KUNZ, J., & FINKEL, A. J. (Eds.). (1987*). The American Medical Association family medical guide.* New York: Random House.

LAIRD, B. (1991, August 9). How live-in partners fared. *USA Today.*

LANG, F. R., & CARSTENSEN, L. L. (1994). Close emotional relationships in late life: Further support for proactive aging in the social domain. *Psychology and Aging, 9,* 315–324.

LATTEN, J. J. (1989). Life course and satisfaction equal for everyone? *Social Indicators Research, 21,* 599–610.

LAUMANN, E. O., GAGNON, J. H., MICHAEL, R. T., & MICHAELS, S. (1994). *The social organization of sexuality: Sexual practices in the United States.* Chicago: University of Chicago Press.

LAZARUS, A. S. (1981). *The practice of multimodel therapy.* New York: McGraw-HIll.

LAZARUS, R. S. (1993). From psychological stress to the emotions: A history of changing outlooks. *Annual Review of Psychology, 44,* 1–21.

LEITENBERG, H., & HENNING, K. (1995). Sexual fantasy. *Psychological Bulletin, 117,* 469–496.

LEONARD, F., & LOEB, L. (1992, January). Heading for hardship: The future of older women in America. *USA Today Magazine,* 19–21.

LEONARD, G. (1991). Abraham Maslow and the new self. In K. G. Duffy (Ed.), *Personal growth and behavior* (pp. 30–36). Guilford, CT: Dushkin Publishing Group.

LEVENTHAL, E. A. (1994). Gender and aging: Women and their aging. In V. J. Adesso, D. M. Reddy, & R. Fleming (Eds.), *Psychological perspectives on women's health* (pp. 11–35). Washington, DC: Taylor & Francis.

LEVIN, W. C. (1988, March). Age stereotyping: College student evaluations. *Research on Aging,* 134–148.

LEVINE, R., SATO, S., HASHIMOTO, T., & VERMA, J. (1995). Love and marriage in eleven cultures. *Journal of Cross-Cultural Psychology, 26,* 554–571.

LEVINE, R. V. (1990, September/October). The pace of life. *American Scientist, 78,* 450–459.

LEVINSON, D. J., DARROW, C. N., KLEIN, E. B., LEVINSON, M. M., & McKEE, B. (1978). *The seasons of a man's life.* New York: Knopf.

LINDSTROM, T. C. (1995). Anxiety and adaptation in bereavement. *Anxiety, Stress, and Coping : An International Journal, 8,* 251–261.

LINVILLE, P. T. (1985). Self-complexity and affective extremity—don't put all your eggs in one cognitive basket. *Social Cognition, 3,* 94–120.

LIU, J. H., CAMPBELL, S. M., CONDIE, H. (1995). Ethnocentrism in dating preferences for an American sample: The in-group bias in social context. *European Journal of Social Psychology, 25,* 95–115.

LOCKE, W. E., & COLLIGAN, D. (1986, March). Stressed for success. *New Age Journal,* pp. 30–31, 63–64.

LONETTO, R., & TEMPLER, D. I. (1983). The nature of death anxiety. In C. D. Spielberger & J. N. Butcher (Eds.), *Advances in personality assessment* (Vol. 3). Hillsdale, NJ: Erlbaum.

LUBOVSKY, L., CRITS-CHRISTOPH, P., MINTZ, J., & AUERBACH, A. (1988). *Who will benefit from pyschotherapy?* New York: Basic Books.

MARANO, H. E. (1992, January/February). The reinvention of marriage. *Psychology Today, 26,* 48–53.

MARBELLA, J. (1989, June 29). Cohabiting won't ensure marital bliss, studies say. *Philadelphia Inquirer,* pp. 1E, 8E.

MARION, M. (1994). Encouraging the development of responsible anger management in young children. *Early Child Development and Care, 97,* 155–163.

MARKUS, H., & KITAYAMA, S. (1991). Culture and the self: Implications for cognition, emotion, and motivation. *Psychological Review, 98,* 224–253.

MARSH, H. W., & BYRNE, B. M. (1991). Differentiated additive androgyny model: Relations between masculinity, femininity, and multiple dimensions of self-concept. *Journal of Personality and Social Psychology, 61,* 811–828.

MARTIN, N. K., & DIXON, P. N. (1994). The effects of freshman orientation and locus of control on adjustment to college: A follow-up study. *Social Behavior and Personality, 22,* 201–208.

MASLOW, A. H. (1968). *Toward a psychology of being* (2nd ed.). New York: Van Nostrand Reinhold.

MASLOW, A. H. (1970). *Motivation and personality* (2nd ed.). New York: Harper & Row.

MASLOW, A. H. (1971). *The farther reaches of human nature.* New York: Viking.

MASTERS, W., & JOHNSON, V. (1966). *Human sexual response.* Boston: Little Brown.

MASTERS, W., & JOHNSON, V. (1979). *Homosexuality in perspective.* Boston: Little Brown.

MASTERS, W. H., JOHNSON, V. E., & KOLODNY, R. C. (1988a). *Crisis: Heterosexual behavior in the age of AIDS.* New York: Grove Press.

MASTERS, W. H., JOHNSON, V. E., & KOLODNY, R. C. (1988b). *Human sexuality* (3rd ed.). Boston: Little, Brown.

MASTERS, W. H., JOHNSON, V. E., & KOLODNY, R. C. (1995). *Human sexuality.* New York: Harper Collins.

MATHES, E. W. (1991). Dealing with romantic jealousy by finding a replacement relationship. *Psychological Reports, 69,* 535–538.

MATLIN, M. W. (1996). *The psychology of women.* Fort Worth, TX: Harcourt Brace.

MATSUMOTO, D. (1992). More evidence for the universality of a contempt expression. *Motivation and Emotion, 16,* 363–368.

MATSUMOTO, D. (1993). Ethnic differences in affect intensity, emotion judgments, display rule attitudes, and self-reported emotional expression in an American sample. *Motivation and Emotion, 17,* 107–123.

MAY, R. (1977, April). Freedom, determinism, and the future. *Psychology Today, 11.*

MCAULEY, E. (1991). Efficacy, attributional, and affective responses to exercise participation. *Journal of Sport and Exercise Psychology, 13,* 382–393.

MCCANN, I. L., & HOLMES, D. S. (1984). Influence of aerobic exercise on depression. *Journal of Personality and Social Psychology, 46,* 1142–1147.

MCCONATHA, J. T., LIGHTNER, E., & DEANER, S. L. (1994). Culture, age, and gender as variables in expression of emotions. *Journal of Social Behavior and Personality, 9,* 481–488.

MCCRAE, R. R., & COSTA, P. T. (1994). The stability of personality: Observations and evaluations. *Current Directions in Psychological Science, 5,* 173–175.

MCDONOUGH, E. M., & MUNZ, D. C. (1994). General well-being and perceived adult friendship behaviors. *Journal of Social Behavior and Personality, 9,* 743–752.

MCGONAGLE, K. A., KESSLER, R. C., & SCHILLING, E. A. (1992). The frequency and determinants of marital disagreements in a community sample. *Journal of Social and Personal Relationships, 9,* 507–524.

MCGUIRE, T. W., KIESLER, S., & SIEGEL, J. (1987). Group and computer-mediated discussion effects in risk decision making. *Journal of Personality and Social Psychology, 52,* 917–930.

MCKAY, K. A., & KUH, G. D. (1994). A comparison of student effort and educational gains of Caucasian and African-American students at predominantly white colleges and universities. *Journal of College Student Development, 35,* 217–223.

McLean, C. (1988). The graying of America. *The Oregon Stater,* 11–17.

Meadows, D. H. (1991). *The global citizen.* Washington, DC: Island Press.

Meichenbaum, D. (1977). *Cognitive-behavior modification.* New York: Plenum.

Meichenbaum, D. (1985). *Stress inoculation training.* New York: Pergamon.

Meindl, J. R., & Lerner, M. J. (1984). Exacerbation of extreme responses to an out-group. *Journal of Personality and Social Psychology, 47,* 71–84.

Michalos, A. C. (1991). *Global report on student well-being: Vol. 1. Life satisfaction and happiness.* New York: Springer Verlag.

Mikulincer, M., Florian, V., & Weller, A. (1993). Attachment styles, coping strategies, and posttraumatic psychological distress: The impact of the Gulf War in Israel. *Journal of Personality and Social Psychology, 64,* 817–826.

Milgram, S. (1974). Obedience to authority. *Human Relations, 18,* 57–76.

Mirowsky, J. (1995). Age and the sense of control. *Social Psychology Quarterly, 58,* 31–43.

Mischel, W. (1986). *Introduction to personality* (4th ed.). New York: Holt, Rinehart & Winston.

Montepare, J. M., & Zebrowitz-McArthur, L. (1988). Impressions of people created by age-related qualities of their gaits. *Journal of Personality and Social Psychology, 55,* 547–556.

Moorhead, G., Ference, R., & Neck, C. P. (1991). Group decision fiascoes continue. Space Shuttle Challenger and a revised groupthink framework. *Human Relations, 44,* 539–550.

Moorhead, G., & Griffin, R. (1995). *Organizational behavior: Managing people and organizations.* Boston: Houghton Mifflin.

Moreland, R. L., & Beach, S. R. (1992). Exposure effects in the classroom: The development of affinity among students. *Journal of Experimental Social Psychology, 28,* 255–276.

Morinaga, Y., Frieze, I. H., & Ferligoj, A. (1993). Career plans and gender-role attitudes of college students in the United States, Japan, and Slovenia. *Sex Roles, 29,* 317–334.

Morreal, J. (1991). Humor and work. *Humor International Journal of Humor Research, 4,* 359–373.

Morris, C. G. (1988). *Psychology: An Introduction* (6th ed.). Englewood Cliffs, NJ: Prentice Hall.

Morrow, L. (1985, September 2). Advertisements for oneself. *Time.*

Murphy, M. C., & Archer, J., Jr. (1996). Stressors on the college campus: A comparison of 1985 and 1993. *Journal of College Student Development, 37,* 20–28.

Murray, S. L., & Holmes, J. G. (1994). Storytelling in close relationships: The construction of confidence. *Personality and Social Psychology Bulletin, 20,* 650–663.

Muuss, R. E. (1986, Summer). Adolescent eating disorders: Bulimia. *Adolescence, 21,* 257–267.

Myers, D. G. (1993). *The pursuit of happiness.* New York: Avon Books.

Myers, D. G., & Arenson, S. J. (1972). Enhancement of dominant risk tendencies in group discussion. *Psychological Reports, 30,* 615–623.

Myers, D. G., & Diener, E. (1995). Who is happy? *Psychological Science, 6,* 10–19.

Nah, K. (1993). Perceived problems and service delivery for Korean immigrants. *Social Work, 38,* 289–296.

National Victim Center. (1992, April 23). *Rape in America.* Fort Worth, TX: Author.

Neck, C. P., & Moorhead, G. (1995). Groupthink remodeled: The importance of leadership, time pressure, and methodological decision-making procedures. *Human Relations, 48,* 537–557.

Neto, F. (1992). Loneliness among Portuguese adolescents. *Social Behavior and Personality, 20,* 15–22.

Neugarten, B. L. (1986). The aging society. In A. Pifer & L. Bronte (Eds.), *Our aging society.* New York: W. W. Norton.

NIETZEL, M. T., BERNSTEIN, D. A., & MILICH, R. (1991). *Introduction to clinical psychology.* Englewood Cliffs, NJ: Prentice Hall.

NOCK, S. L. (1995). Spouse preferences of never-married, divorced, and cohabiting Americans. *Journal of Divorce and Remarriage, 22,* 91–108.

NOLEN-HOEKSEMA, N., PARKER, L. E., & LARSON, J. (1994). Ruminative coping with depressed mood following loss. *Journal of Personality and Social Psychology, 67,* 92–104.

NORCROSS, J. C., & PROCHASKA, J. O. (1988). A study of eclectic (and integrative) views revisited. *Professional Psychology, 19,* 170–174.

OETTINGEN, G., & SELIGMAN, M. (1990). Pessimism and behavioral signs of depression in East versus West Berlin. *European Journal of Social Psychology, 20,* 207–220.

OGGINS, J., VEROFF, J., & LEBER, D. (1993). Perceptions of marital interaction among Black and White newlyweds. *Journal of Personality and Social Psychology, 56,* 219–227.

OHANNESSIAN, C. M., McCAULEY, C., LERNER, R. M., LERNER, J. V., & VON EYE, A. (1994). A longitudinal study of perceived family adjustment and emotional adjustment in early adolescence. *Journal of Early Adolescence, 14,* 371–390.

OLAH, A. (1995). Coping strategies among adolescents: A cross-cultural study. [Special issue: Adolescent research: A European perspective.] *Journal of Adolescence, 18,* 491–512.

OLIVERO, M. (1989, November/December). The "unretired"—seniors are returning to work and loving it. *St. Raphael's Better Health, 10,* 31–37.

OSGOOD, C. E. (1962). *An alternative to war or surrender.* Urbana: University of Illinois Press.

OVERHOLSER, J. C. (1993). Ideographic, quantitative assessment of self-esteem. *Personality and Individual Differences, 14,* 639–646.

PARKER, S., & DEVRIES, B. (1993). Patterns of friendship for women and men in same and cross-sex relationships. *Journal of Social and Personal Relationships, 10,* 617–626.

PARROTT, W. G., & SMITH, R. H. (1993). Distinguishing the experiences of envy and jealousy. *Journal of Personality and Social Psychology, 64,* 906–920.

PATTISON, E. M. (1977). The experience of dying. In E. M. Pattison (Ed.), *The experience of dying.* Englewood Cliffs, NJ: Prentice Hall.

PERLMAN, D. (1991). *Age difference in loneliness: A meta-analysis.* Vancouver: University of British Columbia. (ERIC Document Reproduction Service No. ED 326767)

PERRY-JENKINS, M., SEERY, B., & CROWTER, A. C. (1992). Linkages between women's provider-role attitudes, psychological well-being, and family relationships. *Psychology of Women Quarterly, 16,* 311–329.

PETERSON, A. C., COMPAS, B. E., BROOKS-GUNN, J., STEMMLER, N., EY, S., & GRANT, K. E. (1993). Depression in adolescence. *American Psychologist, 48,* 155–168.

PETERSON, C., & SELIGMAN, M. E. P. (1984). Causal explanations as a risk factor for depression: Theory and evidence. *Psychological Review, 91,* 347–374.

PETERSON, C., & STUNKARD, A. J. (1988). Personal control and health promotion. In C. Peterson, *Personality.* New York: Harcourt Brace Jovanovich.

PILISUK, M., & ACREDOLO, C. (1988). Fear of technological hazards: One concern or many? *Social Behavior, 3,* 17–24.

PLOMIN, R., & RENDE, R. (1991). Human behavioral genetics. *Annual Review of Psychology, 42,* 161–190.

POMERLEAU, O. F., & RODIN, J. (1986). Behavioral medicine and health psychology. In S. L. Garfield & A. E. Bergin (Eds.), *Handbook of psychotherapy and behavior change* (3rd ed.). New York: Wiley.

POPENOE, D. (1989). *Sociology* (7th ed.). Englewood Cliffs, NJ: Prentice Hall.

PORTER, N., GEIS, F. L., COOPER, E., & NEWMAN, E. (1985). Androgyny and leadership in mixed-sex groups. *Journal of Personality and Social Psychology, 49,* 808–823.

POWELL, A. D., & KAHN, A. S. (1995). Racial differences in women's desires to be thin. *International Journal of Eating Disorders, 17,* 191–195.

POWELL, G. E., & LINDSAY, S. J. E. (Eds.). (1987). *A handbook of clinical adult psychology.* Aldershot, England: Gower.

PTACEK, J. T., & DODGE, K. L. (1995). Coping strategies and relationship satisfaction in couples. *Personality and Social Psychology Bulletin, 21,* 76–84.

PUGH, D. N. (1993). The effects of problem-solving ability and locus of control on prisoner adjustment. *International Journal of Offender Therapy and Comparative Criminology, 37,* 163–176.

RALL, M. L., PESKOFF, F. S., BYRNE, J. J. (1994). The effects of information-giving behavior and gender on perceptions of physicians: An experimental analysis. *Social Behavior and Personality, 22,* 1–16.

RAPE IN AMERICA. (1992, April 23). (Available from National Victim Center, Crime Victim's Research and Treatment Center, 307 W. Seventh Street, Suite 101, Fort Worth, TX, 76102.)

RAVEN, B. M., & RUBIN, J. Z. (1983). *Social psychology* (2nd ed.). New York: Wiley.

REED, G. M., TAYLOR, S. E., & KEMENY, M. E. (1993). Perceived control and psychological adjustment in gay men with AIDS. *Journal of Applied Social Psychology, 23,* 791–824.

REICH, C. A. (1995). *Opposing the system.* New York: Crown Publishers.

REMPEL, J. K., & HOLMES, J. G. (1986, February). How do I trust thee? *Psychology Today, 20,* 28–34.

RENDON, L. I. (1992). *Minorities: The coming majority. Your college experience: Strategies for success.* Belmont, CA: Wadsworth.

RICHARDSON, J. D. (1991). Medical causes of male sexual dysfunction. *The Medical Journal of Australia, 155,* 29–33.

RICHEY, C. A., LOVELL, M. L., & REID, K. (1991). Interpersonal skills training to enhance social support among women at risk for child maltreatment. *Children and Youth Services Review, 13,* 41–59.

ROBERTS, B. W., & DONAHUE, E. M. (1994). One personality, multiple selves: Integrating personality and social roles. *Journal of Personality, 62,* 199–218.

ROBERTS, M. (1988, March). Be all that you can be. *Psychology Today, 22,* 28–29.

ROBINS, L., & REGIER, D. A. (Eds.). (1991). *Psychiatric disorders in America.* New York: Free Press.

ROBINSON, I., ZISS, K., GANZA, B., & KATZ, S. (1991). Twenty years of the sexual revolution, 1965–1985: An update. *Journal of Marriage and the Family, 53,* 216–220.

ROGERS, C. R. (1951). *Client-centered therapy.* Boston: Houghton Mifflin.

ROGERS, C. R. (1961). *On becoming a person.* Boston: Houghton Mifflin.

ROGERS, C. R. (1980). *A way of being.* Boston: Houghton Mifflin.

ROGERS, C. R. (1985, March 7). *Toward a more human science of the person.* Paper presented at the conference on A Quarter Century of Humanistic Psychologies, San Francisco.

ROSEN, R. C., & LEIBLUM, S. R. (1995). Treatment of sexual disorders in the 1990's: An integrated approach. *Journal of Consulting and Clinical Psychology, 63,* 877–890.

ROSENFELD, I. (1986). *Modern prevention.* New York: Bantam Books.

ROTHMAN, A. J., SALOVEY, P., ANTONE, C., KEOUGH, K., & MARTIN, C. D. (1993). The influence of message framing on intentions to perform health behaviors. *Journal of Experimental Social Psychology, 29,* 408–433.

ROTHERAM-BORUS, M. J., WALKER, J. U., FERNS, W. (1996). Suicidal behavior among middle-class adolescents who seek crisis services. *Journal of Clinical Psychology, 52,* 137–143.

ROWE, D. C. (1990). As the twig is bent? The myth of child-rearing influences on personality development. *Journal of Counseling and Development, 68,* 606–611.

RUBIN, J. Z., PRUITT, D. G., & KIM, S. H. (1994). *Social conflict: Escalation, stalemate, and settlement.* New York: McGraw-Hill.

RUBINSTEIN, C., SHAVER, P., & PEPLAU, L. A. (1982). Loneliness. In N. Jackson (Ed.), *Personal growth and behavior* (pp. 82–83). Guilford, CT: Dushkin Publishing Group.

RUDIN, M. M., ZALEWSKI, C., & BODMER-TURNER, J. (1995). Characteristics of child sexual abuse victims according to perpetrator gender. *Child Abuse and Neglect, 19,* 963–973.

RUSBULT, C. E. (1987). Responses to dissatisfaction in close relationships: The exit-voice-loyalty-neglect model. In D. Perlman & S. W. Duck (Eds.), *Intimate relationships: Development, dynamics, and deterioration.* Beverly Hills, CA: Sage.

RUSSELL, D., PEPLAU, L., & CUTRONA, C. (1982). The Revised UCLA Loneliness Scale: Concurrent and discriminant validity evidence. *Journal of Personality and Social Psychology, 39,* 472–480.

RUSSELL, J. A., LEWICKA, M., & NIIT, T. (1989). A cross-cultural study of a circumplex model of affect. *Journal of Personality and Social Psychology, 57,* 848–856.

RUSSELL, S. H., FAIRWEATHER, J. S., HENDRICKSON, R. M., & ZIMBLER, L. J. (1991). *Profiles of faculty in higher education institutions.* 1988 (NCES 91-389). Washington, DC: U.S. Department of Education, Office of Educational Research and Improvement.

SACKETT, S. A., & HANSEN, J. I. C. (1995). Vocational outcomes of college freshmen with flat profiles on the *Strong Interest Inventory. Measurement and Evaluation in Counseling and Development, 28,* 9–24.

SAENZ, D. S. (1994). Token status and problem-solving deficits: Detrimental effects of destructiveness and performance monitoring. *Social Cognition, 12,* 61–74.

ST. CLAIR, M. (1986). *Object relations and self psychology: An introduction.* Pacific Grove, CA: Brooks/Cole.

SALOVEY, P., & RODIN, J. (1986). The differentiation of social-comparison jealousy and romantic jealousy. *Journal of Personality and Social Psychology, 50,* 1100–1112.

SALTZBURG, S. (1996). Family therapy and the disclosure of adolescent homosexuality. *Journal of Family Psychotherapy, 7,* 1–18.

SANCHEZ-BERNARDOS, M. L., & SANZ, J. (1992). Effects of the discrepancy between self-concepts on emotional adjustment. *Journal of Research in Personality, 26,* 303–318.

SANDAHL, C., LINDBERG, S., & ROTTENBERG, S. (1990). Efficacy expectations among alcohol-dependent patients: A Swedish version of the situational confidence questionnaire. *Alcohol and Alcoholism, 25,* 67–73.

SAVISHINSKY, J. (1991, March). A new life for the old: The role of the elderly in the Bahamas. *The World and I, 6,* 617–629.

SCARR, S. (1987). Personality and experience: Individual encounters with the world. In J. Aronoff, A. I. Rabin, and R. A. Zucker (Eds.), *The emergence of personality* (pp. 49–78). New York: Springer.

SHEIER, M. F., & CARVER, C. S. (1993). On the power of positive thinking: The benefits of being optimistic. *Psychological Science, 4,* 26–30.

SCHOLING, A., & EMMELKAMP, P. M. G. (1990). Social phobia: Nature and treatment. In H. Leitenberg (Ed.), *Handbook of social and evaluation anxiety* (pp. 269–324). New York: Plenum.

SCHOR, J. B. (1992). *The overworked American.* New York: Basic Books.

SCHROF, J. M. (1994). Brain power. *U.S. News & World Report, 120,* 88–92, 94, 97.

SCHULZ, R., & HECKHAUSEN, J. (1996). A life span model of successful aging. *American Psychologist, 51,* 702–714.

SCHWARTZ, A., & SCHWARTZ, R. M. (1993). *Depression: Theories and treatments.* New York: Columbia University Press.

SCHWARTZ, S. (1994). Are there universal aspects in the structure and contents of human values? *Journal of Social Issues, 50,* 19–46.

SEDIKIDES, C. (1993). Assessment, enhancement, and verification determinants of the self-evaluation process. *Journal of Personality and Social Psychology, 65,* 317–338.

SEGELL, M. (1991). The American man in transition. In K. G. Duffy (Ed.), *Personal growth and behavior* (pp. 91–92). Guilford, CT: Dushkin Publishing Group.

SEGURA, D. A. (1992). Chicanas in white-collar jobs: "You have to prove yourself more." *Sociological Perspectives, 35,* 163–182.

SELIGMAN, M. E. P. (1981). A learned helplessness point of view. In L. P. Rehm (Ed.), Behavior therapy for depression. New York: Academic Press.

SELIGMAN, M. E. P. (1988, October). Boomer blues. *Psychology Today, 50*–55.

SELIGMAN, M. E. P. (1992). *Learned optimism.* New York: Knopf.

SELYE, H. (1974). *Stress without distress.* Philadelphia: Lippincott.

SELYE, H. (1980). The stress concept today. In I. L. Kutash et al. (Eds.), *Handbook on stress and anxiety.* San Francisco: Jossey-Bass.

SELYE, H. (1991). History and present states of the stress concept. In A. Monat & R. S. Lazarus (Eds.), *Stress and coping: An anthology* (3rd ed., pp. 21–35). New York: Columbia University Press.

SHARMA, V., & ROSHA, J. (1992). Altruism as a function of self-actualization and locus of control of benefactor. *Psychological Studies, 37,* 26–30.

SHAVER, P., & HAZAN, C. (1993). Adult romantic attachment: Theory and evidence. In D. Perlman & W. Jones (Eds.), *Advances in personal relationships* (Vol. 4, pp. 29–170). London: Jessica Kingsley.

SHAWN, R. M. (1995). Applicability of the goodness-of-fit hypothesis to coping with daily hassles. *Psychological Reports, 77,* 943–954.

SHEEHY, G. (1995, June 12). New passages. *U.S. News & World Report, 121,* 62, 64, 66, 69.

SHEFFIELD, M., CAREY, J., PATENAUDE, W., & LAMBERT, M. J. (1995). An exploration of the relationship between interpersonal problems and psychological health. *Psychological Reports, 76,* 947–956.

SHELDON, W. H. (1954). *Atlas of man: A guide for somatotyping the adult male of all ages.* New York: Harper & Row.

SHERER, M., MADDUX, J. E., MERCANDANTE, B., PRENTICE-DUNN, S., JACOBS, B., & ROGERS, R. W. (1982). The self-efficacy scale: Construction and validation. *Psychological Reports, 51,* 663–671.

SHERMAN, C. (1987). Friends. In K. G. Duffy (Ed.), *Personal growth and behavior* (pp. 87–88). Guilford, CT: Dushkin Publishing Group.

SIEVER, M. D. (1994). Sexual orientation and gender as factors in socio-culturally acquired vulnerability to body dissatisfaction and eating disorders. *Journal of Consulting and Clinical Psychology, 62,* 252–260.

SILEO, C. C., & BAUM, C. (1989, November). Briefing: Self-enhancement and self-verification: New findings about self-esteem. *High School Psychology Teacher, 20*(5).

SIMONTON, D. K. (1987). *Why presidents succeed: A political psychology of leadership.* New Haven, CT: Yale University Press.

SIMPSON, J. A., CAMPBELL, B., & BERSCHEID, E. (1986). The association between romantic love and marriage: Kephart (1967) twice revisited. *Personality and Social Psychology Bulletin, 12,* 363–372.

SIMPSON, J. A., & GANGESTAD, S. W. (1992). Sociosexuality and romantic partner choice. *Journal of Personality, 60,* 31–51.

SINGH, D. (1995). Female judgment of male attractiveness and desirability for relationships: Role of waist-to-hip ratio and financial status. *Journal of Personality and Social Psychology, 69,* 1089–1101.

SMEDES, L. B. (1984). *Forgive and forget.* New York: Harper & Row.

SMITH, D. E., & COGSWELL, C. (1994). A cross-cultural perspective on adolescent girls' body perception. *Perceptual and Motor Skills, 78,* 744–746.

SMITH, M. L., GLASS, G. V., & MILLER, T. J. (1980). *The benefits of psychotherapy.* Baltimore: Johns Hopkins University Press.

SMITH, P. B., & BOND, M. H. (1993). *Across cultures.* Boston: Allyn & Bacon.

SMITH, R. E., SMOLL, F. L., & PTACEK, J. T. (1990). Conjunctive moderator variables in vulnerability and resiliency research: Life stress, social support, and coping skills, and adolescent sport injuries. *Journal of Personality and Social Psychology, 58,* 360–370.

SNYDER, R. A., VERDERBER, K., LANGMEYER, L., & MYERS, M. (1992). A reconsideration of self- and organizational-referent attitudes as "causes" of the glass ceiling effect. *Group and Organization Management, 17,* 260–278.

SOUTH, S. J., & LLOYD, K. M. (1995). Spousal alternatives and marital dissolution. *American Sociological Review, 60,* 21–35.

SPEARS, R., ABRAHAM, C., SHEERAN, P., & ABRAMS, D. (1995). Students' judgments of the risks of HIV infection as a function of sexual practice, sex of target and partner, and age and sex of student. *Journal of College Student Development, 36,* 103–111.

SPECTOR, P. E. (1996). *Industrial and organizational psychology: Research and practice.* New York: Wiley.

SPICER, J., & HONG, B. (1991). Interpreting coronary-prone behavior: Relationships among Type A behavior, hopelessness, anger management, and social contact. *Psychology and Health, 5,* 193–202.

SPICER, J., JACKSON, R., & SCRAGG, R. (1993). The effects of anger management and social contact on risk of myocardial infarction in Type A's and Type B's. *Psychology and Health, 8,* 243–255.

SPURLOCK, J. (1995). Multiple roles of women and role strains [Special issue: Sixth International Congress on Women's Health Issues]. *Health Care for Women International, 16,* 501–508.

STANLEY, D., & FREYSINGER, V. J. (1995). The impact of age, health, and sex on the frequency of older adults' leisure activity participation: A longitudinal study. *Activities Adaptation and Aging, 19,* 31–42.

STARK, E. (1988, February). For love or money? *Psychology Today, 22,* 18.

STAUFER, M. (1992). Technological change and the older employee: Implications for introduction and training. *Behavior and Information Technology, 11,* 46–52.

STEELE, C. M. (1992). Race and the shooting of Black Americans. *The Atlantic Monthly, 69,* 68–78.

STEINHAUER, S. (1995, April 10). Big benefits in marriage, studies say. *New York Times,* p. A10.

STERNBERG, R. J., & GRAJEK, S. (1984). The nature of love. *Journal of Personality and Social Psychology, 47,* 312–329.

STONE, W. F., LEDERER, G., & CHRISTIE, R. (Eds.). (1993). *Strength and weakness: The authoritarian personality today.* New York: Springer-Verlag.

STRICKLAND, B. R. (1988). Sex-related differences in health and illness. *Psychology of Women Quarterly, 12,* 381–399.

STROH, L. K., BRETT, J. M., & REILLY, A. H. (1992). All the right stuff: A comparison of female and male managers' career progression. *Journal of Applied Psychology, 77,* 252–260.

STRUBE, M. J., LOTT, C. L., HEILIZER, R., & GREGG, B. (1986). Type A behavior pattern and the judgment of control. *Journal of Personality and Social Psychology, 50,* 403–412.

STRUCKMAN-JOHNSON, C. (1988). Forced sex on dates: It happens to men, too. *Journal of Sex Research, 24,* 234–241.

STRUPP, H. H. (1986). Psychotherapy: Research, practice, and public policy (How to avoid dead ends). *American Psychologist, 41,* 120–130.

SUE, S., FUJINO, D., HU, L., TAKEUHRI, D., & ZANE, N. (1991). Community mental health services for ethnic minority groups: A test of the cultural responsiveness hypothesis. *Journal of Consulting and Clinical Psychology, 59,* 533–540.

SUGARMAN, D. B., & HOTALING, G. T. (1989). Dating violence: Prevalence, context, and risk markers. In M. A. Pirog-Good & J. E. Stets (Eds.), *Violence in dating relationships* (pp. 3–32). New York: Praeger.

SWANN, W. B., JR., DE LARONDE, C., & HIXON, J. G. (1994). Authenticity and positive strivings in marriage and courtship. *Journal of Personality and Social Psychology, 52,* 881–889.

SWANN, W. B., JR., PELHAM, B. W., & KRULL, D. S. (1989). Agreeable fancy or disagreeable truth? Reconciling self-enhancement and self-verification. *Journal of Personality and Social Psychology, 57,* 782–792.

TALAMANTES, M. A., LAWLER, W. R., & ESPINO, D. V. (1995). Hispanic American elders: Caregiving norms surrounding dying and the use of hospice services. Special issue: Hospice care and cultural diversity. *Hospice Journal, 10,* 35–49.

TANFORD, S., & PENROD, S. (1984). Social influence model: A formal integration of research on majority and minority influence processes. *Psychological Bulletin, 95,* 189–225.

TAVRIS, C. (1987). You are what you do. In K. G. Duffy (Ed.), *Personal growth and behavior* (pp. 87–88). Guilford, CT: Dushkin Publishing Group.

TAVRIS, C. (1989). *Anger: The misunderstood emotion* (2nd ed.). New York: Simon & Schuster.

TAYLOR, S. E., & ASPINWALL, L. G. (1990). Psychological aspects of chronic illness. In G. R. Vandenbos & P. T. Costa, Jr. (Eds.), *Psychological aspects of serious illness* (pp. 7–60). Washington, DC: American Psychological Association.

TAYLOR, S. E., & BROWN, J. D. (1994). Positive illusions and well-being revisited: Separating fact from fiction. *Psychological Bulletin, 116,* 21–27.

TAYLOR, S. E., & CLARK, L. F. (1986). Does information improve adjustment to noxious events? In M. J. Saks & L. Saxe (Eds.), *Advances in applied social psychology* (Vol. 3, pp. 1–28). Hillsdale, NJ: Erlbaum.

TERRY, R. L., & MACY, R. J. (1991). Children's social judgments of other children who wear eyeglasses. *Journal of Social Behavior and Personality, 6,* 965–974.

THOMAS, E. (1986, May 19). Growing pains at 40. *Time, 138,* 22–41.

THOMPSON, L. (1991). Information exchange in negotiation. *Journal of Experimental Social Psychology, 27,* 161–179.

THORESON, C. E., & POWELL, L. H. (1992). Type A behavior pattern: New perspectives on theory, assessment, and intervention. *Journal of Consulting and Clinical Psychology, 60,* 595–604.

THORNTON, B., LEO, R., & ALBERG, K. (1991). Gender role typing, the superwoman ideal, and the potential for eating disorders. *Sex Roles, 25*(2), 469–484.

TIEFER, L. (1991). Historical scientific, clinical, and feminist criticisms of "the human sexual response cycle" model. *Annual Review of Sex Research, 2,* 1–23.

TING-TOOMEY, S. (1988). Intercultural conflict styles: A face-negotiation theory. In Y. Kim & W. Gudykunst (Eds.), *Theories in intercultural communication.* Newbury Park, CA: Sage.

TING-TOOMEY, S., GAO, G., TRUBISKY, P., YANG, Z., KIM, H. S., LIN, S. L., & NISHIDA, T. (1991). Culture, face maintenance, and styles of handling interpersonal conflict: A study in five cultures. *International Journal of Conflict Management, 2,* 275–296.

TOFFLER, A. (1971). *Future shock.* New York: Bantam Books.

TOFFLER, A. (1980). *The third wave.* New York: William Morrow.

TOFFLER, A. (1990). *Power shift.* New York: Bantam Books.

TOUFEXIS, A. (1988, January 11). Dark days, darker spirits. *Time, 140,* 66.

TRIANDIS, H. C., BRISLIN, R., & HUI, C. H. (1988). Cross-cultural training across the individualism-collectivism divide. *International Journal of Intercultural Relations, 12,* 269–289.

TUCH, S. A., & MARTIN, J. K. (1991). Race in the workplace: Black/White differences in the sources of job satisfaction. *The Sociological Quarterly, 32,* 103–116.

TUCKER, L. A. (1983). Muscular strength and mental health. *Journal of Personality and Social Psychology, 45,* 1355–1360.

TUCKER, M. B., & TAYLOR, R. J. (1989). Demographic correlates of relationship status among Black Americans. *Journal of Marriage and the Family, 51,* 3655–3665.

TUCKER, P., & ARON, A. (1993). Passionate love and marital satisfaction at key transition points in the family life cycle. *Journal of Social and Clinical Psychology, 12,* 135–147.

TURK, D. C. (1994). Perspectives on chronic pain: The role of psychological factors. *Current Directions in Psychological Science, 3,* 45–48.

UCHINO, B. N., KIECOLT-GLASER, J. K., & CACIOPPO, J. T. (1992). Age-related changes in cardiovascular response as a function of a chronic stressor and social support. *Journal of Personality and Social Psychology, 63,* 839–846.

U.S. BUREAU OF THE CENSUS. (1990). *Statistical abstract of the United States, 1990* (110th ed.). Washington, DC: U.S. Government Printing Office.

U.S. BUREAU OF THE CENSUS. (1991). *Statistical abstract of the United States, 1991* (111th ed.). Washington, DC: U.S. Government Printing Office.

U.S. BUREAU OF THE CENSUS. (1992). *Statistical abstract of the United States, 1992* (112th ed.). Washington, DC: U.S. Government Printing Office.

U.S. BUREAU OF THE CENSUS. (1995). *Statistical abstract of the United States, 1995* (115th ed.). Washington, DC: U.S. Government Printing Office.

U.S. DEPARTMENT OF COMMERCE. (1992). *1990 census of population and housing: Summary population and housing characteristics.* Washington, DC: U.S. Government Printing Office.

U.S. DEPARTMENT OF LABOR, BUREAU OF LABOR STATISTICS. (1994). *1993 Handbook on women workers: Trends and issues.* Washington, DC: U.S. Government Printing Office.

U.S. DEPARTMENT OF LABOR, BUREAU OF LABOR STATISTICS. (1990). *Occupational outlook handbook,* 1990–1991. Washington, DC: U.S. Government Printing Office.

U.S. DEPARTMENT OF LABOR, BUREAU OF LABOR STATISTICS. (1996). *Occupational outlook handbook 1996–1997.* Washington, DC: U.S. Government Printing Office.

VAILL, P. B. (1996). *Learning as a way of being. Strategies for survival in a world of permanent White Water.* San Francisco: Jossey-Bass.

VALOIS, R. F., & KAMMERMANN, S. (1992). *Your sexuality: A self-assessment.* New York: McGraw-Hill.

VODANOVICH, S. J., & KASS, S. J. (1990). Age and gender differences in boredom proneness. *Journal of Social Behavior and Personality, 5,* 297–307.

VOLKOV, S. (1995). *St. Petersburg: A cultural history.* New York: Free Press.

WALKER, J. I. (1982). *Everybody's guide to emotional well-being.* San Francisco: Harbor Publishing.

WALLIS, C. (1986, March 31). To feed or not to feed? *Time, 112,* 60.

WARD, C., & SEARLE, W. (1991). The impact of value discrepancies and cultural identity on psychological and sociocultural adjustment of sojourners. *International Journal of Intercultural Relations, 15,* 209–225.

WARD, M. L. (1995). Talking about sex: Common themes about sexuality in the prime-time television programs children and adolescents view most. Special issue: Adolescents' uses of the media. *Journal of Youth and Adolescence, 24,* 595–615.

WATERS, E., MERRICK, S. K., ALBERSHEIM, L. J., & TREBOUX, D. (1995, April). *Attachment security from infancy to early adulthood: A 20-year longitudinal study.* Poster presented at the Society for Research in Child Development, Indianapolis, IN.

WATKINS, E. C. (1993). What have surveys taught us about the teaching and practice of vocational assessment? *Counseling Psychologist, 21,* 109–117.

WEINDRUCH, R. (1996). Caloric restriction and aging. *Scientific American, 138,* 48–52.

WEISINGER, H., & LOBSENZ, N. M. (1981). *Nobody's perfect*. New York: Warner Books.

WEISS, J. C. (1995). Cognitive therapy and life review therapy: Theoretical and therapeutic implications for mental health counselors. *Journal of Mental Health Counseling, 17,* 157–172.

WEISZ, J. R., ROTHBAUM, F. M., & BLACKBURN, T. C. (1984). Standing out and standing in: The psychology of control in America and Japan. *American Psychologist, 39,* 955–969.

WELDON, E., & GARGANO, G. M. (1988). Cognitive loading: The effects of accountability and shared responsibility on cognitive effort. *Personality and Social Psychology Bulletin, 14,* 159–171.

What the world's teenagers are saying. (1986, June 30). *U.S. News & World Report, 112,* 68.

WHEELAN, S. A., & VERDI, A. F. (1992). Differences in male and female patterns of communication in groups: A methodological artifact? *Sex Roles, 27,* 1–15.

WHEELER, L., REIS, H. T., & BOND, M. H. (1989). Collectivism-individualism in everyday social life: The middle kingdom and the melting pot. *Journal of Personality and Social Psychology, 57,* 79–86.

WHISMAN, M. A., & KWON, P. (1993). Life stress and dysphoria: The role of self-esteem and hopelessness. *Journal of Personality and Social Psychology, 65,* 1054–1060.

WHITBECK, L. B., & HOYT, D. R. (1994). Social prestige and assortive mating: A comparison of students from 1956 and 1988. *Journal of Social and Personal Relationships, 11,* 137–145.

WHITE, J. L., & PARHAM, T. A. (1990). *The psychology of Blacks: An African-American Perspective* (2nd ed.). Englewood Cliffs, NJ: Prentice Hall.

WIEBE, D. J. (1991). Hardiness and stress moderation: A test of proposed mechanisms. *Journal of Personality and Social Psychology, 60,* 89–99.

WIEDENFELD, S. A., O'LEARY, A., BANDURA, A., BROWN, S., LEVINE, S., & RASKA, K. (1990). Impact of perceived self-efficacy in coping with stressors on components of the immune system. *Journal of Personality and Social Psychology, 59,* 1082–1094.

WILCOX, D., & DOWRICK, P. W. (1992). Anger management with adolescents. *Residential Treatment for Children and Youth, 9,* 29–39.

WILLS, T. A., VACARO, D., & McNAMARA, G. (1994). Novelty seeking, risk taking, and related constructs as predictors of adolescent substance use: An application of Cloninger's theory. *Journal of Substance Abuse, 6,* 1–20.

WILSON, G. T. (1990). Clinical issues and strategies in the practice of behavior therapy. In C. M. Franks, G. T. Wilson, P. C. Kendall, & J. P. Foreyt, (Eds.), *Review of behavior therapy* (Vol. 12, pp. 271–301). New York: Guilford Press.

WINSLOW, R. W., FRANZINI, L. R., & HWANG, J. (1992). Perceived peer norms, casual sex, and AIDS risk prevention. *Journal of Applied Social Psychology, 22,* 1809–1827.

WOLPE, J. (1973). *The practice of behavior therapy.* New York: Pergamon Press.

WORCHEL, S., & LUNDGREN, S. (1991). The nature of conflict and conflict resolution. In K. Duffy, J. Grosch, & P. Olczak (Eds.), *Community mediation: A handbook for practitioners and researchers* (pp. 3–20). New York: Guilford Press.

WORDEN, J. W., & PROCTOR, W. (1988). What's your PDA? In A. Arkoff (Ed.), *Psychology and personal growth.* Boston: Allyn & Bacon.

YANKELOVICH, D. (1981). *New rules.* New York: Bantam Books.

YARAB, P. E., & ALLGEIER, E. R. (1997, April). *Just don't have sex! Acceptability, disclosure, and forgiveness of extradyadic relationships.* Paper presented to the annual meeting of the Eastern Psychological Association, Washington, DC.

YOVETICH, N. A., DALE, J. A., & HUDAK, M. A. (1990). Benefits of humor in reduction of threat-induced anxiety. *Psychological Reports, 66,* 51–58.

ZEIDNER, M. (1995). Adaptive coping with test situations: A review of the literature. *Educational Psychologist, 30,* 123–133.

ZIMBARDO, P. G. (1986). The Stanford Shyness Project. In W. H. Jones, J. M. Cheek, & S. R. Briggs (Eds.), *Shyness: Perspectives on research and treatment* (pp. 17–25). New York: Plenum.

ZUCKERMAN, M. (1990a). The psychophysiology of sensation-seeking. *Journal of Personality, 58,* 313–345.

ZUCKERMAN, M. (1990b). Some dubious premises in research and theory on racial differences: Scientific, social, and ethical issues. *American Psychologist, 45,* 1297–1303.

ZUMMUNER, V. L., & FISCHER, A. H. (1995). The social regulation of emotions in jealousy situations: A comparison between Italy and the Netherlands. *Journal of Cross-Cultural Psychology, 26,* 189–208.

Photo Acknowledgments

CHAPTER 1 Page 1, William R. Sallaz/Gamma-Liaison, Inc.; p. 5, David Young-Wolff/PhotoEdit; p. 7, Garry McMichael/Photo Researchers, Inc.; p. 9, Bill Losh/FPG International; p. 23, Bob Winsett/Tom Stack & Associates.

CHAPTER 2 Page 29, Tony Demin, International Stock Photography Ltd.; p. 34, Austrian National Tourist Office; p. 43, Albert Bandura; p. 44, Michael Newman, PhotoEdit; p. 48, Carl Rogers Memorial Library; p. 51, Brooks/Cole Publishing Company.

CHAPTER 3 Page 59, Dusan Vranic/AP/Wide World Photos; p. 61, Chuck Savage/The Stock Market; p. 65, PhotoDisc, Inc.; p. 73, Barbara Penoyar/PhotoDisc, Inc. (top, left), Tony Freeman/PhotoEdit (top, center), Rob Lang/FPG International (top, right), Alain Evrard/Photo Researchers, Inc. (bottom, left), Michael Philip Manheim/International Stock Photography Ltd. (bottom, center), Ron Chapple/FPG International (bottom, right); p. 75, Shirley Zeiberg/Simon & Schuster/PH College.

CHAPTER 4 Page 88, Adam Nadel/AP/Wide World Photos; p. 90, John Huber; p. 96, Chuck Mason/International Stock Photography Ltd.; p. 99, ATC Productions/The Stock Market; p. 110, Will Hart.

CHAPTER 5 Page 115, Roberto Soncin Geromett/Photo 20-20; p. 124, Eugene Gordon/Simon & Schuster/PH College; p. 126, Michael Newman/PhotoEdit; p. 142, Laimute E. Druskis/Simon & Schuster/PH College; p. 143, Will Hart.

CHAPTER 6 Page 149, Laurie Bayer/International Stock Photography Ltd.; p. 151, Tony Freeman/PhotoEdit; p. 157, Robert Brenner/PhotoEdit; p. 161, Spencer Grant/Photo Researchers, Inc.; p. 163, T. Michaels/The Image Works.

CHAPTER 7 Page 175, Stephen Simpson/FPG International; p. 180, Robert Fox/Impact Visuals Photo & Graphics, Inc.; p. 187, Richard Hutchings/Photo Researchers, Inc.; p. 189, M. Antman/The Image Works; p. 192, Michael Krasowitz/FPG International (left), Gary Conner/PhotoEdit (right).

CHAPTER 8 Page 202, Beatriz Schiller/International Stock Photography Ltd.; p. 204, The Stock Market (top, left), Bill Bachmann/Photo Researchers, Inc. (bottom, left), Al Stephenson/Woodfin Camp & Associates (right); p. 211, Jon Feingersh/The Stock Market; p. 215, Tom McHugh/Photo Researchers, Inc. (left), Paul Shambroom/Photo Researchers, Inc. (center), Wesley Bocxe/Photo Researchers, Inc. (right); p. 222, Bill Biggart/Impact Visuals Photo & Graphics, Inc.; p. 225, Carolina Kroon/Impact Visuals Photo & Graphics, Inc.

CHAPTER 9 Page 230, Telegraph Colour Library/FPG International; p. 232, Steve Goldberg/Monkmeyer Press; p. 240, Teri Leigh Stratford/Simon & Schuster/PH College; p. 243, Ken Karp/Simon & Schuster/PH College; p. 248, Elyse Lewin/The Image Bank.

CHAPTER 10 Page 257, Major Morris/Simon & Schuster/PH College; p. 261, Alan Carey/The Image Works; p. 264, Charles Gatewood/Simon & Schuster/PH College (top), Giovanni Lunardi/International Stock Photography Ltd. (bottom); p. 276, Michael Newman/PhotoEdit; p. 281, Andrew Savulich/AP/Wide World Photos.

CHAPTER 11 Page 290, Michael Paras/International Stock Photography Ltd.; p. 293, Dion Ogust/The Image Works; p. 295, PhotoDisc, Inc. (left), Thomas Brummett/PhotoDisc, Inc. (right); p. 307, PhotoDisc, Inc.; p. 311, Anita Duncan/Simon & Schuster/PH College.

CHAPTER 12 Page 319, Keith Gunnar/FPG International; p. 327, James Schnepf/Gamma-Liaison, Inc.; p. 331, A. Brett Wallis/Masterfile Corporation; p. 333, Chuck Savage/The Stock Market; p. 335, United Nations/UN/DPI PHOTO.

CHAPTER 13 Page 344, George Rizer/AP/Wide World Photos; p. 348, Mary Ellen Mark Library; p. 353, Jany Sauvanet/Photo Researchers, Inc.; p. 356, AP/Wide World Photos; p. 367, Eugene Gordon/Simon & Schuster/PH College.

CHAPTER 14 Page 375, Shirley Zeiberg/Simon & Schuster/PH College; p. 387, Bob Daemmrich/The Image Works; p. 389, Paul S. Howell/Gamma-Liaison, Inc.; p. 398, James King-Holmes/W Industries/Science Photo Library/Photo Researchers, Inc.

CHAPTER 15 Page 405, Siluk/The Image Works; p. 408, Larry Fleming/Simon & Schuster/PH College; p. 409, Paul Sequeira/Rapho/Photo Researchers, Inc.; p. 418, Nashville Tennesean (left); AP/Wide World Photos (right); p. 425, Ken Karp, Sirovich Senior Center/Simon & Schuster/PH College.

CHAPTER 16 Page 431, Ester Shapiro/Photo Researchers, Inc.; p. 435, Judy Gurovitz/International Stock Photography Ltd.; p. 436, UPI/Vince Mannino/Corbis-Bettmann; p. 442, Tony Freeman/PhotoEdit; p. 443, Simon & Schuster/PH College.

Name Index

Subject Index